2d EDITION

MANAGEMENT and ORGANIZATION

HENRY L. SISK, Ph.D.
Professor of Business Administration
North Texas State University

Published by

G41 **SOUTH-WESTERN PUBLISHING CO.**

CINCINNATI   WEST CHICAGO, ILL.   DALLAS   PELHAM MANOR, N.Y.
BURLINGAME, CALIF.   BRIGHTON, ENGLAND

PREFACE

Several assumptions are implicit to the writing of a textbook about management. First, it is assumed that there are aspects of the practice of management that can be taught to others. Such a statement runs counter to the belief that managers are born or that experience is the only teacher; yet the belief that managers can be taught minimizes in no way the value of experience and practice in the development of managerial skills and insights. It is believed, however, that those who enter managerial positions with knowledge and concepts gained from a formal study of management require less time to develop an acceptable level of managerial performance than those who have not studied management as a discipline. Second, it is assumed that management is best defined as a process of coordinating all the resources of an organization in order to achieve organizational objectives. The definition of management as a process permits the description and analysis of that process, thus making it possible to develop and organize the concepts and techniques of management in a systematic way. Third, there is the implied assumption that the management process is present in and necessary to all formal organizations—business, governmental, educational, social, religious, and charitable—if they are to achieve their respective organizational objectives effectively. Because of the universality of management and the consequent demand for managers, the study of management fulfills an important educational need.

This book is intended for use as a textbook in the introductory management course in four-year colleges and universities and in those community colleges offering a mid-management curriculum. The book may also be used in company management development programs.

During the four years since publication of the first edition, many studies relevant to an understanding of management have been published. In order to incorporate this new material, a significant reorganization of content has been necessary. The separate chapters treating planning for finance, sales, and production have been combined. Planning for the functions of finance and sales now appear in Chapter 5, and Chapter 6 combines planning for production and personnel. Personnel planning was formerly considered with organization development in Chapter 20, but is now included in Chapter 14, "Organizational Change—Analysis and Development." As a result of this internal rearrangement of topics, two new chapters have been added without increasing the total. Chapter 15, "Organizational Behavior," is now the first chapter of Part Three, The Leadership Function. Also, Chapter 23, "A Summing Up," is a new concluding chapter which presents an integrative overview of the management process and is intended to be read in conjunction with Chapter 1. A new comprehensive case concerning the operation of a motel is included in Appendix B. This case may be assigned to integrate each of the five major parts of the text, or it may be assigned as a comprehensive case. In each chapter an effort has been made to introduce new materials appearing in the literature.

As in the first edition, two case problems are presented in each chapter as an integral part of the text. These cases offer the student an opportunity to relate the material in the text to an actual situation. The cases are also helpful in securing maximum student participation in class. Each chapter begins with an opening case problem that describes a business situation. In most of the chapters the case is referred to in the text material, thereby utilizing the case as a practical example to make the discussion in the text more meaningful. Generally the closing case for each chapter draws upon concepts presented in the latter part of the chapter for its solution. The case is related to the text by means of a bridge paragraph at the end of the chapter.

Many persons contribute to the writing of a book; however, for a revised edition there is a special debt of gratitude to the professors and students who have written to the publisher and to the author. Many of their comments have been incorporated in the revision, and it is hoped that the feedback provided by professors and students will continue during the current edition. A special note of thanks is due Mr. M. W. Isbell, Chairman of Ramada Inns, Inc., for his cooperation and interest in the development of the comprehensive case. In addition to the many colleagues in other institutions who have read portions of the revised manuscript, the author wishes to thank his associates at North Texas State University—Professors Elvis Stephens, J. D. Dunn, and Frank Rachel—who have provided the organizational climate and intellectual stimulation necessary to complete this revision.

Henry L. Sisk

CONTENTS

PART THREE   □   **The Organizing Function**

PART FOUR   ☐   **The Leadership Function**

PART FIVE ▢ **The Control Function**

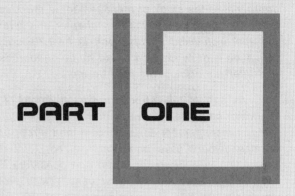

PART ONE

Introduction

What do you think of when you hear or read the word <u>management</u>? Do you think of management as a group, as a profession, as a science, or as an art? How widespread is management and when is it needed? What does a manager do when he manages? These are the questions that form the framework of the discussion concerning the nature of management. From the discussion a definition of management as a telic, or purposeful, process is developed. One of the approaches, the modern or systems approach, to the study of management is introduced briefly. Though systems theory is introduced in the first chapter and referred to throughout the text, the approach used in this book is best described as eclectic; that is, information is drawn from a broad range of sources so that the differing needs and interests of students may be met.

As part of the introduction to any field of study a brief statement of the historical development of that field is helpful. In Chapter 2 the development of management concepts is traced. From time to time different aspects of management have been emphasized. First there is an emphasis upon production, not surprising when one considers the industrial revolution and the need to know how to best utilize mass production facilities. Then the emphasis shifts to the administration of the entire enterprise.

Some refer to an emphasis of one aspect of management in preference to another as a school of management. The emphasis upon production and administration is often referred to as the classical school. Another area of emphasis is human relations. There are so many schools or approaches to the study of management that they have been termed a jungle and their proponents have been accused of engaging in inky warfare. Some of the brush in this jungle is cut away and an integrative view is presented.

The introduction closes with a discussion of two subjects that may seem, at first glance, unrelated. These topics are objectives and ethics. Objectives are goals, and without stated goals formal organizations are doomed to failure. As managers do those things necessary to achieve objectives they interact with other people and this interaction is often described as being either ethical or unethical in nature. Personal values are one of the major determinants of ethical behavior. The personal value systems of managers and the problem areas requiring ethical judgments are discussed.

CHAPTER 1

Management Defined

CASE PROBLEM
1-A

A PROBLEM IN
MANAGEMENT
DEFINITION

"Are we ready to begin now?" Mr. White, president of the J. B. White Company, asked as he mentally noted that all were present for the regular Thursday morning staff meeting. Seated on his left were the chief engineer, the vice-president in charge of sales, and the vice-president in charge of manufacturing. On his right were the controller and the director of research. At the opposite end of the long table was Mr. Peterson, the personnel director.

"As you know," Mr. White continued, "we have discussed from time to time the formation of a management club, but have never quite gotten around to actually starting one. The main problem seems to be in determining who should belong to the club. Let's see if we can't get this settled by next week and schedule the first meeting. Mr. Peterson, would you summarize from your minutes of these meetings our past discussions?"

Before Mr. Peterson could commence, Mr. Riley, the sales vice-president, interrupted, "I would like a clearer picture of what is to be gained by this sort of club. Personally, I don't see much need for my men to attend, although if you wanted someone, the man in charge of the sales order department could come. The others are too busy."

"We'll get to the purpose in just a minute," Mr. Peterson replied, "but first let's discuss the following criteria for membership that have been suggested: (1) every person whose name appears on the published organization chart; (2) all those who have supervisory responsibility; (3) all persons exempt from the provisions of the Wages and Hours Law; and (4) everyone whose earnings are over $500 a month. Mr. Burke, the vice-president in charge of manufacturing, has stated that he thinks the only ones who should belong are the foremen in the factory who supervise. It has also been recommended that membership be limited to our plant here in Cleveland and not include any of the personnel in the branch plant, which is 25 miles away. As you know, Mr. Riley doesn't feel that any of his salesmen or district managers should belong."

Mr. Davis, the controller, spoke up and said, "I've been thinking about the suggestion that I made regarding the salary cutoff, and after looking at some of the earnings of the draftsmen in the engineering department, I think that we had better say 'salary' rather than 'earnings.' "

"That's right," agreed Mr. Johnson, the chief engineer. "I have draftsmen making more money than some of my junior engineers and trainees because these fellows don't get overtime pay since they are classified as professional employees."

"The same is true for me," said Mr. Brewer, the director of research. "Yet I feel that some of my research men would benefit from such a club as they might get a better feel for what we are trying to do as an organization."

There was a pause at this point and then Mr. White spoke, "I know that some of you were critical when I insisted that every person who does not receive overtime pay for extra hours worked be listed on the organization chart by name. I still think that the fact that a person is exempt from overtime pay should be the basis for membership in the management club."

"The heart of any club of this type is the foremen," argued Mr. Burke, vice-president in charge of manufacturing. "These are the people who should be represented. We should have a management club and call it that, even if there are only foremen in it. These men are the company to the employees in the shop, and I think that we should treat them accordingly. Also, we should tell them of our plans, and that way they could find out ahead of time what's going to happen instead of learning it from the union."

Mr. White saw that there had not been much change in the position of any of his staff since the last time the question of having a management club was discussed. He decided that the best course would be to present a specific proposal and ask them to either accept it or reject it. With this thought in mind, he made the following request of Mr. Peterson, the personnel director.

"Mr. Peterson, I would like for you to prepare a summary recommendation for consideration at our next meeting. Include in your report the name of the club, those who are eligible for membership, and a statement of the objectives of the club."

PROBLEMS

1. Assume that you are Mr. Peterson, the personnel director. Write a brief memo to Mr. White as requested.

2. Mr. Burke mentioned the fact that a management club would enable top management of the company to keep the foremen better informed in regard to company plans. Is there any possibility that top management might receive information from the foremen? Discuss.

3. *Research Assignment.* Mr. White indicated that if an employee did not receive overtime payment for extra hours worked, he was eligible for inclusion on the company organization chart. Such employees are normally termed *exempt,* since they are exempt from the overtime provisions of the Fair Labor Standards Act, commonly called the Wages and Hours Law. Consult your nearest wages and hours office, either in person or by letter, and review those publications which discuss the basis for exemption. Discuss briefly whether exemption from overtime payment serves as a valid criterion for membership in a management club.

Seemingly, each person has his own ideas concerning the meaning of the term "management." Some use the word "management" as a collective noun and refer to management as a certain group of persons within an organization. Others define management as a process calling for the performance of specific functions, and there are those who view management as a profession, a science, or an art. Management is also regarded as an academic discipline and field of study. Each of these concepts of management reflects a different aspect of the nature of management. Serious study of management requires a relatively precise definition, and as a means of developing such a definition, let us examine more closely the nature of management.

THE NATURE OF MANAGEMENT

It is said that the lead sentence of a news story should answer the following questions: who, what, when, where, why, and how? These are questions that must also be answered in respect to management so that a precise definition can be developed. In Case Problem 1-A, A Problem in Management Definition, one question to be resolved is the *who* of management: Who is considered a member of management? However, before the *who* of management can be determined, it is necessary to know *what* management does, *how* it is done, *when* management becomes necessary, *where* management is found, and *why* management is necessary. These key questions form the broad organizational outline of the first part of this chapter.

The Need for Management

Our discussion of the need for management answers two of the key questions: *why* and *when?*

One of the best illustrations of the need, or the *why*, of management is found in an announcement reporting a change in the management of a given company. Typically, it is stated that the president of the company has been replaced, though the word "resigned" may be used, and that several vice-presidents have also "resigned." These changes result in the formation of a new management team. One can infer from these changes that something happened which incurred the displeasure of some of the stockholders or the directors of the company. The reasons for the dissatisfaction vary with each situation and range from personal misconduct on the part of the officers replaced to downright ineptness in their handling of the affairs of the company.

Assuming the reason is incompetence, one might raise the question, "Why weren't all of the company's workers fired instead of the president and a few of the other officers?" The answer to this question, in part, defines one facet of the nature of management: *Management is responsible for the success or failure of a business.* If such were not the case, the owners (stockholders) might well have decided to discharge all the workers. Thus, it is apparent that a management is needed to direct the affairs of a company. This need for management is succinctly stated in the phrase, "to run the business." The statement that management is responsible for the success or failure of a business tells us *why* we need a management, but it does not indicate *when* management is needed.

Whenever men form a group, which by definition consists of more than one person, and that group has an objective, it becomes necessary for the group to work together in order to attain their stated objective. Members of the group must subordinate their individual desires to some extent to attain the group goal, and management should provide leadership for group action.

It can be argued that management exists even in the coordination of the efforts of only two individuals. Assume that you and a friend have been driving and run out of gas a few blocks from a service station. You decide it is much quicker to push the car to the station rather than walk to the station and carry the gas back to the car. You then agree that the strength of both of you is required to push the car. Further, you agree that the effort must be exerted at the same time. Once this determination has been reached, your efforts must be coordinated, and both of you must push at the same time. An agreement that one person is to give the signal, "push," makes that person a manager at the time he gives the command. Thus, the question *when* is answered by stating that management is needed whenever there is a group with stated objectives.

The Functions of Management

An analysis of the functions of management tells us *what* management does. Also, an analysis of the functions of management provides the first step in the development of a precise definition of the word "management."

When studying management as an academic discipline, it is necessary to consider management as a *process*. When management is regarded as a process, it can be analyzed and described in terms of several major functions. However, a word of caution is necessary. In discussing the process of management, it is convenient, and even necessary, to describe and study each function of the process separately. As a result, it may seem that the management process is a series of discrete functions with each function fitting neatly into a separate compartment. Nothing could be further from the truth, yet the process must be subdivided with each component part discussed separately so that it may be readily understood. In practice, a manager may, and often does, perform simultaneously, or at least as a part of a continuum, all of the following four functions: planning, organizing, directing, and controlling.

Planning. When management is viewed as a process, planning is the first function performed. Once objectives have been determined, the means necessary to achieve these stated objectives are presented as plans. An organization's plans determine the course it takes and provide a basis for estimating the degree of probable success it will have in fulfilling its objectives. Plans are prepared for activities that require many years to complete; they are also necessary for short-term projects. Examples of long-range planning are found in product development programs and in the plans that guide the financing of a company. At the other end of the time scale, a production supervisor plans the output of his department for a period of one day and for a whole week. Each of these examples represents extremes in the time span covered by the planning process, and each is necessary for the achievement of stated company objectives.

Organizing. In order to carry out plans after they have been prepared, it is necessary to create an organization. It is a function of management to determine the type of organization required to execute stated plans. The kind of organization that is developed determines to a large extent whether or not the plans are fulfilled. In turn, the objectives of an enterprise and the plans required to meet these objectives have a direct bearing upon the characteristics and structure of the organization. A company whose objective is to provide food and shelter to the traveling public requires an entirely different organization than a firm whose objective is to transmit natural gas through a pipeline.

Directing. The third function of management—directing—has been termed motivating, leading, guiding, stimulating, and actuating. Although each of these words has a different connotation, any one of these terms indicates clearly that this function of management is concerned with the human factors of an organization. It is as a result of the efforts of each member of an organization that goals are attained; hence, a major function of the management process is to direct the organization so that objectives may be achieved.

Controlling. The last phase of the management process is the control function. The control function measures present performance in relation to expected standards of performance, and as a result of such comparison, it can be determined whether or not corrective action is needed to bring present performance in line with the expected performance expressed as standards. The control function is exercised continuously, and, although related to the functions of organizing and directing, it is more closely associated with the planning function. The corrective action of control almost invariably calls for a restatement of plans. As a result, many students of the management process consider the planning and control functions as part of a continuous cycle of planning-control-planning.

Management as a Group

One of the questions asked at the beginning of the chapter is whether or not management may be regarded as a group of people— the *who* of management. To some it is unfortunate that the word management is used as a collective noun to designate a group of managers instead of limiting the use of the word to describe the specific processes of planning, organizing, directing, and controlling. Nonetheless, reference to management as a group is deeply imbedded in our everyday language, and clarification of who is normally considered a member of management is needed.

Managers are those persons in an organization who accomplish their work primarily by directing the work of others. Some of the managers of the J. B. White Company, Case Problem 1-A, are seeking an answer to the question, who is eligible to join the management club? Stated another way, who are the persons in the J. B. White Company performing any or all of the functions of planning, organizing, directing, and controlling?

In a typical corporation there are a board of directors, a president, a group of vice-presidents or major executives, managers of divisions or departments, and supervisors of specific areas or functions who report to the manager of that department. Reporting to a departmental supervisor are workers whose function is the performance of specific duties assigned by the supervisor. There is general agreement that those persons who direct the work of others are a part of management. In addition, there are some who do not direct the work of others, yet participate in planning, organizing, or controlling. These people are usually referred to as staff specialists, rather than managers, and are also considered a part of management. Persons who perform relatively specific and routine duties under the direction of a manager or a staff specialist are called operative personnel and are not classed as a part of management.

As a rule, the distribution of a manager's time spent in the performance of each of the four functions of management—planning, organizing, directing, and controlling—is a function of his position in the organization. The major executives of a company devote much of their time to planning and organizing. They are charged with policy making, a form of planning, and they must also determine the organization necessary to execute these policies. On the other hand, a departmental supervisor directs the operative personnel in his department and is responsible for the amount and quality of work produced. Consequently, a large portion of his time is spent in directing and controlling the efforts of his subordinates.

Is Management a Profession?

The question is often asked: Is management a profession? It is also frequently asked whether management is a science or an art. If a profession is defined as an occupation that serves others, it is possible to consider management a profession. However, if a profession is thought of as a vocation requiring licensing and graduate study, such as medicine and law, then management is not a profession. It is not particularly important to categorize management as either a profession, a science, or an art; but there are certain characteristics implied by each of these designations that are worth discussing.

There is a body of knowledge that is peculiar to the study of management. Over the years certain concepts of management have been developed, and there is a vast amount of technical information related to the management of specialized areas such as production, sales, finance, and personnel. Thus, in respect to specialized knowledge, management is a technical field that requires mastery. One of the reasons for studying an introductory course in management is to become acquainted with some of this information. However, neither a license nor a degree is required in order to practice as a manager. The absence of formal licensing and educational requirements is essentially sound because it places the emphasis where it belongs: on performance rather than on academic training. Although academic training is to be highly regarded, access to the field of management should not be limited only to those persons who have completed a prescribed course of study. Nonetheless, a trained manager usually performs better than his untrained counterpart, particularly in today's complex industrial society.

Is Management a Science or an Art?

A discussion of management as a science or an art seldom resolves the question conclusively to anyone's satisfaction. However, since the question is raised frequently in management literature, it is well to establish a point of reference so that each student may answer the question to his own satisfaction. Frederick W. Taylor is usually considered the father of "scientific management." His contributions to management, along with those of other pioneers in the field, are discussed in the following chapter. The use of the phrase, scientific management, in connection with the work of Taylor implies that there is some other form of management. Is the type of management that is not scientific the management described by the phrase, "art of management"?

Historically, scientific management is defined as management that uses the methods of science in making its decisions and evaluating its subsequent courses of action. Every effort is made to obtain complete, valid, reliable information pertinent to the problem under consideration before a decision is made. Under these conditions the decision is consistent with and derived from the obtained information, and subsequent courses of action are subject to rigorous control procedure as a further check upon the correctness of the original decision. The antithesis of the scientific approach is management that operates "by the seat of its pants." It is an approach to management that places emphasis upon sources of information such as personal experiences, intuition, and hunches—all of which have unknown reliability and validity.

The art of management refers specifically to the practice of management. There are many phases of business operations that are not readily amenable to rigorous examination and control. Consequently, information developed in these fields is less precise than information obtained by means of the scientific method. As a result, a greater emphasis is placed upon the individual manager's past experience and judgment than is placed upon his knowledge resulting from a technical course of study, such as engineering or accounting. The solutions to problems involving human relations call upon skills developed primarily through experience. When these skills are practiced smoothly and successfully by a manager, they are often regarded as an art; yet in their development and acquisition, they differ only in degree, not in kind, from skills and knowledge acquired through the more critical methods of science.

A Definition of Management

The basic questions raised at the beginning of this chapter concerning the nature of management have been discussed and partially answered. It is shown that a definite need for management exists if a group is to obtain its desired objectives. The major functions of management—planning, organizing, directing, and controlling—are outlined. Those persons in an organization who are normally considered managers and referred to as members of management are differentiated from nonmanagerial employees because they perform in some measure the four managerial functions of planning, organizing, directing, and controlling and because they share the responsibility for meeting organizational goals. There is a clarification of the use of such terms as science, art, and profession as applied to management.

It is necessary to develop a precise definition of management as a basis for our study of the principles of management. There are three parts to a definition of management as a process: first, the coordination of resources; second, the performance of managerial functions as a means of achieving coordination; and, third, establishing the purpose of the management process. Each part is discussed separately.

1. The first aspect of a definition of management is coordination. Remember the elementary example mentioned earlier of the two students who agree that together they can push a car but that individually they cannot. The coordination required in that situation is the coordination of effort so that both can push at the same time. What does the manager of an enterprise coordinate? He coordinates the resources of the organization; namely, money, materials, and men.

   In a business enterprise, and for that matter in most organized groups, a prime requirement is money. There is seldom an organization without some measure of capital, a requisite for fraternal, social, and religious groups as well as for business organizations. Materials include the physical properties of a business, such as production equipment, plant facilities, and inventories. The people who are members of the organization are the third element. These three elements form a convenient mnemonic device: the three M's of management—money, materials, and men. And, although an oversimplification, this device is an aid in remembering the coordinative aspect of management.

2. The coordination of the resources of an organization is achieved by means of the managerial functions of planning, organizing, directing, and controlling.

3. A definition of management as the coordination of resources through the utilization of the functions of the management process is not complete. Management is a *telic,* or purposive, process; it is directed toward the attainment of stated goals or objectives. Without an objective, there is no goal to reach nor can there be a path to follow. The concept of goal orientation and the subsequent statement of that goal as an objective provide the purposive characteristic of management.

From the above discussion a definition of management may be stated: *Management is the coordination of all resources through the processes of planning, organizing, directing, and controlling in order to attain stated objectives.*

The Universality of Management

The definition of management as a purposive, coordinative process is universal in its application to all forms of group endeavor. It is not confined to business enterprises alone, but is applicable whenever man attempts to reach a stated goal through group effort. The concept of universality of management is also applicable to all levels of managers within an organization and is not confined to the top echelon only. Every manager and every staff specialist of an organization participates in the coordination of resources, the exercise of one or all of the managerial functions, and all are working to achieve the stated objectives.

A MODERN APPROACH TO THE STUDY OF MANAGEMENT

In Chapter 2, "The Development of Management Concepts," major historical approaches to the study of management are reviewed, and an integrative view, referred to as modern organizational theory, is presented.[1] The distinguishing characteristic of modern organization theory is that it utilizes the concepts of a system in the study of management and organizations. Although the components and functioning of management and organizational systems are discussed in Chapter 2, the following introductory statement to the systems concept is timely.

Systems Theory

Systems theory is a way of interpreting objects and events.[2] The definition of a system is relatively simple and easy to understand. In its simplest form, *a system is composed of parts that are interrelated in a manner that forms a unified whole that is more than a mere summation of the parts.* A table or a chair may be considered a system since the parts are arranged in a manner that forms a whole that is *more than* a simple summation of the parts. *More than* means

---

[1] See Chapter 2, pp. 29-59.

[2] Robert Chin, "The Utility of Systems Models and Developmental Models for Practitioners." From Warren G. Bennis, Kenneth D. Benne, and Robert Chin, *The Planning of Change* (New York: Holt, Rinehart, and Winston, Inc., 1961). Mr. Chin presents a sound discussion of several types of systems and develops models for each type of system. He also discusses developmental models and their application.

that the distinguishing characteristic of the whole is a configuration which is dependent upon the interrelationships of the parts rather than being derived from the characteristics of each individual part. Tables are recognized as such because at least three legs support a plane surface in a way that provides the utility factors normally ascribed to a table. It makes no difference whether the shape of the surface is round, square, or hexagonal, or whether the legs are carved, metal, or six in number; if they are arranged in a certain way, we recognize the whole as a table. A slightly more complex example of a system is an automobile. The idea is the same—the parts are arranged and function in a manner that produces a unified whole.

Thought processes are events that can be reduced to writing and arranged in logical patterns. As a result, there are philosophical systems, economic systems, and number systems. Other events that are described as systems are the relationships between people; e.g., social systems, governmental systems, and legal systems.

A still more complex example of a system incorporates features that permit the system to modify its normal way of functioning so that the system adapts to changes as they occur in any of its parts (sometimes called subsystems) or to changes that occur in the larger external environment in which the system operates. Such systems are self-correcting and are called *servo systems*. The corrective action of a servo system is dependent upon the existence of one or more "feedback loops" that provide contact with the external environment or between the component subsystems. The thermostatically controlled household furnace is an example of a simple servo system. The wall thermostat is the feedback loop (and a subsystem) that maintains contact with the external environment (the temperature of the room), and the thermostat in the plenum chamber is the feedback loop (also a subsystem) that prevents the entire system from overheating.

Management and the Systems Concept

The management process occurs within an organizational system. Any organization—whether it be a business firm or a religious, educational, or social institution—is in turn a part of a larger socioeconomic system. As yet there is no single systems category that adequately describes a business firm. To the economist the firm is an economic system, but a treasurer or financial analyst may regard the firm as a system of "cash flow." To others a company is best described as a social system, a production system, or an information-decision-making system. There is evidence to support each point of view.

Regarding a company as a system has several far-reaching implications. For the major executives of a company it means that larger systems must be identified and understood and that the relationships of their company to these larger systems must be defined. Usually such recognition and definition lead to the conclusion that any one firm is, in effect, a subsystem. The company itself is composed of many subsystems with each subsystem having its own goals and objectives. Further, each subsystem within a company is part of a larger external system, not necessarily the same system defined by the major executives. For the chief executive the primary external system may be the government, but the head of the industrial relations department is more closely tied to union organizations as an external system. The sales manager may consider his external systems environment the purchasing departments of the company's customers. The systems concept stresses the dynamic nature of an organization and prevents the manager from viewing his job as one of managing static, isolated elements of the organization.[3]

The four functions of the management process may be considered a system, and each of the functions—planning, organizing, directing, and controlling—may be regarded as a separate subsystem. The functions are interrelated, and the effectiveness of any one managerial function is dependent upon the execution of the other three functions. Planning requires information from the activities of organizing, directing, and controlling, and when plans are developed they may result in change in the organization structure; those who direct the organization must be aware of plans, and provisions must be made for proper controls to determine whether or not these plans are properly executed. Similarly, changes in organization structure may call for a modification of plans, new tasks for those who direct the organization, and the modification of controls to fit the requirements of the new organization.

Each function is a subsystem dependent upon a constant feedback of information from internal and external sources. Planning requires close communication with the external environment and continuous information concerning the capabilities of the organization and the potentialities of control systems so that the feasibility of plans may be determined. The organizing function needs information descriptive of present and future manpower requirements and must interpret this information in the light of projected plans. The resultant organization

---

[3] Seymour Tilles, "The Manager's Job: A Systems Approach," *Harvard Business Review,* Vol. XXXXI (January-February, 1963), pp. 73-81. Mr. Tilles defines the manager's job as one of managing systems. He must define the company as a system, establish system objectives, create formal subsystems, and integrate all subsystems.

must also provide a basis for a sound control system. The same interchange of information is needed for the functions of directing and controlling.

The effectiveness of the management process is not dependent upon success in the performance of any single managerial functional area, such as finance, sales, or production. Rather, the success of managerial action is dependent upon achieving a balanced interrelationship between the functions of the process of management and the attainment of stated goals in each of the major functional areas.[4]

ABOUT THIS BOOK

An introductory course to the study of management is by its very nature a survey course drawing data and observations from many sources and disciplines. Thus, some may term the approach of this book eclectic. At the same time, the approach is integrative and may be classed as a modern approach in that the systems concept is utilized in the analysis of certain aspects of the process of management. Utilization of the systems concept in the study of management does not call for a radically new organization of content. An analogy from the study of medicine shows why a marked departure from the traditional content pattern of management texts is unnecessary.

We no longer question the conclusion that the human organism is a system composed of many interrelated subsystems. In our everyday speech we refer to the skeletal system, the circulatory system, and the central nervous system. Yet modern textbooks of medicine reveal a judicious blending of the use of the term *system* and the study of special systems with traditionally recognized disease processes. For example, some of the major topics discussed in one outstanding medical textbook are the infectious diseases, diseases of allergy, diseases of the skin, diseases of the bronchopulmonary system, diseases of the cardiovascular system, and diseases of the kidneys.[5]

The systems concept can be applied in the same way to a textbook of management. Where pertinent, systems theory is presented and discussed so that a concept of the management process as a system gradually unfolds.

---

[4] Ernest C. Miller, *Objectives and Standards: An Approach to Planning and Control* (New York: American Management Association, AMA Research Study 74, 1966). See pages 9-21 for a discussion of the management process and an interpretation of the management process as a system.

[5] Paul B. Beeson and Walsh McDermott, *Textbook of Medicine*, 13th ed. (Philadelphia: W. B. Saunders Company, 1971).

Although the concepts of management are applicable to the management of religious, social, charitable, and educational groups, our primary concern is with the management of business enterprises, in a political climate relatively free of governmental controls. Consequently, the illustrative material of the text and the case problems are based upon situations that occur in business organizations. Each chapter of this book, except the last one, begins and ends with a case problem, a descriptive statement of a business situation.

Case problems portray an incident or a brief series of related incidents, in contrast to the comprehensive case or case study that generally describes most of the events that occur in a company or other form of organization over a relatively long period of time. The difference between a case problem and a comprehensive case is one of degree, not of kind. Case problems are used as an integral part of this textbook for two reasons. First, case problems are a way of making the text more meaningful; and second, they provide a means of improving one's ability to solve business problems.

Case problems make the information presented in the text more meaningful by relating that information to a specific business situation. As a result, the student has before him an example that shows how the concepts of the text can be transformed from an abstract statement to a practical situation. The abstract concepts of management are more readily remembered when they are described in the context of an easily remembered business experience. Case problems also make the text more meaningful by offering an opportunity to apply management concepts and principles as tools in the solution of specific business problems —another method of facilitating learning. In addition, case problems simulate a real business situation and provide the basis for improving one's skill in problem solving—a requisite for the successful manager. Thus it is necessary to learn how to analyze a case problem.

THE ANALYSIS OF CASE PROBLEMS

Although there is no one way of analyzing a case problem, the following suggestions have proven to be of value in developing skill in the analysis of cases. Before reading the case in its entirety, note the title of the chapter and the title of the case. The title of the chapter tells you what the chapter is about. For example, the title of Chapter 1, "Management Defined," should convey to you that the chapter deals with the definition of management. Similarly, the title of Chapter 2, "The Development of Management Concepts," lets you know that the chapter is concerned with the historical development of management. Since the case problems in this textbook are an integral part of the chapter in which they appear, identifying the subject matter of the chapter often reveals the central theme of the case.

Second, the title of the case itself is of significance. Unlike many case problems, the name of the company in which the incidents described in the case occurred is not used as the title of the case. Instead, the title is a descriptive phrase related to the central theme of the case. Thus, the title of Case Problem 1-A, A Problem in Management Definition, informs you immediately that the problem is one of defining management. The title of Case Problem 2-A, Symptoms or Causes?, infers that the problem is one of differentiating between symptoms and causes. Since the case problem is a part of the chapter concerned with the presentation of the historical development of management thought, one might reasonably expect the solution to lie within the framework presented in the historical development of management concepts.

Reading the Case

After noting the clues offered by the titles of the chapter and of the case, read the problems at the end of the case so you will know what is expected. Then read the entire case rapidly to gain a first impression of the total situation. Next, a careful reading and a detailed analysis are necessary.

Knowledge of the structure of case problems is helpful in the detailed analysis of the case. Usually the first and second paragraphs are a statement of the setting in which the incidents described in the case occur. In these paragraphs the central characters of the case are introduced, the name of the company is given, and if relevant the product or services and the geographical location are mentioned. Information required for the definition and solution of the problem is presented in differing ways. Sometimes data are presented in the form of exhibits at the end of the case. Exhibits may be financial statements, organization charts, tables, or similar summaries designed to present a large amount of information in concise form. However, in most of the case problems the relevant facts of the situation are presented in the form of discussions among the central characters of the case. Thus, the titles of the persons described are significant since the title of the position one holds in a company indicates the role that may be expected. For instance, the title of president or general manager indicates that the major functions, and consequently the role that may be expected, are those of planning and coordinating. On the other hand, a title that designates a person as being in charge of one of the functional areas, such as finance, sales, production, or personnel, indicates that that person is responsible for a given function and may be expected to have that specific function as his major concern—sometimes to the detriment of other functions and to the achievement of overall organizational objectives.

There will be times, even after having read the case thoroughly, when you will say that more information is needed to define the problem and develop a solution. Admittedly, limitations of time and space require that the situation be described in broad strokes and rarely does a student reading a case have at his disposal the same information possessed by a manager of a company. Yet, every effort has been made to provide all the information needed for the definition and solution of the problem. All too often the criticism that a case does not contain sufficient information may become an automatic excuse for not coming to grips with the problem. It must be remembered that in practice the executive rarely has all the information that he would like to have prior to making a decision, but the exigencies of the situation require a decision despite the incompleteness of the information upon which that decision is based.

Analyzing the Case

The following specific steps aid in the systematic analysis of a case.

1. State the Problem. After reading the case thoroughly and after studying the problems at the end of the case, write a statement of the problem—what is the case about, what is there to be done, what action has to be taken, or what questions have to be answered. It may be necessary to state several problems; and, if this is required, you must then decide which of the problems is the most important. For example, in the last paragraph of Case Problem 1-A a request is made of the personnel director that he prepare a report indicating the name of the proposed management club, a definition of who is eligible to join the club, and a statement of the objectives of the club. Thus, there are three problems: title, membership, and purpose. Which of these is the most important? In this instance the last item is the most significant since the objectives, or the purpose, of a club may well determine the title and the membership of the club. The right answer to the wrong problem is of little value.

2. Collect Data. In most instances the data required for the definition and solution of the problem are contained in the case. Marginal notes and underlining are helpful in identifying and summarizing relevant data. Occasionally it may be necessary to prepare a summary on a separate sheet of paper.

3. Analyze Data. In order to analyze and evaluate effectively the data presented in the case, the data must be arranged in a systematic manner. Figure 14-5, Checklist of Organizational Effectiveness (page 415), and the accompanying discussion, "Evaluating Organizational Effectiveness," (pages 414 to 419), present one way of arranging such information. Read this section of the text *now*. Even though you are not expected to be thoroughly familiar with all the terms and concepts used in the discussion, there is much that you can understand and apply. Note that many problems can be categorized within one of eight problem areas, ranging from overall planning to provisions for control. Reviewing the checklist on the right-hand side of Figure 14-5 provides a quick way of identifying problem areas.

4. Formulate Tentative Solutions. It is well to develop the habit of regarding initial solutions as tentative. By so doing the danger of assuming a rigid position is minimized and at the same time the door is left open for other, and sometimes better, solutions. In Case Problem 1-A there are four possible solutions in regard to membership—all persons whose names appear on the published organization chart, all who have supervisory responsibility, all exempt personnel, and all who have earnings greater than $500 per month. The range of objectives and the proposed names of the club should also be regarded as tentative. All tentative solutions available should be given due consideration.

5. Select a Recommended Solution. From the list of tentative solutions, a single solution has to be selected. The final solution should offer the best answer to the problem as stated in Step No. 1, and it should be based upon the data collected in Step No. 2. However, of greatest importance in the selection of a recommended solution is the extent to which that solution is capable of execution. Ultimately solutions to business problems require the commitment of company resources if they are to be executed.

Preparing Written Reports

When a student prepares a written report for a case problem, the report should be regarded as a project assigned by an employer rather than a class assignment. As a task to be performed as part of your job, the report will have its effect upon pay and advancement within the company. The mechanical aspects of the report—spelling, punctuation, neatness, and grammatical style—should be above reproach; yet the format of the report may vary considerably. It may take the form of a memo as requested in Case Problem 1-A. If so, the memo should indicate clearly the person to whom it is directed, its origin (including the name and title of the author of the memo), and the subject of the report. The body of the report is then presented in narrative form. When reports exceed one or two pages in length, it is well to present the conclusions or recommendations on the first page, with the body of the report containing the substantiating data from which the conclusions were drawn.

Case Problem 1-B [6] affords an opportunity to apply the techniques of analysis described above. The title of the case, Anatomy of a Fall, indicates that all did not go well with this particular management. Your task, with the advantages often inherent in hindsight, is to determine why.

CASE PROBLEM
1-B

ANATOMY OF
A FALL

LONDON—Sir David Huddie, it turns out, probably earned Britain's costliest knighthood.

In 1968 Sir David was knighted for "services to export"—that is, for landing Rolls-Royce the big contract to supply Lockheed Aircraft Corp. with engines for its TriStar airliner. At the time the feat was hailed as a triumph for Britain and as proof that the American competition could be outfoxed and underbid on its home ground. Other British industries were urged by the government to learn a lesson from Rolls-Royce and expand exports.

The British "victory" in 1968 has proved disastrous. In less than three years the contract has directly produced these results:

—The collapse of Rolls-Royce Ltd., Britain's fourth largest employer and an automobile and aircraft-engine concern whose name has been a synonym for prestige, superb quality and British pride.

---

[6] Felix Kessler, "Anatomy of a Fall," *The Wall Street Journal,* Vol. XLVII, No. 26 (February 8, 1971), pp. 1, 11. Mr. Kessler is a staff reporter for *The Wall Street Journal.*

—A crisis for Britain's entire aerospace industry. Perhaps 100 contractors, suppliers and other concerns linked with Rolls-Royce were jeopardized when the big company went into receivership last week because it couldn't fulfill the Lockheed engine contract.

—A threat to Lockheed, already saddled with the loss of $200 million on the C5A military-transport contract and now, because of Rolls-Royce's collapse, forced to absorb the probable loss of millions of dollars more.

WORKERS FACE LOSS OF JOBS

Britain hastily began taking steps to nationalize certain divisions of Rolls-Royce deemed necessary to protect the country's vital interests. But up to 20,000 workers at Rolls-Royce may still lose their jobs and perhaps that many more employees at other British companies. And, with Rolls-Royce in part nationalized, creditors like Lockheed and stockholders may recoup little from the bankruptcy proceedings.

Not least important, relations between Britain and the U.S. haven't benefited from what Lockheed described as the "sudden withdrawal" of the Tory government's financial aid for Rolls-Royce.

Britain's biggest bankruptcy proceeding in decades has produced a political, economic and psychological depression as profound as the devaluation of the pound sterling in 1967. Leaders of both the Labor and Conservative Parties describe the failure as a national tragedy, a disaster and a nightmare.

"It's causing shock waves here like the Penn Central did in the U.S.," an American executive says. "Everyone seems to be wondering what else will go."

Some Britons worry that the country's reputation has been tarnished throughout the world. They expect British industries and products to suffer as a result. Others say Britain will have to scale down its efforts from the "euphoria" of world competition.

PRESTIGE vs. PROFITS

"This proves there's a big difference between prestige and profits," says Lord Thomas, former chairman of British Overseas Airways Corp., one of Rolls-Royce's biggest customers. In Rolls-Royce's collapse

Lord Thomas sees "this lesson for government and business—not to be so avidly concerned with exports as to sacrifice profits."

The full dimensions of the collapse won't be known for some time. And the possibility remains that U.S. financing will be found for Rolls-Royce to rescue the engines for Lockheed's civilian airliner. But the California company, which had been scheduled to receive its engines next November, wouldn't get them for at least an extra year. Such a delay could prompt some airlines to switch purchases from the Lockheed TriStar to the rival McDonnell Douglas DC10.

At Rolls-Royce's aircraft-engine plant in Derby, a despondent worker wonders how the company whose car was everybody's status symbol could so quickly "be headed for the scrap heap." Many others here and in the U.S. are asking the same question. The answer lies in a blend of mismanagement, financial miscalculations and overambitious salesmanship—in short, the Lockheed contract.

THE STORY OF A FIASCO

Things began going wrong at Rolls-Royce from the time it decided in 1966 to open a campaign for the Lockheed contract on what a British industry leader says was an "unprecedented" scale. The effort was lavish by any standards. Over an 18-month period, Rolls-Royce officials spent more than $200,000 in transatlantic air fares alone. David Huddie, the managing director of the aero-engine division, moved his operations to the U.S. and personally directed the 20 Rolls-Royce technical and sales experts in their quest for the contract.

Rolls-Royce is estimated to have spent $1 million just compaigning for the engine contract against its rivals—General Electric Co. and the Pratt & Whitney division of United Aircraft Corp. But it all seemed worthwhile when in March 1968 it was announced that Rolls-Royce had won. It would develop an engine that would be more powerful, more efficient, quieter, lighter and—most important—cheaper than anything offered by American rivals.

The engine was called the RB211. Rolls-Royce predicted that its cumulative sales would in time total the equivalent of $2.4 billion. And Britain's government encouraged Rolls-Royce. Of the $156 million the company estimated as the cost of engine development, the government supplied $105 million in financing.

Aided by hindsight, a British aviation-industry official says the promises made by Rolls-Royce in obtaining the 400-page RB211 contract were "highly unusual" at best. The company, he says, committed itself to "design and produce a revolutionary new engine under a tight time schedule and at a very low price." He observes that under the contract Rolls-Royce now would be subject to $120 million in penalties for late delivery.

Others say Rolls-Royce wasn't helped by the fact that its top management—from Chairman Sir Denning Pearson to Sir David Huddie—consisted almost entirely of engineers. Every time the engineers were confronted with figures that showed earlier cost estimates were wrong, they tended to claim the new figures were incorrect, according to a director appointed to the Rolls-Royce board last year.

But the RB211 ran into more than just cost problems, the critics say. Unlike practically every other tough engineering problem that had confronted Rolls-Royce in its 65-year history, this basic engine design still hasn't been solved. Rolls-Royce management was disturbed by the engineering failure perhaps even more than its financial troubles.

Plans called for the use of a new material—lightweight carbon fiber—for the RB211's fan blades. This was to enable the large engine to conserve considerable weight, consume less fuel, operate at high temperatures and still develop the needed thrust of 40,000 pounds. That is more than double the 18,000 pounds of thrust of each Boeing 707-321B engine and is more powerful even than the 35,000 pounds of thrust of the supersonic Anglo-French Concorde's jet engine.

ABANDONING A NEW MATERIAL

But, after many months of development and after numerous announcements that it had achieved new technical breakthroughs, Rolls-Royce gave up on carbon fiber. The blades couldn't meet stress requirements; they weren't strong enough to absorb birds sucked into the seven-foot-diameter engines. Rolls-Royce had to design another engine using titanium blades—adding to the cost and the weight and cutting down on fuel efficiency.

In a vague announcement by the company that it was still six months to a year from production, there still wasn't any assurance that the engines would meet contract specifications. "It goes to show that you can't gamble all your eggs on one product, especially not a new one," says the president of a U.S. company's international operations.

Other aerospace companies, of course, have also suffered through similar unhappy fates. The F-111 and the C5A are aviation-industry projects that won't be remembered with joy in the U.S. "In aerospace, it's hard to know always what you're getting into," one U.S. official says. "You sometimes have to take a flyer. And you only hear about your failures—not the successful gambles that paid off."

But British industry leaders are shocked at the Rolls-Royce situation. Some say Rolls-Royce should have known that its engine bid was far underpriced. An engine that Rolls-Royce had worked on 10 years earlier with 10,000 pounds of thrust cost $72 million to develop. Anyone with a slide rule should be able to figure that a new engine four times more powerful would cost more than twice as much to develop, one source says.

TOP OFFICIALS RESIGN

Last November, after months of optimism, the scope of the failure began to emerge. Rolls-Royce announced that its development costs had risen from $156 million to $344 million. Both the chairman, Sir Denning Pearson, and Sir David Huddie resigned. And a big rescue operation was undertaken by the government and London banks.

And for almost the first time in its history, Rolls-Royce began a cost-cutting campaign; one of the first savings was $1.4 million in annual traveling expenses. But even after the shakeup, veteran Rolls-Royce executives couldn't understand the company's position. One was recently dismayed when his request for an additional $18 million in engine test beds was rejected. "After all," he observed, "what was 7.5 million more pounds?"

Ironically, Rolls-Royce owes its existence to the noise and inefficiency of another engine—that in the second-hand car of Henry Royce. In 1903 he decided he could make a better car and soon began proving it. In 1906 he and a wealthy racing-car driver named Charles S. Rolls became partners in a car factory and produced their first auto, the Silver Ghost.

Rolls-Royce cars over the years have suggested the supernatural in their names—Silver Cloud, Silver Wraith, Silver Shadow and Phantom. And the company's most famous advertisement claimed that at 60 m.p.h. the loudest noise to intrude on a passenger was the ticking of the car's clock.

Rolls-Royce called its first Silver Ghost "the best car in the world." The company hasn't abandoned its modesty since, although some car buffs think the most superlative feature of the Rolls-Royce is its price of $21,000. The company's Bentley cost several hundred dollars less.

RENOWNED BUT NOT POPULAR

But while Rolls-Royce cars are renowned the world over, only about 2,000 are sold annually. A Rolls-Royce official estimates that the auto division, though profitable, probably contributes no more than 5% to total revenue.

Even the car division, which some British and foreign manufacturers are already seeking to buy, is confronted with the loss of confidence that surrounds Rolls-Royce. The British Leyland Motor Corp. said it would stop supplying bodies to Rolls-Royce until the situation is clarified.

Many people still can't understand how an aircraft engine could cause the collapse of the company that boasts that its "engines have been chosen by more than 200 airlines and 70 armed services around the world." Rolls-Royce engines powered the World War II Spitfire, and at that time the company was already working on experimental jets.

Charles Rolls was himself an aviation enthusiast who flew with Wilbur Wright. He became the first Englishman to die in an air crash. That was in 1910, five years before the company began making aircraft engines.

Of course, Rolls-Royce's collapse isn't bad news for everyone. The French aviation industry, a member of the European airbus consortium, may have lost a competitor—and gained a partner. Frederick Corfield, the Conservative minister of aviation supply, said a cooperative Anglo-French aircraft-engine venture might be sought after Rolls-Royce is nationalized. And the British government has given assurances that the Concorde will receive its Rolls-Royce engines as promised.

GOVERNMENT BACKS DOWN

But the government has also made clear that it won't back the $144 million in additional financing that was pledged to Rolls-Royce last November. Mr. Corfield said that "hundreds of millions of pounds" were required to keep Rolls-Royce afloat, including $400 million just for the Lockheed engine.

Some observers think that the government's withholding of financing now is part of international maneuver designed to bring about a renegotiation of the Lockheed contract and produce American funds for the RB211. Others say that after government nationalization proceedings begin this week in Parliament, Rolls-Royce should continue to play a major role in world aviation.

The RB211 is the "workhorse aero-engine of the future," says Anthony Wedgwood Benn, the former Labor government minister who played a leading role in negotiating the Rolls-Royce contract. Mr. Wedgwood Benn, now an opposition member of Parliament, thinks Britain must see that a nationalized Rolls-Royce "gets the backing it needs to restore the world's confidence— and our own as well."

Some Britons even believe that after the current psychological depression has lifted, beneficial effects will stem from the collapse. Lord Thomas, the former BOAC chairman, says: "We're a very resilient people. We tend to learn from very tough lessons."

PROBLEMS

1. What is the primary cause of the difficulties of Rolls-Royce expressed in terms of the management process?
2. What type of experience did Rolls-Royce have that might have led the company to believe that it had underplaced its bid on the RB211? How do you interpret this past experience?

3. Evaluate the plan of nationalizing Rolls-Royce as a
solution to its problems.

Chapter Questions for Study and Discussion

1. Should a marked decline or a sharp increase in company earnings always
be attributed to the management of that company?
2. What connotations are frequently attached to the word "management"?
Are any of these connotations contradictory?
3. What are the four major functions of management? Give an example
of each. Which of these functions, in your opinion, is the most important
in each of the following types of business: an oil pipeline transmission
company, a door-to-door sales organization such as the Fuller Brush
Company, a large retail discount store, and a complex multiproduct
company such as General Motors?
4. Differentiate between an owner and a manager. Give an example of a
manager who is also an owner and an example illustrating the separation of ownership and management.
5. Do you agree with the statement made in the text that it would be undesirable to require a prescribed course of study as a requisite for a
management position? Why?
6. What is meant by the phrase "universality of management"?
7. What is the definition of management given in the text? What are the
three major factors included in the definition of management? Develop
a series of definitions using only two factors for each definition. Evaluate
each definition thus developed in respect to its completeness.
8. Many analogies have been drawn between a business organization and
an athletic team. Examples of this analogy are reflected in such phrases
as "get on the team" and "let's pull together." In what respects are the
jobs of a head football coach and the president of a company similar?
How do their jobs differ?
9. The thermostatically controlled household furnace is cited as an example
of a servo system. Describe several other familiar servo systems, and
explain why each is a servo system.
10. Considering each of the functions of management as a system, describe
a specific change in the control system that might occur and describe
the effect of this change on each of the other functions. Be specific in
your descriptions. Give specific examples of changes in planning, organizing, and methods of directing. Show how changes in any one of these
functions affect the other three.

CHAPTER 2

Development of Management Concepts

It was six o'clock in the evening on the last Friday in April as Marsh Saunders sat at his desk organizing the impressions he had gained during his first month as plant manager for Excellent Foods, Inc. Though he had been a plant manager for Excellent Foods for more than five years, this was the first time he had managed a can manufacturing plant for the company; his previous experience had been in food processing plants. He jotted down a list of his major observations on a sheet of paper. Following each "symptom" he listed possible causes. The following is a copy of his notes with the "causes" in italics.

1. Production—in all operating departments—assembly, shipping, lithography, and press room—operating in the red as measured by engineered standards. Losses range from —20% to —5%; average monthly loss for plant is —15%.

   Machines not properly maintained. Personnel not capable, need more training. Applies to all four departments.

2. Labor relations—poor.

   Every effort to increase efficiency called a speedup. Too many grievances, 150 last year. (Is this the cause of Symptom No. 1, or is it the result of poor performance?)

3. Quality—very poor, many complaints.

   Operating personnel and supervisors don't seem to care. Improperly maintained and poorly adjusted equipment.

4. Housekeeping—lousy.

29

Entire plant dirty with nothing ever in its right place. Machine shop has no idea of spare parts inventory.

5. Quality of supervision—probably technically competent as they all came up from the ranks. Seem to be beat down, no spirit, poor human relations in all departments.

Do not consider themselves a part of the management team. Afraid to do anything, seem fearful of losing job. Would a guarantee of no personnel changes for six months be a good move?

6. Manager's staff—all heads of staff departments (industrial, engineering, personnel, purchasing, quality control, production control, and accounting) have been in their respective jobs for at least three years. No one willing to exercise authority or take responsibility—all seem mediocre in ability.

Is poor performance of this group due to lack of native ability or would additional training help? Should training be in respective technical fields or general management? Though mediocre, these people know the organization.

7. Low morale at all levels from the hourly production workers, through the clerical help, to supervision and staff.

The plant seems to lack a common purpose or goal. An esprit de corps is completely lacking.

As he looked at this list, Mr. Saunders wondered if Symptom No. 7, poor morale, should not be listed as the number one problem in place of low production. He knew that the list was incomplete and that another 10 to 15 items could be added without much difficulty. He also knew that before he could start the much needed management training program he envisioned, he would have to group his problems, or symptoms, into several major areas.

PROBLEMS

1. Assume that you are Mr. Saunders. How would you group the seven symptoms so that a training program could be directed toward three major subject matter areas?
2. Do you think that the words "symptoms" and "causes" are better choices than "problems" and "solutions"? Why?
3. In his notes on the probable causes for Symptoms No. 2 and No. 5, Mr. Saunders raised several questions. How would you answer these questions?
4. Is there any significance in the fact that this is the first can plant that Mr. Saunders has managed?

As you read this chapter, you will discover that the
problems confronting Mr. Saunders are neither new nor
unique to his plant; they are as old as management itself.

There is considerable evidence that effective management of complex social groups has existed for well over 6,000 years. The early
civilizations of the Egyptians, the Greeks, and the Roman Empire
could not have existed for centuries had there not been well-developed
administrative organizations and procedures. Even before these civilizations, there is reason to believe that considerable thought and effort
had been expended on studying and formulating the management
process.

One of the earliest analytical statements of management concepts
appears in the Bible, Exodus 18:13-26. This passage tells how Jethro,
Moses' father-in-law, observed Moses spending an entire day listening
to the complaints and problems of his people. Following this observation, Jethro told Moses that what he was doing was too much for one
man and suggested specific steps that should be taken to relieve him
of his burden. His first recommendation was that "ordinances and laws"
should be taught to the people. The modern counterpart of this advice
is an organization's policy statement. Secondly, he recommended that
leaders be selected and assigned "to be rulers of thousands, and rulers
of hundreds, and rulers of fifties, and rulers of ten." The process of
appointing leaders, each of whom is responsible for a given number of
subordinates, is referred to as delegation of authority. Jethro's third
point, that these rulers should administer all routine matters and
should bring to Moses only the important questions, forms the basis for
a well-known control procedure. This procedure of attending to the
exception that does not conform to expected results is known as the
principle of the exception and is discussed in Chapter 20.

The recounting of Jethro's advice to Moses illustrates the fact that
interest in management as a process existed in antiquity. However, the
systematic study and the development of the formal literature of management appears at a much later date, and can be divided conveniently
into four separate approaches. The first of these approaches emphasizes
management and its relationship to the *production* process. The group
of managers and students who follow this approach believe that managers should direct their attention and energy to increasing the efficiency
of the production process. A second approach to the problems of
management consists of those writings that emphasize the *administration*

of the entire organization. Third, there are those who emphasize the importance of establishing sound practices of *human relations* as a means of improving the management process. Those who stress the importance of human relations are concerned with the human element in management. This point of view is convincing for there are many instances where improved relationships between management and the workers and among the workers themselves have solved the problems of a particular company. As might be expected, there are many instances where conflict arises between those who regard a company's problems as primarily questions to be resolved through the application of practices intended to improve human relations and those who believe that the company's problems are to be solved by increased efficiency in the production process. Finally, there are several contemporary approaches to the study of management that emphasize either the social system, the decision making process, the application of quantitative methods, or the systems approach to the study of management. These may be grouped together as *modern* approaches to the study of management.

These four approaches to the study of management are discussed in the following order:

1. A discussion of some of the work that emphasizes production.
2. A summary of the importance of administration.
3. A review of some major writings in the human relations field.
4. Modern approaches to the study of management.

THE EMPHASIS UPON PRODUCTION

The industrial revolution with its development and utilization of semi-automatic and automatic machinery made possible the mass production of goods and also created the modern industrial organization. These new organizations with their vast potential for production were little understood and the need for knowledge about the management of such organizations soon became apparent. It is not surprising that the first approach to the study of management emphasized the dominant characteristics of these new industrial organizations—production. The contributions of Charles Babbage and Frederick Winslow Taylor, two pioneers in the study of the production function, are examined.

Charles Babbage

Charles Babbage laid the groundwork for much of the work that later became known as "scientific management." A project which

he worked on throughout his life and, unfortunately, was never successful in fully developing was the "Difference Engine," an invention considered to be the forerunner of our modern data processing equipment.
His interest about production problems resulted in two contributions
that are as valid today as when they were first presented. The first contribution stresses the importance of dividing and assigning labor on the
basis of skill. The second contribution provides a means of determining
the feasibility of replacing manual operations with automatic machinery.

Division of Labor. In 1832, in his "On the Economy of Machinery
and Manufactures," [1] Babbage presented a keen analysis of the alternative methods then available in making pins. In his analysis of making
pins by hand, he offers convincing and complete data showing that a
division of labor on the basis of skill is an economic necessity. He cites
as advantages of dividing labor by its level of skill the fact that the
learning time is reduced, since any one worker has to learn only one
skill rather than all. Secondly, in the actual process of manufacturing,
there is a saving because less time is lost as the result of changing from
one set of skills to another. He also points out that a high degree of
precision can be acquired by each workman, for he is learning only
one task and repeating it many times. In addition, since the job is
broken down into its component parts on a basis of the skills required,
there is the obvious possibility of developing specialized tools and equipment to further aid the process. All of these observations result in the
conclusion that dividing a job into its component levels of skill enables
the manufacturer to acquire and pay for only the exact amount of skill
required for each operation.

Manual vs. Automatic Operations. Following his discussion on the
art of making pins by hand, Babbage then mentions briefly a new
(remember, 1832) American process of making pins by machine. He
suggests several questions, the answers to which determine whether or
not the introduction of machine methods is desirable:

1. To what defects pins so made (i.e., by machine) are liable?
2. What advantages they possess over those made in the usual way?
3. What is the prime cost of a machine for making them?
4. What is the expense of keeping it in repair?
5. What is the expense of moving it and attending to it? [2]

---

[1] Charles Babbage, *On the Economy of Machinery and Manufactures* (Philadelphia: Carey and Lea, 1832), Chap. 17, pp. 121-40, "On the Division of Labour"
reprinted in H. F. Merrill (ed.) *Classics in Management,* (New York: American
Management Association, 1960), pp. 29-44.
[2] H. F. Merrill, *ibid.,* p. 43.

These questions are as important today as they were when originally asked by Babbage more than 100 years ago in that they raise
questions concerning quality, the original cost of the machine, and the
cost of operation including manpower and maintenance. Much of
management's effort is directed toward obtaining an answer to these
questions.

Frederick Winslow Taylor

By far the ablest exponent of the probing, analytical attitude
expressed by Babbage was Frederick W. Taylor, commonly regarded
as the father of scientific management. All of you have without
doubt heard the phrase "scientific management" before reading it
in this book, yet how many of you can offer a satisfactory definition
of the phrase? Let us approach the problem of defining scientific management by stating what scientific management is not. There is no
better source than the words of Taylor himself.

> Scientific management is not any efficiency device, nor a device
> of any kind for securing efficiency; nor is it any branch or group of
> efficiency devices. It is not a new system of figuring costs; it is not a
> new scheme of paying men; it is not a piecework system; it is not a
> bonus system; it is not a premium system; it is no scheme for paying
> men; it is not holding a stopwatch on a man and writing things down
> about him; it is not time study; it is not motion study nor an analysis
> of the movements of men; it is not the printing and ruling and unload-
> ing of a ton or two of blanks on a set of men and saying, "Here's your
> system; go use it." It is not divided foremanship or functional
> foremanship; it is not any of the devices which the average man calls
> to mind when scientific management is spoken of. The average man
> thinks of one or more of these things when he hears the words "scien-
> tific management" mentioned, but scientific management is not any one
> of these devices. I am not sneering at cost-keeping systems, at time
> study, at functional foremanship, nor at any new and improved scheme
> of paying men, not at any efficiency devices, if they are really devices
> that make for efficiency. I believe in them; but what I am emphasizing
> is that these devices in whole or in part are not scientific management,
> they are useful adjuncts to scientific management, so are they also useful
> adjuncts of other systems of management.[3]

---

[3] H. F. Merrill, *ibid.,* p. 77. The above passage is an exerpt from testimony of
Frederick W. Taylor at hearings before the Special Committee of the House of Representatives to Investigate the Taylor and Other Systems of Shop Management, January
25, 1912, p. 1387.

The list of what scientific management is not is rather complete, but if it is not any of these techniques, all of which in some form or other have been designed to render the management of a shop more efficient, then what is it? Other questions that come to mind at this time refer specifically to the phrase "scientific management." Who coined the phrase and why was it applied to the systems developed and espoused by Taylor? And what did Taylor do that resulted in his testifying before a special committee of the House of Representatives? The answers to these questions shed much light upon some of the problems still facing management today.

Scientific Management—A Mental Revolution. Consider first the words "scientific management," which to some epitomize the best of our modern industrial society, and to others, the undesirable aspects of the same. The name was not an accident; it was the result of a deliberate choice made during a meeting held in the apartment of one of Taylor's friends and associates, H. L. Gantt, a short time before the congressional hearings began. Other names were considered, such as the Taylor system, functional management, and shop management; but the group decided that henceforth, and particularly during the hearings, the system developed and typified by Taylor's work would be referred to as scientific management.

Taylor, after stating what scientific management was not, went on to state clearly the main characteristic of scientific management. To him, "a complete mental revolution" was necessary for scientific management to come into being. Further, and this is important because it points up the fact that Taylor was far more than a capable technician, this mental revolution must occur in the *workman's* mind as well as in the mind of management. Taylor's analysis of industrial problems existing between management and labor concluded that, to a large extent, it was an argument over the division of the surplus created by industry. Indeed, this still remains one of the major issues in current collective bargaining. The first part of the mental revolution, according to Taylor, is that both parties stop quarreling about how the surplus should be divided and unite to increase the size of the surplus so that the need for hairsplitting in this area becomes less acute.

The second phase of the mental revolution is that the scientific method must be the sole basis for obtaining information to determine the proper procedure to be used in performance of each job and to establish the proper level of output per man-hour. It is the second phase of scientific management that has caused most of the criticism of the Taylor system. The reason is that the application of the scientific method requires so much detailed work and time that the original goal of increasing the surplus is never realized. An example of the extensive work necessary in some areas to determine the scientific basis for the performance of an operation is found in the series of experiments conducted by Taylor extending over a 26-year period to determine the best methods of machining or cutting metals. In the process, high-speed tool steels were developed, and the science of cutting metals was broken down into 12 interrelated variables. These interrelationships were expressed mathematically by formulas, and slide rules were developed so that the optimum conditions for any given task could be computed. It is no wonder that a person becoming immersed in the mathematical analysis of production problems loses sight of the first great mental revolution required; namely, a change in attitude.

The Need for Scientific Management. Scientific management was developed to solve two major problems: to increase the output of the average worker and to improve the efficiency of management. To a degree, increasing the productivity of the average worker is the same problem that challenged Elton Mayo, an able exponent of the human relations approach, at a later date. But the approaches used by each of these men were different. Mayo sought the answer in terms of the social forces that affect the worker as a member of a group while Taylor considered each worker as a separate economic man motivated by financial needs.

Taylor believed that the basis of a worker's tendency to restrict output was his fear of displacement, not too unlike the fear expressed in some quarters today in regard to automation. He suggested two methods of minimizing the fear of displacement expressed by the workmen. One approach was to educate the worker to understand that his economic salvation lay in producing more at a lower cost. The other method was to prove to the worker the effectiveness of this argument by placing him on a piecework system and thereby permitting him to earn more.

Taylor's Principles of Management. The second major problem, improving the efficiency of management, was to be solved through the application of Taylor's four principles of management. The first of these principles urged a gathering, analysis, and codification of all "rule-of-thumb" data existing in the business. The second principle urged careful selection and a thorough study of the workman so that he may be developed to his maximum capabilities. Third, was the persuasive principle of educating, or more properly "inspiring," men to use the scientific principles derived from the careful analysis of all data and methods used in each job. Lastly, he urged that management organize in such a manner that it could properly manage and carry out its duties.

Underlying the whole approach of scientific management is the belief that there is a one best way of doing everything, whether it be using a shovel or making a complex cut on a piece of metal. There was much resistance to the methods espoused by Taylor. It was the strike at the Watertown Arsenal against the Taylor System which led to the congressional investigation. As a result of the investigation, piecework rates were banned from all government jobs at that time; nonetheless, the hearings afforded Taylor an opportunity to bring clearly before the public the meaning of scientific management.

THE EMPHASIS UPON ADMINISTRATION

The second approach to the study of management emphasizes the administrative aspects of management. The emphasis is an overall approach to the problems of management.

The task of management has been summarized in a single word, *coordination,* by Mary Parker Follett; but in order to understand this concept it is necessary to know what is being coordinated and to review suggestions as to how coordination can best be accomplished.[4]

Fayol's Principles of Management

Henri Fayol, a French engineer and geologist, was the first to state a series of principles of management that provide guideposts for successful management coordination. Concurrent with Taylor's study of management through a detailed analysis of the individual worker, Fayol, manager of a large French mining and metallurgical company, analyzed the problems of top management. He modestly believed that his success was not due to any personal characteristics of leadership, but was the result of applying a set of general administrative principles that could be isolated and taught to others. In his book, *General and Industrial Management,* Fayol lists the following 14 principles of management: [5]

---

[4] Mary Parker Follett, *Freedom and Coordination* (London: Management Publications Trust, Ltd., 1949), H. F. Merrill, *ibid.,* pp. 337-52.

[5] Henri Fayol, *General and Industrial Management* (London: Sir Isaac Pitman and Sons Ltd., 1949), pp. 19-42. H. F. Merrill, *ibid.,* pp. 217-41. The copyright date, 1949, is the date of the English translation. Fayol's "General Principles of Management" first appeared in 1916 in an industrial association bulletin published in France.

1. Division of work
2. Authority
3. Discipline
4. Unity of command
5. Unity of direction
6. Subordination of the individual interest to the general interest
7. Remuneration
8. Centralization
9. Scalar chain (line of authority)
10. Order
11. Equity
12. Stability of tenure of personnel
13. Initiative
14. Esprit de corps

Five of Fayol's 14 principles are concerned primarily with the improvement of human relations. One of his principles emphasizes production efficiency, and the remaining eight are directed toward administration of the organization. Those principles contributing to the improvement of human relations are discussed first.

Principles Emphasizing Human Relations

The five principles applicable to problems in the field of human relations are: No. 6, subordination of individual interest to the general interest; No. 11, equity; No. 12, stability of tenure of personnel; No. 13, initiative; and No. 14, esprit de corps. In the first of this group, subordination of individual interest to the general interest (No. 6), Fayol states that individuals and small groups within the overall organization should make their needs secondary to those of the firm. He also emphasizes that it is necessary for the firm to place its interests second to those of the society in which it operates. Recognition of the fact that the administrator of an organization is dealing with a number of groups, as contrasted to a number of individuals, is fundamentally the same group concept of Elton Mayo. Fayol suggests that the attainment of subordination of interest can be achieved by close supervision, good examples of subordination of personal interest by supervisors, and by making agreements with various employees and groups of employees as fair as possible.

In Principle No. 11, equity, he defines what is meant by fair agreements. To him, equity is composed of two ingredients: kindliness and justice. The equal application of policies and practices to all groups and individuals within an organization is certainly a concept difficult to quarrel with, yet also difficult to apply at all times. Fayol applies the concept of desirability of stability of tenure to all levels of the organization. The production worker must have some feeling of security in order to learn his job so that he may perform it well, and he must also have some feeling of psychological security.

Stability of tenure for top management is necessary, for it takes time to get to know the organization, its problems, and its personnel. Fayol even suggests that it might be better for a concern to have a mediocre manager with long tenure rather than have a succession of brilliant managers. In this connection, the following interesting question is raised: Is the poor performance of a company that is experiencing a high turnover of managerial personnel the result of the turnover; or, is the poor performance of managerial personnel the cause of the turnover? It is a question that plagues many companies today, and they are no nearer the answer than was Fayol.

One of the chief reasons for the success of Mayo's work with the textile production problems was that the workers themselves defined the problem, offered a solution, and saw their solution carried through to its success. To Fayol, participation in the solution of problems is represented by the principle of initiative. The principle is with us today and is illustrated by the efforts of companies to establish suggestion systems at all levels of the organization so that the ideas and energies of all workers may be tapped in the solution of common problems. Effective employee suggestion programs utilize the principle of initiative, for they enable an employee to see his ideas carried through to a successful conclusion.

In his last principle, esprit de corps, Fayol states his belief that in union there is strength and warns against a system of divide and conquer in an organization. While dividing and conquering may be a good way of eliminating the opposition, it does not work within a single group such as a business organization. The manager's task is not to eliminate the opposition, but rather to unify all divergent groups and individuals.

Production Efficiency

The first of Fayol's principles, division of work, is similar to the thesis that Charles Babbage presented in "On the Division of Labour." [6] Fayol offers the same reasons for dividing work and creating groups of specialists. He mentions the resulting increased skill,

---

[6] Babbage, loc. cit.

the reduction in learning time, and the increased efficiency that results from not having to change from one task to another. But he goes further than Babbage and applies the principle of the division of work to all levels of management, not limiting its application to the hourly worker. Also, the first principle is an expression of the same interest shown by Babbage and Taylor; namely, an emphasis upon the production process with a desire to increase the efficiency of that process. It is the only one of his 14 principles which can be classed as solely emphasizing production. However, there are two principles of such breadth that production processes are included in their application: remuneration and order. These are discussed later.

Principles Emphasizing Administration

The principles discussed thus far restate much that has been said by other writers in the field who have stressed the improvement of either production efficiency or human relations. The remaining principles are new in concept, for they deal with the problems of top management—administration and organization.

Fayol's second principle, authority, is the first of this group. Authority is defined as the right to give orders and is discussed with its corollary, responsibility. The granting of authority to a manager implies that in accepting that authority, he has also accepted responsibility. It is organizationally unsound and inefficient to assign responsibility without, at the same time, granting authority commensurate to this responsibility. Fayol recognized that authority is misused and suggests that preventing the abuse of authority is dependent upon the integrity of the individual having authority.[7]

Discipline, the third principle, is regarded as the respect shown by all members of the organization toward the written agreements, or policies, governing their conduct in the firm. Fayol proposes that good discipline be achieved by having all agreements between the company and the employees presented as clearly and as fairly as possible, that all supervisors throughout the organization be thoroughly capable, and that if the need for penalties or discipline arises, such penalties should be as fair as possible.

The fourth and fifth principles, unity of command and unity of direction, respectively, are similar and closely related. Yet there is sufficient difference in their purposes so that two separate principles are warranted. The first of these, unity of command, states that orders

---

[7] The problem of integrity is discussed in Chapter 3, "Objectives and Ethics."

should originate from one source only. Thus, from a subordinate's point of view, he is assured that he will have only one superior in the organization from whom he can receive orders. Unity of direction is not directed toward the individual, but refers to the plan or work activities of the group and emphasizes that for one plan there should be one head or director. Thus, these two principles complement each other; the former assures the employee that there will be only one superior, and the latter assures organizational effectiveness in that for every group of workers carrying out a plan, there shall be only one director.

These principles of organization—authority, discipline, unity of command, and unity of direction—leave little room for deviation or individual choice. Because of their nature they appear to be an "all or none" proposition. However, not all of Fayol's principles dealing with organization are as rigid as illustrated by his eighth principle, centralization, and the ninth, scalar chain or line of authority. (Though not stated in the title of the eighth principle, both principles deal with the problem of authority.) The ninth principle urges that definite lines of authority be established from the bottom of an organization to its very top in such a manner that the exact lines of authority relationships between the successive levels of management are unmistakably clear. When it becomes necessary for individuals in different sections of the organization to work directly with each other in order to attain speed of action, the formal chain of command should be short-circuited, provided all persons concerned are properly informed.

The same type of flexibility is evident in determining the optimum degree of centralization in an organization. In general, those actions that tend to reduce the authority and responsibility of subordinates and place more in the hands of a superior may be considered as actions which lend to a greater degree of centralization of authority, while those acts that increase responsibility and authority at lower levels result in what is termed a greater degree of decentralization of authority. With the concept of varying degrees of centralization of authority there is no recommended absolute level of centralization or decentralization. The desired level or degree is dependent upon the situation and includes such factors as the nature of the organization, the problem of the department at hand, and the capabilities of the subordinates in question.

The remaining two principles describe operating procedures of such breadth that they are difficult to classify within the framework of either human relations, production, or administration. These principles, remuneration and order, encompass all three areas. Since they are expressed as problems of top management rather than problems in human relations or the improvement of production, the principles of remuneration and order are considered among those principles contributing to the administrative efforts of management. One of these, the principle of remuneration, starts with the assumption that the wages paid to personnel should be based upon concepts of equity and should be satisfactory both to the employee and the company. The various methods of paying hourly employees are listed, and Fayol shows that he was thoroughly familiar with the piecework system advocated by Taylor. He also mentions the problems involved in profit-sharing plans and bonuses, not only for hourly workers, but for all members of the organization. Again, Fayol develops the same flexible conclusion that he did in principles eight and nine—the method of payment selected should be the one that works best for the particular situation, and the definition of "best" should include the point of view of all interested parties.

The other principle, also broad in scope, is that of order. At first glance, the meaning of order may seem to be the same as Taylor's admonition that the placement of materials and tools should be the result of a methods study to assure efficient production. Fayol's principle does include the concept, "A place for everything and everything in its place." However, it means much more than the neat arrangement of physical materials of an organization. Fayol's idea of order also applies to the human element of the organization. An application of this principle is the organization chart, a device which literally shows the place of every person in the organization and the relationships of each to the other. In addition to knowing personnel as they appear on the organization chart, Fayol recommended they be considered as human resources expressing different capabilities and desires.

THE EMPHASIS UPON HUMAN RELATIONS

The works of two proponents of the human relations school are reviewed briefly. The first statement, expressed by Robert Owen, appeared in 1828 and is regarded as one of the first formal writings in the field of management. Although considered a proponent of the human relations approach to management, Owen's views are now regarded as highly paternalistic in nature. Secondly, a brief view of the work of Elton Mayo, who is considered the founder of the human relations approach to management, is presented.

Robert Owen

Robert Owen, a successful textile mill manager in Scotland from 1800 to 1828, made some remarkable observations concerning the factors which influenced the productivity of the personnel in his plants. He referred to his employees as "vital machines," and in describing how they should be regarded and treated, he compared the importance and nature of "vital machines" with the "inanimate machines" of the factory. A summary of his position was presented in "An Address: To the Superintendents of Manufactures, and to those Individuals generally, who, by giving Employment to an aggregated Population, may easily adopt the means to form the Sentiments and Manners of such a Population." The date of publication of this address was 1813, and in some ways it foreshadows the conclusions of the famous Hawthorne Studies of Mayo which were not undertaken until more than a century later.[8]

Owen stated that it was generally accepted that mechanical equipment kept in a state of good repair more than paid for itself by its increased productivity and longer life. Reasoning by analogy, he concluded that if this were true for the "inanimate machines," it should also be true for the "vital machines." He applied this conclusion to his own plants in New Lanark, Scotland, and claimed that as a result of attention to his personnel, he was receiving more than a 50 percent return on any money so spent. The summation of his position follows:

> And when it was perceived that inanimate mechanism was greatly improved by being made firm and substantial, that it was the essence of economy to keep it neat, clean, regularly supplied with the best substance to prevent unnecessary friction, and, by proper provision for the purpose, to preserve it in good repair, it was natural to conclude that the more delicate, complex, living mechanism would be equally improved by being trained to strength and activity; and that it would also prove true economy to keep it neat and clean; to treat it with kindness, that its mental movements might not experience too much irritating friction; to endeavor by every means to make it more perfect; to supply it regularly with a sufficient quantity of wholesome food and other necessaries of life, that the body might be preserved from being out of repair, or falling prematurely to decay.[9]

George Elton Mayo

Closely related to the work of Owen, though separated by slightly more than 100 years, are the efforts of George Elton Mayo

---

[8] Robert Owen, *A New View of Society* (1st American ed. from the 3d London ed.; New York: E. Bliss & F. White, 1825), pp. 57-62. Reprinted in H. F. Merrill (ed.), *Classics in Management* (New York: American Management Association, 1960), pp. 21-25.

[9] H. F. Merrill, *ibid.,* pp. 23-24.

and his team of Harvard researchers. Mayo was born and educated in Australia, came to the United States in 1922, and was first associated with the University of Pennsylvania. In 1926, he joined the faculty of Harvard University, where he remained until his retirement in 1947. One of his early studies, completed while he was at Pennsylvania, illustrates clearly the results that may be expected by following Owen's admonition "to treat it (the vital machine) with kindness, that its mental movements might not experience too much irritating friction." Appropriately, the title given to this work is "The First Inquiry." [10]

"The First Inquiry." Mayo and his group were asked to solve an industrial problem, the symptoms of which were an excessive turnover of employees in a certain department of a Philadelphia textile mill. The department in question was that of the mule-spinners, whose annual turnover rate was nearly 250 percent while that of other departments in the mill was between 5 and 6 percent. Several consulting firms, then called efficiency engineers, had previously worked on the problem and, among other things, had established a financial incentive plan. The reasoning behind this approach assumed that man is an economic animal, and, as such, he will respond to financial incentive or reward. However, this was not the case, for not once had the men in the department produced enough to earn the rewards of the financial incentive plan. The morale of the department was low. There were many complaints of foot trouble, neuritis, and other miscellaneous aches and pains. The men were working five 10-hour days each week with the day being broken only by a 45-minute lunch period at the end of the first five hours. There were no rest periods during the day, and since the men were on their feet continually, there was reason to believe that fatigue might be playing an important part in creating their general feelings of depression.

The experiment began with the introduction of rest periods for some of the workers in the mule-spinner's department. But rest alone was not the only changed condition in the experiment. The problem had been discussed with all employees in the department, and, as a result, they were made to feel a part of the whole program. In addition, these men were fondly attached to the manager of the plant, a colonel with whom many had served in World War I. They were confident that if the rest periods worked for the experimental group, about one third

---

[10] Elton Mayo, *The Social Problems of an Industrial Civilization* (Boston: Division of Research, Graduate School of Business Administration, Harvard University, 1945). Portions of this work and the Hawthorne Studies are reprinted in H. F. Merrill, *ibid.*, pp. 407-36.

of the workers, all of them would soon have rest periods because of the essential fairness of "The Colonel."

The results of the experiment were almost immediate, not only for the third who received the rest periods, but also for the two thirds who served as the control group and did not receive rest periods but who had taken part in discussing the problem. For the first time since the installation of the incentive bonus plan by the efficiency engineers, the mule-spinners earned incentive pay. This continued for a period of four and one-half months, until February 15, 1923. Then, within a period of seven days the entire department had returned to their initial pessimism and production dropped to its former low level.

What had happened? Nothing that had not happened thousands of times in industrial plants prior to this experiment and thousands of times since this study. There was a sudden demand for the product of the textile mill, and, as a result, the supervisor in the department simply ordered the abandonment of all rest periods. The results were immediate and well-nigh disastrous. The sequel to this supervisor's ill-advised, albeit typical, act is often overlooked. The Colonel, the manager in whom the men had complete personal confidence, took immediate charge. He reinstated the four rest periods and guaranteed that every employee would have two 10-minute rest periods in the morning and two in the afternoon. Practically everyone, except the Colonel himself, doubted that this loss of 40 minutes a day per man could be made up since the machines could not be speeded up. However, the Colonel was right. During the month of April the men made a bonus, and the rate of production continued to climb until the efficiency figures were well above 85 percent, a considerable change from the March low of 70 percent. In addition to reestablishing the rest periods in a manner which had left no doubt in anyone's mind as to what the management believed, the Colonel had done something else of great significance. He had delegated responsibility to the men themselves. Each group of three men was to determine the exact time when the group would take its individual rest periods, but each knew that, without fail, the group would receive four such periods a day. Thus, a guaranteed policy of management and the fact that the workers themselves were to participate to some extent in the decisions involved had turned the tide.

The Hawthorne Studies. Shortly after completing his work, "The First Inquiry," Mayo joined the faculty of Harvard University where, as head of the Industrial Research Department, he led a series of pioneering studies at the Hawthorne plant of the Western Electric

Company.[11] Initially, the purpose of the study was to determine the effect of illumination upon the output of workers; however, at a later date, the studies sought to determine methods of establishing teamwork and continuing cooperation in industrial groups.

In the illumination study, workers were divided into two groups— an experimental group and a control group. Lighting conditions for the experimental group were varied from 24 to 46 to 70 footcandles in intensity while the lighting of the control group remained constant. As expected, the output of the experimental group increased with each increase in light intensity, but the performance of the control group was not expected. Their production increased at about the same rate as the production of the experimental group. Later, the light of the experimental group was reduced from 10 to 3 footcandles. Again, the output of the experimental group continued to increase, and so did the output of the control group. Finally, a decline in productivity of the experimental group did occur, but only when the intensity of light was low enough to approach the level of moonlight. Clearly, something other than illumination was the cause of changes in productivity.

Similar results were obtained in the relay assembly test room experiment, only this time the variable was the amount of rest, rather than lighting, to determine the effects of fatigue on productivity. First, normal production was established, then rest periods of varying lengths and frequency were introduced. Production increased with the increase in frequency and length of rest periods. Finally, in Period XII of the experiments, it was decided to return to the original conditions: no formal rest periods, no lunches, and a full 48-hour week. The return to the original conditions did not result in the expected drop in production; instead, production stayed at its usual high level.

The Hawthorne Effect. The Hawthorne Studies show quite clearly that factors other than working conditions and the physiological state of the worker have a marked influence on productivity. These factors are recognized as social and psychological in nature. The workers of

---

[11] There have been several major books published by Mayo and his coworkers describing the extensive work completed at Western Electric. Among them are the following:

Elton Mayo, *The Human Problems of an Industrial Civilization* (Boston: Division of Research, Harvard Business School; 2d ed.; New York: Macmillan, 1946).

F. J. Roethlisberger and W. J. Dickson, *Management and the Worker* (Harvard University Press, 1939, 10th printing, 1950).

F. J. Roethlisberger, *Management and Morale* (Harvard University Press, 1942).

F. J. Roethlisberger, *Man-in-Organization* (Cambridge: Belknap Press of Harvard University Press, 1968). This book is a series of essays by F. J. Roethlisberger, several of which are concerned with Elton Mayo and the Hawthorne studies.

these studies were the subjects of experiments of interest to the managers of the plant and to their immediate supervisors. Further, they knew that they were participating in experiments that were of interest to management. They responded to this interest, a social force, rather than to the experimentally induced changes in the external physical environment. This phenomenon of responding to the social and psychological aspects of the situation on the part of individuals participating as subjects of the experiment has come to be known as the *Hawthorne Effect*. Because of this phenomenon it is sometimes very difficult to determine whether the subjects of an experimental study are responding to the environmental factor that is being varied by the experimenter or whether they are responding to the knowledge that they are the subjects and participants of an experiment.

The Hawthorne Effect is demonstrated quite clearly in the results of Period XII of the studies concerned with the effect of fatigue. As a result many consider this study a turning point in our understanding human relations because the importance of attitudes toward work, toward management, and toward the work group is recognized as vitally significant.

Summary

Robert Owen urged his contemporaries to concern themselves with the social well-being of their employees both in the community and on the job. In doing this, he recognized that man is essentially a social being. He also stated that if the personal and social needs of employees were attended to, the economic repayment for such attention would take care of itself. Indeed, he claimed that he was receiving a payment on money so invested in excess of 50 percent and soon expected a return of 100 percent. When Mayo first entered the textile mill in Philadelphia, the men were not behaving as the economic creatures that the incentive plan implied or assumed they were. When their personal needs were attended to—their physical condition recognized and corrected—and when they were viewed as social beings, through a discussion of their problems with them, the results were almost immediate. True, the rest periods helped, but the key to the solution is the fact that initially all employees in the department showed an increase in production. And, the increase was not limited to the one third receiving the rest period.

Several conclusions from Owen and Mayo can be drawn at this time. First, man is essentially a social being, not economic, and should be regarded as such. Second, as a social being he is a member of a group; therefore, it is the group that should be approached to participate in discussing their problems and in determining the solution. There is a third conclusion to be drawn from a study of these two works. Mayo touches on this point only lightly and Owen not at all, although in the case of the latter it might have been considered immodest if he had. In both instances, the men running the company (Owen in New Lanark, Scotland, and the "Colonel" in Philadelphia) were leaders and were even perceived as such by the employees. Both were men who "knew" when they were right, and both were sincere in their desire to do the best that they could for the physical well-being of their employees. However, these attributes on their part were not sufficient without a reciprocal feeling on the part of the employees. In each instance, the employees had strong feelings of confidence regarding the ability and sincerity of their leader. Therefore, it is clear that for any successful program in human relations there must be a leader with ability and sincerity, and these traits must be recognized by his employees.

MODERN APPROACHES TO THE STUDY OF MANAGEMENT

In addition to the approaches to the study of management that emphasize production, administration, and human relations there are other areas that have been stressed in the development of management concepts. Indeed, there have been so many ideas concerning the central problems of management that one writer has referred to "The Management Theory Jungle" [12] and another writer has called the sometimes vituperative statements of the proponents of the various management schools a form of "inky warfare." [13] Let us examine this "jungle" so that we might obtain a broader view of management concepts. Also, though not fully developed, there is the beginning of an integrative point of view in management theory. The diverse theories or schools of management are presented as the "jungle," which is followed by an integrative point of view.

The Jungle

Professor Harold Koontz in his now famous article, "The Management Theory Jungle," describes briefly six major schools of management. He groups Taylor and Fayol together and refers to their

---

[12] Harold Koontz, "The Management Theory Jungle," *Academy of Management Journal,* Vol. IV (December, 1961), pp. 174-188.
[13] Lyndall F. Urwick, "The Tactics of Jungle Warfare," *Academy of Management Journal,* Vol. VI, No. 4 (December, 1963), pp. 316-329.

approach as the "management process" school. The work of those who emphasize human relations is recognized separately as the "human behavior school." In addition he recognizes four other schools or theories of management: the empirical school, the social systems school, the decision theory school, and the mathematical school.[14]

The Empirical School. The empirical school studies management through an analysis of the experience of successful managers. The purpose is to permit the formation of generalizations concerning the nature of management. An example of this approach is found in Ernest Dale's, *The Great Organizers,* a review of the operations of such companies as Du Pont, General Motors, National Steel, and Westinghouse Electric Corporation as seen through the eyes of the chief executive of each of these organizations.[15]

In a sense this approach to management is saying, "Let us look at several successful operations, their chief executives, and how they did it, and as a result we will be able to transfer this information to another situation." To a degree the empirical school of management is closely related to the management process school of Taylor and Fayol. Each of these men was a highly successful manager in his own right and much of the writings of each is a distillation and reporting of his own experience as a manager, while Dale's work is a reporting of the experience of others. Thus the two approaches are closely related, the difference lying in who is doing the reporting, with both schools hoping to derive a set of concepts or principles to serve as the basis for managing organizations.

The Social Systems School. Closely related to, but distinct from the behavioral school is the social systems school. The behavioral school has its origin in the work of academicians, such as Mayo, but the social systems school is attributed to Chester Barnard, formerly president of the New Jersey Bell Telephone Company. It has been said that Barnard writes "with authority about authority" and perhaps he should, having been president of a major corporation. Yet Barnard viewed the organization primarily as a social system.[16]

---

[14] The discussion that follows is based on Koontz, *op. cit.*

[15] Ernest Dale, *The Great Organizers* (New York: McGraw-Hill Book Company, Inc., 1960). In addition to the experiences of the "organizers" of each of these four companies, Professor Dale examines concepts of organizational theory in the first chapter and in the concluding chapter discusses the accountability of management.

[16] Chester Barnard, *The Functions of the Executive* (Cambridge: Harvard University Press, 1938).

One of the major contributions of this point of view is recognition of the importance of the informal organization and its impact upon the formal organization as portrayed by the organization chart. Another contribution concerns the nature of authority. The management process school views authority as being derived from ownership and flowing downward throughout the organization; however, Barnard sees authority as originating in the extent to which it is accepted by members of the organization. This view concerning the origin of authority, known as *subordinate acceptance,* is discussed and reconciled with the institutional view of authority of the management process school in Chapter 11.

The Decision Theory School. The decision theory school is concerned with the making of a choice, or decision, between one or more alternatives and considers decision making as one of the primary activities of management. Decision theory is not as narrow as it might seem at first glance; instead, it can and does study not only the decision but also the decision-making process and the behavioral aspects of the decision maker himself.

The Mathematical School. Intertwined with the decision-making school is that group referred to as the mathematical school. The relationship between these two schools is very close because many of the decisions made by management may be expressed as mathematical models and subsequently solved by mathematical processes. In earlier years, the mathematical approach has been called operations research or operations analysis, but presently the term *management science* seems to predominate. Significantly the emergence of mathematics to a dominant position among the approaches to the study of management has coincided with the development of the high-speed electronic computer; thereby permitting the management scientist to construct mathematical models containing as many as one thousand simultaneous equations.[17]

An Integrative View

The divergence of opinion concerning the central issue of management is reminiscent of the three blind men, each of whom described

---

[17] A discussion of management science for the student interested in learning more about this field may be found in Harvey M. Wagner, *Principles of Manaegment Science; With Applications to Executive Decisions* (Englewood Cliffs: Prentice-Hall, Inc., 1970). Note that the subtitle shows the close relationship between the mathematical and the decision theory approach to the study of management.

in turn an elephant as a rope (the one who touched the tail), a snake (the one who found the trunk), and a tree stump (the one who touched a leg). The question arises whether there is a sighted one amongst us who can describe management in its entirety rather than describing a single aspect of the process. There are those who believe that there is such a theoretical framework available at the present time; however, there are discrepancies concerning the details of this framework. Professor Scott has supplied us with a fine summary of an integrative approach to the study of management that is generally referred to as *modern* organization theory.[18] Scott has noted that modern approaches to the study of management have one thing in common—the utilization of the systems concept as a means of describing the total organization rather than emphasizing a specific function such as decision making (the decision theory school) or an elaboration of a method (the mathematical school) to solve organizational problems. The following questions are asked in the systems approach to understanding the management of organizations: [19]

1. What are the strategic parts of the system?
2. What is the nature of their mutual dependency?
3. What are the main processes in the system which link the parts together and facilitate their adjustments to each other?
4. What are the goals sought by systems?

The Parts of the System. The individual is the fundamental unit of the organizational system. The individual is considered in terms of his personality, defining personality as the sum total of his experiences and abilities. One of the significant aspects of the individual's personality is that it sets forth his expectations as an individual and as a member of the organization.

The second part of an organization is the arrangement of the individuals and the functions they perform into what is termed the *formal* organization, often portrayed—albeit inadequately—by the formal organization chart. A fundamental question arises at this point: to what extent are these two parts of the organization in conflict? Some students of management believe that the extent of the conflict is

---

[18] William G. Scott, "Organization Theory: Overview and an Appraisal," *Academy of Management Journal*, Vol. IV, No. 1 (April, 1961), pp. 7-26.

Professor Scott reviews briefly earlier theories of management and classifies them as the classical doctrine. The human relations movement is classified as neoclassical theory of organization. However, the major portion of the article is devoted to modern organization theory. The discussion that follows is based upon this article.

[19] *Ibid.*, p. 16.

considerable; that is, the demands of the formal organization are contrary to the nature of its individual members.[20]

The third part of the organizational system is known as the *informal* organization. The informal organization, not shown on the official organization chart, is composed of informal groups that arise out of the work situations. Sometimes the informal groups develop as a means of completing the assigned work of the formal organization. When this happens the goals of the two groups are frequently in accord; however, there are instances where the expectations of the formal organization are in conflict with the desires of the informal organization. When this happens the individual is frequently torn between the conflicting demands of the formal and the informal organization.

The fourth part of the organization derives from the study of social processes and consequent recognition of the demands of both the formal and informal organization. One of the demands of the organization, formal or informal, is that the individual assume a *role*—prescribed and expected patterns of behavior—that is a result of his position and function in the organization. A specific concept of role that has developed is that of the role at the interface, the demands that are made of the person who is figuratively in the middle and has the task of bringing together two segments, or interfaces, of the organization.[21]

Finally, the last part of the system is the *physical setting* within which the individual or the group, performs its respective duties. It is a setting that is not limited to the physical factors and working conditions such as those investigated by the Hawthorne illumination studies. Instead, it is a concept that seeks the optimum relationship between man and his environment and attempts to allocate the resources and capabilities of man so that they mesh effectively with those of the physical settings of his environment. This method of viewing man in relation to his environment is described as a *man-machine-system,* a concept that strives to optimize the capabilities and performance of both man and the machine.

In summary, the individual, the fundamental building block of the organization, is a member of and is influenced by the formal organization. The requirements of the formal organization determine the composition and nature of work groups. The work groups in turn may

---

[20] Chris Argyris, *Personality and Organization* (New York: Harper & Brothers, 1957). Of a special interest in regard to the question raised above are chapters 2, 3, and 7.

[21] For a discussion of the role at the interface see Chapter 15, p. 461.

form the basis for the informal organization, which is composed of individuals who are simultaneously members of the formal and the informal organization. Both the formal and the informal organization have goals that do not necessarily coincide. In addition, the goals of the formal and the informal organization are related to the expectations and goals of the individual. Also, there is the role that is demanded of the individual as a member of the formal organization and the role that is demanded of him as a member of the informal organization. Finally, there is the realization that all organizational functions occur within a physical setting that evolves beyond the man-machine-systems concept to a man-organization-systems concept.

The Linking Processes. It is easy to state that the parts of the organization are interrelated, simply because they appear to be so. However, the student of organizational theory must do more than make the statement; he must designate, describe, and show the ways in which the processes link the various parts of the organization. One of the linking processes is the *role*, or actions, performed by the individual member of the organization which serves as a means of relating to other persons and to other groups in the organization. *Communication* is another means of linking the parts of the organization. The term, communication, includes not only verbal expressions, both written and oral, but also all information necessary for the effective operation of the organization. When communication is used in this sense, the organization is viewed as a total "information system." Thus there is concern for the flow of information from one subsystem to another subsystem so that the parts are linked together. Closely related to the concept of an organization as an information system is the concept of *balance* or homeostasis. This concept, sometimes referred to as a steady state, is one of the fundamental aspects of systems theory; that is, there is a normal state for the system and when the system is out of balance there is a tendency for it to return to its normal homeostatic state. Another linking process is *decision making*. The process of making decisions may be used to change the direction or goal of the organization, or the decision may be designed so that it restores balance to the system.

Organizational Goals. Scott has stated that the "organization has three goals which may be intermeshed or may be independent ends in themselves. They are growth, stability, and interaction." [22] He points out that the last goal refers to those organizations which exist primarily

---

[22] Scott, *op. cit.*, p. 20.

as vehicles that permit their members to interact with other members—
for example, professional societies and certain social organizations. In
setting the goals of organizations, it is necessary not only to seek a
balance between potentially conflicting organizational goals, but also
to relate these goals to those of the individual and to the goals of the
informal organization. Thus the problem of establishing congruent
goals for all components of an organization becomes highly critical.

The Next Development

It has been suggested by several persons, among them Professor
William C. Frederick, that the next step in the study of management
is the development of a general systems theory.[23] His reason for making
this statement is that a review of the development of management
concepts indicates that five components of a potential general theory
of management have been developed. In discussing these components,
Frederick first points out that the classical management of Fayol and
Taylor resulted in the establishment of management principles, including a delineation of the functions and processes of management. The
human relations school, a second component, stresses that the formal
organization is at the same time a human and social organization and
as such should serve these purposes as well as fulfilling purely economic
ends. The third component is the contribution made by the decision
theory school, including mathematical approaches to management processes, and recognition that decision making performs a linking function in the organization. The fourth factor is the behavioral sciences.
Though quite similar to the human relations school and in the opinion
of some an extension of the work of Mayo, this group stresses that individuals may be regarded as systems and function within larger social
systems. Finally, the fifth component is value theory, a means of
establishing the social responsibility of organizations and managements
and placing in perspective the diverse contributions of the classical,
human relations, decision theory, and behavioral approaches to the
study of management.

The conclusion is inescapable. Modern approaches to the study of
management or organizations are pointing toward the development of
what will someday be a general systems theory of organizations and

---

[23] William C. Frederick, "The Next Development in Management Science: A
General Theory," *Academy of Management Journal*, Vol. VI, No. 3 (September, 1963),
pp. 212-219. The discussion that follows is based upon the five major components of a
general theory of management as described by Professor Frederick.

their management. The next theory of organization will stress the systems concept. Such a theory is presented in Chapter 9, "Organization Theory," as a first step in the development of a systems theory of organization.

SUMMARY OF PRINCIPLES   *Learn.*

Four separate approaches to the problems of management have been reviewed. Each approach emphasizes a different aspect of management and each draws its own conclusions as to what factors

Taylor's Principles of Scientific Management

1. Management must gather, analyze, and codify all existing rule-of-thumb data pertaining to the business in order to develop a science.
2. Workers must be carefully selected and thoroughly studied so that each one may be developed to his maximum capabilities.
3. Workmen must be inspired or trained to use the scientific methods developed as the result of analyzing and codifying rule-of-thumb data.
4. Management must organize in such a manner that it can properly manage and carry out its duties.

Fayol's Principles of Management

Human Relations

Subordination of individual interest to the general interest   Initiative
Esprit de corps
Equity
Stability of tenure of personnel

Production Efficiency

Division of work

Administration

Authority   Centralization
Discipline   Scalar chain (line of authority)
Unity of command
Unity of direction   Remuneration
Order

Figure 2-1
PRINCIPLES OF MANAGEMENT

are of significance in the management process. Conclusions that are fundamental to their nature and basic to the management process have been termed principles of management. Neither Robert Owen nor Elton Mayo, who both designated the development of sound human relations as the primary task of management, stated their conclusions as principles of management. Frederick W. Taylor, representative of the approach that emphasizes production efficiency, and Henri Fayol, who stressed the administrative aspects of management, have stated fundamentals basic to the management process and referred to these conclusions as principles of management.

Taylor's principles of scientific management stressed the need for increased efficiency, whereas Henry Fayol's stressed the administrative aspects of management. Fayol also recognized the need for sound human relations and the importance of production efficiency. The principles stressed by Taylor, as well as those stressed by Fayol, are summarized in Figure 2-1 on page 55.

In this chapter we have reviewed a few of the major concepts in the literature of management, and have shown that the development of management concepts expressed in the literature has taken well over a hundred years. Of what value is such information to the present-day manager? Marsh Saunders (Case Problem 2-A), the new plant manager facing the challenge of creating an effective organization, may not find the specific answers he desires in the literature, but he will discover established principles that will serve as guideposts for any action he takes.

In Case Problem 2-B, Manual vs. Automatic Equipment, a modern counterpart of making pins by hand is described. As a building manager, you are asked to answer and evaluate the worth of the questions posed by Charles Babbage in reaching your decision concerning the advisability of purchasing new equipment in order to convert a manual operation to one that is fully automatic. You may want to review the questions posed by Babbage on page 33 before you read the case.

CASE PROBLEM   The home office of the Diamond Insurance Com-
2-B   pany occupies the fourth, fifth, and sixth floors of the
                       12-story Diamond Building, which was built in the early
MANUAL vs.   thirties. The building has been well maintained through-
AUTOMATIC   out the years, and in 1950 was completely air condi-
EQUIPMENT   tioned. It is well located, with easy access to downtown

stores and other office buildings, with the result that the occupancy rate has been well over 90 percent of capacity until the current year when it dropped to 85 percent. The costs of operating the building have risen steadily for the past 15 years. Though there have been several increases of rental charges in the past to offset rising costs, a readjustment of rates seems out of the question at the present time because several new buildings are nearby and their space costs little more than the Diamond Building.

H. W. Canton, vice-president of the Diamond Insurance Company, who is responsible for the operation of the building, was acutely aware of the declining occupancy rate and the impracticality of raising rental charges as he spoke to Mr. Thomas, the building manager.

"I wish you would look into the feasibility of installing automatic elevators. Find out the cost of installation, maintenance cost, and whether the service to our tenants will be as good as the service we now provide with the elevator operators. We might be interested in converting to automatic elevators if we could pay for them in less than ten years without spending any more than we now spend for operator service."

"What about interest rates?" asked Mr. Thomas.

"Don't worry about that at present. We can always add that amount to the cost that you find." As the building manager started to leave the room, Mr. Canton added, "In determining present costs, use the hourly rate we are now paying the operators. We all know that it is going up, but by using the present rate we'll be on the safe side."

Mr. Thomas began his assignment by collecting all available cost data for the present operation. For the past five years, maintenance costs on the present equipment have averaged $2,300 each year. There are five girls employed as operators for the four elevators, and one employed as working supervisor who schedules the operators, acts as starter, and provides information to visitors from her position at a desk in front of the elevators. Mr. Thomas assumed that she would be retained in order to provide information.

The girls operate the elevators from eight in the morning until 5:30 p.m., Monday through Friday, and from eight to twelve noon on Saturdays. Service on Saturday afternoons, evenings, and Sundays is provided by either the watchman or the night porter. All operators receive $1.70 an hour, and the starter receives $2.00 an hour. Overtime at the rate of time and one half is paid for all hours worked over eight in any one day and for any hours in excess of 40 in any one week. Two of the girls work nine hours Monday through Friday and receive nine and one-half hour's pay, since the ninth hour is paid at the overtime rate. Three of the operators, one of whom acts as relief operator, work eight and one-half hours each weekday and receive eight and three-fourths hour's pay. The starter also is paid for eight and three-fourths hours since her normal work day is eight and one-half hours, Monday through Friday. On Saturdays, two of the operators and the starter each work four hours, and since they all work more than 40 hours during the week, they receive overtime pay for the entire four hours. Work schedules are rotated so that the earnings of the operators are equalized. Fringe benefits, including group insurance, social security taxes, and uniforms, are estimated to be 30 cents an hour (using a 40-hour week) or a total of $72 a week for the six employees. No replacements are hired during the summer when vacations are normally taken.

After consolidating the above information into an annual cost figure, which includes maintenance and labor costs for a 52-week year, Mr. Thomas contacted several elevator companies for estimates on the cost of converting to automatic elevators. The best estimate he received was $110,000 for the cost of installation, with an annual maintenance charge of 5 percent of the installation cost. The elevator manufacturer assured him that automatic service would be superior to their present manual service. This opinion was confirmed by several building managers who had made the conversion.

PROBLEMS

1. Prepare a summary report and recommendations for Mr. Canton.
2. Which of the questions raised by Charles Babbage in 1832 are applicable to the problems stated in this case?
3. What is your answer to each of Babbage's five questions?

4. Can you think of any additional questions that should be answered before a decision is made?

Chapter Questions for Study and Discussion

1. What major conclusions can be drawn from the work of Mayo and Owen? *Human relations*

2. Give an example from your own experience that illustrates the importance of personal leadership.

3. What modern industrial operation best illustrates the division of labor by levels of skill?

4. What responsibilities of management change as the result of changes in methods and time studies of hourly production jobs? Why?

5. Would Mayo have been successful in raising the output of the mule-spinners had he used the methods of Taylor? Do you believe that Taylor would have been successful in raising the output of the labor gang of the Bethlehem Steel Works had he employed the methods of Mayo?

6. In what respect does Fayol's concept of the division of work differ from Babbage's concept as expressed in "On the Division of Labour"?

7. Which of Fayol's principles emphasize human relations? Which of his principles emphasizes production, and which ones emphasize the organizational or administrative aspects of management?

8. Why is it unsound for a manager to approach his organization with a "divide and conquer" philosophy?

9. Differentiate between Fayol's principles of unity of command and unity of direction.

10. What is meant by the term "centralization" as applied to a company's organization structure? What is meant by the term "decentralization"? Give an example of each.

11. Two of Fayol's principles are so broad in their application that they cannot be conveniently classified as falling entirely within any one of the three areas discussed; i.e., human relations, production, or administration. One reason was presented in the text for their consideration as principles contributing toward the administrative aspect of management. What are the principles in question, and what was the reason offered for their being classified as administrative principles?

12. What reasons can you develop to justify the classification of the two principles mentioned in Question 11 as principles contributing primarily to either human relations or production efficiency?

13. A phrase that has been used to describe scientific management is that it is a search for the one best way. Is there such a thing as a one best way in view of modern organization theory?

CHAPTER 3

Objectives and Ethics

At the turn of the century in 1901, a group of civic-minded citizens of Golden City formed a public corporation and received from the city a franchise "to operate a public transportation system." The Golden Transit Company, the corporation thus formed, grew with Golden City; and in 1946 at the close of World War II, its annual statement showed a capital surplus of $1,200,000 in the form of cash and negotiable securities. In addition, the corporation owned substantial real estate holdings, including a 12-story office building.

The end of the war also marked a turning point in the fortunes of the Golden Transit Company. Golden City expanded from its postwar population of 300,000 to more than 700,000 by 1960 and, in the process, the geographic area of the city grew from an area of 30 square miles to more than 120 square miles. The length of existing bus routes had to be increased and, in many cases, new routes were established. With the advent of a system of freeways, Golden City residents contributed their share to the booming automobile market. The transit company had to purchase additional rolling stock, some of which was an overdue replacement of equipment worn out during the war years when replacements were impossible. Much of the equipment, however, was to serve new bus lines and was purchased in an effort to make public transportation more convenient and to attract new customers. In addition, a continuing spiral of rising costs and subsequent fare increases began. The seeming result was that with each fare increase, the number

CASE PROBLEM 3-A

A PUBLIC TRUST

of passengers declined. Though the frequency of service was greatly reduced on many routes, no routes were completely eliminated. The earnings of the company were poor; as a result the stock of the company was traded on the local over-the-counter market at $11 per share, despite the fact that financial analysts estimated a book value of $23 per share.

In the spring of 1961, sales of the stock became more active, and during the remainder of that year it traded at prices ranging between $12 and $14 per share. By the year's end, the reason for the increased market activity of the stock became apparent. It was revealed that National Busways, an out-of-state corporation, had purchased 60 percent of the outstanding stock. Early in 1962, National's slate of directors was elected and a new management for the Golden Transit Company was appointed. In 1962 the following events occurred:

1. Two requests were submitted to the Golden City council for fare increases. The new management stated that it was a public corporation entitled to make a profit, and that if the fare increase were not granted, it would be necessary to further reduce service and eliminate unprofitable routes. The first request was denied by the city council, with the result that ten relatively new routes serving suburban areas were discontinued. The city council was still considering the second request for a fare inrcease.

2. The real estate holdings, including a 12-story office building, were transferred to a holding company controlled by National Busways. The income from this property was no longer available to offset the operating losses of the Golden Transit Company. A large part of the capital surplus was used to purchase another transit company in an adjacent state.

3. Golden Transit Company had been somewhat tardy in establishing adequate retirement and disability insurance plans. However, they recognized these obligations to their employees and devised a plan whereby disabled persons and some of those who had retired could continue working with the company on a part-time basis performing light duty. A total of 51 persons were employed in this category. All of this group were discharged by the new management with the comment "We're running a bus line—not a charity."

4. A citizen's group, whose chairman was a prominent Golden City attorney, was investigating the steps necessary to revoke the charter under which National Busways was operating the Golden Transit Company.

PROBLEMS

1. What were the objectives of the Golden Transit Company when it was first organized? *Service*

2. State the objectives in order of apparent importance of National Busways, the company now operating the Golden Transit Company. *profit, then service*

3. Assume that the citizen's group follows the necessary legal steps and is successful in revoking the charter under which National Busways is operating. Is this action justified? *yes* If so, on what grounds can it be justified? *Failing to supply the service to the public*

4. What problems in the field of ethics (fairness and equity to others) have resulted from National's reducing the frequency of service, eliminating entire routes, and discharging long service employees?

In Chapter 1, management is defined as the coordination of all resources through the processes of planning, organizing, directing, and controlling in order to attain stated objectives. Case Problem 3-A brings into sharp focus the changing objectives of the Golden Transit Company after the management of National Busways gained control of the company. Prior to the change in management, the chief objective seemed to be service. There are public utilities formally known as public service companies, and the Golden Transit Company could have been named quite properly the Golden Public Service Company.

The stage is set to determine whether the primary objective of Golden Transit should be service or profit. Case Problem 3-A also illustrates that the existence of a business firm is sanctioned by the society in which it exists; society, in this case, is represented by the Golden City council. In addition to these questions which relate to the objectives of a business, serious doubts are raised concerning the propriety of the methods used by the new management in obtaining its objectives. The judgment as to whether the actions of the new management are proper or improper is an evaluation of the ethical standards of that management. The determination of the objectives of a firm defines the framework within which the management processes take place. The methods used to attain these objectives, to the extent that these methods affect various groups of people, reflect the ethical standards of a company. This chapter will discuss, first, the objectives of business; and, second, review some of the problems encountered in analyzing and establishing ethical standards for businessmen.

OBJECTIVES

In the discussion of objectives it is necessary to understand the nature of objectives so that purposeful activities such as the management of an organization are most effective. In the chapter that follows, an objective is defined and its significance is stated in concise form. The *classification* distinguishing characteristics of objectives are examined and a taxonomy suggested for their classification. Finally, since most organizations have multiple objectives, areas which need stated objectives are delineated.

Definition

Managing a firm without stated objectives is as frustrating and meaningless as sailing a ship without destination. For management, there is no direction to its efforts or effective coordination of resources; nor can there be needed direction and effective coordination until there is a stated purpose or goal. Thus, an *objective* may be defined as *the end point or goal toward which management directs its efforts.* The statement of an objective is in effect a statement of purpose, and when applied to a business organization, becomes the statement of that firm's reason for existing. In order to gain maximum effectiveness from a statement of objectives, an organization must state its objectives prior to initiating the management processes of planning, organizing, directing, and controlling. Stating an objective may require considerable research, yet it is not a part of the planning process. The planning process is put into effect, along with the other three management processes, for the purpose of achieving stated objectives.

Principle of the Objective

The requirement that the objective should be predetermined is considered of such significance that it is referred to by many as the *Principle of the Objective.* The principle of the objective is stated concisely by John F. Mee: *"Before initiating any course of action, the objectives in view must be clearly determined, understood, and stated."* [1]

---

[1] John F. Mee, "Management Philosophy for Professional Executives," *Business Horizons* (Bureau of Business Research, School of Business, Indiana University, December, 1956), pp. 5-11.

The principle of the objective stresses the outstanding characteristic of an objective. This characteristic is that an objective is *predetermined,* an act which thereby sets it apart from the processes utilized in reaching the objective. A second characteristic of an objective is that it is stated. Generally, stating an objective implies that the statement be in written form. The process of writing a thought contributes to its clarification and, in addition, creates a degree of permanence. One of the chief reasons that written assignments are given to students is that the act of writing forces a clarification not usually achieved in oral presentations. Companies that are reluctant or unable to state their objectives in writing reflect either an inability to reach accord on their goals or a fear of criticism that might be engendered by such a statement. The third characteristic of an objective expresses a duality that, on the surface, appears to be contradictory. An objective should be well within the reach of the organization, yet difficult to attain. If an objective is not attainable, it will be disregarded. When this happens, there is no goal. At the same time, an objective must be sufficiently difficult so that it presents a challenge to everyone concerned; otherwise, its potential as an incentive is not realized.

Value of Objectives

There are four outstanding benefits that result from a statement of objectives. Stated objectives fulfill a need for direction and also serve as motivators for the personnel of an entire organization. In addition, objectives contribute to the management process and form the basis for a sound management philosophy.

Objectives Provide Direction. The primary need for objectives is implied in the definition of an objective as an end point or goal toward which management directs its efforts. That need is the need for direction and is felt throughout the entire organization. Not only should there be a statement of objectives for the company as a whole, but there should also be a statement for each organizational unit of the company. Each unit of the business should have its own related objectives so that its efforts may be coordinated and unified toward a common goal.

Objectives Serve as Motivators. Ideally, objectives serve as motivators in addition to providing direction. Examples of the motivating value of an objective are the monetary rewards used in industry. Incentive plans for hourly workers assume, to some degree, that one of the objectives of a worker is to earn more money. When this assumption is true, it follows that the creation of a situation making it possible for a person to increase his earnings motivates him toward achieving that immediate goal or objective. The desire for economic gain underlies the concept of behavior held by Taylor and others who have installed incentive plans. The creation of corporate profit is often stated as one of the major objectives of business; however, a subtle problem of differentiation exists in determining whether profit is in fact a goal or whether it is primarily a motivator of managers.

Objectives Contribute to the Management Process. The third value to be gained from a statement of objectives is that such a statement makes a significant contribution to the management process. Clearly understood and realistic objectives form a basis for the control process, the measurement of the firm's present position in relation to its desired goal. Objectives are important in that they influence the size and characteristics of an organization and affect the type of leadership required; however, the closest relationship is between objectives and the processes of planning and control. Plans are formulated in order to reach specific goals, and the control process measures the extent to which these plans are achieved. Neither is possible without a prior statement of objectives.

Objectives Are the Basis for a Management Philosophy. Lastly, the statement of objectives forms the basis for a management philosophy. It makes possible the creation of a management by objective rather than management in response to "crash programs" and "special drives." When objectives are not formally stated, the solutions of immediate emergencies are dignified as objectives, and, as such, they become a series of short-term projects that lack cohesiveness and are frequently contradictory in purpose. An example of management by drives in response to emergency situations is the company that exerts all efforts during the month of January toward reducing the number of hourly workers; in February, the drive is directed toward improving the quality of its product; March finds management trying to increase the total number of units produced, with the result that when April comes, there is the same number of employees as in January. Nor has there been any significant change in either the quality or the quantity of the product. Management by drives makes it virtually impossible to achieve Fayol's "esprit de corps," or singleness of purpose, for the simple reason that there are no cohesive objectives. The organization is continually shifting its attentions and efforts in first one direction and then another, with no opportunity to achieve a goal or objective that would result in a feeling of singleness of purpose.[2]

Types of Objectives

There is no single objective for a business organization. Some objectives are primarily of interest to persons and organizations not a part of the organization itself. Other objectives are of especial interest to the organization and of concern to those who are members of or owners of the firm. It is not a question of determining which objectives are most important—those external to the firm or those internal to the firm—but, rather, how to fulfill each set of objectives to the maximum degree.

---

[2] The following bibliography on management by objectives is presented for those students who wish to explore the topic in depth. This bibliography was published in *Management Research,* Vol. III, No. 1 (January, 1970).

Books
Drucker, Peter. *Managing for Results.* New York: Harper & Row, Publishers, 1964.
Hughes, Charles L. *Goal Setting.* New York: American Management Association, 1965.
Odiorne, George S. *Management by Objectives.* New York: Pitman Publishing Company, 1965.
Odiorne, George S. *Management Decision by Objectives.* Englewood Cliffs: Prentice-Hall, Inc., 1969.
Schleh, Edward C. *Management by Results.* New York: McGraw-Hill Book Company, 1969.
Wikstrom, Walter S. *Managing by—and with—Objectives.* New York: National Industrial Conference Board, 1968.

Articles
Glasner, Daniel M. "Patterns of Management by Results," *Business Horizons.* Vol. XII (February, 1969), pp. 37-40.
Howell, Robert A. "A Fresh Look at Management by Objectives," *Business Horizons.* Vol. X (Fall, 1967), pp. 51-58.
Ivancevich, John M. "The Theory and Practice of Management by Objectives," *Michigan Business Review.* Vol. XXI (March, 1969), pp. 13-16.
Scalan, Burt K. and Stanley Sloan. "MBO: It Doesn't Always Work," *ASTME Vectors.* Vol. IV, No. 6 (November-December, 1969), pp. 19-24.
Sloan, Stanley and David E. Schrieber, "What We Need to Know About Management by Objectives," *Personnel Journal.* Vol. IL, No. 3 (March, 1970), pp. 206-208.
Smith, Robert D. "MBO: A Management Strategy," *ASTME Vectors.* Vol. IV, No. 6 (November-December, 1969), pp. 13-18.
Tosi, Henry L. and Stephen J. Carroll, "Managerial Reaction to Management by Objectives," *Academy of Management Journal.* (December, 1968), pp. 415-426.
Tosi, Henry L. and Stephen J. Carroll, "Some Structural Factors Related to Goal Influence in the Management by Objectives Process," *M. S. U. Business Topics.* Vol. XVII, No. 2 (Spring, 1969), pp. 45-50.
Wickens, J. D. "Management by Objectives: An Appraisal," *Journal of Management Studies.* Vol. V (October, 1968), pp. 365-379.
Wikstrom, Walter S. "Management by Objectives or Appraisal by Results," *Conference Board Record.* (July, 1966), pp. 27-31.

External Objectives. National Busways in Case Problem 3-A states that its objective is to make a profit, and judging from the action taken, the implication is a profit at all costs. However, a group of aroused citizens is asking that the charter which permits National to operate the Golden Transit Company be revoked. The request is being made, not because the group objects to the company making a profit, but because the company is ignoring its primary function; namely, providing adequate service to its customers. Therefore, it seems that in this instance, service to customers is a primary objective, and making a profit is a secondary or subsidiary objective. Admittedly, a transit company is a special situation; that is, a public utility chartered to serve the public.

The question arises whether the same emphasis upon service to customers holds true for those firms that are not utilities, but are engaged in manufacturing a product for public consumption. The answer is the same as it is in the case of a utility, although the issue may not be as sharply defined. No organization can exist unless a portion of the public becomes its customers and buys its service or its product. The legendary manufacturer of buggy whips serves as an example. Of what value is it to make a good buggy whip if no one is interested in buying it? But, you say, this is an extreme example. True, however, the same concept applies to the distribution of those products and services currently in demand by customers. Unless a product or service is comparable in respect to price, quality, and utility to that of competing products or services, it will not be purchased in sufficient quantities to generate a profit large enough to permit staying in business. The desire to make a profit and the hope of sharing that profit motivate all employees, particularly managers; but in order to create profit, an organization must serve a customer. Thus, a primary objective of any organization is a service objective—to serve the needs of a customer.

Another implication to be drawn from the Golden Transit Company is that business is sanctioned by the society in which it exists. It is particularly clear in this case since the city granted the charter that permits the company to operate; and by the same token, the city can revoke that permission when the company fails to discharge its obligations. There are many types of businesses that are prohibited by law. For example, most states prohibit gambling. There are federal laws that are restrictive in nature, such as the antitrust laws. Consequently, another objective of business is to render a service sanctioned by society. The objectives of an organization must be in accord with the wishes of society or that organization is not permitted to continue operations.

Internal Objectives. The two objectives, service to a customer and service to society, are objectives *external* to the firm. At the same time these objectives are being fulfilled, an organization is interested in satisfying certain objectives that are of particular interest to the firm itself. These objectives are *internal* objectives. The first of the internal objectives is the overall position of a firm in relation to its competitors. A company may desire to be the largest, to be the most profitable, to show the greatest growth, or to produce the greatest number of new products.

Secondly, there are objectives related to employee groups. The firm may be desirous of attracting and holding the finest type employee possible; or depending upon the nature of the business and the objectives of its management, it may seek an employee with minimal qualifications. In addition, various employee groups may have subobjectives of their own. An example of this is the desire for wages and fringe benefits as expressed by unions.

A third group of objectives is directed toward satisfying the stockholders and is considered internal since stockholders are a part of the firm and are not necessarily the customers nor representatives of the society that sanctions the firm. These objectives usually define profit as a goal so that the stockholders may receive a return on their investment in the firm. Profits are also necessary to provide funds that permit the attainment of the first of the internal objectives, the desired relative position of the company with respect to its competitors.

In summary, the objectives of a firm are classed as external and internal. External objectives are service objectives. Business firms, if they are to survive, must provide a product or a service that is acceptable to customers. Also, the service or product provided must be sanctioned by society. Internal objectives are of particular interest to the firm itself. These objectives define the position of a firm in respect to its competitors and state specific goals in respect to employee groups. There are also internal objectives directed toward satisfying the needs of stockholders. Profit, the lifeblood of a business firm, functions as both an objective and a motive; but profit is not possible unless the needs of customers are satisfied and unless the objectives of the firm are sanctioned by society.

Statement of Objectives

So that objectives may be meaningful and perform the dual role of goal and motivator, they must be stated in a manner that is easily understood. Since there are two types of objectives, those external to the firm and those internal to the firm, which are at times in conflict with each other, it is highly unlikely that a satisfactory statement of goals can be accomplished by setting one single objective. Therefore, it is necessary that objectives be stated for each of several areas of performance. Peter Drucker suggests that objectives be stated for each of the following eight areas of accomplishment:

1. Market standing *product lines*
2. Innovation *research.*
3. Productivity
4. Physical and financial resources
5. Profitability *maximize (most) optimize (best)*
6. Manager performance and development
7. Worker performance and attitude
8. Public responsibility [3]

Objectives for the first five areas are susceptible to quantitative measurement and statement and may be expressed as a numerical value. For example, market standing may be expressed as a rank position in the industry—i.e., first in its field. Standing may also be stated in terms of specific dollar volume—i.e., $10 million sales for the past year. Innovation, or technological development, in respect to the management of the business and in the processes of production, as well as in respect to the product itself, is also susceptible to relatively precise measurement and expression. Productivity may be expressed in terms of total units or in a manner that measures the efficiency of the production process, such as units per man-hour or units per dollar of capital expenditure. Physical and financial resources and profitability may also be expressed in dollars. These are the traditional measures of the growth and well-being of a firm, but unless these objectives are properly supported by stated objectives in the last three areas—manager performance and development, worker performance and attitude, and public responsibility—they become meaningless and the entire structure of objectives will collapse like a house of cards.

It may be argued that the last three objectives relating to the performance of management, the workers, and the meeting of public responsibilities are not objectives but in reality a statement of policy; that is, a broad framework within which the organization operates.

---

[3] Peter F. Drucker, *The Practice of Management* (New York: Harper and Brothers, 1954). These eight areas for which objectives should be set are of significance not only in the setting of objectives but also in determining the areas for which controls must be provided. Seven of these areas appear again in Chapter 20 as those areas needing controls.

Be that as it may, an organization is composed of people, and unless plans are made for the perpetuation of the organization and its improvement as a functioning unit, the organization will not be capable of maintaining or advancing its position in respect to market position, technological development, physical resources, and profitability. It is also necessary that broad social responsibilities be recognized and stated as objectives since society sanctions, or permits, business to exist.

Figure 3-1 is an example of how the Continental-Emsco Company has stated its objectives. Notice how these objectives follow the pattern of the eight areas suggested by Peter Drucker. Objectives Nos. 1 through 4 relate to innovation, including both technological development in existing product lines and the establishment of a character willing to innovate in order to meet changing conditions. Market standing is inferred or determined by objectives Nos. 5 through 8, which relate to product quality, price, the finding of new customers, and the maintenance of a position of leadership. Productivity is covered in objectives Nos. 17 and 18, with the recognition that the degree of productivity is based upon the teamwork of employees and the conditions under which they work. Objectives in regard to physical and financial resources are stated in the last objective, No. 22, and profitability as an objective is found in No. 21. Profitability is recognized as one of the major factors that determines growth and it is stated in the first objective.

Objectives Nos. 9 through 16 set objectives in regard to manager performance and development, and worker performance and attitude. In addition, these objectives suggest to some extent how the desired performance is to be achieved and motivated. Note that there is no differentiation in these objectives in respect to their applicability; they apply equally to the worker and to management. Objectives clarifying the company's social responsibilities are stated in terms of being a good citizen, No. 19, and in encouraging health, education, and good government in objective No. 20.

These are the overall objectives of the entire Continental-Emsco Company. To insure that all levels of management are aware of the stated objectives of the company, a personnel development program is conducted in each plant. Management personnel in each plant develop the statement of objectives for that plant. Since plant objectives are formulated by each plant, they reflect the particular needs and capabilities of that plant, thus permitting maximum contribution to overall company objectives by each unit. Also, having each plant state its own objectives fulfills one of the requisites stated in the principle of the objective; namely, that the objective must be clearly understood.

CONTINENTAL-EMSCO COMPANY *

(A Division of the Youngstown Sheet and Tube Company)

1. To be a growth organization to the degree that is permitted by the profitableness of our current operations.
2. Further the diversification of Company operations.
3. Maintain a formalized advanced planning program.
4. Through research and development and/or acquisition acquire proprietor type products for manufacturing and distribution. When necessary improve existing products.
5. To manufacture quality products at the lowest possible cost utilizing modern manufacturing practices, facilities, tools, and equipment.
6. To sell quality products competitively priced.
7. Find new profitable sales markets for existing product lines and services.
8. To develop and maintain a position of leadership in the industries in which we operate.
9. To instill in each employee pride in the policies, products, and progress of his Company.
10. Continue the development of an aggressive, capable, visionary, and versatile organization, and in so doing develop employees in accordance with their natural capacities.
11. To make it possible for employees to earn promotion and promote from within the Company whenever possible.
12. To provide fair and reasonable salaries equitably applied.
13. To furnish employees adequate knowledge of the Company and what it is doing.
14. To give each employee the opportunity to express his opinion freely regarding policies, working conditions, etc.
15. To provide for each employee an opportunity to be prepared in case of sickness, accident, disability, or death, and to assure an income for his declining years.
16. To deal with each employee fairly and with respect for his human dignity.
17. Develop good employee relations and teamwork, plus good work climate permitting attainment of the greatest possible employee productivity.
18. To provide safe and pleasant work environments.
19. To build good public relations and be a good citizen in the areas of our operations.
20. To promote health, education, and good government.
21. To return our owners a reasonable profit on their investment.
22. To maintain and increase the value of our owners' investment in the Company.

* Reproduced by permission of Continental-Emsco Company, Dallas, Texas.

Figure 3-1
COMPANY OBJECTIVES

ETHICS

Once the objectives of a firm have been established, and assuming that these objectives are sanctioned by society, the manner in which objectives are achieved falls within the province of ethics. The word, ethics, as it is used today, comes from the Greek root, "ethos," and in its original form referred to habitual practices and customs. At a later date the concept of character became a part of its meaning. *Ethics* is defined as the study of conduct between individuals—what are the standards governing their interrelationships? The problem of ethics is concerned with the behavior of individuals; therefore, such terms as "business ethics," "corporate ethics," and "corporate morality" become vague and meaningless. Furthermore, a person's impression of the state of "business ethics" is actually his judgment of the behavior of individuals employed in the business community. Specifically, is the Golden Transit Company behaving in an unethical fashion, or is it the behavior of its managers that is subject to criticism? A business firm may have policies that govern to some extent the conduct of its executives, but the firm itself is a legal entity, not an individual. Thus, a firm is incapable of those personal interrelationships that characterize individuals.

There is a second concept implied in the definition of ethics in addition to the interrelationships between individuals. The additional concept is that the word clearly indicates a desirable standard of performance as demonstrated by the existence and use of the word *unethical,* which denotes behavior that does not meet desired standards.

The Nature of Ethical Problems

There are two approaches to the determination of ethical standards for businessmen. First, there are writings that record examples of behavior in order to classify and synthesize observations into a meaningful arrangement. This method provides a series of philosophical essays as guides. Second there are several empirical studies that analyze current ethical practices in American business. Both approaches are examined and recommendations are made to describe how an individual firm can aid in controlling the ethical standards of its management.

No two writers have described the questions of ethics for businessmen in exactly the same way. However, analysis of the literature results in at least three distinct problem areas:

1. Problems related to the making of decisions that are based on personal values rather than upon factual data.

2. Problems that are best described as a conflict of interest within the individual which arise because he is simultaneously a member of several groups that often have conflicting goals.
3. Interpersonal relationships; that is, relationships with other individuals or groups of individuals.

Let us look at each of these problem areas in turn.

Problems Relating to Decision Making. Not all decisions resolve into ethical problems. Some questions are neatly solved by the application of an impersonal mathematical formula. Examples are plentiful and can be found in all areas of business and at all levels within the organization. The production foreman decides which machine will be used in making a certain part, after analyzing the relative merits of the machines with respect to availability, cost, quality, and amount of time the operation will require. Likewise, the decision to buy a given piece of equipment in preference to another can be made in the same manner. But there are many areas where computations are not applicable. Such an analysis has been presented by Louis W. Norris in his discussion of the "Moral Hazards of an Executive." Mr. Norris presents the following six types of decisions that utilize ethical concepts in their resolution:

1. Living with the necessity of compromise—but never compromising too much.
2. Being free to disclose parts of the truth on many occasions, yet needing to see the whole truth.
3. Having to make final decisions but on the basis of incomplete facts.
4. Accepting the responsibility for the mistakes of subordinates while not allowing them to make too many mistakes.
5. Living up to the image that the public and his associates demand of a man in a high office, but not becoming the victim of it.
6. Succeeding as a man of thought as well as a man of action.[4]

These moral hazards fall within the province of ethics because the resolution of any one of the above-mentioned situations has its impact upon other people; yet this is not the critical factor in making these decisions. In each case the executive is asked to make a judgment, and the reference point for determining the soundness of the decision is a personal value held by the decision-maker himself. Compromise, for example, is essential to success and may be accomplished by modifying the goal or the means of obtaining the goal. The question is one of

---

[4] Louis W. Norris, "Moral Hazards of an Executive," *Harvard Business Review*, Vol. 38 (September-October, 1960), pp. 72-79.

determining when a given compromise becomes too much compromise. In a sense, a personal value is being compromised. Also, it is a judgment based on personal values that guides the executive in determining how much of the truth in any given situation should be revealed, whether a decision should be made even though all the necessary facts are not available, and in determining the upper limits of the number of mistakes on the part of a subordinate that may be tolerated. In addition, a manager must retain a degree of individuality in his personal life, and he must strive to broaden and deepen his intellectual horizons even though the image of his office calls for a man of action. The abovementioned situations are not susceptible to quantification, and mathematical analysis, but must be viewed as questions of personal values.

Conflict of Interest Problems. Much has been said about conflict of interest as it applies to high-ranking government officials. It is now customary for the President of the United States and Defense Department officials to divest themselves of the shares they hold in public corporations, or to establish a trust fund in such a manner that they are not aware of the specific shares held and have no control over the purchase or sale of their equities. Such action has been considered necessary in order to minimize or eliminate situations that might lead to a conflict of interest. It is only normal that a potential conflict of interests exists when an individual is simultaneously a member of one or more groups. Potential conflict is present because a person as a member of a group is expected to perform those actions necessary for the support of that group. Thus, it seems reasonable to assume that the possibility of conflicting interests may be controlled by limiting the number of groups in which an individual may participate at any given time.

The typical conflict of interest situation that arises most frequently originates when an official employed by one company has interests in a second company that either supplies or purchases from the employing firm. This possible conflict of interest is illustrated by the following questions: If an executive has a major financial interest in a firm that supplies parts to the company that employs him, will he, as an employee, be sufficiently forceful in demanding the best price and quality? Will he be more forceful in demanding the best for his employer if he has no personal financial interests in the profits of the supplying firm?

Let us see how one company has answered these questions. The Gillette Company, in its annual report for 1960, answers two specific questions relating to the control of conflict of interest. In answer to a question requesting the company's practice in regard to outside business interests of key employees, the following statement was made: "No member of the management group is permitted to hold a paid position anywhere else which might interfere with his duties or responsibilities to the Company. Questions of directorships, paid or otherwise, are discussed with and approved by the Chairman and President." [5]

This statement, properly applied, does much to control the development of potential conflict of interest situations resulting from an executive's acceptance of pay from outside sources. The statement covers only one aspect of conflicting loyalties in that it mentions only those instances where services are paid for by another company. It does not touch upon the problem of gifts or gratuities. In answer to the specific question concerning the company's practice in regard to avoidance of conflict of interest that might arise from the acceptance of gifts, the following position is quite clear: "No member of management of the Company is allowed to accept any gift or gratuities from third persons which might conceivably tend to induce him to violate his duties to the Company or to have any appreciable interest in any business enterprise which is a supplier or has business relationships with the Company." [6] These statements by the Gillette Company indicate the extent to which control may be exercised in order to minimize the possibility of conflicting or divided loyalties.

Interpersonal Relationships. Ethical problems recognized primarily as matters of interpersonal relationships are closely related to company objectives since the interpersonal contacts of an executive arise to a large extent as the result of actions intended to assist the company in meeting its objectives. One writer, Mr. Charles Kendrick, who is chairman of the board of directors of Schlage Lock Company has defined the problems of business ethics entirely within a framework of interpersonal relationships, and offers the following areas requiring ethical judgments on the part of the businesssman: (1) ethical relations with customers, (2) with the company, (3) between companies, (4) with employees, and (5) with shareholders. [7] Mr. Kendrick limits the fourth area of ethical judgments—interpersonal relationships with employees —to relationships between superior and subordinate and implies that the responsibility for ethical behavior rests solely with the superior. In addition, there are relationships between a subordinate and his superior that call for ethical judgment on the part of the subordinate;

---

[5] The Gillette Company, *1960 Annual Report* (Boston: 1961), p. 16.
[6] *Ibid.*

[7] H. B. Maynard, (ed.), *Top Management Handbook* (New York: McGraw-Hill Book Company, 1960), pp. 1145-1158.

therefore, a sixth relationship—ethical relationships between subordinate and superior—is added to make the analysis logically complete.

The six ethical areas of interpersonal relationships may be grouped as relationships with those persons who are *external* to the firm, and relationships with those persons who are *internal* or part of the firm. Relationships with customers and with society, including the governmental units representing that society, and with other companies, are external to the firm. Relationships with employees, with shareholders, and between subordinate and superior may be considered as internal to the firm. Let us examine the influence of company objectives upon relationships with those persons outside the firm and, then, with those persons who are part of the firm.

EXTERNAL RELATIONSHIPS. A person who represents a company that has adopted a policy of *caveat emptor*—let the buyer beware—has a difficult time in maintaining a continuing relationship with customers that may be judged as satisfactory and within the limits of good business behavior and ethics. Fortunately, most companies are more than willing to stand behind their products and, in many instances, they do so far beyond the demands of any written guarantee. In addition to the desire of individual companies to be fair and equitable with their customers, certain governmental agencies have been established to force compliance with minimum standards in this respect. One example is the Fair Trade Commission, which has much to do with the control and elimination of false and misleading advertising.

A company does much to insure ethical behavior on the part of its representatives in relation to society when it spells out specific objectives that define its relationship with the community in which it exists. For example, the Continental-Emsco Company provides objectives in this area in its objective No. 19, page 71, which specifies that the company desires to be a good citizen, and in objective No. 20, which states the firm's desire to promote health, education, and good government. These objectives imply in broad terms the kind of behavior toward society that may be expected of company executives in fulfilling the requirements of their jobs. Consider, on the other hand, the relationship that exists between an executive of National Busways and the community in which he lives after he has discontinued some of the bus routes and decreased the frequency of service on others. He, too, is doing what is required of him in order to meet company objectives.

Underlying business relationships between competing companies is the assumption that all firms should be allowed to compete on equal terms in a free society. Over the years, a body of regulatory law at the national level has developed, the purpose of which is to define those actions that are not considered as fair and equitable relationships between competing companies. Basic statutes in this area are the Sherman Antitrust Act of 1890 and the Clayton Act of 1914, which were passed to control the formation of monopolies and other activities such as price-fixing, which would tend to result in a restraint of trade. These are but two of the many laws that have been passed to regulate the conduct of businessmen, not only in their relationships with each other, but also in respect to their relationships with society and their customers.

INTERNAL RELATIONSHIPS. There are three areas of interpersonal relationships with individuals and groups internal to the firm that require ethical judgments. These relationships are with employees, shareholders, and superiors. Relationships with the first two groups are more likely to be considered ethical if an executive is fulfilling company objectives that are well stated and have the approval of society. Although company objectives that call for equitable relationships with employees and stockholders guide an executive in making ethical judgments, such objectives do not offer much help when there is an honest difference of opinion as to what constitutes fairness in a specific situation. Examples are the periodic negotiations a company has with the union representing its employees in those matters pertaining to wages and other conditions of employment. Likewise, an honest difference of opinion may arise when shareholders, as owners of the business, desire a greater return on their investment. In addition to resolving these two conflicting requests, management is asked to determine what part of earnings should be retained in the business in order that the company might continue to maintain, or possibly improve, its competitive position. The apportionment of company earnings is not an easy decision to make and requires an ethical judgment concerning the validity of the claims of each segment of the business: the employees, the shareholders, and the needs of the business itself to fulfill its stated objectives.

In addition to relationships between employees and shareholders that are based on principles of equity, a manager's relationship with his superior often calls for ethical judgments. One phase of the subordinate-superior relationship, in which the subordinate is forced to rely upon his own ethical standards in determining proper conduct, is the subordinate's decision that defines proper action on his part in obtaining promotions. Can he establish a reputation for honesty and integrity and at the same time be an opportunist who takes advantage

of others in order to advance himself? Another decision dependent upon
a subordinate's ethical standards centers around his judgment as to what
constitutes an honest, workmanlike job in the completion of duties
assigned him. The other phase of this relationship—from superior to
subordinate—has been touched upon in the discussion of those decisions
that must be made that are dependent upon an ethical judgment as a
criterion. In particular, it is mentioned that a superior is faced with the
problem of determining to what extent he can permit a subordinate to
make mistakes and at the same time accept responsibility for those
mistakes. A superior also faces ethical problems in determining how
much he should compromise with a subordinate and the extent to which
he can reveal all the facts of a situation to those reporting to him.

Value Systems of Managers

The personal value system of the individual manager has a strong
influence on his perception of a situation and his consequent behavior
in that situation. Decisions are often made where the reference point in
determining the soundness of the decision is a personal value held by the
decision maker himself. Compromises almost always represent to some
extent the compromise of a personal value. Consequently, values and
the extent to which an individual adheres to these values are a major
determinant of his ability to compromise. Personal value systems also
influence the way in which a person looks at other persons and groups
of persons thereby influencing his interpersonal relationships. Also,
one's concept of what is or is not ethical behavior is determined largely
by his personal value system. A personal value system may be viewed
"as a relatively permanent perceptual framework which shapes and
influences the general nature of an individual's behavior." [8]

Though similar to attitudes, values are regarded as being broader
in scope, unrelated to specific objects or events as are some attitudes,
and more stable in nature. A personal value system is a series of concepts with each concept having a degree of personal worth and meaning.
Personal value systems determine for an individual what is right or
wrong, good or bad, successful or unsuccessful, pleasant or unpleasant,
or any other similar bi-polar evaluation.

---

[8] George W. England, "Personal Value Systems of American Managers," *Journal
of the Academy of Management,* Vol. X, No. 1 (March, 1967), pp. 53-68. Professor
England examines the personal value systems of 1,072 American managers. He also
presents a theoretical model for analyzing the effect of values on behavior. A detailed
analysis of data obtained is presented. The definition of a personal value system quoted
above is taken from page 54. The discussion that follows is based upon this paper by
England.

In a recent study the personal value systems of 1,072 American managers selected from Poors 1965 Directory of Corporations, Executives and Directors were obtained from a personal values questionnaire (PVQ). Professor England based his research upon an underlying theoretical model shown in Figure 3-2. As shown in the figure, two sets

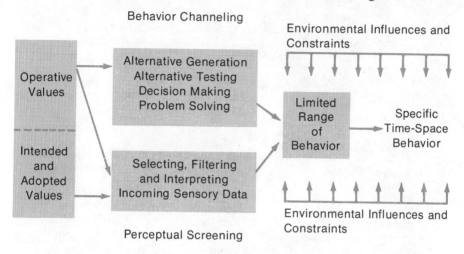

Behavior Channeling

Environmental Influences and Constraints

Operative Values

Alternative Generation
Alternative Testing
Decision Making
Problem Solving

Limited Range of Behavior

Specific Time-Space Behavior

Intended and Adopted Values

Selecting, Filtering and Interpreting Incoming Sensory Data

Perceptual Screening

Environmental Influences and Constraints

Source: George W. England, "Personal Value Systems of American Managers," *Academy of Management Journal*, Vol. X, No. 1 (March, 1967), p. 55.

Figure 3-2
THEORETICAL MODEL OF SPECIFIC TIME SPACE BEHAVIOR

of personal values are recognized. The operative values, those having the greatest influence on behavior, play a significant role in the development of alternative solutions to problems and in decision making. The intended and adopted values serve primarily as a means of screening incoming information, commonly referred to as perceptual screening, and have little direct effect upon behavior. Also, the model recognizes that there are environmental constraints influencing the effective range of behavior.

The 66 concepts of the personal values questionnaire (PVQ)— concepts about which most individuals have a personal value judgment —are reproduced in Figure 3-3 and are arranged into the following five groups: goals of business organizations, personal goals of individuals, groups of people, ideas associated with people, and ideas about topics. The managers completing the PVQ were asked to make four value judgments for each of the concepts shown in Figure 3-3. The first evaluation is known as a *power mode,* an evaluation of the concept on an important-unimportant scale. Next, it was necessary to determine

Goals of Business Organizations	**Personal Goals of Individuals**
High Productivity	Leisure
Industry Leadership	Dignity
Employee Welfare	Achievement
Organizational Stability	Autonomy
Profit Maximization	Money
Organizational Efficiency	Individuality
Social Welfare	Job Satisfaction
Organizational Growth	Influence
	Security
	Power
	Creativity
	Success
	Prestige

Groups of People	**Ideas Associated with People**	**Ideas About General Topics**
Employees	Ambition	Authority
Customers	Ability	Caution
My Co-Workers	Obedience	Change
Craftsmen	Trust	Competition
My Boss	Aggressiveness	Compromise
Managers	Loyalty	Conflict
Owners	Prejudice	Conservation
My Subordinates	Compassion	Emotions
Laborers	Skill	Equality
My Company	Cooperation	Force
Blue Collar Workers	Tolerance	Liberalism
Government	Conformity	Property
Stockholders	Honor	Rational
Technical Employees		Religion
Me		Risk
Labor Unions		
White Collar Employees		

Source: George W. England, "Personal Value Systems of American Managers," *Academy of Management Journal,* Vol. X, No. 1 (March, 1967), p. 61.

Figure 3-3
CONCEPTS USED TO MEASURE MANAGER'S VALUES

why individual managers rated a given item as important or unimportant; therefore, three secondary modes of evaluation were utilized. The three secondary modes selected were a *pragmatic* mode of evaluation using a successful-unsuccessful scale, an *ethical—moral* mode using a right-wrong scale, and an *affect,* or feeling mode of evaluation using a pleasant-unpleasant scale. Thus by using the secondary modes of evaluation one can determine why a given concept is rated as either important, of average importance, or of low importance.

The Value Profile. The results of the survey are shown in Figures 3-4 and 3-5. The first part of Figure 3-4 shows that 29 concepts are assigned high importance because they are successful thus indicating the pragmatic bent of the managers. Note that no concept is assigned high importance because it is pleasant although 10 of the 39 concepts considered of high importance are so ranked because they are right, an ethical-moral judgment. The lower part of Figure 3-4 shows that 562 managers, over one-half of those surveyed, responded with a high importance-successful ranking to more of the 66 concepts than to any other possible response category. It should be noted that 276, approximately one-fourth, have a moralistic and ethical orientation as shown by their rating of concepts as high importance-right.

As a total group, Managers' primary orientation is pragmatic
As a total group, Managers' secondary orientation is moralistic and ethical
Supporting data:

	High Importance	Average Importance	Low Importance
Successful 1st Ranked	29	7	2
Right 1st Ranked	10	11	0
Pleasant 1st Ranked	0	6	1
			66

The 66 concepts are assigned to one of the nine categories (cells) by a joint modal frequency method for the total group of managers. For example, more of the total group of managers responded "high importance-successful" than in any other category of response to each of 29 concepts. Thus, 29 concepts are assigned to the "high importance-successful" category.

	High Importance	Average Importance	Low Importance
Successful 1st Ranked	562	101	0
Right 1st Ranked	276	87	0
Pleasant 1st Ranked	12	29	5
			1072

Each of the 1072 managers is assigned to that category (cell) that contains the highest number of concepts for him. For example, 562 managers responded "high importance-successful" to more of the 66 concepts than to any of the other eight response categories.

Source: George W. England, "Personal Value Systems of American Managers," *Academy of Management Journal,* Vol. X, No. 1 (March, 1967), p. 61.

Figure 3-4
GENERAL VALUE ORIENTATION OF MANAGERS

Figure 3-5 shows the value profile of the managers and the concepts that are ranked as successful with high importance, average importance, low importance; those that were ranked as right with high importance, average importance, and low importance; and those that were ranked as pleasant with high, average, and low importance.

High Importance | Average Importance | Low Importance

Successful 1st Ranked

High Productivity	My Boss	Ability	Labor Unions	Prejudice
Industrial Leadership	Managers	Skill	Aggressiveness	Force
Organizational Stability	Owners	Cooperation	Influence	
Profit Maximization	My Subordinates	Achievement	Power	
Organizational Efficiency	My Company	Job Satisfaction	Compromise	
Organizational Growth	Stockholders	Creativity	Conflict	
Employees	Technical Employees	Success	Risk	
Customers	Me	Change		
My Co-workers	White Collar Employees	Competition		
Craftsmen	Ambition			

Operative Values

Adopted Values Situationally Induced

Right 1st Ranked

Employee Welfare	Social Workers
Trust	Laborers
Loyalty	Blue Collar Workers
Honor	Obedience
Dignity	Compassion
Individuality	Tolerance
Government	Authority
Property	Caution
Rational	Conservatism
Religion	Equality
	Liberalism

Intended Value Socio-culturally Induced

Values with Low Behavioral Relevance

Pleasant 1st Ranked

Leisure	Conformity
Autonomy	
Money	
Security	
Prestige	
Emotions	

Figure 3-5
MANAGERIAL VALUE PROFILE

England summarizes his interpretation of Figure 3-5 as follows:

1. The 29 concepts which are rated as "high importance" and are viewed as "successful" represent the operative values for these managers. They are considered important and fit the primary orientation (pragmatic) pattern of the group and should influence the behavior of the managers more than the ideas and concepts in any other cell in the Value Profile. For example, the fact that managers value the characteristics Ambition, Ability, and Skill more than they value the characteristics Loyalty, Trust, and Honor would be reflected in their own behavior and in their expectations about others' behavior.

2. The 9 concepts found in the cells labeled "Adopted Values—Situationally Induced" are those that have been observed as being successful in the manager's organizational experience but which he finds difficult to internalize and view as being of high importance. Managers seem to be saying, for example, that Labor Unions are successful (they do have a large impact on what goes on in organizations) but that they should not be considered as important as other groups such as Customers or Managers or Owners. The values represented by these 9 concepts would not be expected to influence the behavior of managers to the extent that operative values would, since managers are not as wholly committed to adopted values as they are to operative values.

3. The 10 concepts found in the cells labeled "Intended Values—Socio-culturally Induced" are those that have been considered as highly important by the manager throughout most of his life do not fit his organizational experience (*sic.*). Here the interpretation would be that managers, for example, have viewed "rationality" as an important criterion for behavior but that their organizational environment has not always rewarded "rationality." It is as if they were saying that we have always considered it important to be rational but don't see it as being highly useful in our organizational life. The complexities of organizational requirements do not square with individual notions of what is and what is not rational. These intended values where there is conflict between what one has learned to believe and what one sees in his accepted environment have been termed professed or talking values by a number of authors. Employee Welfare, for example, is viewed as highly important as an organizational goal by managers but it may not affect their behavior greatly because it doesn't fit their primary pragmatic orientation. It is a professed value but not one that is operative or directly influential of behavior to any large extent.

4. Finally, the 18 concepts found in the cells labeled "Low Behavioral Relevance" are those that would not be expected to influence a

manager's behavior to any large extent since they are not considered important and do not fit the pragmatic orientation of managers.[9]

Significance of Personal Value System. The results of this study show that values, even though complex, may be measured. Clearly, a general value system emerges and is best described as pragmatic; that is, a value system measured in terms of whether or not a concept is successful or unsuccessful—does it work or does it not work in operation. At the same time there are individual differences in managers in respect to the number of operant values held and the specific nature of these values. Personal values are significant not only as determinants of one's own decisions, but are also significant as determinants of corporate objectives and strategy. Differences in personal values may account for much of the conflict in organization. It is suggested that accommodation may occur more readily between individuals who have compatible value systems. Finally, personal value systems, both the operative system and the intended and adoptive values, determine one's perception of the ethical content of a situation and the subsequent evaluation of a specific action as being either ethical or unethical.

How Ethical Are Businessmen?

In an earlier study 1,700 representative executives were questioned to determine their attitudes toward ethical problems.[10] The survey establishes four problem areas: the extent to which businessmen are aware of their social and ethical responsibilities, current practices in industry that are accepted yet recognized as unethical, a description of specific areas requiring ethical judgments, and an analysis of the determinants of ethical standards and practices in industry.

Awareness of Social and Ethical Responsibilities. Awareness of ethics as related to business is illustrated by the overwhelming number of executives, 99 out of every 100, who indicate complete agreement with the following statement: "Sound ethics is good business in the long run." In addition, there is considerable evidence that businessmen recognize the multiple nature of business objectives. Five out of six believe that it would be unethical to act in the interest of shareholders only and exclude the interests of employees and consumers. However,

---

[9] *Ibid.*, pp. 60-62.

[10] R. C. Baumhart, "How Ethical Are Businessmen?" *Harvard Business Review,* Vol. XXXIX (July-August, 1961), pp. 6-12, 175. The discussion following is based upon the questionnaire and findings reported by the Reverend Raymond C. Baumhart, S. J., Doctoral Candidate, Harvard Business School. The study reports a wealth of detailed material that is of unique value in that it is a statement of how businessmen define ethical problems and how they react to problems involving ethical concepts.

one out of six, or approximately 16 percent, does not agree that sound ethics is good business.

When the statement, "Sound ethics is good business in the long run," is paraphrased so that it becomes "Whatever is good business is good ethics," 15 percent of those queried indicate agreement with the paraphrased statement. In conclusion, it appears that the vast majority of executives are acutely aware of the social and ethical implications of their actions, but there is also evidence that approximately 15 percent of those included in the survey have a different value system.

Current Practices: Accepted, Yet Unethical. Within many industries there are practices that are tolerated and sometimes even accepted though they fall far short of ideal standards of ethical behavior. In order to obtain direct information on accepted, yet unethical practices, the following question was asked: "In every industry there are some generally accepted business practices. In your industry are there any such practices which you regard as unethical?"

Actions intended to buy loyalty for the company and its products are mentioned most frequently as the one practice that should be eliminated. Among the methods used to secure preferential treatment for the company and its products are gifts, gratuities, lavish entertainment, and outright bribes. Twenty-three percent of those queried indicate that these practices ranked first among those that should be eliminated. Unfair practices in pricing, such as price discrimination, are listed as the next most undesirable practice, with 18 percent indicating that these practices should be eliminated. Dishonest advertising ranks first on the list of practices to be eliminated by 14 percent of those queried. Miscellaneous unfair competitive practices; cheating customers, unfair credit practices, overselling; price collusion by competitors; dishonesty in making or keeping a contract; and unfairness and prejudice in hiring are mentioned, but in no case did more than 10 percent rank any one of these practices as the one practice that should be eliminated.

The preceding information is important for several reasons. First, it illustrates the extent of unethical practices, along with a detailing of these practices. Second, the practices of an industry form the "ethical climate" in which an executive must operate and, as such, influence his behavior. And lastly, the existence of unethical, yet accepted, practices sets the stage for a certain degree of conflict within the executive himself, as he may be required to do things to be accepted by his industry that he recognizes as unethical in the light of his own standards.

Problem Areas Requiring Ethical Judgments. The giving of gifts, gratuities, and lavish entertainment, all of which are intended to obtain loyalty for a company or its products, are ranked as the number one unethical practice that should be eliminated. Thus, it would seem that the problem situation most frequently giving rise to conflict would be in connection with these activities. However, such is not the case. Instead, problems of interpersonal relationships ranked first as the business situation causing the deepest source of concern. Interpersonal problems create a conflict within the individual executive between what is expected of him as a profit-conscious businessman and what is expected of him as an ethical person. Yet it must be noted that only 75 percent of the executives participating in the study indicate that there are any ethical problems. Apparently the 25 percent who do not perceive any problems do not regard the following interpersonal problems as having an ethical content. This 25 percent has a personal value system that differs from the majority and may be best described as one that has "hard" operative values. The problem areas considered as causing the deepest concern for the majority surveyed are firings and layoffs; honest communications; collusion and sharp practices in pricing; gifts, entertainment, and kickbacks; and pressure from superiors.

FIRINGS AND LAYOFFS. The problem mentioned most frequently as creating the deepest concern is that of firings and layoffs, a situation related to an earlier observation concerning the general awareness that exists in regard to the social and ethical responsibilities of businessmen. In this connection, it is noted that five out of every six persons believe that it would be unethical to act in the interest of shareholders alone to the exclusion of the interests of employees and customers. The ethical content of interpersonal problems arising from firings and layoffs is shown by the following comment supplied by a personnel director: "It has always concerned me that the industry's regular (periodic) reduction in work force should always bear so heavily on the 'little people'— particularly when adversity has not always been equally shared by stockholders and top management." [11]

HONEST COMMUNICATIONS. The second category of ethical situations—honest communications—is an example of those problems relating to the making of a decision based upon personal values rather than upon factual data. The question to be answered is essentially the same as that mentioned by L. W. Norris.[12] The problem in respect to honest communications is not the determination of what the truth is nor whether the truth should be told; it is a matter of determining

---

[11] *Ibid.,* p. 163.
[12] Norris, *loc. cit.* Mr. Norris' "Moral Hazards of an Executive" are discussed on page 73.

how much of the truth should be revealed. In reaching this decision, the final judgment is based upon one's own personal values.

COLLUSION AND SHARP PRACTICES IN PRICING. The third category centers around interpersonal relationships with competitors. Particular reference is made to the opportunity for collusion in pricing the company's products. Problems expressed in this area range from the pressure put on small companies to fix prices in line with those of large competitors to the establishment of price differentials for those who buy because of price alone—yet not giving the same advantage to their loyal customers. Also included is the question of determining a fair price for those who purchase goods on an installment plan.

GIFTS, ENTERTAINMENT, AND KICKBACKS. Though the use of gifts and lavish entertainment is designated most frequently as the one practice that should be eliminated, these practices rank fourth as a source of ethical conflict. There seems to be a recognition that customers who are retained by means of lavish entertainment are capable of being bought by someone else who is willing to pay a higher price. Also, questions are raised concerning the propriety of expensive trips for company personnel and other practices that represent an unwise use of the company's money; in short, a breach of trust with the shareholders.

PRESSURE FROM SUPERIORS. The last, and perhaps the most important, situation creating interpersonal conflict is the result of pressures from one's superiors in the company. Such pressures may range from a normal feeling that one is being asked to accomplish too much in too short a time to a frantic attempt to please everyone as a means of advancing within the company. Excessive pressure may also come from a drive for increased production, increased sales volume, or greater profits without regard for the actions necessary to meet these goals. Undue influence from superiors may also extend to expecting an individual to conform with practices that are a violation of law; for example, the establishing of prices that may be in restraint of trade.

Determinants of Ethical Standards and Practices. The degree of awareness of social and ethical responsibilities has been reviewed; current practices—accepted, yet unethical—have been examined; and the five problem areas causing concern because the decisions required involve ethical judgments have been discussed briefly. Though this information is significant, the major contribution of the Reverend Baumhart's study is that it points the way toward the development of a principle of ethics. Before the principle can be developed, it is necessary to know the factors determining the degree of ethical behavior in the business community. The executives included in the survey were asked to rank the influences which, in their opinion, contribute most to ethical behavior and the influences contributing most to unethical behavior. The results of the ranking are shown in Figure 3-6.[13]

Factors Determining Ethical Decisions	
Factor	**Average Rank**
A Man's Personal Code of Behavior	1.5
The Behavior of a Man's Superiors in the Company	2.8
Formal Company Policy	2.8
Ethical Climate of the Industry	3.8
The Behavior of a Man's Equals in the Company	4.0
Factors Determining Unethical Decisions	
Factor	**Average Rank**
The Behavior of a Man's Superiors in the Company	1.9
Ethical Climate of the Industry	2.6
The Behavior of a Man's Equals in the Company	3.1
Lack of Company Policy	3.3
Personal Financial Needs	4.1

Figure 3-6

DETERMINANTS OF ETHICAL BEHAVIOR

When answering the question calling for influences that create ethical behavior, the factor given first rank is the individual's personal code of conduct. Tied for second place in importance as determinants of ethical behavior are two factors in the executive's immediate business environment; (1) the behavior of his superiors in the company, and (2) a formal statement of company policy. Though the ethical climate of the industry and the behavior of his equals in the company are important, they are not as significant in determining ethical behavior as the first three factors—his own ethical standards, the standards of his superiors, and the standards of his company as reflected in its policy statement.

What are the influences leading to unethical decisions? Moving to first rank in importance in determining unethical behavior is the behavior of a man's superiors. The climate of the industry, in reality a composite of the behavior of all the executives of that industry, is second in importance as a determinant of unethical actions. The remaining three factors—behavior of a man's equals, lack of company policy, and personal financial needs are of significance, but in each case the ranked value is greater than three.

[13] R. C. Baumhart, *ibid.*, p. 156.

Thus, it seems that regardless of the manner in which the question is worded; i.e., whether the emphasis is placed upon ethical or unethical behavior, two factors stand out as major determinants of ethical behavior. They are: (1) the individual executive's personal code of conduct and (2) the behavior of his superiors. In the last analysis, the superior's behavior is governed, in turn, by his own personal code of conduct.

The above conclusion, which indicates the ultimate dependence upon a personal code of conduct and ethics, has a familiar ring. In Chapter 2, in the discussion of Fayol's principle of authority, it is mentioned that the solution to questions concerning the abuse of authority lies in the integrity of the person holding that authority. Fayol's full statement concerning this point is as follows: "The best safeguard against abuse of authority and against weakness on the part of a higher manager is personal integrity and particularly high moral character of such a manager, and this integrity, it is well known, is conferred neither by election nor ownership." [14]

A Concluding Concept

Fundamental to the development of a clear concept is the recognition that the business community is composed of many industries which, in turn, are made up of many companies. Each company has its own management, and each and every member of that management is at the same time an individual, a subordinate, and a superior. As an individual, his own personal code of conduct exerts the greatest influence in determining the degree to which his behavior is judged as ethical. As a subordinate, his own code is reinforced and supported by the actions of his superiors. As a superior, he exerts a great positive influence in encouraging ethical behavior on the part of subordinates and has potentially an even greater influence in contributing to a subordinate's unethical behavior. The conclusion is clear: *The ethical standards of any industry are determined by the ethical standards of individual executives of each member company in that industry.*

Code of Ethics

Though the ethical standards of a group are dependent upon the standards of each individual member of the group, the establishment of a code of ethics may serve a useful purpose. The chief value obtained from the establishment of a code is that it offers

---

[14] Henri Fayol in H. F. Merrill (ed.), *Classics in Management* (New York: American Management Association, 1960), p. 220.

a framework within which individual members of the group may work. Guides are provided that offer aid in reaching decisions on those problems having a high ethical content. Ethical codes tend to be an expression of the ideal and, as such, they have the effect of raising the level of conduct of the group governed by the code. There have been many criticisms of codes of ethics. Chief among these criticisms is that, for the most part, such codes are established voluntarily and are difficult to enforce. Usually the penalty for violating a code is expulsion from a group, which has the effect of leaving the violator free from further criticism. Codes are also criticized as being at best an expression of good intentions and not an accurate statement of conditions as they are.

Nonetheless, several industries and groups associated with industry have developed codes of ethics. In 1957 the AFL-CIO formulated a statement called the AFL-CIO Ethical Practices Code. This code lists six ethical practices to be followed by members of the AFL-CIO. Included are regulations governing the issuance of charters for local unions, the honest administration of trust funds, and the conduct of honest elections for union officials. Also mentioned are conditions limiting eligibility to hold office in the AFL-CIO or any affiliated union, limitations on outside financial interests of union officials, and provisions designed to insure maintenance of accurate and honest records of all union transactions. In 1958, the National Association of Manufacturers (NAM) issued a two-part statement setting forth the beliefs of management in regard to moral and ethical standards. The first part of the statement outlines the beliefs of the NAM in regard to the type of political economy that industry should support and suggests the proper relationships between industry and government, suppliers, customers, and stockholders. The second part of the statement outlines the beliefs of the NAM with respect to employer-employee relationships.[15]

In the opinion of many, the two codes of conduct have fallen short of their goals. Neither all unions, nor all managements, conduct themselves according to the standards set forth by their respective groups.

There are instances where self-regulation, the alternate to government regulation, has worked effectively, and demonstrate that self-regulation is possible and effective provided the group sincerely wishes to enforce ethical standards. An illustration of self-regulation is provided in Case Problem 3-B.

---

[15] *Moral and Ethical Standards in Labor and Management* (New York: National Association of Manufacturers, 1958), pp. 1-7.

This case is based upon two press releases issued on the same day by the New York Stock Exchange.[16] Press Release No. 1 is a statement by Mr. Edward C. Werle, chairman of the Board of Governors of the New York Stock Exchange. Mr. Werle's statement presents a detailed statement of an action, and the reasons for that action, taken by the Board of Governors of the New York Stock Exchange. Press Release No. 2, by the president of the New York Stock Exchange, Mr. G. Keith Funston, emphasizes the "moral responsibilities" of the New York Stock Exchange.

PRESS RELEASE NO. 1

Edward C. Werle, chairman of the Board of Governors of the New York Stock Exchange, this morning (September 28) made the following announcement from the rostrum overlooking the trading floor of the Exchange:

"A charge was preferred against Anton E. Homsey, a member of the Exchange and a partner of DuPont, Homsey & Company, a member organization, under Section 1 of Article XIV of the Constitution. The charge was considered by the Board of Governors at a special meeting on September 27, 1960.

"The charge stated that he had committed fraud or fraudulent acts. The substance of the charge was as follows:

"Anton E. Homsey, the managing general partner of DuPont, Homsey & Company, was responsible for the supervision and administration of the firm's back office operations and for surveillance of the firm's capital position.

"Mr. Homsey had delivered to him, on his instructions to the firm cashier or by delivery from the customer, securities from the accounts of three of the firm's customers between March and June, 1960. Mr. Homsey pledged all or most of these securities as collateral for loans without the knowledge of the customers. None of the loans was made in the name of DuPont, Homsey & Company or in the name, or for the benefit, of any of the three customers. Total market value of the securities was approximately $503,000.

"Mr. Homsey also personally removed two 100-share stock certificates from the firm's security box and

---

16 News Bureau, New York Stock Exchange (New York: September 28, 1960). Both releases were issued on the same day and both are reproduced in full.

pledged them as collateral for loans. These loans were not made in the name of the firm.

"Mr. Homsey certified to the Board of Governors that, to the best of his knowledge and belief, answers to financial questionnaires from the Exchange, as of February 29 and July 31, 1960, represented true and correct financial statements of DuPont, Homsey & Company. On each date, however, Mr. Homsey failed to report that he had borrowings on securities in excess of $200,000. The answer to the July 31 questionnaire also failed to disclose the apparent liability to the customers with respect to the securities withheld or withdrawn from customers' accounts.

"The Board found Mr. Homsey guilty of the charge and determined that he be expelled."

PRESS RELEASE NO. 2

Keith Funston, president of the New York Stock Exchange, said today the Board of Governors authorized the following statement regarding the expulsion of Anton E. Homsey, a member of the Exchange and a partner in DuPont, Homsey & Company:

"The Board of Governors has expelled Mr. Anton E. Homsey from membership in the New York Stock Exchange—an action which means that the firm of DuPont, Homsey & Company is no longer a member firm of the Stock Exchange.

"The New York Stock Exchange is shocked that one of its members should have violated the trust placed in him by his associates and clients and is also dismayed that Mr. Homsey, by his action, placed in jeopardy the solvency of a New York Stock Exchange member organization.

"This is the first time in 22 years that the Exchange's Board of Governors has found it necessary to expel a member for fraudulent acts which endangered a member firm's financial position. As part of the vigorous financial supervision to which all member firms are subject, Exchange examiners, in the course of an examination, discovered a condition which suggested that DuPont, Homsey & Company could not be permitted to continue as a member firm with safety to its creditors. Consequently, the firm was suspended promptly from the Stock Exchange and the appropriate regulatory agencies were notified. Continued investigation by the Stock Exchange uncovered evidence that fraudulent acts had been committed by Mr. Homsey and charges were quickly brought against him.

"At the present time a temporary court-appointed receiver is determining the exact financial position of DuPont, Homsey & Company. Pending a complete audit of the firm's affairs which we are advised should be completed in about two weeks, the exact nature of the losses—if any—which might be sustained by the firm's customers cannot be stated.

"While each member firm of the New York Stock Exchange bears the complete responsibility for its obligations to its customers, the Stock Exchange recognizes, nevertheless, that the expulsion of Anton E. Homsey does not solve the problem of protecting the interests of investors—particularly those of modest means—who dealt in good faith with DuPont, Homsey & Company. More than that, the New York Stock Exchange feels that its moral responsibilities to these investors are not ended with the act of expulsion.

"At this time, while awaiting results of the final audit, and of current negotiations by the receiver to resolve outstanding financial problems, the Stock Exchange is studying ways of assisting the receiver in order to help protect the interests of the firm's customers."

PROBLEMS

1. Why should the New York Stock Exchange feel that it has a moral responsibility in this case?
2. What immediate steps would you recommend be taken to protect the interests of those who invested with DuPont, Homsey & Company?
3. What long-range recommendations would you make to insure the interests of investors who invest with member firms of the New York Stock Exchange?
4. Why was it significant that the New York Stock Exchange discovered the irregularity of a member firm and then took the action described in this case?
5. Does this case illustrate the principle of ethics developed in the text? How?

Chapter Questions for Study and Discussion

1. One of the characteristics of an objective is that it should be well within the reach of an organization, yet difficult to obtain. With this in mind,

comment on the following statement: The difficult we do today; the impossible we do tomorrow.

2. Why is the creation of profit a good example of an objective that simultaneously gives direction and motivates?

3. Why is it necessary for a firm to have an objective that states its desired overall position in relation to its competitors?

4. Why is it necessary to state several objectives for a firm rather than one general objective?

5. Continental-Emsco Company, in its statement of objectives, follows the recommendations of Peter Drucker, but separate objectives are not stated for managers and for workers. If you were preparing a statement of objectives for a company, would you differentiate between manager performance and development, and worker performance and attitude?

6. Of what value are the statements of company practice as stated by the Gillette Company concerning outside financial interests of key employees?

7. Is it significant that the classification of interpersonal relationships follows the same general pattern as the classification of objectives; i.e., internal and external interpersonal relationships which correspond to those objectives that are internal to the firm and those objectives that are external to the firm?

8. Define in your own terms Personal Value System. Give an example showing how one's personal value system can influence his perception of the ethical content of a situation.

9. England's study shows quite clearly that the primary personal value system for most American managers is best described as pragmatic. What is meant by the term, pragmatic, and is this an appropriate value for managers? Discuss.

10. Comment on the following statements: "Sound ethics is good business in the long run," and "Whatever is good business is good ethics."

11. On page 86 there is a quotation from a personnel director who recognizes an ethical problem in the effect of periodic layoffs upon workers when adversity has not been equally shared by stockholders and top management. Does the same problem in ethics exist if the company continues to grant wage increases to the extent that it cannot pass on the gains obtained from increased productivity to stockholders in the form of increased dividends and to customers through a reduction in price?

12. The conclusion regarding ethics is worded with reference to an industrial situation; that is, the ethical standards of an industry and the standards of the companies that make up that industry. Does this principle apply equally to professional groups such as teachers, physicians, and lawyers?

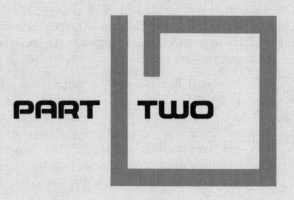

PART TWO

The Planning Function

classification

The planning function is given the primary position among the four functions of the management process since logically it is the function that occurs first. Planning is also regarded as pervasive as it shapes the other three functions of organizing, leading, and controlling. A taxonomy of plans is presented which results in plans being classified in respect to duration, function, or scope. Scope, or breadth, is divided into three subgroups— policies, procedures, and methods. Chapter 4 closes with a discussion of the criteria that may be used to evaluate plans. Two approaches are used in developing criteria. The first approach develops criteria from a procedural analysis and the second provides an evaluation of plans in terms of economic effectiveness.

The next two chapters introduce the major business functions and discuss the development of a certain type of plan for each of these functions. In Chapter 5 the range of policy statements for finance and sales is outlined, and in Chapter 6 the area of policy statements for the functions of production and personnel is presented. The interrelationships between policy statements for each of the four functional areas are summarized in tabular form and are also integrated within the context of a servo system.

Effective planning requires timely and complete information; consequently, it is necessary to study the functions of a management information system. The development of electronic data processing is traced and the steps necessary for the design and installation of a completely integrated data processing information system are set forth. The case problems of Chapter 7 are of particular interest. Case Problem 7-A, The Parable of the Spindle, shows clearly that an information system breakdown can create employee behavioral reactions that are normally considered to arise as the result of poor practices in human relations. Case Problem 7-B, The Short-Order Economy, describes an application of a large scale electronic data processing system and shows how this application affects the organization and relations with customers.

As part of the planning process it is usually necessary to select one plan from several alternatives; in short, a decision must be made. Since many business problems can be expressed as mathematical equations, some of the frequently used quantitative aids for decision making are described. The behavioral aspects of decision making are considered because all decisions are influenced by the individual characteristics of the decision maker. Chapter 8 closes with a consideration of the creative aspects of decision making, and tested methods for encouraging creativity in the solution of business problems are summarized.

CHAPTER 4

Planning

The Bojo Corporation is an established manufacturer, located in a small town in southwestern New York State. The Company was founded about 90 years ago and initially served both the railroad industry and the oil fields of nothern Pennsylvania. At the present time, a large part of its business is still associated with the oil industry. In recent years, however, it has branched into other fields and has been able to develop applications of products originally used in the oil fields to other areas. The Bojo Corporation is a subsidiary company of a large national firm with headquarters in St. Louis. The national headquarters controls all capital expenditures, reviews operating budgets developed by the subsidiary corporations, follows up to insure the meeting of budgetary goals, and also exerts strong influence in the labor relations area. All labor contracts and labor policies are determined by the headquarters staff.

In recent years, the Bojo Corporation developed a new type of pipe coupling that is used to join two pieces of pipe without having to thread the ends of the pipes being joined or cutting them to an exact length. The coupling saves time and money and has experienced a remarkable sales volume from municipalities since it is used primarily to replace existing water and gas lines. There is every reason to believe that the market will expand and that the Bojo Corporation will receive a large share of the increase. Since the coupling is particularly useful in the replacement market with the oldest water

CASE PROBLEM 4-A

SELECTING A PLANT SITE

97

and gas systems on the eastern seaboard, the greatest potential market for the immediate future is in this area.

Present manufacturing facilities, a department in the main plant, are now running at capacity; and in order to meet the anticipated increase in demand, new facilities are needed. Since the present plant location does not permit expansion, it has been decided that a new plant should be built to house the present coupling department and to provide for future increases in volume. A member of the St. Louis controller's staff, Mr. Johnson, has been assigned the task of conducting a plant location survey and submitting subsequent recommendations to the president of the Bojo Corporation and the officials of the parent company.

In preparing for his assignment, Mr. Johnson contacted several executives, among them the executive vice-president responsible for the Bojo Corporation and other subsidiaries in Pennsylvania, New York, and Massachusetts. It was the executive vice-president's wish that the plant be located on a direct route between Pittsburgh, Pennsylvania, and their present location, or between Buffalo, New York, and their present location. His reason for desiring the plant in these areas was that it would be convenient for him as a company executive to fly into either the Buffalo or Pittsburgh airport, rent a car, and drive directly to the plant.

A conversation with the home office vice-president, industrial relations, revealed that the company, as a matter of policy, wished to have a different international union in the new plant rather than have the employees represented by the same union that organized Bojo's New York plant. The reason for the policy was that by having a different union in each plant it would lessen the possibility of all plants closing as the result of a strike, since no one international union would represent more than one plant. The vice-president indicated that it would be necessary to locate at least 100 miles from the present plant in order to be assured of a different union. He also recommended analyzing the labor rates of any community proposed as a location for the new plant so that maximum savings might be realized from low initial labor costs. He stated further that by starting operations with labor rates as low as possible, the company would be in a better position to increase rates in the future.

When Mr. Johnson contacted the president of the Bojo Corporation and reviewed the wishes of the two central office executives, he found the president had a few ideas of his own to add to the picture. The president indicated that it was mandatory that the new location have complete rail facilities, since raw materials were received most economically by rail and many of the finished product shipments could be made by rail. He wanted the plant located east of the present facility to minimize transportation costs by establishing a direct flow of materials from Pittsburgh to the East Coast markets. He was also insistent, as operating head of the company, that the new plant be located in an area where there is a well-defined, stable tax structure. He felt that tax stability was necessary to predict long-range profits with some degree of accuracy. Another requirement was that the site chosen be large enough to permit future expansion of the proposed plant to twice its initial size. The president of Bojo placed no exact limitations in regard to construction costs provided such costs were in line with typical costs for the area selected.

PROBLEMS

1. Assume that you are Mr. Johnson. Prepare an initial determination of the relative significance of the factors considered to be important by:

   a. The executive vice-president of the home office.
   b. The vice-president, industrial relations, home office.
   c. The president of the subsidiary Bojo Corporation.

2. Indicate in detail the steps that you would follow in conducting a study to evaluate alternate sites for the new plant.

3. Prior to Mr. Johnson's receiving his assignment, certain decisions had been made by the Bojo management. What were these decisions? What additional decisions must be made after a satisfactory location for the new plant has been found?

Planning is generally considered the first function performed in the management sequence of planning, organizing, directing, and controlling. The need for planning is not limited to the development of plans for the attainment of organizational objectives. Planning is required to develop plans for the organization necessary to implement those plans designed to achieve overall organizational objectives. Planning is also necessary to determine the methods and types of controls as well as the kind of direction best suited to the organization. Yet, the success or failure of an enterprise or the success or failure of specific plans is dependent upon the way in which the other three functions of the management process are performed, as well as upon the quality of the planning function, since planning is but one function of the management process cycle.

In our study of the planning function we shall examine some of the fundamental concepts of planning and develop a definition of planning. The different types of plans are reviewed and classified, and in the last part of the chapter, criteria are developed for the evaluation of plans.

FUNDAMENTAL CONCEPTS OF PLANNING

In order to understand the nature of planning, the meanings of three terms—planning, the plan, and decision making—must be clarified. We also need to know the purpose of planning and why planning is important to the management process. First, let us clarify the meaning of the terms, *planning, the plan,* and *decision making.*

Planning

Planning is an activity performed by all levels of management. Differences in the complexity of the planning process and the resultant plans are, to a large measure, determined by the organizational level of the person who initiates the planning process. Mr. Johnson (Case Problem 4-A) has been asked to develop and analyze alternatives available to the Bojo Corporation in the selection of a new plant site. There are many factors that he must consider, among which are availability of land, cost of land, cost of building, availability of transportation, and location in respect to raw materials and markets for the finished product. He is required not only to list these factors but also to evaluate them in respect to their relative importance, which in turn means that value criteria must be developed. These are the kinds of managerial activities normally associated with planning.

The outstanding concern of planning is the future, and as a process it probes into the future, literally attempting to foretell the effects of coming events, thereby enabling a firm to meet the future with some degree of success. Less apparent is planning's concern with the past. To develop a sound plan, it is necessary to review the past and evaluate information relevant to the present and the future. Analysis of forces of the present—both internal and external to the organization requiring planning—must also be considered. Thus, the planning function is defined as *the analysis of relevant information from the present and the past and an assessment of probable future developments so that a course of action (plan) may be determined that enables the organization to meet its stated objectives.*

The Plan

Planning, the process of evaluating all relevant information and the assessment of probable future developments, results in the statement of a recommended course of action—a *plan*. Plans should be regarded as blueprints for action. The kinds of plans commonly used in business operations are discussed in the next major topic of this chapter, "Types of Plans." The characteristics of plans and the effect that these characteristics have upon the probable success of plans are discussed in the section, "Criteria for Evaluating Plans."

Decision Making

Decision making is an activity that permeates the entire planning process. *Making a decision is making a choice between two or more alteratives.* The alternative selected is the decision. Planning requires the continuous collection, evaluation, and selection of data. Some data are rejected as not being pertinent to the problem at hand; other data are retained and used to formulate a recommended course of action. Selecting some information and rejecting other information constitute a choice, or a decision. Ultimately one proposed course of action is recommended as being superior to an alternate course as a means of attaining desired objectives. Again, a decision has been made. These are the decisions of a planner as he develops a plan.

Decision making is also used to describe an activity that is characteristic of executive positions. The responsible executive either accepts or rejects the plan. If he accepts the plan, the next step is its implementation. Plan implementation requires commitment of company resources, an action that initiates a chain of events which are sometimes irreversible. The difference between an executive's decision and a planner's decision is one of degree—not kind—since both are making choices. The executive's decisions are overt in nature and are recognized because they commit company resources, but the planner's decisions are covert and can be retracted and reevaluated at will.

Purpose of Planning

The operation of a business does not occur under conditions of complete *certainty,* nor does it occur under conditions of complete *uncertainty.* Conditions of complete certainty exist when more than 99 percent of all the relevant factors are known. Conditions of complete uncertainty exist when less than one percent of all the relevant factors are known. The concepts of uncertainty and certainty represent a range from one percent to 99 percent rather than a range of 0 percent to 100 percent. Business operations occur under conditions that lie between the extremes of uncertainty and certainty—an area on the scale from 1 to 99 percent that is known as *risk.* Risk is defined as knowledge of the probability that a given event will either occur or not occur.[1]

The purpose of planning is to provide information concerning the conditions surrounding a proposed course of action so that the element of risk is known and stated as a probability. Planning does not eliminate the element of risk, but planning does provide the basis for stating the degree of risk in more precise terms. As knowledge of the facts that influence the success or failure of a proposed plan approaches the level of certainty, the degree of risk declines.

Importance of Planning

Planning is of importance for two reasons: its *primacy* from the standpoint of position in the sequence of management functions, and its *pervasiveness* as an activity that affects the entire organization.

Primacy of Planning. Planning has a position of primacy among the management functions. The reason for designating planning as the first of the management processes is that in some instances planning may be the only managerial function performed.[2] Planning may result in a decision that further action is not required or possible. When this happens, there is no need for the subsequent processes of organizing, directing, and controlling. Had the Bojo Corporation, as a result of

---

[1] A discussion of the concepts of uncertainty, risk, and certainty is found in M. H. Spencer, *Managerial Economics* (3d ed.; Homewood, Illinois: Richard D. Irwin, Inc., 1968), Ch. 1, pp. 1-19.

[2] L. F. Urwick, "Management and Human Relations," in R. Tannenbaum, I. R. Weschler, and F. Massarik, *Leadership and Organization* (New York: McGraw-Hill Book Company, 1961), pp. 416-28. On page 423 Colonel Urwick states that planning must be considered a separate function, one which precedes an organization, because one of the possible results of planning is that there is no need for subsequent organization.

early planning, determined that they could manufacture couplings economically and in sufficient quantity by rearranging their present facilities, the present plant location study would not have been initiated, nor would the need arise to organize, direct, and control a new plant.

spread through every part

Pervasiveness. When need for further action is indicated, the pervasiveness of the planning function is revealed. Implementing the results of planning has its effects upon the functions of organizing, directing, and controlling. In addition, planning is an activity that is required to perform the functions of organizing, directing, and controlling. The effect of planning on the other managerial functions is discussed below.

ORGANIZING. Plans, the result of planning, have their effects upon the structure and functioning of an organization. Assume that there is a plan designed to raise a company's sales volume to $500 million. Further, the desired volume requires the acquisition of companies producing related products as well as increasing the sales volume of products now being produced. Acquiring other companies may necessitate establishing a special staff group to study and evaluate potential acquisitions. Also, permanent organizational units must be created to administer and coordinate the companies purchased as a part of the plan to increase sales volume. To increase the volume of sales produced by the present organization, a realignment of the duties of key executives may be required to establish broad geographic divisions, with each division having the capabilities of attaining its own specified share of the expected increase.

Planning is required to define structure, authority relationships, and proper scope for each of the newly created or modified organizational units arising from the implementation of an accepted plan.

DIRECTING. The results of planning have their effects upon the direction of an organization. As we shall find in Chapter 16, "Leadership Patterns," the methods of directing subordinates range from those methods considered as highly participative to techniques of direction regarded as authoritarian in nature. The closeness of direction varies from extremely close supervision to direction that exemplifies a "hands off" policy. Several factors determine the kind of direction that is best suited to meet organizational objectives. Some of these factors are the size of the organization, the capabilities and needs of the members of the organization, the goals of the organization in relation to the goals of its members, the need for an interchange of information between members of the organization, and the extent to which the organization is meeting its stated objectives. All of these conditions—each having its effect upon the kind of direction that is most effective—are the results of planning and the implementation of plans.

CONTROLLING. Planning is closely related to the control process in that plans often serve as the basis for control. A fully developed plan incorporates a timetable that shows, in proper sequence, the activities necessary to reach a stated objective and includes an estimate of the time required to complete each step. Also, a well-presented plan includes a statement of organizational responsibility. Thus, with checkpoints defined and responsibility clearly designated, there is a framework for the control process. The checkpoints provide a basis for comparing present performance, and the designation of organizational responsibility facilitates and makes more effective the corrective action of control. The proper exercise of the control function frequently requires the formulation of new plans or the modification of existing ones—and again, the new or changed plans serve as the basis for continuing control. The continuing relationship between planning and control is frequently described as the planning-control-planning cycle.

TYPES OF PLANS

We have seen that the primary purpose of planning is to reduce the degree of risk in business operations and that planning is important because of its position of primacy and its pervasiveness in influencing the other management functions. The emphasis has been placed on planning as a function. Let us now examine the result of planning—the plan—in respect to its characteristics and application.

The following outline classifies plans in respect to characteristics and use or application:

1. Classification by time or duration
   a. Long-range plans
   b. Short-range plans
2. Classification by business function or use
   a. Plans concerning the sales function
   b. Plans concerning the production function
   c. Plans concerning the personnel function
   d. Plans concerning the finance function
   e. Plans concerning any other major function
3. Classification in respect to breadth or scope
   a. Policies
   b. Procedures
   c. Methods

The above outline provides a useful basis for discussing the various types of plans. However, it must be remembered that any given plan includes more than one of the characteristics or uses shown in the outline. For example, a policy statement in the area of finance is considered a policy because of its breadth; it may also be a long-range plan if it pertains to the means of securing financial resources; and it is a plan concerned with a specific business function, finance. Similarly, a short-range plan may be applicable to any given business function and also classified by its breadth or scope; e.g., a procedure to guide the preparation of a physical inventory.

Classification by Time

When plans are classified in respects to their duration, they are recognized as either long-range plans or short-range plans.[3] Examples of long-range planning are numerous and almost always include financial plans. It is not unusual for companies to issue bonds with a 25-year maturity date as part of a long-range plan to develop desired financial strength. Research and development programs are planned for many years, and the long-range plans for research frequently emphasize the research of "pure science" as well as the development of new products. Research not directed specifically toward new products must be continued on a long-range basis since it has been demonstrated many times that the "pure" research of today leads to the development of products for tomorrow. Corporate public relations programs are also planned on a continuing basis since one of their express purposes is to create a stable public image. General Electric's slogan, "Progress is our most important product," capitalizes on long-range research plans as a means of establishing a corporate image.

---

[3] Long-range plans may be further subdivided in a manner that has proven to be useful in many instances. They may be regarded as being either *strategic* or *operational* in nature. Strategic plans are those plans that are concerned with the long-term well-being of the corporation; for example, financial plans. Operational plans are those plans primarily concerned with the allocation of company resources; for example, finances, plant facilities, or manpower. Generally these operational plans extend for a period of three to five years and are consequently regarded as long-range in nature. For a further discussion of some of the characteristics of long-range planning and the characteristics of organization for long-range planning, the following are recommended:

Robert J. Litschert, "Some Characteristics of Organization for Long-Range Planning," *Academy of Management Journal,* Vol. X, No. 3 (September, 1967), pp. 247-256.

Robert J. Litschert, "Some Characteristics of Long-Range Planning: An Industry Study," *Academy of Management Journal,* Vol. XI, No. 3 (September, 1968), pp. 315-328.

As might be expected, plans that encompass a relatively short period of time are referred to as short-range plans. There is, unfortunately, no precise cut-off point in time which enables one to designate categorically all plans extending beyond a given duration as long range and all plans up to that duration as short range. Short-range plans are best understood in their relation to long-range plans. Examples are found in the daily and even annual operations of a company. Typical short-range plans are production schedules for a period of a day, a week, or perhaps a month. Actually, production schedules may be considered short-range plans even though they extend over a period of a year, provided expanded facilities are planned for the foreseeable future. Thus, the designation of a plan as either short range or long range depends, to some measure, upon whether the plan considered as short range is part of a larger plan. Generally, if a plan is part of a large plan, it may be considered as a short-range plan.

The time span or duration of a plan is significant, not only as a basis for classifying plans, but also as an index of difficulty in evaluating its success. As a rule, it is more difficult to evaluate long-range plans than short-range plans because their duration is sometimes longer than the life span of their originator, or the life span of any one observer. Many times a treasurer retires or dies before his mistakes are discovered. Since the duration of long-range plans makes a determination of their ultimate success difficult, if not impossible, extreme care must be taken to insure highest standards in performing the planning function.

Classification by Function

Another basis for classifying plans is in respect to their function or use. Classification by business function considers planning as applied to the sales function, to the production and procurement function, and to financial and personnel areas. Grouping plans by functions is particularly useful when analyzing the operations of specific areas in an organization. Consequently, many companies find it convenient to develop policy statements in reference to four major functional areas—finance, sales, production, and personnel. Functional grouping of plans enables one to determine more clearly the interaction and interdependence that exist between major areas of operations, and emphasizes the need for determining these interrelationships before plans are approved and put into effect. Specifically, a sales department considering the installation of a sales order procedure should be aware that any such procedure will probably have a marked effect upon production and accounting procedures.

Classification by Scope

Classification in respect to breadth is the third way of grouping plans. Three distinct groups of plans are recognized when scope
or breadth is the basis for classification. They are policies, procedures, and methods. Interestingly enough, this classification not only
permits an immediate determination of the breadth of the plan but
also reveals the organizational level that initiated the plan and the extent
that the plan is utilized in the organization.

Policies. Company policies are broad in their application, and, as
a result, they often appear to be vague and nonspecific in their wording.
They are intended to serve as guideposts that define the scope of activities necessary and permissible to reach desired objectives. In origin,
policies are usually developed by the board of directors or by the
executive committee of a company. It is rare for a department head
to develop policy. He may recommend policy statements for approval
by either the executive committee or the board, but policies emanate
from the highest levels of a company. Another characteristic of policies
is their stability in that they do not change rapidly. They are not im-
mutable, however; but their change is slow. Examples of change can
be found in company policies relating to credit and methods of distribution. The J. C. Penney Company ultimately changed its credit
policy from one of strictly cash to one that permits and even encourages
customer charge accounts. Sears Roebuck, over the years, has shifted its
emphasis from distribution by means of mail-order houses to distribution through retail stores.[4]

Procedures. There is considerably more variation among procedures
in respect to both origin and scope than there is among policies. For
the most part, procedures are interdepartmental or intradepartmental
in their breadth. They do not affect the entire organization to the same
extent that policy statements do, even though they may be observed
on a company-wide basis. The phrase "standard operating procedure"
typifies the fact that procedures are more closely related to the daily
operations of a company than policies. Examples of procedures are
found in every major department of a company, with their origin and

---

[4] The following two sources offer a comprehensive review of corporate policies.
Management Policies I presents the development, formulation, and administration of
corporate policies, and *Management Policies II* offers a source book of policy statements drawn from major United States corporations.

M. Valliant Higginson, *Management Policies I: Their Development as Corporate
Guides* (New York: American Management Association, 1966).

M. Valliant Higginson, *Management Policies II: Sourcebook of Statement* (New
York: American Management Association, 1966).

application confined to one department, such as production, sales, or personnel. Procedures are, by definition, of sufficient breadth to have an impact upon the operations of related departments. Production control procedure, which has as its goal an organized flow of materials through a plant, by its nature modifies and, in turn, is modified by the procedures of the sales department governing the receiving and entering of orders, and by procedures of the accounting department utilized to determine production costs.

Methods. Another group of plans, more specific in scope than procedures, are methods. Methods are applied within a given operating department and are regarded as plans that detail the manner and sequence of performing those individual tasks necessary to complete given assignments. A method is designed to influence the behavior of an individual; for example, there is a prescribed method for the completion of employment application forms. Likewise, there is an approved method for the assembly of a given product or the grinding and finishing of a machined part.

In conclusion, the classification of plans by breadth ranges from policies, which are the broadest of all plans and originate at the highest levels of an organization, through procedures, which are concerned with the operations of major functional departments and are interdepartmental in their effect, to methods, which are specific and stated as a guide to direct the performance of individuals.

CRITERIA FOR EVALUATING PLANS

Two approaches are available in developing criteria for the evaluation of plans. One approach, designated as *Approach A,* is a review and analysis of the procedures followed and the resultant characteristics that differentiate successful plans from unsuccessful plans. These criteria are descriptive in nature and serve as a checklist against which the plan under consideration may be judged. *Approach A* is a procedural analysis of the plan that is being evaluated.

A second approach to the development of criteria for judging plans, designated as *Approach B,* is the determination of the degree to which the plan under consideration is economic. The word "economic" is used here in its broadest sense; i.e., the effective utilization of resources. In order to determine the economic worth of a plan, it is necessary to use a technique that permits describing any plan in economic terms and to utilize this technique to the extent that it becomes a "way of thinking" about plans. *Approach B* is referred to as an economic evaluation of plans. We consider first those criteria developed from a procedural analysis and, second, the evaluation of plans in terms of economic effectiveness.

Approach A—Procedural Analysis

The problem of developing characteristics for use as criteria for judging plans necessitates an analysis of the elements or dimensions of the planning process and the resultant plan. A comprehensive study has listed the following 13 dimensions or factors:

1. Complexity	8. Frequency
2. Significance	9. Confidential nature
3. Comprehensiveness	10. Formality
4. Time	11. Authorization
5. Specificity	12. Ease of implementation
6. Completeness	13. Ease of control [5]
7. Flexibility	

It is apparent that these characteristics or dimensions may be worded to provide a basis or measure against which a plan may be evaluated. It is possible to summarize under three major headings the characteristics that may be considered as criteria for evaluating the probable success of plans. These characteristics are objectivity, degree of structuralization, and flexibility. To apply these characteristics as criteria, it is necessary to discuss more fully the meaning of each term and to present specific examples showing the application of the term to the planning process and to the resultant plan.

Objectivity. Objective findings or conclusions, such as plans, are subject to verification by another observer. The greater the degree of objectivity, the greater is the likelihood that another observer will reach the same conclusion. The antithesis of objective findings is known as subjective and is based upon one's own feelings and beliefs. Conclusions based upon personal experiences and beliefs are not subject to verification by outside observers.

---

[5] P. Le Breton and D. A. Henning, *Planning Theory* (Englewood Cliffs, New Jersey: Prentice-Hall, Inc., 1961), p. 23. This comprehensive work treats planning as it is performed at all levels in the industrial firm. The student is referred to Part 5, pp. 320-44, in which the authors present an excellent summary that shows the relation of each of the above-mentioned dimensions of a plan to one another and the effect of each dimension on the other.

Ralph C. Davis, *The Fundamentals of Top Management* (New York: Harper & Brothers, Publishers, 1951), p. 46. Davis lists the following eight characteristics of a plan: objectivity, logical soundness, security, flexibility, stability, comprehensiveness, clarity, and simplicity.

Objectivity results from the precise observation, recording, analysis, and interpretation of pertinent data, a form of analysis and reasoning known as the *scientific method*. The managerial process of planning can be accomplished by either subjective or objective means. The extent to which the scientific method is followed in the planning process determines the degree of objectivity of that process and the consequent objectivity of the resultant plans. The scientific method, as applied to planning, consists of the following six steps:

1. Statement of objective
2. Statement of problem
3. Designation of planning authority
4. Collection and interpretation of data
5. Formulation and testing of tentative plan
6. Statement of final plan

The application of each of these steps to the process of planning is discussed separately.

STATEMENT OF OBJECTIVE. A strict definition of the scientific method does not include a statement of the objective. Yet it is necessary that a planner have before him, at all times, a clear concept of the broad objectives of the firm and the specific objectives of any given plan. A plan should contribute to meeting these objectives. Having stated objectives available for the planner minimizes the possibility of developing plans that are inappropriate for the attainment of specific objectives.

STATEMENT OF PROBLEM. When planning is required, there is the implication that the organization is not completely meeting its objectives, for if it were, there would be no need for additional or new plans. The discrepancy between present performance and desired performance constitutes the problem area. The problem to be resolved by the planning process must be clearly stated. Stating the problem clearly and setting forth the limiting factors and conditions that must be met define the extent of the planning process and the scope of the resultant plan. In Case Problem 4-A the problem is clearly defined. There is a need for a plant to manufacture a known product. Further, limiting conditions, such as shipping costs of raw materials and finished products, the cost and availability of labor, land requirements, and transportation facilities, are clearly stated. In contrast, a poorly defined problem fails to direct the planning process toward a specific goal and frequently results in inappropriate and ill-conceived plans.

DESIGNATION OF PLANNING AUTHORITY. As part of the planning process, there must be a designated planning authority. After a company has stated the problem and is convinced that a plan or course of action should be developed as a solution to the problem, it is necessary that an individual or group be given the authority necessary to carry out an effective planning process and develop alternate plans. The planner's authority should be granted by that level of the organization that normally has the responsibility for performing those functions included in the approved plan. For example, a plan requiring a large capital outlay, such as the construction of a plant, is normally approved by the president or the executive committee. Determining the appropriateness of the source of the planner's authority provides an estimate of the extent that the recommended plan will be approved and implemented.[6]

COLLECTION AND INTERPRETATION OF DATA. The next step in the planning process is the collection and interpretation of available data. As stated in the definition of planning, consideration must be given to pertinent information from the present and the past, and an assessment must be made of probable future events.

Generally, the data used in planning fall into two broad categories —external data and internal data. Information pertaining to the national economy and the industry in which the company is operating is typical of *external data*. The financial resources of the firm, the past performance of the firm in the attainment of similar objectives, and the ability of personnel charged with executing the plan are representative of *internal data*. Available information from both sources along with estimates of probable future developments must be utilized and interpreted to insure a successful plan.

FORMULATION AND TESTING OF TENTATIVE PLAN. Whenever possible, a tentative plan should be formulated and initiated on a trial basis. Although this step is not always feasible, it is desirable since a trial run reveals strengths and weaknesses and offers a basis for predicting the probable success of a plan. Training programs are sometimes adopted on a trial basis before being applied on a company-wide basis. New products may be introduced to a single geographic region to test the acceptability of the product and the effectiveness of the proposed marketing techniques before making a final decision concerning national distribution.

---

[6] The matter of designating a planning authority specifically for long-range planning is discussed in R. L. Mason, "Developing a Planning Organization," *Business Horizons,* Vol. XII, No. 4 (August, 1969), pp. 61-69.

Daniel D. Roman, "Technological Forecasting in the Decision Process," *Academy of Management Journal,* Vol. XIII, No. 2 (June, 1970), pp. 127-138. Professor Roman has advised that technological forecasting, the assessment of future technology transfer, be assigned a specific function separate from other planning functions.

If plans can be presented as a mathematical formula, changes that would result from altering the value of any one factor or condition can be determined with precision. Analyzing the effect of change by using a model is called *simulation*. The effect of changes in proposed production schedules may be simulated, and the effect of changes in price and volume upon profit may also be predicted accurately. When plans are expressed in quantitative terms, the effects of changing conditions may be simulated as a way of testing a plan's potential success without having to commit company resources.

STATEMENT OF FINAL PLAN. The last step in the planning process is the statement of the final plan. If a plan is to be considered objective (that is, capable of being developed by another planner following the same procedure), it must be derived from the data developed and analyzed. In this sense, a plan is a conclusion. The extent to which the analysis and reasoning of the scientific method have been followed in developing the final form of a plan indicates the degree of objectivity of the stated plan.

Degree of Structuralization. The determination of the degree of objectivity of a plan is essentially an analysis and evaluation of the planning process used in the development of the plan. The *degree of structuralization* is a criterion for evaluating the format of the plan and the extent to which the plan structures the actions of the organization that are necessary for its successful implementation. Well-structured plans are capable of precise execution. Factors considered in determining the degree of structuralization are: comprehensiveness, time span, assignment of duties, and control features.

COMPREHENSIVENESS. When evaluating the structure of a plan, one consideration is the degree of comprehensiveness. The complexity and the breadth of a plan are not necessarily measures of comprehensiveness. Simple plans that are well stated may be comprehensive. A production plan for a departmental supervisor may be for a period of one day and affect the work of only two people; yet it answers his needs. Similarly, a plan requiring 100 people for its execution and a time span of one year is not comprehensive unless it answers fully all the questions raised in the original problem. A plan is comprehensive to the degree that it provides solutions to the original problem raised in the planning process.

TIME SPAN. A well-structured plan has a definite statement of the length of time required for its completion. The statement of dates for the start and the completion of a plan should be specific; in addition, complex plans specify intermediate time goals. For example, a building construction plan should state the date for the first activity on the building site, usually commencing with surveying, the time that grading begins, the date that foundation work starts, and beginning and completion dates for all other events including an expected occupancy date. It is recognized that there are factors which may delay the completion of any intermediate goal; however, the sequence and the relationship of these intermediate points should be clearly stated in the original plan. When a delay occurs, full information concerning the sequence and relationship of all phases of the project facilitates the task of revising the plan.[7]

ASSIGNMENT OF DUTIES. The characteristics of comprehensiveness and time span refer to the structure of the plan itself. One of the expected results of a plan is that it structures the behavior of the organization responsible for carrying out the plan. In order to implement a plan effectively, it is necessary to assign specific duties to designated personnel in the organization. The mere listing of activities to be performed is not sufficient. Activities must be expressed as job duties and assigned as responsibilities to individual members of the organization.

CONTROL FEATURES. Another factor indicating the degree of structuralization is the extent that a plan includes features which facilitate control. One method of controlling the execution of plans is the utilization of logical time-oriented control points. Budgets, a type of financial plan, generally provide for quarterly reviews as an integral part of the plan. Another aspect of control is the designation of personnel to review progress and recommend necessary control action. Also, it is desirable to indicate the amount of variance from the original plan that can be tolerated. Provisions should be made for reporting these exceptions to the responsible manager.

Flexibility. Paradoxical as it may seem, the characteristic that contributes most to the stability and probable success of a plan is its flexibility. Rigid plans may appear to offer stability and firmness; however, rigidity also leads to an inability to meet the requirements of changing conditions.

Flexibility does not mean, nor imply, vagueness or instability. Flexibility results from the development of alternate courses of action.

---

[7] See Case Problem 21B, page 672, for an example of a plan stating specific dates throughout its duration.

Developing plans that include alternatives has several advantages. First, flexibility permits management to meet changing external conditions rapidly and effectively. A plan without an alternate can result either in a blind-alley venture or reaching a point of no return, thereby dooming the plan to failure. Second, if a series of alternate actions is included in the plan, alternates are available immediately and avoid the delay that would result from having to develop a new plan. Lastly, it is much easier to gain approval for a plan in its initial stages when alternate courses are indicated. The presence of several choices implies that a fairly complete analysis of the problem has been made, and that one path has not been chosen and followed blindly. When a plan is being submitted to a group having varied interests and goals, the inclusion of alternate choices increases the possibility of compromise; but when only one course of action is presented, the result may be a rejection of the entire plan. For example, if a plan is presented proposing that a quality control program be established and the only recommendation concerning its administration is that it be placed under manufacturing, and a strong personal conflict exists between the vice-presidents of manufacturing and engineering, an impasse may develop resulting in the cancellation of the entire program. However, the inclusion of an alternate form of organization—the creation of a separate department reporting directly to the president—provides a ready compromise and the achievement of the goal of the original plan.

The preceding discussion—an analysis of the characteristics of plans—presents three criteria for judging the probable success of a plan. These criteria—objectivity, degree of structuralization, and flexibility—serve not only as a measure of the probable success of a given plan but also reflect the effectiveness of the planning process. The relationship between planning and plans is summarized as follows: *Effective planning results in plans that are objective, structured, and flexible, and the extent to which resultant plans possess these characteristics is a measure of their probable success.*

Approach B—Economic Effectiveness

Over a period of years it has been observed that good plans have the aforementioned characteristics. However, it is quite possible that a plan carried through to its successful completion may not have been the most appropriate plan for that specific situation. There is a concept that has been widely used in the field of economics that may be applied to determine whether or not a plan makes the maximum contribution to company objectives. This concept is *economic effectiveness*.[8] Its application as a management tool rests upon two basic assumptions:

1. Management of a business enterprise is primarily an economic activity, and the principles and techniques of economics should be applicable and transferrable as principles and techniques of management. The word *economics* means the effective utilization of all resources.

2. The primary objective of any organization is to maximize the units of return (output) in relation to the effort (units of input) expended. This premise is stated in broad terms because the concept of maximization of return applies not only to capital invested, sales, or production, but also to the management of a charitable foundation seeking the best (most economic) distribution of its funds; to a religious organization seeking converts; or to a labor union demanding increased benefits for its members.

The Law of Diminishing Returns. It is implied in the second assumption that the units of return are compatible with organizational objectives. If so, the problem is one of determining the amount contributed by the last unit of input in relation to the amount contributed by the next to last unit of input. The method of making this determination can be accomplished in several ways, but all methods have one common characteristic—they represent a certain way of looking at input-output relationships. An example frequently presented in economics to illustrate input-output relationships assumes a unit of land (usually an acre), a man who is a worker, and corn, the product. The one man works the one acre and is able to produce 100 bushels of corn with the tools given him. It is reasonable to expect that, with the same tools, by increasing manpower there will be an increase in the yield of corn *up to a point*. Eventually, however, there are enough men so that additional manpower does not result in additional product. This phenomenon has been stated variously as the *law of diminishing returns,* or the *law of variable returns*.

Now, translate the classic economic example into a problem in production. Columns A, B, and C of Table 4-1 indicate the three

8 C. J. Hitch and R. N. McKean, *The Economics of Defense in the Nuclear Age* (Cambridge: Harvard University Press, 1960), pp. 422-vii. This book represents combined staff efforts of the Rand Corporation and presents an economic anlaysis of the problems of defense. It ranges from an analysis of resources available, through concepts of efficiency, and a detailed presentation of specific problems and applications to military research, logistics, and the development of policies for the choice of military deterrents. The underlying economics are applicable to the management of business firms.

elements of our first example. Assume that the tools (that is, the plant and the facilities), the product, and the methods remain the same. One unit of input is the work of one man for an eight-hour day. This one unit of input produces 10 units of output, the total produced. In this instance the average produced is also 10. Average production is obtained by dividing total units produced by the units of input. When another man is added, the economic effectiveness of each man increases and the total produced reaches 24; the average goes up to 12. The addition of the third man results in total production of 39, with an average of 13. So far everything is increasing. When the fourth man is added, total production continues to rise; but the average drops to 12. With the addition of a fifth man, the production goes up and the average slips to 11; and with the addition of the sixth man, the average is down to 10 again; however, the total number of units produced is 60, or six times as much as that produced by one man. After the seventh, eighth, and ninth men, the average production per man is reduced to seven; and, by adding the ninth man, the phenomenon of diminishing returns appears and the total production declines from 64 to 63.

Table 4-1

**THE RELATIONSHIP BETWEEN UNITS OF INPUT, TOTAL PRODUCED,
AVERAGE PRODUCED, AND MARGINAL PRODUCT**

A Units of Input	B Total Produced	C Average Produced	D Marginal Product
1	10	10	—
2	24	12	14
3	39	13	15
4	48	12	9
5	55	11	7
6	60	10	5
7	63	9	3
8	64	8	1
9	63	7	—1

This relatively simple example poses a problem that recurs as the central theme of many managerial decisions. Managers, in making their decisions, are asked to answer the following question: What combination of resources results in the greatest economic return consistent with the objectives of the organization? If it can be said of a plan that it represents the best (most economic) combination of resources resulting in the achievement of desired objectives, the plan can then be considered appropriate. Obviously, both aspects of the test must be met. If the plan does not result in the achievement of desired objectives, it is not appropriate; nor is it appropriate if in achieving the desired objectives, there is anything less than the most economic utilization of resources.

   The Concept of Marginal Product. How can it be determined when there is the most efficient use of available resources? The data presented in the first three columns of Table 4-1 do not provide sufficient information, but they do indicate some difficulty as reflected in the average units produced per man. Note that the average starts falling when the fourth man is added. A second indication that all is not well is revealed by the amount of total production. This measure drops when the ninth man is added. Since our concern is with input-output relationships, does it not seem logical to study these relationships more carefully and find out what happens each time an additional person is added? It is necessary to determine exactly how much *additional* output results from each *additional* unit of input. Economists refer to this incremental relationship between additional units of input and resultant additional units of output as *marginal product.* The terms marginal productivity, marginal revenue, or marginal profit, may be interpreted as *additional* productivity, *additional* revenue, or *additional* profit in relation to an *additional* unit of input.

   In Table 4-1, Column D shows the marginal (additional) product resulting from each additional unit of input. The first man working for eight hours (one unit of input) forms the base of the problem. His marginal productivity cannot be computed because prior to him there was no production. With the addition of the second man, 24 units were produced, a gain of 14 units over that produced by the first man alone (24-10). The marginal production for each additional man is shown in Column D. The addition of the third man results in the production of 39 units, 15 units more than the amount produced by the previous two-man team. The addition of the fourth man yields only nine additional units, compared to the 14 added by the second man and the 15 added by the third man. The average production also drops by one unit from 13 to 12. The incremental increase in production resulting from additional units of input continues to drop and at a more rapid rate than the decline in average production. With the addition of the ninth man, the results are negative, a marginal (additional) increase of -1; and the total number of units produced also declines by one. An inspection of Column D shows that there are increasing amounts of additional production until the fourth man is added; thus, it seems that the maximum utilization of available resources occurs when the third man is added. Prior to this point, the operation is not at maximum efficiency since the cost of additional units of input is more than offset by the value of additional units of output. Beyond this point the operation loses efficiency as each additional unit of input results in the production of a smaller and smaller amount of additional product. The phenomenon of decreasing efficiency in the use of resources is revealed by the marginal product rather than by measures of average or total production. The average production is 12 when the second man is added, and it is also 12 when the fourth man is added; but in the first instance the marginal productivity is increasing while in the second case; i.e., with the addition of the fourth man, it is decreasing.[9]

The concept of marginal output, or incremental changes in the rate of production in relation to each additional unit of input, is a means of determining how efficiently available resources are employed. Efficiency increases as long as the additional units of output increase at a faster rate than the rate of additional units of input. When the point is reached where an additional unit of input results in a smaller rate of increase in output than that resulting from the addition of the previous unit of input, the maximum, or most efficient, utilization of resources no longer exists.

The management of any organization must continuously ask if its action, or its proposed plan, maximizes the efficient utilization of resources in meeting its goals. When a choice must be made between two or more plans, each of which possesses to the same degree the characteristics of objectivity, structuralization, and flexibility, it is apparent that another measure is needed in order to reach a decision. *Economic effectiveness* is the fourth criterion for use in judging the worth of plans and provides a basis for selecting the

---

[9] The student who has had calculus will understand that the curve for marginal productivity is the derivative of the equation for the total product curve. The problem can be expressed as $MC = MR$, or marginal costs equal marginal revenue. In addition to standard calculus texts, the following references are suggested for the student interested in a better understanding of the mathematical expression of the concept of marginal product. Hitch and McKean, *op. cit.*, pp. 362-405. The appendix headed "The Simple Mathematics of Maximization" presents fundamental concepts of calculus as used in maximizing returns in relation to inputs. Herbert G. Heneman, Jr. and Dale Yoder, *Labor Economics* (2d ed.; Cincinnati: South-Western Publishing Company, 1965), pp. 793-809. Heneman and Yoder discuss marginal wage theory. The discussion is directed to problems of marginal productivity as they affect wages; however, the concepts are applicable to any situation of input-output relationships. Spencer, *op. cit.*, pp. 171-179. This discusses the relationships that exist between simple production functions.

appropriate plan. The importance of economic effectiveness as a criterion for evaluating plans is stated in the *Concept of Economic Effectiveness: Economic effectiveness in planning results in plans that maximize achievement of company objectives through the most efficient utilization of available resources.*

Benefit-Cost Analysis

The above discussion of economic effectiveness provides a conceptual framework for evaluating the economic worth of a plan, and as stated on page 115 its application as a management tool rests upon two basic assumptions. The first assumption is that we are dealing with the management of a business enterprise that is primarily economic in nature with the result that the principles and techniques of economics should be applicable and transferable as principles and techniques of management. Implied in this assumption is the quantification of inputs and outputs so that marginal product may be determined. The second assumption is that the primary objective of any organization is to maximize the units of return (output) in relation to the effort (units of input) expended. However, there are many instances where these two assumptions are not appropriate with the result that the concept of economic effectiveness is not applicable to the evaluation of specific plans. These instances may occur in business firms and, in addition, there are non-profit organization—governmental units, educational institutions, and religious and charitable organizations—unable to evaluate plans in respect to their economic effectiveness. For these situations the utilization of benefit-cost analysis techniques offers an analytical framework similar to that provided by the concept of economic effectiveness.[10]

---

[10] An easy to understand introduction to the concept of benefit-cost analysis is the discussion by Harley H. Hinrichs entitled, "Government Decision Making and the Theory of Benefit-Cost Analysis: A Primer," which appears in Harley H. Hinrichs and Graeme M. Taylor, *Program Budgeting and Benefit-Cost Analysis: Cases, Text, and Readings* (Pacific Palisades, California: Goodyear Publishing Company, Inc., 1969), pp. 9-20. Hinrichs' work is used extensively as the basis for this discussion of cost-benefit analysis.

For a discussion of a related concept, cost-effectiveness analysis, the following book published under the auspices of the Washington Operations Research Council is recommended: Thomas A. Goldman (ed.), *Cost Effectiveness Analysis: New Approaches in Decision Making* (New York: Frederick A. Praeger, 1967), pp. 17-32.

The following article includes a 90-item bibliography for those who wish to explore the subject of benefit-cost analysis in depth: A R. Prest and R. Turvey, "Cost-Benefit Analysis: A Survey," *Economic Journal*, Vol. LXXV (December, 1965), pp. 638-735. This paper is reprinted in *Surveys of Economic Theory*, Vol. III: Resource Allocation (New York: MacMillan and St. Martin's Press, 1966).

Quantification Problems. Benefit-cost analysis, sometimes referred to as cost-benefit analysis, is utilized when it is difficult to measure either the value of or the distribution of benefits and when it is also difficult to determine those costs that should be included, as well as determining those that should be excluded, in establishing the cost of a given plan. Difficulties in measuring benefits and establishing costs are encountered often by the non-profit organizations mentioned above and by business firms in evaluating specific programs. Benefit-cost concepts have long been used by the United States Government in the development of river and harbor projects (The River and Harbor Act of 1902) and extensively in the allocation of water resources and the building of dams (Flood Control Act of 1936).[11] Benefit-cost analysis may also be used in evaluating urban renewal projects; in determining a state's allocation of financial resources among a university system, four years colleges, and community colleges; and in determining benefits to be derived from each of several types of executive compensation plans.[12]

All of these problems have two charactistics in common: First, the costs in these situations are difficult to determine and second, anticipated benefits are extremely resistant to quantification. In fact, the quantification of benefits often results in an unrealistic oversimplification. Thus a value judgment must be made concerning the worth of anticipated benefits in relation to what amounts to, at best, an educated estimate of costs. Projected benefits may be expressed as statements which are, in turn, evaluated in respect to their desirability and assigned relative weights, a process of making value judgments. Or the method employed by England, described in Chapter 2, may be used if desired.[13]

---

[11] Hinrichs and Taylor *op. cit.,* p. v.

[12] The following two references are reprinted in Fremont J. Lyden and Ernest G. Miller, (ed.) *Planning, Programming, Budgeting: A Systems Approach to Management* (Chicago: Markham Publishing Company, 1967), pp. 199-241. The paper by Professor McKean shows clearly the impact of personal value systems in the analysis of relative benefits and costs while the article by Professor Maass discusses the application of benefit-cost analysis in making public investment decisions.

Roland N. McKean, "Cost and Benefits from Different Viewpoints," in Howard G. Schallar (ed.), *Public Expenditure Decisions in the Urban Community* (Washington, D. C.: Resources for the Future, Inc., 1963), pp. 147-163.

Arthur Maass, "Benefit-Cost Analysis: Its Relevance to Public Investment Decisions," *Quarterly Journal of Economics,* Vol. LXXX, No. 2 (May, 1966), pp. 208-226.

The following article discusses the application of benefit-cost analysis to problems of executive compensation: George W. Hettenhouse, "Cost/Benefit Analysis of Executive Compensation," *Harvard Business Review,* Vol. XLVIII, No. 4 (July-August, 1970), pp. 114-124.

[13] The use of qualitative judgments is suggested as one of the means of determining the scope of standards to be used as a basis for control, pp. 620-624 and the use of appraisal as a means of setting standards, p. 625. The method used by England is described on pp. 78-84, Chapter 3.

Maximization Dilemma. Even if it were possible to quantify all costs and all benefits, thereby removing the implicit constraint of the first assumption, that inputs and outputs be expressed in quantitative terms, there would still remain the problem of maximization. Since we do not live in a simplistic world, problems seldom can be stated as one of "maximizing the goodies and minimizing the baddies." Frequently, the objectve is not to "maximize"; instead, to use a term of Herbert Simon, it is to "satisfice."

For example, if the objective of a governmental agency or a business firm is to maximize welfare (defining welfare as a subjective state of well-being or the achievement of one's desires), can either the government or the business realistically maximize the benefit, *welfare,* for either its citizens or its employees, as the case may be? Aside from the problems inherent in the quantification of costs and benefits (welfare) several difficult choices must be made to achieve this elusive maximization.[14] First, the government can ignore ethnic groups and the needs of special social classes; disregard political entities such as states, cities and counties; and concentrate its efforts toward maximizing the welfare of each and every citizen. In the same manner, a corporation could ignore divisions, plants, departments, customers, and stockholders; thereby devoting its energies to maximizing the welfare of each of its employees. Should the maximization of benefits for each and every individual prove too difficult, for either the government or the corporation, a second choice is open: Forget maximization; instead, make it possible for everyone to gain something. The third alternative is to arrange events so that some group (either citizens or employees) gains in benefits, but nobody loses. Fourth, should either of the first three choices prove unsatisfactory or unworkable, there is the possibility of having the winners, those who gain in benefits or welfare, outnumber the losers. Admittedly, the concept, welfare, is next to impossible to either quantify or maximize. For that matter so are the normal business objectives of innovation, manager performance and development, worker performance and attitude, and public responsibility.[15]

Thus the problem of analyzing benefits, within the context of cost-benefit analysis becomes a problem of re-examining objectives and making a comparative value judgment concerning the relative worth of stated objectives. A copper mining company may state as one of its major objectives the desire to fulfill its obligations in respect to public responsibility. Undoubtedly, there are also objectives in regard to

---

[14] The following discussion is based upon Hinrichs, *op. cit.,* pp. 10-13.
[15] See Chapter 3, pp. 63-71 and Chapter 20, pp. 619-635.

profitability. What are the benefits to be derived from the installation of a several million dollar device to control the pollutants from its smelter—surely a public responsibility—in comparison to maintaining its dividend to its stockholders and its position as an attractive investment? Though quantification and economic analysis may be helpful, the solutions to this and similar questions are based upon personal value systems, the essence of cost-benefit analysis.

Case Problem 4-B [16] reports the experience of Hooker Chemical Corporation with long-range planning (LRP) as applied to marketing. Also, the relationship between the setting of objectives, Chapter 3, and the planning process is shown.

CASE PROBLEM
4-B

MARKETING
PLANNING
THAT GETS
THINGS DONE

In today's complex world, how can a business organization make itself relevant in its environment, productive in its output, and highly profitable in its operations? How can it develop a "gut feeling" of greatness, an eager spirit of achievement that can combine hundreds—or thousands—of individual talents into an exciting business success?

Much of the methodology of management seems a poor fit for the problems of today, and a looser fit still for the opportunities of tomorrow. Yet from the vast learning and experience of recent years can be formulated concepts that do create such business successes.

At Hooker Chemical Corporation over the past ten years, we have experimented with many approaches and methods. The most successful can be summarized in three fundamental concepts:

1. Concept of mission.
2. Concept of perspective.
3. Concept of management style.

As they have evolved in my company, these concepts have conclusively demonstrated a power to make old organizations young, lazy organizations productive, poor organizations profitable, and good organizations better still. They can be applied to a unit, department, division, subsidiary, or company as a whole. Best, of course, is their application to all groups, so that they

[16] William F. Christopher, "Marketing Planning That Gets Things Done," *Harvard Business Review*, Vol. 48, No. 5 (September-October, 1970), pp. 56-64. © 1970 by the President and Fellows of Harvard College; all rights reserved.

are appropriately related to other company groups, and also to the economic-political-social environment. In such a situation, a group becomes future-oriented, constrained by needs, opportunities, and the individual talents focused there, rather than by organization pressures and yesterday's methods.

In this article I shall describe these three concepts as Hooker has developed them, with examples of their application. As with many methods or techniques, these work successfully only when they are wisely used. But they offer a way of combining leadership skills with technology, business sciences, and motivation principles to develop a competitive advantage for the enterprise.

CONCEPT OF MISSION

This is the most fundamental of all, because here are expressed the motivating ideas that make the enterprise go. Such ideas should not be conceived on Olympus and declared via the corporate policy manual. Instead, they should be conceived broadly throughout the organization, summarized in writing, and promulgated in every word and action of all employees. How can this be done?

Historical Evolution

At Hooker, after several false starts during the past decade, we arrived finally at an approach that gets results where they really count—in the operating statement. We started by developing written "charters" for our operating divisions. Essentially, each charter was a two- to four-page written document prepared by division management, and reviewed and approved by corporate headquarters. Its content included such elements as a general overview of the business; product, market, and process scope; and general and specific goals.

During the time these written documents were being developed, we changed the name from "charter" (it sounded too much like the king bestowing a grant on a favored subject) to "business definition and goals." But this change did not overcome what proved to be their real shortcomings. They read well. They did define the businesses well. And they did state challenging goals.

But they were descriptive and static, and consequently could not direct and energize performance.

These business definitions had two other serious drawbacks: (a) at the corporate level, there was no articulated overall strategy that these definitions could individually relate to; and (b) at the division level, there was inadequate participation from all areas. In short, this was too much a division management response to a corporate headquarters request.

Checklist Form: Despite these shortcomings, the business definitions were helpful in sorting out overlapping areas among divisions, and also in pointing out that we needed to do some homework at the corporate level to develop an overall strategy which would cultivate and encourage talent to high levels of achievement. The first part of this important "homework" we undertook by helping all operating units to do a better job of one-year and five-year planning, with strong emphasis on situation analysis and strategy development.

Situation analysis proved hard to cope with. We used workshops, lectures, special studies, lists of questions, bibliographies of data and information sources, industry advisory services, and even established a corporate library to maintain a data base of industries, products, and markets important to our divisions. However, when decisions had to be made, there always remained the problem of having the appropriate information at hand, and this continued to be pretty much the accumulated information, experience, and judgment resident in the minds of the decision makers.

From several years' experience with situation analysis, we made a checklist of the information areas most important to business planning and decision making. We then divided these areas into two groups: (a) those dealing with the environment, or the market; and (b) those dealing with the competition.

As it developed in its present format, the checklist took the form of a matrix: market data by market sector, and competitive data by competitor, as shown in *Exhibit I.* When filled in, this form provides an excellent summary of the situation for a business area and reviews where needed information is lacking or inadequate. (The form can also be used as a review checklist,

Exhibit I

CHECKLIST MATRIX FOR DEVELOPING LONG-RANGE SITUATION DATA

SITUATION ANALYSIS WORK SHEET (1)

LRP business area _____ Date _____
Prepared by _____

SITUATION ANALYSIS WORK SHEET
COMPETITIVE FACTORS

	Hooker
Competing companies	
Share of market	
Trend of market share	
Reason to change	
Cost position	
Number of salesmen	
How is sales dept. org	
Pricing policy	
Quality of technical se	
Product quality	
Research department	
Important recent inno	
Major strengths	
Major weaknesses	
Strategy used	

SITUATION ANALYSIS WORK SHEET (2)

LRP business area _____
Prepared by _____

SITUATION ANALYSIS WORK SHEET
MARKET FACTORS

Major market sectors
Market size & growth trend
Seasonal sales pattern
Sensitivity to business cyc (ups & downs in general business conditions)
Type & size of customers
Degree of concentration by size
Geographical concentratio (within U.S.A.)
Are there important foreign markets?
Price trends
Profit opportunity
Key buying influences (Who must we sell or influ to get the business? List in order of importance.)

SITUATION ANALYSIS WORK SHEET (3)

LRP business area _____

SITUATION ANALYSIS WORK SHEET
MARKET FACTORS (continued)

Innovation: (a) Significant new products & processes commercialized in last three years
(b) Approximate life cycle for new product
Integration trends—How do they affect our business?
Technological trends—How do they affect our business?
What alternative products or processes are now or potentially able to serve this market?
What are the major needs and problems of this industry?
What are customers' major markets
Is knowledge of these markets important to Hooker? Where answer is "yes," fill out situation analysis work sheet for customers's market.

without putting anything in writing, or for a more detailed report, or for programming information into a computer data bank.)

Interestingly, we found this approach to situation analysis useful to managers with many years of experience, as well as to younger men with limited experience. It helped both to improve the quality of their decisions.

Strategy Development

Overall corporate strategy proved difficult and time consuming to develop. Probably most helpful in arriving at our present strategy were four management workshops held over a period of two years—the first on "management of change," the second on "motivation," and the third and fourth on "strategy." The workshops brought in outside authorities, but they were focused on the company situation with participation by all managers attending—largely through preplanned assignments.

Follow-up programs were worked out at each conference for appropriate implementing action. In addition, we found discussion sessions at general managers' meetings and special task-force assignments helpful in working out our present "statement of mission," which contains these eight basic points:

1. Definition of the broad business areas in which the company will operate, with ample room for future growth and development.
2. Strategy for organizing the total business of the company into divisions and subsidiaries, with responsibility assigned to each for developing its own business definitions, goals, strategies, and programs.
3. Definition of relationships between the divisions and subsidiaries and the corporate headquarters.
4. International strategy.
5. Specific goals for profitability, market position, public responsibility, new business areas, competitive abilities, facilities, motivation, and management skills.
6. Strategy principles to be implemented in business planning throughout all operations.
7. Company commitment to the development of human resources through participative management-by-objectives concepts, broad delegation of authority, high performance standards, and opportunities for increasing education and job experience.
8. Provision for change to keep the statement of mission always current.

The statement of mission can relate to every problem, every action, every opportunity; and it is easy to apply. It makes time and effort more productive. It is in the hands of every management and professional employee and, through company publications, is offered to all employees. It is frequently reviewed at company meetings. But most important of all in its communication is the constant reference to it by top corporate, division, and subsidiary managers in their daily operations and decision making.

Essential Elements

An articulated concept of mission for the company as a whole, or in part, provides the powerful motivating ideas on which the career and the success of the organization can be built. Such a concept, as we now use it, includes three vital elements: a definition of the business, a statement of goals, and a statement of the strategies to be followed to achieve the goals.

Business Definitions: The concept of mission begins with a carefully thought through and explicitly stated answer to the question: "What business are we in?" Although the question is simple, a good answer comes hard. Usually, it takes a combination of long experience with much hypothesizing, evaluating, analyzing, revising, and testing. We have found that the most productive business definitions cover, *first,* some product or service as the output of the enterprise, most likely augmented with related products and services; and *second,* specific targeted markets or market segments. In my company, examples of business definition are . . .

— not the production and sale of supported film, but *synthethic fabrics for apparel.*
— not chemicals for plating, but *metal finishing systems for the automotive industry;* not phenolic resins, but *synthethic fabrics for apparel.*
—not furnaces, but *process heating systems for industry.*

These are not complete definitions. They are summary concepts from business definitions within my company illustrating the product-to-market approach to defining a business.

One word of caution: a definition is not improved just by making it broad and all-encompassing. We might lose far more than we gain if we were to say, "I'm not in the lead pencil business but in the communications business." Our definition must be narrow enough to provide direction, yet broad enought to provide inspiration, room for growth, and room to respond to our changing environment. Many businesses falter or die mainly because they do not really answer the question, "What business are we in?"

Specific Goals: If we do not know where we are going, all roads lead there, and most likely the organization will be running down all of them. In a statement of goals lies a powerful source for motivation, inspiration, and coordination. To be effective, we find that goals must be specific, they must be communicated, and they must be relatable by each employee to his job assignment. This can be accomplished if goals are set for sales volume and market share, profitability, organization development, management style, innovation, and productivity.

Many businesses have short-range goals for sales volume, profitability, and perhaps market share. However, a short-range goal is not an end in itself; rather, it should be but one step toward achieving a long-range goal. Only in consideration of our long-range goals can we truly measure current performance and wisely choose our best options and trade-offs. Thus we need long-range goals not only for volume and profit, but also for all the key performance areas that will determine the success of our business.

Strategic Approaches: These are the generalized concepts of the ways in which the enterprise will deploy its resources to achieve its goals. Business definitions tell us "what we are"; goals tell us "where we are going"; and strategies lay out the general direction of our efforts "to get us there." Here are the strategies for the business definition examples I mentioned earlier, stated in terms of product, distribution, and marketing approach:

Synthetic fabrics for apparel—product innovation responsive to consumer needs; fabrics and finish styling to meet specific requirements of individual merchandisers;

intensive and specialized development selling; and trademark identification.

Metal finishing systems for the automotive industry —innovations in plating systems; nickel conservation; and engineering assistance to provide and maintain a total operating system in the customer's plant that will reliably and economically meet his operating specifications.

Bonding resins for foundry sands—uniquely formulated resins to meet the operating requirements of each foundry; sold directly by a sales and service organization technically competent to assure that the desired operating results are achieved.

Process heating systems for industry—total systems designed to meet individual customer's production requirements and engineered from standardized elements; specialized sales and engineering competence in selected industrial market segments.

Situation Analysis

For an enterprise to be really successful, its management must be sure that it has a clear and relevant concept of mission—namely, a definition of the business it is in, the goals it seeks to achieve, and the strategic approaches by which it will achieve these goals. To make a concept of mission right for an enterprise and relevant to the business situation requires rare insight, or—more probably—difficult and thorough analysis.

It is necessary to know the past, the present, and the trends and new developments that will become significant in the future for:

- Products and services offered by the company.
- Markets served.
- Relevant technologies that serve those markets.
- Business organization itself.
- Competitors of the company.
- Economic environment.
- Social-political environment.

For most companies today, such analysis cannot be limited by regional or national boundaries. Rather, it must be international in its perspective since, increasingly, markets, competition, technology, and economic and social change are not limited by national boundaries.

At Hooker, situation analysis provides the factual framework for our concept of mission and helps us keep it up to date by making changes in it as appropriate. Situation analysis also provides the intelligence needed to plan and control the shorter-range marketing action plans.

In situation analysis, we identify and measure change in all areas affecting our business past, our business present, and our business future. We observe change, we use change, we encourage change, we cause constructive change, and we change our company in response to, and as agents for, the change around us. Situation analysis can and does identify opportunities that we can lock onto for future growth.

No wonder, then, that situation analysis appears mistakenly to be long-range planning itself; it can help us peer into the future and pluck from it those plums that will pay profits five years hence. But the overall direction of any one company's situation analysis, and the disciplines and techniques used, must relate to its own special concept of mission.

Once a concept of mission is developed, it must be put into every facet of all operations in order to minimize conflict and wasted effort, and to stretch the whole organization to new levels of achievement.

The approach becomes practical and results-oriented for two reasons: (a) the concepts are valid, and (b) the work is done, rather than by professional planners and staff groups, by all management personnel at all organization levels. Planning becomes an important part of doing the job—for a president, general manager, sales manager, product manager, salesman, marketing research analyst, and everyone else in the organization.

The Current System

The concept of mission provides a framework for all managers and employees to relate their efforts to specific goals which, in their accomplishment, will result in the achievement of company goals. We spell this out and practice it, at Hooker, in what we call our "LRP-CSP Planning System." This system, which focuses on long-range and customer sales, covers all activities of the company from broad top management policy and resource allocation to specific actions at the point of sale in each customer location.

In all, there are six steps that constitute the *long-range planning* (LRP) phase we have developed to achieve Hooker growth and profit objectives in all operations:

1. Selection of division "business areas" and "product/market segments" for growth and profit improvement.
2. Evaluation of the market and competitive situations.
3. Establishment of goals.
4. Determination of strategy to achieve those goals.
5. Implementation of strategy through action plans that include specific programs, completion dates, and responsibility assignments.
6. Aggressive and goal-centered leadership plus measurement and control of progress to achieve established goals.

The division forward planning just outlined is then applied at the point of sale through *customer sales planning* (CSP). This is the framework for field sales operations, and consists of five steps:

1. Territory examination to develop planning data about accounts, prospects and competitors.
2. Selection of planning accounts and sales volume goals for major customers and prospects.
3. Individual customer sales plan, containing such elements as customer profile, sales goal, sales strategy, and programs and actions.
4. Evaluation of sales plan to assure that it is a sound investment of effort and resources, with a high probability of success.
5. Implementation and measurement by field sales representatives.

CONCEPT OF PERSPECTIVE

To be most effective, the concept of mission described in the previous section requires a new concept of perspective to measure and control progress. The perspective in which we look at the business should include much more than financial measurements for fiscal months and years. All key performance areas— not just dollars—should be measured. And we need a much broader time span in our view than just the current fiscal period.

Most businesses have developed satisfactory reports to provide financial measurements for a month, quarter, or fiscal year. However, since these reports are all specific periods abstracted from the continuum of time, as a rule they do not reveal trends or changes in trends. Thus, although they may be excellent for operating needs on a day-to-day or other short-term basis, they relate hardly at all to long-range marketing plans.

Critical Areas

In most businesses today, many key performance areas that determine long-range success go unmeasured, unobserved, unconsidered. In fact, in only a few businesses today are measurements made on a time scale which is appropriate to long-range marketing planning. We are getting snapshots, when what we need are motion pictures.

Peter Drucker has identified eight key areas where performance and results determine the survival and prosperity of the enterprise:

1. Market standing.
2. Innovation.
3. Productivity.
4. Physical and financial resources.
5. Profitability.
6. Manager performance and development.
7. Worker performance and attitude.
8. Public responsibility.[1]

How many companies set goals for themselves in these eight areas? How many measure performance in all of these areas? My company, at present, does not; but we have a management project now in development that does provide a measurement of seven of these eight on a time scale that shows change and direction of change over a period of time.

I recommend starting with a ten-year time scale— five years past to see where we have come from, present performance as the midpoint, and five years into the future where our goals ahead are set. This presents quite a different perspective from the typical control report that is oriented to the short-range measurement of financial performance versus budget. For example, in our pilot study, we developed similar ten-year measurements for capital resources, for profitability, for productivity, and—over a shorter time span—for innovation and organizational development.

---

[1] *The Practice of Management* (New York, Harper & Row, 1954), p. 63.

This kind of perspective, and this kind of measurement and reporting, make possible "predictive control" of business operations—that is evaluating current performance in relation to environment and to past performance and future goals; projecting the probable future results of current performance; then taking the appropriate current actions that will optimize future results.

On the one hand, for long-range marketing plans, "management by exception" is inadequate. It results in corrective actions which are taken too late.

On the other hand, predictive control enables us to take creative actions early to prevent or minimize what would otherwise become unfavorable exceptions. Moreover, it also enables us to take advantage of every opportunity available to us in the favorable exceptions.

CONCEPTS OF MANAGEMENT STYLE

Along with a concept of mission and a concept of perspective, we need yet a third concept to breathe life and vitality into our long-range marketing plan. This calls for a concept of management style. While long-range marketing planning is the responsibility of top management, there certainly must be participation and involvement by every member of the enterprise in the short-range plans and programs that make it all come true.

An authoritative, production-oriented management cannot use effectively the kind of long-range marketing planning I am advocating. It requires for its success a participative management-by-objectives style, with all the motivations that such a climate of achievement and recognition can provide.

These ideas are attractive to most business people that I have worked with, and especially among those who have a track record of success. But there can be problems. The traditional management fuel is the business cliché—the apt but out-of-date summary of a business principle that "everybody knows." The only thing that such traditional phrases as this do is to put a straitjacket on management thinking.

The concepts described here are not traditional. They do not fit the business cliché. They demand unrestricted attention to the business situation. They are experimental, but pragmatic. They demand hard work, sophisticated skills and knowledge, and high performance standards.

A Case Example

My company's experience illustrates the results achievable with this kind of a business program. A few years ago, as a part of an acquisition, Hooker acquired a business that had a strong market position in its industry. For the previous ten years, its sales volume had been steady with good profit margins, but overall the business had experienced a declining trend in total profits.

The management had a clear but narrow vision of its business. The organization was technically competent and aggressive, but because of its narrow field of concentration had actually been losing market share. Management was oriented to current problems, with little concept of future goals or strategies to achieve them. It had good current data, but only forecasted results up to the close of the previous day's business.

Within the organization, however, there was knowledge on which a bigger and more profitable future could be built. Moreover, there was desire for greater achievement.

Immediately following the acquisition, meetings were held to familiarize the managers of the new division with the long-range planning concepts described in this article, and to help them develop these concepts in their business. Within a few months time, enthusiasm grew within the division for this approach to running their business. The managers raised their sights from yesterday's practices and performance, and focused on tomorrow's opportunities.

As part of this "rebirth," they conceptualized a broader definition of their business, and in their first five-year LRP draft proposed that, while not having grown in volume over the past ten years, they could see a 6½% per year growth over the next five years. More work was needed, however, since the new division was felt to have still greater potential for growth.

Opportunities for growth in existing products and market segments were analyzed. New product-line opportunities were investigated. The result of this planning work—all done within the division—was the establishment of two task force work groups, each to expand a segment of the division's business that showed unique opportunity for growth. The business manager in charge of each group had product management, technical service, and field sales reporting to him. In addition to these two task forces concentrating on segments of the existing business, a third group similarly organized was established to develop and market a new product line.

Within a year's time after the merger, the new division, using a broadly participative management style and with help and support from corporate headquarters, has established these planning principles:

- o An articulated definition of the business providing direction and room for growth.
- o Goals, strategies, and action programs covering eleven key product/market segments.
- o Specialized organizations servicing two major existing business areas and one new business area.
- o A forecasting, measurement, and control system focusing on future goals.
- o A more participative management style involving all employees in the determination and achievement of goals.

The overall result is shown in *Exhibit II.* Here, we see that after ten years of no growth in sales volume, volume in the next five years increased at a rate of 14% per year—doubling in volume and reflecting all growth from within. Whereas for ten years profit had been declining slowly at a rate of 3½% per year, with the successful application of the planning principles just described, in the next five years profits almost tripled, increasing at a rate of 21% per year. Admittedly, we have no objective measurement of organizational morale; however, it is quite apparent that our LRP-CSP planning system has not only made this division bigger and more profitable, but also a much better place in which to work.

CONCLUSION

The three concepts summarized here all too briefly have, in my company, provided the kind of long-range marketing planning that can inspire and motivate great success:

Exhibit II
MARKETING LRP'S IMPACT ON SALES AND PROFITS

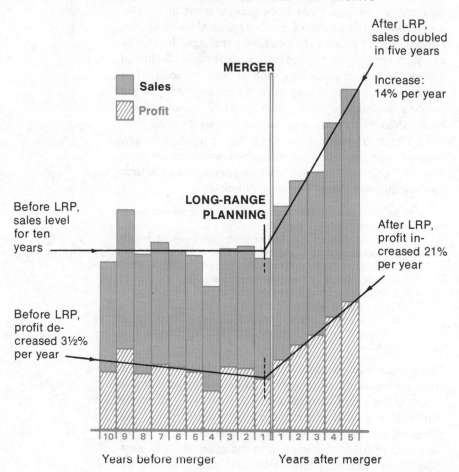

1. Concept of mission—deciding what the business is, where it is going, and the strategy by which it will get there.
2. Concept of perspective—viewing all the key performance areas on which long-range success depends, with current performance measured as the midpoint of a long-range time scale—past and future.
3. Concept of management style—creating a participative management-by-objectives environment which can develop the talent, the will, and the group effectiveness to accomplish the mission.

Let me emphasize that I have not described long-range *marketing* planning—but rather, long-range *business* planning. But marketing has the broad assignment to relate the capabilities of the company to the needs of the market so that both profit. Accordingly, the long-range marketing plan and the long-range business plan must be one and the same. By whatever name we call it, the long-range plan built on these three concepts can tap the full measure of the human potential of the business organization and focus it on the achievement of desirable goals.

Long-range marketing planning, as I have described it, requires a significant reorientation of management's traditional role. The successful manager by his nature loves to solve problems, answer questions, make decisions. He is good at it. But long-range marketing planning forces him to devote his major effort (a) to developing a concept of system for his area of responsibility, and (b) to making this system function effectively.

The manager must keep the system simple—one that is characterized by its concepts, rather than ruled by its regulations. Therefore, he becomes a developer and operator of such a business system, and no longer an ad hoc problem solver. Problems, then, are solved at all levels throughout the organization, and the whole enterprise prospers. It knows where it is going and how it will get there, and all members of the organization are very much involved and participating in getting there.

This kind of long-range marketing planning is not done by professional planners and then imposed on the organization. It is done by everyone throughout the organization, all the time, as a part of the person's job. The whole enterprise is stretched to greater achievement, for long-range marketing planning done this way is energizing and creative, not enervating and constraining.

PROBLEMS

1. Hooker Chemical Corporation places emphasis upon three concepts: the concept of mission, the concept of perspective, and the concept of management style. Which of these concepts is more closely related to the setting of objectives than the other two? Why?

2. Discuss the relationship between setting objectives and planning. Can these two functions be considered one and the same?

3. Why is it necessary to introduce the concept of management style into a discussion of planning?

4. This problem is entitled, Marketing Planning That Gets Things Done. In your opinion is this title too narrow;

that is, does the case illustrate marketing planning
or does it illustrate the long-range planning for the
growth of a corporation?

Chapter Questions for Study and Discussion

1. Determining the objectives of a business was discussed in Chapter 3.
   Some writers include the determination of objectives as a part of the
   planning process and discuss objectives as a part of planning. Develop
   several reasons for the inclusion of objectives as a part of planning and
   several reasons for considering the determination of objectives as a function that precedes planning.
2. Develop an example that shows how the planning function can be applied to the other managerial functions of organizing, directing, and
   controlling.
3. Comment on the statement, "Good decision makers are good planners."
4. Give an example of a decision made by a planner. How does this decision differ from an executive decision? Why?
5. Define the concepts of risk and uncertainty in your own terms. Why is
   the concept of risk important in understanding the environment of business operations? Does good planning reduce risk?
6. What are meant by the concepts of primacy and pervasiveness as applied to planning?
7. Give several examples of "pure" research that have developed into
   today's products. What are some of the products of tomorrow that may
   develop from today's research?
8. Develop a policy statement for a specific functional area. Next, describe
   the procedures and methods necessary to implement the stated policy.
9. What is meant by the concept, objectivity, when used to describe plans
   or the planning function?
10. What is simulation? Give an example of simulation and describe the con-
    ditions that must be met before simulation is possible.
11. Define in your own terms the concept, marginal productivity. Give an
    example of marginal product.
12. What are some of the circumstances that might make it advisable to
    continue production even though the marginal product is declining?
13. Discuss the relationship that exists between personal value systems and
    the determination of benefits within the context of cost-benefit analysis.
14. Discuss the relationships between objectives and cost-benefit analysis.

CHAPTER **5**

Planning for Profit and Sales

CASE PROBLEM 5-A

DEVELOPING A PROFIT PLAN

Assume that you are president of The Specialties Company and own 60 percent of the outstanding common stock. Other members of your family own 20 percent; the other 20 percent is held by outsiders. You have before you the current condensed operating statement.

For the past five years, the operating statements of your company have been very similar. There have been only a few unforeseen expenses and, as a result, a substantial surplus has accrued. Your product, a power lawn edger, has been especially successful and has been distributed on a regional basis. The current building lease is due to expire in six months and you have been notified that the annual cost of rental will be increased $20,000, thereby increasing fixed costs that much. However, the building is adequate in that it houses both office and plant facilities, and there seems little chance of renting for less. Most of the advertising has been conducted through local newspapers and radio and television stations. The advertising agency has informed you that space rates have increased and that it would be well to budget another $5,000 for this expense, which has been charged as a fixed selling expense.

There are approximately 50 hourly employees whose wages are charged as direct labor. If present policy is continued, each will receive an additional five cents an hour, making an increase of about $5,500 in variable direct labor costs. Early indications are that direct material costs will increase four percent in the next year.

The Specialties Company
Condensed Operating Statement

Net sales (60,000 units @ $20 ea.) $1,200,000
Less costs and expenses:

	Variable	Fixed
Direct material	$195,000	
Direct labor	215,000	
Mfg. expense	100,000	$200,000
Selling expense	50,000	150,000
Admin. gen. expense	160,000	50,000

Total costs and expenses 1,120,000

Net profit before taxes .... $ 80,000

PROBLEMS

These are the questions you are asking yourself:

1. What will company expenses be next year?
2. What is the present break-even point and how will it be affected by these changes?
3. What is the present level of profitability as measured against sales, and what will it be next year?
4. Can these relationships be presented graphically so other members of management will understand them?
5. What level of sales must be reached so that the company will still net $80,000?
6. What level of sales has to be reached so that the net profit expressed as a percentage of sales will be the same as it is now?
7. What is the present P/V ratio with current expenses; what is the P/V ratio if projected expenses materialize?

In Chapter 4 the fundamental concepts of planning are discussed, a method for classifying plans is developed, and criteria for evaluating plans are presented. In this and the following chapter the planning process as applied to the major functional areas of management—finance, sales, production, and personnel—is presented. In Chapter 5, financial planning and planning for sales are presented and in Chapter 6 the planning process is applied to the functional areas of production and personnel.

PLANNING FOR PROFIT

In Case Problem 5-A, a brief picture of an organization is presented in terms of its operation and the resultant profit. Despite rising costs, there are several alternatives open to the company so that the level of profit will remain the same. But how is profit to be measured—as an absolute number of dollars, or as a percentage of sales? Before profit can be measured it is necessary to develop a satisfactory definition of profit. The first part of this chapter discusses the meaning of profit; then, the scope of financial policies (plans) is outlined. Next, one of the basic tools of profit planning, the break-even chart, is presented. In the second half of the chapter the same approach is used in discussing planning for the sales function: Basic concepts and definitions of the sales function are presented as determinants of demand, the development of sales policies (plans) is presented, and one of the methods of analysis used by the sales function, market research, is discussed.

The Meaning of Profit

There has been much discussion concerning the *nature* of profit. Profit has been viewed as a form of compensation to either the individual or to the suppliers of the capital necessary to form and operate an industrial firm. Profit has also been defined in reference to an economic process, with the concept that profit within a firm is the result of that firm's operating in an economic environment that is not perfect; i.e., there are *frictions* operating. Differences in the desirability of location or in the possession of a patent on a manufactured product are examples of frictions, or inequalities, that result in one company earning more than its competitors. Another view holds that profit may be the result of innovations, either in respect to the product or to the method in which the business is being operated.[1]

Definition of Profit. There is little dispute concerning the definition of profit, for it is generally agreed that profit is the amount remaining after all expenses associated with conducting a business have been met. Yet, this definition leaves much to be desired as it is passive in nature and can lead one to believe that profit is something that normally happens. Furthermore, there is the implication that profit is something left over. While it is undoubtedly true that there are many prior claims on the apportionment of the sales dollar, profit should not be viewed as that part remaining; rather, profit must be regarded as an integral portion of the sales dollar and as a management goal that can be realized through proper planning.

---

[1] M. H. Spencer, *Managerial Economics,* (3d ed.; Homewood, Illinois: Richard D. Irwin, Inc., 1968), pp. 77-115. In this discussion, the author presents advanced analytical techniques for profit management, in addition to a brief summary of profit theory.

For the entrepreneur who owns and operates his own business, profit may be considered as compensation for the risk involved in ownership and the time required to operate the business. While the concept of profit as payment for time and risk is useful when applied to the entrepreneur, the concept is of limited value as a basis for understanding the significance of profit in a corporation. In a publicly held corporation, members of management are employees and are compensated for performing the functions of management. For the public corporation, profit is necessary in order to repay those persons who have invested their capital in the company; and, in addition, profit creates new capital to provide for expansion. The continuance and growth of any industrial enterprise depend upon its ability to produce profit, for without profit the industrial firm as we know it in our society cannot survive.

Measurement of Profit. There are two measurements commonly used in expressing the amount of profit earned. One measurement expresses profit as total dollars earned for a specified period of time. The other measurement is a ratio that expresses profit as a percentage of either sales or capital invested in the business.

TOTAL DOLLARS EARNED. Total dollars earned for a specified period of time is commonly used in stating company profit; yet unless additional related information is known, this measure may not be too meaningful. Knowledge of past performance adds meaning to a statement of dollars earned, because it provides a basis for comparing a company's present performance with its own past record. Thus it may be determined whether the trend of profit is upward, downward, or static.

Also, the profit for a given firm must be considered in the light of the performance of its industry so that its relative profitability may be ascertained. The meaning of the statement that a company has earned $100,000 for the current year, up 10 percent when compared with its profit for the preceeding year, changes significantly when it is known that the average profit of other companies in the same industry also increased 10 percent. A different meaning would appear, however, if the industry average had decreased 10 percent or remained constant during the period that the company reported a 10-percent increase.

PROFIT RATIOS. In addition to expressing profit as total dollars earned, the following two ratios, or percentages, are normally used to express profitability: (1) percentage return on invested capital, and (2) percentage return on sales.

Percentage return on invested capital is, in the opinion of many, by far the most important measure of management's performance. Return on invested capital indicates the effectiveness of management's stewardship and has a marked effect on the company's ability to attract new investment capital, thereby directly influencing its rate of growth. When profit is expressed as a rate of return on invested capital, management is judged not only in respect to its capability as compared to the management of other companies within the same industry group, but also, it is compared with the managements of other firms. If the return on capital invested in a given company or industry declines, the question is raised as to whether or not it would be wiser to invest new capital in another company or another industry where the return, expressed as a percentage, is greater.

Percentage return on sales is a measure closely associated with the operating statement of a company and is affected directly by changes in operating costs. If costs increase 5 percent, the percentage of sales retained as profit must necessarily decrease; conversely, if costs decrease 5 percent, profit increases by that amount. The answer to Problem 3, Case Problem 5-A, illustrates the effect of rising costs upon the percentage of sales retained as profit. Likewise, profit expressed as a percentage of sales decreases 5 percent when sales volume declines by that amount unless costs are also reduced 5 percent; and when sales volume increases, profit shows the same percentage increase provided all operating costs remain constant.

SUMMARY—MEASUREMENT OF PROFIT. Ratios of profitability are not directly dependent upon the size of the company as measured by the dollar volume of sale. Medium- and small-size companies may show a greater degree of profitability expressed either as a percentage of sales or of invested capital than a larger company that produces a greater volume of profit. This statement does not imply that very large companies are incapable of producing profit that represents satisfactory and comparable rates of return on sales and invested capital.

Planning Financial Policy

Financial policies are plans that provide for the utilization of the money necessary for a company's operation. The acquisition of needed money, the utilization of money in producing and selling the product or service of the organization, and the distribution of the resultant profit form a continuous cycle. The first step of the cycle is the acquisition of needed funds, usually in the form of cash. Next, these funds are used in meeting payrolls, paying taxes, creating reserves for unforeseen expenses, or are converted into fixed assets such as plants and equipment necessary for the production process. Some of these funds will be spent for raw materials and supplies that are ultimately converted into the product or service desired. The third step of the cycle occurs after the product is sold and money is received in payment. All indebtedness incurred is paid, provisions are made for the continuation of the production process or the service, as the case may be, and the resultant profit may be distributed or retained according to plan.

Financial policies are grouped to correspond to the three steps of the cycle, but the broader term "capital" is substituted for the word "cash." The three groups of financial policies provide a basis for the effective performance for each of the three following functions of financial management: (1) acquisition of capital, (2) employment or utilization of capital, and (3) distribution of profit. The scope of policies to guide action in each of these three areas is discussed in turn below.

Acquisition of Capital. For the individual starting a business, savings are one of the major sources of capital, and there is the possibility that he may be able to borrow from friends or if he has sufficient collateral, he may borrow from an established financial institution such as a bank. Generally, the same sources used by the individual—savings, or prior earnings, and borrowed capital—are available to a corporation. The savings of a corporation provide additional capital when needed. Capital acquired from outside sources may be classified in respect to the length of time for which the financing is desired. Usually, financing required for periods greater than one year is referred to as *long-term capital* and that capital required for a period of less than one year is referred to as *short-term capital*.

LONG-TERM CAPITAL. The sources of long-term capital are: stock, bonds, mortgages, and long-term notes, each of which has distinct advantages and disadvantages as shown below.

Stock represents a share of ownership, and the sale of stock is the most widely used means of raising capital for a corporation. Stock is usually classified as *preferred stock* and *common stock*. The rights and privileges accorded the stockholder of each kind of stock vary with the conditions set forth at the time of issuance. As might be expected, certain preferential treatment is accorded preferred stockholders. A fixed rate of return in the form of a dividend is established. Such dividends have first claim on the profit of a corporation and must be paid before making the declaration of any dividends on common stock which does not carry a contractual rate of return. If the company is expanding and its profit is increasing, substantial dividends may be paid on common stock; however, if the earnings of the company decline and the forecast for future earnings is dismal, common stock dividends usually decline or may even become non-existent.

In formulating policies concerning the acquisition of capital through the issuance of preferred stock, a company must consider whether or not it wishes to obligate itself to the payment of dividends on preferred stock. Further, the concept of equity must be considered. Without a corresponding growth in fixed assets, such as land and buildings, the issuance of additional stock, either preferred or common, results in a dilution of stockholder equity. Also, consideration must be given to determine whether or not the payment of a dividend on common stock is necessary to make the purchase of such equities an attractive investment.

Bonds are another means of long-term financing. A company that issues bonds agrees that it will repay the face value of the bond on a specified date and that a fixed rate of interest will be paid until the maturation date. Secured bonds are those that have a portion of the physical assets of the company pledged as security, while unsecured bonds (sometimes called *debentures*) do not have assets pledged as security. Some utilities and railroads have used secured bonds as a means of raising additional capital since such capital is typically spent for real property that may be used as security. Issuing debentures offers advantages to a company with a well-established reputation of performance and integrity.

One advantage of bonds is that management's control of the company is not jeopardized as it may be when additional stock with voting rights is issued. Also, the fixed rate that a company pays for a bond issue is an expense item and not taxed as income; however, dividends paid to stockholders come from profit after the payment of income taxes. A disadvantage resulting from the issuance of bonds is the obligation to pay interest which represents an additional fixed charge to the company, while common stock issues carry no such burden.

Mortgages, secured by a part or all of the company's real property, offer another means of obtaining money. Usually, a fixed interest rate is specified, along with predetermined dates for repayments of the principal. Most modern mortgages enable a company to retain its present management and control as long as payments on principal and interest are met as agreed upon.

Long-term notes have become increasingly popular in recent years due to funds made available by life insurance companies as a means of raising long-term capital. As in the case of bonds and mortgages, interest payments are an expense item and are tax deductible. Usually funds procured from long-range borrowing are spent for additional assets intended to increase the earnings of the company, thereby making it possible for the note to be repaid. However, distinct disadvantages may result if the lender places restrictions on the payment of dividends or the purchase of additional assets. Lenders may also require representation on the board of directors which may or may not be an acceptable condition.

SHORT-TERM CAPITAL. Short-term capital is borrowed for a period of one year or less and, unlike long-term capital, is not used to acquire additional fixed assets or to improve existing assets. Short-term capital supplements the company's existing cash and may be used for such things as to purchase additional inventory for resale, or to take advantage of cash discounts and of quantity purchase discounts. The following are the most frequently used sources of short-term capital.

Commercial credit is similar to an individual's charge account. Vendors of goods and services may extend to a customer with a good credit rating the privilege of deferred payment just as a department store does to a charge account customer. Payments may be deferred for 30, 60, or even 90 days, thus establishing valuable short-term credit. However, cash discounts, which may represent a considerable sum if the volume purchased is large, are sacrificed.

Bank loans represent the most frequently used source of short-term capital. The degree to which banks are used as a source of credit depends upon the company's reputation and the relationship established with the banking community. Bank loans may or may not require collateral depending upon the individual company and the bank.

Commercial factors are firms that specialize in short-term financing usually through the purchase of a company's accounts receivable. In some instances, factors prepare the required invoices and perform all the paperwork necessary to collect the accounts receivable. To firms short on capital and without an adequate clerical staff, the use of a commercial factor may offer an attractive solution for acquiring short-term capital.

Utilization of Capital. Financial policies in the second group serve as guides for the employment or utilization of capital after it has been acquired. Elements to be considered in determining the most effective utilization of capital are the amount of capital to be converted into fixed assets, the ratio between fixed assets and working capital, the amount of inventory, credits, and collections, and depreciation. Each of these elements demands cash and, unless there are policies that specify the amount to be allocated for each use, a serious imbalance may result and thereby impair the firm's position.

FIXED ASSETS. The determination to be made is the extent to which capital is converted into fixed assets. In its simplest form, the question is one of leasing or buying. Among the factors to be considered are problems of obsolescence, maintenance, replacement, and the rate of return on the specific assets. It is also necessary to consider the effect of buying versus leasing in respect to tax liability. Usually money paid for rentals or leases is considered an expense and hence is tax deductible. On the other hand, if assets are purchased a depreciation allowance is permitted which may or may not offset the additional tax liability. Fixed assets may be sold and converted into cash, a move that may be proper if the assets are not fully utilized and if additional cash is needed.

WORKING CAPITAL. Policies must be developed to determine the amount of capital to be retained for the operation of the business and how this capital is to be utilized. This capital, called working capital, is used for the purchase of materials and services, for payment of payrolls, and for contingencies. There should be a balance maintained between fixed assets, all of which require money to operate, and the working capital available for their operation. Policies define the proper relationship for a given company. When fixed assets become too great in relation to available working capital, excessive borrowing may result in order to remain in operation; or if additional funds are not obtainable, a curtailment in production may be necessary. Working capital not fully used should be invested so that a greater return on resources may be realized.

INVENTORY. One of the major uses of capital is that of establishing an inventory of goods in process and ultimately finished goods. Without specific policy statements in this area, it is possible for a company to place too large a portion of its capital into inventories. Such practice is particularly hazardous if there is a possibility of obsolescence due to a change in the product on the part of a competitor or in those situations where there is a marked variation in the price of raw materials used in the product. Thus, policy statements in regard to inventory should include a determination of the size of inventory of both in-process and finished goods, expressed as a unit portion of annual sales; and a determination of the rate of inventory buildup and turnover in order to take advantage of price fluctuations of raw materials and to minimize the risk of obsolescence.

CREDITS AND COLLECTIONS. Virtually every business is forced to extend some credit to its customers. The extent to which credit is granted may be determined by general industry practices, or it may be the result of attempting to secure a better competitive position. In either event, clear-cut policies are needed to determine the amount of credit that should be extended. Closely allied to credit policies are policies governing the collection of accounts receivable and the granting of discounts from list price for prompt payment. Accounts receivable, unless closely watched, may become abnormally large as a percentage of current assets.

DEPRECIATION. Policies are needed to determine the method to be used in calculating the rate of depreciation of capital expenditures. Certain types of equipment may be useful considerably longer than the normal or expected life; and in this case, other things being equal, the straight-line method of depreciation might prove unsatisfactory. However, in industries where there is rapid technological change and improvement in manufacturing methods, along with changes in the product itself, it might be well to use any one of several methods of accelerated depreciation so that sufficient capital will be available to replace equipment as changing conditions make replacement necessary.

Distribution of Profit. The third area in which financial policies serve as a guide is the distribution of profit. As mentioned before, profit is absolutely vital as a means of continuing a business; therefore, it is necessary that policies be developed concerning the amount of profit to be retained and in order to operate the business. Obviously, too large a portion may be retained to the long-run detriment of the firm. There are many who facetiously referred to the "Bank of Montgomery Ward" during the period of time that the retail chain was under the direction of Sewell Avery. During this period, huge cash reserves were built up because of Mr. Avery's stated belief that another severe depression was in the offing.

DIVIDENDS. Policy must be established regarding the payment of dividends. Such a statement is necessary to assure a fair return on investment to those who have invested in the firm and to make the purchase of equities in the firm an attractive investment. When policies express the amount to be paid out in dividends as a percentage of profit earned, there is the possibility of increasing dividends and consequently increasing the rate of return on money invested.

REINVESTMENT. After the establishment of adequate cash reserves and the payment of dividends, the disposition of the balance of earnings must be determined. Questions to be answered are: What portion of the profit is to be reinvested in the firm, and how is this money to be reinvested? It can be invested in fixed assets, a means of placing capital in those channels that results in expanded sales. Another means of expanding sales, not ordinarily classified as an investment is to direct capital into an expanded advertising program or to establish sales territories not currently serviced by the company. Another major direction for the utilization of capital is in the area of research and product development.

Analysis of Profit

Without stated financial policies to guide management in the acquisition and utilization of capital and the subsequent distribution of profit, it is highly unlikely that the level of profit achieved by a business ever approximates its potential. Often, before a final determination can be made regarding the establishment of financial policies, it is necessary to analyze more closely the nature of the process of predicting and measuring profit. One analytical method used to show the interrelationship of the factors affecting profit is break-even analysis. The following section discusses the steps necessary to complete a break-even analysis, the dynamics, or interrelationships, of those factors influencing profit, and an evaluation of break-even analysis as an analytical technique.

Break-even Analysis. A break-even analysis reveals the operating conditions that exist when a company "breaks even"; that is, when sales reach a dollar volume equal to all expenses incurred in attaining that level of sales. Beyond this point, or level of volume, the company has the potential to make a profit on additional sales. It is the purpose of break-even analysis to clarify the dynamic relationship existing between the total costs of a company and unit volume.

The following condensed operating statement includes information needed for a break-even analysis:

Ace Manufacturing Company

Condensed Operating Statement
for the Fiscal Year, 19—

Revenue from sales (20,000 units @ $50 ea.) $1,000,000
Less costs and expenses:
    Variable costs $500,000
    Fixed costs 400,000
        Total costs and expenses 900,000
Net profit before taxes .... $ 100,000

    The operating statement shows clearly the two variables needed for
break-even analysis—a measure of input, costs; and a measure of output, unit volume or sales. The problem is to present the relationship
existing between these variables in such a fashion that the break-even
point, the point at which the Ace Manufacturing Company had sales
sufficient to defray all expenses, may be readily determined. These
variables are presented graphically in Figure 5-1.

    In Figure 5-1, sales volume is plotted on the x, or horizontal axis,
and expense items are plotted on the y, or vertical axis. Note that the
costs for the Ace Manufacturing Company have been separated into
two major types—those costs that are *fixed*, or relatively unchanging
as a result of unit volume; and those costs that are *variable* and vary
primarily as a function of unit volume. Usually fixed costs are costs
that remain relatively stable and independent of unit volume and
that accrue whether or not anything is being manufactured or sold.
These costs normally include real estate taxes, insurance, depreciation,
certain administrative overhead expenses such as executive and clerical
salaries, and interest on indebtedness. They are similar in nature to the
fixed costs of owning an automobile—insurance and depreciation—
and have little to do with the number of miles driven. Gasoline costs,
however, are a direct function of the number of miles driven and are
thus considered variable costs. Likewise, certain costs of business,
usually materials and the cost of labor that works directly on the
product (called direct labor) vary with the number of units produced
and are classified as variable costs.

    There are always some cost items that cannot readily be classified
as either fixed or variable. Typical of these are the costs of supervision,
power costs, and some forms of indirect labor such as inspection and
shipping. In a strict sense these costs are variable, but they are variable
costs that behave as fixed costs; i.e., they move very slowly, and within

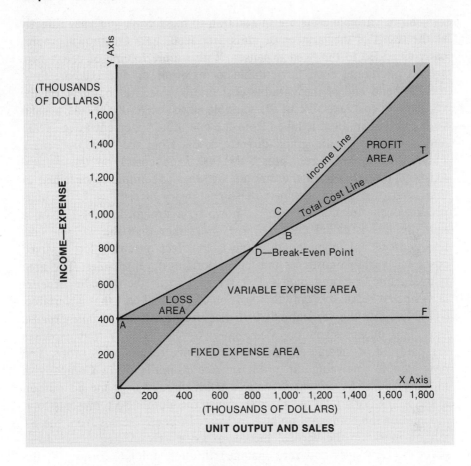

Figure 5-1
BREAK-EVEN ANALYSIS FOR THE ACE MANUFACTURING COMPANY

broad ranges of units produced they do not change. For example, a supervisory staff of 10 foremen may direct the work of 150 men and this work force may be doubled before it becomes necessary to add another supervisor. It is usually safe practice to classify as fixed those costs that are not clearly variable.

At a level of $1 million sales, fixed costs for the Ace Manufacturing Company are $400,000. This value becomes point *A* on the *y*, or vertical, axis. Since this amount does not vary as a result of the number of units produced, it is expressed graphically as a straight line parallel to the *x* axis and is interpreted as constant for all sales up to and including $1 million. The area below the line *A-F* is referred to as the *fixed expense area*.

Since variable costs are in addition to fixed costs and vary directly as the result of the number of units produced, they are shown graphically as added to the fixed expenses. With a unit volume of zero, there are no additional costs attributable to materials or direct labor; thus, the left-hand end of the variable cost line is placed at point A on the vertical or cost axis. Point B, variable costs of $500,000 at a sales volume of $1 million, is taken from the operating statement (page 150) and is entered on the graph directly across from the $900,000 mark ($500,000 variable costs plus $400,000 fixed costs) on the vertical axis and directly above the amount of sales ($1 million) obtained at that level of expense. Because these costs vary directly with the units produced, the relationship can be shown by a straight line, A-T. Notice that this line is called the *total cost line* rather than the variable cost line because any point on this line is in effect a summation of fixed costs and variable costs for that corresponding level of sales. The area between line A-F and line A-T is referred to as the *variable expense area* since it represents only that portion of the total cost that is variable.

Note that the vertical axis 0-IE has been called an *income-expense* line. This dual designation is necessary to show clearly that expenses are paid out of income and that the difference remaining is profit. The next step in analyzing the profit of Ace Manufacturing Company is to locate point C, current income, a point directly over the $1 million mark on the horizontal or sales axis. Since this point also represents total income for the company, point C is located directly across from the $1 million mark on the vertical income-expense axis. A line drawn from point 0 (zero sales and zero income) through point C forms 0-I, the *income line*. The line crosses the total cost line at point D, the break-even point, a sales volume of $800,000. The area enclosed by the triangle IDT represents the *profit area*, while the area enclosed by the triangle $AD0$ represents the *loss area*. Thus, the break-even chart shows graphically the relationships that exist among fixed costs, variable costs, unit price, and unit sales for the Ace Manufacturing Company.

Profit to Volume Analysis. Another analytical technique used in predicting the level of profit is the analysis of the relationship existing between profit and volume beyond the break-even point, referred to as *profit to volume analysis* or *profit to volume ratio (P/V ratio)*. The relationship between profit and volume beyond the break-even point is stated precisely in the following formula:

$$\text{P/V Ratio} = \frac{\text{Marginal Income}}{\text{Sales}}$$

In the preceding formula:

Marginal Income = Sales —Variable Costs, and
Sales = Total Dollar Volume of Sales.

In order to understand the relationships expressed in the formula above, let us apply it to the operating statement of Ace Manufacturing Company where fixed costs are stated as $400,000. As goods are manufactured and sold, variable costs (labor and material) must be paid. After variable costs have been paid, the remainder, *marginal income,* is applied to paying the fixed costs of the business. Since the variable costs of the company are $500,000, when sales are $1,000,000 variable costs represent 50 percent of the sales dollar. Assume that each unit manufactured sells for $50; thus $25 of the money received for each unit is paid out for material and labor. The marginal income remaining, also $25, is applied to fixed costs. This distribution of sales dollars continues until all fixed costs, in this case $400,000, have been paid at which time the break-even point is reached. Beyond the break-even point there are no more fixed costs to be paid, the only costs to be met are the variable costs of material and labor for each additional unit made. Thus the profit for each additional unit beyond the break-even point is determined by subtracting the variable costs from the sales price. The remainder, $25 marginal income, is divided by the sales value of each unit, $50, in order that the relation may be expressed as a ratio or a quotient. The quotient for this example is .50, or 50 percent. Since the P/V assumes a constant variable cost per unit and a constant price per unit, the same result, .50, may be obtained when the totals from the operating statement are used rather than analyzing the fixed and variable costs of each unit made and sold. When totals are substituted in the formula, marginal income, $500,000 ($1,000,000 sales minus $500,000 variable costs), divided by $1,000,000 (sales) yields .50, and can be interpreted as meaning that a profit of 50 percent can be expected on each unit sold beyond the break-even point.

Once the P/V ratio, or more simply P/V, is determined the break-even point may be computed algebraically, thereby permitting an accurate determination of the company's profit plan. One function of profit planning is to predict the effect of anticipated or probable changes on company profit. Case Problem 5-A requires a determination of the present break-even point and the expected break-even point created by rising costs so that plans may be formed to retain profit at its present level. Given the fixed expenses of a company and the P/V, the break-even point is determined by the formula on the following page.

$$\text{Break-Even Point} = \frac{\text{Fixed Expenses}}{P/V \text{ Ratio}}$$

In the case of the Ace Manufacturing Company, fixed expenses of $400,000 divided by the P/V of .50 results in a break-even point of $800,000, the same value obtained by graphic analysis in Figure 5-1. To understand the reasoning behind the second formula, one must remember that every dollar earned below the break-even point is divided two ways—one part is used to pay current variable costs and one part is used to pay established fixed costs. For the example given, an equal amount is distributed to each type of cost.

Dynamics of Profit. Four factors—unit volume, fixed costs, variable costs, and unit price—stand out as having an influence upon profit and emphasize the dynamic nature of profit, thereby stressing that profit cannot be viewed as something left over after all expenses have been paid. A change in any one of these factors has a predictable effect upon the profit of a company, and if the amount of the change is known or can be anticipated, as in Case Problem 5-A, the effect upon profit can be computed. The influence of each factor upon profit is discussed below.

EFFECT OF VOLUME. Although volume, expressed either as units or sales dollars, does not affect the break-even point, it has a direct relationship to the profitability of a company. If the volume is not sufficient to produce a revenue capable of meeting all fixed and variable expenses (the break-even point) then there is no profit but rather a loss as shown in Figure 5-1. However, if the volume of sales is greater than the total expenses incurred, a profit is the result. Additional volume beyond the break-even point has a marked effect upon the profitability of a company, since the P/V is normally far greater than the ratio of profit to total sales volume. Herein lies one of the great advantages of computing the P/V, because it places an emphasis on attaining additional sales thereby increasing the overall level of profitability.

EFFECT OF FIXED COSTS. A company should examine with care any move that results in an increase in fixed costs. Fixed costs by their very nature are extremely difficult to lower as they are literally "fixed." A change in the amount of fixed costs in either direction changes the break-even point and the amount of profit earned for a given level of sales volume. But it does not change marginal income. (Marginal income is equal to total sales minus variable costs.) Fixed costs must be paid out of marginal income; therefore, should fixed costs increase too much, the remainder is negative and appears as a loss rather than a profit for a stated volume.

EFFECT OF VARIABLE COSTS. Unlike a change in fixed costs, a change in variable costs produces a change in marginal income and, as the variable cost of direct labor and materials increase, marginal income decreases. Since fixed costs must be paid out of marginal income, the effect is a definite "squeeze on profit." The inherent characteristics of fixed costs, making them relatively unyielding to change, and the realization that they must be paid out of marginal income go a long way toward explaining the behavior of management during a typical cost-cutting drive. Emphasis is placed upon personnel costs, both direct and indirect, material costs, expense accounts, and a host of seemingly relatively unimportant items. Why? Simply because these items are controllable, or variable, and the truly large cost items of depreciation, taxes, and interest either remain stationary or move slowly. Furthermore, every dollar saved in variable expense is an additional dollar of profit.

EFFECT OF PRICE. A change in dollar sales volume may be accomplished in one of two ways: by producing a greater number of units of volume and selling at the same or original price, or by producing the same number of units of volume but selling at a higher price per unit. A change in price per unit results in a change in marginal income —total sales minus variable costs. In addition, the degree of change in marginal income can be predicted before a price change is made by multiplying the expected difference in price by the number of units produced. Since an increase in price, with all other factors remaining constant, causes a lower break-even point and correspondingly increased profit, the need for experimental pricing practice is evident. There are undoubtedly many instances where modest or even substantial price increases can be accomplished without a decline in the total number of units sold. Too often, firms dealing in consumer products assume that a lower price results in an increased volume, or that an increased price would decrease volume but are hard pressed to produce data to support their assumption.

Evaluation of Profit Analysis Techniques. Obviously there is considerable advantage to the analytical techniques of break-even analysis and P/V analysis since they permit a prediction of profit under varying conditions of volume, fixed costs, variable costs, and price. Nonetheless there are many criticisms of both break-even analysis and P/V

as analytical techniques. If one were to choose a single word to describe the objections, it would be that the techniques are *static* in nature and consequently are not appropriate for use in describing the dynamic situation that is typical of the business environment. Specifically, criticisms have attacked both the reliability and the validity of the concepts of variable and fixed costs stating that neither is a truly reliable measure, other than for the instant from which it is drawn, and that they are not valid measures since they are not what they purport to be. Break-even analysis is also criticized because it implies that all costs contribute directly to production. A third criticism is that break-even analysis is not an accurate reflection of the effect of company pricing practices. And fourth, it is charged that break-even analysis cannot be applied accurately to a company that manufactures more than one product. Even so, the advantage to be gained from such analysis as an aid in decision making are considerable despite the limitations set forth in the criticisms of the techniques.

PLANNING FOR SALES

Case Problem 5-B describes a company that must make a policy decision about the method to be used in distributing its product. Selecting the appropriate channel of distribution for the goods or services of a company is but one of several major policy decisions required in planning an effective sales program. Also, it is necessary to evaluate some of the analytical tools available for analyzing proposed sales practices. The major topics discussed in this section are, first, the determinants of demand; second, the scope of sales policies; and third, a brief review of one of the analytical tools available in planning sales policies and practices.

Determinants of Demand

The sales or marketing function of a business organization encompasses those activities necessary to persuade a buyer to purchase the products or services of the organization. Many factors determine the efficiency and effectiveness of a sales organization. Some of these factors are economic in nature and beyond the control of any one company; yet, a firm must operate within an economic environment that cannot be controlled. The task is to examine those factors of the environment that may be modified and the marketing techniques available to create the desired changes. In order to understand the framework in which selling takes place, it is necessary to review the factors that determine the demand for consumer goods and to consider briefly those factors that influence the demand for capital goods.

Demand for Consumer Goods. There are three elements necessary for the completion of any marketing transaction. One of these elements is a buyer, a person or an institution desirous of purchasing a given product or service; second, a seller who is able to provide the desired product or service; and third, a price that the buyer is willing to pay and that the seller is willing to accept. The economist's approach to the marketing process, described above, is directed toward a better understanding of the relationship that exists between the supply (available quantity) of a product or service and the demand (amount purchased) for a product or service. The conclusion reached from the analysis of these relationships has been stated as the *law of supply and demand*. This law holds that an increase in the supply of a given product tends to decrease the price, thereby increasing the demand for the product; and conversely, if the supply of the product decreases, the price ultimately becomes higher with a resultant decrease in demand.

While the economist places a great deal of emphasis upon the supply of goods available and seeks to determine the effect of supply upon the price of a given product or service, the businessman is concerned with determining how he can influence the consumer to buy at a specified price level and in sufficient quantities so that an adequate return can be realized on invested capital. In the classical portrayal of supply and demand the buying power of the consumer is not mentioned explicitly; yet it is self-evident that a purchaser must have money in some form in order to buy. Buying power is one of the major determinants that affects the sales of an individual business firm. Supply, a major concern of the economist, is in most instances not a critical determinant of the price of manufactured consumer goods over the long run in the United States, since our manufacturing facilities are capable of producing more than can be consumed. To a degree, manufacturers of consumer goods operate in an economy that can be characterized as a constant state of oversupply. Consequently, in the discussion that follows, supply is not considered as a determinant of the demand for consumer goods. *Consumer goods,* those items consumed by individuals in contrast to certain items purchased by industry, are traditionally classified as either nondurable or durable. Each type of consumer goods is discussed separately.

CONSUMER NONDURABLE GOODS. Consumer nondurable goods include those perishable items, such as beverages, foods, and other products consumed in a single act. Also included are items such as household supplies consumed in a matter of months. Characteristically, the unit price of consumer nondurables is less than the unit price of durable goods. The following factors are important in determining the demand for consumer nondurables: buying power, demography, price, sales effort.

Consumer buying power is the net amount of money available for discretionary spending after all fixed charges have been paid. Thus buying power is equal to current income from wages, plus available credit, savings, and income from investments. From this amount must be subtracted payments on life insurance, cost of housing, debt repayment, contribution to company pension plans and payment on other retirement annuities, and direct taxes such as social security, income, and property taxes. The remainder, after subtracting all fixed expense items from gross income, is net buying power, the amount of dollars available for purchase of those items considered as discretionary purchases.

Demography, the personal characteristics of a segment of the population, modifies any one industry's share of the buying power described above. If a disproportionally large number of persons in a given market is over 65 years of age, the brewing industry cannot expect to sell as much as they might otherwise because that segment of the population between the ages of 18 and 45 provides the best market for the sale of beer. On the other hand, a manufacturer of geriatric foods would have a distinct advantage since his market is that portion of the population over 65 years of age. Other examples of demographic characteristics that may influence the sale of any given product are the number of automobiles owned, the number of pre-school children, or the educational level of the adult population.

The monetary price charged for consumer nondurables is important as a determinant of demand. Yet price cannot be measured solely in terms of dollars; it must also be interpreted in relation to buying power and the price of competing and substitute products. The price of an article is in effect lower (in terms of a percentage of income) when price remains constant and the amount of discretionary income increases. On the other hand, if buying power decreases and price remains constant, the effect is the same as an increase in price. A manufacturer of cans for consumer nondurables not only competes with other manufacturers of cans, but also with the makers of glass and plastic containers since these items may be substituted for cans.

Sales effort—unlike buying power, demography, and price which function concomitantly as determinants of demand that are economic in origin and for the most part cannot be modified by the seller—is within the control of the seller. In many instances sales effort is the most important single determinant of demand for consumer nondurables. Sales effort has literally created entire industries; for examples, the chewing gum and cigarette industries are primarily the result of sales effort expressed in advertising. Further, the sales effort of an individual seller is a significant factor in determining his share of the total market.

CONSUMER DURABLE GOODS. In contrast to consumer nondurable goods, *consumer durable goods* are consumed over a period of years, rather than being consumed in a single act or in a short period of time. Examples of durable goods are the appliances used in the home: washing machines, dryers, dishwashers, refrigerators, and household furniture. The serviceable life of these products may extend for many years. The same factors of buying power—demography, price, and sales effort are determinants of demand for consumer durables, but their effect as determinants is modified by the long life of the product, the relatively high unit price, and the need for additional facilities in order to use certain durables. These characteristics of the product and the need for additional facilities all combine to influence the effectiveness of sales effort.

Long life, an outstanding characteristic of consumer durables, modifies the significance of buying power as a determinant of demand. Since many persons have appliances with the expectancy of useful service that may exceed ten years, they become potential customers only when it is necessary to replace present applicances; thus, one part of the market for consumer durables is termed a replacement market. The other segment of the market for consumer durables results from the formation of new family units. Typically, a consumer durable is shared by a family unit; hence, the formation of new household units is necessary for the creation of an additional market for durables. Information concerning the size of the new market and the replacement market, combined with buying power (including credit), offers a means of predicting the demand for a given consumer durable good.

Credit lessens the impact of high unit price since the purchaser of consumer durable goods may extend his payment for the product over a period of time. Thus the availability of credit becomes an important factor in determining the demand for durable products. An increase in unit price may drive some potential purchasers from the market, not because the total cost of the unit is too much, but because an increased price requires a larger down payment. Increased unit prices may be offset by a combination of a low down payment and smaller monthly payments extended over a longer period of time.

Related facilities are required by some consumer durables in order that they may be used effectively. For example many household appliances require the additional facilities of gas or electricity for their operation, and the continuing sale of automobiles may be affected by the availability of highways and provisions for adequate servicing and parking facilities. The demand factors of buying power, demography, price, and sales effort are all negated unless the proper supplemental facilities are present.

Demand for Capital Goods. Those items bought for the express purpose of creating more products or services for the consumer are called *capital goods.* Examples of capital goods that produce products are the machine tools that make equipment used in the production process, such as the huge presses that stamp out automobile body panels or parts for refrigerators and other household appliances. The rolling stock of the railroads and the trucking industry is regarded as capital goods in that it provides service for the consumer by transporting the products he uses. Without capital goods, consumer products and services as we know them would not exist. Since capital goods and consumer goods are closely related, almost a cause-and-effect relationship, the question naturally arises whether the same factors that determine the demand for consumer goods also determine the demand for capital goods.

A survey article by Charles F. Roos provides an understanding of the factors that influence the demand for capital goods.[2] As is the case for consumer goods, purchasing power plays an important role; however, the purchasing power of a corporation is defined somewhat differently than the purchasing power of an individual. *Corporate purchasing power* is composed of profits from current operations, accumulated capital from earlier profits, funds available from new financing, and the amount of money accumulated in depreciation accounts. Also of importance are the prices of metals and metal products, the basic

---

[2] Charles F. Roos, "Survey of Economic Forecasting Techniques," *Econometrica,* Vol. XXIII (October, 1955), pp. 363-95. As the title suggests, this is a survey article. The part of the discussion concerned with the forecasting of capital requirements begins on page 391.

materials that go to make up capital goods. Long-term interest rates are significant, and the ratio of production output to capacity is important. The extent of the contribution of each of the factors above must be determined for each industry, and it is necessary to go one step further and determine the needs of each company within its industry. A proposed program of highway construction may create a demand for the capital goods used in making cement, but an individual company within that industry may not purchase additional capital goods as the result of not having sufficient purchasing power or as the result of having recently refurbished its plant equipment.

Planning Sales Policies

From the preceding discussion, it is evident that broad socio-economic factors are the chief determinants of demand; the sales efforts of a single company have little, if any, effect upon the total demand for a given product or service. Nonetheless, it is important that these factors be recognized and understood since they are part of the economic environment within which sales objectives are determined. In practice, these objectives are expressed in terms of relative achievement within the industry or in comparison to the individual company's past record. For a firm to achieve its sales objectives, it is necessary to formulate policies to serve as plans for each of the four functional areas of sales management. First, it is necessary to state policies that define the characteristics of the product to be sold. Second, the basis for pricing the product must be stated; and third, a channel of distribution must be selected. Finally, effective means of sales promotion must be determined. Each of these areas of sales policies is discussed in turn.

Product Policies. The determination of policies concerning the product or service to be sold is a decision that includes not only the sales function but also the functions of finance, production, and personnel. It is necessary to consider the adequacy of available financing, the production facilities needed for the manufacture of a given product, and the qualifications of personnel in respect to technical knowledge and skills required to make the product. The unique contribution of the sales department in forming product policies is its estimate of the potential market. There are four policy determinations that affect the product's market potential. They are: (1) product diversification, (2) product obsolescence, (3) quality, and (4) product standardization.

PRODUCT DIVERSIFICATION. *Product diversification* refers to the number of products produced and distributed and the extent to which these products differ from each other in respect to physical characteristics, size, manufacturing processes, and selling methods. At one end of the scale of diversification are companies manufacturing a single product, such as Electroware, Case Problem 6-B, prior to the decision to make stoves in addition to electric hot water heaters. At the other end of the scale are companies such as General Motors and General Electric that manufacture and distribute a range of products having little or no common ground in respect to physical characteristics, use, manufacturing processes, or selling method. The phrase, product diversification, implicitly refers to the acquisition of additional products. However, diversification policies should serve not only as guides for the acquisition of additional products but also for showing the need for reducing the number of items in an existing product line. The acquisition of new products must be considered in the light of available financing, the production facilities required, and the expected method of distribution. The qualifications of available personnel, particularly their ability to perform continuing research and development work, is a necessary consideration if a position of leadership is desired. Anticipated market size is also important, for it indicates potential contribution to sales and profit. Predetermined levels of sales volume and profitability serve as effective guides in determining when an existing product should be dropped from the product line.

OBSOLESCENCE AND STYLE. Durable goods may become obsolescent; that is, reach a state of not being usable for any one of several reasons. Products are sometimes termed obsolete when they are worn out and have served their useful life. Obsolescence due to wear forms part of the replacement market for consumer durables, and consequently, the replacement of worn equipment creates demand for capital goods. While obsolescence due to wear may be directly the result of a policy decision concerning product quality, *forced obsolescence* is the direct result of a policy decision. Continued product improvement or change may be used to create consumer dissatisfaction with the product in its present form. Changes in style, for example the periodic model changes of the automobile industry, offer another means of inducing forced obsolescence. Policy statements about product obsolescence determine the extent and frequency of changes in mechanical design and style in order to force obsolescence of earlier products by creating a desire for the model that is new in appearance or better in performance.

QUALITY. Quality refers to those characteristics that are relevant in measuring the degree to which a product meets predetermined standards of performance. Quality is not an absolute value, yet there is an implied relationship between quality and excellence of design, workmanship, and materials. Usually, there is a direct relationship between quality and price. One of the policy questions that must be resolved is the determination of how many levels of quality are to be produced or sold. Most companies have one level of quality; however, Sears, Roebuck & Company describes the quality of many of its products as good, better, and best. There are hazards in selling multiple levels of quality because a customer who purchases an item described as "good" with full knowledge that there are two higher grades of quality available may nonetheless expect the "best" standard of performance. Another policy consideration concerning quality is determining whether or not truly outstanding quality can be used ås a basis for sales promotion.

STANDARDIZATION. The existence of several grades of quality increases the complexity of the product line and can be justified when each gradient of quality taps an additional segment of the market. Likewise the production of several models, all meeting a uniform standard of quality, assumes that each additional model captures its share of the market. A reduction in the number of levels of quality or the number of models produced or distributed is a move toward product *standardization* and usually results in a lowering of manufacturing and distribution costs. Hence, a policy statement setting forth the optimum degree of standardization of a given product line, either in respect to quality levels or the number of models, is a choice between potentially lower costs and the possibility of increased market potential.

Pricing Policies. It is recognized that the cost of manufacturing and distributing has a direct bearing upon price. However, cost is but one of several factors that must be considered in establishing pricing policies; for example, the action of competitors. In addition, when pricing a new product it is necessary to consider the proposed price in relation to the price structure of the entire product line. Finally, the terms of sale, including the availability of credit and discount privileges, modify the significance of the stated price. Each of these factors— product cost, competition, pricing, new products, and terms of sale—is discussed.[3]

---

[3] *Pricing: The Critical Decision* (New York: American Management Association, 1962), Management Report No. 66, p. 96. This report presents a series of articles selected from papers presented at the American Management Association Special Conference on Pricing held in New York City in 1961. Included are discussions on the role of pricing in the American business system and the influence of competitive and economic factors in pricing.

PRODUCT COSTS. Product costs include not only direct material and labor costs but also the indirect costs of administration and distribution. In addition, the expected profit contribution must be included in the final price. If the resulting price is one that the consumer is willing to pay, there is no problem; however, if the price is too high, several alternatives are available. First, every effort must be made to reduce manufacturing costs and the costs of administration and distribution. Second, the possibility of a more effective sales effort should be examined; perhaps a different method of promotion and presentation of the product will permit its sale at the desired price. If neither of these steps results in a price that is acceptable to the customer and at the same time recovers full product costs and contributes to profit, a decision must be made whether to market the product at a loss. Occasionally retailers adopt the practice of promoting a *loss leader,* an item that does not meet its full share of costs, because it is believed that customers are attracted and subsequently buy more profitable items. It is doubtful that the loss leader concept is workable at the manufacturing level for any length of time; however, occasionally manufacturers sell at a price that does not recover full costs in order that all direct costs and a portion of overhead may be recovered. Certain products within a product line may be sold at prices too low to recover all costs in an effort to maintain a competitive product line and to prevent all competition from entering the market. The policy question can become one of determining when "half a loaf is better than none."

COMPETITION. Product cost and profit contribution are considerations internal to the firm; *competitive factors,* external to the firm, must also be considered in establishing pricing policies. Consistent pricing below competitive prices reflects a marketing philosophy which emphasizes price as the most important factor in persuading customers to buy. Alternates to this approach are the emphasis of quality, including performance and long life, and excellence of service.

Anticipating the results of actions of competitors who either raise or lower prices is another phase of competitive pricing. The lowering of price implies that the demand for the product is elastic; that is, for every 1 percent decrease in price there is an increase in sales greater than 1 percent. Before deciding to meet lower competitive prices, it is well to determine the elasticity of demand and project the profit that may be expected at a new level of sales. By the same token, knowledge of price elasticity is important in determining whether to follow a competitor's lead in increasing prices. If demand is inelastic in relation to price, a significant reduction in sales volume does not follow a price increase; however, if demand is price-elastic, the company that retains the lower price may experience a substantial gain in sales volume at the expense of the competitor who raises the price.

PRICING NEW PRODUCTS. Production costs are usually at their highest level when a new product is first introduced. Thus the pricing decision is one of determining whether the initial price should reflect current costs or whether the price should anticipate lower future costs associated with volume production and improved manufacturing techniques. The prices of existing items in a product line also influence the price of any new product. If the new product is smaller or simpler in construction than similar existing items, the price should be recognizably lower; but if the product is of better design and uses more expensive materials, the price should be sufficient to recover these additional costs without creating a barrier that prevents the customer from moving up to a new product. Finally, consideration must be given to competing products, for example household appliances that are similar in design or construction. Or as is true in the packaging industry, the competing products may use different materials and designs, yet perform the same function.

TERMS OF SALE. The preceding discussion implies that price is an absolute monetary value. However, some of the effects of price changes may be obtained without any change in the monetary price of a product or service by altering the terms of sale and may have a marked effect upon sales volume. The availability of credit is an important determinant of consumer buying power. The effect of a price increase in consumer durables may be offset by reducing the amount of a down payment or extending the period of time for repayment. A lease-purchase agreement, usually calling for no down payment and the payment of a monthly charge with an option to purchase at a predetermined price at the end of a specified period of time, is another means of extending credit. Offering cash discounts for prompt payment has the advantage of reducing credit and collection costs, as well as price, yet allows the seller to maintain a firm price structure.

Channel of Distribution Policies. Since customers and consumers are not necessarily synonymous, policy statements outlining methods for product distribution are decisions that determine who is the customer. For the restaurant owner, the customer who buys a meal is also the consumer; yet as an owner he is the customer of a wholesaler or a distributor, but he is not the consumer. The decision to sell either directly to the consumer or through a series of intermediaries to the consumer is the selection of a *channel of distribution. Market penetration,* closely related to and sometimes dependent upon the channel of distribution, is that portion of the potential of a given market, usually defined geographically, that is realized. The scope of policies governing the distribution of products, the channel of distribution, and market penetration, are discussed below.

CHANNEL OF DISTRIBUTION. Certain functions inherent in the process of distribution must be performed. Orders are received, the product drawn from stock, shipments are sent to the customer, a statement of the amount due is prepared, and provisions for collection are provided. Any of these functions may be combined or transferred to another position in the distribution cycle, but the function itself is not eliminated. A company selling directly to the consumer performs all of these functions; however, if one or more intermediaries, called variously jobbers, distributors, or wholesalers, are introduced into the cycle some of these functions may be transferred to the intermediary. In many instances the selection of the channel of distribution is determined by industry practices, that are dependent upon the nature of the product as well as the practice established within the industry. Even so, the selection of a market channel offers an opportunity for innovation. Avon, for example, sells directly to the consumer through its own field sales force, while competitors distribute products through wholesalers, to retail stores, and then to the consumer. The factors to weigh in selecting one channel of distribution in preference to another, assuming that the nature of the product and industry practices permit such a choice, are (1) the cost incurred as the result of performing the functions of the distribution cycle and (2) the advantages gained by controlling the selling effort of the company's own sales force and direct contact with the consumer. One of the problems to be resolved by Electroware, Case Problem 5-B, is that of deciding whether more than one channel of distribution should be used. The use of more than one channel of distribution may permit a company to realize the advantages gained by controlling the selling effort of its own sales force and at the same time, receive the benefits of reduced distribution costs and risks usually associated with intermediaries.

MARKET PENETRATION. Closely related to the choice of channel of distribution are policies expressing a company's desired position in respect to market penetration, the extent to which a company attains the potential of a specified market. Usually, markets are defined in geographic terms such as a city, a state, or a region; however, a market may be defined in terms of demographic groups; e.g., rural, urban, sex, or age group. Market share, or market penetration, is expressed quantitatively by defining present sales as a percentage of potential sales.

Electroware is distributing its water heaters to one thousand retail stores located throughout the midwest and the east at a rate of four each month, and the store owners are dissatisfied since they are not receiving a quantity sufficient to meet demand. If the company decides to sell its stoves through the same channel of distribution, its penetration of the market will be less than it is at present. The importance of the desired degree of penetration in the choice of a channel of distribution becomes more evident when we examine one of the alternatives for distributing electric stoves. If Electroware chooses four distributors, each located in a major city, the penetration of each city market would be much greater than the penetration realized in the vast geographic territory served by retail outlets.

Slight penetration of a market usually results in higher distribution costs per unit, less return per dollar for advertising, and the risk of losing customer good will; whereas, deep market penetration usually results in a position of strength within a given area and an ability to withstand a substantial decline in sales volume. The desired extent of market penetration should be stated clearly as a primary sales objective with policies established to implement this objective.

Sales Promotion Policies. The areas of sales policies discussed thus far consider the product, the pricing of the product, and the method of distribution. The final question to be considered is determining an effective means of persuading the customer to buy the product. One method used is *direct selling,* a method that utilizes salesmen to persuade the customer to buy the product. *Advertising* permits the seller to contact many people simultaneously through mass media. The use of *special promotional devices* to supplement direct selling efforts and advertising is the third method employed to encourage customers to buy.

DIRECT SELLING. The process of persuading a customer to buy a product is commonly called *selling.* Two dimensions of selling are particularly relevant in formulating sales promotion policies. The first is establishing the importance of the role of sales personnel in persuading the customer to buy a given product. At one extreme are those persons—such as those employed by variety chains and supermarkets—who function as salesclerks and whose only contribution to the selling process is at the request of the customer. At the other end of the broad spectrum of the selling activity are the agents of life insurance companies who often seek and locate a prospect, create a felt need for the product, and finally persuade the prospect to buy an intangible item that may never offer a tangible reward to the buyer himself. If it is concluded that the role of a salesman is of minor importance to a specific selling process, the company may direct its efforts to those factors that are of greater importance, such as advertising, packaging, or point-of-sale displays. However, if it appears that the salesman plays a key part in the sales process, attention must be directed toward the selection and training of sales personnel. Thus, an analysis of the contribution of sales personnel to the selling process enables a company to direct its sales promotion efforts more effectively.

The second dimension of direct selling is that of establishing the optimum degree of control necessary to realize the greatest results from the sales personnel. A close degree of control is usually possible when those who sell the product are employees of the company making the product. Many industrial products, such as machine tools, are sold in this manner, but relatively few consumer products are sold by a sales force employed by the manufacturer. Typically, most consumer products—clothing, food, and appliances—are sold through the efforts of employees of the retailer. There is a direct relationship between the degree of control exercised over a sales force and the significance of the role of sales personnel in the selling process. If the efforts of sales personnel are incidental to the selling process, such personnel are usually not employed or controlled by the producer of the product; emphasis is placed upon advertising and special promotional devices. However, if salesmen are the decisive factor in persuading the customer to buy, the company making the product employs and exercises close control over its sales force; the emphasis upon advertising and other promotional devices is relatively less.

ADVERTISING. The ultimate objective of advertising is to persuade potential customers to buy a given product or service. Immediate objectives may be to establish an awareness of a particular brand name, to state the price and describe other attributes of the product, or to create a need for the product. The sale of many consumer products, particularly those that are displayed in conjunction with competing products in supermarkets and drugstores, depends to a large extent upon the kind and amount of advertising used. Typical media used in advertising are television, radio, newspapers, outdoor posters, magazines, and direct-mail pieces.

SPECIAL PROMOTIONAL DEVICES. Special promotional devices are used as a means of augmenting the selling effort of salesmen and advertising. One such familiar device is the point-of-sale demonstration used in department stores and other retail outlets. Personnel for these demonstrations are usually trained by the manufacturer to demonstrate the outstanding features and proper use of the product to prospective customers. Another promotional device is the distribution of free samples as a way of introducing a product. Trial offers with money-back guarantees, coupons redeemable in cash or merchandise, testimonial letters, and advertising novelties such as pens and pencils, are promotional devices or attention-getting actions to induce the customer to make the initial purchase or trial with the expectation that the knowledge of the product thus gained will lead to repeat sales.

Market Research

Greater effectiveness in planning a sales program is possible through an analysis of those factors that influence the sale of a given product. The various techniques that have been developed to analyze market factors and predict probable sales success are known as *market research*. There are many techniques available for market research that are applications of the scientific method to the solution of specific sales problems. Each technique defines the problem under consideration, collects and utilizes data that are as objective as possible, and draws tentative conclusions. In some instances it is possible to test resultant hypotheses by conducting trial marketing programs and, if successful, a final full-scale sales plan is developed and put into effect. Let us examine more closely some of the techniques of market research in order to have a better understanding of effective planning for the sales program. First, the sources of information used in market research are considered, and second, the scope of market research is discussed.

Sources of Market Research Information. There are two sources of information frequently used in market research. One source, called *primary,* is obtained directly from those persons concerned with the marketing or use of the product or service in question. Such persons include customers, potential customers, and all who participate in the distribution system, including the wholesaler and the retailer. In using these sources, the method employed is generally one of asking specific questions regarding the product and observing reactions to the product. It is a polling technique similar to that employed by the political pollsters. The other source of information is *secondary* in nature and draws upon broad social and economic factors of significance to marketing.

Scope of Market Research. Since the primary purpose of market research is to analyze those factors that affect a company's sales so that an accurate forecast may be made regarding the probable success or failure of a given sales plan, the study of any situation or group of factors which might affect sales is within the province of market research. The areas susceptible to market research are the same areas for which sales policies are formulated. Remember, sales policies are broad plans, and market research is the collection and interpretation of data so that sound plans may be formulated; hence, the areas of application of market research are the same as those for which sales policies are developed. Market research may be applied to the product, to price, and its effect on sales; to determining the most effective means of distribution; and to assessing the effectiveness of promotional methods. In practice, most market research efforts touch upon several areas to study.

Case Problem 5-B describes a company, Electroware, that must clarify its policy in regard to channel of distribution. Closely related to the selection of a channel of distribution is the related problem of determining the desired degree of market penetration.

CASE PROBLEM 5-B

CHANNEL OF DISTRIBUTION

In 1920 Electroware began manufacturing electrical household appliances in Toledo, Ohio. From its founding until 1930, its product line was limited to small appliances such as electric irons, toasters, waffle irons, portable ovens, and percolators. These items were sold directly to retail stores, which in turn sold to the consumer. Approximately 1,000 such retail outlets in midwestern and eastern states are customers of Electroware. In 1930 the company introduced a line of electric hot water heaters designed for residential use; and, without giving the matter much thought, the existing channel of distribution from manufacturer to retail outlet to consumer was continued. Several years ago the company discontinued the manufacture of small appliances and devoted its full attention to manufacturing and selling electric hot water units.

Recently John Miller was promoted from the position of vice-president, manufacturing, to president. While in charge of the manufacturing function, he had

served as chairman of a product diversification committee. The committee recommended that the company
manufacture electric stoves to supplement its existing
line of hot water heaters. The recommendation was
adopted and, during his first year as president, Mr. Miller's
attention was directed toward the completion of a new
addition to the plant and the installation of necessary
equipment so that electric stoves could be produced.
Reliable estimates from the production planning department indicated that the stove line would be in operation
by the end of the year and that a total of 26,500 units
could be assembled during the next calendar year. Production of electric hot water heaters is expected to remain constant at 40,000 units per year, or slightly more
than 150 a day.

Tom Andrews, vice-president, sales, had opposed
the expansion of facilities in order to manufacture electric
stoves; instead, he had urged that the output of hot water
heaters be increased. He pointed out that the present
annual production of heaters amounts to less than four
heaters per month for each of the 1,000 retail outlets and
that the store owners and managers are becoming dissatisfied since they are not receiving a quantity of heaters
sufficient to meet customer demand. One store owner
described the situation as follows: "People don't come
in here to buy hot water heaters only; usually they want
something else for their home at the same time. If they
can't buy all the things that they want in one place, most
of them will go to a store that will sell them everything
that they want at the same time. Not having enough
heaters is costing me sales in those items that I do have
in stock." Andrews also argued that the projected volume
of electric stoves would be adding insult to injury because each dealer would receive an average of only two
stoves a month. Mr. Miller then suggested that the stoves
be sold through a different channel of distribution, such
as selling direct to the builders of apartments and large
housing projects. Andrews objected to this approach and
insisted that the company should be loyal to its present
dealers since they had stood by Electroware during the
lean years. Furthermore, he feared that many dealers
would refuse to handle the hot water heaters unless they
received a commission on all Electroware products sold
in their community.

Mr. Miller discussed the problem of selecting a channel of distribution with Ted Donham, the controller, and asked for his suggestion. Donham recommended that a distributor, or wholesaler, be appointed for each of the following cities: Chicago, Detroit, Cleveland, and Cincinnati. He did not like the idea of selling direct to the building contractors because he felt that many of them might prove to be poor credit risks and that the cost of contacting each contractor individually would be excessive. He was against extending the present method of distribution to electric stoves because it would require the shipment of one or two items a month to each of the 1,000 retailers, thereby creating a great deal of paper work. He believed that the selection of four distributors would permit the company to ship in carload lots and reduce freight costs. He also emphasized that the production rate of electric stoves would be sufficient to satisfy the needs of four carefully selected distributors.

PROBLEMS

1. Define the problem that Electroware is attempting to solve.
2. State the policy that you believe Electroware should adopt in order to solve its current problem.
3. Would you recommend that both products be sold through the same channel of distribution? Why?
4. Do you subscribe to Mr. Andrews' point of view that the company should be loyal to its present dealers?
5. While Mr. Miller was vice-president, manufacturing, he served as chairman of a product diversification committee. Would Mr. Andrews, vice-president, sales, appear to be a more logical candidate for the chairmanship of such a committee?

Chapter Questions for Study and Discussion

1. Why is a definition of profit as something that is left over after meeting all expenses considered inadequate as a definition from the viewpoint of a professional manager? How would you, as a student of management, define profit?
2. What measures are commonly used to measure profit, and how does each contribute to an understanding of a company's financial position? In your opinion, which measure is the most important?
3. How are financial policies related to the concept of cash flow?

4. What are the advantages and disadvantages of the commonly used sources of long-term capital and of short-term capital?
5. Why is the allocation of capital important? Discuss the effects of various types of imbalances in the allocation of capital.
6. What are the dangers of distributing profit on a fixed-percentage basis? Do these shortcomings apply to other means of distributing profit on a fixed-dollar basis?
7. Why do manufacturers of consumer durable goods expend large sums of money on advertising despite the statement that the efforts of a single company manufacturing consumer durable goods cannot significantly change the demand for those goods?
8. Why must a manufacturer of consumer nondurables consider all three economic determinants—buying power, demography, and price—when planning a marketing program?
9. How does a company define the demand for its products?
10. Is there a relationship between the rate of consumption of consumer durable goods and the demand for capital goods? If so, how is this relationship modified by other factors that influence the demand for capital goods?
11. How can the advertising of capital goods in a medium read by the general public, such as *Time* or *Newsweek,* be justified?
12. Assume that a company has established a policy of making major engineering changes in its product every five or six years. Shortly after one of these major product changes has been made, the engineering department develops a major breakthrough that would make all former models obsolete. What are the arguments for and against introducing the revolutionary model ahead of schedule?
13. As a special research project, determine the comparative costs of financing an automobile through a bank, a credit union, a finance company, and a plan offered by the dealer. Exclude the cost of insurance but note the variations in total interest charges for 12-, 18-, 24-, and 36-month contracts.

CHAPTER 6

Planning for Production and Personnel

Tim Jones, owner-manager of Kwickie Kar Klean, sat in his office mulling over the results of his first year's operations. Before entering the automatic car wash business, Tim had investigated carefully the claims of several manufacturers of automatic car wash equipment and found considerable variation in what was considered the optimum amount of automatic equipment necessary for a successful business. One manufacturer suggested an installation costing over $50,000 exclusive of land and buildings, and pointed out that the savings in labor would soon pay for the equipment. At the other extreme, there was a unit for $12,000 but it required almost twice as much labor on high-volume days. Tim chose the latter course; however, the equipment was designed to permit adding fully automatic units later.

He considered himself fortunate in being able to rent a building for $500 a month on a busy through street in the center of a large residential area. Thus, his only capital outlay was for equipment capable of washing at least 600 cars a week. A summary statement of average monthly expenses for Kwickie Kar Klean during its first year's operations appears on the following page.

Tim regarded most of these expenses as fixed since there was little he could do to control the first five items. Therefore, he decided to direct his attention to controlling the amount of money spent for labor and improving output per man-hour.

The conveyor that pulls the cars through the washing process is 80 feet long. At the front of this line there is a portable vacuum cleaner used in cleaning the

Expense	Average per month
Heat, light, and power	$ 80
Water	100
Supplies (towels, detergents, etc.) ..	50
Depreciation and repairs	125
Building and land rent	500
Labor	1,800
Total expenses	$2,655

interior of the car. Next, there is a steam cleaning unit used to steam the wheels, bumpers, and grill; and following this is the mitting area where one man on each side washes the entire car with detergent as it is pulled through by the conveyor. The next three operations are automatic: a side and top brush unit (including automatic pre-rinse) washes the top and sides of the car; an automatic rinsing unit removes detergent and loosened dirt left by the washing unit; a drying unit completes the automatic process. The car is moved forward to the front of the building to be wiped and finished manually.

Tim carefully studied the time required for each operation and concluded that the production bottleneck was at the end of the line where the cars are manually wiped. He discovered that two men could wipe one car in three minutes and concluded that his total daily production should be 20 cars per hour, or a total of 200 cars per day since the auto laundry remained open 10 hours each day. However, such was not the case because customers did not appear on a regular schedule. He decided to record the total number of cars washed during a 10-hour day for varying crew sizes. Here is a summary of the production records:

Number of men	Total cars washed in 10 hours
3	90
4	120
5	155
6	180
8	230
10	270
12	350

When using three men, one man at the front of the line operated the vacuum cleaner and the steam cleaner, while the other two men worked in the mitting area, one on each side of the car, and washed the car. Then, as the car moved through the automatic units of the line—the side and top brush unit, the rinsing unit, and the drying station—the two mitters moved to the end of the line and served as wipers after Tim drove the car from the conveyor to the front of the building. When the crew consisted of four men, the additional man was placed on the end of the line to help the mitters in wiping the car. The addition of a fifth man meant that there was still one man at the front of the line, two mitters now remaining in the mitting area, and two men functioning solely as wipers. Though this arrangement of manning yielded the highest average per man for a 10-hour day, it was found that there were times during the day, for example, during the lunch period, when the effective crew was actually four men. Also, if one of the men was absent, the result was a definite undermanning, and if it were a good day for business, Tim felt that he lost customers when they drove by and saw a line of cars waiting to be washed. Consequently, he decided that for the weekdays, Monday through Friday, he would man the crew regularly with six men, which almost always assured him of an effective crew of five, thus allowing him to handle peak periods on these days with ease. With a crew of six, one man vacuumed, one operated the steam cleaner, two were in the mitting area, and two wiped.

During the first year Kwickie Kar Klean washed, on the average, 500 cars a week, but the number of washed was not distributed evenly throughout the six working days. Usually by Friday evening only 40 to 60 percent of the week's total had been completed, which meant that in order to reach the weekly average of 500, it was necessary sometimes to wash as many as 350 cars on Saturday. The addition of two more wipers, making eight, could handle 250 cars, but this was not enough for the busy days. And increasing the total crew to 10 men, with six of them wiping, enabled Tim to turn out only 20 more cars per man in a 10-hour day. After analyzing the production of a 10-man crew, Tim decided that the cars were not being prepared fast enough for the conveyor line, so he decided to put two men on the vacuum cleaning, two on the steam cleaning, and, of course, two in the mitting area. These six on the front of the line seemed to be able to keep the six wipers supplied with cars even during rush periods.

PROBLEMS

1. Evaluate Tim's original decision to man with a crew of six men during weekdays.
2. If the price charged for washing a car is $1.50, how many cars must be washed during a month in order for Kwickie Kar Klean to break even?
3. There were many weeks during the year when the total output, Monday through Friday, was 300 cars with the standard manning of six men. It is possible for these six men to wash approximately 200 cars on Saturday, thus bringing the weekly total to 500. Yet, Tim called in six additional men on Saturday to raise the possible output to 350, or 650 for the week. How much is it costing Tim to be prepared for the additional 150 cars? Would you recommend that this practice be continued? Why?
4. Under what circumstances would you recommend that fully automatic equipment be purchased, assuming that the purchase of such equipment would eliminate four men—the two in the mitting area and the two in the steam cleaning area?

In Chapter 5 the concepts of planning are applied to the functional areas of finance and sales. In this chapter these concepts are developed for the areas of production and personnel. The first part of the chapter is devoted to planning for production, followed by a discussion of planning for the personnel function. Finally, the four functional areas of finance, sales, production, and personnel are integrated within the context of a servo system.

PLANNING FOR PRODUCTION

As a nation we are noted for both effectiveness and efficiency in our production processes. The effectiveness of production, that is, the providing of those goods and services desired by consumers, is the result of a close liaison between the demand side of the business, sales, and the supply side of the business, production. The efficiency of our industrial enterprise results from the production manager continually seeking answers to the following two questions: (1) What is the maximum attainable output with a given set of inputs? (2) What are the minimum inputs required to achieve a stated level of output? These questions form the framework within which policy decisions are made in regard to the production function. Before examining the scope of production policies, it is necessary to review the nature of the production function, then to develop the areas of production policy.

The Production Function

The production function is present in all business enterprises; however, it is easier to recognize that function in businesses that manufacture a product. The factors of input in manufacturing are the physical facilities, which include both plant and equipment used in making the product; the raw materials that are converted into a final form; and the human resources needed to produce the product. The output of the manufacturing firm is a tangible product with physical characteristics of size, weight, color, and form. Kwickie Kar Klean, Case Problem 6-A, is a service organization and, as a service organization, has as its function the production of clean cars. In this instance the customer supplies the product, an automobile, but the company changes the form or appearance of that product by cleaning it. A firm of certified public accountants works with data supplied by its clients and offers as an end result an interpretation of that information based upon its members' professional training and judgment. An airline has as its function the moving of passengers from one city to another, an operation that requires the utilization of airport facilities, ground crews, aircraft, and a flight crew—all factors of input necessary to transport the customer to a desired new location within a specified period of time. Finally, the wholesale distributing organization, typically considered a part of the marketing process, performs a function similar to that of the airlines in that the products to be distributed must arrive at a specified place at a given time.

The discussion above serves to emphasize the variety of activities that may be defined as production and raises a question concerning the classification of these various activities into a meaningful arrangement. A second question to be considered is whether or not there is a predictable relationship between factors of input and the resultant output; and, if there is such a relationship, how may it best be described. Each of these questions is discussed in turn.

Types of Production. One might reasonably ask what is to be gained by developing a classification system for the production function. First, there is a definite relationship between the type of production and the characteristics of the inputs required. Classifying a given production process enables one to draw certain inferences concerning the nature of the physical facilities, the raw materials, and the human resources required for that specific production function. Second, knowledge of the type of production affords insight into the degree of planning required for the production process with particular reference to the planning required in establishing and controlling inventories. Production is classified within a two-dimensional frame of reference, one reference point being the quantity produced, and the other point of reference, the immediacy of customer demand.[1]

REFERENCE TO QUANTITY. The classification of production with reference to the quantity of product produced results in the categories of jobbing, continuous, and intermittent. Production classified as *jobbing* is usually in small quantities, ranging in number from the unique product, such as a bridge, to a lot size that rarely exceeds 50 in number. In addition to the small quantity produced, another characteristic of production classified as jobbing is that the product specifications often vary with the demands of each customer. Typical of the job-shop operation is the printing firm that produces a limited quantity of business forms for a customer. *Continuous production* implies that the product is being produced in large quantities meeting one set of unchanging specifications. The production of steel, chemicals, and paper often fall into this category. *Intermittent production,* as the name implies, lies somewhere in between the extremes of jobbing and continuous production, both in respect to the rigidity of product specifications and the quantity produced. The production of soft drink cans is an example of intermittent production; the quantity is large—usually several hundred thousand—and the structural specifications of the can remain constant; yet the external lithographed label varies for each customer.

There is a definite relationship between each of the above types of production output and the nature of the required inputs. Jobbing utilizes a variety of raw materials, facilities must be flexible so that a wide range of product specifications can be met, and production personnel are usually highly skilled and versatile. In continuous production the facilities permit only a limited variation in product specification, as evidenced by a steel mill or a paper mill; raw materials usually

---

[1] Howard L. Timms, *The Production Function in Business* (2d ed., Homewood, Illinois: Richard D. Irwin, Inc., 1966), pp. 21-31. Professor Timms discusses the classification of the production function in the following types of businesses: manufacturing, marketing, financial, transportation, professional service, and miscellaneous service.

meet rigid specifications; and the majority of the workmen are trained to perform specific jobs that are usually highly repetitive in nature. Again, intermittent production is between these two extremes. There is a greater variation in the raw materials used in intermittent production than in continuous production since the demands of several customers must be met. Physical facilities are also more flexible, and there are many highly skilled workmen whose function is to adjust and adapt the manufacturing equipment so that it can produce the required variations in the product.

REFERENCE TO IMMEDIACY OF CUSTOMER NEEDS. The types of production classified with reference to the immediacy of customer needs are: (1) production to order and (2) production to stock. These classifications enable one to infer the characteristics of product specification and the probable importance of planning inventory requirements. In addition, further insight is gained in regard to the kind of raw materials, production facilities, and human resources required by the business. Jobbing, continuous, or intermittent production may be produced either in direct response to a customer's order or it may be produced and placed in stock in anticipation of future orders.

An important factor in determining whether or not goods should be produced for stock is the degree of variation in product specification. When product specifications are unchanging from one customer to another, it is feasible to build a stock of finished goods inventory from which the orders of many customers may be drawn; however, when the specifications of the product vary with the demands of each customer, goods are usually produced to order. As a result, the establishment of finished goods inventories with the attendant problems of planning and controlling the size of inventories is usually connected with production for stock. Producing goods for stock usually implies that the quantity produced is greater than the amount produced for a single order, thereby making possible reduced costs associated with longer production runs. Also, when the quantity produced and placed into inventory is sufficient to meet the demands of future customer orders, the production facilities, provided they are flexible, may be used to produce other products—a capability that requires more highly trained human resources and a broader range of raw materials.

Planning Production Policies

Sales policies, discussed in Chapter 5, are developed to guide management in making decisions in regard to the product, channel of distribution, pricing, and the method of sales promotion. Decisions concerning the product are also responsibilities of the production function as well as of the sales function since production is charged with producing the required product or service. The guides used in determining appropriate physical facilities are another phase of production policy, and the selection of sources of supply, or vendors, is the third area of production policy. Each policy area is discussed in turn.

Product Policies. In the preceding chapter, we found that sales policies concerning the product encompass product diversification, obsolescence and style, quality, and standardization. Production policies cover these aspects of the product, with the exception of policy statements on obsolescence and style—an area usually reserved for the sales department because of its close contact with the needs of the market. In addition to considering the policies for product diversification, quality, and standardization, the production function is interested in establishing policies governing the control of inventories.

DIVERSIFICATION. We have seen in Chapter 5 that sales policies relating to questions of product diversification confine the meaning of the word, diversification, to the acquisition of new products. Production policies relating to product diversification also utilize this meaning and, in addition, extend the meaning of diversification to include the problem of integration and the question of whether to make or to buy a component part of the end product. The implication of each meaning —new products, integration, and make or buy—is examined below.

New Products. Production policies relating to the acquisition of new products must be closely coordinated with the efforts of the sales department in establishing guidelines for acquiring new products so that the end result is a cohesive set of company policies. In addition, there are questions peculiar to the production process itself that must be considered. Will the new product utilize present production facilities or will it require new or additional facilities? Will the same raw materials be used and the same human skills be required in its production? Will the knowledge gained, as the result of research and development work on the new product, benefit existing products? Almost every business has the opportunity to acquire new products or offer additional services that conform with existing sales and production capabilities.[2] For instance, the automatic car wash service described in Case Problem 6-A can offer to its customers the additional service of polishing and waxing.

---

[2] Joel Dean, "Product-Line Policy," *Journal of Business,* Vol. XXIII, No. 4 (October, 1950), pp. 248-58. This article presents a synthesis of sales, production, and financial criteria to be utilized in selecting new products.

Integration. The combining of a sequence of distinct production processes, sometimes existing in the form of separate companies, is referred to as *vertical integration.* As an example, a Wisconsin company manufacturing glassine paper bags used for packaging potato chips formerly purchased the paper from a nearby mill that produced only glassine paper. When the mill owner died, his heirs decided to sell, and the Wisconsin company bought the mill in order that the company might be assured an uninterrupted source of raw materials. As a result of the acquisition, the bag manufacturer had a new product, glassine paper, some of which was used as raw material in manufacturing its bags and the remainder was sold to other users of glassine paper. This example illustrates the acquisition of earlier stages of production, but the same process is applicable when moving in the other direction; that is, continuing the production process so that present products, currently used by other manufacturers as raw materials, can be converted into finished consumer goods. Some steel companies have integrated in both directions. These companies have acquired raw material sources, iron ore mines, and have also directed the expansion of their operations so that they are able to convert their basic product, steel, into finished consumer goods such as steel pails and even prefabricated houses. The result is a single company with vertically integrated production processes that mine ore, produce steel, and fabricate the finished consumer products.

Make or Buy. The make-or-buy decision is a miniature of the integration decision. When the make-or-buy question is raised, it usually refers to whether a company should make or buy a specific component part that is used in its product. Ball bearings are a typical example of a part that may be purchased from an independent source of supply or manufactured by the user. In formulating a policy that outlines the course of action to follow, the questions to be answered are the same as those raised when considering whether or not a company should adopt a policy of integration. The following questions are a useful checklist in formulating policies concerned with whether or not a company should integrate other related production operations into its present structure and in resolving the make-or-buy decision:

1. Can present facilities be used, or are new facilities required?
2. What new technical skills and knowledges are required?
3. Is the present source of supply satisfactory in respect to quantity, quality, cost, and reliability of service?
4. Will making the new product result in an excess quantity that must be sold by the sales department?

QUALITY. In addition to formulating policies concerning product diversification, the production function (along with the sales function) is concerned with the formulation of policies concerning the quality of the product. Production policies concerning quality emphasize the cost of quality rather than the sales potential associated with the level of quality. Figure 6-1 is a model showing the relationship of the three variables to be considered in formulating policies that define the desired level of quality for a given product or service. The general term, "corrective action," is used since the model is a statement of the factors that must be considered when taking any action designed to improve performance. The vertical axis is a measure of cost, and the horizontal axis indicates units of corrective action. Assume that the quality of a given product can be improved when additional inspectors are added to an assembly line. The cost of additional inspection is shown by line *A*, the rising diagonal line—the cost of corrective action inputs.

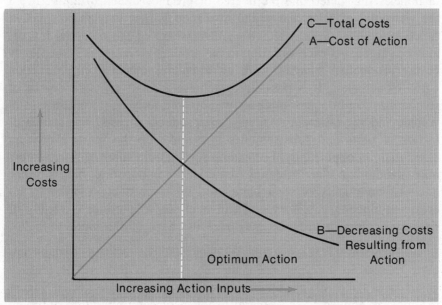

Figure 6-1
MODEL SHOWING THE EFFECT OF MANAGEMENT ACTION

Line *B*, a downward sloping curve, shows the decreasing costs resulting from the corrective action (in this case, the use of additional inspectors). Total costs, line *C*, form a U-shaped curve. When there is no inspection, the cost of that function is zero, but the cost resulting from poor quality due to excessive scrap, replacement of defective parts, and loss of sales is high; consequently, the total cost of producing the product is also high. As additional inspection is added, the cost of such inspection increases, but this rising cost is being offset by the decreasing costs attributable to poor quality, with the result that total costs decline until an optimum point is reached. Beyond that point, total costs again rise since the cost of inspection is greater than the decreasing costs resulting from improved quality.

The cost of additional inspection has been used as an example; however, the same reasoning applies when considering the purchase of new precision equipment as a means of improving quality or the utilization of more uniform or expensive raw materials. One must continually balance the cost of corrective action against the cost of not taking that action to determine the total cost of the plan being considered.

STANDARDIZATION. There is need for close coordination between the sales department and the production department in the formulation of policies that determine the degree of product standardization. From the viewpoint of sales, the addition of models that vary in size, color, function, or quality means that a greater share of the potential market may be gained; yet each variation in the product increases the complexity of the production function with an attendant increase in production costs. Nonetheless, it is possible to achieve a relatively high degree of standardization in some instances without seriously compromising sales volume and yet maintain relatively low production costs. The standardization of parts and subassemblies that make up the finished product offers such an opportunity. For example, a manufacturer of refrigerators may standardize the insulating materials, compressors, hinges, door latches, and quality of steel plate used in its product in order to increase production efficiency and still continue to produce a variety of sizes and colors in order to maximize its share of the market.

INVENTORY. Inventory policies determine the practices that a company follows in carrying raw materials, parts in process, or finished goods in order to fill customer orders. The model presented in Figure 6-1 may be applied to the general problem of determining an optimum inventory level. Since establishing a given inventory level is the result of management action, let the horizontal axis represent increasing amounts of inventory and the rising diagonal, line A, the increasing cost of carrying an inventory. The downward sloping curve, line B, shows the decreasing costs that might be expected as the result of fewer stock-outs. When stock-outs are frequent, total costs, line C, are also high since stock-outs may mean either a loss in sales volume as the result of not being able to fill customer orders, or increased production costs as the result of frantic efforts to fill a succession of small orders. As the amount of inventory increases, so does the cost of carrying that inventory increase, line A; but the cost of inventory is offset by the decreasing number of stock-outs which enables the company to fill customer orders promptly and to increase the efficiency of the production process through longer production runs. The optimum level of inventory, as measured by total cost, is reached when the total cost curve, line C, reaches its lowest point. Beyond this point the cost of carrying additional inventory is greater than any advantage gained as the result of further reduction in the number of stock-outs, and total costs again begin to rise.

Though it is impossible to carry a stock of finished goods on hand in a service business, a similar decision is made in determining the total quantity of service to be offered. Kwickie Kar Klean's manager, Tim Jones, makes such a decision when he decides to carry a reserve of manpower on Saturdays in order to meet the peaks of customer demand, thereby minimizing stock-outs; i.e., customers driving away because the waiting line is too long.

Facility Policies. The physical facilities of production include the land, buildings, and all equipment used in the production process. The nature of some processes—for example, paper making—offers relatively few degrees of freedom to the manager in selecting either equipment or location; and some production, such as steel-making, is so technical that only those persons who are highly trained in the industry can appreciate the problems involved. For these reasons a discussion of the selection of specific facilities for a given industry is beyond the scope of this book. Nonetheless, these are three aspects of facility policies that are broad in scope and applicable to most business firms. These are policies that aid management in determining the best location for production facilities, the proper capacity of such facilities, and the subsequent plan for maintaining plant and equipment.

LOCATION. For many businesses the location decision has been made and usually little can be done about it; but for those that are contemplating expansion or establishing a new business, the decision may be crucial, particularly when choosing the location of a new retail or service establishment. The location of Kwickie Kar Klean, Case Problem 6-A, on a busy thoroughfare surrounded by a large residential area, illustrates the importance of two factors that are significant in choosing a location. The factors are availability of raw materials and ready access to market; in this instance, as is true in many service businesses, the customer also supplies the raw material. Other factors that must be considered in choosing a location are availability and cost of space, cost of construction, and the cost of services such as heat, light, and power. Another consideration of significance in determining the effectiveness and cost of subsequent operations is the availability and cost of labor.

CAPACITY. Again, Kwickie Kar Klean illustrates the essential features of the problem present in determining proper size, or capacity, of production facilities. If facilities are too large, waste is evident; if too small, loss in sales volume and inefficiencies in the production process may result. Tim Jones compensates for the normal capacity of his car wash by doubling the size of the labor force on Saturdays, and though the results may not be the most efficient or profitable, his policy does offer a means of satisfying and retaining customers. The alternative is the installation of fully automatic equipment, thereby permanently increasing capital outlay and depreciation charges (fixed costs) in order to meet periods of peak demand more efficiently. Policies relating to capacity for production should provide for maximum flexibility so that variations in output may be handled in the most efficient manner possible.

MAINTENANCE OF FACILITIES. Figure 6-1 provides the basis for determining the policy to be followed in the proper maintenance of production facilities. In this application the management action is a predetermined scheduled maintenance program, known as *preventive maintenance,* designed to minimize lost production time as the result of equipment failure. The reduction of losses due to breakdown is shown by the downward sloping curve of line *B*. As action inputs, sound preventive maintenance, increase, the cost of such maintenance also increases (shown by line *A*). But this cost is offset by the decreasing costs of production failures that are reduced by the maintenance program. Consequently, total costs are also declining as shown by the U-shaped curve of total costs, line *C*. When total costs are at the lowest point, the optimum degree of preventive maintenance is attained. When total costs rise excessively as the result of an extensive maintenance program that becomes necessary to keep worn equipment in operation, consideration should be given to replacing existing facilities with new equipment requiring less maintenance.

Selection of Vendors. Policies relating to the selection of vendors are developed to insure an uninterrupted flow of materials and supplies vital to the production process. Usually the factors of quality, service, and price are of prime importance in selecting a vendor; however, attention must be given to the number of vendors, and in some instances it is necessary to consider the question of reciprocity.

NUMBER OF VENDORS. Many companies attach great importance to those policies that govern the number of vendors selected to provide needed products or services. Frequently, vendors are pitted against each other by the purchaser as a means of improving the quality of the item purchased and insuring prompt service if the need arises. Multiple sources of supply are also used as a means of providing a continuing source of materials in the event that one supplier is unable to make delivery due to difficulties arising from strikes or mechanical failure.

On the other hand, small companies frequently find it advantageous to patronize a single source of supply. The reason is that the volume purchased by a small company is such that if it were divided among several suppliers, the amount of business for each supplier would not be large enough to warrant special attention and service. In addition, the vendor may offer credit, provided he receives the entire account. In formulating policies concerning the number of vendors, a company must be able to view itself as a customer as well as analyze its own needs as a purchaser.

RECIPROCITY. Reciprocal agreements are possible when the purchaser of a given item produces a product or service that can, in turn, be used by the vendor. For example, the ABC company, a printer of office forms and stationery, may agree to purchase the services of an industrial catering company to operate its plant cafeteria provided the caterer agrees to purchase its office forms and stationery from the ABC company. The existence of reciprocity between purchaser and vendor does not imply collusion or unethical conduct. There is no reason to develop a policy statement barring reciprocity provided such agreements are evaluated in respect to quality, service, price, and strategic position.

THE PERSONNEL FUNCTION

The functions of finance, sales, or production are usually managed by an executive who is assigned sole responsibility for the performance of that particular function. If the organization is large enough, there is also an executive assigned responsibility for the performance of the personnel function; but, unlike his counterparts, he shares with them the performance of the personnel function. The reason for the shared responsibility in the performance of the personnel function is inherent in the nature of the function itself.

The personnel function includes all of the activities associated with the management of personnel. Since organizations are composed of people and the work of organizations is accomplished by and through people, managers of operating units by necessity manage personnel. In addition, historically managers have performed, and still do in small companies, all of the duties normally associated with the management of personnel—including selection, training, compensation, and administering any additional benefits associated with employment. It has only been within the last 50 or 60 years that personnel management has emerged as a separate function with a manager charged with the responsibility of administering the personnel function for the entire organization. Even so, many of the functions of personnel are still performed by other managers. For example, in most companies the responsible manager still retains the final decision as to whom he will employ, makes recommendations concerning promotions and level of pay, and is responsible for much of the training.

Several factors have contributed to the emergence of the function. First, as companies grew in size and complexity it became increasingly more difficult for the unit manager to continue successfully the performance of the personnel functions. Second, knowledge developed from two divergent sources had a direct bearing upon the management of personnel. One source of this additional knowledge was the result of the scientific management movement led by Frederick W. Taylor. This group stressed the importance of measuring work, the need for selection and training, and a more complex method of determining the amount of compensation to be received for performing a job. Knowledge was also gained from the human relations approach to management for it was this group that pointed out that the worker was motivated by sociological and psychological factors as well as by purely economic interests. Finally, the development of labor unions, supported by a strong statement of public policy, with their interest in bargaining for wages, hours, and other terms and conditions of employment forced companies to set up a counterpart to bargain with the unions. Indeed, the mere threat of unionization has forced many a company, and is now forcing many non-profit organizations, to develop a competitive personnel program. These factors have combined to formalize the personnel function and, like the other functions of management, the development of plans in the form of policy statements is necessary if the function is to be performed effectively.

Planning Personnel Policies

Perhaps the most obvious area of policy formulation is the process that creates employees—recruitment and selection. However, the problem is broader than the recruitment of new employees, for it also includes the placement of present employees in positions that are new for them; hence, the broader term, *staffing,* is used to designate the first area of personnel policies. After a person becomes an employee or is assigned to a new position, there is need for *training* or *development,* the second area of policy determination. Third, employees must be *compensated* for the work they perform; and for those organizations whose employees are represented by unions it is necessary to develop policy statements concerning *labor-management relations.* These four aspects of personnel management—staffing, development, compensation, and labor-management relations—define the scope of personnel policies.[3]

Staffing. Staffing policies have their effect upon an organization in two ways. First, effective staffing reflects itself by increasing the general level of competence of employees in the performance of their assigned duties. Secondly, staffing policies have a direct bearing upon the mobility of employees from one position to another within the organization, a factor that can contribute significantly to the motivation of employees. Three facets of the staffing process are significant in determining the effectiveness of the staffing process as reflected by the assignment of personnel qualified to fulfill assigned positions and in providing opportunity for mobility within the organization. *Selection* is a term that refers for the most part to the selection of new employees; yet it must be remembered that present employees are often selected to fill vacancies. Thus policies concerning *promotion* become significant. Finally, provisions for the *termination* of employees must be considered if a predetermined level of competence and opportunity for mobility are to be maintained.

SELECTION. We must assume that a company has knowledge of the requirements necessary for the successful performance of jobs in respect to training, education, and prior experience, for without this information the selection process is little more than a game of chance. Knowing the qualifications for jobs to be filled, a company has three

---

[3] William H. Newman and James P. Logan, *Strategy, Policy, and Central Management* (6th ed.; Cincinnati: South-Western Publishing Company, 1971), pp. 93-349. In Part 2 of their text, Chapters 5 through 15, Professors Newman and Logan present a detailed discussion of problems encountered in defining policies for production and personnel, discussed in this chapter, and for the areas of finance and sales, discussed in Chapter 5. Much case material is included in the Newman and Logan presentation.

choices provided its compensation and employee benefits are at competitive levels: (1) It may select employees who are underqualified for the job—this usually happens when compensation and benefit plans are below par. (2) It may select employees qualified for the present job but limited in potential. (3) It may select employees who are overqualified for the current job vacancy. If those selected are underqualified, excessive turnover may result from terminations due to poor performance, and those who do remain are rarely capable of being promoted within the organization. The same restrictions on mobility develop if candidates are selected to fit the requirements of the current vacancy but are limited in potential. Companies that select overqualified candidates may experience excessive turnover if these people become restless because they are not progressing rapidly enough. Also, it may be necessary to pay more than the entering job is actually worth in order to attract overqualified people. The recruitment of college graduates is a good example of hiring overqualified candidates in order to have personnel with potential for growth. At the hourly level it may be wise to hire candidates with one or two years of training beyond high school to insure a supply of potential supervisory personnel. When establishing selection policies, a company has to determine the degree of qualification desired—one of the three choices listed above—and the policy should be flexible for differing organizational levels and units.

PROMOTION. Strictly defined, promotion is vertical movement upward in the organizational hierarchy and usually is associated with an increase in pay. In practice, however, the concept of promotion includes lateral transfers to other positions at the same organizational level since such transfers may be part of a long-range training plan. Also included in the concept of promotion are increased responsibilities in a current position with or without an increase in compensation. In any event, whether the new job is called a promotion, a transfer, or simply increased responsibilities, all represent a form of employee mobility and consequently all are potential motivators since they may satisfy the needs for growth, achievement, increased responsibility, and recognition. The effectiveness of policy statements encouraging promotion from within is dependent upon the selection policies of a company. Such statements are effective only if there is a sufficient number of employees with the potential for promotion; otherwise, it becomes necessary to fill vacancies by hiring from outside the company.

TERMINATION. Policies governing the termination of employment have a marked effect upon the mobility of employees. When the phrase "termination of employment" is mentioned, we usually think of discharge for cause, such as failure to report for work or resignation, but there are other and increasingly more frequent reasons for the termination of employment. Among the reasons for termination that are important in the formulation of personnel policy is retirement. Policies calling for retirement at a stated age definitely provide opportunities for mobility since positions in the organization become available as incumbents reach the stated age limit. However, there are factors other than those of providing an opportunity for mobility to be considered in the statement of retirement policies. A mandatory retirement age, such as age 65, may result in some employees, particularly executives, being forced to retire despite their potential contribution to the company. At the same time other employees may have to work several years beyond their period of effective contribution in order to comply with the mandatory retirement age of 65. For these reasons retirement policies should be flexible with provisions for extended service on a part-time or consulting basis and with provisions for early retirement.

Development. Policy statements concerning the development of personnel are dependent in large measure upon the policies established for promotion. If an organization has decided to make every effort to promote from within, then the development of employees follows as part of a logical sequence; however, if promotion from within is not given a high priority, it follows that the development of personnel also receives a correspondingly low priority. For those organizations committed to promotion from within, the development of personnel is viewed as a vital function as it provides the means for continued organizational development and performance; but for those organizations that elect to fill vacancies from outside, development may be regarded as a chore that should make minimal demands in respect to time and expense. These two extremes define the range of values within which policy statements concerning development are formulated.

Either term, *training* or *development,* refers to the same process; i.e., learning. However, the term training is used with greater frequency when the development of hourly employees is discussed while the term development is used more often when referring to the development of managers; for example, management development. This distinction in terminology is observed in the discussion that follows.

TRAINING. Training begins with first impressions. *Orientation* programs are designed to control those first impressions. The extent of employee orientation may range from no formal program whatsoever, with the employee being directed to his work place and not even knowing his supervisor's name, to a carefully structured introduction to the organization. A well-planned orientation not only familiarizes an employee with all aspects of his immediate work situation, but also acquaints him with the nature of the organization, its objectives, and his role in the attainment of these objectives. Orientation affords the organization an opportunity to create a lasting favorable first impression.

The area of greatest concern in the training of hourly employees, both clerical and operative, is the development of *job skills*. The methods used in developing these skills vary considerably and include on-the-job training, vestibule training, and a combination of on-the-job experience and formal classroom training. The choice of training method varies with the nature of the job in question and the experience and training of the employees. By far the most widely used method is that of on-the-job training which may take the form of informal, and sometimes casual, instruction by the supervisor or a carefully planned sequence of activities with a formal assessment of achievement. Reliance upon on-the-job training as a means of developing skills requires that supervisors be trained as trainers if the method is to be most effective.

Vestibule training takes its name from the location of the training site—in a separate room apart from the area where the job is normally performed. It is used most frequently in those situations where the employee has no knowledge of the job to be performed and where there are stringent demands for either quantity or quality. Skills in operating high-speed automatic equipment are best acquired by receiving instruction and gaining experience in operating equipment in a training situation where the speed of the machine can be controlled to fit the level of skill of the trainee. Proofing operations, such as those performed in a bank, are best learned in a situation where initial errors are not critical. Generally, vestibule training requires considerable investment in equipment and a formal staff of trainers; however, these costs are largely offset by the quantity and quality of production on the job.

Training for some jobs is acquired from experience obtained on the job in combination with formal classroom instruction. Many apprentice programs of trade unions combine on-the-job experience with a planned classroom instructional program offered by vocational high schools. Interne programs of community colleges combine experience gained while working on the job, usually on a part-time basis, with formal instructional programs related to the work experience.

Related to training for job skills is the decision to encourage employees to prepare themselves for advancement within the organization.

When there is a stated policy of promotion from within, encouragement is often given employees to develop knowledge and skills in areas other than those in which they are presently working to prepare themselves for promotion. Policy decisions in this area are concerned with the determination of the extent of the encouragement; i.e., should the additional training be subsidized in full, including tuition and other costs such as books. Also to be considered is whether work schedules should be modified to provide opportunity for such additional training.

MANAGEMENT DEVELOPMENT. Three terms are used, often interchangeably, to designate programs that fall under the general heading, development. These terms are: *executive development, management development,* and *organization development*. However, each descriptive term carries with it a slightly different connotation. "Executive development" emphasizes the development of the individual executive; "management development" indicates a plan for the development of all members of management, and "organization development" implies that the entire management structure is involved, not as individuals, but as members of the organization, so that the organization can function in a different or improved manner. Regardless of the program undertaken there is a twofold responsibility for its success. First there are the responsibilities of the organization and second there are certain responsibilities that fall upon the individual participating in the program.

Responsibilities of the Organization. The responsibilities of the organization in the development of management are threefold. First, and it may be argued that setting objectives is not properly a policy area, is the development of a clear statement of the objectives of a management development program expressed in terms of the behavior and attitudes necessary to perform as a successful manager. Implied in this step is the belief that managerial skills can be transmitted to others through an educational process, in contrast to the belief that good managers, like cream, will rise to the top. A concise statement of objectives forms the substance of a management development program. Second, the scope of the program, defined in terms of the levels of the organization must be determined. Are all personnel in the organization, including hourly clerical and production workers to be included and regarded as potential managers; or is management development to be confined to certain levels of supervision and a few key administrators? Third, in order to execute the broad policy decisions regarding the objectives and scope of the management development program, provision must be made for adequate procedures to administer the programs and to determine the extent to which objectives are met.

Responsibilities of the Individual Manager. The responsibility for the ultimate of management development efforts is shared by both the organization and the individual manager who participates in the program. There must be readiness on the part of those who participate in management development to put forth their best efforts in order that the desired change may be effected. Readiness to learn is characteristic of any successful educational process. Students are aware that universities fall short of their goals unless the students have clear personal objectives and a readiness to learn. Evidence indicates that one of the most frequent reasons for the shortcomings of management development programs is that those participating in such programs do not have clearly defined goals. They do not know what they want to achieve in the business world, nor do they have a clear concept of the position they expect to achieve within the organization. Some would like positions of responsibility and the prestige and money associated with such positions; yet many are unwilling to make the sacrifices that are sometimes necessary in the early years of corporate life. For example, frequent moves from one town to another are often necessary in order to gain the experience necessary for promotion and increased responsibility.

Top management must recognize the dual responsibility of the organization and the individual for the success of management development plans and consequently should be wary of formulating a policy requiring all managers to participate in a development program. Another result from recognition of the responsibility of the individual manager is the statement of management development objectives so that they may ultimately be adopted as the personal objectives of each individual manager—only then may the objectives of the organization be fulfilled.

Compensation. Compensation is defined as money paid for work performed. In establishing compensation policies, there are three major considerations. First is the selection of criteria to determine the level or amount of compensation, and second, is a determination concerning the method of payment. In addition to payment received for work performed, referred to as a wage or salary, employees also receive other benefits—vacations, holidays, insurance, sick leave—that are economic in nature and may be considered a part of the total compensation plan. Thus, in addition to the determinations concerning the level of compensation and the method of payment, consideration must also be given to employee benefit plans.

AMOUNT OF COMPENSATION. Determining the amount of money to be paid for a given job is not an easy task since there is no single criterion applicable to all companies or even to the same company over a period of time. At least three criteria are used by most companies in determining the level of compensation; however, the significance assigned each criterion varies considerably. The three criteria most frequently used are: area rates, industry rates, and internal rate structure equity.

For many businesses the rates paid in a given geographic area are the controlling factor in determining wage levels. The geographic area encompasses the labor market that a company draws upon; thus, it may consist of a single, small community or a vast metropolitan complex. The prevailing rates for each of several key jobs, usually 15 to 25, are determined by means of a wage survey. A company can thus determine what it must pay to attract and retain the type of employee it needs. When rates higher than those paid in the immediate area are established, it may be possible to secure a better class of employee; when rates lower than those of the area are adopted, increased turnover, absenteeism, and poor performance may result. Area rates are the chief determinant in setting the level of payment of many clerical workers and for those employed in local retail establishments.

For larger industrial firms the prevailing rates of the specific industry may be the factor given the most weight. Industry patterns are prevalent in the manufacture of steel, autos, chemicals, and aircraft. To a large extent, industry rates are the result of collective bargaining agreements between the member firms of an industry; for example, the automobile companies, and the United Automobile Workers, which represents a large number of employees in each company in the industry.

Wage levels determined by either area or industry rates utilize criteria external to the company; however, there is an internal criterion that also must be satisfied. Within each organizational unit, such as a plant or a corporate headquarters office, there should be an equitable relationship between the amounts paid for jobs requiring different levels of skill, responsibility, and training. For example, what should the mail clerk's rate of pay be in comparison to the rate paid an accountant, and what should the accountant's pay be in comparison to that of a programmer for an integrated data processing system? The same questions arise at the plant level. What are the proper relationships for the rate of pay for the janitor, a skilled machine-tool operator, and a tool and die maker? Equitable pay structures are developed through the use of *job evaluation* procedures, a technique of weighting the various factors necessary for the performance of each job.

Thus, the amount of pay is a policy decision resulting from the weighting of three separate criteria: area rates, industry rates, and an internally equitable rate structure between each of the several jobs. In addition, some companies reward employees for above-average performance of their jobs and for length of service on the job. Policies governing these practices, usually referred to as merit and length of service increases, must also be determined.

METHOD OF PAYMENT. Once the amount of compensation has been determined as the result of a judicious weighting of internal and external criteria, a method of payment must be selected. Fundamentally there are two methods of payment. One method is to pay for *time* spent on the job; the other is to pay for the *amount* of work produced. There is, of course, the possibility of a combined payment for both time and amount produced. However, such combinations are usually regarded as payment for work and are classed as incentive plans.

Payment for time is applicable to all levels of the organization, even though the unit of time varies considerably. Production workers are paid for the actual number of hours worked, and the amount earned is usually computed and paid on a weekly basis. Time for non-exempt clerical employees, those who must be paid for overtime, is computed on a weekly basis and payment may be received weekly, biweekly, or semimonthly. Although clerical workers are expected to work a predetermined number of hours each week, policy decisions determine whether or not pay is received for time not worked due to absence or tardiness. Those employees who are exempt from the provisions of the law requiring payment of overtime are called salaried employees, and their time is computed on a monthly basis with payment either monthly or semimontlhy.

Payment for work performed, whether it be the piece rate of the garment industry with no hourly guarantee for time spent on the job or an hourly rate with additional pay for work produced in excess of a stated standard, rests upon two assumptions. First it is assumed that the worker has control over the amount of work that can be produced; and second, that he will respond to the monetary incentive and earn more money by increasing his output. The second assumption leads to the designation of compensation based on the work produced as incentive compensation plans, or more simply, *incentive plans*. The validity of the first assumption can be determined only by a systematic analysis of each work situation. The extent to which the second assumption is applicable is in dispute with some sources stating that only 10 percent of hourly production workers respond fully to monetary incentive.[4]

---

[4] This subject is discussed fully in Chapter 18, pp. 550-555.

EMPLOYEE BENEFIT PLANS. The amount of compensation received is directly related to the job performed. Employee benefits are not directly related to the job itself; instead, they are peripheral to the job and are aptly called "fringe benefits." Included among the many fringe benefits are retirement plans, educational plans, and tuition rebates; various forms of insurance; sick leave; recreation programs; supplemental unemployment compensation; and other items intended to improve the welfare of the employee.

Fringe benefits are important to the employer and the employee alike. For the former, fringes are an important cost of doing business but unfortunately benefit programs do not motivate employees to higher levels of productivity, better quality, or innovations. In addition, benefits must be maintained at competitive levels in order to attract and retain desired employees. For the employee, benefit plans are a normal, expected part of the job. When absent or not present in sufficient quantity in a present job, fringe benefits are a source of annoyance that may color the entire work situation. If the benefit programs of a potential employer do not meet preconceived minimal levels of acceptability, that employer has little chance of attracting discriminating personnel.

Formulating policies governing employee benefit plans is primarily an economic matter. As is the case in setting compensation levels, surveys of the area and the industry should be used as a guide to determine current practice. A company has little to gain by offering the most expensive benefit plan, but there is much to lose if the plan is too little and too late. A sound communications program on a continuing basis is an aid in keeping employees informed of the value received from the many benefit programs.

Labor-Management Relations. The above discussion of staffing, development, and compensation is presented in a manner which implies that these are policies to be determined solely by the management of an organization. Such is not the case, particularly when employees are represented by a labor union, since unions are entitled to bargain for "wages, hours, and other terms and conditions of employment." [5]

In addition, unions can and do use the economic strike as a weapon to obtain demands presented to management. Though not participating formally in the development of personnel policies, labor unions have a marked impact upon policy statements. Such impact is not limited to those organizations whose employees are union members but extends to non-union employers competing in the same labor market or industry.

---

[5] Labor Management Relations Act of 1947 as amended, Sec. 8, (d).

The threat of unionization has forced many employers to meet or exceed union gains in wages and benefits in an effort to avoid unionization.

ORGANIZATIONAL CLIMATE. The major policy consideration is that of determining the organizational climate within which a given set of labor-management relations are to occur. Frequently the nature of these relationships is described as ranging from open hostility to one of cooperative effort between management and labor. Open hostility will most likely occur during union organization and negotiating of the initial labor agreement. During this stage of development of labor-management relations, management's attitude is manifested by an intense resentment toward any infringement upon management rights. It is also possible that during this initial period management may take the course of least resistance and follow the pattern set by other companies and other unions in the community or industry with little regard for the ultimate effect of such practice upon the welfare of the company or its employees. Such acceding to the pressures of the union represents an attitude of fear and resignation.

A more mature relationship between labor and management is often described as a business relationship and is similar in many respects to the relationship that exists between a company and its suppliers and customers. The open hostility has disappeared and each side recognizes the responsibilities and rights of the other. The ultimate in labor-management relations is evidenced by complete cooperation and understanding on the part of both the union and the company. It is recognized that a mature cooperative relationship between a company and a union depends on factors other than the establishment of organizational climate; for example, the goals and strength of the union and the economic condition of the company. The organizational climate established by management, however, sets the upper limits of the extent to which cooperative efforts may be realized not only in the negotiation of successive labor agreements but also in the manner of their administration.

Once an organization has determined the organizational climate within which its labor-management relations will occur, there are other policy areas which must be considered. Among these are union security, bargaining tactics, and treatment of non-union employees.

UNION SECURITY. Unions desire provisions in the labor agreement that provide for their security such as the union shop and the checkoff of union dues. The union shop provides that all employees must maintain membership in the union in order to remain in the employment of the company. The checkoff is a device whereby a company, usually after an employee has signed an authorization card, deducts from each employee's pay his monthly union dues and then submits the total amount to the union in a single check.

BARGAINING TACTICS. In a large measure the bargaining tactics of an organization should derive from the other policy areas of finance, sales, and production. The needs and goals established in these areas determine whether or not a company assumes a firm posture in bargaining or whether it assumes a "follow the leader" approach. Financial exigencies or stated policies directed toward the expansion of production and sales may make a strike intolerable, yet long-term plans in these areas may make acquiescence to union demands equally intolerable. Either way, a company should prepare its position on major issues before negotiating and determine the limits within which it is willing to negotiate. Consistency in preparedness at the bargaining table provides the basis for a settlement satisfactory to both parties.

RELATION WITH NON-UNION EMPLOYEES. Closely related to bargaining tactics is the decision concerning the treatment of non-union employees. It is seldom that all hourly employees, both clerical and production, belong to a union. Often the production workers are unionized while the hourly clerical employees are not, and in those instances in which clerical employees are unionized they rarely belong to the same bargaining unit as the production employees. When clerical employees are not unionized and hourly production workers are, it should be decided beforehand whether any improvement in wages or benefits extended to production workers should be granted to clerical employees. Or a company may decide to extend to its non-union employees those increase in wages and benefits that it believes can honestly be made for all employees, union and non-union alike. Further, the extent to which increases in hourly benefits should be extended to supervisory personnel must be decided. Decisions in these areas may modify or even determine the bargaining tactics of a company.

INTEGRATING POLICY STATEMENTS

In Chapter 5, the major areas for which policy statements, or plans, must be made for the functional areas of finance and sales are discussed. In this chapter we examine the scope of policy statements for the functional areas of production and personnel. The scope of policy statements for each of the four functional areas—finance, sales, production, and

FINANCE	SALES	PRODUCTION	PERSONNEL
Acquisition of Capital	Product Selection	Product Selection	Staffing
Long-Term Capital	Diversification	Diversification	Selection
Stock	Obsolescence and	New Products	Promotion
Bonds	Style	Integration	Termination
Mortgages	Quality	Make or Buy	Development
Long-Term Notes	Standardization	Quality	Training
Short-Term Capital	Pricing the Product	Standardization	Management Development
Commercial Credits	Product Costs	Inventory	Compensation
Bank Loans	Competition	Facility Policies	Amount of Compensation
Commercial Factors	Pricing New Products	Location	Method of Payment
Employment of Capital	Terms of Sale	Capacity	Employee Benefit Plans
Fixed Assets	Channel of Distribution	Maintenance of	Labor-Management Relations
Ratio of Working	Selecting the Channel	Facilities	Organizational Climate
Capital	Market Penetration	Selection of Vendors	Union Security
Inventory	Sales Promotion	Number of Vendors	Bargaining Tactics
Credit and Collections	Direct Selling	Reciprocity	Relation with Non-
Depreciation	Advertising		union Employees
Distribution of Profit	Special Promotional		
Dividends	Devices		
Reinvestment			

Figure 6-2

SUMMARY OF SCOPE OF POLICIES FOR EACH FUNCTIONAL AREA

personnel—are summarized in tabular form in Figure 6-2. A cursory examination shows that there is a high degree of interrelationship between each of the functional areas. The availability of capital and the manner in which capital is employed have their effect upon the production process especially in reference to the ability to diversify as the result of new product development and in regard to the nature and capacity of production facilities. There is also a close relationship between the policies governing the production function and the sales function. There is common interest concerning the product which is produced by one function and sold by the other, since the quantity and quality of the product or service produced sets the upper limits of the level of achievement of the sales function. Well formulated and properly executed personnel policies have their effect upon both sales and production since effective staffing is necessary for both functions to operate efficiently. Likewise, personnel policies in the areas of development, compensation, and labor-management relations are felt throughout the entire organization.

However, an integration of the functional areas is best achieved by examining them within the context of a servo system as shown in the schematic diagram, Figure 6-3. Financial inputs to the production process supply the raw materials and the physical facilities necessary to produce the product. Personnel inputs furnish the required skills, knowledge, and judgment. The sales function is charged with the responsibility of selling the product to the customer. At this point, a feedback of information occurs which is interpreted and then relayed to production. If the customer buys the product in sufficient quantity the cycle continues, and production signals for a continuation of financial and personnel inputs. If the demand is greater than the quantity produced, production requests additional inputs. When customers do not buy, the signal from sales calls for a reduction of inputs.

Note that there are both internal and external feedback loops. The loop between sales and the customer provides information relating the efforts of the company to its external environment, specifically the customer. Information provided by this loop enables the firm to modify its product or service so that customer demand may continue. If these efforts are not successful, the level of production can be modified to prevent excessive inventory buildup. The other feedback loops are internal to the organization and relate financial and personnel inputs with the functions of production and sales. Should either of these inputs be inadequate in any respect the initial impact is felt in the production function, usually a diminution of that function. The extent and nature

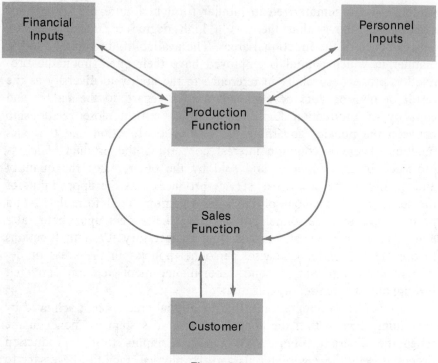

Figure 6-3
INTEGRATING FUNCTIONAL AREAS—A SERVO SYSTEM

of the needs for financial and personnel inputs are the result of information obtained from the combined production-sales cycle.

In summary, Figure 6-2 summarizes the content of policy statements
for each of the four functional areas while Figure 6-3 shows the dynamic
interrelationships of these functional areas within the context of a
servo system.

Case Problem 6-B, "Formulating Personnel Policies," provides an
opportunity to develop a set of consistent policies for a specific organization.

CASE PROBLEM
6-B

FORMULATING
PERSONNEL
POLICIES

Joe Beck, vice-president of industrial relations for
Diversified Manufacturing, has just completed some notes
that he had been preparing for his conference with Bob
Cox, the personnel director who reports to him.

"Bob," he began, "we have been asked to prepare
a draft of proposed personnel policies to be submitted
to the board of directors when they have their annual

meeting here in Chicago next month. It seems that we are being criticized because of what appears to be a lack of consistency in some of the decisions made concerning the personnel function."

"Is that criticism true?" Bob asked.

"I believe there is a good basis for it. Here are some of the incidents that have been brought to my attention." Joe handed Bob the notes he had been preparing. The following is a copy of Joe's notes.

1. In the western division's Los Angeles plant, there was a 45-day strike because the company insisted that an incentive plan be installed as a way to raise average earnings of employees. The union had proposed a general wage increase to bring the rates up to the average of the area. As the strike progressed, it became clear that the real issue was one of permitting union participation in setting time standards. The company stated that determining standards was a company prerogative and no concern of the union. Yet, in a New York plant a job evaluation plan had been installed with joint union-management participation.

2. The general manager of the eastern division responsible for both manufacturing and sales had attended several management development seminars at the request of the president. These seminars emphasized the need for the establishment of a cooperative organizational climate as the backdrop for labor-management relations. Later he sent many of his new managers to similar programs. Some of these managers were then transferred to the western division and have reported that they feel as though they were working for a different company. One even said that if he could not return to the eastern division he would resign.

3. The basis for determining wage levels is not clear. In the eastern division the company's position is that the area wage should be the basis for determining the wage level; yet, in the western division the company argues that the average of the industry, rather than the geographic area average should determine the wage level. The union says the company is inconsistent.

4. Employee benefit programs are uniform throughout all plants in both divisions. As a result, there are locations where hospitalization benefits adequately cover the cost of hospitalization, and there are locations where the benefits received are inadequate. Uniform practices are also followed in respect to vacations, holidays, and leaves of absence, and, as in the case of the hospitalization benefits, there are instances where company practices are more liberal than those of other companies in the area and there are situations where company practices fall short of area standards.

5. The eastern division reimburses all employees for expenses for tuition and books after the completion of any course in an accredited school or college. This includes trade courses, secretarial courses, and degree courses. In addition, employees with five or more years' seniority are granted leaves of absence with one-half pay for periods of one year in order to complete their college work. The manager of the eastern division contends that such programs contribute to the division's ability to promote from within. The western division has no subsidies for self-improvement.

6. In the eastern division the plant supervisors, along with other members of the management, attend a regularly scheduled monthly dinner meeting to discuss production schedules and methods for the coming month and to review performance of the past month. No supervisory meetings are held in the western division.

After reading these six incidents, Bob returned the list to Joe and commented, "It almost seems as though we are talking about two different companies."

"It certainly does, and our job is to develop some policies that will bring these two divisions together. Try and get a draft of such policies for me within the next couple of days."

PROBLEMS

1. What key determination must be made before any policies can be developed for this company?

2. Is it necessary, or even desirable, for a company to have consistent personnel policies within separate operating divisions? Give reasons to support each point of view.

3. Develop a proposed set of personnel policies.

Chapter Questions for Study and Discussion

1. What is the production function? What are some of the production problems encountered in each of the following types of companies: a bank, an insurance company, a public utility, and a restaurant?

2. Would you classify the production of aircraft as jobbing, continuous, or intermittent? Why?

3. Compare the meanings of the phrase "product diversification" when used in reference to sales policies and when used in reference to production policies. Which meaning is broader?

4. Show the application of Figure 6-1, The Effect of Management Action, to areas other than quality control (for example, the cost of advertising or the optimum number of salesmen for a company).

5. In Figure 6-3 the policy areas discussed in Chapter 6 and Chapter 7 are presented as parts of a servo system. The relationship between the sales function and the customer is considered a feedback loop. Is it possible to consider the financial and personnel interests also as feedback loops? If so, how would you differentiate between the feedback loop formed by sales and the customer and the feedback loops formed by production and the inputs of finance and personnel?

6. Figure 6-3 shows a feedback loop between a sales function and the external environment, the customer. Prepare a similar feedback loop between the personnel function and its external environment.

7. Prepare a similar feedback loop between the functions of finance and its external environment.

8. In addition to the inputs of the financial function to the production process what are its inputs in regard to the personnel function? To the sales function?

9. Support the thesis that organizational climate is the result of all other personnel policies rather than an area for which policy can and should be stated.

10. Discuss the significance of each of the areas of personnel policy. Which seems to be the most important in your opinion? Why?

CHAPTER 7

Management Information Systems

Once upon a time the president of a large chain of short-order restaurants attended a lecture on "Human Relations in Business and Industry." He attended the lecture in the hope he would learn something useful. His years of experience had led him to believe that if human relations problems ever plagued any business, then they certainly plagued the restaurant business.

The speaker discussed the many pressures which create human relations problems. He spoke of psychological pressures, sociological pressures, conflicts in values, conflicts in power structure, and so on. The president did not understand all that was said, but he did go home with one idea. If there were so many different sources of pressure, maybe it was expecting too much of his managers to think they would see them all, let alone cope with them all. The thought occurred to him that maybe he should bring in a team of consultants from several different academic disciplines and have each contribute his part to the solution of the human relations problems.

And so it came to pass that the president of the restaurant chain and his top-management staff met one morning with a sociologist, a psychologist, and an

---

[1] Elias H. Porter, "The Parable of the Spindle," *Harvard Business Review*, Vol. 40 (May-June, 1962), pp. 58-65. The parable presented in this article, pages 58-61, is attributed to Professor William Foote Whyte of Cornell University. The remainder of the article, pages 61-65, discusses the spindle in the light of current systems theory. Mr. Porter is a member of the research staff of System Development Corporation, Santa Monica, California.

anthropologist. The president outlined the problem to the men of science and spoke of his hope that they might come up with an interdisciplinary answer to the human relations problems. The personnel manager presented exit-interview findings which he interpreted as indicating that most people quit their restaurant jobs because of too much sense of pressure caused by the inefficiencies and ill tempers of co-workers.

This was the mission which the scientists were assigned: find out why the waitresses break down in tears; find out why the cooks walk off the job; find out why the managers get so upset that they summarily fire employees on the spot. Find out the cause of the problems, and find out what to do about them.

Later, in one of the plush conference rooms, the scientists sat down to plan their attack. It soon became clear that they might just as well be three blind men, and the problem might as well be the proverbial elephant. Their training and experience had taught them to look at events in different ways. They decided that inasmuch as they couldn't speak each other's languages, they might as well pursue their tasks separately. Each went to a different city and began his observations in his own way.

First to return was the sociologist. In his report to top management he said:

"I think I have discovered something that is pretty fundamental. In one sense it is so obvious that it has probably been completely overlooked before. It is during the rush hours that your human relations problems arise. That is when the waitresses break out in tears. That is when the cooks grow temperamental and walk off the job. That is when your managers lose their tempers and dismiss employees summarily."

After elaborating on this theme and showing several charts with sloping lines and bar graphs to back up his assertions, he came to his diagnosis of the situation. "In brief, gentlemen," he stated, "you have a sociological problem on your hands." He walked to the blackboard and began to write. As he wrote, he spoke:

"You have a stress pattern during the rush hours. There is stress between the customer and the waitress. . . .

"There is stress between the waitress and the cook. . . .

"And up here is the manager. There is stress between the waitress and the manager. . . .

"And between the manager and the cook. . . .

"And the manager is buffeted by complaints from the customer.

"We can see one thing which, sociologically speaking, doesn't seem right. The manager has the highest status in the restaurant. The cook has the next highest status. The waitresses, however, are always 'local hire' and have the lowest status. Of course, they have higher status than bus boys and dish washers but certainly lower status than the cook, and yet they give orders to the cook.

"It doesn't seem right for a lower status person to give orders to a higher status person. We've got to find a way to break up the face-to-face relationship between the waitresses and the cook. We've got to fix it so that they don't have to talk with one another. Now my idea is to put a 'spindle' on the order counter. The 'spindle,' as I choose to call it, is a wheel on a shaft. The wheel has clips on it so the girls can simply put their orders on the wheel rather than calling out orders to the cook."

When the sociologist left the meeting, the president and his staff talked of what had been said. It made some sense. However, they decided to wait to hear from the other scientists before taking any action.

Next to return from his studies was the psychologist. He reported to top management:

"I think I have discovered something that is pretty fundamental. In one sense it is so obvious that it has probably been completely overlooked before. It is during the rush hours that your human relations problems arise. That is when the waitresses break out in tears. That is when the cooks grow temperamental and walk off the job. That is when your managers lose their tempers and dismiss employees summarily."

Then the psychologist sketched on the blackboard the identical pattern of stress between customer, waitress, cook, and management. But his interpretation was somewhat different:

"Psychologically speaking," he said, "we can see that the manager is the father figure, the cook is the son, and the waitress is the daughter. Now we know that in our culture you can't have daughters giving orders to the sons. It louses up their ego structure.

"What we've got to do is to find a way to break up the face-to-face relationship between them. Now one idea I've thought up is to put what I call a 'spindle' on the order counter. It's kind of a wheel on a shaft with little clips on it so that the waitresses can put their orders on it rather than calling out orders to the cook."

What the psychologist said made sense, too, in a way. Some of the staff favored the status-conflict interpretation while others thought the sex-conflict interpretation to be the right one; the president kept his own counsel.

The next scientist to report was the anthropologist. He reported:

"I think I have discovered something that is pretty fundamental. In one sense it is so obvious that it has probably been completely overlooked before. It is during the rush hours that your human relations problems arise. That is when the waitresses break out in tears. That is when the cooks grow temperamental and walk off the job. That is when your managers lose their tempers and dismiss employees summarily."

After elaborating for a few moments he came to his diagnosis of the situation. "In brief, gentlemen," he stated, "you have an anthropological problem on your hands." He walked to the blackboard and began to sketch. Once again there appeared the stress pattern between customer, waitress, cook, and management.

"We anthropologists know that man behaves according to his value systems. Now, the manager holds as a central value the continued growth and development of the restaurant organization. The cooks tend to share this central value system, for as the organization prospers, so do they. But the waitresses are a different story. The only reason most of them are working is to help supplement the family income. They couldn't care less whether the organization thrives or not as long as it's a decent place to work. Now, you can't have a noncentral value system giving orders to a central value system.

"What we've got to do is to find some way of breaking up the face-to-face contact between the waitresses and the cook. One way that has occurred to me is to place on the order counter an adaptation of the old-fashioned spindle. By having a wheel at the top of the shaft and putting clips every few inches apart, the waitresses can put their orders on the wheel and not have to call out orders to the cook. Here is a model of what I mean."

When the anthropologist had left, there was much discussion of which scientist was right. The president finally spoke. "Gentlemen, it's clear that these men don't agree on the reason for conflict, but all have come up with the same basic idea about the spindle. Let's take a chance and try it out."

And it came to pass that the spindle was introduced throughout the chain of restaurants. It did more to reduce the human relations problems in the restaurant industry than any other innovation of which the restaurant people knew. Soon it was copied. Like wildfire the spindle spread from coast to coast and from border to border.

PROBLEMS

1. In your opinion, which of the three scientists offered the most plausible explanation of the restaurant's problems?
2. Are the personnel problems observed by the owner "problems" or are they "symptoms"? Defend your answer.
3. In recommending the spindle, the scientists are tacitly admitting that the restaurant is a form of system. Name the kind of system they are thinking of and show how the restaurant meets the requirements of a system.
4. Prepare a chart showing the flow of information in the restaurant and designate the major steps in this process.

Figure 6-3 of Chapter 6, "Planning for Production and Personnel," depicts the business firm as a servo system. In the discussion of this figure it is stated that management receives and interprets information from both internal and external sources and designates the corrective action necessary for the firm to continue operating successfully. Since management must receive, interpret, and transmit information in order to accomplish its stated objectives, the planning of an effective information system is an important management task. In order to design an information system it is first necessary to establish the meaning of the phrase, information system, and to determine the major functions of such a system. Second, it is necessary to understand fundamental electronic data processing techniques in order to design and evaluate an integrated data processing information system.

FUNCTIONS OF AN INFORMATION SYSTEM

The concept of a *system* implies a dynamic relationship between the components of a larger whole and at the same time permits the recognition of each part as a separate *subsystem* which makes its own unique contribution to the function of the whole. The human organism is an excellent example of a system composed of many subsystems. There is a gastro-intestinal system with its function of converting food into energy so that the larger whole may survive. The circulatory system carries the nutrients thus provided to every part of the body, supplies needed oxygen to the tissues, and removes waste materials. The nervous system, a communications network, is composed of several subsystems. The autonomic nervous system monitors and controls the gastro-intestinal and circulatory systems. The peripheral nervous system receives stimuli, such as heat or cold, from the external environment and warns of impending danger by transmitting a signal of pain. The central nervous system performs an integrative function by coordinating the many subsystems of the body.

In many respects an *information system* is analogous to the human nervous system. Patterns of information flowing from production and sales may be likened to the impulses transmitted by the autonomic nervous system in controlling the vital functions of the body. Messages from the sales force, field engineers, and buyers are similar to the stimuli transmitted by the peripheral nervous system in that they represent contacts with an environment external to the organism. Management, like the central nervous system, must interpret the data received and transmit directions so that corrective action may be taken. Unlike the human organism, however, a company is not created with a complete information (nervous) system; therefore, management must design its own system so the firm may function properly. What are the components of such a system, and how does each part contribute to the operation of the complete system?

Components of an Information System

Information systems range in degree of complexity from the very simple as described in Case Problem 7-A, "The Parable of the

Spindle," to the extremely complex system utilized by Westinghouse, which is described in Case Problem 7-B. Regardless of the simplicity of the system, an effective information system has the following five parts: (1) *input device*—a means of placing information into the system, (2) *storage unit*—provides for the accumulation of information (performs a memory function), (3) *control unit*—selects the proper information from the storage unit and controls the operations of the (4) *processing unit*—the part that handles and interprets the data, and the (5) *output device*—presents the original information in usable form after it has been processed.

Contribution of Each Part

Before discussing the contribution of each part of an information system to the functioning of the total system, it is well to recognize that all organizations have some form of information system. When the system functions imperfectly, as illustrated in Case Problem 7-A, the symptoms of such malfunction may become so acute that they appear to be the problem. Each of the three scientists consulted by the restaurant owner determined that the problem arose during rush hours; however, each presented a different interpretation of the causes. The sociologist described the situation in terms of stress patterns coupled with the concept of status; the psychologist saw ego involvement arising from a disregard of classic familial authority relationships; and the anthropologist couched his explanation of the problem in terms of values. Fortunately, all agreed on one solution—an improved information system—though none of the three defined the basic problem as one resulting from the imperfect functioning of an inadequate information system. Let us determine the contribution of each part of the recommended system.

Input Device. The input device recommended as the first step of the new information system is a ticket on which the waitress writes a description of the desired order. Formerly the waitresses called their orders to the cook, a method that invites error and confusion. In addition to decreasing the possibility of misunderstanding, a written record provides a means of checking the accuracy of the eventual output and serves as a basis for correcting errors should they occur. When written records are used, it is possible to designate the point of origin; in this instance the initials of the waitress serve that purpose. Further, an input record may serve more than one purpose. When the ticket is returned with the prepared order, it may be used as a bill to be presented to the customer and then retained by the manager as a permanent record of the day's activities. Thus, written inputs minimize the introduction of error, provide a basis for correcting errors when they do occur, indicate the origin of the input, and serve as a permanent record.

Storage Unit. The main contribution of the spindle to the flow of information is the effect it has upon the cook's work. With orders of the waitresses attached to the revolving spindle, it is no longer necessary for the cook to remember each order. The spindle is performing a function formerly performed by the cook's memory; consequently, a storage unit is frequently referred to as a *memory unit*.

Rarely does information enter a system at a uniform rate; instead, the flow of information during a normal business day forms a chart with many peaks and valleys. The introduction of a storage unit into an information system makes it possible to control the rate of flow to subsequent units. The spindle storage unit has another important feature in that data may be drawn from it without reference to the sequence followed in putting information into the system. Storage units that permit the withdrawal of information without regard to the sequence of input are called *random access* units. If the tickets had been placed in a box rather than on a spindle, the cook would be relieved of remembering each order and could control the rate of flow of information from the box by selecting one or two tickets at a time. However, he would see only the top ticket; consequently, he could not combine several orders so they might be filled more efficiently. The visual display of the spindle allows random access without regard to the sequence in which the orders are received. At a single glance, the cook has access to all written tickets and can determine the number of steak dinners on order, thus enabling him to prepare similar orders simultaneously. The spindle adequately performs the functions of a storage unit in that it stores, or remembers, the information; aids in regulating the flow of information to subsequent units in the system; and permits random access to the stored information.

Control Unit. In an information system the influence of the control unit is felt throughout the entire system. Though the unit cannot control the rate at which information enters the system, it can reject those items not suitable to the system or that are incapable of interpretation. The cook, who functions simultaneously as a control and a processing unit, may reject an order that is not on the menu; i.e., not suitable for the system, or ask that a ticket be rewritten because it is illegible. However, he cannot control the rate at which waitresses enter the orders. Also, in exercising his power of control the cook may determine the sequence in which orders are selected from the random access memory unit. The control unit also determines the method to be used in processing the order and checks the final results to make sure that the original input request is fulfilled. In addition, the output of the processing unit is monitored in respect to quality, quantity, and rate of output. In complex systems employing electronic data processing equipment, the control unit and the processing unit are separate pieces of electronic equipment; yet the control function remains the same—checking the flow of information into the system, determining the sequence in which material will be drawn from the memory unit, setting up the methods to be used in processing, and controlling output in respect to quality, quantity, and rate of output.

Processing Unit. The chief task of the processing unit is one of interpreting information so that the output of the system conforms to requirements laid down by the control unit. Since the cook is performing the processing function as well as the control function, it is his task to interpret the symbols on the tickets and translate these symbols into action that produces the specified output—orders of food. Simple arithmetic computations are necessary to determine the number of orders on each ticket, and on occasion the cook may compute the total number of identical orders capable of being prepared at the same time, thereby increasing efficiency of output. In more sophisticated systems, such as the one used by Westinghouse in Case Problem 7-B, advance-design computers form the processing unit. However, the function remains the same—the interpretation and manipulation of symbolic data to produce the desired output.

Output Device. The output of an information system is the final step in the sequence of input, storage, control, and processing of information. Frequently the output of the processing unit is additional information, usually directions requiring action on the part of subsequent elements in the system. The cook could, for example, interpret the information stored on the spindle and give directions to his assistants, indicating the work that each is to perform. Or immediately after interpretation, the information may be converted into action that fulfills the objectives of the system, in this instance, the preparation of food. In any event, the end result of the system, either additional information or action that fulfills the objectives of the system, should be capable of being checked against the original input so that the reliability of the entire process is insured. In our present example the original ticket may be placed with the prepared food, which enables both the cook and the waitress who placed the original information (order) into the system to check the accuracy of the final result.

In addition to providing a basis for discussing the major parts of an information system, "The Parable of the Spindle" points up the value of viewing business problems as occurring within a system rather than isolated problems to be analyzed and solved as separate entities. Suppose that none of the scientists had recommended the installation of a spindle, but that one had recommended a more tolerant cook; another, a more stable manager; and the third, the selection of waitresses with a higher degree of emotional stability. Such recommendations represent an approach that emphasizes the strength of each element rather than the design of the system itself. The solution that was adopted, the installation of a spindle, illustrates the systems approach to the management process. Seymour Tilles has suggested that the manager's job is essentially one of managing systems and that a manager should define the company as a system, establish objectives for the system, create formal subsystems, and then integrate all such systems.[2] The chief advantage to be derived from regarding the manager's job as one of managing systems is the recognition of the interdependence and contribution of each part to the whole system and the realization that failure to meet objectives may be due to an improper design of the system itself rather than the result of shortcomings attributable to the individual components of the system.

INTEGRATED DATA PROCESSING

"The Parable of the Spindle" serves a useful purpose since it provides a means of illustrating the components of an information system and the importance of recognizing the management of systems as an important element of the manager's job. Obviously, the

---

[2] Seymour Tilles, "The Manager's Job—A Systems Approach," *Harvard Business Review*, Vol. 41 (January-February, 1963), pp. 73-81.

R. A. Johnson, F. E. Kast, and J. E. Rosensweig, *The Theory and Management of Systems* (New York: McGraw-Hill Book Company, 1963), pp. viii, 350.

Both of these works emphasize the business organization as a complex of systems and the manager's job as a manager of systems. *The Theory and Management of Systems* relates the systems concept to the management functions of planning, organizing, controlling, and communication.

F. E. Kast and J. E. Rosensweig, *Organization and Management: A Systems Approach* (New York: McGraw-Hill Book Company, 1970), Chap. 12, pp. 340-370. Chapter 12 of *Organization and Management* discusses the characteristics of and the problems encountered in the design of information-decision systems.

number of business situations in which a spindle may be used as a storage unit is limited; also, most business situations are so complex that an information system that relies solely upon human capabilities for the functions of control, interpretation, and output of data would be extremely limited in its effectiveness. Fortunately, there are techniques available for the design of effective communication systems for those situations too complex for the spindle and the powers of human memory and reasoning. An increasing number of modern communication, or information, systems rely upon the use of electronic data processing (EDP) equipment which may be combined into an integrated data processing (IDP) system. In discussing integrated data processing, we will touch upon the development of electronic data processing, the steps in the design of an integrated data processing system, and an evaluation of integrated data processing.

Before discussing the development of electronic data processing, it is necessary to define some commonly used terms. *Data processing* refers to the act of handling information or data, either *manually* or *automatically*. Typical of the manual methods of handling data is the work of clerical employees such as bookkeepers, accountants, billing clerks, and payroll clerks. *Automatic data processing (ADP)* is the handling of information by machines rather than by human beings. The punch card equipment, discussed below, is an example of automatic data processing. The phrase, *electronic data processing (EDP)*, means that the data are processed at high speed by electronic equipment. When the word electronic was first used to describe data processing equipment, it designated equipment that utilized the vacuum tube rather than the earlier electromechanical devices. The term electronic is still used to describe data processing units that are completely transistorized and no longer use vacuum tubes. Since the computer is the best known example of an electronic data processing unit, the phrase EDP also implies that a computer is part of the electronic data processing system. *Integrated data processing (IDP)* refers to the integrated collection, transmission, handling, and use of all data needed for the operation of a business. It is an integrated management information system. It must be recognized that there are varying degrees of integration and that technically IDP is not dependent upon any form of automatic equipment. For example, "The Parable of the Spindle" described an integrated flow of information that is manually operated. However, as the term IDP is now used, it almost always means that EDP is being utilized, but the emphasis is upon the integrative aspects of management information rather than upon the means of processing the data.

Development of EDP

The origin of automatic data processing may be traced to Charles Babbage, who in 1823 conceived the idea of a "Difference Engine" to compute and print mathematical tables.[3] Though he worked on this project for 10 years, it was never completed due to difficulties encountered primarily in its manufacture. The next major step in automatic data processing occurred in 1890 when Dr. Herman Hollerith developed the now familiar punch card as an aid in tabulating the results of the 1890 census. Information was coded by means of holes punched in the cards, and an electrical contact completed through the holes activated mechanical counters. The first computer, started in 1937 by Professor Howard Aiken of Harvard University in conjunction with the International Business Machines Corporation, was placed in operation in 1944 and is still in use. The computer, the Automatic Sequence Controlled Calculator—Mark I, operated on electromechanical principles with the counters controlled by electrical relays. The first electronic computer, completed at the University of Pennsylvania's Moore School of Engineering in 1946, was called the Electronic Numerical Integrator and Calculator (ENIAC). This computer replaced the relays and counters of Mark I with 18,000 vacuum tubes. By 1950 there were approximately 20 different types of computers in use and in 1960 this number had reached at least 300.[4] Table 7-1 on page 218 shows actual sales for computers, peripherals, and software for 1960 and projections for 1975.[5]

Computers are only one part of the present-day electronic data processing equipment used in electronic data processing systems. The components of an electronic data processing system are the same as the components of the information system described in "The Parable of the Spindle." Inputs into the system are in the form of electrical impulses placed in the system by means of punched cards, punched paper tape, magnetic tape, or magnetic ink characters such as those used by banks in the processing of checks. Paper tapes may be prepared as a by-product of conventional typing and may be fed into the system at speeds in excess of 500 characters per second. The information is usually

---

[3] See Chapter 2, page 33.

[4] It is beyond the scope of this chapter to present a detailed analysis of the construction of electronic data processing equipment. The student is referred to the following reference as a broad source of information concerning the principles of electronic data processing equipment and its application to the behavioral sciences.

Harold Borko (ed)., *Computer Application in the Behavioral Sciences* (Englewood Cliffs, New Jersey: Prentice-Hall, Inc., 1962).

[5] "160,000 Computers in Use By 1975, Says Diebold," *Administrative Management*, Vol. XXXI, No. 2 (February, 1970), pp. 58-62.

Table 7-1

EDP GROWTH FROM 1960 TO 1975
(Computers, Peripherals, and Software)

	1960	1965	1970	1975
Number of Computers in Use	4,500	30,000	90,000	160,000
Installed Value of CPUs Shipped *	$280	$1,300	$3,400	$4,500
Number of Computers Shipped—				
Total	1,000	7,000	18,500	46,000
Monitoring Control Computers	(Negl.)	800	5,000	22,000
Sales of Peripheral Equipment *	$120	$1,350	$5,100	$10,500
Terminal Devices	(Negl.)	100	1,600	5,500
Other Peripherals	120	1,250	3,500	5,000
Terminal Devices in Use	(Negl.)	30,000	60,000	700,000
Total Software Sales *	$300	$650	$1,500	$2,600
Contract Programming *	190	520	1,100	1,850
Proprietary Packages *	10	130	400	750

* Millions of dollars

Source: "160,000 Computers in Use By 1975, Says Diebold," *Administrative Management*, Vol. XXXI, No. 2 (February, 1970), p. 58.

stored in the "memory unit" of the computer as an electronic charge on a magnetic core, a magnetic drum, or magnetic discs. Most modern systems permit random access to any bit of information, and storage capacities of two or three million alphanumeric characters are not at all unusual. The computer is the arithmetic processing unit and performs all arithmetic operations—addition, subtraction, multiplication, and division—at extremely high rates of speed by using the binary system, which expresses all numbers and letters in various combinations of either 0 or 1. The control unit, equipped with a console, offers a means whereby the operator communicates with the computer and enables the computer to inform the operator of any errors that may be encountered or mechanical breakdowns that may occur. The control unit directs the operation of the arithmetic processing unit by means of a predetermined program that sets forth each step to be performed and the sequence of that step in relation to other operations. Also, the control unit decodes incoming information, places it in proper form in the storage unit, and regulates the form and rate of output. Due to the tremendous speed of the arithmetic processing unit, original output is placed on magnetic tape which may be transcribed onto punched paper tape and then fed through a typewriter or a printer, or transferred to punched cards which are processed through a printer. Or, high-speed electronic printers, capable of printing up to 5,000 lines per minute, may be used.

Designing an IDP Information System

Electronic data processing is a powerful tool capable of handling large quantities of information in very short periods of time. Integrated data processing usually employs electronic data processing techniques and combines the various applications of EDP into an integrated flow of information to and from all levels of the organization so that management has relevant and timely information for decision making. The following discussion outlines five major steps in designing an IDP information system, reviews some of the problems encountered in each step, and offers suggested ways of overcoming these problems.[6]

State Objectives. Normally company-wide objectives are expressed in terms of accomplishments in specific functional areas and do not specify the information needed to achieve these goals. Objectives should be reexamined and expressed as information needed for their achievement. For example, the sales department might specify the need for additional economic information in order to improve the accuracy of sales forecasts. A way of gathering the information required to meet objectives is to ask each department manager to develop the information needs required to improve the performance of his department. This approach, in addition to aiding in restating objectives, serves to acquaint the organization with the benefits to be derived from IDP and helps to allay fears associated with the introduction of automatic, high-speed processes. Stating information objectives carefully also avoids the tendency of indiscriminately collecting and processing large masses of information simply because the equipment is capable of handling a huge volume of work. Remember, the ultimate purpose of IDP is to aid in decision making; the preparation of irrelevant information confuses the issue and hinders the manager in making a decision. Too, the accumulation of unnecessary information is wasteful.

---

[6] M. K. Evans and L. R. Hague, "Master Plan for Information System," *Harvard Business Review*, Vol. XL (January-February, 1962), pp. 92-103. A similar analysis of five steps is presented in this article.

Designate Authority. When the information needs of the company have been stated and it has been decided to install an IDP information system, it is necessary to designate authority for the planning of the system and its later administration. Usually it is best to choose one person to be responsible for both planning and administration since the knowledge gained of the organization and its information needs during the planning phase of the program is invaluable in administering the program. If possible, the person chosen should have a thorough knowledge of the company and a reputation that merits the confidence of the company's top officials. In small and medium-size firms the controller is usually designated, since he generally has a broad knowledge of the company and usually administers a large part of the present information system. In large companies—with several plants, a diverse product line, and several sales offices—it is best to create an information function independent of the controller's office. Frequently the manager of IDP carries the title of vice-president, administrative services. Regardless of title, the person in charge of planning and administering IDP should report to the chief operating head of the company.

Analyze Present Systems. There are two divergent theories concerning the extent to which present information systems should be examined in order to develop a new IDP system.[7] One of these theories holds that there should be a detailed analysis of present systems even though the information gained is not completely relevant. Most companies have established procedures to describe a series of related tasks, such as payroll procedures, employment procedures, or accounting procedures. Procedures are usually implemented by methods, a descriptive statement of the precise way to perform a given job, such as detailing the steps to be completed in preparing an invoice. Procedures and methods are examples of the flow of information; however, it is information flowing primarily in one direction since the major emphasis in developing procedures and methods is that of describing the manner in which a given task or job is to be accomplished.[8] Since the

---

[7] James D. Gallagher, *Management Information Systems and the Computer* (New York: American Management Association, 1961), Research Study No. 51, p. 127. Mr. Gallagher's research study surveys the problems generally associated with information systems and contains two case studies of information systems of special interest: the American Airline Sabre System and the system used by Sylvania Electric Products, Inc.

[8] The following references present sound discussions of business procedures:
Ralph C. Davis, *The Fundamentals of Top Management* (New York: Harper & Brothers, Publishers, 1951), Chap. 20, "Business Procedure," pp. 744-84.
William H. Newman and James P. Logan, *Business Policies and Management* (4th ed.; Cincinnati: South-Western Publishing Company, 1959), Chap. 24, "Operating Methods and Procedures," pp. 637-665.

purpose of procedures and methods is to accomplish work, rather than develop information for an integrated system, a detailed analysis of an existing system is of questionable value. Detailed analysis of present systems may build mountains of data that obscure real information needs.

The second theory holds that only information pertinent to the meeting of company information objectives should be analyzed and recorded. Selecting only pertinent data not only reduces the amount of work but also avoids one of the dangers inherent in the first theory— unconsciously trying to fit powerful electronic data processing techniques to existing procedures and methods that were originally designed to direct manual operations. In practice, a middle ground is usually chosen. Thorough knowledge of present information is required, but the collection of voluminous data is avoided since the purpose and techniques of IDP differ from those of the existing system.

Install Short-Range Improvements. There are those who say that a complete system must be developed before making any changes in present procedures; yet there is much to be gained by installing short-range improvements provided such steps mesh with the goals of a total IDP information system. Critics of short-range improvements state that until the entire systems analysis is complete, there is no way of knowing ultimate equipment requirements; however, modern EDP equipment is of modular design, and units acquired at a later date are usually compatible with existing units. Further, early experience with IDP influences the design of subsequent systems and demonstrates early the benefits resulting from an integrated approach to information handling. In some instances it is possible to realize an immediate reduction in costs, for example, applications of IDP to inventory control procedures, payroll procedures, or the processing of sales orders. The Westinghouse installation of EDP, Case Problem 7-B, illustrates the realization of immediate gains that are also a part of an overall IDP information system.

Prepare for Organizational Change. Despite the many technical problems encountered in the installation of a company-wide information system, the greatest difficulties experienced by many firms are the effects of IDP upon the organizational structure of the company. George Fleming of the Boeing Company states that installation problems are more people oriented than machine oriented.[9] One factor contributing

---

[9] *Advances in EDP and Information Systems* (New York: American Management Association, 1961), Management Report No. 62, George J. Fleming, "Developing a Practical Data Collection System at Boeing," pp. 82-87. The article by Mr. Fleming is one of 21 reports based on material originally presented at AMA's Seventh Annual Data Processing Conference held in March, 1961.

to Fleming's statement is the obvious fear and resistance on the part of employees who might be displaced by electronic data processing equipment. Yet, in many respects, the major problems with people come from middle and top management. Organizational structures usually conform to and are derived from the work patterns of the organization. People doing similar work are grouped into units that may develop into departments. For example, those persons engaged in scheduling the product through production form the production control department, and those who keep financial records make up the accounting department. Supervisors of departments tend to develop a proprietary interest in the work performed in their departments and the people performing this work. An IDP system, by automating manual operations, frequently eliminates the need for entire departments and their respective supervisors. Consider the plight and attitude of the employees and the supervisor of a payroll department when it is learned that an IDP system will record the hours worked for each production worker, accumulate the total number of hours for each worker during the pay period, and at the close of the period compute all necessary extensions and deductions and print individual checks for the net amount due.

As yet, very few companies are organized to take full advantage of an IDP information system; but it appears certain that if maximum advantage is realized, it will occur in those companies that are organized to conform with the capabilities of the system rather than in those companies that have planned the system to fit current organization structure.[10]

Evaluation of EDP

Few companies have completely integrated data processing systems. However, most EDP installations are hopefully a first step toward an integrated management information system. A question that normally arises whenever the design and installation of EDP is being considered is the matter of cost. It is extremely difficult to develop meaningful figures because each company has its own unique information needs. Also, rental charges for equipment, depending upon the kind selected and the number of units required, range from a low of $1,000 per month to approximately $200,000 per month. Should

---

[10] The following two references are recommended for their discussion concerning the impact of computer technology and EDP upon management organizations.

Harold J. Leavitt and Thomas L. Whisler, "Management in the 1980's," *Harvard Business Review* (November-December, 1958), pp. 41-48.

William E. Reif, *Computer Technology and Organization* (Iowa City, Iowa: Bureau of Business and Economic Research, The University of Iowa, 1968).

the user decide to purchase the equipment, the sales price is roughly equivalent to the rental charges for a four-year period.

There have been isolated instances where the installation of EDP resulted in marked reductions in the number of clerical personnel, as illustrated by the Treasury Department's installation of a computer, programmed to reconcile the government payroll and print the checks, which resulted in a reduction of clerical workers from 755 to 270. In addition, Federal Reserve banks were able to eliminate some 400 employees as the result of this move.[11] However, the personnel reductions experienced by the government are not typical of industry's experience since personnel reductions of this magnitude occur only when an extremely large volume of repetitive clerical work is mechanized. For most companies the number of clerical workers remains the same and many firms have been forced to increase their clerical staff. The reasons for this paradox are not due to the inefficiencies of EDP but are attributable to normal expansion of and the accumulation and use of data not readily available when manual information systems are used.

Although there is a wide variation in information needs among companies and in charges for EDP equipment, there is a fairly stable, predictable pattern of costs.[12] Prior to ordering any electronic equipment a feasibility study, which normally takes about six months to complete, is usually made. At the end of this time, equipment may be ordered, with delivery usually promised in one year. During this year between 15- and 30-man years, at a cost of $10,000 to $12,000 per man-year, may be spent in systems analysis, training, and programming. Also occurring during this period is the necessary remodeling or building of physical facilities to house the EDP installation. The cost of physical facilities may range from $50,000 to $250,000. When the equipment arrives, rental charges begin and for a few months there is little produced, and duplicate manual and electronic systems work side by side. With a machine rental of $30,000 a month, it is possible to have a total of $780,000 invested in feasibility studies, training personnel, programming, physical facilities, magnetic tapes, and the overlap period when both electronic and manual operations are in use. Assuming that the installation is expected to earn $30,000 a month, or $360,000 a

---

[11] *Use of Electronic Data Processing Equipment,* Hearing before the Subcommittee on Post Office and Civil Service, House of Representatives, 80th Congress, 1st Session (Washington, D. C.: U. S. Government Printing Office, 1959) Appendix A, pp. 34-40.

[12] E. W. Martin, Jr., "Practical Problems of Introducing a Computer," *Business Horizons,* Vol. III (Fall, 1960), pp. 4, 6, 8, 10, 12, 14-16, 84-86. The illustration of cost patterns that appears in the text is taken from this article and is typical of what might be expected to occur as the result of a large installation.

year, it is at least a year and a half after the initial study before the break-even point is reached. Another two years beyond the break-even point are required to recover the $780,000 spent prior to the equipment's effective use. Thus, the total recovery point may be at least three and one-half years after the initial feasibility study. The example above is typical of a large installation and it must be recognized that though the dollar amount varies from one installation to another, there is a period of approximately one and one-half years before an installation can be expected to reach the break-even point in respect to current operations, and another two to three years before the total costs are recovered. Thus, it is usually three to four years before any profit may be realized as the result of installing an EDP information system.

In addition to potential earnings resulting directly from a well-planned EDP information system, the major value to be derived from such an installation is the improved effectiveness of the business organization as an information-decision system. Peter Drucker expresses the value of an improved information-decision system as follows: [13]

> The new organization, whether an army or a business, is above all an information and decision system. Information, ideas, questions, flow from the outside environment as well as from people within. They not only have to be perceived and transmitted; the relevant has to be separated from the merely interesting. Then somebody has to make a decision which in turn has to flow back to the places where it can become effective action. Information and decision systems are around us everywhere; every living being is one, and so is every machine. But the organization is probably the most complex.

As you read "The Short-Order Economy," Case Problem 7-B,[14] try to trace the information-decision flow in Westinghouse.

CASE PROBLEM   On the outskirts of Pittsburgh, in an old warehouse
7-B   that once housed transformers, switchgear, and hundreds
                          of other products made by Westinghouse Electric Corp.,
THE SHORT-   sits a little machine with a fabulous memory. It is an
ORDER ECONOMY   I.B.M. 1401 computer hooked up to a random-access

---

[13] Peter Drucker, *Landmarks of Tomorrow* (New York: Harper & Brothers, Publishers, 1959), p. 92.
[14] Carl Rieser, "The Short-Order Economy," *Fortune*, Vol. LXVI (August, 1962), pp. 90-94. Reprinted from the August, 1962, issue of *Fortune* Magazine by Special Permission; © 1962 *Time*, Inc. In addition to the detailed account of Westinghouse's application of electronic data processing, the article presents other applications of data processing.

memory bank that holds some 20 million bits of information. To the observer, the bank is merely a stack of flat disks about the size of long-playing phonograph records. At one side of the stack, working up and down on a spindle, is a long stylus that flicks in and out among the disks faster than the eye can follow. That little machine is busier than a couple of hundred salesmen, order clerks, stenographers, traffic men, and switchboard operators.

It knows more about the territory—indeed, about scores of territories—than the oldest salesman. It has more information about sales than the smartest sales manager. It remembers far more accurately than the stock clerks where the nuts and bolts can be found in any warehouse. It is a wondrous combination of traveling salesman, mathematical genius, and the Sears, Roebuck catalogue. With affectionate pride, the people who work with it call it their "monster." It is revolutionizing distribution at the producers' level, just as the discount merchants discussed earlier in this *Fortune* series have revolutionized retailing. The distribution of goods has finally begun to get the full benefit of the accumulated technology of the Western world, which for two centuries has been miraculously transforming the production of goods.

What the monster is doing to old Westinghouse is awe-inspiring. It knows all the pertinent facts about some 15,000 customers who buy Westinghouse industrial products directly from the company, including about 500 distributors who in turn supply many thousands of smaller customers. The computer knows each major customer's address, what normal trade discounts he is entitled to. The memory bank stores data about some 60,000 finished industrial products, from large electric motors and line transformers to tiny replacement parts—prices, shipping weights, discount structures, production schedules, and the number of units presently in stock in each of twenty-six field warehouses and nineteen factory warehouses across the U.S. The equipment handles an average of 1,800 orders a day, and on busy days the total may go up to 2,400.

From the moment a salesman in, say, the Seattle office gets an order for an integral horsepower motor and hands it to a clerk, the whole order process is almost completely mechanical. The clerk looks up the number for the motor in a code book thick as a small telephone directory, supplies the customer's code number and the necessary details about the order, and teletypes it to Pittsburgh. From there on the computer takes over. Aside from some handling of data-processing cards, no human hands touch the order until the motor is shipped.

When the order comes in from Seattle, the monster first searches its memory to find the warehouse nearest the customer that has the item in stock. It then adjusts the inventory record. If the stock has now fallen to a predetermined danger point, the electric-motor factory in Buffalo gets the word to put the model back into production. Next the computer reaches into the memory bank for the customer's normal trade discount, figures out the state sales tax, shipping charges, and so forth, and types out an invoice. Finally the computer transmits the order to the proper warehouse, where it emerges a few seconds later from the teletype machine complete with bill of lading, addressed labels for the carton, and instructions telling the order picker what bin to go to.

All this takes no more than fifteen minutes on the average. By startling contrast, before Westinghouse installed the system in 1959, it used to take an average of five days that were often filled with worry and confusion. First the salesman had to waste precious time checking around to see where the item was in stock. (Now all he has to do is put a query on the teletype and the computer will have word back to him within ten minutes.) If the order was mailed to the warehouse or factory, that took a couple of days, and two or three days more were spent by the clerks figuring out the prices and processing the paper work. In the course of this, likely as not, the impatient salesman got on the phone or the teletype to see if the order had been shipped, and all that accomplished was to help jam up Westinghouse's communications system.

"We were always dealing with history," says David C. McAlister, who is manager of distribution, accounting, and procedures and the chief architect of the computerized ordering system. No one ever quite knew the state of inventories on a national basis because both sales and inventory figures were weeks behind time. The tendency therefore was to keep large "protective" inventories on hand in order to guard against the danger of running out of stock, which is anathema to a sales manager. Because the whole system was so slow, sales managers also pressed the company to maintain a large network of warehouses so as to be near as many customers as possible. Even so, Westinghouse found itself out of stock on a quarter of the orders received.

The speedy little monster has drastically altered all this. Westinghouse can now ship its orders from any point no matter how far away—even from the factory itself— and still get the goods to the customer faster than it once did. In many instances it can assure overnight delivery. The company has been able to close five of its field warehouses—one of them has been converted into a home for the computer—and some of the remaining twenty-six are scheduled to go. It has also slashed overall inventories, and has cut stocks of one line of products from $5 million to $1,700,000. Yet Westinghouse now is out of stock on only one out of every twenty orders.

The treasurer's office has been made happy by all kinds of savings. Cash flow has been speeded up by five days because the invoices are mailed out to the customers the day the orders are received. Since the monster does all the bookkeeping, costs have been cut sharply; one factory has reduced its operating costs by more than $200,000 a year. And there has been at least one unexpected financial boon. Westinghouse, like any large industrial company, has a melange of normal trade discount structures for its thousands of products. ("You name it; we've got it," says McAlister.) It is also changing prices constantly. In precomputer days, there was always a lag between the time a price change was announced and the time the news got to the 100-odd Westinghouse sales branches. Now the computer gets the news immediately and applies the new price at once. As a result, Westinghouse realizes an average of about one-half of one percent more on the price of each item.

The sales force has mixed feelings about the new system. McAlister contends that "the salesmen never had it so good." They can assure faster service, and as one sales manager puts it, "We are able to ship when we say we are going to ship." On the other hand, the monster has automated the whole process of selling to a degree that is unsettling to many an older salesman. It used to be that the customer had several days' leeway if he placed an order, then decided to cancel. Now, with lead time down to fifteen minutes, the order has been invoiced and shipped by the time he changes his mind. The salesman then has the unhappy choice of reconvincing the customer that he needs the product—which may be difficult—or of having the goods returned.

McAlister has recently bypassed some salesmen altogether by putting teletype machines right into the offices of a few of Westinghouse's larger industrial customers, enabling them to order directly through the Pittsburgh computer center. "I give 'em a catalog and let 'em buy," says McAlister. "I tell the salesmen that in the future all they will have to do is to carry an oilcan and keep those sending machines well oiled."

For major appliances (washing machines, refrigerators, etc.), Westinghouse has a second ordering system, located at a central shipping point in Columbus, Ohio. The problems here are different, and there is a somewhat lesser degree of automation. One of the important logistical considerations is to save freight costs by assembling full rail carloads of various appliances for pooled shipments to several dealers. Human brainwork is still required for putting together the mix. But the system has achieved enormous gains, similar to those for the industrial goods. The computer has speeded up the time needed to process an order from seven days to three days, has cut overall inventories by 25 percent, and has leveled out seasonal peaks and valleys on the production lines.

Sometime late this fall Westinghouse will cap four years of work by opening a glittering new Tele-Computer Center a few miles from Pittsburgh, built around one wonderfully versatile computer that will handle the work now done by both the Columbus and the present Pittsburgh ordering systems. This newest monster, a Univac 490 Real-Time computer, will be the brain for Westinghouse's entire teletype communication system, linking some 265 offices, factories, warehouses, and sales branches throughout the U.S. and Canada. More than 15,000 messages of all kinds each day will flow directly into Univac, which will sort out the 2,000 to 3,000 specially coded orders for industrial goods and appliances and put them through an even more highly automated process than now exists. (It will eliminate the need for using data processing cards for the industrial goods.) And as a sideshow, the Univac will also be turning out sales, financial, and engineering data for corporate and divisional staffs. "My worst nightmare," says McAlister, "is that someday the machine is going to goof and I'm going to deliver a carload of line transformers to a corner drugstore."

Westinghouse was one of the first corporations to experiment with the application of the computer to the day-to-day problems of distribution, and in four years it has advanced so far with its system that it has become a mecca for U.S. and foreign businessmen who are fascinated by the new possibilities of the electronic era. But many other companies have installed similar systems —General Foods, Armstrong Cork, Clark Equipment, Scott Paper, Chemstrand, and Pittsburgh Plate Glass, just to name a few. Throughout a broad segment of industry, engineers like Westinghouse's McAlister are shaking up sales and order-filling procedures, inventory handling, and production scheduling.

PROBLEMS

1. Is the computer thinking or making decisions when it notifies a factory to start production when the stock of a given item has fallen below a specified point? Defend your answer.
2. What are the major advantages realized by cutting the time required to fill an order from 5 days to 15 minutes? Are there any disadvantages?
3. Do you believe that the Westinghouse installation has paid for itself? Why?
4. What organizational problems and changes do you foresee resulting from the use of the "monster"?

Chapter Questions for Study and Discussion

1. Is it possible for an information system to function with one or more of the five components missing? If so, which components could be omitted? If not, why not?
2. Does EDP eliminate the possibility of human error? If not, where is human error most likely to occur?
3. What is meant by "random access" and why is it a desirable feature of a management information system?
4. What is meant by the statement that failure to meet objectives is more often due to an improper design of the system rather than to the short-comings of the separate components of the system?

5. State what is meant by and give an example of each of the following abbreviations: ADP, EDP, and IDP.
6. When are the meanings of EDP and IDP synonymous?
7. How does EDP aid the manager in making decisions? Does this necessarily mean that the manager's decisions are easier to make?
8. What is meant by the statement that the major problems of installing an information system are people oriented rather than machine oriented?
9. Comment on the statement: Most companies experience a sharp reduction in the number of clerical personnel as the result of an EDP installation.

CHAPTER 8

Decision Making

John Anderson, a design engineer for Apex Valve Company, believes that he has a secure future with his present employer and expects to continue until his retirement when he hopes to spend more time in his home shop and perhaps develop some patentable ideas. John is 45 years old and has had 15 years of service with Apex. Although there is little chance of his being promoted to chief engineer, he is next in line for the job of chief of the design section, a promotion that would raise his annual salary from $10,000 to $12,000. He likes his present position and has turned down several job offers in defense industries that would have paid more money because, in his opinion, the positions offered were not permanent.

Recently John inherited Anderson's Clothing Store, a men's specialty shop formerly owned by his uncle. The store has a good downtown location, a parking lot next door, and no outstanding major debts. After reviewing his uncle's records, John believes that the store is as profitable as the average for that industry. For the past three years average sales volume has been $100,000; average value of inventory, $25,000; and a net profit of $3,500 a year before taxes. Currently a temporary manager is employed at $500 a month. Prior to his death, the uncle had drawn a salary of $6,500 a year, which is typical for stores of this size.

In some respects John would like to operate the store as manager; however, he is reluctant to do so as it would mean quitting his present position. He realizes that in order to increase the dollar volume of sales, it is necessary to increase inventory, a step that would necessitate expanding the present building. Expansion is possible because the uncle owned both the store and the parking lot, and the local bank has indicated that the present building can be mortgaged to finance the new construction. But as a matter of good business policy, the bank prefers that any additional inventory be handled on a cash basis. If John leaves Apex Valve Company to manage the store, he can withdraw approximately $7,500 from the retirement fund; the cash value of his life insurance and savings amounts to another $10,000.

Although John has made no attempt to sell the store, he believes that the building, the property including the parking lot, inventory, and goodwill are worth at least $75,000.

PROBLEMS

1. What decision do you recommend for Mr. Anderson?
2. What courses of action are available for Mr. Anderson to follow?
3. How does Mr. Anderson's personal value system affect the ultimate decision?
4. Develop a means-end analysis for your recommended solution.

Chapter 7, "Management Information Systems," concluded with Peter Drucker's observation that organizations are information and decision-making systems. We have examined in some detail the nature of information systems. Now it is necessary to study the decision-making phase of the information and decision-making cycle. In this chapter we analyze the decision-making process, examine quantitative aids to decision making, consider some of the behavioral aspects of the decision-making process, and conclude with some suggestions to enhance the creative aspects of decisions.

THE DECISION-MAKING PROCESS

Decision making is frequently defined as the selection of one course of action from two or more alternate courses of action. This definition has the advantage of brevity, is easy to remember, and focuses attention upon the essential element of decision making—making a choice. There are also disadvantages in this definition, for it does not emphasize the making of a decision as only one of several steps that occur in sequence as part of an intellectual process. Nor does it indicate that business decisions, if they are to be effective, must be executed or translated into a course of action. However, the definition is satisfactory provided we understand that making a decision is part of a process which includes the following four steps: Definition of the Problem, Analysis, Development of Alternate Solutions, and Selection of a Decision. A fifth step—although technically not a part of the decision-making process itself—must be included if management decisions are to be effective in meeting company objectives. That fifth step is Execution.[1, 2]

Definition of Problem

The intellectual process that culminates in making a decision is referred to as *problem solving* or *reasoning*. It is an activity undertaken by an individual to resolve tensions created by a situation that thwarts his normal course of activity. Problems are personal in their nature in that they thwart the activity of an individual. Herein lies an explanation of the difficulty frequently encountered by managers in securing employee participation in solving company problems—there is no problem for the employee unless the situation creates tensions which may be resolved through problem-solving activity. Employee suggestion systems are an attempt to elicit problem-solving activity through the creation of a problem—how can I get the money?—and offering a suggested means of attaining the goal—suggesting an improvement in company operations. Suggestion plans are successful only to the extent that they create within employees tensions that are capable of resolution as the result of problem-solving activity.

---

[1] Most present-day analyses of problem solving, or decision making as it is called in management literature, are based upon John Dewey's analysis of thinking which includes the following five steps: a felt difficulty, its location and definition, suggestion of possible solution, development by reasoning of the bearings of the suggestion, and further observation and experiment leading to its acceptance or rejection. These steps are discussed in detail in the following work: John Dewey, *How We Think* (Boston: D. C. Heath & Co., 1910), pp. 68-78.

[2] Peter Drucker, *The Practice of Management* (New York: Harper & Brothers, Publishers, 1954).

For a more recent discussion by Peter Drucker on the decision-making process the following is recommended: Peter Drucker, "The Effective Decision," *The Harvard Business Review,* Vol. XLV, No. 1 (January-February, 1967), pp. 92-98.

No amount of care and effort in the subsequent steps of analysis and development will yield a decision capable of reaching desired objectives unless the problem is properly defined. It is a common error in the diagnosis of problem situations to confuse obvious symptoms, usually those characteristics that attract attention, with the problem itself. Poor decisions are many times correct solutions to the wrong problem and are considered poor because they do not contribute to stated goals. We have seen in "The Parable of the Spindle," Case Problem 7-A, how an inadequate information system may result in poor human relations. Excessively high manufacturing costs may be attributable to too many people; yet an excess number of workers is a symptom, not a cause. The cause may be poor product design, poor scheduling, or excessive equipment breakdown. Likewise, unsatisfactory sales volume may be the result of factors such as incompetent salesmen, an excessively high sales price, an improper channel of distribution, or poor quality of product. It is not easy to differentiate between symptoms and problems. A good way of getting behind the symptom and to the problem itself is to ask *why*: Why are the people upset? Why are manufacturing costs too high? Why is sales volume too low? This approach usually involves listing all the possible causes and consumes considerable time and effort; nonetheless, it is better than solving the wrong problem.

Also, it is helpful to ask the following question: Would the solution to the problem as diagnosed provide an effective means to the desired end or goal? This question is stated diagrammatically below.

Problem ——→Solution = Means ——→End

When enlisting the help of others in solving a problem, it may be necessary to restate the problem in terms understandable to those asked to participate. A sales manager would be well advised to restate the problem of attaining a desired percentage of the market in terms that present a challenge to each salesman. This may be done by having the individual salesman define the problem in his territory and develop a plan that will result in increased sales volume from existing customers and the acquisition of new customers.

Analysis

When the problem has been satisfactorily defined and there is reasonable assurance that its satisfactory solution provides a means to a desired end, the next step is the analysis of available information. At first glance, it may seem that this step implies the gathering and analysis of facts not presently at hand, an assumption which is correct in most instances; however, there are at least two classes of problems that require no additional information for their correct solution. First, there are those problems that clearly fall within the scope of existing policies. One of the major purposes of a policy statement is to provide a predetermined course of action, in effect, a solution to a multitude of similar problems. A personnel director, when asked to decide whether or not an employee's request for early retirement should be granted, has a ready answer after the question is properly defined and it is determined that it falls within the province of the company's retirement policy. The second class of problems not requiring the acquisition of additional information consists of those problems that fall within the decision maker's range of experience. He may possess, as the result of prior experience and training, the factual information and conceptualizations necessary to resolve the question and make a decision. Man's ability to synthesize past experiences so that they form a cohesive network of information that can be used in solving current problems is one of the primary reasons for the emphasis placed upon past experience as a factor in the selection of managers.

For those situations that do not fall within the range of existing policies or within the decision maker's experience background, it is necessary to acquire additional information, a process of "getting the facts." One step that has been taken to assure proper information for analysis is the building of information systems such as the one used by Westinghouse (Case Problem 7-B). When information systems provide a timely flow of relevant information to management, they become information-decision-making systems. Such systems are of particular value in providing the information necessary for decisions concerning production schedules or optimum inventory levels, for they provide up-to-date and accurate information. Even so, there is need for judgment. Too much information may be gathered, with resultant masses of data, not relevant facts. Judgment is also required in determining when it is advisable to make a decision even though all necessary facts have not been acquired or analyzed.

Development of Alternate Solutions

Having defined the problem and analyzed the available information, the decision maker is now ready for the third step, the development of alternate courses of action. Logicians refer to this step as the formulation of hypotheses—tentative explanations or conclusions.

Alternate solutions come as the result of weighing the concepts derived from the analysis of data in the preceding step. Concepts are weighed and interpreted in the light of past experience; and continuing effort should be made to rearrange the information of the second step, analysis, so that new concepts emerge and, in turn, may be examined and evaluated. Both inductive and deductive reasoning processes are used, and the validity of the tentative conclusions may be tested against the rules of logic.[3] The development of alternatives is usually regarded as the central step of the decision-making process, for it is during this step that creative, or original, solutions to problems come into being. Suggestions for the encouragement of creative solutions to problems are discussed later in this chapter. Operations research techniques and other applications of the computer have been developed as special aids in the development of alternate courses of action. These, too, are discussed later in the chapter.

Selection of Decision

The selection of a decision is the process of making a choice between two or more alternatives. The number and quality of choices available are dependant upon the degree of productiveness and originality employed in the third, or developmental, stage. It is unusual for a manager to have only two alternatives from which he must make his selection; rather, his problem is that of selecting one from many. In addition to the choices that represent new courses of action, there is always one other alternative—to do nothing. Volkswagen's decision not to change body styles is in every sense of the word as much a decision as Detroit's annual selection of one body style, from among many, to be adopted for the coming year.

Making the correct choice is not easy. Seldom is there only one correct choice with all others classed as incorrect. Instead, business decisions are neither black nor white; for the most part they are grey. Part of the difficulty in making the final or correct decision stems from the element of risk. It is difficult to assess the probable success or failure of a projected plan since the environment in which business operates is continually changing. In addition to the element of change, incomplete and unavailable data often limit the number and quality of

---

[3] Robert W. Morell, *Managerial Decision-Making* (Milwaukee: The Bruce Publishing Company, 1960). The student is referred particularly to Chapters 4 through 9, which discuss in considerable detail the rules and application of logic to the solution of business problems.

concepts developed during the third stage of the decision-making process. Because of the difficulties encountered in selecting the best decision, the development of criteria for determining the worth of decisions is very important. The following three questions form a basis for judging decisions:

Does the decision contribute toward the attainment of stated objectives? Implied in this question is recognition that a course of action is but a means to an end, and if a proposed solution to the problem does not further the stated objectives, it should not be adopted.

Does the decision represent the maximum degree of economic effectiveness? The decision selected should represent the maximum utilization of all available resources; anything less than this would not contribute toward maximum economic effectiveness.

Is the decision capable of execution? Here we are asking whether or not it is possible to develop a plan to make the decision effective.

The use of the above questions to judge the worth of a decision is another application of the Concept of the Objective, the Concept of Economic Effectiveness, and the Concept of Planning. These concepts are also used as criteria in the formulation of policies, and they are useful in evaluating any projected course of action. The act of deciding does not stand for long by itself as a single act; it rapidly merges into a series of actions designed to implement the decision.

Execution

The fifth and final step of the decision-making process, execution, converts the selected decision into action. Unlike the problem solver who has completed his task when he has found the correct solution to a problem, the manager must follow through to make his choice effective. When measured in terms of contribution to company objectives, there is no difference between no decision at all and an ineffective decision that is not feasible. A decision has been made possible as the result of utilizing the flow of information from both within and without the firm; now the information-decision-making cycle must be completed with information flowing to those persons in the organization who will translate the decision into action. It must be recognized that the current decision is but one of a series and when translated into action, additional problems will arise that will demand solutions and subsequent decisions. The decision to build a new plant in Chicago provides an answer to two questions, whether or not a plant should be built and where it should be located; but it also opens the door to a flood of new questions related to the construction of the plant.

When communicating a decision, every effort must be made to use clear, concise terms understandable by those who will translate the decision into action. Perhaps it will be necessary to point out the logic of the decision and state the reasons for making it. The extent to which such persuasion, or selling, is necessary serves as a measure of the probable success of the decision, since it reveals the degree of participation on the part of those directly affected by the decision. Group participation in both decision making and creative thinking is discussed in the last section of this chapter.

Quantitative Aids in Decision Making

In our discussion of the second step in the decision-making process, analysis, we mentioned that policies may serve as an aid to decision making provided the problem under consideration falls within the scope of the existing policy. For this reason, policies have sometimes been called *standing plans,* and as such provide the means for making these decisions effective. However, policies and other standing plans are of assistance only in the solution of recurring problems. During World War II, certain mathematical techniques were developed to aid in the resolution of complex military problems and in recent years have been applied to aid managers in their decision making. A general term used to describe these rather sophisticated mathematical techniques is "operations research." [4] The following discussion defines operations research, reviews some of its major techniques and applications, and suggests limitations.

Definition of Operations Research

Operations research (OR), like automation, is a term that apparently means different things to different people. It is, above all else, an application of the scientific method to problem situations; however, the scientific method is not the distinguishing characteristic of OR. Frederick W. Taylor advocated the use of the scientific method as a fundamental approach to management problems, yet we do not consider him a forerunner of operations research. Nor is the decision

---

[4] The phrase, management science, is frequently used as a synonym for "operations research." Harvey M. Wagner, *Principles of Management Science; With Applications to Executive Decisions* (Englewood Cliff, N.J.: Prentice-Hall, Inc., 1970) p. 1.

maker who faithfully follows the five steps of the decision-making process, an application of the scientific method, using operations research techniques. In OR the scientific method is applied to the analysis of the operations of a system rather than to the solution of a specific problem.

The phrase, operations of a system, implies that the problems undertaken by OR are much broader than those susceptible to solution by other decision-making techniques. Examples of operating systems that have been analyzed by operations research are weapons systems, man-machine systems such as aircraft, and business organizations. Further, the research on the system being studied is directed toward an understanding of the functioning of the entire system and ultimate improvement of the degree of control over the operation of the system. The specific techniques of OR demand that the system be represented as a mathematical model; that the solution to the problem be obtained by solving the mathematical equations representing the system (i.e., the model); and in addition, that the obtained solution be tested and recommendations made for its application.

Operations research may be defined as: *(1) an application of the scientific method to (2) problems arising in the operations of a system which may be represented by means of a mathematical model and (3) the solving of these problems by resolving the equations representing the system.*[5]

The following examples are illustrative of applications of operations research to industrial problems.[6]

Locating Warehouses.

A company with a number of products made at three different locations was concerned about the items to be produced at each location and the points at which the items would be warehoused. Freight costs constituted a substantial part of the delivered cost of the material. Operations research showed that what appeared to be a complex and involved problem could be broken into a series of rather simple components. Adaptations of linear programming methods were used to find the warehousing schedule which would minimize freight costs. The study is now being extended to determine the best distribution of products among manufacturing plants and warehouse locations in order to minimize net delivered cost in relation to return on investment.

---

[5] C. West Churchman, Russell L. Ackoff, and E. Leonard Arnoff, *Introduction to Operations Research* (New York: John Wiley & Sons, Inc., 1957), p. 18.

[6] C. C. Herrmann and J. F. Magee, " 'Operations Research' for Management," *Harvard Business Review,* Vol. XXXI, No. 4 (July-August, 1953), p. 102. This article presents a complete discussion of the application of OR to management problems.

Allocating Advertising Budget.

A manufacturer of chemical products, with a wide and varied line, sought more rational or logical bases than the customary percentage of sales for distributing his limited advertising budget among products, some of which were growing, some stable, and others declining. An operations research study showed that advertising effectiveness was related to three simple characteristics, each of which could be estimated from existing sales data with satisfactory reliability: (a) the total market potential; (b) the rate of growth of sales; (c) the customer loss rate. A mathematical formulation of these three characteristics provided a rational basis for distributing advertising and promotional effort.

Determining Value of Missionary Sales Effort.

In a company making a line of light machines, the executive board questioned the amount of money spent for missionary salesmen calling on customers. Studies yielded explicit mathematical statements of (a) the relation between the number of accounts called on and the resulting sales volume and (b) the relation between sales costs and manufacturing and distribution costs. These were combined by the methods of differential calculus to set up simple tables for picking the level of promotion in each area which would maximize company net profits. The results showed that nearly a 50% increase in promotional activity was economically feasible and would yield substantial profits.

Setting Time Standards.

An industrial products manufacturer wanted to set time standards as a basis for costs and labor efficiency controls. The operations research group studied several complex operations; expressed the effect of the physical characteristics of products and equipment and the time required to produce a given amount of output in the form of mathematical equations; and then, without further extensive time study or special data collection, set up tables of production time standards according to product characteristics, equipment used, and worker efficiency, which could be applied to any or all of the production operations.

Setting Inventory Levels.

A company carrying an inventory of a large number of finished items had trouble maintaining sound and balanced stock levels. Despite careful attention and continued modification of reorder points in the light of experience, the stock of many individual items turned out to be either too high for sales or inadequate to meet demand. The problem was solved by a physical chemist who first collected data on the variables, such as size and frequency of order, length of production and delivery time, etc.; then set up an assumed system, which he tried out against extreme sales situations, continually changing its characteristics slightly until it met the necessary conditions—all on paper (a technique well known to physical scientists); and thus was able to determine a workable system without costs of installation and risk of possible failure.

Each of the above applications of operations research to industrial problems requires an analysis of the functioning of a system, the construction of a mathematical model, and a solution—obtained by solving the mathematical equations representing the system—which results in greater control over the operations of the system.

OR—Techniques and Applications

The following introduction to operation research techniques and applications indicates a few major applications of OR and touches briefly upon some of the underlying mathematical techniques.

Linear Programming—Allocation Problems. *Linear programming* techniques are most useful in those situations requiring an optimum allocation of resources. As the name implies, linear programming is concerned primarily in analyzing those relationships capable of being expressed mathematically as linear functions, and in most instances there are several such linear functions operating simultaneously.

One of the classic applications of linear programming is of assistance in determining the location of an additional plant within an existing complex of plants and warehouses. Assume that a company has existing plants in Milwaukee and Philadelphia and that the single product of these plants is being distributed to warehouses in Chicago, St. Louis, New York, and Atlanta. Further, preliminary studies have narrowed the choice of a possible new plant site to Memphis or Indianapolis. If optimum allocation of resources is defined as least cost, including both manufacturing cost and the cost of transporting the finished product from plant to warehouse, a partial statement of the problem is determining which location offers the lower cost. However, the introduction of a new plant into the existing system of plants and warehouses necessitates revision of the allocation of the output of present plants to warehouses; therefore, the problem stated in its entirety is determining which of the two proposed systems offers the lower cost.

In addition to providing solutions to location problems, linear programming also aids in determining the most profitable product mix, whether to make or buy, and economic inventory levels. *Quadratic programming*, like linear programming, is an algebraic technique developed for analyzing those systems whose functions are nonlinear in nature.

Queuing Theory—Intermittent Servicing Problems. *Queuing theory,* sometimes called *waiting-line theory,* is of value in determining the correct balance of factors necessary for the most efficient handling of intermittent service. There are costs involved in having a waiting line, whether it be customers waiting for service in a restaurant or machines waiting to be repaired and returned to production. Time lost in waiting, particularly the downtime of machines needing repair, is also a factor of cost; and if the line is one of impatient customers, sales volume is reduced. In order to eliminate the line or decrease its length, thereby reducing waiting-line costs, it is necessary to increase servicing capacity. In turn, there is an increase in the cost of physical facilities and labor necessary to perform the desired service. The restaurant has to enlarge its seating capacity and hire more waitresses, cooks, and bus boys to reduce its line of waiting customers; the industrial plant needs more maintenance men and a larger stock of repair parts to minimize production losses resulting from idle machines waiting for repair.

Another important factor in determining the optimum size of servicing facilities is time of arrival. Occasionally, actual observations may be made and a tally kept of the exact number of units requiring service during each hour of the workday. In many instances, such observations cannot be carried on for a long enough period of time to produce a stable pattern of work load. The *Monte Carlo* technique is used to produce a sample of random arrivals for those situations where actual observation is impracticable or impossible. Essentially, the Monte Carlo technique provides a large sample of random numbers that may be generated by a computer. From the large Monte Carlo sample, rather precise determinations may be made in regard to the expected servicing load for each hour of the day. Queuing theory is of value in reaching decisions concerning the optimum balance between the cost of service and the cost of having a waiting line; and when combined with the Monte Carlo technique, projections may be made for those situations where the work load varies in a random fashion.

Game Theory—Simulation of System Operation. "War games" have been used for many years as a means of training personnel and testing plans and equipment under field conditions. The process of obtaining the essential qualities of reality without reality itself is known as *simulation.* "Management games" have been developed to provide training in decision making by providing laboratory situations that simulate as nearly as possible real-life operations. The development of management games is incredibly complex, particularly if it is a game involving a situation in which there is a competitor aware of changing conditions—an increase in price or volume of goods produced—who responds with counter moves. At the moment, the application of game theory to business problems has been used primarily for training purposes rather than for solving competitive problems because of the complexities in analyzing and programming the many variables as they exist in real life.

Another example of simulation is the analysis of an actual system through the use of a simulated system programmed into a computer. United Air Lines has simulated the operations of aircraft at New York's LaGuardia Field by running a program of a "station model" on an IBM 704 computer. The elements included in this program are time of day, week, and year; weather conditions; maintenance required; type and length of repair job; availability of spare aircraft; delays in landing or take-off; absenteeism of personnel; and number of maintenance personnel. By varying any one or a combination of factors, the functioning of the system may be observed under changed operating conditions, and subsequent analysis reveals operating efficiencies and cost.[7] Though game theory and simulation are still in the developmental stage, these techniques offer a means of training managers and analyzing the operations of a system under changing conditions.

Probability Theory—Determining Degree of Risk. Statistical techniques in their simplest form provide a descriptive statement of the characteristics of a group. For example, a wage survey may show that the average wage for tool and die makers in an area is $5.00 an hour. Further analysis, an application of *probability theory,* results in a measure of the reliability or accuracy of the obtained average. A probable error of ±5 cents an hour is interpreted to mean that the chances are 50-50 that the true average wage of all tool and die makers in the area falls between $4.95 and $5.05 an hour. A probable error of ±3

---

[7] Elizabeth Marting (ed.), *Top Management Decision Simulation* (New York: American Management Association, 1957), pp. 50-51. In addition to United Air Line's "station model," a simulated distribution and inventory control model used by Imperial Oil Limited of Canada is presented. There is also a description of the development of the AMA game.

cents an hour indicates that the chances are 50-50 that the true average wage lies between $4.97 and $5.03. Thus, the smaller the probable error, the greater the degree of confidence that can be placed in the average. Measures of probable error are significant when dealing with a sample, or a part, of an entire population by not only showing the reliability of the obtained data but also by revealing whether or not additional time and money should be spent in securing more information.

Predictions concerning the probable outcome of future events are inferences based upon careful statistical analysis of existing data. Life expectancy tables used by insurance companies in setting their rates are statements of the probable death rate expected for each age group of the entire population during the present year. Statistical quality control is another application of the theory of probability. The volume of goods produced in high-speed manufacturing is so great that the cost of inspecting each item produced would be prohibitive. But a detailed inspection of a small sample, say one of every thousand, and periodic checking of the production equipment make it possible for a quality control supervisor to predict with high accuracy the number of defective products that may be expected in every thousand produced.

Limitations of OR

Operations research is a direct aid to the decision-making process through its contribution to the steps of analysis and development, and, indirectly, OR forces a clearer statement of the problem. It does not, however, make the final choice nor translate the decision into action. The effectiveness of OR is limited to the analysis and comparison of relationships that may be expressed quantitatively and transformed into a mathematical model. Even so, there are times when the subjective judgment of the decision maker must override the recommendations of OR. Operations research may set the economic level of raw material inventory for an auto manufacturer, but in the face of an impending steel strike, the judgment of the individual executive should control. As yet, OR techniques are not adaptable to the prediction of customer reactions to a given style or color, nor do they clarify alternatives in human relations problems.

BEHAVIORAL ASPECTS OF DECISION MAKING

The preceding discussion of the sequence of the decision-making process and the brief review of quantitative aids describe the decision-making process as an exercise in logic—purely cognitive, or intellectual, in nature. However, there are other behavioral factors significant to the decision-making process. One group of factors is the personal characteristics of the decision maker himself. Also, most business decisions are rarely made by a single individual; instead, they are the result of the interaction between individuals who function as members of one or more groups. Consequently, the behavioral aspects of decision making may be conveniently classed as those factors attributable to the characteristics of the individual decision maker and those that are the result of group behavior.

Individual Factors

One of the fundamental observations of psychology is that individual differences exist in virtually every measurable human characteristic. Decision making is no exception. These differences are manifested in the way in which different persons define the problem, the extent and breadth of the search for and the analysis of relevant data, and the number and kinds of alternative solutions developed. Also, differences between individuals determine the characteristics of the solution, or decision, ultimately chosen and influence the degree of vigor and decisiveness shown in its execution. Though there are many behavioral characteristics influencing the decision-making process, the following three seem most significant. First, there is the way in which the person perceives the problem; second, there is the matter of ability and willingness to process information in the search for and the analysis of data, a prerequisite for the development of alternate solutions; and third, there is the personal value system of the decision maker, a factor of great significance in determining the final choice or decision.

Perception of Problem. *Perception* is a psychological process utilizing both incoming data from the sense organs and information learned from past experience so that meaning is attached to incoming data. Perception may be visualized as being midway on a continuum with direct sensory awareness (hot, cold, pain) at one extreme and thinking (not requiring external stimulation) at the other extreme.[8]

The process of "making sense" out of what we see, hear, feel, taste, or smell obviously depends to a great degree on the nature of the external

---

[8] Floyd L. Ruch, *Psychology and Life* (7th ed.; Glenview, Ill.: Scott, Foresman and Company, 1967). See pp. 300-324 for a complete discussion of the phenomenon of perception. The above description of perception appears on p. 300.

stimuli; however, of equal importance, if not more so for our purposes, is the past experience of the person receiving the stimulation. When the same objective data are given to persons of differing backgrounds there is always the likelihood that each will perceive a different problem. For example, Case Problem 7-A (pp. 206-210) tells of a restaurant owner who observes that his waitresses break down in tears, that the cooks walk off the job, and that his managers become so upset that they summarily dismiss employees. His statement of the symptoms of the problem was verified by each of three consultants—a sociologist, a psychologist, and an anthropologist. Each observed and reported the objective data describing the behavior of the waitresses, cooks, and managers as reported by the restaurant owner. Yet each perceived a different problem; for one it was a sociological problem, for another it was psychological in nature, and for the third the problem was anthropological in nature. Given the same data each consultant perceived the problem in the light of his own professional background.

In addition to influencing how one perceives the problem, the first step of the decision-making process—the perceiver's experience—operates in a similar manner in subsequent steps of the decision-making process. Of significance is the manner in which alternative solutions are perceived. The same background factors that influence the perception of one aspect of a problem as being more significant than another may also influence the perception of one solution as being more desirable than another. If perception of one solution as being more desirable than another occurs early in the development of alternatives, there is the likelihood that other alternatives will not be fully developed; therefore the quality of the final solution to the problem will be strongly influenced.

Ability to Process Information. In addition to differences in how problems are perceived, there are also wide individual differences in the ability to process and store information. The effect of these differences is most evident in the second and third steps of the decision-making process—the search for and analysis of data and the development of alternative solutions. Some decision makers make decisions with relatively little data and the development of few alternatives because they are incapable of handling large quantities of data and wish to avoid the discomfort and confusion occasioned when confronted with new and unfamiliar information. The inability to handle information may result in an extreme stance either to the right or to the left of broad social issues as indicated in the following quotation from Boulding.

There is also a considerable relationship between the capacity of a decision maker to handle large quantities of information and his ability to widen his agenda. People who have narrow agendas, the bigots, the Birchers, the Marxists, the Nationalists, and the schizophrenics, are by and large people whose information processing capacities are highly limited. They retreat into narrow agendas because they cannot bear the information overload which would seem to result from the wide ones.[9]

The breadth of a person's agenda is frequently characterized as either open-mindedness or closed-mindedness. If one is open-minded there is a flexibility in approach and a willingness to consider a wide range of data and alternative solutions, but the closed-minded person tends to consider only those data and those solutions supporting his preconceived position. Thus the process of search is undertaken only to verify an *a priori* position. There are many characteristics of open-mindedness; however, the three suggested by Rokeach seem most useful in understanding managerial decision making.[10] First, there is ability to remember information, including new data, relevant to the solution of the problem. Second, there is a willingness to consider and explore various alternate solutions; and third, the breadth of one's past experience is an index of willingness to accept new ideas. The broader one's range of past experience the greater is the likelihood that new ideas can and will be accepted since breadth of experience is a measure of past encounters with new ideas.

In addition to the ability to process and store information and the willingness to accept new ideas (open-mindedness) there are also differences in the characteristic way in which information is handled. For some their *forte* is the gathering and analysis of data, while others excel in the synthesis and interpretation of information. These differences may have a marked effect upon the quality and type of decision eventually developed. The ability to synthesize, in contrast to data gathering and analysis, tends to improve the quality of the final decision and enhances the probability of creative decisions. Thus the ability to handle information, the willingness to accept new information, and the proclivity to either analyze or synthesize are all behavioral characteristics of the individual decision maker that profoundly influence the outcome of the decision-making process.

---

[9] Kenneth E. Boulding, "The Ethics of Rational Decision," *Management Review,* Vol. 55, No. 2 (February, 1966), p. 167.

[10] M. Rokeach, *The Open and Closed Mind* (New York: Basic Books, Inc., Publishers, 1960), pp. 392-393.

Personal Value System. Since a personal value system is a series of concepts with each concept having a degree of personal worth and meaning, the individual values of the decision maker influence the decision-making process.[11] Values are significant determinants, not only in the selection of the final choice from among several alternates, but also as determinants of the statement of the problem. The ultimate decision for Mr. Anderson (Case Problem 8-A, problem 3) is based on his personal value system.

In Chapter 4 (pp. 119-122) benefit-cost analysis, a technique used in those situations where anticipated benefits or costs are either difficult or impossible to quantify, is discussed. Frequently cited business objectives such as innovation, manager performance and development, worker performance and attitudes, and public responsibility are examples of hoped for benefits not readily amenable to quantification. When alternate solutions are developed with each intended to increase benefits in any one of the above mentioned areas, the final choice is often based upon the personal values of the decision maker. If, for example, alternatives are proposed for a manager development program, the decision maker's personal values concerning the relative merits of each of several types of educational activities may form the basis for decision.

Personal values are important in initiating the course of the decision-making process. Problems frequently arise as a result of the general question, "What must be done to achieve a stated objective?" Objectives are often the organizational counterparts of personal objectives. Personal objectives, by their very nature, are a reflection of what is important to a person. The individual's desire for achievement, growth, excellence, or originality indicates that these attributes are significant to the person holding such values. A manager has the opportunity of fulfilling his personal objectives through the instrumentality of the organization. Thus the organizational problems that emerge and the subsequent decisions to be made are shadows cast by the personal values and objectives of the manager.

Group Factors

In formal organizations it is rare for an individual to complete the entire decision-making process without functioning as a member of a group. Even in those instances where an individual is designated as

---

[11] See Chapter 3, pp. 78-84 for a discussion of the value system of American managers.

being responsible for solving a specific problem, the execution of the decision requires the participation of other persons. The observation that more than one person is required for the execution of a decision is significant because it implies that there is a need for commitment on the part of others. The participation of groups in the earlier steps in the decision-making process introduces factors that may either enhance or inhibit the decision-making process. The following are observations concerning the major advantages and disadvantages inherent in group participation in decision making.[12]

Advantages of Groups. One of the greatest advantages of group decision making is that potentially the group has a wider range of knowledge than any single member of the group since each individual brings to the group a different experience background. The extended range of knowledge should be of benefit in the definition of the problem and in the development of a broader search for alternatives, and should result in a more critical analysis of the alternatives developed. Further, participation in decision making usually results in a better understanding of the decision reached. When commitment on the part of the group is needed in the execution of the decision, the fact of having been participants increases the probability of a resultant increased commitment by each individual member of the group.

Disadvantages of Groups. The major limiting factor in determining the effectiveness of group participation in decision making arises as a result of social pressures.[13] In formal organizations there is the superior-subordinate relationship that may result in no real participation on the part of the subordinate; instead, there may be mere acquiescence. Or the subordinate, in order to enhance his position with his superior, may elect not to participate in developing the decision but rather to go along with the wishes of his superior. Even though hierarchical pressures are not normally present in informal groups, there are nonetheless definite

---

[12] Norman R. F. Maier, *Problem-Solving and Creativity in Individuals and Groups* (Belmont, California: Brooks-Cole Publishing Company, 1970), pp. 431-444. Study Number 37 was originally published in the *Psychological Review,* 1967, Vol. 74, pp. 239-249. This volume brings together the results of 15 years of study on individual and group problem solving conducted in Professor Maier's laboratory. Most of the studies have been published in other sources. The summary presented above is based upon study 37.

[13] Chris Argyris, "Interpersonal Barriers to Decision Making," *Harvard Business Review,* Vol. 44, No. 2 (March-April, 1966), pp. 84-97. This study reports the findings of an analysis of the decision-making process in six companies. It analyzes the behavior of 165 top executives in these companies during the decision-making process.

social pressures. Sometimes the desire for acceptance by the group prevents a significant contribution to the decision-making process, thus having the same effect as hierarchical pressures. Questions are also raised concerning the quality of group decisions. Often a proposed solution is accepted without thorough evaluation in respect to quality simply because there is a concensus favoring that solution. In addition, there is the potential of individual domination of a group with a resultant diminution of group activity. Further, on occasion members of groups become engrossed with winning the argument rather than seeking the highest quality decision. Also, groups generally require more time, measured in total man hours, to reach a decision than that required by an individual.

Evaluation of Group Decision Making. There are two aspects of group decision making that may be considered advantageous under certain circumstances; yet those same characteristics may be liabilities under other conditions. First, there is a tendency for those holding extreme positions to move toward the norm of the groups when that norm represents a middle ground. Second, there is a tendency for a group to select a decision representing a higher degree of risk, defining greater risk as increased uncertainty in respect to the probability of achieving expected outcomes. The tendency for extremes to approach the mean is desirable if an extreme position interferes with the execution of the decision or does not contribute significantly to any step of the decision-making process; however, if the extreme position represents the highest quality decision, such movement toward the center automatically impares the quality of the final decision. Likewise, the degree of riskiness of the decision varies in its desirability. When there is an increased payoff associated with increased risk, the greater risk may be desirable; but if the payoff appears to be no greater, the increased risk may not be desirable.

Although the potential benefits of group participation in decision making is great, such potential is seldom achieved in actual practice.[14] Membership in a group does not insure participation; hence, the knowledge that each might contribute to the decision-making process is not always tapped. In addition, the social pressures that develop, even in informal groups, seriously impair the quality of the decision-making process. The answer to the effectiveness of group decision making is dependent upon the quality of leadership. The leader of the group must

---

[14] Chris Argyris, *ibid.*

be skilled in creating an environment that encourages each member to make his full contribution. The leader must help individuals in recognizing, and in placing in proper perspective, conflicting individual and group goals, and he must guide the discussion so that the highest quality decision, consistent with the stated objectives, is reached. In effect, the leader must function as the central nervous system so that each member of the group makes his maximum contribution to the group effort.[15]

CREATIVITY IN DECISION MAKING

In spite of the saying, "There is nothing new under the sun," we all recognize the results of creative thinking. Creativity may range in content and quality from a child's finger painting to Einstein's theory of relativity. Whatever the line of endeavor, creativeness is measured by the end result—a new idea, a new product, a new way of doing something, or a new application of existing ideas and products—something new and different.

Creativity is a much sought after talent in the business world, for there is a continual need for a quantity of fresh and original solutions to existing problems. The nature of business problems continually changes, and when a competitor discovers a different and better way of solving these problems, present solutions become obsolete. The environment of any given industry is essentially the same for all companies within that industry. Therefore, in order to gain a competitive edge, it is necessary to develop a better way of doing those everyday things which must be done, or develop something new to do—manufacture a new product. The constantly changing environment, resulting in new and different problems, and the continual pressure of competition among companies form the basis for the demand for creative decision making.[16]

In considering creativity in decision making we will first relate the steps of creative thinking to those of the decision-making process and include suggestions to improve creativity. Second, we will discuss group participation as a means of stimulating creative thinking.

---

[15] Maier, *op. cit.* See Maier's discussion in study number 37 in which he develops the analogy of the leader of a group and the central nervous system in the starfish.

[16] For a different point of view the student is referred to the following article: Theodore Levitt, "Creativity Is Not Enough," *Harvard Business Review,* Vol. XLI, No. 3 (May-June, 1963), pp. 72-83.

Steps in the Creative Process

Creative thinking is closely related to the decision-making process; indeed, there is a distinct advantage in considering creative thinking as a special case in the decision-making process. Though slightly different terminology is used to describe the creative process, the number and sequence of steps are the same as those of decision making; however, each process emphasizes a different aspect of the same type of thought processes. Decision making emphasizes the choice, the act of making the decision and its subsequent execution so that there is a commitment of resources and ensuing action. The creative process, on the other hand, emphasizes the uniqueness of the solution, its newness, and to a certain extent, the step immediately preceding the solution, Illumination, thereby stressing the highly individual and personal nature of creativity. When decision making and creative thinking are considered as variations of the same underlying thought processes, we increase the opportunity for truly creative decisions. The following tabular arrangement of the steps of these two processes demonstrates their similarities: [17]

Creative Thinking	*Decision Making*
1. Personal need	1. Definition of problem
2. Preparation	2. Analysis
3. Incubation	3. Development of alternate solutions
4. Illumination	4. Selection of decision
5. Verification	5. Execution

Personal Need. The adjective, "personal," stresses the individual aspect of the creative thinking process; and, as in the case in decision making, there must be a motivating force to initiate the creative thought process. The motivation of the poet, the artist, or the essayist may be an obscure inner urge, an urge similar to the motivation of the hobbyist who spends countless hours at his bench creating furniture, or the gardener who raises orchids under adverse conditions. The hobbyist and the gardener are mentioned to illustrate that creativity is latent within all of us; the problem, from an industrial point of view, is one of

---

[17] Graham Wallis, *The Art of Thought* (New York: Harcourt, Brace, and Company, Inc., 1926). Mr. Wallis identifies the four steps of the creative process as Preparation, Incubation, Illumination, and Verification. The first step, Personal need, has been added since creative thinking is the resolution of a problem.

As indicated in the following more recent reference concerning the steps normally included in the creative thinking process, the number ranges from four to seven. Andrew Crosby, *Creative Thinking as a Process*, (London: Travistock Publications, 1968), pp. 52-63.

stimulating the innate urge to be creative and channeling creativity into areas of value to the organization. The question arises concerning the ability of an individual to be creative on request, and fortunately the answer is in the affirmative. Advertising agencies produce their creative work on assignment, industrial research departments have been very productive, and many of the outstanding works of literature and art have been produced to meet the demands of externally imposed goals. The decision maker does not seek a solution until confronted with a problem; nor does creative thinking appear until the individual is motivated, either by the need of self-expression or as the result of an externally imposed problem situation.

Preparation. Preparation and the last step, Verification, may properly be called the *work* stages of the creative process. Contrary to popular belief, creative ideas do not come as a "bolt out of the blue." Instead they emerge from an intensive period of preparation. Einstein's theory was developed by Einstein the physicist, not by a musician or a novelist. The Salk vaccine was developed by a physician, not by an architect; and though Coleridge's *Kubla Khan* is said to have appeared to him in a dream, it was preceded by 25 years of study and travel. Preparation is not only a period during which one becomes saturated with information, it is also a period of trying to perceive a new and meaningful relationship so that an original solution to the problem may be obtained. The originality of the solution depends on the number of avenues explored and the extent to which possible interrelationships and solutions have been examined. Taking notes on materials read and keeping a file of clippings prove helpful in providing source materials for constant review so that all possible combinations may be developed. Perhaps emphasis upon the need for creativity is due to the fact that most decisions are the result of only cursory preparation and examination, with the result that only a few commonplace solutions are available. Aside from technical libraries for engineering and research groups, few companies maintain libraries so that an executive may saturate himself with the literature of marketing, production control, or quality control prior to undertaking a major decision in one of these fields. If only obvious bits of information are analyzed superficially, it is difficult to visualize a truly creative solution.

Incubation. The intellectual processes that occur during the third step of the creative process, Incubation, mark the difference between a good decision and an original or creative decision. The difference is inferred to a certain extent by the descriptive terms used to describe the third step of the processes of creative thinking and decision making. The word, "development," as applied to the decision-making process, implies the logical sequences of either inductive or deductive thought processes and emphasizes the perception of logical relationships. Seemingly there is an "either or" quality to the choices that must be made, a concept substantiated by the mathematical approach of OR, a process of finding the one best solution and eliminating all other alternatives by measuring each against an objective criterion such as cost. The logical aspects of evaluation provide an accurate and adequate description of the development stage when measurable criteria are available; but when considering an original or creative solution, there are no preconceived objective criteria against which the solution may be tested. In fact, there is no solution in the sense of making one choice from among several apparent choices. Instead, it is a process of finding a new solution, a new arrangement and interpretation of information acquired during the period of preparation. True, it is possible for an original solution to be found immediately or as the result of a relatively brief analysis of information, but this is rare. There is a definite need for the concept of incubation, a period of mulling the problem over, sometimes consciously and sometimes totally unaware of the thinking process. It is during this period of incubation when the creative person may be described as absent-minded; note that the adjective *absent* is used, not *empty*-minded. His mind is absent from the mundane affairs of the world, but present and working on the problem. Some writers ascribe an important role to the "unconscious mind" during the period of incubation. Whatever the nature of the process, it is clear that the period of incubation is a period of gestation and may result in a fully developed creation, or illumination, that solves the problem.

When should one set a problem aside and allow it to incubate? After intensive periods of study and reflection, the phenomenon of *perseveration* often appears. Perseveration is easily recognizable because thoughts seem to go around in circles, with no new ideas or interpretations occurring, an indication of fatigue. This is the time when the subject should be dropped momentarily and attention turned to something else, thus permitting incubation to take place. However, it is wise to set a deadline; and if the solution does not appear within a matter of days, review the problem once again and reexamine the notes and other materials acquired during preparation.

Illumination. One of the earliest and most famous illuminations is attributed to Archimedes. We have all heard the story that Archimedes, a Greek mathematician of the third century B.C., shouted, "Eureka" (I've found it), while sitting in his bath, upon discovering that his body displaced its own volume in water. But how many of us remember the problem that had been occupying his mind during the period of incubation? Archimedes had been assigned a problem by King Hiero of Syracuse who had received a new crown and had reason to believe that not all the gold delivered to the goldsmith had been used in the crown. But how does one determine the volume of an object with the irregular shape of a crown? Archimedes' illumination solves the problem; if gold is adulterated by a lighter metal, the bulk of the crown must be increased to equal the original weight of the gold, and as a result displaces a greater amount of water than an equivalent weight in gold.[18] The story of Archimedes illustrates the suddenness that characterizes creative solutions to problems. There is a period of insight, and the answer appears in a flash. The story also supports two statements made earlier. First, the solution came to one well prepared; the king went to Archimedes, the mathematician and scientist, not to a leading poet of the time; second, truly original and creative solutions are possible when working on an assigned project. When solutions appear, it is suggested that they be jotted down immediately so that every detail may be remembered.

Verification. For most creative thinking, verification represents the second of the "hard-work" stages, the first being Preparation. It is rare that the final solution, even though appearing suddenly and apparently complete, is sufficiently polished to be adopted without further change and modification. For the writer, verification may be a period of vacillation between one mode of expression and another, and changes made may seem to be the result of trial-and-error behavior not unlike that of the laboratory rat seeking its way through a maze. For the inventor, verification is a period of refinement and elimination of minor defects that may mar an otherwise ideal invention. This last stage of creative thinking transforms the insight of illumination into finished form, whether it be an artistic effort, a new product, or a better way of performing everyday tasks. Charles Babbage's Difference Engine is conceptually the same as the computer, but it remained only an idea, for he was unable to transform it into an operative machine.

Verification implies a willingness to experiment, to modify, and to improve. A good antidote for pride of authorship, which may cause resistance to suggested changes, is to assume the role of the devil's

---

[18] The goldsmith had alloyed the gold with baser metals and was executed.

advocate by trying to anticipate and answer potential criticism. We should also recognize that ideas, like mechanical devices, evolve over a period of time and that the solution adopted today may be improved in years to come. How many times have you said to yourself, "Why, I had that idea two years ago"? The difference between the idea and the implemented creative thought is verification, a period of change, improvement, and sometimes compromise to make the idea acceptable. In the last analysis, creativity is judged by quality and quantity of completed work; without verification creativity, in effect, does not exist.

Group Participation in Creative Thinking

Thus far, our discussion presents creative thinking as an individual undertaking; certainly illumination is experienced only by the creator of an idea. However, man is a social animal and one of the characteristics of his gregariousness is the influence exerted on him by a group and the effect that he, in turn, has upon other members of the group. Each of us is acquainted with someone who in private conversation is rather quiet and reserved, yet when present at a social gathering blossoms forth and becomes the life of the party. The capacity to be stimulated by a group, and at the same time contribute to shaping the group's behavior is called *social facilitation* and forms the basis for successful group patricipation in creative thinking.[19]

Several techniques have been developed as group aids to creativity and their success is dependent upon the following two basic psychological phenomena:

1. Free association of ideas is a process of producing ideas in rapid succession with a minimum of inhibiting or restraining action. The original stimulus word is presented by the group leader and immediately the free associations thus produced function as additional stimuli for the group.
2. Social facilitation, as defined above, increases the productivity of each individual and his increased productivity further stimulates other members of the group.

A summary of the rules and suggestions for conducting two different types of group sessions in creativity is presented in Figure 8-1.[20]

---

[19] Robert J. Zajonc, "Social Facilitation," *Science,* Vol. 149, No. 3680 (July, 1965), pp. 269-74. In this paper Zajonc reviews the conditions under which the social facilitation occurs.

[20] Charles S. Whiting, "Operational Techniques of Creative Thinking," *Advanced Management* (October, 1955), pp. 24-30. In addition to the Osborn and Gordon techniques, Mr. Whiting discusses several forced-relationship methods.

Osborn Brainstorming
Rules:
1. Judicial thinking or evaluation is ruled out.
2. Free wheeling is welcomed.
3. Quantity is wanted.
4. Combinations and improvements are sought.

Suggestions for the Osborn technique:
1. Length: 40 minutes to one hour, sessions of 10 to 15 minutes can be effective if time is short.
2. Do not reveal the problem before the session. An information sheet or suggested reference material on a selected subject should be used if prior knowledge of a general field is needed.
3. Problem should be clearly stated and not too broad.
4. Use a small conference table which allows people to communicate with each other easily.
5. If a product is being discussed, samples may be useful as a point of reference.

Gordon Technique
Rules:
1. Only the group leader knows the problem.
2. Free association is used.
3. Subject for discussion must be carefully chosen.

Suggestions for the Gordon technique:
1. Length of session: two to three hours are necessary.
2. Group leader must be exceptionally gifted and thoroughly trained in the use of the technique.

General Suggestions That Apply to Both Techniques
1. Selection of personnel: a group from diverse backgrounds helps. Try to get a balance of highly active and quiet members.
2. Mixed groups of men and women are often more effective, especially for consumer problems.
3. Although physical atmosphere is not too important, a relaxed pleasant atmosphere is desirable.
4. Group size: groups of from four to twelve can be effective. We recommend six to nine.
5. Newcomers may be introduced without disturbing the group, but they must be properly briefed in the theory of creative thinking and the use of the particular technique.
6. A secretary or recording machine should be used to record the ideas produced. Otherwise they may not be remembered later. Gordon always uses a blackboard so that ideas can be visualized.
7. Hold sessions in the morning if people are going to continue to work on the same problem after the session has ended; otherwise hold them late in the afternoon. (The excitement of a session continues for several hours after it is completed, and can affect an employee's routine tasks.)
8. Usually it is advisable not to have people from widely differing ranks within the organization in the same session.

Source: Charles S. Whiting, "Operational Techniques of Creative Thinking," *Advanced Management* (October, 1955), p. 28.

Figure 8-1
SUMMARY OF RULES AND SUGGESTIONS FOR GROUP SESSIONS

Each one of these types, Osborn's brainstorming and the Gordon technique, is discussed below.

Brainstorming. Brainstorming was developed by Alex F. Osborn as an aid in producing ideas for an advertising agency; however, since that time the technique has been applied in many other situations where there is a need for the production of a large number of new solutions in answer to a specific problem. In order to develop the desired quantity of ideas, an atmosphere conducive to the free flow of ideas is created. The group leader informs the participating members of the desired objective and the quantity of new ideas, and cautions them against being critical of their ideas. He encourages "free wheeling," and usually all criticism of ideas is barred. Occasionally checklists and suggestions for developing new ideas are distributed to the group. One such list, developed by Osborn, is as follows: [21]

1. Put to other uses	6. Substitute
2. Adapt	7. Rearrange
3. Modify	8. Reverse
4. Magnify	9. Combine
5. Minify	

One of the major criticisms of brainstorming is that, by its very nature, it tends to produce rather superficial ideas since the problem is worded in specific terms and thus limits the development of broad free association. Also, the technique may be very time-consuming; for in addition to the man-hours spent in the session itself, time is required to evaluate the ideas produced. Nonetheless, it is a valuable group aid to encourage creative thinking, particularly in those situations where a specific answer is desired such as a name for a new product or an advertising slogan. Above all else, it tends to create an atmosphere within the organization that encourages individual creative thinking long after the session has ended.

Gordon Technique. William J. J. Gordon developed a technique to meet the needs of Arthur D. Little, Inc., a consulting group specializing in industrial research and other technical problems. The participants of a Gordon session, unlike those of a brainstorming group, are not aware of the specific problem under consideration. For example, if the desired result is an improved method of dehydrating food, the

---

[21] Alex F. Osborn, *Applied Imagination* (New York: Charles Scribner's Sons, 1953), p. 284.

key word selected might be preservation, a stimulus which would elicit suggestions for the preservation of many items other than food. Also, it must be remembered that the Gordon technique was developed for the highly trained staff of the Arthur D. Little organization. Proponents of Gordon's approach to conducting group sessions in creativity claim that the technique results in a higher quality of ideas since the generic key word does not tend to limit ideas, nor is there the likelihood of a member developing pride of authorship because he has no information concerning the application of his idea. In addition, many of the ideas produced may be of value in later projects even if they are not applicable to current problems. If the leader is highly skilled and the participants have both depth and breadth of knowledge in the field in question, the Gordon method is an excellent means of generating new ideas.

Continuing Conditions for Creativity

The real lesson to be learned from brainstorming and the Gordon technique is that ordinary people under proper circumstances may create new ideas. The free association device employed by both techniques is applicable to individual problem-solving situations; the only factor absent is the stimulation of a group. Companies can contribute a great deal to continuing creativity by developing an atmosphere that encourages new ideas. Organizations that discourage new ideas with the comment, "We tried that 20 years ago and it didn't work," are in effect telling their employees not to think. In the next major part of this book, "The Organizing Function," some of the benefits derived from group participation in creative thinking and other forms of decision making are discussed.[22]

Case Problem 8-B offers an interesting opportunity for a group to use either the Osborn or the Gordon technique in finding a creative solution to a business problem.[23]

---

[22] For a discussion of the organizational conditions that enhance creativity, the following article is recommended. Larry Cummings, "Organizational Climate for Creativity," *Academy of Management Journal,* Vol. VIII, No. 3 (September, 1965), pp. 220-232.

[23] Theodore Levitt, "M-R Snake Dance," *Harvard Business Review,* Vol. XXXVIII, No. 6 (November-December, 1960), pp. 76-84. Mr. Levitt presents an interesting analysis of the sameness that appears in much advertising. "M-R Snake Dance" provides a good background for Case Problem 8-B.

CASE PROBLEM 8-B

ANOTHER MENTHOLATED CIGARETTE

For many years, Dordon, Dobson, and Duke, Inc., a large and well-known advertising agency, has retained the Sea Captain Tobacco account. Sea Captain is manufactured and distributed by the Carolina Tobacco Company, and its slogan, "The Captain's Choice," is well known to pipe smokers throughout the world. In addition to its pipe tobacco, Carolina manufactures and distributes an established brand of snuff. As part of a planned expansion program, now two years old, the company is ready to introduce a mentholated cigarette. In a recent conference with Mr. Dordon, senior partner and founder of the advertising agency, Mr. Walter Davis, the president of the Company, made the following remarks:

"It seems to me that when people buy cigarettes, or for that matter any other item at a drugstore counter, they are buying on impulse until they firmly decide upon a particular brand. This is one of the reasons why we want to enter the mentholated cigarette market; as yet, with the exception of Kools, all the brands are relatively new and none are as firmly established as, say, Camels are in the nonmentholated field.

"I can't make any special claims for our cigarette; it is no better, nor is it any worse than any of the others. We have no secret process in making it, and we can hardly claim that it is good for anyone's health. We do think that people will enjoy it as much as they do any other cigarette of the same type.

"Yesterday when I stopped at a drugstore counter, I was overwhelmed by the number of mentholated cigarettes on display. All the packages seem to be green or blue, with ice or waterfalls, and with beautiful young girls on the point-of-sale display smiling as though they were refugees from a toothpaste advertisement. I don't think we have the money to buck that kind of advertising; anyway, we don't want to be just one more green-packaged waterfall. Frankly, one of the reasons for the success of our Sea Captain is that it is packaged in an octagonal can, while every other can on the market is square or round. People can recognize our product for what it is. Also, as you know, our snuff is packaged in a triangular shaped tin which makes it distinctive. And, thanks to you people, our copy for these products has been different."

PROBLEMS
1. Working within the framework suggested by Mr. Davis, develop a name, a package design, and the initial advertising copy for Carolina Tobacco Company's mentholated cigarette.
2. Do you agree with Mr. Davis' desire to develop a new and different approach for advertising mentholated cigarettes? (The article mentioned in footnote 23 will be of help in formulating your answer to this question.)
3. How much originality is evident in the advertising of competitive products within the same price range; e.g., Cadillac, Lincoln, and Imperial?

Chapter Questions for Study and Discussion

Commits resources.

1. Why is the fifth step, Execution, included as part of the decision-making process even though it may be argued that execution is not a part of decision making? —*Decision maker acts — Planner only plans.*
2. In defining a problem, how does one distinguish between the symptoms resulting from the problem and the problem itself?
3. Give an example of a correct decision to an improperly defined problem.
4. Give several examples of the need for restating problems in terms that are understandable to those who are asked to help in solving the problem.
5. What is the relationship between established policies and decision making? Give an example of a recurrent business decision that could be eliminated by establishing a policy.
6. Why is experience valuable in making decisions? What are some of the dangers in relying too heavily on experience in decision making?
7. What is meant by the term operations research? What is the relationship between OR and the scientific method?
8. Discuss the following statement: Most modern applications of OR would be impossible without the aid of the computer.
9. Which of the three personal characteristics of the decision maker—perceptual characteristics, ability to process information, personal value systems—do you consider to be most important? Why? Which of these three characteristics is most closely related to intelligence?
10. What are the similarities and differences that exist between the creative-thinking process and the decision-making process? Give the arguments for and against the thesis that creative thinking is a special case of the decision-making process.
11. Give an instance from your own experience when you have said, "I thought of that." Was your failure to complete the creative process the result of not verifying your solution or the lack of adequate preparation?

12. In Figure 8-1 a summary of the rules and suggestions for the Osborn and Gordon group sessions is presented. Note that Osborn calls for sessions of 40 minutes to one hour in length while the Gordon technique requires a session length of two to three hours. Also, Osborn requires a clear statement of the problem, but Gordon requires that only the group leader know the problem. Are these differences contradictory in nature, or do they merely serve to limit the usefulness of each technique to a certain class of problem? Under what circumstances would you recommend Osborn's brainstorming? When would you recommend the Gordon technique?

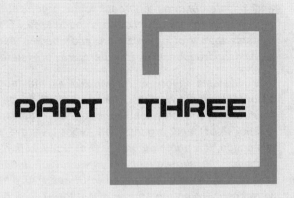

PART THREE

The Organizing Function

Underlying organization theory are assumptions, often implicit, concerning the structure and functions of organizations. One set of assumptions concerning work and the people performing that work is known as the work-centered, or classical, theory of organization. Another approach, with different assumptions concerning work and people, is people centered and sometimes called neo-classical theory. The third approach to understanding organizations is a system theory. The concepts of the work-centered and people-centered approaches to organization theory and resultant organizational characteristics are compared. Chapter 9 concludes with a systems theory of organization, and specific parameters, all appearing with significant frequency in the literature, are stated.

Systems theory is recognized as the modern approach to the study of organizations; however, there is much to be learned from the past. For this reason the classical concepts of organization structure, organization relationships, and organization processes are examined carefully. Departmentation, the prime determinant of organization structure, and recommendations for the subsequent arrangement of departments into effective spans of management are discussed in Chapter 10. There are two widely divergent views concerning the source of authority. One holds that authority is derived from an institutional, or societal, source; the other states that authority is derived from acceptance by subordinates. Both views concerning the source of authority and the authority relationships between line and staff personnel are discussed. The analysis of the processes of transferring authority within organizations, delegation and decentralization, also considers the behavioral aspects of delegation and offers guides to determine the optimum degree of decentralization.

Although organizations are composed of individuals, much of the work accomplished is the result of group effort. The strengths and weaknesses of committees are evaluated, and the keystone committee of formal organizations, the board of directors, is given special attention.

Since social organizations are not static, it is necessary to prepare for the inevitable change that is certain to occur. One form of change may be rather sudden in nature and stems from an organization analysis setting forth specific recommendations for change; the other form of change is evolutionary in nature and is the result of planned organization development. The tools for organization analysis and the steps necessary to establish an effective organization development program appear in Chapter 14.

CHAPTER 9

Organization Theory

"Good morning, gentlemen." Robert Billings, vice-president for manufacturing of Centroid Corporation, paused and briefly surveyed the group of five management trainees reporting to the manufacturing division for a two-month training period. "I note here that your previous assignment was in the personnel department," he continued as he shuffled a sheaf of personnel folders. "Now, let me tell you how personnel really works in the manufacturing division of this company."

"First, each of you men will be assigned to a general foreman who is in charge of one of the major areas of the shop. You will report directly to the general foreman. If, for any reason, you want to see me you must first go to the general foreman and ask his permission; he will, in turn, send you to the plant manager, and if he can't answer your question, arrangements will then be made for you to see me on Saturday mornings or after 5 o'clock on weekdays.

"This is a large plant, about 1,500 employees, and we have a problem with absenteeism. We also have a provision for sick pay in our union contract. When a man calls in and says that he is sick, I want you to get in touch with the industrial relations department immediately and have them send one of the industrial nurses out to the man's home.

"The third point I want to make with you fellows is in regard to shop rules. We're known around here as

CASE PROBLEM
9-A

WHAT KIND OF
ORGANIZATION?

'tough but fair' and I want it kept that way. If you see any workman breaking one of the rules, give him a verbal warning if it is the first time—and be sure and make a written record of the fact that you gave him a verbal warning. If it is his second offense, issue a written reprimand; and if it is the third time, suspend him for five working days. The fourth offense usually means discharge. Turn these cases over to your general foreman.

"Grievances are next. We have a lot of them, and we go by the book in the way we handle them. According to our labor contract a foreman has 24 hours before he has to answer a grievance. I expect you to take the full 24 hours. The plant manager has three days in which to give his answer, and I have one week after that before writing my answer. We intend to take all of the time allotted to us in handling grievances; that way it discourages the filing of petty complaints.

"Fourth, you are going to have to watch quality. Quality is very important to us, so the first thing you should do every morning is find out whether or not the quality control inspector is in your area. If any questions arise during the day, turn the problem over to him. He knows how the machines should be set and he will tell the operators what to do.

"We have a suggestion system here in the plant. If any of your men come up with a suggestion, have him put it in writing on the proper forms. Sign these forms, then forward them to the industrial engineering department. They will check them out and write a letter to the worker telling him whether or not his suggestion is accepted. Usually it takes from 60 to 90 days to get an answer from them. Incidentally, foremen do not participate in the suggestion program; it's part of your job to have new ideas so you don't get paid extra for them. One or two foremen, who are no longer with us, gave their ideas to men working for them and then split the award. Don't try it.

"Number 6 on my list of things to cover with you concerns job openings. Keep your eyes open for good, hard workers; these are the men we want to promote. We notify the man chosen for promotion when an opening occurs; and if the union thinks that we have not followed seniority, they file a grievance. We don't allow people to transfer from one department to another, so if a man starts in the shipping department, where the rates aren't too high, that's his tough luck. In this company you live and die in the department in which you start.

"Finally, I want to say that we have openings on our manufacturing team for two or three of you fellows. Those of you who demonstrate true leadership ability and originality will be kept on permanently. Good luck!"

PROBLEMS

1. Does the manufacturing division of Centroid Corporation subscribe to the tenets of Theory X, Theory Y, or Theory Z?
2. Which assumptions regarding the nature of work and/or the nature of human beings underlie each of the seven points made by Mr. Billings?
3. How would you, as a management trainee, demonstrate originality and leadership in this situation?
4. How can an hourly production worker develop personally in his job at Centroid Corporation?

It is a truism that organizations are a major force in determining the course of our lives; yet few of us recognize the extent to which organizations shape our behavior. We are born in hospitals and immediately the process of adapting to formal organizations begins; for the hospital, an organization, imposes a schedule of eating, sleeping, and bathing. There is a brief respite from formal organizations during the next five years; then at the age of six, when school begins, we become members of a succession of formal organizations—grade and high school, college, and the places where we work. Retirement from active employment does not mean retirement from all organizations, for usually memberships in social clubs, civic organizations, and churches continue.

The word, organization, has two distinct meanings, one of which refers to *an* organization as an *entity* in itself, and the other one which refers to organization as a *process*. Some of the more common organizations, as entities, are mentioned above—schools, places of employment (including industrial organizations, governmental agencies, or private institutions), social clubs, civic service organizations, and churches. There are three characteristics common to each of the organizations above: first, each is composed of people; second, each has a distinct purpose or goal to achieve, thus offering a reason for its existence; and third, each has a degree of formality in the structure of the organization that results in a definition and limitation of the behavior of its members. *Thus, as an entity, an organization is a group of people bound together in a formal relationship to achieve organizational goals.*

The second meaning of organization is that it is a *process of structuring, or arranging, the parts of the organization;* a meaning exemplified by the phrase, "what this place needs is more organization." The question arises, what is being organized? There are three possible answers to this question; first, *work* is being organized; second, *people* are being organized; and third, *systems* are being organized. The answer you choose as being most descriptive of the process of organization is dependent upon certain fundamental assumptions in regard to the nature of work and the behavior of human beings in a work situation. These assumptions, known as theories of organization, are important for they determine the structure of an organization and the methods used in administering the organization. The theoretical framework leading to the conclusion that organization is a process of organizing *work* is known as *Theory X*; those assumptions concluding in the belief that *people* are the central theme of organization form *Theory Y*; and an approach that emphasizes the organization of a *system* is designated as *Theory Z.*

THEORY X—A WORK-CENTERED APPROACH

Underlying every management action is a set of implicit assumptions concerning the nature of work and the nature of human beings. Theory X is a group of assumptions that results in what is referred to as the traditional, or classical, approach to organization.[1] In discussing Theory X, let us first examine the basic assumptions concerning work and the nature of human beings in a work situation.

Assumptions of Theory X

Theory X is the traditional, or classical, approach to organization and rests upon four implicit assumptions. The first of these

---

[1] Douglas McGregor, *The Human Side of Enterprise* (New York: McGraw-Hill Book Company, 1960), pp. viii, 246. Professor McGregor summarizes the assumptions of traditional management under the heading, Theory X, and presents those assumptions which result in a human relations approach to management under the heading of Theory Y. The theoretical assumptions of both theories are presented in Part I of the book; Part II is a discussion of Theory Y in practice; and Part III is a discussion of the development of management talent.

assumptions is concerned with the nature of work, and the remaining three describe the behavior of human beings in a work situation.

1. *Work, if not downright distasteful, is an onerous chore to be performed in order to survive.*
2. *The average human being has an inherent dislike of work and will avoid it if he can.*
3. *Because of this human characteristic of dislike of work, most people must be coerced, controlled, directed, threatened with punishment, to get them to put forth adequate effort toward the achievement of organizational objectives.*
4. *The average human being prefers to be directed, wishes to avoid responsibility, has relatively little ambition, wants security above all.*[2]

Briefly, Theory X states that there is no intrinsic satisfaction in work, that humans avoid it as much as possible, that positive direction is needed to achieve organizational goals, and that workers possess little ambition or originality. Let us assume that Theory X is an accurate statement of conditions as they exist today. How do these assumptions affect the structure and processes of an organization?

Effect on Organization

Adherence to Theory X results in a *work-centered* organization. As noted earlier, one of the characteristics of an organization is that it has a goal—a *raison d'être*. It is normal to be concerned about the work of an organization, and when work is distasteful, something to be avoided like the plague, firm steps must be taken to assure its accomplishment. An external force is needed to accomplish organizational objectives under the conditions prescribed in Theory X. This force is dependent upon the traditional concept of authority; indeed, it is so dependent upon authority that organizations which subscribe to Theory X are frequently referred to as *authoritarian* organizations. Once the foundation of an organization has been laid upon the cornerstone of authority, the location of the decision-making process is determined, the organizational structure acquires certain characteristics, and the roles of the supervisor and the individual member of the organization are sharply defined.

---

[2] *Ibid.*, pp. 33-34. Assumptions 2, 3, and 4 are quoted directly from McGregor. Assumption 1 has been added as an explicit statement of the nature of the work to which humans are reacting. For a good treatment of work theory, see Dale Yoder, *Personnel Management and Industrial Relations* (5th ed.; Englewood Cliffs, N. J.: Prentice-Hall, Inc., 1962), Chap. 5, "Theories in Management: Work Theory," pp. 56-77.

Authority. Authority has been succinctly defined as *the right to command and the power to exact obedience,* a definition that raises two questions: (1) the source of the *right* and (2) the method of *power.* One source of authority, used by the early European monarchies, is expressed by the phrase, the divine right of kings. A corresponding point of view applied to the management of industrial enterprises regards authority as emanating from the right to own property and the attendant obligation to manage that property. The power of the monarchist in enforcing obedience is absolute, because he can exact the supreme penalty, death, if it is deemed necessary. In the industrial situation the supreme penalty for disobedience is discharge, a penalty that prohibits an employee from fulfilling his economic needs. It is interesting to note that many arbitrators, when writing decisions concerning the discharge of an employee, equate the death penalty to discharge by an employer. We will see when we discuss Theory Y that there is another concept of authority, But Theory X rests upon an assumption of complete authority as the motivating force directing the course of the organization.

Location of Decision Making. The analogy of a political monarchy and a highly authoritarian industrial organization continues as an effective means of describing the location of the decision-making process. In the monarchy, decision making is highly centralized and located at the apex of the organization, the king, since it is the king who has the divine right to command. For the authoritarian industrial organization, the nominal head of the organization is the locus of the decision-making process; again this is a logical location when the right to manage is derived from ownership. Centralized decision making requires a certain form of organizational structure if the decisions are to be carried out effectively.

Organization Structure. When authority to make decisions is centralized at the top of the organization and its primary purpose is the accomplishment of work, a structure must be designed that permits the ready exercise of authority at all levels of the organization, and maximum effectiveness in the accomplishment of work.

Figure 9-1 is a model showing the structure of the traditional work-centered, or authoritarian, organization. Note that authority to manage flows from the owners through the board of directors to the president who is appointed by the board. Reporting to the president are several vice-presidents, each of whom is in charge of a specific phase of the work of the organization. Figure 9-1 is an exploded diagram of

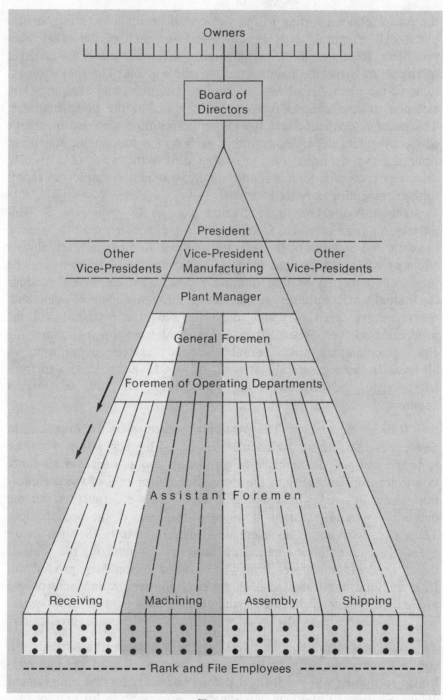

Figure 9-1

PYRAMIDAL STRUCTURE OF TRADITIONAL ORGANIZATION

the organization reporting to the vice-president, manufacturing; similar pyramidal structures could be developed for each of the other vice-presidents. Reporting to the manufacturing vice-president is the manager in charge of a specific manufacturing unit, a plant. The major operations of the plant—receiving, machining, assembly, and shipping—are assigned to four general foremen who report to the plant manager. The general foremen direct the efforts of foremen who are in charge of the operating departments within each of the four major functions. Four assistant foremen, each of whom directs the work of a specific area, report to each foreman; and, finally, production employees report to their respective assistant foreman.

Figure 9-1 refers to production workers as *rank and file* employees, a phrase borrowed from the military expression used to describe the rows and columns of the infantry platoon. Another military phrase, *chain of command,* is used to describe the means of transmitting the president's authority so that ultimately production employees produce the desired work. Authority is transmitted through a chain of command, the successive levels of management, between the president and the production worker. When Figure 9-1 is read from top to bottom, the chain of command, which permits the ready exercise of authority at all levels in the organization, is easily followed; and when viewed from left to right, the division of the organization into units of work is apparent.

Role of Supervisor. The pyramidal structure of the organization determines the role, or function, assumed by the supervisor. First, he is an integral part of the chain of command, and as such it is his function to transmit authority to the succeeding lower level of the organization. Decision making is a minor, if not nonexistent, function, for the authority to make decisions is vested in the head of the organization. Thus, the supervisor is an agent of a higher authority. Second, as an agent of higher authority, he has the function of optimizing the goals of the organization; therefore, he may be expected to emphasize production. If, in addition, that foreman is an agent of an organization built on the premise that work is distasteful and that persons tend to avoid work, is it any wonder that all his efforts are oriented toward production?

Role of Individual. The role of the individual worker is that of a cog in a machine. He is to be directed, coerced if need be, and controlled so that he will put forth the effort necessary for the achievement of organizational objectives. His function is to perform his present job;

there is little encouragement for self-development or advancement. The phrase, rank and file, is used to describe the production worker (Figure 9-1); perhaps an even more descriptive appellation is "hired hand," a term that implies that only the hands, not the complete man, are being hired. However described, the production worker in a Theory X organization is regarded as an individual unit reporting only to his direct supervisor. He is not considered a member of a group, or for that matter a member of several groups; instead, he stands isolated reporting to and influenced only by his supervisor.

The discussion above that outlines the organizational effects implicit in the assumptions of Theory X may seem exaggerated, but before concluding that the Theory X organization has been overdrawn, read Case Problem 9-A again. Surely, you have heard the thoughts expressed by Robert Billings when talking to the management trainees. The propositions of Theory X and the effectiveness of the authoritarian, work-centered organizations are evaluated following the presentation of Theory Y.

THEORY Y—A PEOPLE-CENTERED APPROACH

The assumptions of Theory Y concern the nature of human behavior based upon an interpretation of modern behavioral sciences. The same format used in the presentation of Theory X is used in presenting Theory Y; first, the assumptions of the theory are stated and, second, the consequent effects of these assumptions upon the organization are reviewed.

Assumptions of Theory Y

The assumptions of Theory Y are the antitheses of those of Theory X. The six assumptions of Theory Y are as follows:

1. *The expenditure of physical and mental effort in work is as normal as play or rest.* The average human being does not inherently dislike work. Depending upon controllable conditions, work may be a source of satisfaction (and will be voluntarily performed) or a source of punishment (and will be avoided if possible).

2. *External control and the threat of punishment are not the only means for bringing about effort toward organizational objectives. Man will exercise self-direction and self-control in the service of objectives to which he is committed.*

3. *Commitment to objectives is a function of the rewards associated with their achievement.* The most significant of such rewards, e.g., the

satisfaction of ego and self-actualization needs, can be direct products of effort directed toward organizational objectives.

4. *The average human learns, under proper conditions, not only to accept but to seek responsibility.* Avoidance of responsibility, lack of ambition, and emphasis on security are general consequences of experience, not inherent human characteristics.

5. *The capacity to exercise a relatively high degree of imagination, ingenuity, and creativity in the solution of organizational problems is widely, not narrowly, distributed in the population.*

6. *Under the conditions of modern industrial life, the intellectual potentialities of the average human being are only partially utilized.*[3]

Effect on Organization

Adherence to Theory X results in work-centered, authoritative organizations. Theory Y is an approach to organizational problems that emphasizes human relations and results in an organization characterized as *participative.* The two forms of organization, authoritative and participative, are the extreme points of a continuum. Between these poles are many gradations and shades of organizational behavior. One writer distinguishes the following steps: (1) exploitive authoritative, (2) benevolent authoritative, (3) consultative, and (4) participative group.[4] Thus, when discussing the effect of the propositions of Theory Y on organizational structure and processes, it is well to remember that we are dealing with the other end of the continuum in order to present in clear, sharp lines the differences existing between the two approaches.

Authority. Authority, as presented in Theory X, is the right to command and the power to enforce obedience. However, there is more to authority than right and power as illustrated by the following brief story:

An agent for the Textile Workers Union of America likes to tell the story of the occasion when a new manager appeared in the mill where he was working. The manager came into the weave room the day he arrived. He walked directly over to the agent and said, "Are you Belloc?" The agent acknowledged that he was. The manager said, "I am the new manager here. When I manage a mill, I run it. Do you

---

[3] *Ibid.*, pp. 47-48.

[4] Rensis Likert, *New Patterns of Management* (New York: McGraw-Hill Book Company, 1961), Chap. 14, "A Comparative View of Organization," pp. 222-236. This book is recommended as a summary of research in organizational behavior and leadership.

understand?" The agent nodded, and then waved his hand. The workers, intently watching this encounter, shut down every loom in the room immediately. The agent turned to the manager and said, "All right, go ahead and run it." [5]

Unquestionably the manager has the right to run a plant, and it is possible, under certain circumstances, for him to exercise his power and discharge all workers for engaging in an unauthorized work stoppage. Then he can start anew with a different group of workers, but this seems the hard way to manage a plant. Theory Y presents man as a rational being who is willing to work; in fact, he must work if he is to satisfy deep-seated psychological needs (propositions 1 and 3). Also, he has intelligence and is capable of making his own decisions. Among the decisions that man makes is that of deciding *which* leadership he will accept. The above incident does not portray a situation in which there is no authority; on the contrary, there was a great deal of authority—in the hands of the agent for the union. The workers in the mill had decided to accept one source of authority and reject another source. Thus, *acceptance* of authority, rather than right of authority, is one of the major differences between Theory Y and Theory X.

If authority based upon the concept of the right to command is displaced by authority which must be accepted to be effective, what happens to power? Power, too, is displaced. Look at proposition 2 of Theory Y, which states that "man will exercise self-direction and self-control in the service of objectives to which he is committed." One tool available to management to replace power in gaining an employee's commitment to organizational objectives is *persuasion*; another means is to afford an opportunity for *participation* in setting objectives.

Location of Decision Making. Setting objectives is one form of decision making and, according to Theory X, is retained by the nominal head of the organization. Proposition 5 of Theory Y states that "the capacity to exercise a relatively high degree of imagination, ingenuity, and creativity in the solution of organizational problems is widely, not narrowly, distributed in the population." Under these circumstances it is no longer necessary to retain decision making in the hands of a few. As a result, decision making in the Theory Y organization is widespread and diffuse, and it may occur at any level of the organization. Herein lies the meaning of participation; it is participation in decision making, including the determination of objectives.

[5] McGregor, *op. cit.,* p. 23.

Organization Structure. Figure 9-1 shows the pyramidal structure of the typical traditional organization with successive layers of supervision and the development of work functions for each supervisor. The relationships between superior and subordinate at any level of the organization appear in the usual organization chart as shown below.

Figure 9-2 emphasizes the work-centered aspects of the organization. Each subordinate is in charge of a specific function. It is an organization constructed primarily for the downward flow of authority in order to accomplish work. Communications between superior and subordinates are illustrated in Figure 9-3.

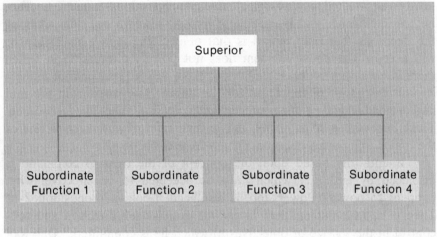

Figure 9-2
**THE TYPICAL RELATIONSHIP BETWEEN SUPERIOR
AND SUBORDINATES**

Figure 9-3 implies that interpersonal face-to-face relationships occur only between a superior and each subordinate in succession. The individual is the basic unit of the organization, and at best there can be no more than two-way communication between superior and subordinate. Earlier in this chapter an organization was defined as a *group* of people bound together in a formal relationship to achieve organizational goals. Theory Y emphasizes that organization has to do with groups and that when an individual accepts organizational goals, he does so as a member of a group. Thus, the group, not the individual, becomes the basic unit of organization. The reasons for recognizing the group as the basic unit are found in proposition 3 of Theory Y. Since the degree of commitment to organizational objectives is a function of the rewards derived from satisfying ego and self-actualization needs, which include participation in and recognition by a group, it is logical that

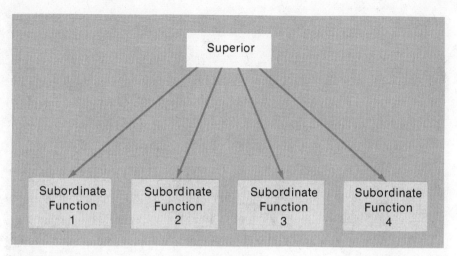

Figure 9-3
INTERPERSONAL RELATIONSHIPS IN THEORY X ORGANIZATION

superior and subordinates be considered a functional group. The large triangle of Figure 9-4 on page 278, enclosing superior and subordinates, is one way of representing the group as the primary organizational unit. Figure 9-4 also illustrates the free communication of ideas between every member of the group.

Role of Supervisor. Under the conditions of Theory X, the supervisor, a vital link in the chain of command, is an agent of higher authority. As such, it is his role to optimize the goals of the organization by directing the efforts of the individuals who report to him. But Theory Y replaces authority with the concept of acceptance and replaces power with persuasion and participation. Also, the supervisor is no longer dealing with individuals; he is now working with a group and in addition he is a member of that group. Thus, he has an *intragroup* function of leading his own group. At the same time he is a member of a supervisory group which means that he has an *intergroup* function to perform —coordinating the efforts of the two groups to which he belongs. Likert refers to this coordinative function as the "linking pin" function.[6] Note the arrows in the heavily shaded areas of Figure 9-5; these are the linking pins which denote that the supervisor has an intergroup and an intragroup coordinative function.

Role of Individual. Theory X regards the individual as an isolated worker whose function is that of a cog in a machine. His responsibility

---
[6] Likert, *op. cit.*, pp. 113-115.

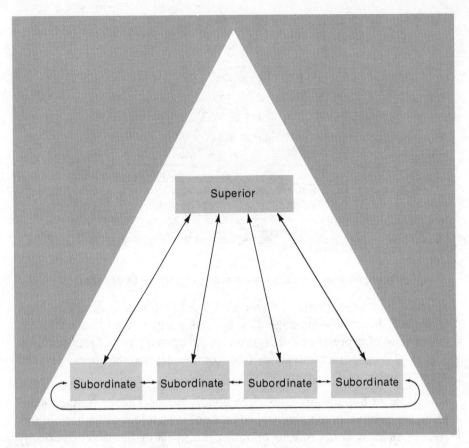

Figure 9-4
SUPERIOR-SUBORDINATE FUNCTIONING AS A GROUP

is limited to quality and quantity of production, control of his work is ever present and from external sources, and there is little opportunity or need for individual growth and development. The assumptions of Theory Y portray an intelligent, willing person functioning as an integral member of a group and contributing to the success of that group; thus, the need arises for maximizing the contribution of each member of the group by encouraging individual growth and development. External control and coercion are replaced by self-control and motivation derived from satisfying ego and self-actualization needs. The individual is creative and should participate in determining the objectives of his group, for it is through the act of participation that the goals of the organization and the goals of the individual become congruent. It must be remembered that although Theory Y encourages individual

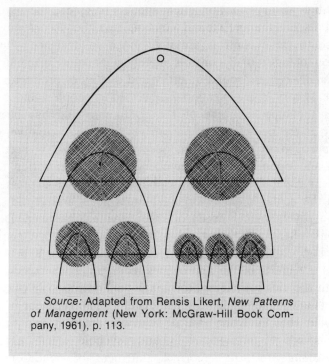

Source: Adapted from Rensis Likert, *New Patterns of Management* (New York: McGraw-Hill Book Company, 1961), p. 113.

Figure 9-5

THE "LINKING PIN" FUNCTION

growth and development, the employee is not an isolated individual; rather, he is a participating member of a group and the group is the smallest functioning unit of the organization.

Evaluation of Theories X and Y

Before presenting a systems approach to organization theory, Theory Z, a summary statement of the positions of Theory X and Theory Y and an evaluation of the two theories are in order. One such summary asserts that Theory X describes "organizations without people," while Theory Y describes "people without organizations." [7]

Describing a Theory X organization as an organization without people is admittedly an overstatement. Organizations using the Theory X approach also have been termed work-centered, traditional, classical, and authoritative. Such characterizations place these organizations at one extreme of a continuum of theoretical approaches to organization

---

[7] W. G. Bennis, "Leadership Theory and Administrative Behavior," *Administrative Science Quarterly,* Vol. IV (December, 1959), pp. 259-301.

theory. Such an organization often appears to ignore the psychological needs of its members. External controls and the accompanying overt resistance to these controls are very much in evidence. Further, the imposition of additional controls merely aggravates original problems which usually center around quantity and quality of production.

The Theory Y organization—described as people without organizations—is the other extreme of the continuum and has been termed variously as the neo-classical, human relations, participative, or democratic approach to organization. Seemingly, all that is needed is the freedom and opportunity for members of the organization to express their latent capabilities. Such an opportunity for self-expression would result in the achievement of organizational goals and at the same time fulfill the psychological needs of the individual member. Despite the limitations inherent in the extreme stance of each theory, acquaintance with the implicit assumptions of Theory X and Theory Y is of value for it defines the limits of the approaches to organization theory.

Both theories suffer from too much generalization in that sweeping statements are made concerning work and human behavior in a manner that implies that all work and all behavior are thus and so. A study of the findings of both sociology and psychology tells us that such generalizations are not a correct statement of conditions as they actually exist. There are marked variations in the demands placed upon persons as the result of work, and what is considered as pleasant work by one individual is boredom and drudgery for another. Likewise, the behavioral characteristics suggested by each theory represent the extremes of the distribution of personality traits in the general population. Few people consistently demonstrate the characteristics postulated by either theory.

A second criticism that applies equally to each theory is that neither Theory X nor Theory Y is consistently in accord with research findings. The "organization without people" description of a Theory X organization is all too familiar to students of management, but not all Theory X organizations have such problems. Yet for those that do, the prescriptions of Theory Y—creation of jobs with intrinsic satisfaction, a democratic form of supervision, and participation in the decision-making process—do not consistently cure the ills of the Theory X organization.[8]

---

[8] Job satisfaction and its relationship to productivity are discussed in Chapter 18, patterns of leadership are presented in Chapter 16, and supervisory practices are evaluated in Chapter 19.

THEORY Z—A SYSTEMS APPROACH

Fortunately there is an approach to organization theory holding promise that eventually the effects of organizational changes and the most effective form of organization for a given situation can be predicted. It is an approach that views the problems of organization as one of organizing a system. The systems concept is first introduced in Chapter 1 as an approach to the study of the management process, and in Chapter 6 (pp. 201-202, Figure 6-3) the major business functions are discussed as a servo system. The concept is presented again in Chapter 7 in connection with information systems and expanded in Chapter 8 into information-decision-making systems. We know that a cybernetic system is a recirculating type of process and is capable of a degree of corrective action, either as the result of internal changes within the system or in response to external environmental changes. A system is usually made up of one or more subsystems, and the capabilities of the entire system depend on the capabilities of each subsystem; in turn, any change in the function or capacity of the larger system requires corresponding changes in the subsystems. Inputs into the total system may originate from outside the system or from the internal subsystems; the same is true of outputs—they may be placed outside the system or fed back into any one of the subsystems.

Parameters of Theory Z

One of the main problems in developing a systems approach of organization theory is determining the parameters of the system; what are the factors (component parts either of the larger system or of the subsystems) that make up the total system? March and Simon in their book, *Organizations,* consider 206 variables as parameters of organization.[9] Many of the variables presented by March and Simon are new and as yet have not been tested by research; in addition, it is almost impossible to comprehend 206 variables and all the possible interrelationships that might arise. Their work stresses the belief that organizational effectiveness depends on recognizing and adapting to many variable and interdependent situational factors, and that what is considered effective organization for one situation may be woefully inadequate for another.

---

[9] James G. March and Herbert A. Simon, *Organizations* (New York: John Wiley & Sons, Inc., 1958), pp. xi, 262. *Organizations* is primarily a systems approach to the study of organizations. The list of 206 variables is contained in the appendix, pp. 249-253. The book is recommended to the advanced student interested in organization theory.

At the other end of the spectrum, Theory X and Theory Y utilize only two factors—work and the nature of people—as the parameters of organizations. A middle ground suggests the following six interacting, situational variables as factors that determine the appropriateness of any given organizational structure or process: (1) size of organization, (2) degree of interaction, (3) personality of members, (4) congruence of goals, (5) level of decision making, and (6) state of the system.[10, 11]

Size of Organization. As size (defined as number of people) increases, organization structure becomes more formal and complex, with the result that the appropriate processes of motivating employees toward the achievement of organizational goals become more formal and directive—rather than informal and participative—in nature.[12]

---

[10] Perhaps the best method of developing the parameters of organization theory would be to use multivariate analysis as a technique for determining the dimensions of organizations. The following studies are suggestive of this approach:

William B. Eddy, Byron R. Boyles, and Carl F. Front, "A Multivariate Description of Organization Process," *Academy of Management Journal,* Vol. XI, No. 1 (March, 1968), pp. 49-61. This study is a multiple factor analysis of 24 performance measures obtained from a firm's records. One group of variables is drawn from monthly financial statements; another group is taken from information concerning the firm's labor force; some reflect the utilization of labor and its costs; and the last group contains ratios pertaining to productivity.

Stanley E. Seashore and Ephraim Yuchtman, "Factorial Analysis of Organizational Performance," *Administrative Science Quarterly,* Vol. 12, No. 3 (December, 1967), pp. 377-395. In this paper the annual performance data of 75 insurance sales agencies over an 11-year period are subjected to multiple factor analysis methods.

D. S. Pugh, D. J. Hickson, C. R. Hinings, and C. Turner, "Dimensions of Organization Structure," *Administrative Science Quarterly,* Vol. 13, No. 1 (June, 1968), pp. 65-105. Measures of the dimensions of organization structure for 52 organizations in England are analyzed by the principle-component method of analysis. The dimensions of organization structure considered are specialization, standardization, formalization, centralization, and configuration.

[11] Raymond A. Katzell, "Contrasting Systems of Work Organization," *American Psychologist* (Washington, D. C.: American Psychological Association, February, 1962), Vol. XVII, pp. 102-108. In this paper, Professor Katzell's presidential address to the Division of Industrial Psychology, American Psychological Association, five situational parameters are presented. They are: size, degree of interaction and interdependence of organization members, personality of organization members, the degree of congruence or disparity between the goals of the organization and that of its employees, and who in the organization has the necessary ability and motivation to take action that will further its objectives. Professor Katzell has suggested the name, Theory Alpha and Omega, for the theoretical approach based upon these variable constructs; however, the designation, Theory Z, is used since it is consistent with the alphabetical names of the two theories presented earlier in the chapter. Several of Professor Katzell's factors are rephrased and a sixth, state of the system, is added by the writer.

[12] The following studies indicate the significance of size as a dimension of organization theory:

Geoffrey K. Ingham, *Size of Industrial Organization and Worker Behaviour* (Cambridge: Cambridge University Press, 1970), p. 170.

Pugh, Hickson, Hinings, and Turner, *op. cit.*

Henry Tosi and Henry Patt, "Administrative Ratios and Organizational Size," *Academy of Management Journal,* Vol. X, No. 2 (June, 1967), pp. 161-168.

(*Continued*)

Degree of Interaction. As the need for interaction between members of an organization increases in order to accomplish the prescribed work, the organization structure should permit a free flow of information and exchange of ideas, and the accompanying processes of motivation should become more participative and informal in nature.[13]

Personality of Members. Effective organizational structure and processes conform to the personality and expectations of members of the organization. Members who do not expect participation and who are dependent upon others for motivation react best to formal patterns of structure and motivation, while those who expect participation and are motivated largely from within react best to participative processes and informal organizational structure.[14]

Congruence of Goals. When the goals of the organization and those of its members are congruent, participative processes and a less formal structure are appropriate; but when organizational goals and members' goals are divergent, greater reliance must be placed upon external controls and formal structure so that adequate control is assured.[15]

Level of Decision Making. The hierarchical level of decision making is primarily a function of the technology of the organization. When technology permits and decision-making functions are retained within the primary work group of an organization, participative processes and informal structure are effective; as the decision-making processes move upward in the organizational hierarchy and away from the work group

---

William A. Rushing, "The Effects of Industry Size and Division of Labor on Administration," *Administrative Science Quarterly*, Vol. 12, No. 2 (September, 1967), pp. 273-295.

[13] The following studies indicate the importance of interaction between members of an organization:

John J. Morse and Jay W. Lorsch, "Beyond Theory Y," *Harvard Business Review*, Vol. XLII, No. 3 (May-June, 1970), pp. 61-68.

Paul R. Lawrence and Jay W. Lorsch, "Differentiation and Integration in Complex Organizations," *Administrative Science Quarterly*, Vol. 12, No. 1 (June, 1967), pp. 1-47.

[14] Victor H. Vroom, *Some Personality Determinants of the Effects of Participation* (Englewood Cliffs, New Jersey: Prentice-Hall, Inc., 1960), p. 91.

William W. McKelvey, "Expectational Noncomplementarity and Style of Interaction Between Professional and Organization," *Administrative Science Quarterly*, Vol. 14, No. 1 (March, 1969), pp. 21-32.

[15] W. Keith Warner and A. Eugene Havens, "Goal Displacement and the Intangibility of Organizational Goals," *Administrative Science Quarterly*, Vol. 12, No. 4 (March, 1968), pp. 539-555.

Lawrence and Lorsch, *op. cit.*

Seashore and Yuchtman, *op. cit.*

George W. England, "Organizational Goals and Expected Behavior of American Managers," *Academy of Management Journal*, Vol. 10, No. 2 (June, 1967), pp. 107-117.

always written

affected by those decisions, formal structure and directive processes are more appropriate.[16]

State of the System. When the performance of an organization is relatively poor in respect to the achievement of organizational goals (thereby creating a state of system imbalance), directive processes of motivation and formalized structure become necessary to initiate corrective action; however, as the organization achieves stated goals, participative processes and informal patterns of organization become more effective and are expected by the members of the organization.[17]

not going well

Theory y why they exist?

The parameters stated above form the framework of Theory Z, a systems approach to the study of organizations. These dimensions are not broad generalizations concerning the nature of work and the characteristics of human beings, nor do they prescribe "the one best way." Instead, the parameters of Theory Z offer a means of analyzing each organizational situation as it arises so that the most appropriate organizational structure and process may be designed to fit the needs of that particular situation. One might well preface each statement with the phrase, "other things being equal," for the parameters expressed in Theory Z function as a system and a change in the value of one factor modifies the significance and function of the remaining five variables.

Case Problem 9-B, Plant Shutdown for Vacation, provides another opportunity to evaluate a type of leadership. It also raises to some

---

[16] The following discussion illustrates the effect of electronic data processing and management information systems (information technology) upon the locus of decision making:

William E. Reif, *Computer Technology and Organization* (Iowa City, Iowa: Bureau of Business and Economic Research, University of Iowa, 1968). See discussion beginning on page 109.

To the extent that organizational structure is a function of technology the following references are pertinent:

L. Vaughn Blankenship and Raymond E. Miles, "Organizational Structure and Managerial Decision Behavior," *Administrative Science Quarterly,* Vol. 13, No. 1 (June, 1968), pp. 106-117.

Joan Woodward, *Industrial Organization: Theory and Practice* (London: Oxford University Press, 1965).

David J. Hickson, D. S. Pugh, and Diana G. Pheysey, "Operations Technology and Organization Structure: An Empirical Reappraisal," *Administrative Scence Quarterly,* Vol. 14, No. 3 (September, 1969), pp. 378-396.

Jerald Hage and Michael Aiken, "Routine Technology, Social Structure, and Organization Goals," *Administrative Science Quarterly,* Vol. 14, No. 3 (September, 1969), pp. 366-376.

Pugh, Hickson, Hinings, and Turner, *op. cit.*

[17] Gwen Andrew, "An Analytic System Model for Organization Theory," *Academy of Management Journal,* Vol. VIII, No. 3 (September, 1965), pp. 190-198.

extent the question of where in the organization certain types of decisions should be made.

CASE PROBLEM
9-B

PLANT SHUTDOWN
FOR VACATION

General Manufacturing Company produces a line of small power tools for home workshops which are distributed nationally through department and hardware stores. The company has grown steadily since its founding, and at the present time there are approximately 500 employees, 400 of whom are directly connected with manufacturing, and about 100 employed in the office, which is located in the same building. Mr. Ransom, founder and president, often refers to the company as "one big happy family."

However, as June 1 approaches each year, the manager of manufacturing raises a perennial question concerning the possibility of closing the plant for two weeks during the summer and having all employees take their vacation at that time. He offers the following reasons for his position:

1. At present, in the plant alone, there are 100 employees entitled to three weeks' vacation, 200 entitled to two weeks, 50 entitled to one week, and 50 who have not earned any vacation. The grand total is 750 man weeks of vacation during a 13- or 14-week period from June 1 to September 1—an average of 50 people on vacation each week during the summer. The result is increased overtime, which is costly, and unskilled summer replacements which increase scrap costs and quality complaints.

2. A plant shutdown affords an opportunity to perform much needed machine repair that otherwise has to be done on an overtime basis and usually results in lost production.

3. A plant shutdown would permit the supervisors to have their vacations during the summer months. Under the present system, they are working either short-handed or have so many new employees as replacements that it is impossible to let them have vacations during the June-to-September period.

Mr. Ransom considers these reasons valid but wants the employees to participate in making the decision. Here is his statement during a recent management meeting:

"As you know, we pride ourselves in our good human relations, and—in my opinion—one of the reasons our relationships are so good is that we encourage our employees to make as many decisions for themselves as possible. For example, each year they elect their own officers and administer the entire employee activity fund, including the determination of how much money is to be allotted to each activity. I suggest that they be permitted to vote on whether or not the plant should be closed for two weeks and all vacations taken at that time."

"Voting is all right for some things," replied John Havers, the manager of manufacturing, "but I'm not sure that they should vote on something that is as important and costly as this is to the company. We have increased our inventory and rented additional warehouse space so that we can close for a two-week period. Also, if your plan is used, how many should be allowed to vote? I feel certain that most of the girls in the office will vote against closing the plant since most are married and want to take their vacations with their husbands. Then, too, we want the 25 men in the various maintenance departments to stay on. Should they be allowed to vote even though it has been decided that they have to work? And what about the new men who are not entitled to vacation? It's hard to imagine their voting themselves out of two weeks' pay. It seems to me that we might even get a majority vote against closing the plant that actually wouldn't be representative of the majority of those involved. I'm for preparing an announcement that the plant will close on such and such a date for a period of two weeks and that vacations will be taken at that time with certain exceptions."

Mr. Riley, director of personnel, added: "This situation is somewhat similar to one that I experienced several years ago in another company. We let the office employees vote on whether or not office hours should be changed for the summer months from the normal eight to five with an hour off for lunch to 7:30 to 4:00 with a half hour for lunch. The margin in favor of changing was only three votes out of the 110 voting, and there was nothing but trouble throughout the entire summer because of the exceptions that had to be made. One thing that stands out is that voting seems to solidify the losing side, with the result that during the summer they always said, 'Well, I didn't vote for it.' Another point to remember is that this situation isn't going to get better; as time goes on, we will have more and more employees entitled to three weeks' vacation, which means that under our present policy each summer is going to become more costly."

The other members of the management committee agreed with Riley and Havers.

PROBLEMS

1. What is your recommendation to Mr. Ransom as the proper course of action?
2. Would there be any inconsistency in Mr. Ransom's behavior if he overruled his management committee and insisted that the employees vote on this question? Discuss.
3. Comment on the following statement: Minorities should be protected from the action of the majority.

Chapter Questions for Study and Discussion

1. Give examples from your experience that illustrate the two meanings of the term, organization. Are these meanings mutually exclusive or is there a degree of overlap between the two meanings? Discuss.
2. After reviewing the assumptions of Theory X, describe a work situation that reflects these assumptions as nearly as possible.
3. Describe a work situation that reflects the assumptions of Theory Y.
4. In your opinion, in our industrial society do most work situations conform more closely to the assumptions of Theory X or of Theory Y?
5. Compare a Theory X organization and a Theory Y organization with respect to the type of authority, the location of the decision-making process, the characteristics of the organizational structure, and the roles of the supervisor and the individual members of the organization.
6. Is it possible to have an organization that conforms to Theory X in some respects and to Theory Y in other respects? Give an example.
7. Describe in your own terms what is meant by a systems approach to organization theory.
8. Theory Z presents six parameters for the characteristics of organizations. If you were to reduce the number to three, which three would you present? If the parameters for a systems approach to organization theory were to be increased, which ones would you add?

CHAPTER 10

Organization Structure

Excelsior Products, originally a sales organization owned and operated by a manufacturer's representative, is now a wholly owned subsidiary of Triumph Chemical Company, a relatively large concern in its industry and engaged in the development, manufacture, and distribution of industrial maintenance chemicals. Excelsior, like the parent company, sells direct to the industrial consumer and counts among its best selling items degreasers, waxes, detergents, insecticides, weed killers, special paints, and liquid fertilizers. All told, there are 85 products currently in the line; new products are added at a rate of about ten a year and usually the five poorest selling items are dropped from the line.

The sales force is composed of commission salesmen who are among the highest paid of any industry. Although the commission rate varies from a low of 20 percent on some items to a high of 35 percent on a very few items, the average rate paid—based on current sales analysis—is 25 percent of total sales volume. Salesmen earn an average gross income of $14,000 a year, and out of this amount they pay their own expenses. However, many salesmen who have been with the company for more than a year earn at least $25,000.

The sales expense of Excelsior Products includes the 25 percent direct selling cost paid to salesmen as commissions and 8 percent allocated to advertising in trade journals, printed specification sheets carried by all salesmen and distributed to customers, semi-annual national sales meetings, and other miscellaneous sales expenses. Thus, from the $56,000 sales volume generated by each salesman, the total sales expense is $18,480, or 33 percent.

During the first complete year of operations following the acquisition by Triumph, all five of the salesmen employed by the former owner of Excelsior remained; true to expectation, they produced a total sales volume of $280,000. During this year no effort was made to expand the sales force by Mr. Thomas Jackson, a former district sales manager for Triumph and the new general manager of Excelsior. In the second year Mr. Jackson hired and trained ten new salesmen, but by the year's end only five of the new men remained; however, sales for that year totaled $375,000. At the beginning of the third year, Mr. Jackson had ten good men, each capable of producing a sales volume of $56,000. The plans for the third year called for hiring and training two new men each month. Actually this goal was not realized, but he did hire 20 men, 12 of whom were still with the company at the end of the third year. Fortunately, none of the ten salesmen working at the beginning of the year quit, and as a group they produced $570,000. This amount, combined with the volume of the new men—none of whom sold for a full year—totaled $810,000. Mr. Jackson is convinced that the 22 men presently employed are capable of producing a sales volume of $1 million in a full calendar year. These 22 men are located in the following areas: Los Angeles, 2; San Francisco, 2; St. Louis, the home office, 5; Dallas, 2; Houston, 2; Florida, 1; New York City, 3; Chicago, 3; Detroit, 1; and Colorado, 1.

Now Mr. Jackson is planning for the coming year and realizes that the growth of Excelsior Products is dependent primarily upon the number of salesmen hired. Most of the men live in relatively large cities and sell not only to customers in that city but also to customers in the small towns in that section of the state. He recognizes that he has only one salesman in the southeastern part of the United States and none in the Northwest or New England.

Mr. Jackson spends most of his time in recruiting and training new salesmen. Some of the new men are referred to the company by present salesmen, but most are recruited through newspaper advertising. Usually a new man is sent out on the road for a period of one week with an experienced salesman; then Mr. Jackson spends a week with the new man in the territory assigned to him. He realizes that the training received under these circumstances is probably inadequate, but it is all that time allows. In addition to recruiting and training new salesmen, Mr. Jackson conducts two national sales meetings a year in order to introduce new products, and these meetings afford an opportunity to brush up on sales techniques. Although the laboratories of the parent company develop new products, it is the general manager's responsibility to choose the product name, approve the package design, and prepare the layout and copy of the specification sheets that describe the product and are carried by all salesmen. In the home office there are three clerical employees who process sales orders as they are received from the field. The billing of customers, the computation of commissions, and the payment of salesmen are performed by personnel of the parent company. Jackson realizes that if Excelsior Products is to continue to grow, he needs more managerial help, but he feels obligated to stay within the 33 percent selling cost imposed by the parent corporation.

PROBLEMS

1. Develop an organization structure for Excelsior Products that will permit the company to attain a sales volume of $5 million annually. Will this structure be effective when sales reach $15 million?

2. Of what significance are the findings of Graicunas in understanding the problems of Mr. Jackson?

3. Is it possible to change the organization structure of Excelsior Products and still remain within the 33 percent overall selling cost? State the reasons for your answer. How does the answer to this question affect the recommendations made concerning organization structure in your answer to Problem No. 1?

Three theories of organization are presented in Chapter 9, each of which emphasizes a different aspect of organizing. Theory X presents organization as centered around the work to be performed, Theory Y stresses the people of the organization, while Theory Z views organization as a system that integrates the requirements of work and the desires and capabilities of the people who make up the organization. The alert student has probably said to himself that the three theories talk more of people than organizations, an observation which has considerable merit, for it is through people that the work of an organization is accomplished. Nonetheless, the structure of the organization—the arrangement of the component parts, people and work—is a major determinant in shaping the behavior of people, and, in turn, determines the extent to which organization goals are realized. One writer makes the following statement about the relationship between organization and people:

> People have about the same relationship to the organization as the driver and passengers in an automobile have to the automobile itself. If we want to improve the effectiveness of the automobile in reaching its objectives, that is, improve it as a means of rapid, safe, and comfortable transportation, we can do a number of things. We can improve the design of the automobile to better adapt it to the people who will probably use it. We can modify it to better conform to the characteristics of the roads it will travel. We can alter the furnishings of the automobile or adjust certain of its mechanical features to human needs. Such flexibility is inherent in good design. The design of the automobile must always be predicated upon the characteristics of the people who will use it and the environment in which it is to be used. The automobile is neither the people nor the environment, but it is inextricably linked with both.[1]

We all know something about the design of an automobile in relation to its purpose and the people who use it. If the automobile is to carry 50 people, it becomes a bus; if it is to enter the Indianapolis 500, there is room only for the driver; and Ford learned as the result of a survey, which surprises no one who has given the matter much thought, that engaged couples do not like bucket seats. We all know something about the structure and design of organizations, even though an organization is not a tangible entity like an automobile. When organizing a group, such as a fraternity, for a social outing, one of the first items to be considered is the part that each person is to play in preparing for and conducting the event. Five members may be chosen to arrange transportation, three more to assume responsibility for providing food and beverages, and a third group to select and make advance arrangements for the site. Each group has a chairman who works closely with the person in charge of special social events, usually a designated officer in a fraternity, so that the efforts of all groups will be coordinated.

---

[1] Louis A. Allen, *Management and Organization* (New York: McGraw-Hill Book Company, 1958), p. 353. This book is a presentation of organization which emphasizes an orientation toward the work to be accomplished. It should be read as a supplement to the concepts of organization presented by Rensis Likert in *New Patterns of Management* and Douglas McGregor in *The Human Side of Enterprise.*

The example of a fraternity preparing for an outing illustrates two characteristics of organization structure. First, the work to be accomplished is divided and then arranged into manageable portions. The word used to describe the process of analyzing, dividing, and arranging work into manageable portions is _departmentation._ Second, the leader of each group works closely with the permanent social chairman so that the efforts of each group may be coordinated. The number of work groups reporting to the chairman is a structural characteristic resulting from the manner in which the work is organized. To the chairman, these are the number of groups that must be coordinated, or managed; hence, the expression, _span of management._ This chapter discusses the two major characteristics of organization structure—departmentation and span of management—and then applies the parameters of Theory Z as guides for selecting the most effective structure.

DEPARTMENTATION

A reservation concerning the use of the term, organization, must be made. For the most part, organization is actually _reorganization._ Seldom is an entire organization projected from scratch; instead, it is a process of changing and refining present structure and personnel. Problem 1 of Case Problem 10-A requests that you develop an organization structure for Excelsior Products and reflects a common use of the word, organization, in management literature. A more precise, though cumbersome, wording would request a reorganization. We will continue to use the expression, organization, as it appears in most management writings, but it is well to remember that in practically all instances we are discussing reorganization.

The need for departmentation, defined as the grouping of work and/or individuals into manageable units, is easily understood, and usually the process of creating manageable units is the first step in building an organization structure. It is conceivable that one man can perform all the work of an enterprise provided he has the necessary skills, knowledge, and time. A one-man hamburger stand is illustrative of a business whose _functions_ are managed by one person. As the business prospers, the owner finds that he does not have the time to perform the work of preparing food and serving customers. Thus, as a first step in organization, he divides the work into units that can be completed by one man. Perhaps a cook who performs all functions associated with the preparation of food is hired, and the owner retains those functions connected with serving customers and managing the business. If

the hamburger stand continues to grow and becomes a restaurant capable of seating 100 customers, the work of the cook is further subdivided. A chef is now in charge of the preparation of food and is
responsible for all work performed in the kitchen. He supervises the
work of several assistants, each of whom is skilled in the preparation
of a certain type food. A supervisor of the dining room directs the
waitresses who serve the customers. The owner is performing the
managerial function of coordinating the efforts of all personnel. Should
a chain of restaurants develop, each restaurant may be regarded as a
manageable unit. Thus, departmentation, the grouping of work and
people, occurs at all levels of an organization. What are the bases most
commonly used in determining departmental structure?

Bases of Departmentation   *Very Important.*

Certain well-recognized and accepted bases for departmentation
have developed over a period of years. These bases, which are common to all types of organizations, appear with such frequency and
consistency that they may be regarded as common denominators of
organization. The units created through the process of departmentation combine to form the total structure of the organization, and are
work-centered in their origin and application since the primary goal is
an effective division of work. The most frequently used bases of departmentation are: (1) function, (2) product, (3) customer, (4) geography, (5) process, and (6) sequence. Each basis for dividing work
is discussed below.

Function. *Function* denotes related activity. It is a relationship
that is apparent because of the similarity of the skills required to perform a given kind of work, or a relationship that binds together a group
of tasks in the accomplishment of a common goal. The fundamental
appeal of function as a basis for dividing work is its logical simplicity.
What is more natural than grouping together all work requiring
the skills necessary to operate machine tools and placing persons
with those skills under the direction of one supervisor? By the same
token, all persons having the required skills to assemble the product
form the assembly department. These and other seemingly unrelated
skills may be grouped together on a functional basis because the application of each skill results in the accomplishment of a specific task; and
when these tasks are combined, a logical relationship may be perceived,
for machining and assembling are activities (functions) necessary to
accomplish a common goal—the production of the product.

The functions usually identified in the top echelon of business organizations are production, finance, and sales. These functions have been described as primary, vital, or organic; the implication is that the absence of any one of the three functions would result in the death of the organization. The terminology used to describe these functions and the significance of these and other functions varies from one type of enterprise to another. Manufacturing firms use the terms production (or manufacturing), finance, and sales; wholesalers recognize the functions of finance and sales, but production takes the form of buying, warehousing, and distribution; and airlines use the word, operations, to describe their production function—the movement of passengers. For some organizations one or more of the functions may be vestigial in nature; for example, hospitals and banks have no sales function per se; rather, these organizations refer to the function of public relations. On the other hand, it is difficult to imagine a function more vital to pharmaceutical firms than research, because over half of their current sales volume results from products which were unknown ten years ago.

In addition to the primary functions, which vary in respect to the terminology used to describe them and their significance and number for different types of enterprises, there are auxiliary functions that must be performed. Traditionally, auxiliary functions—frequently called staff functions—are considered supportive in nature and supplement the primary functions of the organization. Delicate interpersonal relationships between persons performing primary functions and those carrying out auxiliary functions often arise and are discussed in considerable detail in the next chapter.

Product. Companies with diversified product lines frequently create managerial units based upon the product. Three forms of product departmentation are shown in Figure 10-1. Chart 1 shows the division of both the sales and the manufacturing functions into product departments, while Chart 2 shows product departmentation applied to the sales function only. In Chart 3 the manufacturing function is departmentalized according to product, and sales remains as a single unit. Figure 10-1 also illustrates that the process of creating departments quite properly employs more than one basis. In this instance, the bases of function and product are used.

Customer. Retail stores may organize their sales force to meet the needs of a specific class of customer by forming special departments to cater to teenagers, collegians, or brides. An industrial firm manufacturing valves might divide its sales force so that one part of it sells to

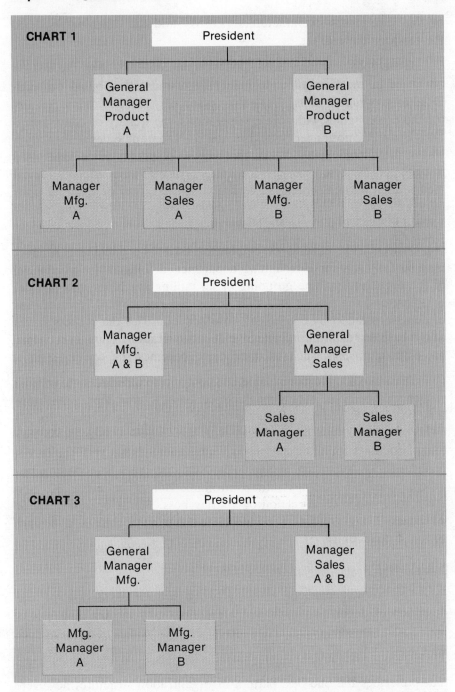

Figure 10-1
**THREE POSSIBLE ARRANGEMENTS OF DEPARTMENTATION
BASED UPON PRODUCT**

original equipment manufacturers (OEM) and the other part sells to the replacement market.

   Geography. At one time, poor communications was the reason advanced in most instances to justify departmentation based on territorial or geographic units. While this reason may still have some validity for those companies with foreign operations, the quality of communications is usually no longer a valid reason for geographic departmentation within the United States. When the number of people to be supervised is large and dispersed over a wide area, territorial units afford a logical means of developing manageable units. The creation of regional units offers a possible solution to the organization problem confronting Excelsior Products, Case Problem 10-A.

   Process. The process or equipment used in producing a product may be the basis for determining departmental lines at the plant level of the organization. The grouping of all milling machines into one department and the placing of lathes in another department is illustrative of departmentation by equipment. In other industries the process serves as the basis for determining effective departmentation. Thus, in a chemical plant a process, such as distillation, becomes the operating unit.

   Sequence. Departments sometime conform to alphanumeric or time sequences. The bookkeeping machine section of a large department store may be subdivided into two units, one of which posts accounts for all customers whose last names begin with the letters A through M; the other unit posts for those customers whose names begin with the letters N through Z. Numerical sequence is often the basis for dividing undifferentiated labor gangs into controllable units; i.e., every 30 men are placed under the direction of a straw boss. Plants operating 16 or 24 hours a day establish separate shifts, and each shift is a distinct administrative unit.

Creating Manageable Departments

   The above bases of dividing work are an extension of the definition of departmentation and a description of the building blocks that make up the organization structure. Creating manageable departments is not an end in itself; instead, it is a means of facilitating the achievement of organizational objectives. There is no set of rules that prescribes the one best pattern of organization structure; however, there are guides, discussed in the last section of this chapter, which are useful in selecting the most appropriate structure.

SPAN OF MANAGEMENT※

Once the bases of departmentation are determined—whether by function, product, customer, geography, process, sequence, or any combination of these criteria—another problem in organization structure immediately arises: How many departments are to be placed under the direction of one individual? This problem is frequently referred to as *span of control*; however, the phrase *span of management* describes the question more accurately because an executive performs the functions of planning, organizing, and leading, as well as the function of control. The span of management has a direct bearing upon the number of hierarchical levels in an organization; the number of levels, in turn, is a measure of the length of that organization's *lines of communications*.

For example, Thomas Jackson of Excelsior Products, Case Problem 10-A, has 22 salesmen and three clerks in the home office reporting to him, a span of management of 25 persons. Let us assume that he names a chief clerk and appoints four regional sales supervisors; his span of management is reduced from 25 to five, but there is now one level of supervision through which communications between him and the salesmen and clerks must pass. Suppose that he appoints an eastern division sales manager and a western division sales manager, each of whom supervises three regional sales managers. Mr. Jackson's span of management is reduced to three persons. While there is one supervisor between him and the clerks, he must now communicate to his salesmen through two levels of supervision, the divisional and the regional managers.

From the discussion above, it is apparent that if the span of management is decreased, the lines of communications are lengthened; and, conversely, if the lines of communication are shortened, the manager's span is increased. Yet, there are instances in the literature of management that advise the chief executive to simultaneously reduce his span of management and shorten the organization's communication lines. Let us review the reasons frequently advanced in support of a limited span of management and then examine the experience of several companies that have deliberately increased the manager's span.

Reasons for a Limited Span

One of the earliest recommendations in support of a limited span of management is found in Jethro's advice to Moses that he establish "rulers of thousands, and rulers of hundreds, and rulers of

fifties, and rulers of tens." [2] In modern literature the development of
the concept that supports a limited span of management is attributed
to the work of three men. First, there is the statement of Sir General
Ian Hamilton; second, the work of A. V. Graicunas; and third, the
formal statement of a principle by Lyndall F. Urwick.

Hamilton's Recommendations. General Hamilton's conclusions are
drawn from his experiences as a military officer. He begins his line of
reasoning with the statement that the average human brain finds its
optimum work level when handling three to six other brains. His observation that a noncommissioned officer is not fully occupied when
directing only three soldiers and that a lieutenant general finds it difficult to direct the activities of six divisional generals is recognition that
the number of persons under the direction of one supervisor should be
greater at the lower levels of the organization than the number supervised at the top of the organization. General Hamilton recommended
that "the nearer we approach the supreme head of the whole organization, the more we ought to work toward groups of six." [3]

The Theory of Graicunas. An important consideration in establishing an appropriate span of management is the number of potential
interactions that might occur between a manager and his subordinates.
A. V. Graicunas, a Lithuanian management consultant, developed a
formula for determining some, but not all, of the relationships inherent
in a given span. [4]

If, for example, one supervisor, S has two subordinates, A and B,
reporting to him, a *direct relationship* may occur between the supervisor S and A, and the supervisor S and B. But there are times when S
talks to A with B present or to B with A present; thus, two *group
relationships* are possible. Further, *cross relationships* may exist between
A and B and between B and A. As shown in Figure 10-2, these three
sets of relationships—direct, group, and cross—combine to form six
possible interactions between one supervisor and two subordinates.
When a third subordinate, C, reports to S, one additional direct relationship is established between S and C; but seven additional group
relationships ($AC, CA, BC, CB, ABC, CBA,$ and BAC) are possible.

[2] See Chapter 2, "The Development of Management Concepts," page 31, for a
more complete analysis of Jethro's recommendations which are contained in Exodus
18: 13-26.

[3] Sir Ian Hamilton, *The Soul and Body of the Army* (London: Edward Arnold
Publishers, Ltd., 1921), p. 221.

[4] A. V. Graicunas, "Relationship in Organization," *Papers on the Science of
Administration,* ed. L. Gulick and L. Urwick (New York: Columbia University, 1947),
pp. 183-87.

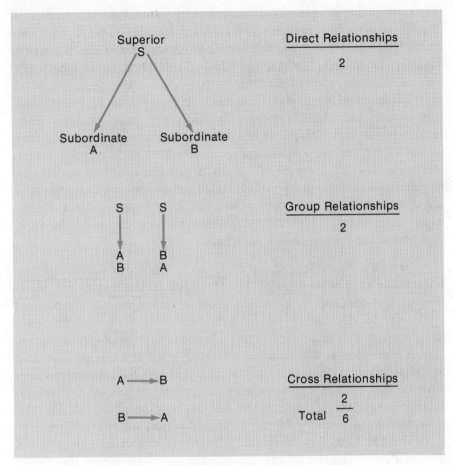

Figure 10-2
DIRECT, GROUP, AND CROSS RELATIONSHIPS THAT MIGHT
OCCUR BETWEEN A SUPERIOR AND TWO SUBORDINATES

Also, four more cross relationships ($A\!\blacklozenge\!C$, $B\!\blacklozenge\!C$, $C\!\blacklozenge\!A$, and $C\!\blacklozenge\!B$) are added, thus bringing the potential number of interactions to 18. A fourth subordinate raises the theoretical interactions to 44, the fifth results in an even 100 relationships, and the executive with eight subordinates is the center of a web of 1,080 potential relationships.[5]

---

[5] The number of relationships, r, may be determined by the following formula, in which n represents the number of subordinates:

$$r = n\,(2^{n-1} + n - 1)$$

As mentioned in the text, Graicunas does not take into account all possible relationships. Any one of the subordinates could conceivably initiate action, which in effect doubles the number of potential direct relationships; in addition, the supervisor could participate as a member of each group, with successive members of that group assuming the dominant role.

Graicunas's mathematical analysis of the potential relationships in a given span of management is significant for two reasons. First, his theory emphasizes the complex social processes that occur between a superior and his subordinates and between the subordinates themselves. Second, the application of his formula stresses the alarming rate at which the complexity of these social processes increases with each additional subordinate. The addition of the fifth subordinate raises potential interactions from 44 to 100, the eighth subordinate moves the potential from 490 to 1,080, and the fourteenth subordinate finds the total relationships soaring to 114,872 from 53,404 with 13 subordinates. Fortunately, the relationships envisioned by Graicunas do not occur on a daily basis, or for that matter may not occur at all; but the warning is clear—somewhere there is one additional subordinate who proves to be the straw that breaks the managerial camel's back.

Urwick's Principle. Lyndall F. Urwick, a noted management consultant who credits Sir General Ian Hamilton as the first to call attention to the concept of a limited span of management, encouraged Graicunas in developing his mathematical analysis of relationships. Urwick offers as a reason to support a limited span the observed psychological phenomenon that man has a limited "span of attention"—a limit to the number of items that may be attended to simultaneously. Other limitations in human spans, such as the amount of energy available to a supervisor in the performance of his job, may be advanced. Further, time may be a limiting factor. Admittedly, not all the relationships recognized by Graicunas develop during the course of a single day, but if only a small fraction of the 1,080 potential relationships that might arise with eight subordinates occurs with any degree of regularity, an executive's span is limited by the amount of time that may be allocated to each personal contact. Graicunas recognizes that the number of cross relationships between subordinates, a major factor in determining the complexity of a supervisor's job, is dependent upon the nature of the work being performed. Colonel Urwick recognizes the variable complexity of a supervisor's job as a function of the work being performed in the following statement of principle:

"No superior can supervise directly the work of more than five or, at the most, six subordinates whose work interlocks." [6]

[6] Lyndall F. Urwick, "The Manager's Span of Control," *Harvard Business Review,* Vol. XXXV (May-June, 1956), pp. 39-47. Colonel Urwick's article is an excellent discussion in support of a limited span of management. The principle stated above first appeared in Lyndall F. Urwick, *Scientific Principles and Organization* (New York: American Management Association, 1938), Institute of Management Series No. 19, p. 8.

Span of Management in Practice

Lyndall Urwick's recommended limitations on the span of management—"five or, the most, six subordinates"—is rather specific; but it must be noted that the suggested limitations are modified by the qualifying phrase, "whose work interlocks." How valid is this precept? One way of determining the validity of the concept of a limited span of management is to examine current industrial practice in this respect. If there are differences between practice and recommendation, why do the differences exist? Two studies, one reported in 1952 and the other in 1967, present a good picture of current practice and trends in respect to existing spans of management.

The American Management Association study (1952) presents the results of a survey of current practices in respect to the span of management of the presidents of 141 companies that are "all known to have good organizational practices." [7] In the 1967 study Ernest Dale conducted a special questionnaire survey for the American Management Association. [8] The results of both studies are presented separately for large companies (over 5,000 employees) and for medium-sized companies (500-5,000 employees). The first two columns of Table 10-1 show the number of executives reporting to the presidents of the 100 large companies participating in the survey reported in 1952. The third column reports the results of the 1967 survey. It should be noted that in 1967 there were only 93 companies with a single chief executive; with the remaining seven companies having a form of group management at the very top with lines of authority leading from this group rather than from a single executive. The fourth column of Table 10-1 shows the number of potential relationships according to the formula developed by Graicunas. [9] Note that the median number of

[7] Ernest Dale, *Planning and Developing the Company Organization Structure* (New York: American Management Association, 1952), Research Report No. 20, p. 56. This research report is divided into two parts. Part I discusses the dynamics of organization in respect to determining objectives, delegating responsibility, span of control, the staff assistant, the staff specialist, group decision making, and decentralization. Part II presents established procedures in the mechanics of organization, including the development of charts and manuals. Many persons consider this work a "handbook" of organization.

[8] Ernest Dale, *Organization* (New York: American Management Association, 1967), pp. 94-96. This study on organization is not a revision of the 1952 study; rather, it is based upon a new survey of practices in large and medium-sized companies. Further, it includes some of the recent behavioral work on organizations.

[9] Walno V. Suojanen, "The Span of Control—Fact or Fable?" *Advanced Management*, Vol. XX (November, 1955), pp. 5-13. The third column of Table 10-1 utilizes the figures computed by Professor Soujanen. Professor Soujanen's paper is an interesting criticism of the concept of a limited span of management and should be read in conjunction with the article written by Lyndall F. Urwick, which is cited in footnote 6.

Table 10-1
NUMBER OF EXECUTIVES REPORTING TO PRESIDENT IN LARGE COMPANIES AND COMPUTED POTENTIAL RELATIONSHIPS

Number of Executives Reporting to Chief Executive *	Number of Companies * (1952)	Number of Companies ** (1967)	Potential Relationships *** (Graicunas Formula)
1	6	2	1
2	—	1	6
3	1	4	18
4	3	1	44
5	7	8	100
6	9	8	222
7	11	13	490
8	8	8	1,080
	Median	Median	
9	8	10	2,376
10	6	7	5,210
11	7	8	11,374
12	10	5	24,708
13	8	4	53,404
14	4	3	114,872
15	1	1	245,974
16	5	1	524,534
17	—	1	1,114,392
18	1	2	2,359,612
19	—	1	4,981,090
20	1	1	10,486,154
21	1	2	22,020,532
22	—	0	46,137,824
23	2	1	96,469,518
24	1	1	201,327,166
	100	93	

* Columns 1 and 2 are from Ernest Dale, *Planning and Developing the Company Organization Structure* (New York: American Management Association, 1952), Research Report No. 20, p. 57.

** Column 3 is from Ernest Dale, *Organization* (New York: American Management Association, 1967), p. 95.

*** Column 4 is from Walno V. Suojanen, "The Span of Control—Fact or Fable?" *Advanced Management,* Vol. XX (November, 1955), p. 6.

executives reporting to the president in 1952 and 1967 is between eight and nine, a number considerably above the limits recommended by Colonel Urwick. In the medium-sized companies, the results are essentially the same. The median number is between six and seven for both surveys; however, in 1952 the range in the number reporting to the chief executive was 1 to 17, and in 1967 the upper limits of this range increased to 22.

It is evident that more than half of the companies in each group do not adhere to the recommendation that "five, or at the most, six" subordinates report to each superior. Nor does it seem possible that the deviation from the recommended five or six is due to work of subordinates that does *not* interlock. Again, there is marked similarity between the two groups of companies with respect to the functions performed by the subordinates reporting to the president. Among those functions most frequently mentioned by both groups that are supervised by the president are production, sales, industrial relations, legal counsel, controller, treasurer, finance, purchasing, research, plant management, and engineering. The nature of these functions is such that there is usually a high degree of interrelationship between them.

Clearly, these companies, "all known to have good organizational practices," are not following Urwick's principle. A systems approach to organizational structure explains to some extent why these studies report such a marked variation from the span of management recommended by Urwick.

A SYSTEMS APPROACH TO ORGANIZATION STRUCTURE

Our concern with organization structure is twofold: first, the creation of manageable work units—the process of departmentation—and second, the corollary stemming from departmentation—the grouping of people and work into effective spans of management. The bases most commonly used for departmentation—function, product, customer, geography, process, and sequence—have been examined. Also, we have reviewed the recommendation of Urwick, based upon the work of Graicunas, and the findings of the AMA study which show that more than half of the firms surveyed exceed the recommended span of management. What are the guides to be followed in determining effective departmentation and efficient spans of management? Each of the six parameters of Theory Z—size of organization, degree of interaction, personality of members, congruence of goals, level of decision making, and state of the system—is applied as a guide for establishing departments and determining effective spans of management.

Size of Organization

There is a direct relationship between the size of an organization, when defined as number of people, and the structure of the organization. As size increases, the need for departmentation, the grouping of people, becomes evident. Consider a small machine shop engaged in the building and repair of metal parts. The owner-manager may be able to effectively direct the work of ten to fifteen journeymen machinists and, in addition, perform the functions of design, cost estimating, scheduling production, and selling the services of his shop. During this period he may develop a strategic, long-range plan to increase the size of his organization, perhaps the manufacture and distribution of a patentable product in large quantities. If successful, the size of the organization may increase to 200 people; and in order for the organization to maintain a high degree of economic effectiveness, the structure of the organization must change to accommodate the enlarged size.[10] One of the characteristics of organizational change is the creation of departments to perform the functions of design, estimating, scheduling, and selling. The sales function may be further departmentalized according to geographic areas or on the basis of product sold. Whatever the basis selected for the creation of departments, whether it be function, geography, product, or any other unifying characteristic, an increase in the size of an organization operates as a major force in creating the need for departmentation.

The size of an organization, again defined as the number of people, is also operative in determining the span of management. Table 10-1, showing the number of persons reporting to the presidents of 100 large corporations (over 1,000 employees), reveals that the median number of executives reporting to the president is between eight and nine and the range in the number reporting is from one to 24. The same analysis for medium-size companies (500 to 1,000 employees) shows that the median number of executives reporting to the president is between six and seven and the range in the number reporting is from 1 to 17 in 1952 and 1 to 22 in 1967. Ernest Dale attributes the reduction in the median and the range of the span of management to size in the following statement: "The reduced median

---

[10] Alfred D. Chandler, Jr., *Strategy and Structure* (Cambridge, Massachusetts: The M. I. T. Press, 1962), pp. 1-17. In this section, "Introduction—Strategy and Structure," Mr. Chandler develops the thesis that organizational form results from growth, and that the growth of an organization is the result of strategic planning. Detailed analyses of DuPont, General Motors, Standard Oil Company (New Jersey), and Sears, Roebuck and Company are presented.

and range reflect the lesser volume of important problems faced by the smaller companies and the smaller number of people required to assist the president in coordination and control." [11] To be sure, factors other than size determine the span of management; nonetheless, the size of the organization is important in determining the manager's span.

Degree of Interaction

An important guide in determining effective departmentation is the need for interaction between members of an organization in order to achieve organizational goals. The need for interaction arises when several persons are solving a common problem, developing and using the same information, or when there is need to communicate with each other. The following example illustrates the effect of interaction upon organization structure: Prior to reorganization, a manufacturer of twist drills, had four separate departments working on various phases of quality control. There was the field engineering department, whose function is to answer customer complaints, aid in solving technical problems, and prepare postmortem reports analyzing the causes of product failure. Field engineering reported to the vice-president, sales. Reporting to the director of quality control was the plant quality control department, which inspects the product during the manufacturing process. Under the direction of the chief metallurgist was a department responsible for metallurgical specifications, and the supervision of the heat-treating process, an important step in manufacturing. Finally, there was a product design department supervised by the vice-president, engineering. The members of these departments were all highly skilled technicians, many having engineering degrees; all were interested in the quality of the product and might have benefited from a free exchange of ideas and information; yet they were located in physically separated departments with little opportunity for interaction or communication. Recognizing the problem, the company located all four departments in one geographic area under the direction of the vice-president, engineering, a move which not only permits interaction between the members of the four departments but also facilitates coordination of effort.

The degree of interaction between persons supervised by one superior may be a factor in determining the limits of an effective span

---

[11] Ernest Dale, *Planning and Developing the Company Organization Structure* (New York: American Management Association, 1952), Research Report No. 20, p. 59.

of management. The geometrically progressive increase in the number of relationships described by Graicunas is a function of the cross relationships between those being supervised, a function recognized by Urwick in the qualifying phrase, "whose work interlocks." However, there is evidence that there are factors which counterbalance interaction and thus make possible the effective use of an increased span of management. James C. Worthy reports the effects of an increased span of management in his study of two groups of Sears, Roebuck and Company stores, each having approximately 150 to 175 employees.[12] The structure of one group of stores followed the conventional limited span of management with a level of supervision between the store manager and the heads of the more than 30 merchandising departments. In the other group of stores, the manager had an assistant manager and the more than 30 merchandising managers reported directly to him. When compared in respect to employee morale, sales volume, and profit, the stores having a large span of management resulting in a relatively "flat" structure were superior to those stores with the smaller span of management and a level of supervision between the manager and the department heads. There is evidence that the flat structure encouraged the department heads to develop into strong managers capable of operating with a minimum of supervision, thereby making a large span of management effective.

Personality of Members

The personality of the members of an organization (defining personality as the sum total of the skills, abilities, interests, and personal characteristics) is an important guide in determining departmental lines. Admittedly, the structure of the organization is not the people, but like the well-designed automobile that conforms to the characteristics of the persons using it, so should the well-designed organization structure adapt to the personalities of the members of the organization. Work is often departmentalized according to the skills employed, an arrangement which encourages specialization and the maximum development of individual skills and abilities. Specialized knowledge concerning a specific product or function may well serve as the basis for defining a department. However, there are dangers inherent in overspecialization. The members of a highly specialized department and their supervisors may become so narrow and engrossed in one limited

---

[12] James C. Worthy, "Organization Structure and Employee Morale," *American Sociological Review*, Vol. XV (April, 1950), pp. 169-79.

aspect of a problem that they fail to recognize broader organizational goals. Also, jobs may become so limited in scope that boredom and monotony are the result. It is essential to maintain a balance between specialization, which often facilitates training and results in a high level of skill, and the enlargement of jobs and departments so that there is maximum utilization of the capabilities of members.

The personality of the members of an organization is an important consideration in determining the extent of an effective span of management. First, consider the personality of the manager. It is axiomatic that there are wide variations in the capabilities of managers in respect to range of interests, breadth and depth of knowledge, and the amount of energy expended on the job. In addition to these characteristics, which are usually recognized without too much difficulty, there is that relatively rare quality—the ability to inspire others. Managers who inspire subordinates to "play over their heads" should have larger spans so their dynamic qualities of leadership are felt by as many as possible.

Second, the personality characteristics of subordinates contribute to the manager's span. It is apparent that if subordinates are well trained, interested in their jobs, and capable of making their own decisions, less supervisory effort is required, thereby making it possible for a superior to increase his span of management. It is suggested by critics of an extended span of management that one of the chief reasons for the large spans in the Sears' stores (discussed above) is the lack of interaction between the merchandising department heads, with the result that there are very few cross relationships. Though this appraisal may be valid to some extent, the primary reason for the success of the large span of management in the Sears retail stores is the effect that a large span has on the members of the organization. The store manager, knowing that he can devote only a limited amount of time to each subordinate, exercises greater care in the selection and training of each department manager. Of equal importance is the effect a large span of management has upon the development of the subordinate. Since he receives less supervision, the subordinate is forced to make his own decisions in the operation of his department, and this experience in managing without close supervision makes it possible for him to develop into a capable departmental manager.

Congruence of Goals *(coinciding or equal)*

Congruence of goals may serve as a guide in drawing departmental lines when the immediate objectives of several diverse activities are similar. Plant maintenance departments usually include personnel who possess the diverse skills of millwrights, electricians, plumbers, steamfitters, and machinists—a variety which at first glance may seem to have little in common. However, all are concerned with the immediate objective of keeping plant facilities in a good state of repair, and the combining of many crafts into a single administrative unit improves the coordination of the many skills necessary for plant maintenance. The placement of salesmen and service personnel under the direction of the sales manager is another example of combining into a single department apparently unrelated activities. In this case, the common objective is customer satisfaction. The chief advantage resulting from the application of congruence of goals as a guide in grouping diverse activities is a structure that permits a high degree of coordination.

Congruence of goals as a guide for departmentation relates primarily to the similarity of objectives that exist between persons who perform apparently unrelated activities. When applied as a guide in determining an effective span of management, congruence of goals refers not only to the similarity of goals of various work groups, but also includes the degree of congruence between the immediate goals of the individual and those of the organization. An illustration of congruence in the goals of several work groups is found in our example of the need for interaction as a guide for determining departmental lines. In this case the need for interaction is resolved by placing the four quality control departments under the direction of the engineering vice-president, a solution that increases his span of management. Yet, it is a tenable arrangement since the four departments all have a common goal—the improvement of product quality. An argument often presented in support of the establishment of incentive plans, which relate the pay of an individual to his productivity, is that the installation of such plans is a means of making the goals of the individual congruent with those of the organization. In general, as the immediate goals of subordinates become congruent with the goals of other subordinates and with the goals of the organization, the span of management may be increased.

Level of Decision Making

In some organizations the power to make important decisions is retained by the chief executive and his immediate subordinates, while in other firms decision making occurs at all levels of the management hierarchy. The hierarchical location of decision making is primarily a function of the technological characteristics of the organization which may result in a need for a high degree of coordination or result in an information pattern where only the top level of the organization possesses sufficient information for sound decisions. Both of these reasons are valid under certain circumstances; for example, purchasing and production planning decisions may be retained by the top echelons of the organization in multiplant companies where there is a need to coordinate the purchase of raw materials from several different sources and the scheduling of production among many plants. However, there are occasions when the creation of managerial units is guided by the need for moving the level of decision making downward in the organization. Departments may be created for the specific purpose of placing decision making at the level where it will be most effective. The creation of geographical units with decision-making powers is an example of the downward movement of decision making. The reasons most frequently advanced for such a move is the need for timeliness of decisions, a better coordination of activities in the geographic region, and the ability to meet and take full advantage of local factors such as the actions of competitors. The determination of the most effective level of decision making is a major consideration in the organizational process known as *decentralization* which, in effect, is the decentralization of authority to make decisions—a topic discussed in full in Chapter 12.

The level at which decisions are made in an organization has a direct bearing upon the breadth of an executive's span of management. The executive who retains the responsibility for making decisions usually reduces his span of management; however, if he permits his subordinates to make decisions, his span of management may be increased. One of the reasons for the success of the extended span of management in the retail stores of Sears, Roebuck and Company is attributable to the development of decision-making capabilities on the part of the departmental managers. However, it must be recognized that the technology of a department store makes it possible to assign broad decision-making functions to departmental managers.

State of the System

The state of the organization in respect to the achievement of organizational goals—in effect, the state of the system—is an important consideration in developing departmental units. The reduction of costs, a continuing goal for most organizations, is frequently achieved by avoiding duplication of effort. A plant manager may desire to have fully autonomous purchasing and payroll departments as a part of his organization; however, if these functions are being performed adequately at a higher level of the company, the creation of duplicate departments at lower levels is not justified. The personnel function and the public relations function may be conducted by separate departments at the corporate level of an organization, and at the plant level these functions may be combined within the personnel department as a means of reducing expenses. Occasionally, the needs of the organization are such that it becomes necessary to emphasize a particular function by creating a separate department which reports to the chief executive. For example, a firm manufacturing electronic equipment may create a separate sales department, reporting to the president, to secure government contracts. The desire to reduce costs or to emphasize a particular function is an example of the organization, viewed as a system, responding to the pressures of its environment.

The extent to which the goals of an organization are stabilized and the degree to which an organization is achieving these goals serve as guides in determining an effective span of management. The recommendation that the span of management be limited is based upon observations of military organizations. Hence, it is well to note two characteristics of military types in order to estimate the applicability of these to business situations. First, the military organization is operating in a situation of continuing emergency during war. Though the long-range goal, the defeat of the enemy, may not change, the pressure and demands of day-to-day tactics combined with shifts in broad strategy make necessary an organization capable of adjusting rapidly to environmental changes. Narrowing the span of management is a means of structuring an organization so that it may be comprehended and controlled by one man, thereby permitting relatively rapid adaptations to changing organizational goals. Second, during periods of war the military is managed by a nucleus of highly skilled regulars, but the vast majority of the organization is composed of relatively unskilled, or at best newly trained, civilians. Because of inexperience, the number that may be supervised effectively declines somewhat; hence, a narrow span is more appropriate than an extended span.

These two characteristics of the military, a continuing state of emergency during war with resulting changes in goals and the relative inexperience of organizational members, are not typical of the average business organization. Though the goals of a business venture change, they do not change with the rapidity of military goals; also, a business grows over an extended period of time, with the result that the proportion of new and inexperienced members is small. The relatively stable goals of business and the high proportion of experienced members contribute toward the effectiveness of extended spans of management.

▬▬▬▬▬▬▬▬▬▬▬▬▬▬▬▬▬▬▬▬

Case Problem 10-B, "Needed—A Plan for Organization," provides an opportunity to apply the bases for departmentation and the guides for determining an effective span of management to a real situation. Like many companies, the Flexopak Company just grew; there is little evidence of organization planning, and the resultant structure is the result of adding a bit here and a bit there over a period of years. When change occurs, occasioned by the retirement of the chief executive and founder, the company may enter a period of reorganization so that the new president can effectively guide the organization.

**CASE PROBLEM
10-B**

**NEEDED—
A PLAN FOR
ORGANIZATION**

Flexopak, founded in 1910 in Madison, Wisconsin, as a printing job shop, soon began to specialize in the printing of flexible packaging materials sold primarily to food processors. During the years immediately after its founding, growth was steady but not particularly rapid; however, with the advent of the modern supermarket and the phenomenal growth of chain stores, the company grew quite rapidly. Flexopak celebrated its 50th anniversary as the largest company in its field, with annual sales in excess of $60 million and with approximately 2,600 employees. Shortly thereafter the president and founder, Thomas Samuels—then in his 70's—decided to step down and turn the active management of the company over to one of the present officers of the company. Recognizing that there had been little organization planning and that a new president, even one from within the company, would find the present structure confusing and unwieldy, he decided as a first step in reorganization to analyze the top management of the company. Exhibit 1 on page 312 shows the present top management of Flexopak.

Reporting directly to President Samuels as an "assistant to" is Thomas, Jr., his 30-year-old son. The younger Samuels works primarily on special projects assigned to him by his father as part of a long-range program designed to groom him for the presidency. At the moment, because of his youth and inexperience, he is not being considered as a replacement for his father. The treasurer, who has 25 years' service, is slated to replace Mr. Samuels as president. There are several reasons for his selection. First, he is thoroughly

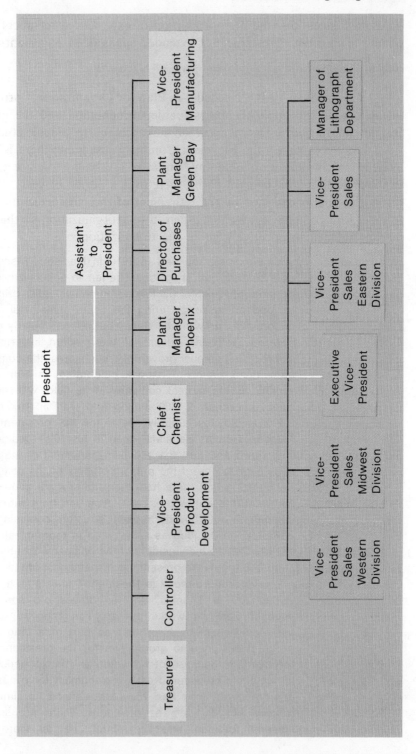

Exhibit I
TOP MANAGEMENT—THE FLEXOPAK COMPANY

acquainted with the financial affairs of the company and has personally arranged all long-term financing. Second, there is the possibility that Flexopak will either "go public" or merge with a larger company seeking diversification. In either case, the major strategic moves of the company seem to lie in the financial field, hence the desire to have a chief executive thoroughly familiar with the company's finances.

The controller of the company actually functions as chief accountant and does not have the necessary breadth to assume the duties of treasurer. There is the vice-president, product development, formerly an outstanding salesman, who directs the work of a small research group. The chief chemist, reporting directly to the president, is responsible for the development, production, and distribution of vinyl film, which is produced in a small Wisconsin plant. The development laboratory is located in the plant and is supervised by the chemist.

The plant managers of the Phoenix plant and the Green Bay plant report directly to Mr. Samuels. The plants in Phoenix and Green Bay are of special interest to Mr. Samuels and, at the time they were founded, he told the managers of these plants that they were his personal representatives in the communities in which the plants are located. It should be noted that the manager of the lithograph department also reports to the president. The lithograph department, in reality a complete operation within the main plant in Madison, is operated on a profit-sharing basis by an old friend of Mr. Samuels. The vice-president, manufacturing, supervises the works manager of the Madison plant; however, his chief function is machine design.

The executive vice-president, also located in Madison, supervises the company's one subsidiary, a paper mill, and has reporting to him, in addition to the president of the paper company, the corporate director of industrial relations. The director of purchases, who joined the company two years ago, performs the purchasing function for the Madison plant only, but hopes in time to purchase for the entire company.

There are four men who have the title, vice-president, sales. Actually, the eastern division and the western division vice-presidents function as general managers. In the eastern division there is an assistant manager who supervises the activities of the 20 salesmen in the eastern states. In addition to the assistant manager, the sales vice-president of the eastern division, whose officers are in New York, has reporting to him the managers of plants located in Philadelphia, Lancaster, and Brooklyn. The western division vice-president, with offices in Madison, has Mr. Samuels' younger son as his assistant sales manager. The assistant manager directs the work of 15 salesmen who are located in the southwestern and southeastern states. The vice-president of the western division also supervises the managers of the Los Angeles and San Francisco plants and the ten salesmen who are located in the western states. The vice-president of the midwestern division is not responsible for any plants. He, too, has an assistant manager who supervises the 15 salesmen of the midwestern region who do not live in Chicago. From his Chicago office the vice-president works closely with the 11 salesmen assigned to the Chicago area. The fourth vice-president, sales, is located in the home office in Madison and has reporting to him four product sales managers, three city salesmen located in Madison, the director of advertising, and the director of the creative art department, a group that designs packages as a customer service.

PROBLEMS

1. Recommend a plan of reorganization for Flexopak. Present the new organization in chart form and justify your solution.
2. Comment on Mr. Samuels' span of management. How can this span be justified?

Chapter Questions for Study and Discussion

1. The quotation from Louis A. Allen on page 291 presents an analogy that compares the design of an organization to the design of an automobile. What is the lesson to be learned from this analogy? What similar analogies can you develop? What are the limitations of such analogies?
2. What is meant by the statement that most of what is called organization is actually reorganization?
3. What is meant by the term departmentation? Give an example of each of the six bases of departmentation.
4. Comment on each of the following statements: (a) The characteristics of people should be given prime consideration in the creation of departments. (b) The characteristics of the work performed should be given prime consideration in the creation of departments.

5. Why is the phrase, span of management, used in the text rather than the phrase, span of control? Which phrase do you prefer? Why?
6. Comment on the advisability of shortening the lines of communication and at the same time decreasing an executive's span of management.
7. Evaluate the reasons presented by Hamilton, Graicunas, and Urwick for a limited span of management.
8. What phrase in Urwick's principle makes possible the justification of increased spans of management? Does this seem a valid reason for increasing the span of management?
9. Summarize in your own words the results of the AMA survey (Table 10-1) and advance several reasons why these companies "all known to have good organizational practices" do not follow Hamilton's recommendations or Urwick's principle.
10. Summarize in your own words how the propositions of Theory Z can be applied as a means of evaluating the bases used for departmentation and for determining the probable effectiveness of a given span of management.

CHAPTER 11

Organization Relationships

The Muskegon Machine Works is a Delaware corporation that operates two plants. One is located in Muskegon, Michigan, and employs 700 people; the other is located in Nashville, Tennessee, and employs 300 persons. The Machine Works, as it is known locally, is proud of its relations with its stockholders and their active participation in annual meetings. At the last meeting the present board of directors was reelected and, in turn, the board reappointed the present officers of the company. A meeting of the board of directors of the Machine Works is now in progress.

"Gentlemen," John Johansen, president of the company and a member of the board, began. "I have asked for a meeting so that we might review our current labor negotiations. We have been negotiating with the local union for the past 60 days in an effort to reach an agreement satisfactory to both parties. Two months ago we met in this same room and authorized our negotiating team to hold the line with a seven cent an hour increase, some slight improvement in the pension plan, and a modification of our group insurance to bring the benefits in line with the daily room charges of the local hospitals. Mr. Lasker, chairman of our negotiating committee, tells me that the union is adamant in its demands: a 12 cent an hour wage increase, one additional holiday which brings the total to nine, and four weeks' vacation for all employees with 10 years' service. The seven cents an hour represents an increase in labor costs of $145,000 a year for the company since we give the same increase to the Nashville plant that we settle for here. The 12 cents that the union is demanding would add another $100,000 to the $145,000. You are well aware that our average hourly rate in Muskegon is 20 cents an hour above the average for the industry and 30 cents more than our average in the Nashville plant. Also, I am told that the union is meeting tonight to take a strike vote on our final offer presented to them this morning and in line with the instructions we gave our committee at the start of these negotiations. We have a meeting scheduled with the union tomorrow, the expiration date of our current labor agreement; if we don't reach an agreement then, the union is free to strike. Shall we stand firm in the face of what promises to be a long and costly strike?"

All issues are discussed thoroughly and the board votes unanimously in support of the company's final offer and instructs the negotiating team not to change its present position.

*   *   *   *

In another part of town a special meeting of the local union is in progress. Norvell Slater, a 39-year old electrician with 20 years' seniority is speaking to the membership. He has been an active member of the union since its certification as the bargaining agent of the employees of the Muskegon Machine Works by the National Labor Relations Board more than 15 years ago.

"I am reporting to you as president of the local and chairman of your bargaining committee. For the past two months we have been meeting with company representatives in an effort to reach agreement on a new contract. So far, not much has been accomplished. We have gained some slight improvement in our pension plan, and the daily room allowance of the hospitalization insurance has been increased so that it now covers the full cost of a hospital room. The real problem seems to be wages. When we started negotiations, we decided that we wouldn't take less than 12 cents an hour. The company says that they won't give more than seven cents. They say that we are getting 20 cents an hour more than the rest of the industry and 30 cents more than Nashville. I don't know about that. All I know is that we are getting 10 cents an hour less than other workers here in Muskegon for the same kind of work and we live here, not in

Nashville." At this point there is a roar of approval from the floor.

"The other things we can't get together on are holidays and vacations. Don Toms, our international representative, tells us it would be a feather in our cap if we could lead the parade for once and get something first in this town. Getting that ninth holiday would put us out in front for a change. And about the four weeks' vacation for you fellows with 10 years' service; you should get that now and not have to wait 20 years for it like I did. Anyway, that fourth week doesn't seem like much to me when you compare it to the three-month vacations that some companies are giving. Any questions?"

Again all issues are discussed thoroughly and the vote to strike is unanimous unless the company meets the union's demands for wages, vacations, and holidays.

At nine o'clock the next morning the negotiating teams meet in a downtown hotel. The meeting ends at 6 p.m. with no agreement. As the meeting closes, Norwell Slater makes this comment: "You know our contract expires at midnight. We have a strike vote backing us up, and since we can't get together we have no choice but to strike. Pickets will be placed around the plant in the morning."

The next morning pickets are at every gate and none of the hourly employees, all members of the union, make any effort to cross the picket line.

PROBLEMS

1. What is the source of authority granted to the board of directors of the Muskegon Machine Works? Did the board exceed that authority in authorizing the company negotiating committee to stand fast in the face of a certain strike?
2. What is the source of authority that permits the local union to enforce its contract demands by striking? Has the union exceeded its authority in the above case?
3. Does the action taken by the union; i.e., an economic strike, negate or cancel in any way the authority of the management to operate the plant? If so, how?
4. What are the obligations of the employees of the Machine Works to (a) the company and (b) the union?

When discussing theories X and Y in Chapter 9, brief statements were made concerning the *source* of authority. It was mentioned that

Theory X assumes that the source of authority is related to the right to own property and the attendant obligation to manage property, while Theory Y states that in order for authority to exist, it must first be accepted by those who are being subjected to that authority. These two positions concerning the source of authority are diametrically opposed; one regards authority as being granted by a source external to the organization and the other views authority as being granted internally by the members of the organization through their acceptance of the exercise of authority. The first purpose of this chapter is to discuss the nature of authority and to reconcile these opposing points of view concerning the *source* of authority. In addition to understanding the sources of authority, it is necessary to appreciate the relationships between two types of authority that are exercised in most formal organizations. These different types of authority are usually called *line* authority and *staff* authority. The second part of the chapter discusses the important organizational relationship of line-and-staff authority.

AUTHORITY

One way of developing an understanding of the differences concerning the source of authority is to present statements representative of each point of view. However, before presenting and analyzing these statements, let us examine various familiar meanings of the word, authority.

Meanings of Authority

There are many different meanings to authority. A board or a commission empowered to act in a specific area may be termed an authority; for example, the port authority. We recognize government as an authority in the phrase, the authority of the state. An individual may be recognized as competent in a given field of learning or as possessing technical qualifications that enable him to speak with authority. Technical writers and expert witnesses are examples of this kind of authority. When we refer to the authority of the president, we are associating authority with an office or a position.

Authority is an abstract concept and, as shown by the above examples, it is a concept applicable to many situations. When used in management literature, the term authority has yet another meaning. Managerial authority may be defined as *the right to act or to direct the action of others in the attainment of organizational goals*. This definition states explicitly two characteristics of authority: (1) authority is a *right* and (2) as a result of possessing this right, one is entitled to *act*, either directly through his own actions or indirectly through the actions of others. Implied, but not stated explicitly, is a third characteristic of authority—(3) the *power* to employ penalties or rewards so that the desired action is completed. Power remains implicit, for there is a great deal of variation in the amount of power associated with managerial authority; in fact, there is one form of authority, staff authority, that may be purely advisory in nature with no power whatsoever. In addition, there are situations in which two or more conflicting or overlapping authorities are entitled to act and the power assigned to one authority may outweigh the power of the others; yet, the authority of those with lesser power remains.

Sources of Authority

Theory X, the work-centered approach, relates the source of authority to the right to own property. The right to own property and the association of authority with that right are dependent upon the organization of the society in which we live. Relating the source of authority to the right to own property and the subsequent management of that property may be termed an *institutional* source of authority since it is dependent upon the institution of organized society. Theory Y, the people-centered approach, regards authority as a situational phenomenon. Authority exists only when the subordinates of a situation accept another individual as having the authority to direct them. Therefore, this source of authority may be designated as *subordinate-acceptance*.

Institutional Source. To state that authority is derived from the right to own private property is a narrow view of the source of authority and not entirely correct since there are instances of managerial authority not dependent upon the ownership of property. To discover the source of authority one must first determine why it is possible to own private property. Our constitutional form of government in the United States rests upon the concept that government represents the will of the people, a will expressed through the action of elected representatives, Congress, and enforced by a judicial system. One aspect of our legal system is that it permits the ownership of private property and the management of that property in accordance with established law. Thus, the real source of managerial authority lies not in the right to own property, but rather in the laws that permit the ownership of property. Case Problem 11-A states that the Muskegon Machine Works is a Delaware Corporation, a statement which indicates that the company is created by law and, as such, possesses the authority necessary for its operation. If further evidence is needed to emphasize that authority is derived from law and not the ownership of property, consider the Tennessee Valley Authority. The managerial authority exercised by the managers of TVA, a publicly owned and operated utility, is derived from an action of Congress, which created the Tennessee Valley Authority. The authority of the management of TVA can come from no other source than law since the ownership of private property is not involved.[1]

Subordinate-Acceptance Source. Do you remember the following story that appears in Chapter 9?

> An agent for the Textile Workers Union of America likes to tell the story of the occasion when a new manager appeared in the mill where he was working. The manager came into a weave room the day he arrived. He walked directly over to the agent and said, "Are you Belloc?" The agent acknowledged that he was. The manager said, "I am the new manager here. When I manage a mill, I run it. Do you understand?" The agent nodded and then waved his hand. The workers, intently watching this maneuver, shut down every loom in the room immediately. The agent turned to the manager and said, "All right, go ahead and run it." [2]

The story illustrates, according to the subordinate-acceptance approach, that the manager has no authority because the subordinates, the men in the mill room, refuse to accept his authority.

Among the first to dissent from the institutional concept of authority was Chester I. Barnard, a successful business executive, who, in the words of Professor Mandeville, "writes with authority about authority." [3]

---

[1] Cyril J. O'Donnell, "The Source of Managerial Authority," *Political Science Quarterly,* Vol. XLVII (December, 1952), pp. 573-88. Professor O'Donnell's article is a skillful presentation of authority derived from institutional sources.

[2] Douglas McGregor, *The Human Side of Enterprise* (New York: McGraw-Hill Book Company, 1960), p. 23.

[3] Morton J. Mandeville, "Organizational Authority," *Academy of Management Journal,* Vol. III (August, 1960), pp. 1960), pp. 107-18. An adaptation of Professor Mandeville's article appears in Paul M. Dauten (ed.), *Current Issues and Emerging Concepts in Management* (Boston: Houghton Mifflin Company, 1962), pp. 199-207. Professor Mandeville presents the entire range of opinion concerning the definition of authority. Immediately following Mandeville's "Organizational Authority," in *Current Issues and Emerging Concepts in Management,* is a reply by C. Edward Weber entitled "The Nature of Authority: Comment" and Mandeville's reply to Weber's comment, pp. 208-12. The original citation for Professor Weber's article is as follows:

C. Edward Weber, "The Nature of Authority: Comment," *Academy of Management Journal,* Vol. IV (April, 1961), pp. 62-66.

Robert Albanese, "Substitutional and Essential Authority," *Academy of Management Journal,* Vol. IX, No. 2 (June, 1966), pp. 136-144.

The student who reads these articles will gain insight into a current management issue that is far from settled.

The following quotations from Barnard present his definition of authority and the related concept that the source of authority is its acceptance by a subordinate.

> Authority is the character of a communication (order) in a formal organization by virtue of which it is accepted by a contributor to or "member" of the organization as governing the action he contributes, that is, as governing or determining what he does or is not to do so far as the organization is concerned.[4]

Barnard's statement concerning the source of authority is as follows:

> If a directive communication is accepted by one to whom it is addressed, its authority for him is confirmed or established. It is admitted as the basis of action. Disobedience of such a communication is a denial of its authority for him. Therefore, under this definition the decision as to whether an order has authority or not lies with the person to whom it is addressed, and does not reside in 'persons of authority' or those who issue these orders.[5]

We now have before us two conflicting views of authority. One, the institutional approach, says that authority is derived from the laws of the society in which we live; the other view of authority, the subordinate-acceptance approach, says that there is no authority unless the person who is the object of that authority accepts the order or directive as authoritative. Thus, it is the subordinate's acceptance, not the laws of society, that is the source of authority.

Effectiveness of Authority

Effective management requires a manager to have a clear understanding of the nature of authority. Managerial authority is not absolute; however, a manager cannot permit himself to be reduced to a state of indecision resulting from self-questioning concerning whether or not he has the right to manage. On the other hand, he cannot blithely assume that his every action or directive will result in the fulfillment of organizational goals. There are three factors that limit the effectiveness of managerial authority—(1) superior authority, (2) overlapping authority, and (3) subordinate acceptance of authority. Note that subordinate acceptance as stated above does not negate or cancel managerial authority; *it merely limits the effectiveness of that authority*. Let us examine each of the three limitations on authority.

---

[4] Chester I. Barnard, *The Function of the Executive* (Cambridge: Harvard University Press, 1938), p. 163.
[5] *Ibid.*

Superior Authority. The actions of the officers of a corporation are subject to review and limitations imposed by the board of directors. In Case Problem 12-A, the president of the company calls for a meeting of the board to review current labor negotiations. In so doing he is recognizing the higher authority of the board and seeking a course of action that meets with their approval. The board, in turn, is subject to the legal authority of the owners, the state and the federal governments. Companies impose limitations on the authority of managers by establishing policies and procedures; for example, a plant manager may be authorized to make capital expenditures up to $1,000 without prior approval, but required to submit for approval expenditures in excess of $1,000. These instances illustrate that authority is not absolute; rather, it is always subject to limitation by higher authority.

Overlapping Authority. Problem No. 3 of Case Problem 11-A asks whether or not the action of the union, i.e., the calling of a strike, negates or cancels the authority of management. If the source of authority lies in the acceptance of that authority by subordinates, then the answer to Problem No. 3 is affirmative. Now, analyze the situation carefully. The company, a corporation created by law, is exercising proper authority in determining what it believes to be best for its economic welfare. The union, too, is created by law and is certified by the National Labor Relations Board as the official bargaining agent for the employees of the Muskegon Machine Works. Also, the union is exercising properly the authority granted by law in enforcing its economic demands by striking. Thus, here is a situation in which both parties are exercising legally constituted authority to determine the wage rates of the employees of the company. Clearly, there is overlapping and dual authority, with each authority having the same source, law, and each authority being properly exercised. The rejection of the company's offer by the union and the subsequent strike do not negate the authority of management; it simply means that at this point in time the power of the union is sufficient to prevent the management from exercising its authority to operate the plant. Later, as the strike progresses, the company may accede partially or fully to the union's demands, or the union may agree to the original offer made by the company. Authority is not cancelled by power conflicts, which arise frequently when authority overlaps; it is only held in abeyance until the forces of power are resolved.

Subordinate Acceptance. Some proponents of the subordinate-acceptance concept of authority leave the impression that disobedience and the rejection of authority are the normal behavior for members of an organization. Nothing could be further from the truth. The institutions of society, including authority, serve a purpose desired by the majority of that society; however, occasions do arise when subordinates refuse to accept the direction of authority. Most authority carries with it rewards and penalties that may be used to encourage compliance. Robert Tannenbaum, who recognizes authority as derived from the acceptance of subordinates, also recognizes that the weighing of rewards and penalties by subordinates is an important factor in their determining whether or not to accept authority.[6] The weighing of rewards and penalties is in effect a recognition of authority. Disobedience does not cancel authority, but it does render it ineffective for that particular situation unless the reward and/or punishment is sufficient to exact compliance.

LINE AND STAFF RELATIONSHIPS

The preceding discussion emphasizes superior-subordinate relationships—the relationships between the managers and the workers of an organization. There is another authority relationship that is equally important—the relationship between two different types of authority exercised by the managers of an organization. These two forms of authority are called *line authority* and *staff authority,* designations of authority that result in the corresponding expressions of *line organization* and *staff organization,* phrases which classify the entire organization according to the predominant type of authority exercised. In discussing line-and-staff authority relationships, we will seek answers to the following four questions:

1. What is line authority and what are its functions?
2. What is staff authority and what are its functions?
3. What are the problems inherent in line-and-staff relationships?
4. Is the line-and-staff concept of authority obsolete?

Line Authority

The concept of line-and-staff authority recognizes that within an organization there are two types of managerial authority. There are also two aspects to the definition of line authority. First, line authority may be defined as a relatively simple authority relationship that exists between a superior and a subordinate. Second, line authority may be defined in terms of the organizational function supervised by a manager. When line authority is defined in respect to organizational

---

[6] Robert Tannenbaum, "Managerial Decision Making," *Journal of Business,* Vol. XXIII (January, 1950), pp. 22-39.

function, the critical characteristic of the function that determines whether it is line or staff is the degree to which the function in question contributes to the direct achievement of organizational objectives. Let us examine each aspect of line authority.

An Authority Relationship. When defined as an authority relationship, *line authority entitles a superior to direct the work of a subordinate; in essence, this is a command relationship.* It is a command relationship extending from the top of the organization to the lowest echelon and is aptly described as the *chain of command.* As a link in the chain of command, a manager has the authority to direct the work of his subordinates, and, in turn, he is subject to the direction of his superior. He reports "in line" to his superior and is a part of the line organization. Figure 11-1 shows the relationships that form the chain of command.

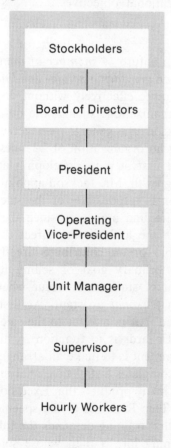

Figure 11-1
**LINE AUTHORITY RELATIONSHIP
AS A CHAIN OF COMMAND**

Contribution to Organizational Objectives. The second definition of line authority does not contradict the above view which holds that line authority is a command relationship between superior and subordinate. It does, however, shift the emphasis of the definition from one of relationship between superior and subordinate to organizational function. This shift in emphasis results in the following definitions.

"Line refers to those positions and elements of the organization which have responsibility and authority and are accountable for accomplishment of primary objectives." [7]
and,

"Line positions in an organization are those concerned directly with the creation and distribution of salable utilities or with the management of such activity." [8]

The key to distinguishing between line and staff is not the function itself,

---

[7] Louis A. Allen, *Management and Organization* (New York: McGraw-Hill Book Company, 1958), p. 206.
[8] William McNair Fox, *The Management Process* (Homewood, Illinois: Richard D. Irwin, Inc., 1963), pp. 78-79.

but rather it is the degree to which the function contributes directly to the achievement of organizational objectives. In an army, the infantry, the artillery, and armored units are known as "line" since they contribute directly to organizational objectives—engaging the enemy in battle; the supporting services—ordnance, medical, engineering, and supply—are regarded as auxiliary in nature and referred to as "staff." In manufacturing organizations, production and sales are regarded as line functions, while purchasing (supplies) is usually classified as staff. Yet, in a department store, the purchasing function, called buying, and sales make up the line organization. Most firms regard finance as a staff function, but for a loan company the acquisition and management of capital is part of the line organization. In each of these examples, the basis for designating a function as line is the contribution of that function to the direct achievement of organizational objectives.

Staff Authority

Staff authority is advisory or service in nature. *A member of management possessing staff authority advises or provides a service for line managers.* An organization may function quite effectively without any designated staff managers, and in small organizations such is the case.

In Case Problem 10-A, Thomas Jackson, the general manager of Excelsior Products, is effectively managing an organization of 22 salesmen and three clerks. Assume that, as a first step in developing an organization structure capable of extended growth, Mr. Jackson appoints five regional sales managers, each of whom is responsible for the sales in his geographic area. These managers are line managers since they report directly to Mr. Jackson. They have the authority to direct the work of the salesmen and are fully responsible for and contribute directly to the achievement of the organization's primary goal of selling its product. The first step in the development of staff might occur when Mr. Jackson employs Tom Richards as a *personal* assistant. At first, the duties of Tom Richards are not specified, but in a letter to the sales managers, Mr. Jackson states that Tom Richards is to function as his personal assistant. Perhaps Tom's first assignment is to make all arrangements for the next sales meeting. Then he completes a statistical analysis of the dollar volume of sales for each of the many products that Excelsior sells. Eventually, Mr. Jackson may assign Tom Richards to the specific job of training new salesmen and discover that training demands the full time of a specialist. As a next step, he may hire a man whose sole function is the training of new salesmen. Thus, the undifferentiated work of the personal assistant may develop into a specialized staff role.

This example illustrates that the need for staff services arises partially as the result of increasing size in an organization with an attendant increase in the work load of the chief executive. Consequently, one of the functions of staff is to ease the load of top management.[9] The personal assistant is frequently engaged as a means of easing the work load. As size increases, operations usually become more complex and the need for specialized services arises and results in the creation of a specialized staff. These two forms of staff, which are termed _personal staff_ and _specialized staff,_ are discussed briefly.

Personal Staff. There is need to define clearly the difference between an _assistant-to_ a manager and an _assistant_ manager. The former, the assistant-to, is a personal assistant to his chief. His duties vary widely from one organization to another and they also vary considerably from time to time within the same company. He receives the necessary authority to perform his duties from his chief and usually the authority is granted on a limited basis; that is, it is extended for a specific job and for a relatively short period of time. The duties of an assistant-to may range from the routine task of opening the chief executive's mail to negotiating a purchase agreement for a new plant site as a personal representative of the chief. Note that the assistant-to usually has no specific function to perform; his duties vary with the assignment at hand. Second, there is no authority associated specifically with the position; it is authority granted only for each individual assignment. Third, the assistant-to does not act in his own behalf; instead, he is acting as a personal representative of his superior.

The assistant manager is not regarded as staff; rather, he is part of the line. As shown in Figure 11-2 (A), the operating executive reports through the assistant general manager to the general manager. In the absence of the general manager, the assistant manager acts in his stead. The assistant-to, Figure 11-2 (B), usually does not have the authority to act as general manager when the latter is absent. If the general manager desires, he may assign certain specific functions to the assistant manager. For example, all activities related to manufacturing may report to the assistant manager, while the general manager supervises those activities associated with sales. Another possible arrangement is for the general manager to oversee the line functions of the organization, while all staff services report to the assistant manager. In each

---

[9] Ernest Dale and Lyndall F. Urwick, _Staff in Organization_ (New York: McGraw-Hill Book Company, 1960), pp. 1-14. The first chapter of the book, entitled "The Load on Top Management," serves to introduce the various applications of staff in management.

of these possibilities we note that (1) subordinates report directly to the assistant manager, (2) the assistant manager has fairly constant, well-defined responsibilities assigned to him, and (3) in the absence of the general manager, the assistant manager assumes the full authority of the general manager's position.

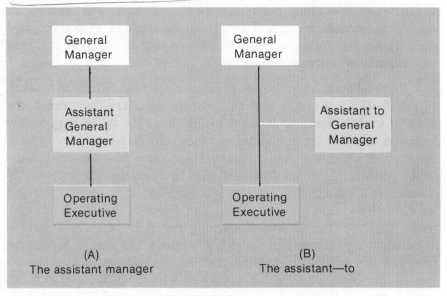

Figure 11-2

**ORGANIZATONAL POSITION OF THE ASSISTANT GENERAL MANAGER
AND THE ASSISTANT TO GENERAL MANAGER**

Specialized Staff. As an organization grows in size and complexity, the undifferentiated role of the personal assistant develops into specialized staff assignments. There is no unanimity concerning the functions that may be performed by specialized staff personnel, nor is there complete agreement concerning the type of authority that may be exercised by staff managers. Nonetheless, the following three types of specialized staff authority appear in business organizations with great frequency:

1. A staff specialist may have the authority to provide a specific *service* for the line organization and thus exercise *service authority.*
2. Not all staff positions are created for the purpose of providing service; some have as their sole function the offering of advice in respect to a special group of problems. Staff men in these positions exercise *advisory authority.*
3. Another type of specialized staff authority is *functional authority,* an authority that provides the staff specialist with considerable latitude and freedom to make decisions in his own functional area.

It must be understood that these three forms of staff authority are not clear cut; there is considerable overlap, and many positions utilize all three forms of staff authority.

Figure 11-3 shows a typical staff organization at the plant level of a manufacturing firm. The supervisor of production planning and control is responsible for planning and controlling the flow of production; the supervisor of purchasing serves by making necessary purchases; and the plant engineer is responsible for maintaining physical facilities. The supervision of each of these functions exercises *service authority* in providing a service for the line organization. The authority of the supervisor of personnel may be either service authority or advisory authority. When performing the employment function of recruiting and screening applicants, the personnel supervisor is clearly rendering a service for the line; however, his duties may also include the administration and analysis of morale surveys with the purpose of advising the line in regard to actions necessary to improve employee morale. The staff supervisor, when offering advice to the line, is drawing upon advisory authority. The industrial engineer, the quality control supervisor, and the head of the accounting department have as their primary function the offering of advice in specialized areas; and though there is a strong element of service in the work that each performs, it is best to regard their authority as *advisory* in nature.

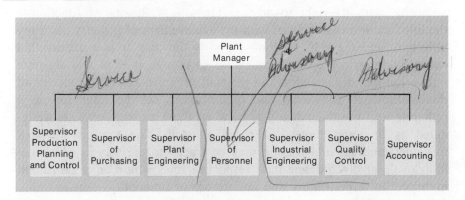

Figure 11-3
TYPICAL STAFF ORGANIZATION AT THE PLANT LEVEL

Functional authority broadens the concept of service and advisory authority so that a staff manager may exercise effective direction and control of his functional specialty. There are two ways of exercising functional authority. First, staff managers may be granted functional authority over their counterparts who are in lower levels of the organization; and second, the particular functional specialty in question may be separated from the line manager's job and assigned to the appropriate staff specialist.[10] Figure 11-4 shows both forms of functional authority. Note that the plant supervisor of each staff function reports functionally (usually indicated by a dotted line) to his staff counterpart at the next higher level. In large organizations this next higher level may be a geographic division, and the managers at the divisional level report to their counterparts on the corporate staff. In addition, the plant staff supervisor performs that portion of the production foreman's job which falls within his specialty. Thus, there are cost clerks in the production department who report to the supervisor of cost accounting and prepare all production costs. The plant industrial engineer supervises time studies and institutes changes in methods, and the quality control supervisor directs the work of inspectors who accept or reject the finished product. Although functional staff authority is limited to a specific function, it may sometimes be quite absolute within that particular function, with the result that the auhority of the line manager may be severely restricted.

Problems in Line-Staff (L/S) Relationships

The duality of the line-staff (L/S) concept inherently creates problems of interpersonal relationships. Two authorities exist within an organization—line authority with its right to command, and staff authority, with its right to advise. There is a duality of function— the line function is associated with the achievement of primary company objectives and the staff function supports the line. It is a duality that results in referring to an organization as though it were two separate units—the line organization and the staff organization. The concepts of dual authorities, functions, and organizations set the stage for some rather serious misunderstandings between those persons who are designated as line and those designated as staff. The reasons for L/S misunderstandings and friction may be traced to the way in which the individuals involved define their respective roles within an organization in respect to responsibility and importance of function.

Responsibility. It is generally agreed that the line manager is responsible for achieving the primary objectives of the organization.

---

[10] Frederick W. Taylor referred to the assignment of the specialized portions of the production foreman's job to the appropriate staff specialist as "functional foremanship." Further, he recommended that all of the "brain work" be eliminated from the foreman's job and that the worker come in contact with many members of management for his directions rather than just one member—the foreman.

Frederick W. Taylor, *Scientific Management* (New York: Harper & Brothers, 1947), pp. 98-99.

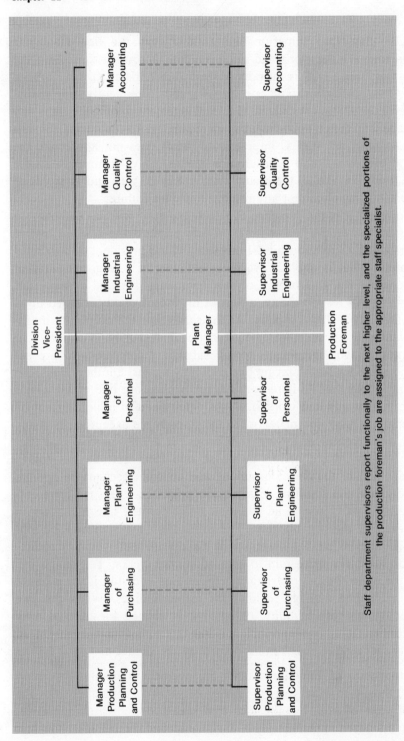

Staff department supervisors report functionally to the next higher level, and the specialized portions of the production foreman's job are assigned to the appropriate staff specialist.

Figure 11-4

THE EXERCISE OF FUNCTIONAL AUTHORITY

When the organization is small and there is no staff, there are no restraints other than superior line authority on the line manager's freedom to make decisions and initiate action necessary to achieve the stated goals. When staff is introduced, restraints appear, for it is implied that the line manager should consult with staff. Frequently, line managers view consultation with staff as an infringement upon their authority to manage, and the resulting resentment toward staff is expressed through such statements as "staff is impractical," "staff does not appreciate the technical problems," and "consultation means delay." Line may accuse staff of trying to take all the credit when things go well and at the same time be unwilling to accept any responsibility for failure.

However, it is the presence of functional staff with its authority to administer its own particular function that presents the severest test of interpersonal L/S relationships. For example, the president of a subsidiary company that is one of several subsidiaries of a large corporation is responsible for the profits of his company; and as a means of emphasizing this responsibility, a part of his incentive pay is based upon the profitability of his company. At the same time the corporate industrial relations staff, empowered by functional authority, is expected to negotiate the labor agreements for all subsidiary companies to prevent the various unions from playing one company against another. Thus, the president is told that he is responsible for profits, but one of the major cost factors—wages and work rules—is determined to a large extent by staff personnel who do not report to the responsible executive. Is it any wonder that resentment toward staff arises? It is only normal that friction builds up in a situation in which one feels that he has lost a significant part of the decision making and control necessary to operate effectively, and the resulting tensions are expressed as a specific resentment toward staff. The same situation holds for the line managers in lower levels of the organization. The production foreman may be told that he is responsible for the costs of his department, yet the requirements of staff may force him to hire additional clerks. To summarize, one of the main sources of friction between line and staff is the manner in which the line manager defines his responsibilities. When the line manager defines responsibility, or when it is defined for him, as *total* responsibility, it is only normal for him to resent any intrusion of authority that tends to weaken his control of the situation.

Importance of Function. Staff's infringement upon the line manager's authority to manage is the major cause of L/S conflict from the point of view of line, but the idea that staff functions are supportive, with the attendant implication that they are secondary and somehow less important, is the main source of L/S conflict as viewed by staff managers. To understand staff's position, it is necessary to state briefly the personal characteristics of staff personnel. As a rule, staff men are highly ambitious and eager to advance, and they are somewhat younger and have a higher level of formal education than their line counterparts.[11] The staff manager is also aware that the reason for his employment is his specialized knowledge, and since he is ambitious and desires to advance, it is only natural that he advance by the avenue which seems most logical to him—advancing his ideas. When his ideas are restricted by line, he is told that it is the function of line to decide and that his role is supportive in nature. To the staff man the statement that line makes the decision is a distortion of what happens in practice, if not pure fiction. The following example supports staff's contention that it is staff, not line, who makes critical decisions or, at the very least, makes it possible for the line manager to decide.

In a typical manufacturing organization, the manager of manufacturing is responsible for producing the product and the sales manager is responsible for distribution of the product. Both are line managers whose activities are coordinated by a higher line authority, a president or a general manager. Who determines how much of each product is to be manufactured and the sequence in which these items are to be produced and sold? As a result of analyzing market trends and customer needs, the staff manager of the market research department recommends the optimum product mix. The manager of production planning and inventory control, another staff department, interprets and translates the findings of market research into production schedules that specify quantity and sequence for manufacture of each product. Though the sales manager approves the recommendations of market research and the production manager approves schedules developed by production planning and inventory control, it is understandable why staff managers of market research and production planning consider that they in effect make the decisions. It is difficult to relegate either staff function to a supportive role when the very nature of these functions influences so greatly the success of the company in fulfilling its primary objectives— the manufacture and the distribution of a product.

Is Line-Staff Obsolete?

Conflict between line and staff has long been recognized as a major deterrent to organizational effectiveness, with the result that

---

11 Melville Dalton, "Conflicts Between Staff and Line Managerial Officers," *American Sociological Review,* Vol. XV (June, 1950), pp. 342-51.

many students of management have offered suggestions to minimize such conflict. One such set of recommendations states that line has the final responsibility for the successful operation of the company and consequently should have the authority to make operating decisions. Staff functions are carefully defined as providing either service or advice to the line; an advice or service that should be presented when requested by line and also when, in the opinion of staff, it is considered necessary. It is stated that whether or not staff's advice or service is accepted depends entirely on the judgment of line, and line is urged to seriously consider staff recommendations. The last recommendation.suggests that both line and staff should have the right of appeal to a higher authority.[12]

The recommendations presented above are helpful in some cases; however, such recommendations are of limited value primarily because they rest upon assumptions that are of questionable validity. These assumptions are: (1) line managers will accept the advice and recommendations of staff and (2) staff is able and willing to accept a supportive-role in the organization and continue to put forth its best effort when in fact its recommendations are generally ignored.[13] Also, recommendations for improving line-staff relationships implicitly assume that the line-staff concept is necessary for organizational effectiveness. There are two alternatives to the line-staff concept that deserve careful consideration.

Functional-Teamwork. Functional-teamwork is an organizational concept presented by Gerald Fisch, a management consultant, as an alternate to the line-staff concept.[14] It is suggested that three functional areas be defined and each area represent a function significant to the well-being of the organization. In addition to defining the functional areas that are grouped under *time, resources,* and *human interrelations,* the task of top management is carefully defined. Let us see how the many activities of a business organization that are classed as either line or staff are treated under the functional-teamwork concept.

---

[12] Louis A. Allen, "The Line-Staff Relationship," *Management Record,* Vol. XVII (September, 1955), pp. 346-49. The recommendations cited in the text are based upon Mr. Allen's suggestions. Also see the set of recommendations found in Ernest Dale, *Planning and Developing the Company Organization Structure* (New York: American Management Association, 1952), Research Report No. 20, pp. 76-83.

[13] Rocco Carzo, Jr., "Organizational Realities," *Business Horizons,* Vol. IV (Spring, 1961), pp. 95-104. See pages 99-100 for Mr. Carzo's analysis of line and staff.

[14] Gerald G. Fisch, "Line-Staff Is Obsolete," *Harvard Business Review,* Vol. XXXIX (September-October, 1961), pp. 67-79. This section is based upon Mr. Fisch's article which states the author's belief that the line-staff concept is obsolete. In place of the line-staff (L/S) concept, Mr. Fisch suggests *functional-teamwork* (F/T). The first part of the article presents a careful analysis of the line-staff concept and the second part presents in detail the functional-teamwork concept.

PROCESS FUNCTIONS. All functions within the business that must be controlled with *time* as a major element are classed as *process functions.* Included as process functions are product design, purchasing, manufacturing, advertising, physical distribution (sales), and billing. Note that in this arrangement the usual line functions of sales and manufacturing are grouped with functions normally regarded as staff to form a functional unit concerned with the movement of the product from its inception in product design, through manufacturing, the distribution system, and the final billing—all related activities accomplished under the pressure of time; hence, they are process functions.

RESOURCES FUNCTION. All resources—physical, monetary, and human—are considered as part of the resources of a company, and it is the function of the resources manager to acquire, maintain, and utilize these resources in the most efficient manner possible. Physical facilities, capital invested in the business, the skills of employees, and patents on products or processes are all considered as resources that should be carefully controlled and utilized.

RELATIONS FUNCTION. The relations function can be summed up in one word, communications, and it includes both internal and external communications. Business in our society has an acute communications problem; and, in most companies, little is being done to present a consistent, coherent picture of the company and its problems to employee groups, shareholders, the community, various government agencies, and to the customer. These are the relations that would be supervised by the director of the relations function.

GENERAL MANAGEMENT. Though not a function in the same sense as the above three functions, general management deserves particular attention under the functional-teamwork concept. With the day-to-day work allocated to the three functional managers, the top management of the organization is free to establish corporate goals and objectives, to offer leadership when needed, to coordinate and realign the functions when necessary, and to control the entire operation.

There are several characteristics of the functional-teamwork concept that differentiate it from the line-staff concept of organization. First, there is only one authority, managerial authority, that is exercised by each of the managers of the process, resources, or relations function within his own functional area. Second, once the goals of the organization are established and the resources determined to be adequate for the project at hand, the decisions concerning the production of the company's product or services fall within a logical framework. Third, a structure encouraging teamwork is stressed so when the actions of one function touch upon those of another function, the problem is one of resolving the question on a teamwork basis rather than determining which party has the superior authority. Also, top management is free to encourage a teamwork solution to problems as they arise.

Task Force Organization. The functional-teamwork concept implies a fundamental redesign of the organization structure. An approach similar to functional-teamwork, though generally much more limited in its scope, is often called *task force organization* or *task force management*. Like functional-teamwork, a task force is essentially a team effort. There are several distinctive characteristics of a task force. First, it is a tightly organized unit under the direction of a manager who usually has broad powers of authority. Second, a task force is organized to accomplish a specific task or goal such as the introduction of a new product or building and placing into operation a new physical facility. A task force is working against a time deadline since its objectives must be accomplished by a certain date. Third, the personnel who make up the task force possess a diverse range of skills and abilities, thus making it possible for each member of the group to make a unique contribution to the solution of the problem.

A good example of the application of the task force concept of organization to the solution of a specific problem is Minneapolis-Honeywell's Polaris Missile task force headed by a manager of the team with a production manager, an account manager, a subcontract manager, and a procurement manager reporting to him. The task force organization is also successfully used in such diverse activities as construction, advertising, military fighting units, and motion picture film production. Whenever there is a need for *concerted* team effort to accomplish a specific goal within a relatively short period of time, the creation of a task force may offer a means of creating an organization capable of accomplishing the desired goals.[15]

---

[15] A. K. Wicksberg and T. C. Cronin, "Management by Task Force," *Harvard Business Review,* Vol. XL (November-December, 1962), pp. 111-18. In this article the authors stress team effort in task force management and offer practical suggestions for the reassignment of personnel after the completion of a specific project.

The following studies, more recent than "Management by Task Force," indicate that there are also problems inherent in the task force or project form of organization that may in some circumstances limit the effectiveness of this form of organization.

Richard Alan Goodman, "Ambiguous Authority Definition in Project Management," *Academy of Management Journal,* Vol. X, No. 4 (December, 1967), pp. 395-407.

Richard M. Hodgetts, "Leadership Techniques in the Project Organization," *Academy of Management Journal,* Vol. XI, No. 2 (June, 1968), pp. 211-219.

(Continued)

There is no universal answer to the question raised at the beginning of this section—is line-staff obsolete? The line-staff concept serves many companies very well, particularly those companies operating in an environment of minimal change. However, when stress situations appear with the accompanying need for prompt action in order to survive, many companies turn to the functional-teamwork concept of organization by creating a task force to solve the immediate problem. Since the application of the concept of functional-teamwork is effective in a crisis situation, it is only logical to consider the possibility of applying the functional-teamwork approach to organization as a continuing form of organizational structure to insure the maximum utilization of resources in meeting the daily challenges of competition. In addition to stress situations with their accompanying need for prompt action, the introduction of integrated information-decision-making systems also calls for a reexamination of the line-staff concept. Such systems cut across traditional departmental lines and functions with a resultant change in the locus of the decision-making function. Modern information systems also result in the creation of large functional units composed of several traditional line-staff departments. Further, when the need for interaction between the members of an organization is high, the functional-teamwork concept offers a structure that makes possible highly effective communications.

Case Problem 11-B offers you an opportunity, as a chief executive, to resolve a typical conflict between a line manager and a staff specialist.

| CASE PROBLEM 11-B

LINE-STAFF RELATIONSHIPS | The Glass Container Company, with headquarters in Chicago, is a large manufacturer of glass containers that operates 18 plants located throughout the United States. The company has three geographic divisions—Eastern, Central, and Pacific—each of which is headed by a vice-president and general manager who is responsible for the sales and manufacturing functions within his division. The Central Division's general manager is a young, aggressive executive who seems destined to become the president of the company. Under his direction the profits and sales volume of the division have grown |

W. A. Meinhart and Leon M. Delionback, "Project Management: An Incentive Contracting Decision Model," *Academy of Management Journal*, Vol. XI, No. 4 (December, 1968), pp. 427-434.

Clayton Reeser, "Some Potential Human Problems of the Project Form of Organization," *Academy of Management Journal*, Vol. XII, No. 4 (December, 1969), pp. 459-467.

each day, a growth due in large part to the successful operations of the Minneapolis plant. The manager of the Minneapolis plant, a graduate engineer, was brought into the company as a plant manager as part of a planned program to strengthen the management of the company. Plans are now being made to transfer the Minneapolis manager to the corporate headquarters in New York, thus making it necessary to select a new manager for Minneapolis.

In Chicago, there is a director of organizational planning who is a member of the corporate staff and reports directly to the president of the company. At the suggestion of the director of organizational planning, the Minneapolis plant manager was recruited from outside the company since a survey of key personnel indicated a need for technically trained managers. Normally the director of organizational planning works directly with the division vice-presidents in an advisory capacity; and when he and the vice-president agree upon a proposed move of key personnel, the move is made without consulting the president of the company. However, when there is disagreement, the matter is usually referred to the president who makes the final decision.

There is still a need for graduate engineers capable of filling top managerial positions that are presently available and those expected to develop within the next five years as the result of expansion and the retirement of present personnel. It is believed by all concerned that sound preparation for top management should include two or three years of experience as a plant manager as a means of learning the technical aspects of the glass container industry.

In regard to the Minneapolis position, there are three possible choices. First, another man can be recruited from outside the company and be assigned to the Minneapolis plant as manager, thus providing a period of training with subsequent assignment to a more responsible position in the corporation. Second, there are several young assistant plant managers who would profit from experience as manager of a large plant; and although it would probably take longer for any of them to develop, they too could be promoted to more responsible positions. The third possibility is to promote the present assistant plant manager, a man who is 50 years old with 25 years' service with the company. The assistant plant manager is responsible to a large extent for the success of the plant since he directly supervises the operating departments and is thoroughly familiar with the technical aspects of glass making. However, he has indicated an unwillingness to move from the Minneapolis area and has expressed a desire to retire upon the completion of 30 years' service at age 55, which is permissible under the terms of the company's pension plan.

In discussing these three possibilities with the general manager of the Central Division, the director of organizational planning recommended either of the first two choices and pointed out that if the third choice were adopted, it would mean the blocking of a valuable training position for at least a five-year period. He also stated that should the assistant plant manager elect to work until normal retirement at age 65, it would mean an even longer period of time before the plant could be used as a training position. However, the division vice-president insists upon promoting the present assistant plant manager. He readily admits that the promotion of the assistant plant manager will effectively block the use of that position as a training position; but he does not want to see any of the younger assistant plant managers in the Minneapolis position, nor will he approve the recruitment of a man from outside the company. To him, either of the first two choices means putting an unknown quantity into an important operating position that markedly affects the profitability of his division. In summing up his position, he tells the director of organizational planning:

"I'm charged with the responsibility of maintaining profitable operations in the plants under my direction, and the extent to which I meet this responsibility determines to a large extent my future in this company. For me to accept either a new man from outside or a younger man from within the company whom I don't know personally is to run the risk of being responsible for a less profitable plant. I realize that you are responsible for planning for corporate organizational needs, but I'm responsible for the operating success of this division."

Since the matter could not be resolved with the vice-president of the division, the director of organizational planning decided to refer the question to the president of the company.

PROBLEMS

1. As president of the company, how would you decide the matter?

2. Should the director of organizational planning be given the authority to overrule the division vice-president in the functional area of organizational planning?
3. Is the concept of functional-teamwork applicable in this situation? If so, how?

Chapter Questions for Study and Discussion

1. Comment on the following statement: Authority emanates from the office or the position that a person holds and not from the person himself.
2. How is the concept of power related to the concept of authority? Is it possible to exercise authority without power? Give an example.
3. What is meant by the statement that managerial authority has its source in law rather than as the result of a right to own property?
4. Under what condition does the quotation on page 321 that describes the relationship between a union agent and a plant manager illustrate the loss or the absence of authority? Is the plant manager still managing the plant even though it is not in operation?
5. In your opinion is the quotation on page 321 illustrative of the absence of authority or the lack of effectiveness of authority? If your answer is lack of effectiveness, why is the manager's authority ineffective?
6. Develop examples that illustrate each of the conditions that limit the effectiveness of authority.
7. Identify, by occupation and function performed, the line organization of the following types of organizations: a manufacturing firm, a bank, a retail store, a hospital, and a university. Why do certain occupations such as accountants and physicians shift from line to staff positions in different types of organizations?
8. Is there a chain of command within a staff department? If so, give an example.
9. Differentiate in your own words between an "assistant-to" and an "assistant" manager. Give an example of each. Which assistant is staff?
10. On what grounds can the concepts of line and staff as applied to industrial organizations be criticized? What are the advantages resulting from utilizing the L/S concept in industrial groups?
11. Under what conditions is the functional-teamwork or the task force type of organization feasible?
12. Is the functional-teamwork or the task force type of organization a play on words, or is it actually a different type of organization? Support your answer.

CHAPTER **12**

Organizational Processes
—Delegation and Decentralization of Authority

Thomas Dayton, now 41 years old, is one of several candidates who are being considered for the position of general manager of manufacturing for Engineering Products, a firm with seven manufacturing plants. A review of Tom's personnel file indicates that he joined the firm as a design engineer immediately after receiving his degree in mechanical engineering from the state university. His first assignment was on the board as a draftsman, and a notation by the supervisor of the drafting department indicates that Tom did this job willingly and well. The notation reads in parts:

"Mr. Dayton is now in his sixth month as a member of the design department. There have been several occasions when he has come in voluntarily on weekends to rework drawings so that they meet the most exacting specifications. It is unheard of for Mr. Dayton to turn in work that is smudged or messy in any way."

At the end of 18 months Tom was promoted to section chief and placed in charge of ten draftsmen. As might be expected, the work from his section was almost perfect. One reason for the high level of accuracy was that Tom actually performed the work of the section checker and personally reviewed all drawings thoroughly and carefully before passing them on to the head of the department. On more than one occasion Tom reworked the drawings of his subordinates in order to meet specified deadlines.

Following these early years in the design section, Tom's rise was steady and sure. During the time that he served as assistant manager of the research laboratory there were several important product modifications, primarily the result of his own work and effort. After several years in research, he was transferred to one of the larger plants as assistant manager in charge of all production departments so that he could supervise the introduction to manufacturing of one of the products which he had developed. He remained in this position for over five years and during most of this time the production costs for the manufacturing departments under Tom's supervision were the lowest in the company. Upon the retirement of the plant manager, Tom was moved up to manager with the honest congratulations of all concerned. There were no reservations concerning his ability to work long and hard in order to get the job done; nor was his loyalty to the company questioned.

It did not take long to realize the success predicted for Tom as plant manager; that is, success measured by the operating statement. Operating efficiency increased slightly, and when combined with the substantial reduction in administrative expenses, the result was a marked increase in the profitability of the plant. However, all was not well with Tom's administration. The chief industrial engineer of the plant resigned and told Tom his reason for resigning was that he had been offered a similar position in another company at considerably more money. Yet, in a conversation with the corporate general manager of industrial engineering, the following remarks were made:

"We no longer have any weekly staff meetings at the plant. These were stopped about a month after Tom became plant manager. He told us then that they were a waste of time and that if we had any special ideas about improving operations we should see him personally. Also, he now approves all changes in pay. As a department manager, I used to be able to approve pay changes for the engineers in my department as long as they were within the provisions of the corporate salary plan; but not now, because he approves all changes in pay, regardless of the amount or whether they are within the terms of the salary plan. As for overtime, he approves all overtime in advance, not only in the general administrative departments but also within the production departments, a responsibility that normally lies within the control of the assistant plant manager. And the cost control program results in his actually running all departments. We are supposed to run our departments within the limitations set by the annual budgets, but not any more. Tom wants all expense accounts sent directly to him; as department managers, we no longer see them. The switchboard operator sends him a daily tally of all long-distance telephone calls with the name of the party called, the name of the person making the call, and the amount of the call. But what really irritates me is that he plans the work of my department and calls my men into his office to check on the accuracy of their work. If he wants to run the industrial engineering department, he is welcome to do so, but he doesn't need a department manager for the job—he needs a chief clerk."

Mr. Thompson, the present general manager of manufacturing, is slated to move to the presidency of the corporation. He is a staunch supporter of Tom Dayton and points to Tom's outstanding record of success in the company. The general manager of manufacturing coordinates the production of all seven plants and is accountable to the president of the company for the performance of the plants. Traditionally there is a substantial degree of delegation of authority to the individual plant managers for day-to-day operations. Such a policy of delegation results, on occasion, in some rather expensive mistakes on the part of plant managers and the attendant temptation to step in and correct things immediately; but the net result is the development of strong plant managers and a highly efficient manufacturing organization. Mr. Thompson realizes that Tom Dayton is not a good delegator, but he believes that as president of the company, he can develop Tom into a good manufacturing manager and teach him how to delegate.

PROBLEMS

1. What are the underlying causes of Tom's failure to delegate?
2. Do you agree with Mr. Thompson that Tom can be taught how to delegate?
3. Why should a manager be criticized for his failure to delegate?

In Chapter 11 the sources of authority were examined and the interpersonal relationships that exist between those persons performing line functions and those who are engaged in staff work were discussed.

Fundamental to the exercise of managerial authority, either as line authority or staff authority, is an organizational process that permits the transmission of authority from superior to subordinate—a process called the *delegation of authority*. It is this process of delegating authority from superior to subordinate that makes it possible for organizations to grow. The extent to which organizations consistently delegate authority downward to lower-level organizational units is called the process of *decentralization of authority*. In this chapter we discuss the nature of the process of delegation of authority with particular emphasis upon the factors that make it difficult for an executive to delegate effectively. The chapter also applies the concepts of Theory Z in determining the optimum degree of decentralization of authority within an organization and examines the potential effect of modern information-decision-making systems upon the extent of decentralization.

THE PROCESS OF DELEGATION

Delegation of authority is an organizational process that permits the transfer of authority from superior to subordinate. There is general agreement that the process of delegation is made up of three distinct steps; however, there is considerable variation in the terminology used to describe each of the three steps. The following quotations illustrate the variation in terminology and emphasize the need for careful definition of terms so that the process of delegation may be understood.

Professors Koontz and O'Donnell describe delegation as follows:

> The entire process of delegation involves the *assignment* of tasks, the *delegation* of authority for accomplishing these tasks, and the *exaction* of responsibility for their accomplishment.[1]

Professor Newman describes the delegation process as follows:

The process of delegation has three aspects:

1. The assignment by an executive of *duties* (planning and doing of specified activities) to his immediate subordinate.
2. The granting of *permission* (authority) to make commitments, use resources, and take other actions necessary to perform the duties.
3. The creation of an *obligation* (responsibility) on the part of each subordinate to the executive for the satisfactory performance of the duties.[2]

---

[1] H. Koontz and C. O'Donnell, *Principles of Management* (4th ed.; New York: McGraw-Hill Book Company, 1968), p. 67. Chapter 4, "Authority and Responsibility," pp. 59-80, discusses the process of delegation in considerable detail.

[2] W. H. Newman, *Administrative Action* (2d ed.; Englewood Cliffs, New Jersey: Prentice-Hall, Inc., 1963), pp. 185-86.

The third quotation from Louis Allen, a management consultant, defines responsibility as work rather than an obligation and introduces the concept of accountability.

> We have now described the three essential aspects of delegation: the entrustment of *work,* or *responsibility,* to another for performance; the entrustment of *powers and rights,* or *authority,* to be exercised; and the creation of an *obligation,* or *accountability,* on the part of the person accepting the delegation to perform in terms of the standards established.[3]

Aspects of Delegation

Although each of the definitions above recognizes three major steps in the process of delegation, there is considerable difference in the terms used to describe each step. In this textbook, the following terms will be used to describe the three aspects of the process of delegation:

1. The assignment of responsibility.
2. The delegation of authority.
3. The creation of accountability.

Assignment of Responsibility. The term, *responsibility,* has been used to refer to either the work that is being assigned or to the obligation created by the assignment of such work. In the first two quotations cited above, responsibility is used to denote an obligation; yet the third statement by Louis Allen defines responsibility as work to be performed. There are several reasons for limiting the meaning of responsibility to duties, or work, to be performed in fulfilling an assignment. In our everyday speech we frequently equate responsibility and duties by referring to the responsibilities of a parent or the responsibilities of a student. Also, many companies in their descriptions of managerial positions state the responsibilities of a given position as duties to be performed. Another reason for limiting the meaning of the word responsibility to assigned duties is that there is a specific term, *accountability,* which is used to describe the obligation created by the assignment of responsibilities.

Thus, responsibility is defined as *all of the duties that must be performed in order to complete a given task.*

Delegation of Authority. Delegation has a precise meaning. One who delegates to another person *empowers that person to act for him.*

---

[3] L. A. Allen, *Management and Organization* (New York: McGraw-Hill Book Company, 1958), p. 116. On pages 116-17, footnote 3, there is a brief discussion of the various terms used to describe the process of delegation.

Two facets of this definition deserve careful attention. First, the delegator *empowers* the delegatee. In Chapter 11, authority is defined as the right to act or to direct others to act. Since responsibilities—or duties—are assigned as the first step in the process of delegation, it is necessary that the person to whom responsibility is assigned either act or direct others to act in the performance of those duties. Authority empowers such action; hence the expression, the delegation of authority, with the result that the delegatee is empowered to act or to direct others to act.

The second facet of the definition deserving careful attention is the phrase, *for him*. A person possessing delegated authority is acting for, or representing, the person who delegated the authority. The implications of acting for another are significant as an organizational process because it means that even though authority is delegated to subordinates so that they may successfully fulfill their assigned duties, the delegator still retains full control over the delegated authority and may recall that authority as the occasion demands. Delegation in no way implies abdication. When a king abdicates, he divests himself of all responsibility and authority; however, an executive who delegates remains responsible for the accomplishment of assigned duties and retains full control over delegated authority.

Creation of Accountability. The moment one accepts a loan from a bank he incurs an obligation to repay the money that he has borrowed. Likewise, when a subordinate accepts responsibility and the authority necessary to carry out those responsibilities, he incurs an obligation—a duty to perform the assigned work and to properly utilize the authority delegated to him. The creation of such an obligation on the part of a subordinate, when viewed as an organizational process, is defined as the creation of *accountability*. The subordinate is *accountable* to his superior for the proper exercise of authority and the performance of assigned responsibilities. An easy way to differentiate between the concepts of responsibility and accountability is to remember that a subordinate is *responsible for* the completion of work assigned to him and is *accountable to* his superior for the satisfactory performance of that work.

Conditions for Effective Delegation

The preceding analysis of delegation presents a process that is relatively easy to understand and seemingly simple in its nature; however, in actual practice a great deal of difficulty is experienced in achieving effective delegation. There is general agreement among students of management and management practitioners that three conditions must be met for the process of delegation to be most effective. These conditions are:

1. Parity of authority and responsibility.
2. Absoluteness of accountability.
3. Unity of command.

Each condition is discussed briefly below.

Parity of Authority and Responsibility. *For effective delegation, the authority granted to a subordinate must be equal to the responsibility assigned to him.*

When a subordinate undertakes assigned duties, it is logical and fair that he be delegated the authority necessary to enable him to act, or direct others to act, so that the assignment may be completed. The concept of parity of authority and responsibility recognizes the need for delegated authority and emphasizes that delegated authority should be of sufficient scope so that the assigned responsibility may be accomplished. Too little authority usually manifests itself by a manager having to consult his superior before making relatively routine decisions. A manager of manufacturing, charged with the responsibility of producing the company's product within specified cost and quality limits, should be able to make decisions pertaining to purchasing raw materials, maintenance of equipment, selection and training of personnel, and the determination of the most efficient methods of manufacturing. In short, the authority granted should be of sufficient scope so that all related activities may be accomplished.

Although the granting of too little authority is a frequent reason for ineffective delegation, failure to fully understand and recognize the limitations normally inherent to managerial authority causes most of the difficulty in the application and interpretation of the principle of parity of authority and responsibility. One limitation, not always understood or appreciated, is that managerial authority seldom carries with it the power necessary for the literal achievement of assigned responsibilities.

For example, a sales manager cannot force customers to buy, nor can a personnel director force a union to cooperate with management; yet, it is not uncommon to say that the sales manager is "responsible" for the sales in his territory and that the personnel director is "responsible" for establishing cooperative relations with the union. Another limitation on managerial authority results from restrictions imposed by the organization itself. Authority is not absolute; instead it is circumscribed by statements of company policy and procedure that have the effect of defining the limits of authority for each level of the organization. A regional sales manager may have a substantial advertising budget and the authority to select the media appropriate for his geographic area, yet the total spent may not exceed the budgeted amount without prior approval from his superior. Restrictions set by higher authority exist for every position within a company.

We have described three conditions that may result in an imbalance between authority and responsibility. First, there may be too little authority granted for the task at hand; second, there are situations in which a manager has little or no power to direct the actions of others; and third, organizational policies and procedures often limit the extent of a manager's authority. With such restrictions on authority, one might reasonably ask whether or not a concept of parity of authority and responsibility is practical. The answer is yes, because knowledge of the difficulties encountered in creating coextensive authority and responsibility should help in developing effective techniques of delegation and in realistically assessing the extent to which an executive should be held responsible for the accomplishment of assigned duties.

Absoluteness of Accountability. *Although responsibility may be assigned to and authority may be delegated to subordinates, accountability to one's superior can neither be assigned nor delegated.*

When the process of delegation is defined as the assignment of responsibilities, the delegation of authority, and the creation of accountability, it is evident that both responsibility and authority may be transferred. Indeed, the continuing redelegation of authority and reassignment of responsibility makes organizations possible. Departmentation, the dividing of work into manageable units, is an example of the assignment of responsibility. When major departments are created, the chief executive is dividing his responsibility—his work load—so that others may more effectvely accomplish the tasks necessary for the achievement of organizational goals. At the same time that responsibilities are assigned, commensurate authority is also delegated so that managers of the newly created work units may effectively act or direct others to act. In turn, the major departmental units are further subdivided, with the managers of the subunits receiving assigned responsibilities and delegated authority. But accountability, the obligation to report to one's superior, cannot be delegated nor assigned. The president of a company, although assigning to a sales vice-president the responsibility and delegating to him the authority necessary to carry out the sales function, remains accountable to his superior, the board of directors, for the successful discharge of the sales objectives. In turn, the sales vice-president, though redelegating authority and reassigning responsibility to division sales managers, remains accountable to his superior, the president, for the successful discharge of the sales function. In theory, the concept of accountability is absolute and cannot be transferred. However, in practice it is recognized that assigned responsibilities are performed by subordinates whose work may fall short of expected standards of performance. For example, the sales vice-president considers the number of new and inexperienced salesmen when evaluating the performance of a division sales manager; and the president considers these facts when appraising the work of the vice-president.

Unity of Command. *Each subordinate should be accountable to one, and only one, superior.*

The unity of command concept states something we all know— no man can serve two masters well. The expression, unity of command, stresses that the sources of command should be so unified that a subordinate receives assigned duties and delegated authority from one superior and is accountable only to that superior. The following four examples represent situations that result in a subordinate having more than one master and serving none well.

UNDIFFERENTIATED ORGANIZATIONS. Occasionally in small organizations there are work groups that are undifferentiated in respect to rank or job assignments. Frequently the head of such a group characterizes his work force as "one big happy family." An employee who is a member of an undifferentiated work group is not certain what is expected of him nor is he sure of the relative powers of the several persons who direct him. As a result, he is forced to select from several job assignments those that he believes to be most effective in placating his several supervisors. Even though an employee may succeed in keeping his job by "greasing the wheel which squeaks the loudest," it is doubtful that organizational objectives are being met effectively. Objectives may be attained much more efficiently when an organization structure is established so that each supervisor knows clearly the subordinates accountable to him and each subordinate knows the supervisor to whom he reports.

INTENTIONAL DISREGARD OF UNITY OF COMMAND. Frequently organizations that have progressed beyond the undifferentiated work-group stage and have established well-defined superior-subordinate relationships intentionally assign one subordinate to two or more supervisors. Such assignments are justified on the grounds that the work load is light and that it is necessary for an employee to work in several departments in order to keep fully occupied. However, it must be recognized that disputes may arise when one supervisor demands more than his share of time. These difficulties can be avoided or minimized by designating in advance a higher authority to determine which department has precedence.

BYPASSING INTERMEDIATE SUPERVISION. A third violation of the unity of command concept arises as the result of leapfrogging or bypassing one or more levels of intermediate supervision. For example, a plant manager who ignores his superintendent and directs a foreman to change a production schedule is bypassing an intermediate level of supervision. Such action is unfair to the foreman who is put into the position of serving two masters and carrying out two sets of conflicting directions. It is also unfair to the superintendent who remains accountable to the plant manager for the performance of his subordinates even though he has lost effective control over their actions. The remedy for the difficulties and misunderstandings which appear as the result of bypassing is not found in recommending that each supervisor have contact only with his immediate superior and his immediate subordinate; rather, it is found in clearly defining the nature of these personal contacts. It is desirable and necessary for an executive to be aware, as the result of personal observation and contact, of the activities of all levels of the organization; however, the actual direction of subordinates should remain the specific responsibility of that subordinate's designated supervisor.

STAFF RELATIONSHIPS. Figure 11-4 on page 330 illustrates the concept of functional staff authority and shows the relationship that may exist between two or more levels of staff personnel and between line-and-staff personnel at the plant level. The exercise of strong functional authority may result in situations that violate the unity of command concept.

Dual command arises when the supervisor of quality control at the plant level receives instructions concerning the establishment of acceptable levels of quality from his functional superior, the division manager of quality control, that conflict with those standards established by the plant manager who is his direct line superior. In the same manner, a production foreman may be placed in the position of receiving orders from more than one source of authority when the plant quality control supervisor sets quality standards in conflict with those previously stated by the plant manager. The potential difficulties resulting from the dual authority sources of line and staff are minimized when the functional authority of staff is clearly defined and it is emphasized that even though staff properly has authority within a given functional area, any direct orders are to be issued only by the immediate line superior.

Practical Suggestions for Successful Delegation

The conditions for effective delegation discussed above provide a basis for understanding more fully the process of delegation and recognizing the conditions that may result in ineffective delegation. Admittedly, a delegation of sorts can occur even though all three conditions are violated simultaneously, yet few deny that observance of the conditions of delegation results in more effective delegation. The following practical suggestions for successful delegation are offered as a means of putting into practice the conditions for effective delegation.[4]

1. Determine Objectives. Remember the principle of the objective: *Before initiating any course of action, the objectives in view must be clearly determined, understood, and stated.* The process of delegation affords an excellent opportunity for the application of the principle of the objective. As a first step, it is necessary to determine the goals expected as the result of a specific work assignment. A statement of goals is important to the process of delegation for two reasons: First, the duties and responsibilities of a job are derived from and directed toward the achievement of stated objectives. Second, the person to whom work is assigned is accountable to his superior for successful completion of those duties; consequently, unless work performed is pertinent to achieving stated goals, the concept of accountability becomes exceedingly vague.

2. Assign Duties and Delegate Commensurate Authority. Determine all the duties that must be performed to complete the task at hand; then assign the whole job—not just parts of it. There are too many instances where supervisors assign only the minor or routine details of a job and retain the key decision-making aspects of the job for themselves. Such assignments are not delegation in the true sense of the word since there is little need for the delegation of authority. Defining the whole job at the very start of a project brings into proper perspective the amount of authority needed to insure parity of responsibility and authority. Also, subordinates are more likely to be better motivated by assignments that encompass the whole job.

---

[4] *Ibid.*, Chap. 7, "Better Methods of Delegation," pp. 134-55. Chapter 7 presents an extensive discussion of specific methods that may be used for more effective delegation.

3. Select Subordinate. Select the man for the job in the light of what is expected. Assigned responsibilities are in effect the duties of a job; and duties, if they are to be completed successfully, require certain skills and knowledge. In addition to possessing the necessary skills and knowledge, the best candidate for the job is the man who is willing to accept full responsibility for achieving stated objectives. Among the many reasons for a subordinate's unwillingness to accept responsibility are lack of understanding of what is expected, fear of failure or criticism, and insufficient motivation. Whatever the reason, if a choice must be made between two subordinates with one possessing the necessary skills and experience but unwilling to assume responsibility, and the other short on experience but willing to assume responsibility, it is probably better to choose the one who is willing to accept responsibility.

4. Establish Necessary Controls. In the discussion of the second step of the process of delegation, the delegation of authority, it is stated explicitly that delegation is not synonymous with abdication. Instead, the delegator retains the right to recall delegated authority and remains accountable to his superior for those responsibilities assigned to others. Thus, it is necessary for the delegator to establish and exercise necessary control over the actions of his subordinates so that he may fulfill his obligations. Essential to proper control is the maintenance of clear channels of communication between superior and subordinate so that a complete interchange of information is possible. Controls also imply that corrective action may be taken if needed to insure the fulfillment of stated objectives. Resentment toward controls on the part of subordinates is minimal when the subordinate participates in establishing the controls to be used.

BEHAVIORAL ASPECTS OF DELEGATION

Thus far, our discussion of delegation includes an analysis of the three steps in the process of delegation, a statement of three conditions that should be observed for most effective delegation, and specific practical suggestions for successful delegation. There has been nothing said about the process of delegation that is not perfectly straightforward and relatively easy to understand. Yet, if this were all of delegation, or even a major portion of the process of delegation, there would be little reason for discussing delegation so extensively in management literature. The real problems of delegation lie not in the observance of the conditions of delegation nor in following the practical suggestions for successful delegation, but rather they are found in the personality of the person doing the delegating.[5]

Usually it is easy to recognize the superior who finds it difficult to delegate. His behavior is characterized by an excessive attention to details, coupled with a marked distrust and questioning of the ability of subordinates. There are many reasons for these two characteristics, which for purposes of discussion, may be grouped into four broad categories. First, there are those persons who seemingly have always been interested in activities and studies that require precision and exactness. These persons seem to often follow vocations requiring and emphasizing precise action. Second, there are those persons who immerse themselves in details as a means of avoiding the central problems of a situation. Third, there are those who refuse to relinquish any part of their job to others because of a deep-seated fear of failure. The fourth group who refuse to delegate and must retain all of a job for themselves are those who have a paranoid (fear of persecution) distrust of others. Let us examine each of these groups separately, realizing that there is considerable overlapping between each group and that most failures to delegate can be traced to one or more of the four categories.

Vocational Choice

Any discussion of personality factors and vocational choice may evolve into the proverbial question of which comes first, the chicken or the egg. In other words, does one enter a given vocation because of certain underlying personality traits or does the specific vocational training received mold the personality? Admittedly, both processes operate simultaneously. There is much in our culture that emphasizes the importance of doing a job well and following it through to completion. Some people have been brought up with the admonition, "If you want a job done well, do it yourself." Whatever the sources of desire for personal accomplishment, we are taught to respect those persons capable of hard and effective work.

There are specific forms of vocational training that tend to reinforce and make even more permanent the normal inclinations of attending to detail. Accounting and engineering are good examples of such vocational training in that both courses of study require a meticulous

---

[5] Ernest Dale, *Planning and Developing the Company Organization Structure* (New York: The American Management Association, 1952), Research Report No. 20, pp. 38-48. Professor Dale presents a discussion of the impact of the chief executive's personality upon the process of delegation.

attention to detail, a liking for exactness expressed in the form of numbers to the third decimal place, and considerable hard work and drudgery to complete the course. Upon graduation, the engineer may find himself in the position of doing exacting work on a drafting board and the accountant may be performing the work necessary for a detailed audit. It is the ability to do this first assignment—close attention to detail—and to do it well that results in promotion. Is it any wonder that a man with a normal liking for detail, reinforced by four years of college training in precise work and subsequently reinforced en route to success and promotions, should find it difficult to let go of the detail part of his job and turn it over to others?

Some of these highly trained persons, and Thomas Dayton of Case Problem 12-A is one of them, are frequently very competent in their field of work, a competency often expressed by the phrase, "I can do it better myself." Although they may not be able to do it better, they usually can perform the work as well. Another characteristic is the 12- to 16-hour day, which with few exceptions is the result of an inability to delegate, rather than due to the press of important affairs. It is difficult to change persons such as Thomas Dayton and make them successful delegators. Basic to the difficulty is their liking for work and their ability to do it well. Admonitions concerning health may fail to encourage them to delegate. Even after the occurrence of physical breakdown, some are still unable to slow down and delegate their work to others.

Avoidance of Major Issues

Attention to detail sometimes offers a security and comfort not possible when one's attention is directed toward the major problems at hand. In extreme cases the ability to attend to detail rather than to the central issue is important for life itself, for were one to face the real problem, he would be overwhelmed and unable to carry on. An example of the extreme is illustrated in the following brief quotation describing the plight of a refugee:

> The refugee was a peasant woman from down San Carlos way. She was complaining of the haste with which she and her family had had to flee. The burden of her complaint was that her husband's new suit and his Sunday gloves had had to be left behind. I had heard exactly the same kind of protest years ago in China; I was to hear it later in Austria and Czechoslovakia. The mind of the refugee, dazed and uprooted, concentrates upon the small, specific losses that it can cling to with understanding. To be homeless and without food or shelter

as a result of the "policy" of foreign dictators and prime ministers—that is a state so terrible that it cannot be taken in all at once. The new suit, the Sunday gloves, these are the losses one can still comprehend.[6]

Although managers may not be faced with problems of such personal magnitude as those confronting the war refugee, there are instances where some managers simply cannot cope with the central issues of their environment and as a result direct their attention to peripheral details that are related to, but are not the real problem. The sales manager who personally reviews each salesman's expense account and then tallies the amount spent on telephone calls may be avoiding the real problem of increasing the number of new customers. The president of a company who reviews every change in salary may hold down payroll costs and then complain that he does not have time for the major task of coordinating the development of new products.

Fear of Failure

Feelings of personal insecurity with the attendant fear of failure may be the cause of inability to delegate. These are not the feelings of insecurity and unsureness associated with lack of knowledge and experience that are normal when one undertakes a new job; rather, it is the unsureness derived from a feeling of personal inadequacy. For some, fear of failure may be very real and imminent, for they may be on the brink of failure and realize that one more mistake can cost them their job or, at the very least, an opportunity for promotion. For others, failure may not be near, but there is the constant fear of what might happen if failure does occur. In either case, whether failure is imminent or imagined, the underlying thought processes are somewhat as follows: This is a very difficult job to be done. It is full of problems and pitfalls; it requires a great deal of attention, hard work, and skill. It is going to tax my abilities to the limit. Since it is such a hard job for me to do, how can anyone else possibly do this job? Whatever the cause of personal inadequacy, the result tends to be the same—a refusal to delegate, with the firm belief that the job is so taxing that it is inconceivable that anyone else can possibly handle it. As expected, it is extremely difficult to persuade these individuals to let go, because the motivating force is a fear of personal failure. It is a fear that immobilizes action since there is a complete inability to take a risk.

---

[6] Vincent Sheehan, *Not Peace but a Sword* (New York: Doubleday Doran, and Company, Inc., 1939), p. 86. Reprinted by permission of Doubleday & Company, Inc.

Distrust of Others

A fourth reason for not assigning duties and delegating authority to subordinates may be the result of a paranoid distrust of the motives of others. The word paranoid is used to describe a person who has delusions or false beliefs of persecution. The phrase, paranoid distrust, as used here refers to a distrust of others based upon the false belief that a subordinate's drive for success is founded upon a desire to displace or discredit his boss. The supervisor who distrusts his subordinates and fears that they intend to displace him refuses to delegate authority to them as a means of countering their threat. Such refusal weakens organizational processes. There is also a long-range effect on the organization, for when a supervisor tormented by fears of distrust has the opportunity to select subordinates, there is understandably a strong tendency to select only those persons who are so submissible that they are incapable of threatening any superior's position.

To summarize, whatever the reasons for failure to delegate, whether it be the highly trained technician with a liking for detail work, a defense against having to face the central issues of a problem, the fear of failure, or the desire to maintain one's own security through the process of weakening competition, the results are essentially the same. First, the refusal to delegate and let subordinates carry projects through to their normal completion results in the elimination of valuable training experiences. If the reason for reluctance to delegate lies in a well-founded belief that subordinates are not trained or capable, the sad fact remains that by not delegating, subordinates never become trained or capable since the opportunity to learn through the experience is denied. Second, refusal to delegate has the effect of stifling initiative, with the result that it is not long until suggestions and new ideas cease entirely. The subordinate is saying to himself, "Why should I say anything? I'm not allowed to do anything around here anyway." The third effect of refusing to delegate is that the better people, defining better people as those who need to develop and accept more responsibility, leave the company at the earliest opportunity. The industrial engineer of Case Problem 12-A is a case in point. The net result is not a pretty picture—a frustrated superior incapable of delegating and surrounded ultimately by subordinates incapable of accepting responsibility, even if it were offered.

DECENTRALIZATION OF AUTHORITY

Delegation of authority is described in the first part of this chapter as a process that transfers authority from superior to subordinate in an organization. The extent to which authority is delegated within an organization is a measure of the degree of decentralization of authority within that organization. The concept of decentralization of authority is relative in its nature; an organization is never completely centralized nor is it completely decentralized. Complete centralization of authority would require one man with no subordinates—hardly an organization— while complete decentralization implies that there is no longer a central authority, again a situation resulting in no organization.

In discussing decentralization of authority, it is first necessary to define decentralization and to establish guides for determining the extent to which a company is decentralized. Second, criteria are developed in the light of Theory Z to determine the optimum degree of decentralization for an organization. Third, the probable effects of the application of integrated information-decision-making systems upon the extent of decentralization within an organization are examined.

Definition of Decentralization   *where do you find authority.*

Before defining decentralization, it is well to differentiate between decentralization and two other processes often confused with it. These two processes are departmentation and geographic dispersion. In Chapter 10, "Organization Structure," *departmentation* is defined as the grouping of work and people into manageable units, and the bases most frequently used in the creation of departments are discussed. These bases are departmentation by function, product, customer, geography, process, and sequence. However, the mere creation of separate departmental units does not constitute decentralization. For example, the vice-president of sales who appoints five sales managers, each in charge of a different product, is further departmentalizing the sales function along product lines, but he is not necessarily decentralizing the sales function. The division of one large manufacturing plant into six widely separated smaller plants certainly results in *geographic dispersion,* but not necessarily in decentralization. The key to whether the appointment of product sales managers or the building of geographically separate plants is decentralization, or merely further departmentation, is revealed by analyzing the effect of such changes upon the decision-making process within the organization.

Decentralization is the delegation of authority to make decisions to the managers of lower echelon organizational units. The decentralization of the decision-making function is relative, and the degree of decentralization is dependent upon the following three characteristics of the decisions made at lower levels of the organization: (1) frequency of the decisions, (2) breadth of the decisions, and (3) the extent of the controls exercised over lower level decisions. Let us examine briefly each characteristic.

Frequency of Decisions. The greater the frequency or number of decisions made at lower levels of an organization, the greater is the degree of decentralization in that organization.

Breadth of Decisions. The broader the scope of decisions made at lower levels of an organization, the greater is the degree of decentralization. The breadth of decision making is determined by the number of functions affected by the decisions. A plant whose manager is limited to making only those decisions directly affecting production is less decentralized than the plant whose manager's scope of decision making includes, in addition, the negotiation of labor agreements with a union.

Extent of Controls over Decisions. The extent of controls exercised over the decisions made at lower levels of an organization is an important measure of the degree of decentralization. Decisions are frequently classified in terms of the number of dollars involved, with dollar limitations placed upon decisions that may be made without prior approval. Thus, an organization that permits a sales manager to approve customer credit up to $5,000 is more decentralized, other things being equal, than the organization that permits approval by the sales manager of only $1,000 credit. Timeliness of approval is also a factor. There is less decentralization when approval is required before the decision is made than when a superior is notified after the decision is made or when higher authority is not even informed. The number of approvals required prior to the making of a decision is also an index of the degree of decentralization. Generally, the fewer the number of persons who must be contacted for approval, the greater is the degree of decentralization.

A Systems Approach to Decentralization

The preceding discussion of the varying degrees of decision making that may exist at lower levels of an organization emphasizes the relative nature of the concept of decentralization of authority. Decentralization is dependent upon the process of delegation of authority, for without delegation there can be no decentralization. Yet decentralization, as an organizational style, is much more than delegation; it is an expression of a basic management philosophy of operation. With such a philosophy of management, the maximum degree of decentralization is achieved when the authority to make decisions is delegated to the lowest possible level of the organization yet consistent with the needs of the organization, the ability and knowledge of the manager in question to make the decision, and the extent to which information necessary for a sound decision is available at that level of the organization. To implement an approach toward decentralized decision making in an organization, it is necessary to examine some of the factors that influence the extent of decentralization.

In Chapter 9, the parameters of a systems approach to organization theory are stated and in Chapter 10 are applied as aids in determining effective departmentation and efficient spans of management. In the same manner the systems approach parameters may be used as guides in determining the optimum degree of decentralization for a given organization.

Size of Organization. There is a direct relationship between the size of an organization, when defined as the number of people, and the number of decisions that must be made. In addition to an increase in the number of decisions resulting from increased size, there is also a tendency for decisions to become more complex. The increased volume of decisions and the additional time required for the analysis of more complex problems may result in an overburdening of top management and may be accompanied by serious delays in the decision-making process. Thus, one of the major goals of decentralization of authority is the creation of effectively sized decision-making units. Among the advantages claimed for the smaller decentralized units is that the total number of decisions to be made is less, with the result that more time can be devoted to each problem. Also, the decision-making authority is closer to the point of operations, which results in a shortening of the lines of communications and a consequent reduction in the amount of time taken to make each decision. Further, the manager close to the point of operations should be thoroughly familiar with local conditions and able to take these factors into consideration when making decisions.

Interaction Between Members. The need for interaction arises when several persons are working on the solution of a common problem, developing and using the same information, or when there is need for communications with each other. Consequently the need for interaction between members may be used as a guide in determining the optimum degree of decentralization. If the quality of the decision-making process is improved as the result of interaction between members of a given level or unit of an organization, it is wise to decentralize the authority to make decisions at that level. Much of the decentralization that appears in sales departments is recognition of the need for close interaction between the customer, the salesman, and the local manager in reaching satisfactory solutions to a common problem. However, when decisions require interaction between members of several different organizational units or different levels of the same organization, it is wise to centralize the decision-making function at a higher level of the organization so that information may be obtained from all sources.

Personality of Members. The personality of the members of an organization (defining personality as the sum total of the skills, abilities, interests, and personal characteristics) is an important consideration in determining the appropriate degree of decentralization. The personality of the chief executive is highly significant as a predictor of the extent and effectiveness of decentralization within an organization since the first step toward decentralization is taken when he delegates authority to his subordinates. If he is insecure or for any other reason is unable to delegate, the concept of decentralization of authority to make decisions is neither encouraged nor understood. If, on the other hand, the chief executive is capable of delegating authority and circumstances permit him to delegate, the first step toward decentralization is assured, for his understanding of the process of delegation enables him to encourage his subordinates to delegate as fully as possible.

Despite the willingness of top management to decentralize authority, there are instances when the degree of decentralization is severely limited by the availability of competent managers at lower levels of the organization. It is interesting to note that the highly centralized company, upon realizing the gains that might be obtained from decentralization, frequently finds its capabilities to decentralize limited by the availability of competent managers. Often it is necessary to recruit personnel from outside the company to secure managers capable of fulfilling the responsibilities of decentralized operations. Decentralization in itself offers the soundest basis for providing a supply of capable managers. Usually decentralized companies provide more middle management positions that serve to challenge and motivate personnel. The positions are challenging because the areas of responsibility are relatively large and well defined. Middle managers are motivated because there is a greater likelihood that achievement will be recognized and that opportunity exists for advancement to even more responsible positions.

Congruence of Goals. Usually decentralized units are much broader than departments and often are referred to as operating divisions. The need for congruency of the goals of the various parts of a decentralized unit is every bit as important as the need for similarity of objectives of the members of a smaller departmental unit. The result is the same as in the case of the department, for when all members of a decentralized unit are working toward the same objectives—by definition, a high degree of congruency of goals—it is much easier to coordinate the efforts and activities of members. One way of helping to assure congruent objectives among the various decentralized units of a company, and within each separate decentralized unit, is through the establishment of clearly stated company objectives and policies intended to implement these objectives. Continuing two-way communications between the highest and lowest levels of an organization is of importance in maintaining consistent goals for all levels of the organization.

Another method frequently used to assure a high degree of congruence of goals between the corporate managers of a company and the managers of decentralized operating units is through the application of the concept of a *profit center* as the basis for defining the extent of and the goals of a decentralized unit. When profit centers are used as the basis for establishing decentralized units, the process is often described as *profit decentralization.* Either expression, profit center or profit decentralization, emphasizes the use of profit as a basis for establishing decentralized units, an emphasis having several marked effects upon the organization. When the responsibilities, or job duties, of the manager of a decentralized unit are defined in terms of profit, the goal established is congruent with the objectives of the top management of the corporation. Also, when a manager is held responsible for the profits of his division, two additional steps must be taken. First, the unit must be carefully defined so that all segments that contribute to profit come under the jurisdiction of the manager; and second, necessary authority must be granted so that the manager may be held fully accountable to his superior for the profits of his unit. The very concept of profit decentralization has a tendency to further the process of decentralization since both the structure of the organization and the responsibilities of the manager are more sharply defined. However, there are limitations to the extent that the concept of profit decentralization may be applied. Generally, the concept is more readily applied to companies having clearly differentiated product lines that may be combined into logical units, relatively independent of each other, and with each unit capable of producing a measurable profit. General Motors with its highly decentralized Chevrolet, Buick, Oldsmobile, Pontiac, and Cadillac divisions is an example of decentralized product divisions, with each manager responsible for the profits of his division.

Level of Decision Making. When discussing the level of decision making as a guide to the optimum degree of decentralization, we are referring to the level in the organizational hierarchy at which a decision should be made in order to most effectively fulfill the needs of the organization. The appropriate level of decision making changes with respect to each of the major business functions—manufacturing, sales, finance, and personnel.

Typically, manufacturing and sales are among the first functions to show some degree of decentralization, since the purpose of the organization is often served best by decentralizing these functions. In manufacturing, the plant is usually considered as an organizational unit and is relatively self-sufficient and capable of performing all functions necessary for its successful operation. Also, separate plants imply geographic dispersion and tend to encourage decentralization. The same factors that lead to the decentralization of manufacturing are also present as forces in the decentralization of the sales function. Many times on-the-spot decisions demanding special knowledge of a particular customer have to be made. The best decisions from the standpoint of correctness and timeliness come from the local level; hence, the tendency to decentralize the authority to make these decisions.

Finance remains a highly centralized function in most companies. There are several reasons why financial decisions remain centralized in the highest echelon of the organization. Problems relating to the procurement of capital and the distribution of earnings as capital expenditures are properly the functions of the highest level of the organization. These functions, upon which the very existence of the corporation depends, cannot very well be delegated to decentralized units.

Although many of the decisions made in the area of personnel may be decentralized to the operational units of manufacturing and sales, there is a growing tendency to make the key decisions of the personnel function at a centralized level in the organization. For example, operating units usually have the authority to hire employees at the local level; yet the range of salaries paid, and the amount and type of pensions, vacations, and other so-called fringe benefits are determined by corporate personnel policy established by top management. The existence of a master labor agreement, i.e., a single contract between an international union and the several plants of a multiplant company, is the key factor in determining whether or not the previously mentioned areas of personnel decision making are centralized at the corporate level of the company rather than being delegated to the local plant level.

In general, those decisions that are best made at a high level of the organization are more costly in their nature, affect a larger number of employees, and are more significant in determining the course of the business than those decisions delegated to lower levels of the organization.

State of the System. The state of the system is an important consideration in determining the optimum degree of decentralization. In addition to including the extent to which organization goals are being achieved, the concept of the state of the system includes the stage of growth of the company, the nature of the company's business, and the availability of controls. As a company succeeds in achieving its financial objectives, it is possible to exercise a more participative, permissive form of leadership. In a large measure such a form of leadership tends to encourage and further the process of decentralization. Although permissive and participative leadership patterns are not synonymous with decentralization, there is considerable relationship since decentralization is the delegation of authority to make decisions, a move that means that subordinates are participating in the shaping of decisions.

The stage of a company's growth cycle is a phase of the state of the system that influences the extent to which decentralization is operative. As a general rule, most companies retain a high degree of centralized authority during their early years. Centralization at this stage of growth is particularly characteristic of closely held businesses where the major stockholder is also the founder of the firm and its chief executive. The Ford Motor Company, while still under the direction of its founder, Henry Ford, provides an example of highly centralized management during a company's early years.

Another aspect of a company's growth cycle is the manner in which growth occurs. Some companies grow as the result of a gradual expansion from within, while others grow by purchasing existing firms. When growth occurs as the result of gradual expansion, there may be relatively little need for further decentralization of managerial authority because additional products and processes are usually homogeneous in nature and readily assimilated into existing methods of operation. On the other hand, growth resulting primarily from acquisition frequently means dissimiliar products and processes. Also, an acquired firm may have its own management and, if management is capable, it may be left intact to operate in a highly decentralized fashion.

The nature of a company's business may force a high degree of centralization even though other factors such as size and the stage of development of the firm point toward a more decentralized form of management. Of specific concern are such factors as the needs of the customer, the source and kind of raw materials, and the location and type of manufacturing facilities. When the industrial customer produces his products in diverse locations; when raw materials are purchased from several sources; and when the supplying company has many plants, all producing the same product, there is a need for coordinating the decision-making process at a high level in all three organizations. For these reasons a firm such as Continental Can Company that purchases its raw material from several steel mills in order to service the many refineries of a company like Humble Oil Company (ENCO) tends to be more centralized in many phases of its decision making than a firm manufacturing a diverse line of products sold to many small localized customers.

Finally, the availability of controls, an index of the state of development of a system, is of great importance in determining the potential success of decentralization. In discussing delegation, we state that delegation is not abdication; nor is decentralization abdication. A manager cannot be expected to decentralize decision making to a lower level of the organization without adequate controls. Adequate controls are the feedback loop of the system, for they provide the information necessary to determine the extent and kind of corrective action which may be needed.

Integrated Data Processing and Decentralization

The preceding discussion of the applications of Theory Z to determine the optimum degree of decentralization serves to emphasize that decentralization is not a concept which calls for one being either for it or against it. The proper degree of decentralization is determined by carefully considering all factors in relation to the objectives of the organization. One factor that causes a great deal of interesting speculation in regard to its effect on decentralization is the introduction of high-speed, integrated data processing equipment. Review Case Problem 7-B, The Short-Order Economy, an account of the application of an IBM 1401 to the information-handling problems of Westinghouse. The 1401, storing 20 million bits of information in its "memory," receives an order for an electric motor from a customer on the West Coast, selects the warehouse nearest the customer, and prepares for the warehouse in printed form the customer's name, address, and pertinent credit information. If the order results in the level of inventory being reduced below a predetermined point, the manufacturing plant is notified and the motor is scheduled for production. There are even instances of large customers placing their orders direct to the 1401 from teletype equipment in their own offices, thereby bypassing the local sales office.

When considering that customers can order directly through the 1401, it is easy to point to the sales office and conclude that the decision-making role of middle management is weakened with the introduction of integrated data processing. With the undermining of middle management's decision making and the centralization of information handling, one can develop the argument that modern information systems are more conducive to a centralized rather than a decentralized style of management. Whether or not this argument is valid depends on the definition of middle management decision making and the basic philosophy of the company in regard to decentralization. If middle management's decisions are defined as the processing of orders, the checking of inventories, and the performance of other routine functions, then in all probability these functions are better handled by electronic equipment. Also, if the basic philosophy of the company is one of centralization—the desire to place as many decisions as possible in the hands of a few top executives—modern information-decision-making systems tend to strengthen that philosophy. But if the underlying philosophy of the company is one of decentralization, it is possible to direct the flow of information to subordinate managers so that they may make better decisions, thereby increasing their contribution to the organization and making their positions more secure. Companies which are frequently centralized because needed information is complex and must be laboriously handled in a central location may find that modern data processing eases the burden of handling such information, thereby making it possible to decentralize. Thus, whether or not integrated data processing strengthens or weakens the trend toward decentralization depends upon the definition of decision making on the part of middle managers and the basic philosophy of the company in regard to decentralization.[7]

The decentralization of authority to make decisions is not an *either-or* proposition as implied by the expression, centralization vs. decentralization. Instead, the extent of decentralization is a point on a

---

[7] William E. Reif, *Computer Technology and Management Organization* (Iowa City, Iowa: Bureau of Business and Economic Research, The University of Iowa, 1968). In this empirical study, Mr. Reif analyzes the effects of the installation of electronic data processing systems upon a bank, a utility, and a manufacturing organization. The effect of computers on the degree of centralization is discussed in full in Chapter 7, pp. 91-108.

continuum with a high degree of centralization and a high degree of decentralization marking the limits of the continuum. Case Problem 12-B illustrates that the definition of the degree of decentralization depends upon one's position in the organization. The chairman of Dynamic Industries honestly believes that there is a high degree of decentralization in the corporation, but the president of a subsidiary company questions that view. The case also illustrates how a few well-chosen corporate controls—capital expenditures, budgets, and centralized industrial relations—effectively limit the degree of decentralization.

CASE PROBLEM 12-B

DECENTRALIZATION —FACT OR FICTION?

Dynamic Industries, a diversified manufacturer of automotive replacement parts, is a company that is growing rapidly as the result of an aggressive policy of acquisition. Board chairman John Rafferty believes that the growth of his company is sound and that the main reason for the extremely rapid growth is due to the operation of the company on a highly decentralized basis. Since growth is the result of acquiring companies that are going concerns, Rafferty encourages the managements of the subsidiary companies to carry on as they had prior to joining Dynamic Industries. At present, discussions regarding merger are being held with Central Electronics, a company that manufactures a broad line of electronic components, many of which have applications in the defense and space industries. Central Electronics is interested in Dynamic Industries because Dynamic could supply the much-needed capital to complete the final stages of the development of a high-performance transformer and the building of a plant in which to manufacture the new product. However, George Owens, the founder and president of Central, realizes the potential dangers of merging with another company in that he might lose control of his own firm and be placed in the position of being an employee for a larger corporation.

But Rafferty continually assures Owens that Dynamic Industries operates on a highly decentralized basis and describes their concept of decentralization as follows:

"We expect you, as the president of a subsidiary company, to manage as you have in the past. You are successful with your own company and there is no reason why you shouldn't continue to be a success operating as a part of Dynamic. The major functions of sales, manufacturing, engineering, and product development are all yours to do with as you see fit. In a sense we are sort of the banker; that is, we supply the money that you need for capital improvements and expansion. Even though the profits of each subsidiary company go into the corporate till, it is still like having your own company because your pay for the year is a combination of a guaranteed salary and a percentage of the net profits of your company."

Thus assured, Owens decided to merge with Dynamic Industries.

During the first six months all went well and Owens saw very little of anyone from corporate headquarters. At the beginning of the seventh month, the corporate controller paid Owens a visit and explained to him in detail the company's requirements for profit planning and requested that Owens develop a profit plan, a detailed forecast of Central's revenues and operating expenses, for the coming year. Though very pleasant, the controller made it quite plain that should the performance of the company deviate significantly from the forecast, a team of cost analysts and industrial engineers would arrive from headquarters to determine the cause of the deviation and to recommend necessary changes.

Shortly after this experience with the controller, the industrial relations vice-president of Dynamic Industries called on Owens and informed him that a member of the corporate industrial relations staff would be on hand to conduct the coming negotiations with the union representing Central's employees. Owens protested, saying that he had been negotiating his own labor contracts for years; however, it was explained to him that because of company-wide employee benefit plans, such as pensions and insurance, and to prevent the unions from pitting one subsidiary company against another in the area of wages, centralized control over negotiations was very necessary. At the time of this visit, the provisions of the company's salary plan were outlined to Owens and arrangements were made for the installation of the corporate clerical and supervisory salary plans by a member of the headquarters industrial relations staff.

The following month Owens called Rafferty and asked what steps should be taken to secure capital for the new building intended for the manufacture of the high-performance transformer. Rafferty answered by saying, "I'll have someone from the treasurer's office call on you and show you how to fill out the forms used in requesting funds for capital expansion. It's quite a process, but remember you are only one of 15 subsidiaries and they all seem to want money at the same time. Whether or not you get it this year depends not only upon your needs but also upon the needs of the other 14 companies.''

PROBLEMS

1. Has Dynamic Industries decentralized its operations as much as possible?
2. As George Owens, president of Central Electronics, would you regard the management policies of the parent corporation as primarily centralized or primarily decentralized?
3. Is Dynamic Industries exerting too much control over Central Electronics? Why or why not?
4. Recommend the optimum degree of decentralization for the situation described in this case.

Chapter Questions for Study and Discussion

1. Several descriptive statements of the process of delegation are given in the text. How do these statements differ from each other and in what respects are they the same?
2. Why is it necessary to define the term *to delegate* precisely? How does such a definition contribute to an understanding of the control exercised by the person who does the delegating?
3. Why is it necessary to have three principles covering the process of delegation? Explain what would happen if accountability were not considered absolute.
4. Should the president of a company be held accountable for the following action of subordinates?

   (a) Price fixing in violation of federal laws and stated company policy.

   (b) Failure to meet stated company sales objectives.

   (c) Loss of competitive position in the development of new products.

5. Why is it possible for the process of delegation to work even though one or more of the conditions of delegation is violated?
6. How valid is the concept that an executive should be held accountable for the performance of his department even though he has no power to control the actions of others? (for example, the sales manager who cannot force customers to buy.)
7. Give an example of each of the four situations that results in a violation of the condition of unity of command.

8. If delegation includes the granting of authority and empowers a subordinate to act, why is it necessary to establish controls to see that the subordinate performs as expected?

9. What is meant by the statement that the real problems of delegation lie not in a violation of the conditions of delegation but rather are found in the personality of the person doing the delegating?

10. How is the concept of decentralization of authority related to the concept of delegation? In what respects do these two concepts differ? In what respects are they the same?

11. Differentiate between decentralization and geographic dispersion. Develop an example of geographic dispersion and show how it can be transformed into decentralization of authority.

12. Discuss each of the criteria used in determining the extent of decentralization.

13. Discuss the following statement: The development of integrated data processing systems tends to centralize authority and limit the decision-making powers of the middle manager.

CHAPTER 13

Group Functions in Organization
–The Committee

Ray Talbert, the president and founder of Electric Manufacturing Corporation (Emcorp), is wondering how he can follow the advice of his doctor, who told him to take it easy after last year's coronary attack. Emcorp manufactures a full line of fractional horsepower electric motors sold to both original equipment manufacturers (OEM) and distributors throughout the country.

At the present time, the company employs approximately 1,000 persons.

Talbert, an engineer, has maintained tight control over all major functions throughout the years; and though each of the heads of the engineering, manufacturing, sales, finance, and personnel departments has the title of vice-president, they come to Talbert for approval before making any changes in procedure. Usually, each of these men sees Talbert several times a day. The personnel director once suggested a weekly meeting, but Talbert vetoed the idea as too time consuming. Now, worried about his health as well as the problems of the company, Talbert is beginning to feel the need for some relief from the constant pressure.

The manufacturing department shows a picture of rising costs, consistent failure to meet delivery schedules, and an increasing number of quality complaints. John Stroud, vice-president of manufacturing, admits to poor performance, but says that the cost figures from accounting are pure history and of no use since they do not reach manufacturing until the 15th of the month following the month in which the work is completed. He states that

CASE PROBLEM
13-A

A PROBLEM IN
COORDINATION

370

his failure to meet delivery schedules is due almost entirely to the fact that the sales department makes unrealistic promises and does not bother to check manufacturing schedules. Stroud attributes most of the quality problems to the incessant flow of engineering changes that come without warning and with no time to work out the production problems present in all new products. Talbert admits to himself that he forgot to tell Stroud that he had approved the last set of engineering changes and that he had asked Frank Smyth, vice-president of engineering, to put all of the approved changes into production immediately.

The vice-president and general manager of sales, Jack Linder, recognizes that he has no knowledge of the manufacturing schedules and realizes that he, too, is being criticized by Talbert for the many broken promises in regard to delivery dates. However, Linder's chief complaint at the present time is the result of having sold a large order of standard motors to a distributor having a supply of replacement parts in stock and then discovering that engineering had changed specifications—a change that made all replacement parts in the field obsolete. Another irritant for Linder is the tightened credit requirements instituted by the finance department without prior consultation with the sales department. Again Talbert admits privately that it is the same engineering change which caused so much trouble in manufacturing that is causing trouble for the sales department and obsoleting the existing stock of replacement parts. He also realizes that at his request, due to an unusually short cash position, the finance department tightened up on credit requirements.

PROBLEMS

1. Define the major problem facing Emcorp's management.
2. Would the formation of a committee be of any value in this situation? If a committee is needed, assign a title to the committee and indicate who should be members of the committee. Is there a need for an outside member on the committee?
3. Would an *ad hoc* committee be of any value?
4. In the event that Talbert decides to retire, would the presence of a committee make it easier or more difficult for Talbert's successor? Discuss.

Up to this point in our discussion of organizational processes and organizational structure, the relationships between individuals are emphasized. In the preceding chapter, the process of delegation is treated as a superior-subordinate relationship, a relationship between individuals. However, there are many instances when functions are assigned to a group rather than to an individual. Frequently a group that has been assigned managerial functions is called a committee since specific functions have been committed, or entrusted, to the group. This chapter is divided into two parts: first, there is a general discussion of committees and, second, there is a discussion of the committee that is the keystone of the corporate organization, the board of directors.

COMMITTEES

Usually a committee is assigned functions that are homogeneous in nature, and the scope of its activities and powers is defined. There is also a chairman, or leader, of the group who may be elected by the committee itself or appointed by the party who creates the committee. Another characteristic of committees is that in most organizations, membership on a committee is a part-time activity. A committee member typically has other organizational functions to perform, and an individual often serves as a member of several committees simultaneously.

Committees are a major part of organizational structure, and most students of management sooner or later serve as a member or chairman of a committee. A study of committees is necessary for a full understanding of the process of organizing and the potential assignment as a committee member. First, let us examine some of the underlying assumptions that are implied when a managerial task is assigned to a committee rather than to an individual, and also evaluate committees to determine those situations that lend themselves best to committee action. Second, the committee is analyzed as it functions in business organizations; and lastly, the concept of the *plural executive* is discussed.

Evaluation of Committees

Before discussing the advantages and disadvantages of the use of committees, it is helpful to examine the underlying assumptions whenever a committee is created as part of an organizational structure. At least one of the following two assumptions is implicit in the creation of any committee. The first of these assumptions is that somehow, as a result of interaction between the members of a committee functioning as a group, the results produced by the committee should be better than the results achieved by an individual. The benefits of inter-action between the members of a group may take one of several forms. If ideas are sought from the group, interaction will hopefully increase either the quantity or quality of ideas produced; and if action is desired as a result of committee deliberation, the fact that all members of the committee have participated in determining the course of action is likely to improve the quality and forcefulness of such action. The assumption that the interaction of the members of a group is beneficial is best described as a *participative belief*—a belief in the efficacy of participa-tion *per se.*[1]

The second assumption implicit in the creation of a committee is that as an organization increases in complexity, primarily as the result of the increased number of delegated functions and the complexity of the individual functions, it becomes necessary to have the managers of these various functions meet periodically to exchange information.[2] The need for an exchange of information between the managers of the major functions of an organization is illustrated in Case Problem 13-A. Committees formed as the result of a need to exchange informa-tion perform not only a message-center function, thereby improving the quality of communications, but they also perform a coordinative func-tion as the result of channeling information.

Advantages of Committees. Advantages resulting from the use of committees are discussed under the following four headings: (1) group judgment, (2) improved motivation, (3) as a check on authority, and (4) improved coordination. The first three of these advantages are at-tributable to the interaction of the members of a committee functioning as a group, while the fourth advantage is attributable to the committee performing a coordinative function made possible by the exchange of information.

GROUP JUDGMENT. The idea that the judgment of a group is superior to that of an individual is expressed in the phrase, "two heads are better than one." We all know that two heads are not necessarily

---

[1] Harold J. Leavitt, "Unhuman Organizations," *Harvard Business Review,* Vol. XL (July-August, 1962), pp. 90-98. The paper by Professor Leavitt examines carefully some assumptions concerning organizations that he terms "participative beliefs." Al-though mentioned only in passing in this chapter, the concept of participative beliefs is reviewed in detail in Chapter 16, "Leadership Patterns."

[2] Ernest Dale, *Planning and Developing the Company Organization Structure* (New York: American Management Association, 1952) Research Report Number 20, pp. 83-93. The above concept is stated by Professor Dale on page 83.

better than one; however, there are certain situations in which the judgment of a group tends to be better than that of a single individual. A problem requiring diverse knowledge and varied experience for optimum solution is ideally suited for group consideration, since it is more likely that a group is able to contribute knowledge and experience broader than the knowledge and experience of an individual. The final determination of whether a given product should be placed in a company's product line is a good example of a situation requiring diverse information from production, finance, and sales. A word of caution is in order, however. Even with problems requiring information drawn from each of the major functions of the company, it is not always necessary that the managers of these functions act as a group to obtain the values derived from such diverse backgrounds. The president of the company can talk to the heads of each department separately and acquire from each manager the breadth of information required for a sound decision. Staff specialists who conduct a survey by interviewing many department heads are gaining the values associated with broad experiences without the necessity of meeting as a group.

In addition to values attributable to breadth of knowledge and experience, group judgments are sometimes improved by the internal self-criticism developed within the group as the result of interaction between its members. Self-criticism may result in a compromise solution containing the best aspects of several solutions proposed by individuals. Impulsive decisions and actions are minimized by the self-criticism generated by the group. A further benefit possible from interaction when meetings are conducted as "brainstorming" sessions, as described in Chapter 8, is an increase in the quantity of ideas produced by the group.

Another valuable characteristic of group judgment occurs when the membership of the group is carefully selected so that all interested parties are represented, thereby increasing the likelihood that the final decision takes into consideration the needs and interests of each member of the group. The daily production meeting of a manufacturing plant usually includes representatives from each production department, shipping, production control, and quality control so that any action taken considers the needs of all participating departments.

IMPROVED MOTIVATION. Although the values received from the pooled knowledge and experience of committee members are often cited as the major contribution of a committee, there is much to indicate that one of the underlying reasons for committees, if not the dominant reason, is to assure cooperation in the execution of any plan developed by the committee. Cooperation, or improved motivation, in the execution of the plan may result from having participated in the work of the committee, for one of the benefits directly traceable to participation is increased knowledge, and, consequently, greater understanding of concepts that were formerly unknown or rejected. Another advantage resulting directly from participation is best described as pride of authorship. It is difficult not to support the execution of a plan developed, at least in part, by one's own efforts. An example of a committee owing its success to the positive values derived from participation is a salary or compensation committee that describes and evaluates all jobs and then develops and administers a plan of compensation.

An additional characteristic of committee participation that contributes toward better motivation is obtained by using membership on a committee as a means of "selling" or persuading a lukewarm member to go along with the majority. Such persuasion may range from the benefits gained by a better understanding acquired through participation to the implied pressure created by the stamp of approval that comes as the result of being a member of the committee.

A CHECK ON AUTHORITY. One of the functions of a committee that may be considered an advantage is its operation as a check on authority. The use of committees in business organizations to limit authority is not frequent, yet committees are used for this purpose in other forms of organizations—governmental, religious, social, and educational—to such an extent that a brief discussion of the subject is warranted. The Supreme Court of the United States is, in effect, a nine-man committee that serves to check the authority of all agencies of the government; and the two houses of Congress serve, not only as a check on the powers of the chief executive, but also as a check and balance upon the powers of each other. Most religious and social organizations such as fraternal groups are governed by boards that effectively restrain the powers of designated officials. In universities we find good examples of restraint through the action of committees. The president of a university is usually restrained not only by the committee that appoints him, often called a board of regents, but also by committees of the faculty that may have authority ranging in scope from determining the curriculum to administering faculty pay increases and determining tenure policy.

The use of a committee as a restraining agent is not as clear cut in business organizations. Perhaps it is because many businesses have their origin as a result of the efforts of a single individual, or it may be the recognition that there are inefficiencies inherent in committee organization. Even so, the board of directors, a committee elected by the stockholders, serves as an effective check on the powers and actions of the president.[3]

IMPROVED COORDINATION. The three advantages of committees described above—group judgment, improved motivation, and a check on authority—are advantages that are believed to be derived from the participation of a group. Improved coordination resulting from committee action is not so much the result of participation *per se*; instead, it is the result of receiving, interpreting, and channeling information. Committees whose purpose is to transmit information and coordinate the activities of the various functions of the organization are formed at the upper levels of an organization and may be called an executive committee or an operating or management committee. Usually these groups are composed of the managers of functional areas such as sales, manufacturing, engineering, and finance. The person-to-person contact afforded by regularly scheduled meetings permits all interested parties to receive and exchange information with considerable savings in time and an improved degree of understanding.

A further strength of committees whose purpose is one of coordination is that such committees may be granted an authority greater than that possessed by any of the individual members. For example, a new products committee, composed of the heads of sales, manufacturing, engineering, and finance, may be granted the authority to accept or reject a given product, thereby exercising an authority greater than that of any of its members. By granting superior authority to the committee, rather than to an individual, the coordinative purpose of the committee is emphasized.

In Case Problem 13-A, the Electric Manufacturing Corporation can achieve improved coordination by creating an executive or management committee whose function is primarily the exchange of information. Such a group, meeting on a regularly scheduled basis, would serve to channel information to Ray Talbert so that he could better coordinate the various management functions. Also, if Talbert's health problems persist, the committee could be delegated sufficient authority to coordinate and administer the affairs of the company.

---

[3] Harold Koontz and Cyril O'Donnell, *Principles of Management* (4th ed.; New York: McGraw-Hill Book Company, 1968). For a more complete discussion of the function of a committee as a check on authority, see 380 and 381.

Disadvantages of Committees. The disadvantages and criticisms leveled at committees often result from the misuse of committees as well as from weaknesses inherent in the committee system itself. The criticism most frequently charged to the committee system is that the cost is greater than the value received. Committees are also charged with not being able to produce good decisions since their very nature tends to develop a compromise decision rather than the one solution that is best for the situation; and lastly, the composition of a committee with its several members and semblance of democratic action makes it difficult to establish accountability. Each of these criticisms is discussed below.

COST. The costliness of committees comes not only from the direct cost of each man-hour spent in committee service but also from the losses incurred when timeliness is a factor in determining the worth of the decision. Committees are very time consuming, since one of the premises upon which they operate is that the committee serves as a forum in which all members have a right to express a point of view no matter how trivial or inconsequential. If there is an important item under discussion, it is highly unlikely that any action will be taken without a review of the written minutes of the meeting by each individual member, an action that results in further delay and expense.

Though it is difficult to determine the cost of committees, particularly when measured against value received, an approach suggested by Ernest Dale forces, at the very least, a critical review of the worth of a committee. First, determine the number of man-hours spent per year in meetings by multiplying the total number of meetings, times the average length of each meeting, times the average number of executives in attendance. Add to this figure the cost of the secretary of the committee and other clerical and staff work; then assign an average dollar cost to the total time spent (remember that the cost of a $25,000 a year executive is about $15 an hour). Review the work of the committee for the past year and place a monetary value on its accomplishments. Balance this value of work accomplished against total cost; then determine whether the work of the committee could be carried on as effectively if the committee were dissolved.[4]

COMPROMISE DECISIONS. Although the value of group judgment derived from varied backgrounds and experiences of the members of a committee is listed as one of its chief values, it is a value realized only under relatively limited conditions. Far too often the decision of a

---

[4] Dale, *op. cit.*, p. 88.

committee may result in a compromise at what appears to be the level of the lowest common denominator. The reasons for poor quality in committee decisions are not hard to find. Committees often develop a belief that they should reflect a unanimity of opinion, and unless a unanimous decision can be achieved, there is a tendency to delay any decision. The desire for unanimity, even though it means compromise, is understandable when there is a decision requiring execution because a recalcitrant member can sabotage the entire action of the committee by refusing to aid in carrying out the plan. Another reason for compromise is that committees within a company are made up of men who must work together in many different capacities, with the result that there is opportunity for a degree of political trading and a reluctance to force unpleasant situations—conditions that encourage compromise.

Still another factor affecting the quality of committee decisions is the control of a committee by a minority, a control particularly effective when there is a tradition of unanimous action. Such control may be exercised by the power of veto, or as illustrated in national politics by the power of the filibuster. Although the filibuster is not operative as a formal institution in business, there are times when a subject is avoided rather than invite what everyone knows is going to be a protracted discussion of an issue.

If decisions are not compromised, either in an attempt to secure unanimity or as the result of minority control, the other extreme may occur, a single dominant person hiding behind the screen of a committee composed of a group of "Yes men." If such is the case, the following question should be raised: Why have a committee in the first place?

LACK OF ACCOUNTABILITY. In discussing the process of delegation in the last chapter, the three steps of the process are set forth: (1) the assignment of duties or responsibilities, (2) the delegation of authority, and (3) the creation of an accountability on the part of a subordinate to his superior. Committees, like individuals, may be assigned responsibilities and may be granted delegated authority. However, the establishment of accountability is very difficult. Theoretically, all members of a committee may be held accountable for the action of the committee, yet this is not a practical point of view when the final position of the committee is a compromise reached as the result of many hours of discussion. One might wish to hold the chairman accountable, but he may have no effective control over the individual members of the committee. The inability to establish accountability clearly and to take any necessary subsequent corrective action makes committees particularly ineffective as an organizational structure when the responsibility assigned is one of action or execution.

Committees in Use

The use of the committee as a part of the organization structure of top management is relatively recent, the first notable example being the top management committee established in 1921 by E. I. du Pont de Nemours & Company.[5] Since 1921 the use of committees has grown extensively; however, before discussing the extent to which committees are used, it is helpful to develop a means of classification because committees vary widely in respect to functions assigned and the degree of authority granted to them.

One method of classification results in committees being grouped by function as either *general management* committees or as *restricted* committees. The major function of a general management committee is policy making and the effect of its work is usually company-wide in scope. Those committees not engaged in general management activities are classified as restricted committees and their scope is limited to one function or, at the most, to a group of related functions. Typically, restricted committees are concerned with such functions as marketing, production, or personnel. Both of these broad categories, general management committees and restricted committees, may be further subdivided in respect to the degree of delegated authority possessed by the committee. If the committee has the power to make decisions and an effective means of carrying out these decisions, it is regarded as an *authoritative* committee. If the committee is not capable of carrying out its recommendations, or if it is organized solely for the purpose of study and advice, the committee is classified as *nonauthoritative*.[6]

Functions of Committees. There are two studies of the extent to which committees are used and the functions assigned to them. M. R. Lohman's survey of 319 top management committees in 93 different companies reveals that 78 of the 93 companies have general management committees. Of these general management committees, two thirds of them receive their authority from the president of the company and the other one third is appointed by and receives its authority directly from

---

[5] M. R. Lohman, *Top Management Committees* (New York: American Management Association, 1961) AMA Research Study 48, p. 5. Research Study 48 of the American Management Association presents information gathered from 93 firms that have a total of 319 management committees of all types and discusses the current status of committees in American industry today.

[6] *Ibid.*, pp. 13-21.

the board of directors. Twenty-five percent of these general management committees are classified as authoritative and 25 percent are classified as nonauthoritative. The remaining 50 percent have some degree of authority in specific areas of operations, but the authority is not of sufficient breadth to warrant their classification as authoritative. It is interesting to note that of those general management committees appointed by the board of directors—one third of the total—83 percent are classed as authoritative, while only 20 percent of the committees reporting to and drawing their authority from the president of the company are regarded as authoritative. Seemingly, the degree of authority granted top management committees is dependent upon and related to the source of authority. Only 12 of the 78 firms reporting the presence of a general management committee are limited to that one committee; 66 of the 78 firms have at least one restricted committee in addition to the general management committee. All the firms surveyed reported some form of top management committee.[7]

The other study, conducted by Rollie Tillman, Jr., is a survey of 1,200 executives in regard to the functioning and extent of committees in their companies. The presence of a regular, or a "standing" committee, is to some extent related to the size of the company defined in terms of total number of employees. Of those firms with less than 250 employees, only 63.5 percent have one or more regular standing committees, while 93.8 percent of those firms with more than 10,000 employees report one or more standing committees. The average for all firms represented by the 1,200 executives who participated in the study shows that 81.5 percent have one or more standing committees.[8] One aspect of Tillman's study is that it presents in concise form the major functions assigned to each of the various types of standing committees. The distinction between standing or regular committees and those that are temporary in nature is that the temporary committee is usually organized for a specific purpose and dissolved when that purpose is satisfied. Temporary committees are generally called *ad hoc* committees. The results of Tillman's study are presented in Table 13-1.

The committees listed by Tillman conform to the classification developed by Lohman. Sixty-seven percent of the executives serving on general management committees report the primary function of the committee as one of setting policy, and the functions of planning and making

---

[7] *Ibid.*, pp. 10-11.

[8] Rollie Tillman, Jr., "Committees on Trial," *Harvard Business Review*, Vol. XXXVIII (May-June, 1960), pp. 6-8, 11, 12, 162-164, 166, 168, 171-173.

Table 13-1
COMMITTEES—WHAT ARE THEIR FUNCTIONS?

Type of Committee	Percent of Executives Serving on Each Type of Committee Who Report This Function				
	Advisory	Operating Decisions	Review	Planning	Policy
General Management	43%	58%	43%	64%	67%
Finance & Control	30	47	39	55	42
Marketing	42	44	76	43	10
Production	34	54	42	63	25
Labor & Personnel	41	43	38	39	39
R & D and New Products	40	38	48	73	38
Public Relations	53	33	31	50	39
Other	45	46	35	52	36

Note: The rows of figures in this table add to more than 100% because respondents report their committee as having more than one purpose and function.
Source: Rollie Tillman, Jr., "Committees on Trial," *Harvard Business Review*, Vol. XXXVIII (May-June, 1960), p. 162.

operating decisions are second and third in importance. The remaining types of committees—finance and control, marketing, production, labor and personnel, research and development and new products, public relations, and the miscellaneous classification of other—correspond to Lohman's classification of restricted committees.

It is interesting to note the variation in the major function assigned to each of the restricted committees. The committees of finance and control, production, and research and development are engaged primarily in the function of planning, while marketing mainly performs a review function. Very few of those serving on marketing committees report a policy function for this committee; apparently the policies of marketing are determined by general management committees. The function most frequently performed by the labor and personnel committee is that of making operating decisions and is probably due to the necessity for these committees to interpret labor agreements as they affect company operations. The committees on public relations most frequently serve in an advisory capacity. Although Tillman's study shows definite trends in the functions assigned to various management committees, it is unwise to generalize concerning the purpose of a given committee since there is substantial variation in the functions assigned to general management committees and to each of the restricted committees. Nonetheless, the study is of value in that it shows succinctly the wide range of activities that may be delegated to various committees.

Du Pont and Committees. In 1921 E. I. du Pont de Nemours & Company, Inc., became the first company to establish committees as a permanent part of its top management structure. A recent organization chart of Du Pont, Figure 13-1, shows that there are four major committees—bonus and salary committee, executive committee, finance committee, and the committee on audit—reporting directly to the board of directors.[9] As a direct result of having these four committees report directly to the board of directors, virtually every function within the company ultimately reports to a committee.

One of the difficulties that arises as a result of Du Pont's committee structure is that of designating, in chart form, the proper position and function of the president of the company. The organization chart shows the president reporting to the executive committee, the finance committee, and the board of directors; but in practice, he is a member of all committees including the board of directors and is not, as shown on the chart, accountable to each committee. The executive committee is composed of the president, who functions as its chairman, and eight vice-presidents, who, unlike their counterparts in most companies, have no other duty than that of serving on the executive committee. Since these officers are not responsible for the functions of an operating department, there is less likelihood for bias and prejudice in their decisions. Reporting to the executive committee are the general managers of the 12 industrial (line) departments and the directors of all auxiliary (staff) departments. The treasurer reports to the finance committee.

How well has the committee system worked for Du Pont? According to Mylander, who asked this and other questions of the 12 top executives of the company, the system has worked well for Du Pont.[10] The advantages of the committee system are listed as giving the strength and security that arise from group decisions, an improved objectivity in

---

[9] K. K. White, *Understanding the Company Organization Chart* (New York: American Management Association, 1963) Research Study No. 56, p. 161. This study includes a discussion of the committees in Du Pont on pages 159, 162-163.

[10] William H. Mylander, "Management by Executive Committee," *Harvard Business Review*, Vol. XXXIII (May-June, 1955), pp. 51-58. Mr. Mylander's article affords excellent insight into the workings of Du Pont's executive committee. Included is an agenda for one of the regular Wednesday meetings, which shows the full range of committee action.

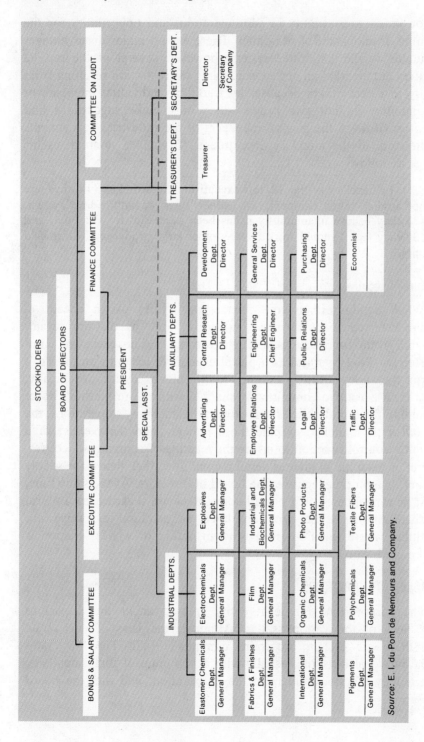

Figure 13-1

ORGANIZATION CHART OF E.I. DU PONT DE NEMOURS AND COMPANY

Source: E. I. du Pont de Nemours and Company.

decision making, continuity in administration, and opportunity for the maximum development of personnel. There are no major disadvantages attributable to the committee system; however, several of the top 12 executives did mention an occasional feeling of frustration resulting from inability to direct others because, by tradition, individual members of the committee do not give orders—they only make suggestions and serve as advisors to the general managers of the industrial departments and directors of the auxiliary departments. Mylander summarizes his findings as follows:

> In conclusion, the 12 top executives stressed that (1) they are not urging other companies to adopt their committee-line system, (2) they believe unanimously it has been successful for Du Pont, and (3) they feel it should work for any other large producer of diversified lines.[11]

The Plural Executive

When committees assume the responsibilities of an executive, they are referred to as a *plural executive*; and, as the phrase implies, the group functions as a single executive. The executive committee of Du Pont operates as a plural executive, for with one voice it performs the duties normally assigned to the chief executive. Specifically, the Du Pont executive committee is charged with the responsibilities of determining the broad policies that govern the company's operations, the selection of personnel to execute those policies, and the exercise of a continuing control function to insure the meeting of company objectives.

Let us examine in greater detail a committee that almost invariably functions as a plural executive, the board of directors. At the same time, it must be remembered that not all committees are regarded as a plural executive. Among those not considered as a plural executive are committees whose function is advisory in nature or whose function is research and study.

THE BOARD OF DIRECTORS

The corporation is a legal entity created under the provisions of the laws of the various states. Although the laws of each state differ, there are certain provisions common to all. The law states that the board of directors, usually with a minimum of three members, be elected by the stockholders of the corporation, and that the board

---

[11] *Ibid.*, p. 58.

is charged with the responsibility of directing the affairs of the corporation as representatives of the stockholders, who are the legal owners. The law, in effect, designates the board as a plural executive, for an action must come from the board as a group and not from the action of any single board member. The line of authority flows from the individual stockholders to the elected board of directors and thence to the officers of the company who are appointed by the board. There is no clear delineation between the activities normally associated with directing the affairs of the corporation and those activities assigned to the officers of the corporation who are responsible for the day-to-day management of the company. In some companies, it is not unusual for the chairman of the board to hold the dual title of chairman of the board and chief executive officer, an example of the overlap that may exist between directing and managing. Despite the lack of separation between functions normally associated with directing and those assigned to the officers of the company, there are certain responsibilities traditionally reserved for the board. In our discussion of the board of directors, we shall examine those functions normally associated with boards of directors, some of the problems that must be considered in determining the most effective composition of the membership of boards, and lastly, the value of boards of directors in small companies.[12]

Functions of the Board of Directors

Before considering the specific functions of the board of directors, it is well to recognize that, in practice, the authority of boards varies considerably. Such authority may range from *making decisions* that affect the life of the corporation, and subsequently assigning the execution of these decisions to the management of the company, to a situation in which the board merely acts as a *rubber stamp* by perfunctory approval of the actions of management. Between these extremes are the exercise of authority that amounts to *confirmation* of action taken by management, *influence* exerted by individual members of the board through counseling with management, and formal *review* of management's handling of the affairs of the company with the

---

[12] The following references are suggested for those desiring a complete treatment of the structure and function of boards of directors:

Harold Koontz, *The Board of Directors and Effective Management* (New York: McGraw-Hill Book Company, 1967).

Stanley C. Vance, *Boards of Directors: Structure and Performance* (Eugene, Oregon: University of Oregon Press, 1964).

Mayer N. Zald, "The Power and Functions of Boards of Directors: A Theoretical Synthesis," *American Journal of Sociology*, Vol. 75, No. 1 (July, 1969), pp. 97-111.

implication that such review may lead to criticism and suggestions for improved performance.

A listing of the functions of the board of directors would include the selection of officers and directors; determination of basic policies in finance, production, sales, and personnel; allocation of the earnings of the company; and the determination of financial structure. However, the many items that come before the board for consideration and action may be grouped under four major headings; (1) determination of objectives, (2) selection of management, (3) financial well-being of the company, and (4) review and stimulation. Each major area of responsibility is discussed below.

Determination of Objectives. Fundamental to the concept of the corporation is that, as a legal entity, the corporation exists in perpetuity; that is, it exists until formal action is taken to dissolve the corporation through liquidation of assets or by merger with another company. The board of directors acts as a steward or trustee of the assets that belong to the owners of the company. Because of the responsibility of stewardship, the major duty of the board is to determine the objectives of the company. Underlying all decisions concerning objectives is the ultimate welfare of the stockholders. Usually the interest of stockholders is considered in terms of long-range potential as well as concern for immediate earnings. Consideration must also be given to the public welfare. An example of the interrelationship between long- and short-range earnings and the public welfare is afforded by the action of the Du Pont board of directors when considering whether to expand existing facilities for the production of neoprene rubber or whether to build a new plant. It was decided that since Du Pont was the sole supplier of neoprene for the free world and that there existed a possibility of the destruction of a single plant through enemy attack, it would be wiser for both the public and the stockholders to build an additional plant even though immediate costs would be greater.

Another duty related to the statement of objectives is the translation of objectives into policies governing sales, finance, production, and personnel to insure the fulfillment of stated goals.

Selection of Management. Closely associated with the function of policy making is the selection of the management necessary for the execution of policy. There are degrees of the extent to which boards participate in determining the choice of executives. Usually the selection of the president is the sole responsibility of the board of directors; however, the extent to which the board participates in the selection of other officers and key officials varies widely. Since it is recognized that the success of the president of a company depends in large measure on the capabilities of the other officers, it is not unusual for the president to nominate, subject to the approval of the board, his associates. Along with the selection of the president and the confirmation of other officers, is the determination of salaries and bonuses of top executives.

In addition, the board of directors plays a prominent role in choosing replacements or additions to the board itself. Again, practice varies. The president, almost always a member of the board, may submit nominations and, if such is the case, the nominees are inclined to be friendly toward management. The same is true if the nominees are presented by other members of the board; they, too, are inclined to be friendly. In either event, the final selection to membership is made by the board. Though it is true that there are occasional proxy battles for control, they are relatively rare and represent the interests of large financial holdings rather than the desires of many small stockholders. Thus, there is a self-perpetuating characteristic of boards and managements.

Financial Well-Being of the Company. The financial well-being of a company is one of the major responsibilities of the board, a responsibility that in most cases is not delegated; and whenever it is delegated, there are tight controls and prescribed limits within which the officers of the company must perform. Figure 13-1 showing the top management of Du Pont stresses the importance of this function, for it shows that the finance committee reports directly to the board. Further evidence of the importance of financial position, including capital budgets, appears in Case Problem 13-B in which the executive committee of Jersey Standard, also members of the board, sets the limits of expenditures for a new refinery. The directors of a company are also responsible for approving or initiating any changes in the capital structure of the organization, and not the least of their responsibility in the financial area is determining the distribution of earnings—the portion that should go to the stockholders, the amount to be retained for cash reserves, and the amount to be ploughed back into the business for replacement of present facilities and expansion to meet new objectives.

Review and Stimulation. In order to assure that objectives are met and policies properly executed, it is necessary that the performance of management be reviewed periodically. Discerning questions at this time may do much toward stimulating management and suggesting possible avenues of improvement. A management that must account to a discerning board is more apt to check its own performance than one reporting to a rubber-stamp board. In addition to the formal review of management's work during scheduled meetings, there is much that can be gained by individual counsel between board members and executives of the company. Although the board's formal action is that of a plural executive, advice and counsel may be given by individual members. Of course, the worth of such advice is dependent upon the qualifications and persuasiveness of the individual board member.

Composition of the Board

In an earlier discussion in this chapter, four advantages are cited that may result from the proper use of committees—group judgment, improved motivation, a check on authority, and improved coordination. Since the board of directors is a committee, a board with properly chosen membership reflects the advantages normally ascribed to effective committee action. The pertinent question to be answered in determining the proper composition of the membership is whether the board should be an *inside* board, composed of employees of the company, or whether it should be an *outside* board, with the majority of its members chosen from outside the company. There are advantages to both types, and no hard-and-fast rule can be stated that favors either form.

Outside Boards. The advantages attributed to outside boards appear only when the members are able men with truly diverse backgrounds and have the time and interest to acquaint themselves thoroughly with the problems of the company. The reasons most frequently cited for wanting to serve on a board are prestige, a sense of obligation to the business community, and an opportunity to make additional business contacts. The pay for services as a board member is nominal, on the average about $100 per meeting. Thus, the medium-size or small company, unable to offer sufficient prestige or business contacts, may find it difficult to attract the caliber of men it should have in order to realize the benefits that come from a well-chosen membership from outside the company.

Inside Boards. The value of group judgments from committee action is dependent upon the knowledge of each member, the time available for preparation, and the diversity of backgrounds of the members. The value is not dependent upon whether or not the board member is an employee of the company. A superficial examination of the problem may lead one to conclude that an external board is more objective in its judgments, but of what use is objectivity if the real requirement for sound judgment is an intimate knowledge of the company and the time necessary to evaluate the mass of information necessary for a decision? Thus, some companies, in order to avoid the problems that arise from having board members who can devote only a small portion of their time to the company and who do not have an intimate knowledge of the company's processes and problems, have turned to inside boards. Du Pont, for example, has a full-time board whose members have formerly served as members of management and when serving on the board have no responsibility other than that of a board member. Jersey Standard has a 15-man board, seven of whom serve as members of the executive committee that oversees the day-to-day operations of the company. Dow Chemical and Bethlehem Steel have inside boards with members who serve both as officers of the company and as directors.

It is worthwhile to examine the conditions that make the functioning of an inside board effective. First, the company must be large enough so that there is a sufficient number of executives to permit a choice from many qualified men. Second, there should be a tradition of promotion from within and, when combined with a large organization, there is opportunity for an executive to mature over a period of years and acquire a diverse background in company operations. Third, there is a tendency for inside boards to appear in companies where the operations are technical in nature and where technical knowledge is a requisite for sound judgments. And lastly, the company must be able to afford and need the services of an inside board that devotes full time to the affairs of the company.

Boards in Small Companies

The selection of a board of directors for a small owner-managed corporation or a medium-size publicly held corporation with professional management poses several problems. In the small owner-managed company, the board of directors in many instances merely meets the legal requirement that there be a board, and frequently it is composed of members of the owner's family. Family boards may be due in part to a fear of having outsiders participate in the management of the company or it may be due to an honest belief that outside help is not necessary.

The small- to medium-size publicly held company faces a dilemma in securing the advantages of an effective board. The small company is unable to offer prestige, one of the main reasons for serving on a board, with the result that those whom it does attract from outside the company may not be fully qualified. Outside boards, even with the best of personnel, suffer from the shortcomings of part-time activity. Nor are inside boards the answer. In all probability, there is no need for the services of a full-time inside board of directors. Inside boards performing the dual role of officer and director may not have the breadth of experience and diversified knowledge necessary for corporate growth in a competitive economy.

The best solution for the small- to medium-size corporation often is the selection of an outside board. True, an outside board presents the part-time problem, but the question of individual competence can be overcome to a large extent through the selection of men well qualified in their respective fields of work. Bankers, attorneys, educators, consultants, and executives from other companies are likely candidates and, when combined with the key officers of the company, the resulting board should provide the stimulation and guidance necessary for survival and growth.

Case Problem 13-B, How Rathbone Runs Jersey Standard,[13] is an interesting account of a meeting of the executive committee of the Standard Oil Company (New Jersey). A brief background of Jersey's chief executive officer is presented and some of the problems encountered in reorganizing the board of a large company are described. The members of Jersey's executive committee are also members of the board of directors.

CASE PROBLEM 13-B	Little knots of waiting men are standing in the paneled boardroom. They are dressed in sober blue or dark gray; here an assertive little flower is pinned to a lapel; there a cuff link, half hidden by a well-tailored sleeve, gleams in the soft fluorescent light. The men are executives of the Standard Oil Co. (New Jersey) and they are waiting for a meeting to begin—or, more precisely, they are waiting for another man, whose appearance
HOW RATHBONE RUNS JERSEY STANDARD	

---

[13] Walter Guzzardi, Jr., "How Rathbone Runs Jersey Standard," *Fortune*, Vol. LXVII (January, 1963), pp. 85-87, 89, 171, 172. The student is urged to read the entire article, which presents in great detail the problems faced by the chief executive of a large corporation.

will mark the beginning of a meeting. The man they are waiting for is Monroe Jackson Rathbone, the president of Jersey Standard and its chief executive officer.

Most of the men now waiting for Rathbone once had their well-tailored sleeves plunged to the elbows in crude oil. They have spent many years with Jersey or one or another of Jersey's 100-odd affiliates that pump crude from the ground, transport, refine, or market it. But now the whole group belongs to Jersey, which strictly speaking is not an oil company at all, but a holding company that invests in the oil business—a kind of Roman Empire of the modern business world. Paramount in the minds of the men now gathered together—on the twenty-ninth floor of Jersey's New York offices at Rockefeller Center, around the boardroom's oval table, beneath a pensive portrait of John D. Rockefeller, Sr.—is the aggregate prosperity of a great and sprawling mosaic of investment. An affiliate may importune from the heat of competitive struggle or the environment of a foreign country, but (as with the Roman Empire) Jersey can never accede to a major request from a family member without considering what the reverberations through the provinces will mean to the larger interest—that of the Jersey company itself.

How Jersey executives manage the affairs of empire make a case study in American management. Over its eighty years, Jersey has developed a highly refined managerial philosophy, which puts primary emphasis on the committee system. Thorough staff work digs out and distills the mountains of facts needed by Jersey's committees. Decisions that reach beyond one committee's scope are passed up to another level of committee management. At the top of the chain sits a seven-man executive committee whose members also serve on Jersey's fifteen-man board of directors. Meeting every day, this committee looks to the general good of Jersey by two major means. First, it governs the finances of affiliates by a detailed review of budgets and contemplated new investments. Second, bearing a different formal designation, the executive committee passes on the selection and promotion of the top officers who run Jersey's companies around the world. On this day, the executive committee is about to hold discussions in both these broad areas of responsibility.

Now the side door opens, and Rathbone, a man with the husky frame of a roustabout and the craggy features of an amiable pugilist, steps from his office into the boardroom. As always, he sits in a chair close to his office door, in the middle of the oval's broad curve. Other chairs are pulled up around the table, beneath the pensive Rockefeller portrait. There is no gavel-rapping. At a nod from Rathbone, the meeting begins. Every executive officer has his style of running things. Let's watch the carefully modulated style of the man who presides over a corporation with assets of almost $11 billion.

REFINEMENTS IN BUILDING A REFINERY

The first matter to come up for decision is a proposal for the construction of a refinery in France. Once the executive committee's controls were so tight that it had to pass on many small purchases contemplated by affiliates. Controls were loosened as Jersey grew. Then, when Rathbone became Jersey's chief executive, he and the board delegated a great deal of financial authority to another Jersey committee, the board advisory committee on investments, headed by company director Marion Boyer; now the executive committee considers only those expenditures over $1 million.

This refinery at Marseille, if Rathbone and the committee approve it, will cost Jersey in the neighborhood of $35 million. Three times before, the committee has been informed of the progress of the plans for the refinery; this time the proposal, to be explained in detail by staff officers, comes to the committee for formal action. Following his usual technique, Rathbone first hears the proposal all the way through, with only an infrequent interruption to clarify a point. He tests the staff work by calling attention to staff studies showing that the excess refining capacity in France will diminish over the next ten years, and asking sharply: "What about the fact that the decrease in that excess capacity depends partly on export markets? Are we sure those markets will still be there in 1966, when the refinery will be finished?" Satisfied with the reply, Jersey's president lets the presentation of details about the refinery run on to its end.

Then he moves in heavily on a matter always foremost in his mind—costs. "What about the estimates of the cost of the refinery—how good are they?" Told that while they were not yet detailed, they seemed good enough so that the cost would probably come within the 10 percent latitude that Jersey allows in such cases, the president bears down: "We allow that 10 percent to take care of emergencies or unforeseen situations. But we don't want to start a project of this size with the idea that cost can be allowed to go to $3 million or $4 million. It's bad psychology to start with the idea that you have that kind of leeway. We've had some horrible overruns on these refineries, and I don't want that to happen in this case. If there is an overrun, the size of the refinery may have to be reconsidered. What we are approving is this: a $35-million refinery at Marseille. If it comes to more, you come back to us. The proposal is approved on that basis."

Chairs are pushed back. The staff men who presented the refinery proposal depart. Presently the executive committee, now sitting in its capacity as the compensation and executive-development committee, turns its attention to the careers and next assignments of top officers. Rathbone has spent forty-one years working for Jersey; he appears to know everyone who comes up for discussion, and listens carefully. Occasionally he drops in a comment. Upon hearing of the good performance of a man on a new assignment, he remarks: "It has taken a long time, but it looks like he has finally found his niche in this company. It's nice to have him in the right place at last."

A Jersey affiliate abroad needs a top manager, and one of the executive-committee members knows just the right man. But the man cannot move into the job for a year. One officer comments: "We'll send him next year. He's the man we want." Nodding of heads. The president (sharply): "But what about leaving that job vacant for a whole year? Can we afford to do it?" There is a small shock, and more discussion; it is decided to keep the job open for the man. But Rathbone has left hanging in the air just a suspicion that so long a delay borders on being unwise.

There is a discussion of a slate of three names for another job. "Don't forget that this spot is a breeding ground for the board of directors," says Rathbone. "When we look over these names, let's keep that in mind. Let's look down the road a way. Which of these men is going to be best for the board?"

Rathbone (on still another Jersey man): "I know he's got three children. But they have a fine nurse who's just like a mother to those kids. The children will get along fine out there. He's making $25,000 a year now— below the minimum for his class. Even after this raise, he'll still be below the minimum. But we can leave him at that level for a while. He's been moved along very well."

The meeting breaks up. A few people drift off. One or two stay behind for a word with Jersey's president. Answering questions or giving curbstone opinions, Rathbone seems consciously to eschew the attributes popularly assigned to the boss: he has no tough bearing, he generates no tension, he affects no elegance. He gives the impression of a willingness to talk every problem through, no matter how long it takes. His language is not incisive; instead he often clothes his positive views in negative syntax: "I'm not sure I'd buy that," or "That may not be the best basis to put it on." Such replies seem to satisfy his interrogators, who hurry away. Rathbone steps back into his own office. His schedule has run late on this particular day and the afternoon is almost over. Rathbone flips through a few documents his secretary brings him. He remembers to give to her the $5.64 that he owes her from the day before. Around 5:30 p.m., with his correspondence signed and his desk cleared, Rathbone goes home. He takes a thick tan briefcase with him.

A SPECIAL STRAIN OF MANAGER

Whether in board meeting, in the privacy of his office, or even at home, Rathbone has come almost automatically to think of Jersey first. Like Frederick Kappel at A.T.&T., Lawrence Litchfield, Jr., of Alcoa, and Frederic Donner of General Motors, Rathbone belongs to a distinct managerial strain—men who mature in one company with the conviction that they or someone else going through the same maturation process eventually will be in charge of it. Rathbone was brought up in the Jersey system, shaped by it and at the same time shaping it. Virtually every Jersey board member has spent most of his working life with Jersey. None has worked for any other oil company. On an average, each board member has served thirty-one years with Jersey or its affiliates. The total time spent in the company by present members of the board comes to over four hundred and fifty years. The company believes that the place to learn the oil business is inside Jersey's family—a belief supported by the performance of system-made men like Rathbone.

The son of a Jersey Standard man, Rathbone studied chemical engineering at Lehigh, and joined Standard Oil Co. of Louisiana after graduation in 1921. He went to work in the big refinery at Baton Rouge. "Rathbone was the first man of a new wave," recalls Henry Voorheis, general manager of the refinery. "Refining oil was a combination of guesswork and art in those days. Jack was the first of a group of educated men who made refining into a science." Rathbone worked "in that old hellhole, the acid plant." Then he went into thermal cracking. "The first time I saw Jack, he was climbing up the ladder of one of the first big cracking units," recollects David Shepard, now an executive vice president of Jersey. "He seemed to be practically running up the ladder. I'll never forget the sight—there went Rathbone, climbing, climbing."

As Jersey measures time, the climb was quick. Rathbone became general superintendent of the refinery at thirty-one, and five years later was president of Standard Oil of Louisiana, the Jersey affiliate whose chief asset was the refinery. In an early test of his diplomacy, Rathbone staved off predatory attacks by Huey Long, who "customarily ran for office against Standard Oil of Louisiana." Then, in 1944, Rathbone took a big step. He left Baton Rouge, to which he now occasionally returns for a vacation at his camp on the Amite River. Taking with him a whiff of the bayous in his accent, Rathbone moved to New York to become president of Esso Standard. Five years later, he became a member of Jersey's board of directors. That took him another long stride forward— out of an operational oil company, and into the broader business of management of the empire. Five years afterward, Rathbone became the president of Jersey. Then, in May, 1960, he succeeded the late Eugene Holman as Jersey's chief executive. By then Rathbone was sixty years old.

Rathbone's accession meant many changes for Jersey. As a colleague says: "Rathbone and Holman worked closely and in harmony for many years. But it was natural that Jack should change some things—he would have been less than human if he hadn't." The first important change lay deep in the psyches of the two men. A friend who knew them both recollects that "Gene was shy and reserved. Jack is outgoing and enthusiastic. Holman solved tough problems by making the partners to the dispute work them out—he kept them coming back to him until they arrived at a compromise. Rathbone's procedure is different. He looks the situation over, figures out what's best, and proposes his solution to both parties. He may adjust it to meet their objections, and like Holman he may end up with everyone satisfied. But the solution comes initially from Rathbone." Another friend who once worked for Jersey adds: "Holman was a softer and a gentler man. He did well at stockholders' meetings, but I think they were an ordeal for him. Jack actually seems to enjoy them."

THE REORGANIZATION MAN

Since becoming chief executive, Rathbone has changed Jersey's organization in various ways. Like his predecessors, he believes in the wisdom of an inside board of directors, all of whose members are full-time executives of the company. As it did before, the board still delegates most of its executive functions to the smaller executive committee. But soon after he became chief executive, Rathbone changed the board's organization and direction. Before his accession, executive responsibilities were parceled out along functional lines. One director, for example, was charged with overseeing marketing, or refining, or transportation. As a collateral responsibility, the same man would oversee a group of affiliates, usually the ones whose principal activity lay within his functional province. But the system had serious deficiencies. At the joints, where the various functions dovetailed—as they did with the big integrated affiliates—Jersey's top-level responsibility tended to blur. Some directors were carrying enormously heavy loads. Others, to relieve the burden, took responsibilities for some affiliates on the basis of expediency; the transportation director, for example, supervised the Scandinavian affiliates. Further, no one was looking at areas broadly enough: people thought about Brazil or Argentina, but no one was encouraged to consider the total problem of Latin America. To give a director experience in more than one function, says a Jersey man, "every couple of years we threw all the papers in the air and sat different men down at different piles. The result of it all was a dilution of the abilities and time of our top executives."

The time of dilution corresponded with a time of deluge. For Jersey was then being caught up in the flood tide of international oil surpluses, which threatened to bring down the whole fancy price structure of international oil. And, abroad, Jersey had never faced bigger or more difficult political complications. In seeking to meet those challenges, Jersey had to move swiftly in two areas. It had to search out and exploit new markets. And it had to bear down hard to reduce the per-barrel cost of oil everywhere in the world. But just when it needed most to move swiftly, Jersey found itself hamstrung by its old organizational patterns.

After he took over in May of 1960, Rathbone made some quick repairs. Atop Jersey's functional groupings Rathbone superimposed a regional grouping—"like an overlay of diagonal streets imposed upon a grid." In addition to their functional assignments, Rathbone gave some board members responsibilities as contact directors of geographic regions. Where two or more functions dovetailed, the new regional contact director now took responsibility for their coordination. The problems of new or difficult areas, like the Common Market or Latin America, could be considered as a whole. By thus breaking up the old compartmentalized approach, Rathbone did a good deal to prepare Jersey for combat in its new and tougher world. "After reorganization," explains David Shepard, "we couldn't point to a new chair or a new job title and say 'There's the answer to our need for new markets or for new economies.' It wasn't that simple. But the emphasis on regional thinking in fact enabled us to do just that."

PROBLEMS

1. How would you classify the executive committee of Standard of New Jersey?
2. In your opinion, why do you believe the executive committee was given the responsibility of overseeing the financial affairs of affiliates and the compensation and selection of the top officers of the company? Would

it have been better to have given the latter function, compensation and selection, to another committee? Discuss.

3. Of what significance is it that the executive committee considered the assignment of a $25,000-a-year-man? Should this problem be delegated to a lesser committee?

4. Could outside board members make a significant contribution to the management of Jersey Standard? Support your answer.

5. Are there dangers of inbreeding that might result from having an inside board in a company the size of Jersey Standard? What about the dangers of inbreeding in a smaller company?

Chapter Questions for Study and Discussion

1. What assumptions are implied whenever a committee is formed? Which assumption is more applicable to the formation of a general management committee? Which is more applicable to the formation of an *ad hoc* or restricted committee?

2. Under what conditions is the judgment of a group likely to be superior to that of an individual? Is the information presented in Chapter 8 concerning brainstorming applicable to the improvement of the judgment of a group? How?

3. Why are committees not used as a check on authority more frequently in business organizations?

4. What problems concerning accountability arise when a committee is granted the authority to make decisions? How can the chairman of a committee be held accountable for the action of the group?

5. Lohman's study indicates that committees appointed by the board of directors are more authoritative than committees appointed by the president of the company. Why is this true?

6. Is there any conflict that might arise as the result of individual board members influencing members of management and the concept of the board as a plural executive? Discuss.

7. In his article, Mylander refers to the committee system of Du Pont as a "committee-line system." What do you think is meant by this phrase?

8. What conditions make it advisable for a company to have a full-time board whose membership is limited to those who have had prior experience with the company?

9. What are the hazards of having an inside board for a small company? Do these same hazards apply to an inside board for a larger company with a sales volume of approximately $500 million a year?
10. How can the shortcomings of an outside board be minimized?

CHAPTER 14

Organizational Change
–Analysis and Development

Twenty-five years ago Stanley Johnson founded the Johnson Valve Company, which has grown and prospered over the years. Mr. Johnson, now 62 years old, realizes that he cannot continue as president indefinitely, but there are no well-formulated plans for management succession. The stock in the company is closely held by Mr. Johnson and members of his immediate family, with only ten percent held by an outsider, the attorney who serves as the only outside member of the board and as general counsel for the corporation. The attorney has suggested that the position of executive vice-president be created and a man brought in from another company with the intention of moving him up to the presidency, if he performs satisfactorily, upon Mr. Johnson's expected retirement at age 65. Currently the organization is as follows.

Reporting directly to Mr. Johnson as an "assistant-to" is a man in his early thirties who has a master's degree in marketing. Although his title is "assistant-to," his primary function is to conduct market research studies in the valve industry and to prepare detailed analyses of current sales. Johnson often refers to his assistant as "my forward planning unit." Also reporting to the president are the treasurer, the vice-president of sales, the purchasing director, the production vice-president, the chief engineer, and the plant manager. The plant manager, now nearing retirement, has been ill most of the past year, so in effect the plant superintendent reports directly to the president.

The treasurer, who for several years was the firm's only accountant, has been with the company since its founding. Reporting directly to the treasurer is the office manager who not only manages the office but also performs the personnel function for all salaried and clerical personnel. The controller, responsible for the cost accounting section, and the supervisor of general ledgers also reports to the treasurer. The vice-president in charge of sales has been an officer of the company for the past five years; however, for many years he was in charge of the field sales force and the entire sales function with the title of sales manager. Although there is now a sales manager reporting to him, the vice-president actually directs the sales force and the sales manager spends most of his time in the office handling the paper work generated by the salesmen. The supervisor of the sales order department also reports to the sales manager.

The purchasing director, with a staff of two buyers and a clerk, reports directly to the president as a result of Mr. Johnson's desire to control the cost of raw materials. Formerly, the director of purchases reported to the production manager, who is a vice-president and Mr. Johnson's brother-in-law, but the only person now reporting to the production manager is the head of the production scheduling department. The chief engineer, also an officer of the company, knows the product well and supervises the section chief of the drafting department, the chief metallurgist, and the director of the research laboratories.

Most of Johnson Valve Company's current problems center in the production area. The plant manager's staff consists of the maintenance foreman, the plant personnel and employment manager, and the foreman of the tool room; but for the past year, as the result of his illness and absence, the plant staff has been reporting directly to the plant superintendent, who also reports on paper to the plant manager. Normally reporting to the plant superintendent are the shipping and receiving foreman, the machining foreman, the quality control manager, the factory stores supervisor, the assembly foreman, and the supervisor of the experimental shop, which is engaged

primarily in carrying out projects assigned by the chief
engineer.

1. Prepare an organization chart showing the present
structure of Johnson Valve Company.

2. Prepare a plan for reorganization. Include a new
organization chart and your justification for the
changes suggested.

Organizations are not static structures; instead, organizations are
made up of dynamic interrelationships existing between people performing those functions necessary for the achievement of organizational
goals. As either goals or people change, the need for modification of
organization structure and function arises. Symptoms calling for organizational change, such as those described below, reflect inadequacies
or inefficiencies in any part of the organization.

1. *Decision making.* Decision making may be too slow to gain full advantage of the situation, or there may be errors in decisions that are
   being made. Perhaps the difficulty in decision making may be traced
   to the placement of the responsibility for decisions at a level of the
   organization not having access to necessary information.
2. *Poor Communications.* Case Problem 13-A, A Problem in Coordination, illustrates poor communications between one man, the president, and his executive group. The Parable of the Spindle, Case
   Problem 7-A, is illustrative of the complete breakdown of an information system with its resultant personnel problems.
3. *Failure in Functional Areas.* There may be failure or inefficiency
   in any one of the major functional areas. Production may not meet
   schedules or it may show excessive costs and quality defects. Sales
   may show a steady loss of customers and failure to achieve expected
   market penetration, while finance may reveal an inability to provide
   for long-range corporate demands. In the area of personnel, the need
   for organizational change may arise as the result of personnel not
   meeting the requirements of changing positions, with poor performance as a result; or the need for change may be highlighted by
   excessive personality clashes between employees (again, the Parable
   of the Spindle).
4. *Lack of Innovation.* There may be a dearth of new ideas, either in
   the form of new products or new and better ways of performing
   present functions. When innovation ceases, growth ceases also.

The presence of any of the above symptoms indicates the need
for organizational change. Such change may occur within a relatively

short period of time as a result of organizational analysis and an evaluation of organizational effectiveness—an approach that emphasizes change in structure. Or organizational change may occur as a result of implementing a long range plan of organizational development that stresses the development of individual managers—an approach that emphasizes change in behavior. Each approach, structural or behavioral, has its place.[1] Discussed first is organizational analysis, including the procedures and techniques usually used in such studies, and a method of evaluating organizational effectiveness. Planned organizational development programs emphasizing the development of executives or managers are discussed in the second part of the chapter.

ORGANIZATIONAL ANALYSIS

When conducting organizational analysis, one is planning for the future of the organization; therefore, it is helpful to follow a procedure based on an objective method. As a result the procedures used in organizational planning follow very closely the procedures discussed in Chapter 4, "Planning" (pp. 97-138).

Procedures for Organizational Analysis

The procedures for sound organizational analysis are an application of the scientific method. They are: (1) assign responsibility, (2) collect data, (3) prepare alternate plans of organization, and (4) install the best plan and follow up.

Assign Responsibility. There are three questions to be answered in the assignment of responsibility for organizational analysis. The first of these questions is, who is to initiate the study; the second, who is to collect the necessary data and develop recommended changes; and third, who is to approve the recommended changes and place them into effect? A study by K. K. White of 118 companies sheds some light on what is actually done by industrial firms in one phase of organizational analysis, preparing the organization chart.[2] White's study shows that the company president initiates the charting of the organization in 42 percent of the companies surveyed; a company vice-president in 22 percent of the companies; and the personnel executive in 12 percent

---

[1] William F. Glueck, "Organization Change in Business and Government," *Academy of Management Journal,* Vol. XII, No. 4 (December, 1969), pp. 439-449. Professor Glueck discusses the approaches to organizational change, both structural and behavioral, and outlines the dimensions of organizational change.

[2] K. K. White, *Understanding the Company Organization Chart* (New York: American Management Association, 1963), Research Study Number 56, pp. 16-17.

of the companies. In most instances, 25 percent of the companies surveyed, the personnel executive compiles the necessary data and prepares
the chart. The president of the company does the charting in 17 percent
of the cases, a company vice-president in 14 percent, or an outside
consultant in 13 percent of the companies. Final approval for any
organizational change must come from top management itself. It goes
without saying that the chief executive, usually the president, must
approve any changes and, to insure maximum cooperation, approval
of other members of top management is much desired.

Collect Data. Once the responsibility for analysis and preparation
of proposed changes is established, it is necessary to collect all pertinent information so that any proposed change is founded on fact, not
upon supposition. The availability and type of information sought varies
from one situation to another. Certain historical records are of interest,
particularly those that show the growth of the company in respect to
the number of people, their titles, their duties, and their personal backgrounds and qualifications. The pattern of growth of the company as
reflected by gross sales is of value, especially when these figures can
be correlated with the need for personnel. In this manner, definite trends
may be established, and personnel needs for expected future levels of
sales may be projected. The analysis of current reports and forms, for
example, the monthly distribution of manufacturing costs, shows the
flow of information within the company. Activity charts showing the
distribution of an employee's time for each day or week may be prepared for key jobs or for all the jobs within a department. When interpreted in the light of information gained from an analysis of existing
reports, the activity chart indicates whether or not the information is
needed. Information gained from the organization questionnaire (discussed below) is of value in defining authority relationships, the nature
of assigned responsibilities, and the extent of authority delegated
to carry out these responsibilities. The gathering of data for an organizational analysis is often a long and tedious task, but it is an important
step for it establishes the factual basis for any proposed change.

Prepare Alternate Plans. Ultimately, any proposed change in organization must be sold to key personnel and alternate plans should be
prepared as a form of insurance. Among these plans, there should be
an "ideal" structure that is theoretically desirable, but not necessarily
attainable. Using the ideal as a starting point, modifications in the plan
may be developed that consider the economic and competitive position
of the company. If only a single plan is presented, it may be rejected

by one displeased executive; an alternate plan is necessary since organizational change is a situation in which "half a loaf is better than none" and the adoption of the alternate plan is at least a step in the right direction.

Install the Best Plan and Follow Up. When the plan is approved, it should be installed and there should be provisions for continuing study and analysis so that any necessary modifications can be made. This task is usually assigned to the group that proposes the initial change. Proper follow-up and modifications of the plan, when needed, emphasize the continuing nature of organizational change.

Tools of Organizational Analysis

There are many tools available for use in organizational analysis. Among those most commonly used are the organization questionnaire, the position description, the organization chart, and the organization manual. Each of these techniques used in studying organizations is discussed briefly.

The Organization Questionnaire. One of the first steps in describing the present organization is to determine the functions and positions of present personnel. Figure 14-1 is an Organization Questionnaire to Executives that has been found useful in securing information from executives, supervisors, and department heads concerning their positions in the organization. The first five items of the questionnaire are for the purposes of identification. The answer given to item 4, title or name of your position, may provide one of the first clues pointing toward the need for clarifying the organization structure. Discrepancies may appear in designating the organizational unit. For example, one department head may describe himself as a section supervisor, cost accounting, while another department head describes himself as supervisor, general accounting; yet both units are at the same level of the organization and report to the same supervisor.

Questions 6 through 10 reveal the nature and extent to which responsibilities have been delegated, the authority granted to meet these responsibilities, and the clarity of the lines of accountability. Note that questions 6 and 8 may be refined to determine the specific degree of authority by specifying those actions that must be reported prior to their occurrence, after the action has occurred, or not reported at all. Question 9 requires a listing of all responsibilities and duties and offers the opportunity for describing the relationships, both internal and external, that must be maintained.

ABC COMPANY
ORGANIZATION QUESTIONNAIRE TO EXECUTIVES
Outline for Describing Your Position

1. Your name.

2. Your department.

3. Your division.

4. Title or name of your position.

5. Your location.

6. To whom do you report?

7. Title or name of the position of the immediate supervisor.

8. Give the names and titles (or names of positions) of those who report to you. In (6) and (8), a distinction might be made of the types of actions which must be reported: (a) actions reported before they take place; (b) after they take place; and (c) those which need not be reported at all.

9. Describe fully the responsibilities of your position as you understand them to be at present. (As part of this description, you should also include your existing responsibilities and relationships with other units within your division and with affiliates and with any outside service agencies.)

10. What is the nature of your authority?
    (a) For establishing policy?
    (b) For incurring expense?
    (c) For personnel changes including selection, promotion, termination, and compensation?
    (d) For establishing methods and procedures?

11. Indicate any committees in the Company or trade groups of which you are a member. If you are chairman, include a description of the purpose, scope of activities and accomplishments of your committee.

12. List by name or title the regular reports which (a) you receive and (b) you prepare, and indicate whether daily, weekly, monthly, etc.

13. List the basic records you are responsible for keeping.

14. Mention anything else of interest in understanding your responsibilities and activities, including any special problems needing attention, any suggestions for improvements or general comments on the overall Company organizational structure.

Source: Ernest Dale, *Planning and Developing the Company Organization Structure* (New York: American Management Association, 1952), Research Report No. 20, p. 135.

Figure 14-1
ORGANIZATION QUESTIONNAIRE

The three questions, 11 through 13, form the basis for an activity analysis and the preparation of flow charts to show the movement and utilization of existing reports and forms. These questions may be modified for use in production departments to trace the movement of the product and the contribution of each production department. The last question, 14, calls for suggestions concerning the improvement of the organization and serves as a means of insuring two-way communications in organizational analysis.

There are two methods of securing the information called for by the questionnaire. One method is to have the incumbent in the position fill out the questionnaire and return it to the person conducting the study; the other method is to secure the information through interview. While the latter method is more costly and time consuming, it is generally agreed that the interview yields much more information and understanding of the organization as a result of aside remarks and nuances of meaning implied in the way in which answers are given. Once the questionnaires have been completed, they are usually reviewed with the next higher level of authority. It is at this stage that significant discrepancies in the opinions of superior and subordinate with respect to the nature of assigned duties, the nature and extent of delegated authority, and the lines of accountability may become apparent.

The Position Description. The data obtained from the questionnaire is the primary source of information for preparing the *position description,* a written statement that describes a specific position in the organization. Whether a written position description merely sketches the major duties of the job or whether it goes into minute detail depends on its intended use. If the purpose is to define the major positions in the organization and show their relationships to each other, the description may be relatively brief; if however, the primary purpose of the description is for training, the job duties may be detailed so that they approach the completeness of a procedural manual.

Most position descriptions usually include the following information. There is a section that *identifies* the job and may range from a statement of the title only, as in Figure 14-2, to the inclusion of statements indicating the title of the immediate superior, the date of preparation of the description with dates of revision, and the number and types of employees supervised. Generally, the name of the incumbent is not included since a change in personnel would necessitate a revision of the description. Next, there is a statement of the major responsibility or *primary functions* of the job, a capsule description of the purpose of the position. A statement of *responsibilities* presents the major tasks

MANAGEMENT GUIDE
SUPERVISOR ACCOUNTING SECTION, MANUFACTURING DIVISION

I. FUNCTIONS

    Furnishes functional guidance to the Plant Superintendents on, and provides services in connection with accounting, auditing, budgets, inventory and stock control, payroll, and tax activities.

II. RESPONSIBILITIES AND AUTHORITY

The responsibilities and authority stated below are subject to established policies.

1. Administers approved policies and procedures pertaining to accounting, auditing, budget, payroll, and tax activities, making such recommendations as he deems necessary to the Comptroller through channels.
2. Administers approved policies and procedures pertaining to inventory and stock control activities, making such recommendations as he deems necessary to the Manager of the Supply and Transportation Department through channels.
3. Consolidates the financial, accounting, budget, inventory and stock control, payroll, and tax reports and statements of the plants, and prepares such reports and statements for the Division.
4. Establishes and maintains necessary accounting records for the Division.
5. Establishes and maintains necessary cost control records for the Division.
6. Maintains necessary inventory and stock control records for the Division.
7. Maintains necessary production records for the Division.
8. Maintains necessary records of receipts and disbursements and has custody of funds on hand for the Division office.
9. Maintains necessary payroll records and accounts; prepares and pays Division office payrolls and confidential payrolls of the Division.
10. Conducts all tax activities for the Division.

III. RELATIONSHIPS

  A. General Manager, Manufacturing Division
     Reports to the General Manager.
  B. Plant Superintendents and Section Supervisors
     As directed, or as requested by the Plant Superintendents and Section Supervisors, advises and assists them in the accomplishment of their respective functions in all matters within his province.
  C. Outside Auditors
     Cooperates with independent auditors.
  D. Others
     Conducts such other relationships as are necessary to the accomplishment of his function.

Source: George Lawrence Hall, *The Management Guide* (2d ed.; San Francisco: Standard Oil Company of California, 1956), p. 63.

Figure 14-2
A TYPICAL POSITION DESCRIPTION

that must be performed in order to fulfill the functions of the job. It is this portion of the description, when developed in great detail, that may serve as a useful training device; but for the most part, executive and supervisory descriptions are limited to a statement of between six and ten major responsibilities. The *authority* delegated to the position in order to perform the required functions may appear as a separate section of the position description or, as in Figure 14-2, it may be combined with the statement of primary responsibilities. The last section of most descriptions is a statement of *relationships*. The reason for stating relationships is twofold. First, it shows the position in its proper relationship to other positions within the company and relationships to persons outside the company such as vendors, auditors, or public relations contacts. Second, a statement of relationships tends to answer criticism often made of position descriptions that descriptions force a man into a narrow role and make him oblivious to other events and persons in the company.

As a general rule, position descriptions do not include a statement of the specifications and qualifications required of incumbents. If such specifications are prepared, they are on a separate sheet and include requirements in respect to age, education, experience, and other personal characteristics. Specifications are of value as an aid in evaluating and selecting potential replacements.

The Organization Chart. An organization chart presents in graphic form the major functions and the lines of authority of an organization as of a given moment in time. Charts range in complexity from the simple chart shown in Figure 14-3 to complex charts that use color and the photographs of the incumbents in key positions. However, for purposes of organizational analysis and reference, it is best to keep charts as simple as possible.

The mechanics of constructing an organization chart are not difficult. Figure 14-4 presents in tabular form ten suggestions for preparing organization charts. These are not hard-and-fast rules and they should be modified when the occasion demands. By far the most common form of organizational charting is the *vertical* chart (Figure 14-3), which shows the organizational hierarchy ranked from top to bottom. A variation of the vertical chart is the *horizontal* chart, which is read from left to right rather than from top to bottom. A more complex form of charting is the *circular* organization chart, which places the chief executive in the center of the circle with the horizontal lines of the vertical chart forming a series of concentric circles around the chief executive. Proponents of the horizontal form of charting contend that

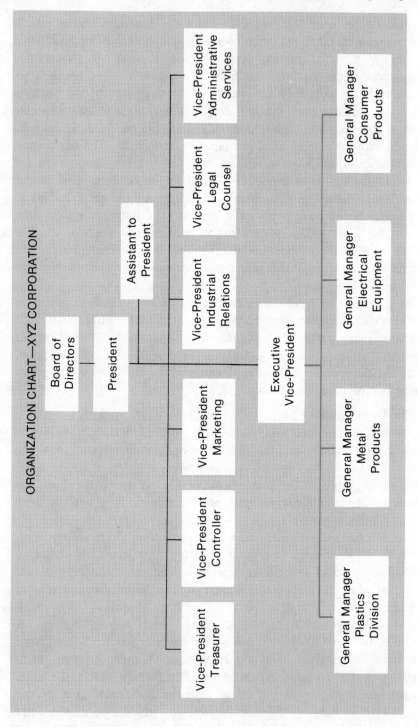

ORGANIZATION CHART—XYZ CORPORATION

Figure 14-3

A VERTICAL ORGANIZATION CHART

SUGGESTIONS FOR PREPARING AN ORGANIZATION CHART

1. Identify the chart fully showing the name of the company, date of preparation, and title of person or name of department responsible for preparation. If the chart is for one division of the company only, include such information as part of the title.
2. Use rectangular boxes to show either an organizational unit or a person. Plural executives and other committees occupy one box. (See Figure 13-1.)
3. The vertical placement of the boxes shows relative positions in the organizational hierarchy; however, due to space limitations, line units are frequently shown one level below staff units. (See Figure 14-3.)
4. Any given horizontal row of boxes should be of the same size and should include only those positions having the same organizational rank.
5. Vertical and horizontal solid lines are used to show the flow of line authority.
6. If necessary, use dotted or broken lines to show the flow of functional authority. (See Figure 11-4.)
7. Lines of authority enter at the top center of a box and leave at the bottom center; they do not run through the box. Exception: the line of authority to a staff assistant or an "assistant-to" may enter the side of the box. (See Figure 14-3.)
8. The title of each position should be placed in the box. The title should be descriptive and show function. For example, vice-president is not sufficient as it does not show function. The functional area; e.g., manufacturing, should be included even though it is not a part of the official title. Titles should be consistent; if necessary, revise titles so they are both consistent and descriptive.
9. Include the name of the person currently holding the position unless personnel turnover is so great that revision of the chart becomes burdensome.
10. Keep the chart as simple as possible; include a legend if necessary to explain any special notations. When preparing a separate chart for an organizational unit, include the superior to whom the unit reports.

Figure 14-4
SUGGESTIONS FOR PREPARING AN ORGANIZATION CHART

we normally read from left to right and that a horizontal chart follows this natural tendency. Those who favor the circular chart claim that dynamic relationships are better portrayed through a series of concentric circles. However, precedent and ease of construction and interpretation favor the continued use of the vertical chart.

The Organization Manual. An *organization manual* is a compilation of descriptive statements usually bound in manual form concerning the organization of a specific company.[3] The content of organization manuals varies widely; however, two of the tools of organizational analysis are included in almost all manuals—position descriptions and organization charts. The combination of these two instruments shows the lines of authority and accountability, the major functions of each position, the responsibilities and authority for each position, and the primary interrelationships between key positions. In addition, organization manuals may include a statement of company objectives and statements of company policy. In large companies, it is not uncommon to find organization manuals consisting of several volumes, one for each of the major functional areas of the company. In such cases, each volume includes a statement of company objectives, policies, and the organization charts and position descriptions for that specific functional area.

Evaluation of Formal Organizational Analysis

Not all companies believe in using the formal tools of organizational analysis. The extent to which formal tools of analysis are used is related to the size of the company as shown in Table 14-1. To be sure, White's study deals only with the use of organization charts; however, it is safe to assume that a company without organization charts has not prepared position descriptions or an organization manual. Note that even in the large companies, 5,000 employees and over, four of the 15 companies in this category do not have organization charts. The absence of charts in small companies may be due to a belief that they

Table 14-1

RELATIONSHIP BETWEEN COMPANY SIZE AND PRESENCE OF ORGANIZATION CHARTS

No. of Employees	No. of Companies with Charts	No. of Companies without Charts	Total Companies	Percent of Companies with Charts
1-249	34	41	75	45
250-499	27	4	31	87
500-999	15	7	22	68
1,000-4,999	28	9	37	76
5,000 and over	11	4	15	73

Source: K. K. White, *Understanding the Company Organization Chart,* (New York: American Management Association, 1963), Research Study No. 56, p. 19.

---

[3] George Lawrence Hall, *The Management Guide* (2d ed.; San Francisco: Standard Oil Company of California, 1956), p. 74. The Standard Oil Management Guide is one of the best known organization manuals and is available in most libraries.

are not needed, a lack of available personnel to prepare charts, or any of a number of similar reasons. However, large companies without charts have not prepared them because it is felt that the disadvantages of charting the organization outweigh the advantages. Let us examine the advantages and disadvantages usually attributed to the use of formal tools of organizational analysis.

Advantages of Formal Organizational Analysis. The advantage most frequently cited in support of preparing a formal analysis of an organization is that the process of analysis itself forces the key executives of the company into critical thinking directed toward organizational problems. The process of analysis leads to a reexamination of present structure and functions and makes possible the correction of organizational defects. Second, charts and manuals are of use in training replacements for present personnel. True, the man holding the position at present may not benefit greatly, but new people coming into the organization or a man moving into a position new to him find charts and manuals helpful during their period of orientation. The third reason advanced for formalizing the organization structure is that charts and position descriptions offer an authoritative source which describes the major functions and responsibilities for each position and thus become a means of settling disputes that may arise concerning lines of authority and accountability.

Disadvantages of Formal Organizational Analysis. Those who prefer not to use formal analysis claim that the formalization of organization structure by charts and position descriptions leads to rigidity and inflexibility in organization structure and function. They point out that a new man coming into a position complete with chart and position description is bound by precedent and does not have the full opportunity to express himself and show how much he can really contribute to the organization. In a sense, these critics of charting are saying "Put a man into a square and you have one." In addition to organizational inflexibility and the stultifying effects that charting may have on individuals, opponents of formal analysis state that formal charting ignores completely the informal organization—the many interpersonal relationships, lines of communications, and influence—which exists among people who work together every day and is often quite different from the formal relationships shown on the chart.[4]

---

[4] Frank J. Jasinski, "Adapting Organization to New Technology," *Harvard Business Review,* Vol. XXXVII (January-February, 1959), pp. 79-86. Mr. Jasinski's article contains an extensive discussion of horizontal relationships.

There is a need for balance. Charting is not intended to stultify or limit the achievement of individuals. It is intended to show in broad strokes major functions and relationships. Nor is charting intended to promote organizational inflexibility; on the other hand, an organization with relationships that change from day to day or with every crisis cannot properly be called an organization.

Evaluating Organizational Effectiveness

The application of the tools of organizational analysis—the organization questionnaire, the position description, and the charting of the present organization—is the second step in the process of organizational analysis. In order to complete the third step of analysis, to prepare alternate plans of organization, and move on to the fourth step of selecting the best plan for a given situation, it is necessary to establish a basis for evaluating present organizational effectiveness. Due to the dynamic nature of organizations resulting from patterns of leadership, the structure of the organization, the types of organizational authority, the efficiency of organizational processes such as delegation, and the utilization of groups to perform organizational functions, any concept of measuring effectiveness must recognize these variables and interpret them in terms of the needs of each specific organization. Figure 14-5, Checklist of Organizational Effectiveness, is a systematic means of checking each major factor contributing to organizational effectiveness. Let us examine Figure 14-5, remembering that the characteristics of organization are not absolutes—either black or white.

Overall Planning. The extent of overall planning lends direction and purpose to an organization and is basic to the effectiveness of any enterprise. In the collection of data for organizational analysis, the examination of company records may determine the extent of overall planning. Two questions are asked in this regard: Is there a written statement of company objectives, and Is there a written statement of company policy? Objectives define the goals of the organization, while policy statements indicate the broad framework within which each of the functional areas of the firm should operate in achieving the objectives. As an absolute minimum, there should be policy guides for each of the major functional areas of finance, production, sales, and personnel. Unless objectives and policies are clearly stated, there is little hope for establishing effective organizational structure and processes.

Patterns of Leadership. Chapter 9, "Organization Theory," discusses Theory X, a work-centered approach to organizational leadership,

1. OVERALL PLANNING
    Written Statements of Company Objectives   _____
    Company Policies
        Sales   _____
        Finance   _____
        Production   _____
        Personnel   _____
        Other   _____
2. PATTERNS OF LEADERSHIP
    Primarily
        Authoritative   _____
        Participative   _____
        Appropriate   _____
3. ORGANIZATIONAL STRUCTURE
    Departmentation
        Function   _____
        Product   _____
        Customer   _____
        Geography   _____
        Process   _____
        Sequence   _____
    Span of Management
        One over One   _____
        Two or Three   _____
        Three to Seven   _____
        Eight or More   _____
    Overall Impression
        Proper Balance   _____
        Proper Emphasis   _____
4. AUTHORITY RELATIONSHIPS
    Factors Limiting Effectiveness of Authority
        Overlapping Authority   _____
        Superior Authority   _____
        Provisions for Subordinate Acceptance   _____
    Line and Staff Relationships
        Use of "Assistant-to:"   _____
        Limits of Line Authority   _____
        Limits of Staff Authority   _____
        Task Force Organization   _____
5. DELEGATION
    Parity of Authority and Responsibility   _____
    Absoluteness of Accountability   _____
    Unity of Command   _____
    Personality Factors   _____
6. DECENTRALIZATION
    Definition of Decentralized Unit   _____
    Scope, Type, and Frequency of Decisions   _____
    Availability of Controls   _____
    Statement of Goals for Unit   _____
    Degree of Decentralization
        Optimum   _____
        Too Little   _____
        Too Much   _____
7. USE OF COMMITTEES
    Committees
        Ad Hoc   _____
        Advisory   _____
        Management   _____
        Composition   _____
        Benefits   _____
    Board of Directors
        Outside Members   _____
        Inside Members   _____
        Contribution   _____
8. PROVISIONS FOR CONTROL
    Definitions of Standards   _____
    Units of Measurement   _____
    Reporting of Exceptions   _____
    Timeliness of Controls   _____
    Strategic Placement of Controls   _____
    Control Information for Line Managers   _____

Figure 14-5

CHECKLIST OF ORGANIZATIONAL EFFECTIVENESS

and Theory Y, a people-centered or human relations approach to leadership. Theory Z, a systems approach to organization theory, holds that the most effective leadership pattern, whether it be predominantly authoritative or participative, is dependent upon the characteristics of the organization and its members. As the organization grows in size, defining size as number of people, there is a tendency for leadership patterns to become more authoritative. The same tendency exists when there is little need for interaction between members, when members of the organization are submissive and dependent, when the goals of individuals and the organization are divergent, when decision making occurs at a high level of the organization, and when the organization is under pressure to survive and meet stated objectives. The converse of the above situation—a small organization or unit, need for interaction, independent members, congruent goals, decision making at all levels in an organization achieving its objectives—calls for a participative form of leadership. Although a judgment concerning the effectiveness of leadership is highly subjective in nature and its worth dependent upon the skill of the person performing the organizational analysis, such a judgment should be made in evaluating an organization.

Organization Structure. When evaluating the structure of an organization, three structural characteristics are considered: departmentation, span of management, and an overall impression of balance and emphasis. The most frequently used bases for departmentation are function, product, customer, geography, process, sequence, and any combination of these. The basis chosen for forming a department varies from one level of the organization to another and there may be variation in the bases for departmentation among units of the same level. The test of proper departmentation is whether or not the result is a grouping of activities that is capable of functioning effectively.

Span of management is the number of departments or functions under the direction of one manager. The checklist in Figure 14-5 provides a basis for grouping the span of management into four broad categories. When a one-over-one arrangement is found, it deserves careful examination. A situation in which a one-over-one arrangement is probably effective and necessary is that of an executive vice-president as the sole person reporting to the president. In this instance, the president's other duties, such as relations with the board of directors and with groups outside the company, may make it mandatory that only one person report to him. However, one-over-one relationships at lower levels of the organization should be regarded with suspicion. The designation of an assistant manager, a line relationship showing only one subordinate, may be justified if there is a clear understanding of those functions to be performed by the manager and those functions to be performed by the assistant manager.

An overall impression of the effectiveness of an organizational structure includes evaluating the structure; *i.e.*, departmentation and span of management, in respect to the *balance* and *emphasis* accorded those functions and activities most closely related to the objectives of the organization. It is helpful to view the structure as components of a system, and the parameters of Theory *Z*, as discussed in Chapter 9, are helpful as a basis for determining whether the departmentation, span of management, and the degree of balance and emphasis represent the optimum for organizational effectiveness.

Authority Relationships. In reviewing authority relationships, our concern is directed toward those factors that limit authority, the clarity of established line-and-staff relationships, and ultimately a consideration of the feasibility of a task force form of organization. When determining the effectiveness of lines of authority, it is necessary to determine the extent to which there is overlapping authority between managerial functions. The source of this information is the questionnaire and the position description. Occasionally authority may be ineffective because provisions for subordinate acceptance of authority are inadequate, and may result in ineffective performance, lack of cooperation, and on occasion, refusal to follow directions. The pattern of leadership is an important item to consider when assessing provisions for subordinate acceptance.

When checking line-and-staff relationships, review any position entitled "assistant-to" and question the practicality of designating a specific staff title more descriptive of the functions performed. In small organizations or in the case of new positions, descriptive titles may not be practical. When determining the authority relationships of established line-and-staff positions, attention is directed toward the degree to which authority relationships are defined—the stating of definite limits of authority for each, and the extent to which each authority understands the role of the other. In some organizations, characterized by changing projects, with well-defined objectives and limiting time tables, it is well to consider the possibility of using a task force organization designed for the specific task at hand. It is necessary that responsibility for the entire project be stated and that provisions be made for the reassignment of personnel upon the completion of the project.

Delegation. Violation of any of the three conditions for effective delegation may result in ineffective delegation. Admittedly, these conditions are ignored on many occasions; but when ignored and when the resultant delegation seems effective, it is effective in spite of the fact that the conditions have been disregarded. Also, poor delegation may be due to personality characteristics of either the superior or the subordinate which make the process of delegation ineffective.

Decentralization. The measure of the effectiveness of decentralization of authority is whether it meets the needs of the organization. The parameters of Theory Z form a useful set of guides concerning the appropriateness of the degree of decentralization. Additional questions may be raised concerning the definition of the decentralized unit, the scope and type of decisions made within the unit, provisions for adequate control, and the statement of goals for the unit. An overall determination of effective decentralization expresses the degree of decentralization as optimum, too little, or too much.

Use of Committees. When properly used, committees may perform quite effectively the managerial functions assigned to them. In rating the effectiveness of committees, it is necessary to determine the extent to which the duties assigned to the committee are in keeping with the functions normally assigned to a given type of committee. *Ad hoc* committees are temporary in nature and are formed to consider a specific question. They are disbanded upon the completion of their assignment. *Ad hoc* groups may appear at any level of the organization and the functions assigned may range from making recommendations to making decisions and taking action necessary for the completion of the assignment. Advisory committees are, as the name indicates, assigned advisory functions with the right to take action reserved for another, usually the person to whom the committee reports. The management committee, whose members are from the top level of the company, offers a means of coordinating the work of individual functional areas and may operate as a plural executive. Benefits derived from the proper use of committees are the value of pooled judgments coming from the diverse knowledge of the individual members, the creation of a favorable training situation, and improved cooperation on the part of individual members as the result of having participated in the work of the group.

In determining the contribution of a board of directors, review the backgrounds of individual members, not only in respect to their status as employees of the corporation which determines whether they are inside or outside members, but also in respect to the amount of time each member is able to devote to the company. The contributions of a board depend on the manner in which they perform their directive functions of setting corporate objectives, selecting management, and subsequently reviewing and guiding management's efforts.

Provisions for Control. Though the control process is not discussed fully until Part Five of this textbook, items concerning the control function are included in the checklist for organizational effectiveness for the sake of completeness. In evaluating control provisions, it is necessary to determine the extent to which standards of performance are clearly defined—particularly for the production and sales functions. The units of measurement employed to measure performance against standard should be appropriate and as objective as possible. Consideration is also given to the degree that controls report the exceptional deviation from standard, to their timeliness, and to their strategic placement. Since the last step of the control process may require corrective action, controls should provide necessary information for the responsible manager so that he may take appropriate corrective action.

ORGANIZATION DEVELOPMENT

As noted in Chapter 6 in the discussion of personnel policy statements concerning management development (pp. 193-194), three terms are used, often interchangeably, to describe the long range process of organizational change that emphasizes the development of executives or managers. These terms, all emphasizing a change in behavior as opposed to structural change, are: *executive development, management development,* and *organization development.* However, each descriptive term carries with it a slightly different connotation. *Executive development* emphasizes the development of the individual executive, *management development* indicates a plan for the development of all members of management, *organization development* implies that the entire management structure is involved, not as individuals but as members of an organization, so that the organization functions in a different or improved manner.

In discussing organization development the following topics are considered. First, there is a review of several points of view now existing in organization development; second, a review of the elements of a formal organization development program; and third, a discussion of one of the major problems in evaluating an organization development program, the measurement of performance. Finally, there is a description of what appears to be a breakthrough in organization development.

Approaches to Management Development

Douglas McGregor describes two extremes in the approaches to management development. The earliest approach to management development regards development as an automatic process requiring little attention on the part of management. This approach assumes that competent managers, like cream, will rise to the top and can be skimmed off when needed. There is much to be said for this view, provided conditions are such that the cream can rise to the top. For most companies the "hands-off" approach did not produce enough qualified managers, with the result that during the last 20 years another way of developing managers emerged. The second method may be called the "manufacturing" approach, in which the development of managers is looked upon as a production problem. When development programs are considered to be a problem of producing managers, people are "assigned the *engineering* task of *designing* a program and *building* the necessary *machinery,* toward the end of *producing* the needed *supply* of managerial talent." [5] The major criticism of the manufacturing approach to executive development is that all too frequently companies become so engrossed in the mechanics of the program that they lose sight of the original objectives of management development—the development of managers for the organization. Let us review briefly the current thinking in regard to management development that lies between the two extremes outlined by McGregor. First, the development of executives is recognized as a process of change; second, the role of the individual being developed or changed is considered; and third, the contributions of the organization are evaluated.

A Process of Change. When a company expresses a need for organizational development, it is in effect saying that change is desired so that the organization may become more effective. Change may be accomplished in several ways. Occasionally it may be necessary to remove an executive from his position by transferring him to another post or by terminating his services with the company. [6] The duties of the position may be modified so that the present incumbent's abilities are sufficient for the changed job requirements, or it may be necessary

---

[5] Douglas McGregor, *The Human Side of Enterprise* (New York: McGraw-Hill Book Company, Inc., 1960), p. 191. Italics are McGregor's. Chapter 14, "Management Development Programs" and Chapter 15, "Acquiring Managerial Skills in the Classroom" pp. 190-226, provide a good general discussion of management development.

[6] Saul W. Gellerman, "When the Job Outgrows the Man," *The Management Review,* Vol. XXVII (June, 1960), pp. 4-8, 68-70. Dr. Gellerman presents the arguments for making a clean break; i.e., removing the executive from his job.

to undertake an extensive reorganization to align job requirements and personnel capabilities. The recruitment of executive talent from outside the company is frequently used as a means of introducing organizational change.[7] However, our concern is the development of management personnel—itself a process of change—as a means of changing organizations.

A question arises concerning the objectives of management development programs—what is it about the executive that needs changing? It could be the acquisition of professional knowledge and skills such as those possessed by engineers or accountants. However, most managers have such skills at the time they are employed; and in those instances where additional knowledge or skill is required, either company or university training programs seem to meet this need satisfactorily. *Development programs are aimed toward producing a set of attitudes that differentiate the competent, professional manager from the incompetent or immature manager.* Part of the difficulty in achieving desired results in management development is due to an unsureness and inability to define the attitudes required, and part is due to our failure to apply consistently what is known about the process of changing an individual member of a social organization—a form of *influence*.[8] Edgar H. Schein, a psychologist at Massachusetts Institute of Technology, offers a model for change capable of being used in evaluating the potential effectiveness of management programs.[9] The model consists of the following three steps: (1) unfreezing, (2) changing, and (3) refreezing.

---

[7] Stephen Habbe, "What About Executive Recruiters?," *Management Record,* Vol. XVIII (February, 1956), pp. 42-44. The operations and services of executive search firms, sometimes called "flesh peddlers" and "body snatchers," are presented in simple question-and-answer form.

For a more detailed discussion of executive recruiting, the following article is recommended: Robert F. Moore, "The Executive Matchmakers," *Business Horizons,* Vol. IV (Fall, 1961), pp. 29-36.

[8] T. A. Mahoney, T. H. Jerdee, and S. J. Carroll, *Development of Managerial Performance, A Research Approach,* Monograph C-9 (Cincinnati: South-Western Publishing Company, 1963). This study directed toward a descriptive statement of the functional aspects of managerial performance illustrates the difficulty of specifying the attitudes necessary for such performance.

[9] Edgar H. Schein, "Management Development As a Process of Influence," *Industrial Management Review,* Vol. III (May, 1961), pp. 59-76. Dr. Schein's article is a well-reasoned statement of the application of current knowledge concerning social influence as a factor in changing attitudes. He applies the model he develops to the brainwashing of the Communists, the training of a nun, and the development of managers.

For a similar approach to the analysis of management development, see the following: Robert J. House, "Management Development Is a Game," *Harvard Business Review,* Vol. XXXXI (July-August, 1963), pp. 130-143.

UNFREEZING. All learning, whether it be the acquisition of skills, knowledge, or changed attitudes, assumes that the learner is ready to learn. He is *set* for the experience and motivated. When attitudes are being changed, it is necessary to "unfreeze" present attitudes so they may be dropped and new ones acquired. Coercion may be used as an aid in unfreezing, as in the case of the "brainwashing" of the Chinese Communists; however, management development assumes that the manager is ready to learn. There is some evidence that such is not the case. One study shows that even top-level executives have ill-defined goals and merely wish "to get ahead" and that many middle- and lower-level managers fail to see the purpose of management development either in terms of company needs or in respect to their own needs.[10] Other factors that aid in the unfreezing of old attitudes to make room for the new include a completely new environment, thus removing the individual from the sources of his old attitudes, a certain amount of punishment and humiliation for holding on to old attitudes, and a carefully planned series of rewards and punishments to emphasize the value of change. The hazing of fraternity pledges offers a good example of removal from an old environment, humiliation, and selected rewards and punishment.

In order to have successful management development programs, companies must communicate their organizational needs to prospective participants to insure an understanding of the aims of the program. The participants themselves must have clearly defined goals congruent with those of the organization and must perceive the need for change on their part. The use of environmental factors that aid in the unfreezing process poses a real problem in developing a planned company program of attitude change. The difficulty is not one of physically removing the executive from his old environment since there are many university training programs that meet this requirement; rather, it is the nature of the change process, the second step of the change model.

CHANGING. According to Schein's model, a change in attitudes is accomplished either as the result of *identification* or *internalization*. The opportunity to identify one's self with a person having the desired attitudes facilitates the acquisition of those attitudes. The executive who, in describing his early years with the company, refers to a superior with

---

[10] Reed M. Powell, "Growth Plans for Executives," *Business Horizons,* Vol. IV (Summer, 1961), pp. 41-50. This report is part of a study on the impact of university-sponsored development programs upon executives. For a more detailed treatment of the study, see the following article: Kenneth R. Andrews, "Reaction to University Development Programs," *Harvard Business Review,* Vol. XXXVII (May-June, 1961), pp. 116-134.

the words, "He treated me like a father," or "He treated me as though I were his son," is expressing identification with his former boss. Herein lies the problem of removing the trainee from his organizational environment—he is prevented from identifying with someone in the company. The same difficulty is present when executive development programs are conducted by staff men. Regardless of how competent staff personnel are, it is rare that a line executive will identify himself with a staff man.

Internalization is the process of trying, adopting, and using the new attitudes as a way of solving problems and learning how to live with them. Training programs away from home grounds usually offer an excellent opportunity for internalization since the environment is relatively controlled and other trainees are going through the same process of experimenting with the new attitudes. Further, rewards in the form of approval by the leader and other members of the group tend to encourage the adoption of the desired changes. It is difficult, if not impossible, to internalize attitudes if training is sandwiched in between the regular course of a day's work. Attitudes must be lived, studied, and experimented with in order that they may finally be accepted and integrated into one's personality.

REFREEZING. Refreezing is the final acceptance and integration of the desired attitudes so they become integrated as a permanent part of one's personality. Time and organizational support are needed for this phase of the process of change. In Chapter 19 the importance of organizational climate is discussed as a factor in the training of supervisors, and it is stated that unless the climate is favorable, training programs may be a complete waste of time and money. An organizational climate that encourages the executive to exercise his newly formed attitudes and rewards him for using them is essential to the process of refreezing.

The Individual and Change. The above discussion presents attitudinal change as a relationship between an individual undergoing the process of change and an organization inducing that change. Let us examine more closely the role of the individual, particularly in respect to those changes desired through the process of management development.

First, there is evidence presented that members of middle and lower management are not ready for change, as evidenced by their lack of understanding of the organization's goals for management development and their failure to perceive within themselves the need for change. Without proper motivation and readiness to learn, the desired change in attitude cannot be reasonably expected. Second, the opportunity for identification with another person seems to be an essential ingredient of attitudinal change. As part of psychological growth a son attempts an identification with his father, also a symbol of authority. If identification is not completed with the father, it may occur with a scoutmaster, a coach, a teacher, or some other adult figure. If the father is rejected as an object of identification, or if he discourages his son from identifying with him, psychological growth is stunted and at the same time the son rejects symbols of authority. One of the characteristics of organizations is that they are authoritarian to some degree. The son who has failed to form identifications with authority figures and who later becomes a manager in an organization has attitudes toward authority that are incompatible with the concept of authority as it operates in business organizations. He usually has difficulty in accepting authority, understanding it, submitting to authority, or using authority wisely when it is delegated to him. The ability to identify and the related attitudes toward authority are well established before a man finishes college, yet management development programs are challenged to change these attitudes five or ten years after a manager has completed his professional training. The difficulty of the task is evident.[11] Third, there is also mounting evidence that success or failure as a manager is dependent to a considerable extent upon personality factors. Again we are dealing with behavioral patterns established early in life, and to change long-established patterns of personality is tedious and difficult.[12]

These three items—the readiness to learn new attitudes, the ability to identify with a person having the desired attitudes (along with the

---

[11] Harry Levinson, "A Psychologist Looks at Executive Development," *Harvard Business Review,* Vol. XXXX (September-October, 1962), pp. 69-75. Dr. Levinson's article presents a point of view similar to that expressed in the text. He evaluates management development programs, particularly appraisals of performance and the opportunity for identification, as a means of encouraging psychological growth.

[12] Thomas W. Harrell, *Manager's Performance and Personality* (Cincinnati: South-Western Publishing Company, Editor's Series, 1961). This book presents a summary of the literature concerning personality and its relation to performance in the upper levels of business management. The following quotation from page 172 supports the concept that authority relationships are dependent upon identification with an adult figure early in life.

"Relations with one's parents seems to offer the best explanation for the development of a personality similar to that of successful managers. Who the parents are, especially what is the father's occupation, has already been discussed. Relations with parents regardless of their socio-economic status are also crucial. Many young presidents have been reported to be comparing with their fathers whom they respected but wanted to match or outdo. The mobile elite, who by definition did not have highly successful fathers, occupationally were still trying to prove themselves worthy of the acceptance they had not had from their fathers, and often had developed an identification with some other father figure who inspired them to great effort."

implications of former identifications), and the significance of personality as a determinant of managerial success—are characteristics of the individual manager who is the object of the desired change. It must be recognized that for one reason or another every manager is not subject to change; and for those who are capable of change, the direction and the degree of change vary with each individual.

The Organization and Change. The role of the organization in the process of change is of utmost importance in the unfreezing of the unwanted or old attitudes and the *refreezing* of the new or desired attitudes. In his analysis of management development as a process of influence, Dr. Schein describes the institution's total control over the environment in the shaping of attitudes. He cites the environmental control exerted by the Chinese Communists in their brain-washing technique and the rigid structure imposed by the convent in the training of nuns. Other less rigorous examples of institutional control over the individual that result in the fixing of attitudes acceptable to that institution would include the internship and residency of a physician, and the various military and naval academies. To a lesser degree the college fraternity system accomplishes the same end. An important element in institutional control of environment is that the administrators of such institutions have been through the same process of influence and change—a condition that goes a long way toward explaining the rigidity of institutions. At the same time these administrators become acceptable objects for identification and thereby facilitate the acquisition of the new attitudes. Their presence, their behavior, and their attitudes serve to reinforce the new attitude during the process of *refreezing.*

Industrial organizations cannot and do not exert the same degree of control over the environment of their managers. Most companies have top managements with no common institutional background with the result that there is no clear attitudinal pattern to transmit to managers, nor is there a uniform image of managerial success as an object of identification.

The practice of *coaching;* i.e., individual counsel and guidance, is used frequently in management development, but its contribution to the development of managers is questionable. Lack of time is usually cited as the reason why coaching is not conducted on a systematic basis; however, the real reasons are a lack of understanding of the dependency needs of subordinates and the need for identification, an environment that tolerates precious few mistakes, and the fact that very few companies include development of subordinates as a major function of an executive's job.

The above outline of the knowledge we have available concerning the optimum conditions required for a change of attitudes shows the difference between industrial organizations and those organizations better suited for instilling a prescribed set of attitudes. Yet the development of managers and organizational planning is a necessity for the industrial firm. The following section describes the major steps in the administration of a management development program.

An Organization Development Program

The steps necessary to establish an organization development program are outlined in Figure 14-6. Step one of the outlined program, the analysis of the present organization, is developed in the first part of this chapter. The determination of the objectives of the program and the establishment of opportunities for development are the result of personnel policy statements in regard to staffing (pp. 405-412) and define the direction and scope of any organization development program. However, the fourth major step of an organization development program, the evaluation of the program itself, relies heavily on performance appraisals and for that reason it is well to discuss in considerable detail the nature of performance appraisals.

Performance Appraisals

The main purpose in evaluating an organization development program is to provide a feedback so that the effectiveness of the program in respect to its contribution to the development of the entire organization may be determined. Evaluation of results is also necessary to revise manpower requirements and to bring up-to-date the information contained in the personnel inventory. Opinion and attitude surveys of those who have participated in the program are of value; however, there is evidence that the information elicited from such surveys may express at best only a general satisfaction with the "broadening effects" of management development rather than provide the specific data necessary for the improvement of such programs.[13] The most common device used to evaluate the development of managers is the

---

[13] Kenneth R. Andrews, "Reaction to University Development Programs," *Harvard Business Review*, Vol. XXXVIII (May-June, 1961), pp. 116-134. The information contained in this article may serve as a guide for the development of a survey of the values received from a management development program.

I. Analyze Present Organization

  A. Preparation of Organizational Charts (Figure 14-1)

  B. Preparation of Organizational Manuals

  C. Completion of Organizational Checklist (Figure 14-5)

II. Determine Objectives of the Program

  A. Management Manpower Requirements
    1. Replacement Needs
    2. Growth Needs
      a. Historic Growth
      b. Planned Expansion
    3. Improved Performance Needs

  B. Management Personnel Inventory
    1. Inventory of Current Capabilities
    2. Appraisal of Current Performance
    3. Estimate of Potential Growth

III. Establish Opportunities for Development

  A. Internal Sources
    1. Training Programs
    2. Job Rotation
    3. Committee Assignments
    4. Coaching
    5. Planned Promotional Sequence

  B. External Sources
    1. University Programs
    2. Professional Meetings
    3. Industrial Conferences

IV. Evaluate Program

  A. Continue Performance Appraisals

  B. Opinion and Attitude Surveys

  C. Feedback to I and II above

Figure 14-6
AN ORGANIZATION DEVELOPMENT PROGRAM

performance appraisal. Since the performance appraisal is used not only as a means of evaluating a management development program but also as a means of supplying information for the management personnel inventory, there is considerable criticism concerning performance appraisals. Although a subordinate's performance is always appraised in some fashion by his superior, the introduction of formal performance appraisals into an organization is invariably met with resistance. Such resistance is usually evidenced by the inability to complete the required appraisals within the allotted time limits. Resistance is due in part to the lack of a clear statement of the purpose of appraisals, a definition of expected standards of performance, and an understanding of the objectives of the appraisal interview.

Purpose of Appraisals. There are two questions to be resolved in determining the purpose of performance appraisals. First, is the appraisal intended to measure current performance, or is it intended to measure the subordinate's potential for promotion? Second, is the appraisal to be used to determine advances in salary, or is it to be used as a basis for self-improvement?

It is difficult enough for a manager to appraise current performance without, as Douglas McGregor phrases it, "playing God" by being required to state his estimate of a subordinate's potential capabilities in the organization.[14] Admittedly, a manager makes such estimates and his estimate of potential is reflected each time a subordinate is selected for promotion, but having to state potential capabilities in writing and perhaps having to reveal and defend his estimate to the subordinate during the interview is one of the major causes of resistance to formal appraisal systems. An appraisal is not only a statement of a subordinate's performance but also a mirror of his superior's personality and concept of adequate performance. If the superior is unsure of himself and perhaps has lost hope of being promoted, it is possible he may reflect these attitudes in the appraisal of his subordinates. Further, few managers have a sound basis for determining the ability required for any position other than their own. Indeed, the question of capabilities and manager performance has only begun to be answered. Thus, it seems wise to limit appraisals to an evaluation of current performance.

Having determined that the appraisal should be limited to an evaluation of current performance, the second question—whether the results of the appraisal should be used to determine salary or used as a basis for self-improvement—remains to be answered. When appraisals are used to determine whether or not a subordinate should receive an

---

[14] Douglas McGregor, "An Uneasy Look at Performance Appraisals," *Harvard Business Review,* Vol. XXXV (May-June, 1957), pp. 89-94.

Another critical summary of performance appraisals is found in: George S. Odiorne, *Personnel Policy: Issues and Practices* (Columbus, Ohio: Charles E. Merrill Books, Inc., 1963), pp. 304-329.

increase in salary, there is a tendency to distort the appraisal of current performance so that the decision in regard to salary may be justified. Performance is only one of several factors determining whether or not an increase in pay should be granted. Availability of funds, length of time on the job, salary ranges, and the subordinate's position within the range are a few of the other factors that must be considered. Since the goal of a management development program is the development of individual managers, appraisals of performance should serve as a basis for improving that performance in the future. Objective discussions of current performance are possible only when salary considerations are set aside and attention is directed toward the improvement of performance and the development of the individual. Decisions concerning salary should be made at a separate time and should include all aspects of the company's salary policy.

Standards of Performance. Another problem encountered in the use of performance appraisals is that of developing criteria for measuring performance on the job. In many appraisal systems the manager is asked to rate his subordinate on a five-point scale in respect to a list of personality traits such as loyalty, promptness, and willingness to work. All too frequently this approach may again become a reflection of the rater's personality. Occasionally a superior is asked to rate the performance of each subordinate against that of each of the other subordinates—a man-to-man rating. The shortcomings of this method are obvious, particularly when subordinates have different jobs requiring different abilities and levels of achievement. A third type of criteria is defined in terms of the goals of the job itself. However, for job goals to be effective standards of performance, they must be clearly stated, measurable, and within the control of the subordinate.

The Appraisal Interview. Most formal appraisal systems require an interview between subordinate and superior. The interview is supposed to offer an opportunity for the subordinate to discover where he stands, at which time his superior should outline steps to be taken for the improvement of job performance and self-development. An extensive study of the typical appraisal interview conducted at General Electric shows that praise has little effect, either positively or negatively, that criticism has a negative effect on future achievement, and that defensiveness results from criticism with no improvement of performance.[15] The

---

[15] Herbert H. Meyer, Emanuel Kay, and John R. P. French, Jr., "Split Roles in Performance Appraisal," *Harvard Business Review*, Vol. XLIV (January-February, 1965), pp. 123-124.

same study indicates that discussions concerning salary should be held at a separate time and not as a part of a performance review. It is questionable whether the typical line manager is capable of conducting a broad evaluative interview in terms of his training or inclination. As McGregor has noted, there is a reluctance to "playing God," with the result that the typical interview is resisted by both superior and subordinate and usually becomes a mere formality, with little of the developmental benefits that should result from it.

Improving Performance Appraisals. The weaknesses of the typical performance appraisal are attributable to failure to define the purpose of the appraisal, the need for a well-defined set of criteria, and the inadequacy of the appraisal interview. Appraisals may be conducted to determine the potential of a member of management, to evaluate performance in his present job, or to develop a plan for self-improvement. Criteria may consist of a list of illusive personality traits, the performance of a subordinate's peers, or a statement of job goals. The inadequacy of the interview may result from the superior's having to evaluate performance and justify salary action at the same time, or from being required to assess personality and potential development—tasks he is not trained to do. The following five-step program eliminates the conflicting points of view in regard to purpose and criteria, and as a result places the appraisal interview on much safer ground.[16]

1. The individual discusses his job description with his superior and they agree on the content of his job and the relative importance of his major duties—the things he is paid to do and is accountable for.
2. The individual establishes performance targets for each of his responsibilities for the forthcoming period.
3. He meets with his superior to discuss his target program.
4. Checkpoints are established for the evaluation of his progress; ways of measuring progress are selected.
5. The superior and subordinate meet at the end of the period to discuss the results of the subordinate's efforts to meet the targets he had previously established.

The five-step program suggested by Kindall and Gatza corrects the major weakness of the usual performance appraisal since the purpose of the appraisal is clearly defined as the appraisal of current performance, the goals of the job are determined and agreed upon by both

---

[16] Alva B. Kindall and James Gatza, "Positive Program for Performance Appraisal," *Harvard Business Review,* Vol. XXXXI (November-December, 1963), p. 157. This article presents a brief statement of the shortcomings of the typical appraisal program and then develops a plan for the installation of the five steps.

superior and subordinate, and the interview is confined to a discussion of performance with superior and subordinate equally interested in improving that performance. General Electric uses an appraisal system, called the Work Planning and Review program, that incorporates these five steps and finds the new program to be far more effective than the traditional approach to appraisals in improving the level of job performance.[17]

A Breakthrough in Organization Development

What would happen if it were possible to have all members of management participate in a program designed to change attitudes towards one's self and toward others? In effect, what would happen if we could achieve *organizational* development as well as individual executive development? In a study that appears to be a major breakthrough in *organization* development, all members of management (a total of some 800 line, staff, and technical personnel) participated in a laboratory training program known as the Managerial Grid.[18] The Managerial Grid program directs attention towards managerial styles. Five basic types of managerial styles, as shown on page 432, are identified:

1,1—Minimum effort to get work done but sufficient to maintain organization.

9,1—Emphasis on work with minimum interference from human factors.

1,9—Primary attention to needs of people, a comfortable place to work.

5,5—Balance between attention to getting work done and attention to people.

9,9—Work is accomplished by people committed to the organization; a high degree of congruence between the goals of the organization and the goals of its members.

---

[17] Meyer, Kay, and French, *op. cit.,* pp. 127-129.

[18] R. R. Blake, J. S. Mouton, L. B. Barnes, and L. E. Greiner, "Break-through in Organization Development," *Harvard Business Review,* Vol. XXXXII (November-December, 1964), pp. 133-155. The first part of the article is a description of the Managerial Grid Program and is written by Drs. Blake and Mouton. As a consultant, Dr. Blake introduced the concepts of the Managerial Grid to a few top managers of the plant known as Sigma. These managers then administered the program to the entire management group. The second part of the article is an independent audit of the program conducted by Dr. Barnes and Mr. Greiner. This is an unusual, comprehensive study well worth careful attention.

For a complete description of the Managerial Grid, see: Robert R. Blake and Jane S. Mouton, *The Managerial Grid* (Houston: Gulf Publishing Company, 1964).

Vera Kohn, *A Selected Bibliography on Evaluation of Management Training and Development Programs* (New York: The American Foundation for Management Research, Inc.). Copies of this annotated bibliography may be obtained by writing directly to the foundation in care of the American Management Association.

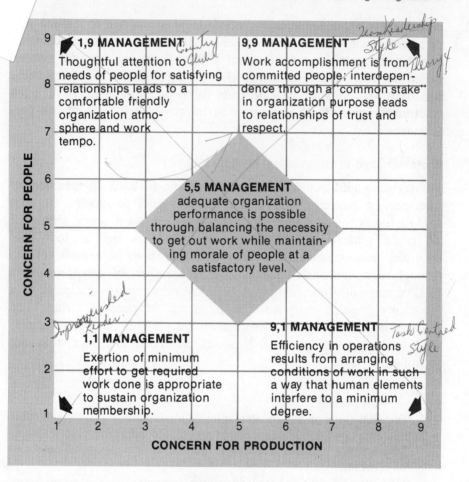

Figure 14-7
MANAGERIAL STYLES OF THE MANAGERIAL GRID PROGRAM

Managerial Grid training can be broken down into six phases; the first two are directed toward *manager* development and the last four are concerned with *organization* development. The first phase is the *laboratory-seminar training* directed toward the analysis of management style, and the second phase is an on-the-job application of phase one resulting in *team development*. The organization development phases, also conducted on the job, are: *Intergroup development, organizational goal setting, goal attainment,* and *stabilization*. In the "breakthrough" study, Dr. Blake, the developer of the Managerial Grid Program, trained four of Sigma's top management, including the plant manager. These four trained 22 instructors chosen from management, and in turn, the instructors trained the remaining 800 members of management. Thus, with the exception of the four trained initially by Dr. Blake, the development program was administered internally by Sigma's management.

The problems involved in measuring organizational effectiveness are complex; nonetheless, the following changes in Sigma's organizational performance are attributable to the Managerial Grid Program of organizational development.

Profit. It must be remembered that profits are a function of some factors that are uncontrollable by local plant management, such as cost of raw materials, taxes, depreciation, and revenues; and factors that are within the control of management—controllable costs. Profits more than doubled during the first full year following the introduction of the Managerial Grid Program. Fifty-six percent of the increase in profits was attributable to noncontrollable factors, but the remaining 44 percent resulted from a reduction in controllable costs. Sixty-nine percent of the reduction in controllable costs came from the elimination of excess manpower—600 employees, with 520 of them accepting early retirement. Those who were laid off did not express bitterness toward the company. The balance of the reduction in controllable costs resulted from a 31-percent increase in productivity per man-hour without the introduction of new machinery or radical innovations in technology. Follow-up projects (phases four and five of the program) were established and are expected to yield substantial savings in the future.

Changes in Management Practices and Behavior. There was a marked increase in the number of meetings held, an indicator of increased group effort in the solution of problems. There was a downward shift in the age of the 50 most valuable managers, thereby emphasizing youth and ability rather than seniority as a criterion of managerial effectiveness. Also, a greater mobility of managers was evidenced by an increase in the number of in-plant transfers and an increase in the number of transfers to corporate units outside the plant. The net result of the increase in transfers was an increase in promotional opportunities, a strong motivational factor.

Changes in Attitudes and Values. A shift in values and attitudes toward the 9,9 style of management as introduced in phase one of the grid program was noted. This shift in values was reflected by the acceptance or rejection of items descriptive of various management practices contained in a questionnaire. Overall ratings of the Managerial Grid program were obtained. Only 16 percent of those participating in the program rated the grid training as somewhat low or very low, while 84 percent rated the program as high or very high. There seemed to be a thoroughgoing respect for, and the establishment of, a set of operational ground rules approaching the 9,9 concept of management.

The organizational development program as conducted at Sigma seems to answer a question that has arisen among behavioral scientists and practicing managers alike: Are the findings of behavioral science applicable to large-scale industrial operations? The answer, based upon this study, is an unqualified "yes." However, for an organization development program—an application of what we know concerning leadership, communications, and motivation—to be as successful as Sigma's program, top management must not only give their enthusiastic support to the program but also become the internal administrators of the program. Only then will there be created an organizational climate that permits the application of our knowledge from the behavioral sciences.

Case Problem 14-B poses a series of questions encountered sooner or later by most companies and offers an opportunity to plan an organization development program. There is an obvious need for the development of a planned approach to the replacement of key executives of a company who are due to retire within the next few years under the provisions of the company's mandatory retirement plan. Contemplated expansion increases the need for a planned program of organization development since the requirements of an expanded organization must be met as well as the needs arising as the result of attrition in the present organization.

CASE PROBLEM 14-B

ORGANIZATION PLANNING

William Evans, president of Toolco, Inc., looked up as Robert Kessler, the director of industrial relations, entered his office and asked, "What kind of progress are you making on the report I asked for last week?"

"Here are some notes I have prepared covering key executives in the company," Kessler answered as he handed Mr. Evans a copy of Exhibit 1 (pages 436 and 437). "It appears that the compulsory retirement plan that went into effect the first of this year is going to create a real need for replacements within the next five years."

"We not only have a replacement problem," Evans rejoined, "we also have some problems coming up as the result of our decision to move into the industrial products area and create a new industrial products division. As you know, our existing product line is purchased by individuals through department and hardware stores; however, the new division means not only manufacturing new products, it also means a new method of distribution."

"There is another factor other than replacement and expansion to be considered," Kessler stated.

"What is that?"

"The information I just handed you pertains only to replacements due to reaching the mandatory retirement age; thus far we have no information about the needs that might arise if we were to evaluate some of these people in terms of the quality of their performance. We both know that some of our managers are not doing the job that we would like to see done."

"Are you suggesting that we get into the area of performance appraisals?" Evans asked.

"We're going to have to get into it sooner or later; otherwise, how are we going to know who is promotable to these key positions when they open up as the result of retirement?"

"Bob, as you know, we have an executive committee meeting at the end of next week. I wonder if you could show our needs in some graphic form that would impress everyone at the meeting. There are still some doubting Thomases who believe that the cream will rise to the top—personally I don't think it will, and even if it does I doubt that we have that much time. When we have this meeting will you also recommend some definite name to designate this program we're going into? You and I have at various times called it executive development, management development, or organization development, and even organization planning. We ought to settle on a title that has meaning to everyone." Mr. Evans returned the notes Bob had given him and closed with, "See me again a day or two before the committee meeting so that I can review the recommendations you intend to present at the meeting."

PROBLEMS

1. Prepare an organization chart that shows clearly the replacement needs of Toolco for the next five years.
2. What title would you choose to designate the program being considered by Toolco? Why?

Exhibit I

President—Age 62, founder of company and the driving force behind the institution of the company's compulsory retirement plan a year ago.

Reporting to the President:

Director of Marketing—Age 40, has been in position only a little over one year, former director of economic research for an advertising agency. Performs economic research; has staff of two: a statistical typist and a statistician—both in early 30's. It was his recommendation that company enter industrial products field.

Legal Counsel—Age 45, functions primarily as liaison between engineering and outside firm of attorneys in patent matters. Occasionally handles real estate transactions; has one legal secretary.

Vice President and Treasurer—Age 50, a CPA who has been with the company 20 years; formerly head of the cost accounting section. Has heads of cost and general accounting sections reporting to him; responsible for all financial affairs of the company. As the company grew, it was his idea that the position of controller be established as a separate function reporting to the president.

Controller—Age 45, has been with the company only three years; has a small clerical staff; is in the process of establishing and refining budgets in the manufacturing plants. Though the chief of the cost section reports to the treasurer , the controller maintains a close working relationship with him.

Director of Industrial Relations—Age 40, has been with the company five years; chief negotiator for the company; his staff consists of a secretary, a clerk, and a research assistant. Each plant has its own personnel director. Administers company-wide salary plan and employee benefits, including insurance and the new retirement plan. It will be his responsibility to administer any executive development program agreed upon.

Director of Purchasing—Age 60, formerly a purchasing agent in one of the plants. Serves in an advisory capacity to plant purchasing agents for the most part, although occasionally does purchase those items that can be used by all plants.

Executive Vice President—Age 62, formerly vice president in charge of manufacturing; over 20 years' service with the company; started as a plant manager in its number 2 plant.

Reporting to the Executive Vice President:

Vice President Manufacturing—Age 55, has been with the company five years; came to company as vice president, manufacturing when the post of executive vice president was created. At that time it was believed that the plant manager of the number 2 plant, then 55 years old, was capable of filling the vice president position, but there was no suitable replacement for him in his plant. Since the

Exhibit I (continued)

number 2 plant is the largest plant in dollar volume and profit, he was kept in that position. Reporting to the vice president, manufacturing, in staff positions are: the Director of Industrial Engineering and the Director of Quality Control. These positions were created shortly after his taking the job. Both men are in their early 40's and well trained for their positions. Both have worked previously with the vice president, manufacturing, in another company.

The managers of the five manufacturing plants report to the manufacturing vice president. Each plant manager has managers of personnel, quality control, industrial engineering, purchasing, accounting, product engineering, and an assistant plant manager. Each staff department head has at least three exempt employees and several clerical employees reporting to him. The assistant plant manager supervises directly the plant engineer (building maintenance), the master mechanic who is responsible for the tool room and the machine shop, and the general foremen in charge of the production departments. The following summary shows the age of the plant manager, the number of hourly employees, and the number of general foremen and foremen for each plant.

Plant No.	Age of Plant Manager	Total Hourly Employees	General Foremen	Foremen
1 (outboard motors)	50	250	3	20
2 (engine plant)	60	700	4	32
3 (power hand tools)	45	400	3	18
4 (lawn mowers and edgers)	50	300	3	15
5 (power tools)	56	500	4	24

Vice President, Engineering—Age 48, has been with the company 22 years. He has been in his present position five years. There are five supervising design engineers who report to him, one for each of the product lines. There is also a chief metallurgist who directs the metallurgical laboratory.

Vice President, Sales—Age 61, has the advertising manager (age 50), the head of the sales order department (age 60), and the assistant general sales manager (age 58) reporting to him. Most of his efforts are devoted to the various advertising programs and promotional campaigns. The head of the sales order department acts as liaison between plants 1 and 4 since these plants purchase 50 percent of the output of the engine plant. The assistant general sales manager directs four regional sales managers. Each regional manager has a clerical staff of two and approximately 15 salesmen reporting to him. The manager of the Eastern region is 62 years old, the manager of the Central region is 58, the Southern regional manager is 50, and the manager of the Pacific region is 55.

3. How many persons would you include initially as a part of any proposed development program?
4. Prepare a set of recommendations to be submitted to Mr. Evans prior to the committee meeting. Outline and justify each step in the proposed program.

Chapter Questions for Study and Discussion

1. What basic similarity exists between organizational analysis and planning for production and sales?
2. Discuss briefly the tools commonly used in organizational analysis.
3. Rearrange Figure 14-3 so that it appears as a horizontal chart and as a circular chart. What are the advantages attributed to each form of charting—vertical, horizontal, and circular?
4. Discuss the strengths and weaknesses of formal organizational analysis. When would the disadvantages of formal analysis outweigh the advantages?
5. Why is it important to evaluate organizational effectiveness? Should this be done before introducing any organizational change or after the change has been introduced?
6. What is meant by the statement that most organizational studies are actually reorganizational studies?
7. Two extreme approaches to the development of managers are described by McGregor. Evaluate each of these extremes and then describe a middle-of-the-road approach.
8. Most of us can agree on some of the basic attitudes necessary for the practice of medicine. Develop a similar set of attitudes for the successful practice of management.
9. Describe in your own terms the change process. What condition must exist prior to the beginning of this process for the change to be most effective? If this condition does not exist, how does the first step of the change process serve to induce a readiness to change?
10. Why are attitudes toward authority significant in determining the manner in which a person adjusts to formal organization? Where are early attitudes toward authority learned?
11. Would it be desirable for industrial organizations to exert the same degree of control over the environment and actions of new managers as that exercised by a convent in respect to noviates or a military academy in respect to cadets? Discuss.
12. Discuss performance appraisals in respect to the following factors: purpose, strengths, weaknesses, and methods of improving performance appraisals.

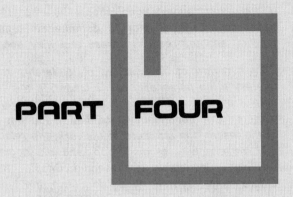

PART FOUR

The Leadership Function

The quality of leadership determines the degree of effectiveness in the performance of the functions of planning, organizing, and controlling. The experimental method and its conceptualization of independent, intervening, and dependent variables offers a convenient way of discussing organizational behavior. Organizational climate—and leadership is a part of that climate—influences the behavior of organizational members; but the effect of climate upon behavior is determined by the individual's perception of the organization. Organizational behavior takes many forms; however, the discussion in Chapter 15 is limited to organizational role, sources of conflict, and the resultant stress that may occur in organizations.

A review of the theories of leadership reveals that there has been interest in the personality of the leader, in the situation, and in the interaction of the situation and the leader as the major determinant of effective leadership. A contingency model of leadership which considers the style of the leader, the structure of the task, the relationship between the leader and the members of his group, and the degree of power accorded the position of leadership is presented. Chapter 16 also makes an important differentiation between leadership style, the type of interpersonal relationship between leader and subordinate, and leadership behavior which includes all of the things a leader does as a manager in the performance of his duties.

Communication is one of the tools of effective leadership. Formal communications within organizations are related to management information systems. However, much of the communication that occurs in organizations is informal in nature; for example, the grapevine and communication between superior and subordinate. The psychological factors in communication are considered and guides for effective communication and listening are presented.

The last two chapters are concerned with problems related to the behavior of employees in organizations. In Chapter 18 motivation is discussed in terms of basic psychological needs. These concepts are applied to problems of motivation in industry, the role of job satisfaction as a factor in performance is examined, and a model developed that relates job performance, the type of rewards received, and the interpretation of those rewards in relation to goal attainment, and consequent job satisfaction. Studies show that there is a consistent relationship between the quality of supervision and productivity. Chapter 19 discusses the supervisor and his role in determining the productivity of employees.

CHAPTER 15

Organizational Behavior

In the chapter that follows, organizational climate is considered to be those relatively permanent characteristics of an organization that influence the behavior of its members. Also, the characteristics of organizational climate serve to differentiate one organization from other organizations. Since most of the users of this text are members of an organization—a college or university—we limit the problem of measuring organizational climate to determining the climate of the school that *you* are attending.

Several approaches may be used in assessing the organizational climate of a college.[1] The demographic characteristics of the institution may be tabulated and classified in respect to size, source of revenue (private or public), location (rural or urban), student/faculty ratio, number of courses and majors, and other similar objective data. Another way of determining climate is to study the students. What are their socioeconomic backgrounds, level of intelligence, values, high school grade point average, and vocational and social aspirations? Third, direct measures of organizational behavior may be obtained by observation or by asking students to report their behavior. Such questions would include the number of blind dates, hours of study per week, hours of work per

CASE PROBLEM 15-A

MEASURING ORGANIZATIONAL CLIMATE

---

[1] C. Robert Pace, *College & University Environment Scales: Technical Manual* (2nd ed.; Princeton, New Jersey: Educational Testing Service, 1969), p. 7. The four approaches discussed in this case problem are outlined in greater detail by Professor Pace.

week, number of classes cut, and other direct accounts of behavior. A fourth, and perhaps the most fruitful approach, is to determine how a member of an organization perceives that organization. The student is asked to report on many facets of the environment as he sees, or perceives, it to be. In so doing, he draws his own psychological map of the organization.

It is the last approach, your perception of the organization, that is used in this case. You are asked to describe the climate, or environment, of the school that you are now attending.

PROBLEMS

1. Complete the college and university environment scales (CUES II) presented in Appendix A, pp. 718-724.
2. What characteristics of the environment do you believe are measured by CUES II? Which of these factors have the greatest influence on your behavior?
3. How would you expect your professor, or dean, to describe the organizational climate of your school? Discuss.

A summarization by Warren Bennis, presented in Chapter 9, "Organization Theory," states that Theory X describes "organizations without people" and Theory Y describes "people without organizations." [2] To many readers it may appear that the chapters subsequent to Chapter 9 concerning the concepts or organization structure, authority processes, committees, and methods of analysis and change, like Theory X, are devoid of people. If such is the impression, it should be corrected in this chapter for here we study the behavior of people in organizations.

As a first step in the study of organizational behavior it is necessary to examine briefly the research methods of the behavioral sciences. There are two reasons for the study of methodology. First, knowledge of the methods employed in a given study enables one to infer and assign a degree of confidence to the results obtained. Second, the experimental method, used in the study of organizational behavior, provides the conceptual framework of independent, intervening, and dependent variables—a useful way of thinking about problems of organizational behavior. Following the discussion of methodology the independent,

---

² W. G. Bennis, "Leadership Theory and Administrative Behavior," *Administrative Science Quarterly*, Vol. IV (December, 1959), pp. 259-301.

intervening, and dependent variables of organizational behavior are examined in greater detail.

BEHAVIORAL SCIENCE RESEARCH METHODS

The behavioral sciences—primarily psychology, sociology, and anthropology—are all concerned with the study of human behavior, yet each discipline emphasizes differing aspects of behavior.[3] As a result it is difficult to develop a classification system of research methods for the behavioral sciences that applies equally well to each discipline; consequently many schemes have been developed. Research may be classified in terms of its purpose, e.g., descriptive, exploratory, or hypothesis-testing studies. The method used in collecting data may be the basis for classification; for example, observation, interview, questionnaire, or the examination of written documents. The locus of the study—in the field or in a laboratory—may be used as a basis for distinguishing between types of research. The degree of scientific rigor, ranging from the observations of a competent observer, very difficult to replicate, to the laboratory experiment which may be replicated, is another method of classification. Any system of classification is largely arbitrary and contains many overlapping categories. For our purposes, the classification of research methods into two broad categories—field studies and experiments—is a useful way of studying organizational behavior.[4]

Field Studies

As the term implies, *field studies* are conducted within the environment of an existing organization. The data used in field studies may be the observed behavior of the members of an organization, recorded by a neutral observer; also, members of the organization may be asked to provide information during an interview or by completing a questionnaire or other similar instruments. Written documents, such as contractual agreements between labor and management and company policy

---

[3] Review Case Problem 7-A, The Parable of the Spindle (pp. 206-210), as an example of differing explanations offered for the same phenomena by a psychologist, a sociologist, and an anthropologist.

[4] A relatively brief discussion of methodology may be found in Peter M. Blau and W. Richard Scott, *Formal Organizations: A Comparative Approach* (San Francisco: Chandler Publishing Company, 1962), pp. 15-26.

The following is recommended for a more complete discussion of research methods. Leon Festinger and Daniel Katz (eds.), *Research Methods in Behavioral Sciences* (New York: Dryden Press, 1953), pp. 13-172.

and procedure statements, along with objective measures of production and quality, are part of field study data.

The purpose and design of field studies vary widely. Some studies are intended to survey current practices within an organization or an industry; some may be designed as case studies to provide comparative data between cultures, industries, companies, or individual members of organizations. Studies that show development and change in organizational behavior over a period of time are referred to as longitudinal studies. A brief discussion of each design reveals the breadth and scope of field studies.[5]

Survey Study. Survey studies are designed to present a broad spectrum of events. Usually, such studies are cross-sectional in nature and represent a sample of organizational behavior drawn from many different individuals who may be representative of many companies and industries. Two survey studies describing the behavior of a large number of American managers are reported in Chapter 3.[6] In the study by England, 1,072 American managers responded to a value system questionnaire; and in the study by Baumhart, 1,700 executives completed a questionnaire concerning the nature of ethical and unethical behavior.

Survey studies are of value in that they may establish statistical indexes of behavior and, when verified by subsequent research, trends may be observed. To draw reliable conclusions, the representativeness of the study sample must be established and the statistical methods used must be appropriate.

Case Study. The purpose of a case study is to provide an in-depth analysis of an industry, a company, or an organizational unit within a company. A case study may, and often does, use many sources of data, including the researcher's observation of the organization, information supplied by the members of the organization during interviews and in questionnaires, and objective indexes of organizational performance such as cost, profits, and the quantity and quality of production. Normally, one thinks of a case, in contrast to the longitudinal study, as a still camera shot in that it portrays an organization during a short time period.

---

[5] For a somewhat different classification of research methods and a review of the effect of environmental variation on organizational behavior see Garlie A. Forehand and B. von Haller Gilmer, "Environmental Variation in Studies of Organizational Behavior," *Psychological Bulletin,* Vol. LXII, No. 6 (December, 1964), pp. 361-382.

[6] George W. England, "Personal Value Systems of American Managers," *Academy of Management Journal,* Vol. X, No. 1 (March, 1967), pp. 53-68. See Chapter 3, pp. 78-84.

R. C. Baumhart, "How Ethical Are Businessmen?" *Harvard Business Review,* Vol. XXXIX (July-August, 1961), pp. 6-12, 175. See Chapter 3, pp. 84-88.

Longitudinal Study. The case study method is well adapted for tracing the development of a particular organization or the behavior of members of an organization over an extended period of time. Such studies are called longitudinal studies and provide insight into the dynamics of organizational behavior and change.[7]

Comparative Study. There are two distinct approaches to the design of comparative studies.[8] First, the researcher may seek two or more organizations that differ in characteristics believed to have an effect on the behavior of its members, and determine whether or not these differences do have such an effect; or the researcher may start with observed differences in the behavior of the members of two or more organizations, then describe and measure the organizational characteristics to determine whether or not there is a relationship to the observed differences in behavior. Among the organizational variables that have been considered as having potential influence on members' behavior are size, style of leadership (autocratic vs. democratic), organization structure, and the interdependence of employees in various work groups. Behavioral differences that have been used as the starting point for organizational studies include quantity and quality of production, absenteeism, turnover rate, accident frequency and severity, and perceived job satisfaction.[9]

Experimental Studies

Field studies provide much information concerning organizational behavior; yet, their very complexity and the absence of controlled conditions makes it extremely difficult to say with assurance that a given form of behavior is the direct result of a specific organizational characteristic. Fortunately, the experimental method overcomes many of the shortcomings inherent in the methodolgy of field studies.

In theory, the concept of the experiment is quite simple. By isolating and manipulating a single variable, and at the same time holding

---

[7] An example of a longitudinal study is the account of the acquisition of Weldon Manufacturing Company by the Harwood Manufacturing Company. The first part of the book is an in-depth case study of the Weldon Manufacturing Company, the second part of the study outlines the change strategies, and the concluding portion of the study describes Weldon after the changes were introduced. The study encompasses a two-year period. Alfred J. Marrow, David G. Bowers, and Stanley E. Seashore, *Management by Participation* (New York: Harper & Row Publishers, 1967).

[8] Forehand and Gilmer, *op. cit.,* p. 363.

[9] The following study is a summary of comparative studies of the cultural effects of given societies upon organizational behavior. Karlene H. Roberts, "On Looking at an Elephant: An Evaluation of Cross-Cultural Research Related to Organizations," *Psychological Bulletin,* Vol. LXXIV, No. 5 (November, 1970), pp. 327-350.

all other variables constant, the experimenter is able to measure the effect that the manipulated (independent) variable has upon the behavior (dependent variable) of the subject of the experiment. In practice, the design and execution of experiments in the behavioral sciences is quite difficult. Formal organizations are complex with many characteristics potentially capable of influencing the behavior of members. While it may be possible to isolate and vary one of the independent variables; e.g., style of leadership or physical working conditions, seldom is it possible to control and hold constant all of the remaining organizational variables that might influence behavior. Also, it is difficult to obtain precise measures of behavior, the dependent variable. The quantity of work performed, absenteeism, resignations, accidents, and job satisfaction are but a few of the dependent variables. Further, experimental studies with living subjects are confounded, or contaminated, by a group of variables known as *intervening* or *moderating* variables. Included as intervening variables are such factors as the degree of motivation, the ability to learn, and the individual's perception and reaction to the changing independent variable.

Despite the difficulties encountered in applying the experimental method to the study of organizational behavior it is regarded as the most rigorous method of the behavioral sciences. However, all experimental studies do not possess the same degree of rigor since there are variations in the degree of control exercised over independent and intervening variables and in the definition and measurement of dependent variables. The natural experiment, the field experiment, and the laboratory experiment, presented in ascending degrees of rigor, are discussed below.[10]

The Natural Experiment. The natural experiment is the result of a series of fortuitous circumstances. It may be argued that the natural experiment is not an experiment since the experimenter does not exercise control, directly or indirectly, over any of the independent variables in the situation.[11] Nonetheless, there are instances where the natural experiment approximates the field or laboratory experiment since only one major independent variable is changed and there are objective and

---

[10] For a complete discussion of laboratory experiments see "Laboratory Experiments" by Leon Festinger. Festinger and Katz, *op. cit.*, pp. 136-172.

[11] The following reference recognizes a natural experiment as distinct from the field experiment and the laboratory experiment. Dorwin Cartwright and Elvin Zander (eds.), *Group Dynamics: Research and Theory* (3d ed.; New York: Harper & Row Publishers, 1968), pp. 32-33.

varied measures of organizational performance and behavior available. The following example illustrates the natural experiment.

Robert H. Guest describes the operation of an automobile assembly plant over a four year period. In 1953, an in-depth case study of a large automobile assembly plant (Plant Y) was undertaken. According to objective measures of performance, Plant Y was not performing as well as other assembly plants in the corporation. Interviews were conducted with all levels of management personnel within the plant, observations were made in production departments, and hourly production employees (a representative sample) were interviewed in their homes. Further, members of corporate management responsible for the operation of the plant were interviewed, and officials of the international union representing the employees in the plant were also contacted. In mid-1953 a fortuitous circumstance, the assignment of a new plant manager to Plant Y, occurred thereby making a natural experiment possible. In 1956, data similar to that collected in 1953 were obtained after the change in a major independent variable, the leadership input by the plant manager.[12]

The Field Experiment. The manipulation of the independent variable in the natural experiment is an event not controlled by the researcher, and seldom are control groups available. In the field experiment the researcher controls the timing and extent of the change in the independent variable; in addition, control groups may be established as further assurance that any change in the dependent variable, organizational performance or behavior, that occurs after the independent variable has been manipulated is the result of that specific change and not the result of extraneous, uncontrolled factors.

A field experiment by Morse and Reimer describes the effect of changing a major organizational variable—the hierarchical location of decision making. Four similar divisions, all engaged in clerical work, of a large industrial firm participated in the experiment. The independent variable was the location of the decision-making process in the organization structure. In two of the divisions (the autonomy program) formal changes in organization structure and decision-making processes were

---

[12] The subtitle of Guest's book indicates the direction of the change following the manipulation of the independent variable. This study started as a case study. When the change in plant leadership provided opportunity for continuing study it became a natural experiment. In addition, there are aspects of the study that are longitudinal in nature. Robert H. Guest, *Organizational Change: The Effect of Successful Leadership* (Homewood, Illinois: Dorsey Press and Richard D. Irwin, Inc., 1962.)

introduced so that rank and file participation in decision making was increased. In the other two groups changes were made so that supervision and upper-level management had an increased role in the decision-making process (hierarchical control). Pre- and post-experimental measurements of productivity, perception of changes by clerical and supervisory personnel, and job satisfaction measures were obtained.[13]

The Laboratory Experiment. The laboratory experiment, more rigorous than either the natural or field experiment, affords the greatest degree of control over independent, intervening, and dependent variables. A *laboratory* is defined as any setting where the variables of the experiment are subject to the control of the experimenter. Ideally, the laboratory experiment isolates and varies only one independent variable at a time. Intervening variables are held constant, or any change is also subject to control, and the effect of the change in the independent variable upon the behavior of the subject is measured with precision.

The most frequent criticisms of laboratory experiments are that they are unrealistic and an oversimplification of organizational behavior. Realism may suffer when subjects are given the task of assembling washers and nuts on a bolt in contrast to the assembly of an automobile, and the study of the behavior of small groups in the laboratory is admittedly an oversimplification of the behavior of large groups of people in a formal organization. Yet it is precisely the capability of taking a complex situation and "cutting it down to size" that is the greatest strength of the laboratory experiment. It enables one to test a specific hypothesis or theoretical construct, to control and analyze the interaction of all variables, and to state with precision the effect of the manipulated variable upon the dependent variable.[14]

A laboratory experiment by Mackworth illustrates the effect of independent and intervening variables upon behavior in a laboratory situation. The environmental working conditions of heat and humidity usually are assumed to have an adverse effect upon the performance of a physical task. It is also assumed by many that a high degree of

---

[13] Although both groups showed an increase in efficiency as measured by reduced costs, the autonomy program produced a higher degree of job satisfaction than did the hierarchical control program. Nancy C. Morse and Everett Reimer, "The Experimental Change of a Major Organizational Variable," *Journal of Abnormal and Social Psychology,* Vol. 52 (January, 1956), pp. 120-129.

See Chapter 2, pp. 45-47, for an account of The Hawthorne Studies, a classic field experiment.

[14] A complete discussion of the application of the laboratory experiment to the study of organizations is found in Karl E. Weick, "Laboratory Experimentation With Organizations," published in J. G. March (ed.), *Handbook of Organizations* (Skokie, Illinois: Rand McNally & Co., 1965), chap. V, pp. 194-260.

motivation tends to offset the effect of hot and humid climatic conditions. In Mackworth's study, the velocity of the air was controlled at 100 cubic feet per minute and humidity and temperature were varied so as to produce effective temperatures ranging from 61° to 92° Farenheit. The intervening variable, motivation, was recognized and varied by establishing two groups, one working under high incentive conditions provided by goal setting, immediate feedback of results, and encouragement from the experimenter. The other group operated under ordinary incentive conditions with no goal setting, knowledge of results, or comments from the experimenter. The task consisted of raising and lowering a 15-pound weight 2 feet every 2 seconds. As might be expected, the group performing under high incentive conditions outperformed the group working under normal incentive conditions, regardless of temperature, thus illustrating the significance of motivation as an intervening variable. However, when the room temperature reached an effective temperature of 79°, both the high and the ordinary incentive groups showed a marked decrement in performance. Thus Mackworth shows that there is a critical level of heat and humidity that results in a drop in physical output regardless of the degree of motivation.[15]

A Concluding Concept

In Chapter 4, we find a concept from economics (marginal product) that provides a useful way of thinking about and evaluating the planning process.[16] Similarly, the experimental method with its conceptualization of independent, intervening, and dependent variables provides a useful way of thinking about organizations and behavior. It offers a means of identifying those characteristics of organizations (independent variables) that influence the behavior of its members (dependent variables). The perceptions, capabilities, and expectations of the members of an organization are recognized as intervening or moderating variables. Thus behavior in organizations, as is true of all behavior, is best described as a function of the interaction between a person and his environment. With this concept in mind, let us examine the major independent, intervening, and dependent variables of organizational behavior.

INDEPENDENT VARIABLES—ORGANIZATIONAL CLIMATE

Case problem 15-A requests that you describe the organizational climate of your college or university; not a simple task since educational

---

[15] N. H. Mackworth, "High Incentives vs. Hot and Humid Atmosphere in a Physical Effort Task," *British Journal of Psychology,* Vol. 38 (1947), pp. 90-102.

[16] See Chapter 4, pp. 117-119.

institutions are complex. In addition, the phrase, organizational climate, has many meanings. However, a definition has been offered that is gaining wide acceptance. *Organizational climate* may be defined as "the set of characteristics that describe an organization and that (a) distinguish the organization from other organizations, (b) are relatively enduring over time, (c) influence the behavior of people in the organization."[17] The limitation in the definition that the characteristics of climate enable one to differentiate one organization from another implies that these characteristics must be measurable; the limitation that the characteristics must be fairly enduring over a period of time eliminates those features of an organization that influence behavior for a relatively short period of time such as cost cutting during economic retrenchment. Finally, the limitation that organizational climate apply only to those characteristics that influence behavior is perhaps the most difficult aspect of the definition to clarify since the list of potential stimuli is varied and lengthy.

Many classifications of the characteristics of organizational climate have been proposed, yet it seems that the grouping of characteristics into three broad areas serves our purposes best. First, and perhaps most obvious, are those formal actions of the executives of a company that are intended to motivate employees. Included are formal systems of rewards and punishments, various employee benefit programs, incentive pay plans, communication programs, and the quality of leadership offered by the top echelon of the organization and the resulting supervision exercised in the middle and lower levels of the managerial hierarchy. Each of these approaches to influencing the behavior of an organization's members are discussed in this section, The Leadership Function.[18] Also, the structural characteristics of the organization influence behavior. Since the first group of organizational characteristics is discussed elsewhere in the text, the following discussion is limited to structural characteristics and their influence on behavior. Structural properties are considered as independent variables and the resulting attitudes and job related behavior are regarded as dependent variables.

In an extensive review of the literature, Porter and Lawler classify the structural properties of organizations into two broad groups: (1) characteristics of the *total-organization* (defining the total-organization as a company with a president and capable of selling its own stock independently of other companies), and (2) characteristics of

---

[17] Forehand and Gilmer, *op. cit.*, p. 382.
[18] See Chapter 16, "Leadership"; Chapter 17, "Communications"; Chapter 18, "Motivating Employees"; Chapter 19, "Supervision and Productivity."

sub-organizational units (which range from subsidiary companies and decentralized divisions in large corporations, through plants in multi-plant companies, down to and including departments and primary work groups within departments).[19] First, we examine the properties of sub-organization, considered as independent variables in the literature, then we examine total-organization characteristics assumed to influence behavior.

Suborganization Properties

The structural characteristics of suborganization units are drawn from the relationships shown in the formal organization chart. The characteristics mentioned most frequently are number of *organizational levels, line and staff functions, span of management,* and *size* of the subunit, defining size as number of people. Though discussed separately, these characteristics should not be considered mutually exclusive. As shown in Chapter 10, there is a relationship between size and span of management which, in turn, has a marked influence on the number of levels within the organization. The effects of organization structure upon its members are measured in two areas—attitude and overt behavior. The term, *attitude,* includes opinions about one's job, company policy, supervision, and perceived satisfaction from the job. Overt behavior includes such measures as absenteeism, turnover rates, accident frequency, productivity, labor disputes, and progression or mobility within the organization.

Organization Levels. Early studies of organizational behavior, for example the Hawthorne Studies, were concerned with the attitudes and behavior of hourly production employees. Next, studies focusing on comparisons between managerial and nonmanagerial employees emerged, and most recently there have been many studies concentrating on differences between hierarchical levels within management. Almost without exception, these studies show a strong positive relationship between organizational level and the degree of perceived job and need satisfaction. Managerial employees of all levels report greater satisfaction with their work than that reported by hourly employees. Further, within the management structure there is a positive relationship between organizational level and satisfaction, with higher levels of management showing greater satisfaction than lower managerial levels.

---

[19] Lyman W. Porter and Edward E. Lawler III, "Properties of Organization Structure in Relation to Job Attitudes and Job Behavior," *Psychological Bulletin,* Vol. 64, No. 1 (1965), pp. 23-51. Much of the material in the text has been drawn from the Porter and Lawler study. Also, their classification and sequence of structural factors are used.

However, there is no such relationship between the perceived needs of organizational members and their level in the organization. Several studies utilizing hierarchically arranged needs—social, achievement, recognition, and fulfillment—show that needs are surprisingly the same for all levels of the organization. Differences are minor with lower levels of the organization being more concerned with aspects of their immediate work environment while the higher levels are more concerned with the entire organization. Consequently it seems that the relative importance of various kinds of needs are constant throughout the organization and not related to organizational level.

The frequently used indexes of overt organizational behavior—turnover, absenteeism, accident frequency, etc.—have been used as measures of hourly employee behavior and have not been used widely with managerial groups. Thus, there is relatively little data that compares managerial and nonmanagerial employees in these respects. Yet within the managerial hierarchy there are indications that face-to-face intra-organizational, interpersonal contacts decrease at the higher levels of management; but interpersonal contacts with individuals outside the organization increase. Decisions at the higher levels of management take longer to make, and a longer period of time for feedback concerning their correctness is evident. However, data are scanty at this time; therefore, any conclusions must be considered as tentative.

Line-Staff Structure. The distinction between line and staff functions and the problems inherent in line-staff relationships are discussed elsewhere.[20] Therefore the following is limited to observing differences in attitudes and behavior between the two groups. The evidence shows that the line manager consistently reports a higher degree of satisfaction with his job than does the staff manager. Also, line managers report a higher degree of need satisfaction, especially those needs related to esteem and self-actualization. For the most part, line and staff personnel express the same needs when stated in terms of desirable working conditions; however, there is a tendency for staff to desire greater autonomy and to perceive themselves as being more oriented toward getting along with others and more directed by others than are line managers.

Studies pertaining to the behavior of line and staff managers are severely restricted, only three in number. Staff's mobility within the organization, the result of the nature of their jobs, makes them more informed than line managers on conditions within the organization. Also, the turnover rate of the staff manager is two to four times that of line

---

[20] See Chapter 11, pp. 324-337.

personnel—in all probability the combined result of two factors. First, as noted, staff reports a lower degree of job satisfaction. Second, staff skills are acquired largely as the result of education, as opposed to experience, and are more readily transferred to other organizations than are the technical skills of the line manager which usually are acquired in a single company or a specific industry.

Span of Management. Span of management is an easily recognized structural characteristic of organizations. As noted elsewhere, there are several interacting factors that determine the optimum span of management.[21] More than twenty years ago, based upon research conducted in Sears, Roebuck & Company, James Worthy stated that flat organization structures with the resultant increased span of management are positively related to morale.[22] Unfortunately, Worthy does not present any empirical data to support his statement. Nor has the study been replicated. Thus, there are no objective data relating span of management to either attitudes or overt behavior.

Size of Subunit. A subunit of the total organization is defined by boundaries that exclude the remainder of the organization. Subunits may consist of a primary work group, a department, a single plant in a multiplant company, a decentralized division of a corporation, or a subsidiary of a conglomerate. With such range in the size and type of subunits, the difficulties encountered in evaluating empirical studies concerning the effect of size are apparent. Nonetheless, some relatively firm conclusions concerning the effect of subunit size upon attitudes and behavior may be drawn.

Generally, small departments and work groups have more positive attitudes toward their work than do large departments and large work groups. But no sweeping generalizations can be made concerning all employees, since the studies reported measure the attitudes of hourly workers in relation to group size and virtually no studies report managerial job related attitudes and group size. The size of the group has its effect upon attitudes other than job satisfaction. Perhaps because of the increased opportunity for interaction, smaller groups show a higher degree of intimacy and less control than larger groups. Group cohesiveness is also more pronounced in smaller groups than in larger groups. However, the larger the group the greater is the willingness to accept leader-directed activities and plans.

---

[21] Chapter 10, pp. 297-303.
[22] James C. Worthy, "Organization Structure and Employee Morale," *American Sociological Review,* Vol. 15 (1950), pp. 169-179.

Most studies show a strong positive relationship between the absentee rates of hourly employees and subunit size; however, the few studies concerned with absenteeism among managerial employees show no consistent relationship between size and absenteeism. Again, there is a strong positive relationship between size and the appearance of labor disputes; but in all probability no causal relationship. Historically the strong militant unions have represented employees in industries where subunit size is large—automobile manufacturing, steel, and mining. The data are inconclusive in regard to turnover rates and productivity. The turnover rate data are equivocal with a slight tendency for turnover rates to be positively related to unit size. In the case of productivity, the data are inconsistent and show no predictable relationship with subunit size— a finding that is not surprising when one considers the many factors that determine the level of productivity.

Total-Organization Characteristics

There are difficulties in interpreting the literature concerning total-organization units because most studies do not state clearly whether the subject is a subunit of an organization or the total-organization itself. For example, many researchers loosely refer to the study of an organization when in reality the unit is but one plant of a multiplant company. An admittedly arbitrary definition is that a total-organization unit has a chief executive with the title of president or its equivalent and can sell its stock independent of other companies, even though it may be part of a larger corporation. Recognizing the lack of a consistent definition, let us continue the discussion of size.

Size of Total Organization. One study that *seems* to relate the size of the total organization to job satisfaction shows a correlation of —.67 between the satisfaction of hourly employees and size.[23] Although the study does include some total-organization units, the difficulty in interpreting the significance of the findings is one of determining whether the dissatisfaction stems from the size of the subunit (known to have a negative relationship with job satisfaction) or whether the dissatisfaction stems from the size of the total-organization unit.

There is a series of studies that sheds some light on the relationship between total-organization size and managerial attitudes. Questionnaire respondents were grouped into three categories based upon the size of the company in which they were employed. Companies with less than a

---

[23] S. Tallachi, "Organization Size, Individual Attitudes and Behavior: An Empirical Study," *Administrative Science Quarterly,* Vol. 5 (1960), pp. 398-420.

total employment of 500 were regarded as small; the medium-size companies ranged in total employment from 500 to 4,900; and those companies with more than 5,000 employees were considered large. Managerial personnel of the small companies showed a greater degree of need satisfaction than those of the larger companies at the lower levels of the organization, but at the upper levels of management the greater need satisfaction appeared in the larger companies. These studies by Porter show clearly the mediating effect of organization level upon size.[24]

It must be noted that we know very little concerning the effect of total-organization size upon the behavior of either managers or workers. For example, we do not know how the total company absentee, turnover, or accident rates of General Motors, Standard Oil of New Jersey, and Ford Motor Company compare to smaller companies with similar technologies and operating in the same geographical areas.

Shape of Organization. Organizations are sometimes characterized as being either tall or flat. Tall organizations have a greater number of managerial levels in relation to total size than do flat organizations. The key to whether a company is tall or flat is span of management. Given the same number of employees, reduced spans of management at each level produce a tall organization while increased spans of management create a flat organization.

Much of the interest concerning the shape of organizations stems from Worthy's statement that "Flatter, less complex structures, with a maximum of administrative decentralization tend to create a potential for improved attitudes, more effective supervision, and greater individual responsibility and initiative among employees." [25] Yet, as noted earlier, Worthy does not present any quantitative data to support his conclusion.

There are very few empirical studies that test Worthy's statement by reporting the effect of the shape of an organization on either attitudes or behavior. In one study, Porter and Lawler show that managerial employees in companies with fewer than 5,000 employees show a higher degree of need satisfaction in flat organizations than in tall ones.[26] However, the reverse is true in companies employing more than 5,000 since the managers in these companies with tall organizations perceive a greater need satisfaction. However, the apparent advantage of the tall

---

[24] Lyman W. Porter, "Job Attitudes in Management: IV. Perceived Deficiencies in Need Fulfillment As a Function of Size of Company," *Journal of Applied Psychology,* Vol. 47 (1963), pp. 386-397.

[25] Worthy, *op. cit.,* p. 179.

[26] Lyman W. Porter and Edward E. Lawler III, "The Effects of Tall vs. Flat Organization Structures on Managerial Job Satisfaction," *Personnel Psychology,* Vol. 17 (1964), pp. 135-148.

organization is limited to those needs relating to social and security needs while the flat organizations are superior in respect to the needs concerning self-actualization. Thus no clear-cut superiority exists for either the tall or the flat organization.

Degree of Decentralization. Another facet of organizational structure is the degree of decentralization, defining decentralization as extending authority to make decisions to lower-level organizational units. Data relevant to the effect of centralization and decentralization upon either attitudes or behavior is sketchy at best. One study of a staff function, industrial relations, shows that those working in decentralized departments prefer. it that way while those in centralized departments prefer centralization.[27] In one of the few other studies in this area Weiss found no significant statistical relationships between the degree of decentralization and grievances, turnover rates, absenteeism, accident frequency, and severity rates, number of white collar workers, and the age of managers. Though the differences were not statistically significant, there was a slight trend for each factor in favor of decentralization.[28]

In summary, the degree of centralization or decentralization and span of management show no signficant measurable effects upon either attitudes or behavior. However, the other five structural characteristics of organizations—organizational level, line-staff organizations, size of subunit, size of total-organization, and shape of organization—show significant relationships to either job related attitudes or behavior, or both. Further, it is shown that these characteristics are interrelated and that one is capable of moderating the effects of another; for example, organizational level has much to do with one's job related attitudes and perceived need satisfaction regardless of the size of the subunit or the total-organization.

INTERVENING VARIABLES—THE INDIVIDUAL

Throughout the above discussion of the effects of organization structure, an independent variable, the individual's *perceived* attitudes toward his job and degree of need satisfaction, is used as a measure of behavior, the dependent variable. Aspects of the organization that stimulate behavior are received and interpreted by the individual; hence, the individual's perceptions of what is "out there" acts as a *moderating* or *intervening* variable between organizational stimuli and resultant

---

[27] Helen Baker and R. R. France, *Centralization and Decentralization in Industrial Relations* (Princeton, New Jersey: Princeton Industrial Relations Section, 1954).

[28] E. C. Weiss, "Relation of Personnel Statistics to Organization Structure," *Personnel Psychology*, Vol. 10 (1957), pp. 27-42.

behavior. Accordingly, knowledge of perception, especially how one person perceives another, leads to a greater understanding of organizational behavior. As a first step in learning more about perception we discuss briefly the nature of perception.

The Nature of Perception

In the early history of psychology much time was devoted to the study of perception. For the most part research concentrated on the perception of sensory stimuli such as sound, color, light, form, odor, and the various means of stimulating the senses of the skin. Soon it became apparent that there were marked differences between individuals in the way in which they perceived sensory stimuli; further, it was noted that the same individual sometimes perceived stimuli having constant physical properties differently from one day to the next. Also, it was found that peripheral or extraneous factors were significant as determinants of the meaning attached to external stimuli. In 1945, D. M. Johnson summarized research on object perception and the influence of so-called extraneous factors.[29]

1. He may be influenced by considerations that he may not be able to identify, responding to clues that are below the threshold of his awareness. For example, a judgment as to the size of an object may be influenced by its color even though the perceiver may not be attending to color.
2. When required to form difficult perceptual judgments, he may respond to irrelevant cues to arrive at a judgment. For example, in trying to assess honesty, it has been shown that the other person's smiling or not smiling is used as a cue to judge his honesty.
3. In making abstract or intellectual judgments, he may be influenced by emotional factors—what is liked is perceived as correct.
4. He will weigh perceptual evidence coming from respected (or favored) sources more heavily than that coming from other sources.
5. He may not be able to identify all factors on which his judgments are based. Even if he is aware of these factors he is not likely to realize how much weight he gives to them.

The above summary should not be interpreted as meaning that we respond only to the peripheral factors of a situation; however, it does mean that peripheral factors can and do influence perceptual judgments.

In 1958, Jerome Bruner summarized the results of a series of experiments concerning the influence of social behavior upon perceptual

---

[29] D. M. Johnson, "A Systematic Treatment of Judgment," *Psychological Bulletin,* Vol. 41 (1945), p. 206.

processes that "came, rather waggishly, to be called the 'New Look' in perception." [30] These studies emphasize the behavioral aspects of perception such as social values, needs, attitudes, and cultural background, rather than the effect of the "out there" that marked the earlier studies. It is now recognized, as a result of the work of Bruner and others, that there is the phenomenon of perceptual readiness, or *set*, arising from the behavioral aspects of perception that largely determines the way in which we perceive social situations. The following study illustrates the effect of set.

In an experiment designed to determine the influence of predisposition, or set, Kelley investigated the effect of labeling a person as having a "warm" or "cold" personality.[31] Students were told that a guest lecturer would conduct the class, and a biographical sketch of the guest was distributed to the class. Two sketches were distributed and were identical except for one statement. One half of the class received a data sheet with a statement that described the guest as being a "very warm" person, and the other half of the class received data sheets that described him as being "rather cold." The guest led the students in a 20-minute discussion and following the discussion was rated by the class on a 15-item rating scale. Those who had received the sketch describing the guest as "very warm" rated him as being more popular, humane, humorous, sociable, and considerate of others than did those who had received the descriptive statement that the guest was "rather cold." Obviously, it pays to have a good press agent.

Factors Influencing Perception

The study by Kelley shows the effect of perceptual readiness and how quickly and easily it may be induced. There are other types of errors in perception some of which are due primarily to the perceiver and some are the result of the characteristics of the perceived.

The Perceiver. In addition to perceptual readiness, there are other predispositions on the part of the perceiver that influence social perceptions. *Stereotyping* is the most frequently encountered source of perceptual bias. Although the term stereotype originally referred to a three-dimensional, relief type face made by a casting process, Walter

---

[30] Jerome S. Bruner, "Social Psychology and Perception," published in E. Macoby, T. Newcomb, and E. Hartley, *Readings in Social Psychology* (3d ed.; New York: Holt, Rinehart & Winston, Inc., 1958), pp. 85-94.

[31] H. H. Kelley, "The Warm-Cold Variable in First Impressions of Persons," *Journal of Personality*, Vol. 18 (1950), pp. 431-439.

Lippmann used the term in 1922 to describe "pictures in peoples' heads." [32] Stereotyping, as a perceptual process, is categorizing a group into a rather simplistic mold with the simplified characteristics ascribed to the group often having no basis in fact. Generally, the stereotyped ideas of a group are widely held within a given culture and are extremely resistant to modification. Stereotypes are frequently associated with ethnic groups, and there are also stereotypes for various professions as well as for other classes of persons.

Stereotypes exist within organized labor in regard to management personnel and *vice versa*. In an experimental study concerning the stereotypes that management and labor hold toward each other, Haire asked a group of labor officials and a group of management personnel to judge the personality of two individuals based upon a short biographical sketch and a photograph. One half of each group, labor and management, received photographs indicating that Person A was a secretary-treasurer of the union and that Person B was a branch manager of a manufacturing company. For both groups the biographical data accompanying each photograph were the same. The other half of the management group and the other half of the labor group received the same biographical data, the same photographs, but the designation of role as being a member of labor or management was reversed. None of the four groups responded to the photographs or the biographical data; instead, they responded to the designation of role as being either a union official or a branch manager. The union officials perceived the secretary-treasurer of the local in a much more favorable light than the branch manager, while management personnel perceived the branch manager as having the more desirable characteristics.[33]

The *halo effect* is a perceptual phenomenon that has received a great deal of attention because of its effect on the rating of subordinates. When rating a subordinate there is a tendency to focus attention on a single trait, either favorable or unfavorable, thereby forming a "halo" that surrounds the rating of other traits. If the dominant trait is favorable, other traits are likely to be classified as favorable; however, an unfavorable dominant trait usually results in unfavorable ratings on all other traits. The halo effect also operates in determining an employee's perception of his company. The clerical employees of a Chicago firm that had been in receivership for a period of six months were surveyed

[32] Walter Lippmann, *Public Opinion* (New York: The MacMillan Company, 1922).
[33] Mason Haire, "Role-Perceptions in Labor Management Relations: An Experimental Approach," *Industrial and Labor Relations,* Vol. 8 (1955), pp. 204-216.

in respect to ten aspects of job satisfaction. As might be expected, they rated their company low in regard to job security; however, the halo spread and the employees perceived working conditions, such as office space and furnishings, pay, and other items not related to job security, as being low. Yet, these characteristics were, by objective standards, superior to those of other offices in the area.[34]

Projection, a defense mechanism, is a means of transferring, or projecting, the blame for one's shortcomings to an object or to another person. The saying, "A poor workman blames his tools," is a good example. Projection also operates as a perceptual bias in the perception of others and can result in unduly favorable or unfavorable impressions. An insecure supervisor with a borderline record of performance has a strong tendency to perceive his subordinates as having these same traits. Thus it is very difficult for him to recognize a subordinate as being ready for promotion. In the same manner, a manager who has difficulty in delegating to his subordinates for reasons of personality usually perceives his superior as also having difficulty in delegating and for the same reasons.[35]

The Perceived. Perceptual biases resulting from stereotyping, the halo effect, and projection are attributable to the perceiver; however, there are errors that are induced by the person being perceived. The organizational position of the person being perceived is significant. Characteristics are attributed to the person being perceived because of his *status*; i.e., his position within the organization. For example, it has been shown that persons with high status are perceived as willing to cooperate, while persons with lower organizational status are viewed as having to cooperate.[36] Closely related to status is *role,* behavior that is expected and prescribed by the organizational position that one holds. Status and role are significant because they provide important cues to the observer who may then place the observed into a predetermined stereotype. The *visibility* of certain traits of the perceived forces one to attend to those traits and possibly ignore more significant characteristics because they cannot be readily visualized and determined. Aggressiveness and level of energy draw one's attention simply because they are visible, but the characteristics of integrity or honesty are not

---

[34] B. A. Grove and W. A. Kerr, "Specific Evidence on Origin of Halo Effect in Measurement of Morale," *Journal of Social Psychology,* Vol. 34 (1951), pp. 165-170.

[35] Chapter 12, pp. 341-369.

[36] J. W. Thibaut and H. W. Riecken, "Some Determinants and Consequences of the Perception of Social Causality," *Journal of Personality,* Vol. 24 (1955), pp. 113-133.

readily visible and often ignored. The high visibility of certain ethnic groups serves as a constant reinforcement of bias and prejudice.

Improving Perception

From the preceding discussion, one is almost tempted to conclude that there is no "real" world; the world is only as it is perceived. For the effective management of organizations, the administrator should learn to recognize the differences between his perceptions and the perceptions of others. First, it is suggested that the perceiver be constantly aware of the sources of perceptual errors. Recognition that such errors do exist and knowledge of the common causes of these errors is helpful. Second, there is mounting evidence that the degree of personal adjustment on the part of the perceiver determines what he will see in others. Those who are well adjusted and secure perceive positive traits in others, while those who are insecure and unable to recognize and accept their short-comings tend to perceive others as having the same characteristics. In other words the recommendation is more than "know thyself;" it also includes "accept thyself."

DEPENDENT VARIABLES—ORGANIZATIONAL BEHAVIOR

There are many dimensions of the dependent variable, organizational behavior. Job related attitudes are mentioned in the discussion of the effects of organization structure and are examined more closely in Chapter 18, "Motivating Employees." Productivity, another significant form of organizational behavior, is discussed in Chapter 19, "The Supervisor and Productivity." Our concern in this chapter is the examination of organizational behavior in broad terms in order to develop a useful basis for understanding behavior. First, every individual who enters a formal organization assumes a role, a form of behavior that is expected of and prescribed by the position. Second, conflict is a normal part of organizational life; to believe otherwise is to engage in wishful thinking. Third, stress, a subjective state perceived in varying degrees by each person, is present in all organizational behavior. These three forms of organizational behavior—role, conflict, and stress—are discussed in turn.

Role

The neat squares and the straight lines of the organization chart may lead one to believe that the organization is a spatial arrangement of physical entities much like the stones of an arch with the president occupying the keystone position. But the squares of the chart do not possess the physical properties of stone; instead, they are symbolic of events and the actions of people. The title, President, in the square of the chart is indicative of the events and actions associated with that position and differentiates that office from the events and actions implied by the title, Controller. When one person leaves a position, another steps in and assumes the mantle of the office; thereby giving constancy and durability to the otherwise ephemeral actions of man. Thus role, expected behavior associated with an office, is central to the concept of enduring social organizations.

It has been suggested that the organization may be likened to a large fishnet with each knot representing an office and the strings of the net showing the functional relationship between the positions.[37] When one picks up the net by a single knot it is possible to visualize immediately adjacent and related positions. Positions closely associated within a given office are those of the immediate superior, subordinates (if any), and peers. Since role is an expected form of behavior derived from the office it is well to understand how such expectations are established. The cycle of the role episode provides such understanding.[38]

Role Expectations. One aspect of role expectations, the first step in the role episode cycle, is presented in Figure 14-2 (p. 408), the position description for a supervisor of the accounting section. Such descriptions usually specify the main functions, responsibility and authority, and the primary interpersonal relationships necessary to accomplish the job. Although descriptions are important and form a part of the basis upon which performance is judged, there are other expectations in the minds of persons closely associated with a given office or position. Influence, in varying degrees, is associated with each organizational office. Also, there are expectations in regard to the kind of authority, the type of leadership pattern, the exercise of power, and general behavioral characteristics of the incumbent.

Role Sending. The second step of the role cycle episode is role sending, the exercise of influence that effects the role behavior of another person in the organization. It may range from a grumpy "good morning" or a wave of the hand to an explicit written memorandum

---

[37] Daniel Katz and Robert L. Kahn, *The Social Psychology of Organizations* (New York: John Wiley & Sons, Inc., 1966), p. 174. This work is recognized as an outstanding theoretical contribution to the study of organizations and social institutions. Most of the discussion concerning the role episode and conflict are drawn from this work.

[38] *Ibid.*, pp. 174-184.

requesting the performance of certain job duties by a subordinate. Roles may also be sent to peers and superiors. Role sending is a process of influence and communication and, as such, it indicates the degree of freedom the receiver, or *focal* person, has in carrying out the assigned (sent) role behavior. Sent roles also vary in the strength of their attempt to influence behavior. Implied in role sending, especially to subordinates, is the use of power; rewards if role expectations are fulfilled and penalties if they are not.

The Received Role. The role received by the focal person is, in effect, a *perceived* role. His perception of the role sent to him has varying degrees of congruence with the sent role as defined by the sender. Yet it is the received role, the person's own psychological map of the organization, rather than any objective description of the organization that directly determines role behavior. It must be recognized that for any one person in an organization there is more than one received role since he may receive roles from more than one superior, from subordinates (if any), and from peers. In addition to complications arising from the reception of multiple roles there is the person's own expectations concerning the roles received. Thus role behavior is a result of forces created by multiple sent roles, multiple received roles (including perceptual errors), and the person's own preconceived expectations for each of these roles.

Role Behavior. Role behavior in an organization ranges from the relatively simple to the very complex. At the simple end of the continuum, there is the assembly line worker who performs a repetitive task determined largely by the work situation and reinforced by verbal communication (role sending) when necessary. The repetition of a single task is the expected role behavior for the office of assembly line worker. Further, the office is occupied by one person. There is a unitary arrangement of one task, one role, one office, and one person. Moving away from the simple end of the continuum, there is a possibility of multiple tasks, typing and filing for example, that combine into a single role, an office held by one person. Multiple roles with implied multiple tasks often combine into a single office. The supervisor carries out the role of a subordinate to his superior, a superior to his subordinates, and that of a peer in relation to other supervisors. These multiple roles combine into a single office held by one person, a supervisor. Finally, there are those situations that combine multiple tasks, multiple roles, and multiple offices all held by one person. The president of a company, in addition to holding the office of president, may hold the office of chairman of the board and also occupy the position of chairman of the United Fund, the presiding office of a completely separate organization. As one moves from the simple to the complex in role behavior it is apparent that conflict may arise in the performance of multiple tasks, the performance of multiple roles, or the holding of multiple offices since in each instance the execution of the required roles is by a single person.

Conflict

The description of behavior within the context of the role episode—role expectations, role sending, the received role, and role behavior—provides a framework for understanding behavior in organizations, particularly the phenomena known as conflict and the attendent sub-jective state, stress. Conflict, like change, is one of the constants of organizational life. The problem is not the elimination of conflict; rather, it is understanding the sources and types of conflict and learn-ing how to cope with conflict in a way that minimizes the resulting stress upon the organization and its members. Katz and Kahn suggest the following four types of conflict associated with organizational roles: intra-sender, inter-sender, inter-role, and person-role.[39] In addition, inter-person conflict is considered.

Intra- and Inter-Sender Conflict. These sources of conflict are con-sidered together because they pertain to the messages sent to the re-ceiver. Intra-sender conflicts have their origin in the sender and arise when the role sender requests conflicting behavioral responses on the part of the receiver. The degree of conflict may range from a situation that requests responses that are incompatible and consequently difficult to perform in conjunction with each other to those instances where the behavioral patterns required are mutually exclusive. The plant manager who requests higher unit production, and at the same time issues direc-tives restricting the amount of overtime, may be requiring responses that are difficult to execute and in some cases the responses may be mutually exclusive.

Inter-sender conflict arises when a person receives messages from one or more sources calling for behavioral responses that again may range from those that are merely incompatible to those that are mutually exclusive. The unity of command concept is the prescriptive statement designed to minimize inter-sender conflict; yet it should be noted that inter-sender conflict arises in situations other than those resulting from attempting to serve two masters. The production worker urged by

---

[39] *Ibid.*, pp. 184-185.

management to respond to an incentive system may also receive pressure from his peer group to restrict output. Similarly, a supervisor is often the "man in the middle" trying to respond to conflicting requests from his superiors and from his subordinates.

Inter-Role Conflict. All organizational members experience inter-role conflict in some degree because every person is simultaneously a member of more than one group. The demand for overtime hours, an organizational role expectation, may conflict with the time demands required by one's role as a member of a family. Simultaneous multiple roles within the same organization are also a source of conflict; for example, the multiple roles of committee chairman and department head often result in conflict. Thus, inter-role conflict may arise from multiple roles within a single organization or as the result of being a member of two separate organizations.

Person-Role Conflict. Inter-sender, intra-sender, and inter-role conflicts describe situations in which the sent role is external in nature and there are situations when conflict arises as a result of conflicting internal and external roles. Internally perceived roles and their expectations are the result of a person's perceptions of himself, his code of ethics, and his values. Externally imposed roles that require a violation of one's self perception create person-role conflict. Being required to offer a kickback in order to obtain a sale or the assumption of a subservient position by one who perceives himself as a professional, are illustrative of person-role conflict.

Inter-Person Conflict. Inter-person conflicts are most frequent between persons whose roles place them at an organizational *interface,* a position that requires interaction with other segments of the same organization or with other organizations. The production manager, typical of a role at the interface, is in frequent contact, and often conflict, with his counterparts in the operating departments. For the most part such conflict is not personal in nature; rather, it is the result of conflicting roles with each incumbent an honest protaganist for his segment of the organization. The purchasing agent often finds that his role conflicts with that of the person representing the vendor, and the industrial relations manager's role is often in conflict with that of the representative of the international union. Though many inter-person conflicts arise solely from the nature of the roles involved, there are situations complicated by personal animosity and dislike.

Stress

The above conflict situations, derived from the role episode, provide an objective analysis of conflict. Conflict situations often result in the subjective state known as *stress*. Stress is defined as a state of tension, strain, or pressure and is a normal reaction resulting from the interaction between an individual and his environment. Those forces that induce stress are known as *stressors*, thus conflict often acts as a stressor. The individual's perceptions of his environment are also significant in determining the degree of the resulting stress; yet, there is evidence that an individual may experience stress without being aware of it. Within the context of organizational behavior the stressors most frequently noted are *role ambiguity* and *role overload*.

Role ambiguities have their origin in the conflicting role situations described above and create doubt, uncertainty, and even frustration on the part of the person receiving the role. The messages sent may be ambiguous; thereby making it impossible to determine with clarity the meaning of the sent role, or the source of the ambiguity may lie in determining the expected and desired role performance. Inability to accept an expected role, not consonant with one's self-image, is another form of ambiguity. Whatever the source, ambiguity functions as a stressor and creates the subjective state of stress for the person experiencing the ambiguity with resulting feelings of doubt, uncertainty, or frustration.

Role overload is another stressor associated with organizational role. Unlike role ambiguity, characterized by uncertainty, role overload occurs when the person receiving the sent roles cannot perform the expected activities within prescribed time limits. More often than not, there is no question concerning the legitimacy of the request, no lack of understanding concerning what is wanted, and no incompatibility between the expected responses. Instead, the problem is one of completing as many expectations as possible within a limited time period. Often quality is sacrificed for quantity, and difficult decisions must be made to determine which responses are most significant and to be performed first with the realization that others must be excluded. More than any other single factor, role overload characterizes the pressures of large formal organizations.

Regardless of the nature of the stressor, role ambiguity or role overload, the individual as an adaptive organism usually attempts to resolve the resulting stress. Much of the problem behavior exhibited in organizations is either exploratory or adaptive and reflects the individual's attempt to resolve the stress created by the conflict situation. Although much has been written concerning the psychology of adjustment there is little agreement concerning the classification of adjustive processes. However, two broad groupings do emerge; those reactions to stress that are characterized by physiological changes and those that are primarily a modification of overt behavioral patterns.

Physiological Reactions. Historically there has been a dichotomy between "mind" and "body." As a result of this dualistic concept, behavior is regarded as a function of the "mind," and changes in physiological functions, especially disease processes, are regarded as a function of the "body." However, in recent years there has been recognition that many of the so-called physical disorders and illnesses, if not having their origin as the result of psychological processes, are profoundly influenced by the psychological make-up and attitude of the person. These illnesses are often called *psychosomatic* disorders, a rather unfortunate choice of terms since it tends to perpetuate the separation of mind (psyche) and body (soma). The term *somatization reactions,* used in the Army psychiatric classification system, is much preferred since it avoids the mind and body dualism. Somatization reactions are differentiated from other reactions by two distinguishing characteristics: (1) they are the result of the interaction between a person, his environment, and organic factors, and (2) demonstrable pathological changes in either the structure or functioning of bodily organs are evident.

Although there is relatively little specific data on the effects of stress resulting from role ambiguity, there is mounting evidence that cardiovascular disorders, particularly suceptibility to heart attacks, is closely associated with role overload.[40] For many years Jenkins and his co-workers have been studying the relationship between the incidence of coronary heart disease and basic personality type. They recognize two broad personality types, designated as Type A and Type B as follows: [41]

> Type A is characterized primarily by excessive drive, aggressiveness, ambition, involvement in competitive activities, frequent vocational deadlines, pressure for vocational productivity, and an enhanced

---

[40] The following study is one of the few that addresses itself specifically to attitudes and behavior resulting from role ambiguity. John R. Rizzo, Robert J. House, and Sidney I. Lirtzman, "Role Conflict and Ambiguity in Complex Organizations," *Administrative Science Quarterly,* Vol. 15, No. 2 (June, 1970), pp. 150-163.

[41] C. D. Jenkins *et al.,* "Development of an Objective Psychological Test for the Determination of the Coronary-Prone Behavior Pattern in Employees," *Journal of Chronic Diseases,* Vol. 20 (1967), p. 371.

sense of time urgency. . . . The converse pattern, Type B, is characterized by the relative absence of this interplay of psychological traits and
situational pressures. The Type B subject is more relaxed and more
easy going, seldom becoming impatient and takes more time to enjoy
avocational pursuits. He is not easily irritated and works steadily, but
without a feeling of being driven by a lack of time. He is not pre-
occupied with social achievement and is less competitive in his
occupational and avocational pursuits.

Many studies, reviewed and summarized by Sales, indicate that
the Type A person is more prone to heart attacks than his Type B
counterpart.[42] Further, there is evidence that each group is different in
respect to biochemical characteristics. With dietary factors held constant, Type A persons show a higher serum cholesterol (closely associated with coronary disease) than a similar group of Type B persons.
Sales has shown that a relatively simple role overload situation
results in a five-percent increase in serum cholesterol as compared to
the statistically insignificant change in serum cholesterol during an underloaded period. The subjects of this experiment, male undergraduates,
solved anagrams for a period of one hour. The overloaded group was
provided with 35 percent more anagrams than they could decode in
each five minute period, while the underloaded group was idle and waiting for additional work for approximately 30 percent of the one hour
experimental period. These results are rather striking when one considers
the short time period of the experiment, one hour, and the simplistic
nature of the overload compared to the duration and type of overload
existing in real organizations. For the objectively overloaded group,
those perceiving a high degree of overload show a greater rise in serum
cholesterol than those that perceived a low overload. Those working
under objectively underloaded conditions, yet perceiving a state of overload, show a decrease in serum cholesterol, while those in the objectively
underloaded group who perceived a low degree of overload show only
a slight increase in cholesterol.
In addition, Sales notes that quite independent of the degree of
overload, measured either subjectively or objectively, those reporting
satisfaction with the task show less increase in cholesterol than those
reporting low satisfaction with the task. Consequently there is experimental support for Wolf's clinical observation that men who work
"without joy" are more prone to coronary disease than those who work

---

[42] Stephen M. Sales, "Organizational Role as a Risk Factor in Coronary Disease,"
Administrative Science Quarterly, Vol. 14, No. 3 (September, 1969), pp. 325-336.

"with joy." [43] Perhaps the industrial psychologist's interest in job satisfaction may gain wide support as a contribution to employee health.[44]

Behavioral Reactions. Stressors and the attendent state of stress do not always result in somatization reactions. In all probability, behavioral evidences of stress are more frequent than somatization reactions. A discussion of behavioral reactions to stressors within the space of a few pages is a virtual impossibility. One survey of eight textbooks of mental hygiene and related fields that discuss behavioral adjustment processes shows that no less than 32 adjustment mechanisms are listed and of these 32 there are only 2 that appear in all eight books.[45] Obviously, the selection of any classification system is essentially arbitrary.

A summary prepared by Costello and Zalkind, Table 15-1, lists 13 adjustive reactions, defines each reaction, and illustrates the reaction by citing recognizable forms of organizational behavior.[46] Careful study of the table and close observation of fellow workers or students provides insight into the causes of many seemingly inexplicable forms of behavior.

In conclusion, it is evident that there is much we do not know about stress. For example, we do not know why some persons react to stressors with the development of cardiovascular diseases while others develop gastric disorders. Nor do we know why some individuals develop behavioral modifications rather than physiological reactions, or why a given behavioral reaction develops instead of another. Stress is one of the normal aspects of life. It cannot be avoided; however, there is evidence that much can be done to reduce the effects of stress. But there is no simple prescriptive statement that, if followed, would guarantee the minimization of stress. The statement by Somerset Maugham in *The Summing Up,* his autobiography, provides a rare insight into one man's perception of his own limitations in relation to his work and may be of value to others.[47]

---

[43] S. Wolf, "Disease as a Way of Life," *Perspectives in Biology & Medicine,* Vol. 4 (1961), pp. 288-305.

[44] Coronary disease is discussed as a physiological reaction primarily because of its significance as a health factor and its lethal nature. The same general observations may be made about gastro-intestinal disorders. An early experimental investigation in this area is S. Wolf and H. G. Wolff, *Human Gastric Functions: An Experimental Study of a Man and His Stomach* (2d ed.; New York: Oxford University Press, Inc., 1947).

[45] Laurance F. Shaffer and Edward J. Shoben, Jr., *The Psychology of Adjustment* (2d ed.; Boston: Houghton Mifflin Company, 1956), p. 158. Part Two is recommended as a highly readable discussion of adjustive reactions, pp. 157-306.

[46] Timothy W. Costello and Sheldon S. Zalkind, *Psychology in Administration: A Research Orientation* (Englewood Cliffs, New Jersey: Prentice-Hall, Inc., 1963), pp. 148-149.

[47] W. Somerset Maugham, *The Summing Up* (New York: Doubleday, Doran & Company, Inc., 1938), pp. 29-30. © 1938 by W. Somerset Maugham. Reprinted by permission of Doubleday & Company, Inc.

Table 15-1

ADJUSTIVE REACTIONS TO FRUSTRATION, CONFLICT, AND ANXIETY

Adjustive Reactions	Psychological Process	Illustration
Compensation	Individual devotes himself to a pursuit with increased vigor to make up for some feeling of real or imagined inadequacy	Zealous, hard-working president of the Twenty-five Year Club who has never advanced very far in the company hierarchy
Conversion	Emotional conflicts are expressed in muscular, sensory, or bodily symptoms of disability, malfunctioning, or pain	A disabling headache keeping a staff member off the job, the day after a cherished project has been rejected
Displacement	Re-directing pent-up emotions toward persons, ideas, or objects other than the primary source of the emotion	Roughly rejecting a simple request from a subordinate after receiving a rebuff from the boss
Fantasy	Day-dreaming or other forms of imaginative activity provides an escape from reality and imagined satisfactions	An employee's day-dream of the day in the staff meeting when he corrects the boss' mistakes and is publicly acknowledged as the real leader of the industry
Identification	Individual enhances his self-esteem by patterning his own behavior after another's, frequently also internalizing the values and beliefs of the other; also vicariously sharing the glories or suffering in the reversals of other individuals or groups	The "assistant-to" who takes on the vocabulary, mannerisms, or even pomposity of his vice-presidential boss
Negativism	Active or passive resistance, operating unconsciously	The manager who, having been unsuccessful in getting out of a committee assignment, picks apart every suggestion that anyone makes in the meetings
Projection	Individual protects himself from awareness of his own undesirable traits or unacceptable feelings by attributing them to others	Unsuccessful person who, deep down, would like to block the rise of others in the organization and who continually feels that others are out to "get him"

Rationalization	Justifying inconsistent or undesirable behavior, beliefs, statements motivations by providing acceptable explanations for them	Padding the expense account because "everybody does it"
Reaction-Formation	Urges not acceptable to consciousness are repressed and in their stead opposite attitudes or modes of behavior are expressed with considerable force	Employees who has not been promoted who overdoes the defense of his boss, vigorously upholding the company's policies
Regression	Completely excluding from consciousness impulses, experiences, and feelings which are psychologically disturbing because they arouse a sense of guilt or anxiety	A subordinate "forgetting" to tell his boss the circumstances of an embarrassing situation
Fixation	Maintaining a persistent nonadjustive reaction even though all the cues indicate the behavior will not cope with the problems	Persisting in carrying out an operational procedure long since declared by management to be uneconomical as a protest because the employee's opinion wasn't asked
Resignation, Apathy, and Boredom	Breaking psychological contact with the environment, withholding any sense of emotional or personal involvement	Employee who, receiving no reward, praise, or encouragement, no longer cares whether or not he does a good job
Flight or Withdrawal	Leaving the field in which frustration, anxiety, or conflict is experienced, either physically or psychologically	The salesmen's big order falls through and he takes the rest of the day off; constant rebuff or rejection by superiors and colleagues, pushes an older worker toward being a loner and ignoring what friendly gestures are made

Source: Timothy W. Costello and Sheldon S. Zalkind, *Psychology in Administration: A Research Orientation* (Englewood Cliffs, New Jersey: Prentice-Hall, Inc., 1963), pp. 148-149.

I discovered my limitations and it seemed to me that the only sensible thing was to aim at what excellence I could within them. I knew that I had no lyrical quality. I had a small vocabulary and no efforts that I could make to enlarge it much availed me. I had little gift of metaphor; the original and striking simile seldom occured to me. Poetic flights and the great imaginative sweep were beyond my powers . . . I was tired of trying to do what did not come easily to me. On the other hand, I had an acute power of observation and it seemed to me that I could see a great many things that other people missed. I could put down in clear terms what I saw. I had a logical sense, and if no great feelings for the richness and strangeness of words, at all events a lively appreciation of their sound. I knew that I should never write as well as I could wish, but I thought with pains I could arrive at writing as well as my natural defects allowed.

Case Problem 15-B, What Killed Bob Lyons?, is a descriptive statement of the interaction of one man and his environment. Although the dynamics underlying Bob Lyons' decision to suicide are not discussed in the text, they are readily available elsewhere.[48] For some persons there would be little stress in the situation described; for others, assuming that there is stress, the reaction might have been a somatization reaction or one of the many behavioral adjustive reactions described in Table 15-1.

CASE PROBLEM 15-B

WHAT KILLED BOB LYONS?

Those who knew Bob Lyons thought extremely well of him. He was a highly successful executive who held an important position in a large company. As his superiors saw him, he was aggressive, with a knack for getting things done through other people. He worked hard and set a vigorous pace. He drove himself relentlessly. In less than ten years with his company, he had moved through several positions of responsibility.

Lyons had always been a good athlete. He was proud of his skill in swimming, hunting, golf, and tennis. In his college days he had lettered in football and baseball. On weekends he preferred to undertake rebuilding and repairing projects around the house, or to hunt,

---

[48] Harry Levinson, "What Killed Bob Lyons?" *Harvard Business Review,* Vol. 41, No. 1 (January-February, 1963), pp. 127-128. © 1963 by the President and Fellows of Harvard College; all rights reserved. The introductory material of this article appears as Case Problem 15-B. Dr. Levinson's statement of the reasons why Bob Lyons' reaction to his environment resulted in suicide and some practical conclusions to be drawn from this study are presented in the *Student Study Experiences.*

interspersing other sports for a change of pace. He was usually engaged, it seemed, in hard physical work.

His life was not all work, however. He was active in his church and in the Boy Scouts. His wife delighted in entertaining and in being with other people, so their social life was a round of many parties and social activities. They shared much of their life with their three children.

Early in the spring of his ninth year with the company, Bob Lyons spoke with the vice president to whom he reported. "Things are a little quiet around here," he said. "Most of the big projects are over. The new building is finished, and we have a lot of things on the ball which four years ago were all fouled up. I don't like the idea of just riding a desk and looking out the window. I like action."

About a month later, Lyons was assigned additional responsibilities. He rushed into them with his usual vigor. Once again he seemed to be buoyant and cheerful. After six months on the assignment, Lyons had the project rolling smoothly. Again he spoke to his vice president, reporting that he was out of projects. The vice president, pleased with Lyons' performance, told him that he had earned the right to do a little dreaming and planning; and, furthermore, dreaming and planning were a necessary part of the position he now held, toward which he had aspired for so long. Bob Lyons listened as his boss spoke, but it was plain to the vice president that the answer did not satisfy him.

About three months after this meeting, the vice president began to notice that replies to his memos and inquiries were not coming back from Lyons with their usual rapidity. He noticed also that Lyons was developing a tendency to put things off, a most unusual behavior pattern for him. He observed that Lyons became easily angered and disturbed over minor difficulties which previously had not irritated him at all.

Bob Lyons then became involved in a conflict with two other executives over a policy issue. Such conflicts were not unusual in the organization since, inevitably, there were varying points of view on many issues. The conflict was not a personal one, but it did require intervention from higher management before a solution could be reached. In the process of resolving the conflict,

Lyons' point of view prevailed on some questions, but not on others.

A few weeks after this conflict had been resolved, Lyons went to the vice president's office. He wanted to have a long private talk, he said. His first words were, "I'm losing my grip. The old steam is gone. I've had diarrhea for four weeks and several times in the past three weeks I've lost my breakfast. I'm worried and yet I don't know what about. I feel that some people have lost confidence in me."

He talked with his boss for an hour and a half. The vice president recounted his achievements in the company to reassure him. He then asked if Lyons thought he should see a doctor. Lyons agreed that he should and, in the presence of the vice president, called his family doctor for an appointment. By this time the vice president was very much concerned. He called Mrs. Lyons and arranged to meet her for lunch the next day. She reported that, in addition to his other symptoms, her husband had difficulty sleeping. She was relieved that the vice president had called her because she was beginning to become worried and had herself planned to call the vice president. Both were now alarmed. They decided that they should get Lyons into a hospital rather than wait for the doctor's appointment which was still a week off.

The next day Lyons was taken to the hospital. Meanwhile, with Mrs. Lyons' permission, the vice president reported to the family doctor Lyons' recent job behavior and the nature of their conversations. When the vice president had finished, the doctor concluded, "All he needs is a good rest. We don't want to tell him that it may be mental or nervous." The vice president replied that he didn't know what the cause was, but he knew Bob Lyons needed help quickly.

During five days in the hospital, Lyons was subjected to extensive laboratory tests. The vice president visited him daily. He seemed to welcome the rest and the sedation at night. He said he was eating and sleeping much better. He talked about company problems, though he did not speak spontaneously without encouragement. While Lyons was out of the room, another executive who shared his hospital room confided to the vice president that he was worried about Lyons. "He seems to be so morose and depressed that I'm afraid he's losing his mind," the executive said.

By this time the president of the company, who had been kept informed, was also becoming concerned. He had talked to a psychiatrist and planned to talk to Lyons about psychiatric treatment if his doctor did not suggest it. Meanwhile, Lyons was discharged from the hospital as being without physical illness, and his doctor recommended a vacation. Lyons then remained at home for several days where he was again visited by the vice president. He and his wife took a trip to visit friends. He was then ready to come back to work, but the president suggested that he take another week off. The president also suggested that they visit together when Lyons returned.

A few days later, the president telephoned Lyons' home. Mrs. Lyons could not find him to answer the telephone. After 15 minutes she still had not found him and called the vice president about her concern. By the time the vice president arrived at the Lyons home, the police were already there. Bob Lyons had committed suicide.

PROBLEMS
1. Describe in your own words the reasons for Bob Lyons' suicide.
2. Was Lyons' reaction a result attributable primarily to his work situation, to his personality, or to an interaction between his personality and his work environment? Explain.
3. How much of Lyons' problem is attributable to this particular work situation? Describe a situation that would minimize stress for him.
4. Is it possible that somatization or adjustive behavioral reactions might appear in a stress situation of this type? Under what conditions?

Chapter Questions for Study and Discussion

1. What is the meaning of the phrase, scientific rigor?
2. In general, which of the two broad types of studies, field studies or experimental studies, is considered the more rigorous? Under what conditions would the type of study that you designate less rigorous become more rigorous than the other type of study?
3. Differentiate between and give an example of each of the following: natural experiment, field experiment, and laboratory experiment. What are the major factors that determine the experimental method to be used in a given study?

4. Define in your own terms the phrase, organizational climate. Drawing from your experience as a member of a formal organization, either a college or an industrial organization, give examples of characteristics of the organization that seem to meet the criteria set forth in the definition.
5. Summarize in your own words the effects of organizational structure upon the behavior of its members. What major factors mediate, or moderate, the effect of organization structure upon behavior?
6. What is meant by the term *perception*? How does readiness or set influence perception?
7. In addition to readiness or set, there are other perceptual biases, some traceable directly to the perceiver and some to the perceived, that influence interpersonal perceptions. Give an example of each of these sources of perceptual error.
8. How does one's degree of personal adjustment influence the accuracy and quality of interpersonal perceptions?
9. What is meant by *role*? Why is the concept of role significant to the study of formal organizations?
10. How does the concept of role relate to the concept of conflict? Is it possible for an organization to exist without conflict? Discuss.
11. What is the relationship between role and stress? Is stress always perceived?

Leadership Patterns

Among the many factors that contribute to the effectiveness of leadership are the behavior of the leader, the nature of the task, the composition of the group being led, and leader's position within the group. In this problem we examine one aspect of the leader's behavior, leadership style. In the chapter that follows criteria are developed for determining the structure of the task, and in Case Problem 16-B measures are presented for the evaluation of the group and the position of the leader.

The phrase, leadership behavior, is broad in meaning and includes the managerial functions of planning, organizing, and controlling as well as the function of leading or directing. Leadership style is a narrower concept. It refers to the characteristic way in which a given leader relates to his subordinates and the task assigned to the group. His style is considered to be primarily a function of his personality. Although many terms have been used to describe leadership style, most classifications result in two broad groups: those who are essentially interested in maintaining good interpersonal relationships and those who are essentially interested in the accomplishment of the task.

There are many ways of measuring style. One method is to ask direct questions concerning the leader's action in a given situation. Another method used to determine leadership style is by inference—asking a person to describe his least preferred co-worker. Your description of the person whom you would least like to

CASE PROBLEM
16-A

MEASURING
LEADERSHIP
STYLE

work with—either someone you now know or have known in the past—is used to measure your leadership style.

PROBLEMS

1. Before describing your least preferred co-worker and computing your average LPC score, do you consider yourself to be a leader who is primarily motivated to maintain good interpersonal relationships with your co-workers or do you consider yourself to be one who is primarily motivated to complete the assigned task, even at the expense of good interpersonal relationships?

2. Exhibit I on pages 479 and 480 provides a way of determining your leadership style. Read the directions, complete the LPC scale presented in the exhibit. Directions for scoring and the rationale of the scale are described on page 496.

3. Does your average LPC score support your own evaluation of your leadership style? Discuss.

Within the framework of independent, intervening, and dependent variables presented in the preceding chapter, leadership is regarded as an independent variable—an input into the organization intended to influence the behavior of the members of the organization. As an independent variable, the function of leadership in formal organizations is the attainment of organizational objectives by means of interpersonal relationships with other members of the group. It is a function that is present at all levels of an organization. The president, by stimulating, directing, and coordinating the functions assigned to his line and staff officers, starts the process of organizational accomplishment. In turn, each key executive serves in the dual role of subordinate and leader. As the result of personal interaction with subordinates, each contributes his share to the attainment of stated goals. At the lowest level of the management hierarchy, a production foreman or a supervisor in the accounting department meets departmental goals by interaction with and the coordination of the efforts of workers who have no supervisory responsibilities.

Despite the general agreement that exists in regard to the interpersonal nature of the leadership function and its presence in all organizations—admittedly in varying degrees of effectiveness—there is no concensus concerning the primary role, or function, of leadership. The various roles ascribed to the leadership function have been termed by

Exhibit I

A MEASURE OF LEADERSHIP STYLE

People differ in the ways they think about those with whom they work. This may be important in working with others. Please give your immediate, first reaction to the items on the following two pages.

Below are pairs of words which are opposite in meaning, such as "Very neat" and "Not neat." You are asked to describe someone with whom you have worked by placing an "X" in one of the eight spaces on the line between the two words.

Each space represents how well the adjective fits the person you are describing, as if it were written:

FOR EXAMPLE: If you were to describe the person with whom you are able to work least well, and you ordinarily think of him as being *quite neat,* you would put an "X" in the second space from the words Very Neat, like this:

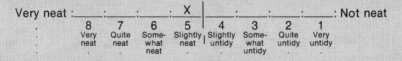

If you ordinarily think of the person with whom you can work least well as being only *slightly neat*, you would put your "X" as follows:

If you would think of him as being *very untidy*, you would use the space nearest the words Not Neat.

Very neat :___:___:___:___|___:___:___:__X__: Not neat
         8   7   6   5   4   3   2   1
       Very   Quite   Some-   Slightly   Slightly   Some-   Quite   Very
       neat   neat   what   neat   untidy   what   untidy   untidy
                  neat   untidy

Exhibit I (continued)

Look at the words at both ends of the line before you put in your "X". Please remember that there are *no right or wrong answers*. Work rapidly; your first answer is likely to be the best. Please do not omit any items, and mark each item only once.

LPC

Think of the person *with whom you can work least well*. He may be someone you work with now, or he may be someone you knew in the past. He does not have to be the person you like least well, but should be the person with whom you had the most difficulty in getting a job done. Describe this person as he appears to you.

	8	7	6	5	4	3	2	1	
Pleasant									Unpleasant

	8	7	6	5	4	3	2	1	
Friendly									Unfriendly

	1	2	3	4	5	6	7	8	
Rejecting									Accepting

	8	7	6	5	4	3	2	1	
Helpful									Frustrating

	1	2	3	4	5	6	7	8	
Unenthusiastic									Enthusiastic

	1	2	3	4	5	6	7	8	
Tense									Relaxed

	1	2	3	4	5	6	7	8	
Distant									Close

	1	2	3	4	5	6	7	8	
Cold									Warm

	8	7	6	5	4	3	2	1	
Cooperative									Uncooperative

	8	7	6	5	4	3	2	1	
Supportive									Hostile

	1	2	3	4	5	6	7	8	
Boring									Interesting

	1	2	3	4	5	6	7	8	
Quarrelsome									Harmonious

	8	7	6	5	4	3	2	1	
Self-assured									Hesitant

	8	7	6	5	4	3	2	1	
Efficient									Inefficient

	1	2	3	4	5	6	7	8	
Gloomy									Cheerful

	8	7	6	5	4	3	2	1	
Open									Guarded

Source: Fred E. Fiedler, *A Theory of Leadership Effectiveness* (New York: McGraw-Hill Book Company, 1967), Table 3-1, pp. 40-41.

some writers as theories of leadership and are discussed first. As might be expected there have been many approaches to the study of leadership. A review of the literature reveals that most of the early studies were directed toward the measurement and description of the characteristics of the leader as a person. The next period shows an emphasis on the nature of the situation in which leadership occurs. Most recently, studies of leadership stress the interaction between the leader, the situation, subordinates, and the task to be accomplished and is known as a contingency, or interactionistic, approach to leadership. Each of these various approaches to the study of leadership is presented. Finally, the studies of leadership show that the behavior of the leader, termed leadership style, is significant in its own right. The last part of the chapter presents a convenient means of classifying leadership behavior according to its style and a basis for selecting the most effective form of leadership for a given situation.

THEORIES OF LEADERSHIP

Defining leadership as a process of interpersonal relationships between the leader and members of the group does not indicate the nature of these relationships nor does it reveal the role, or function, of leadership. In part, the nature of these interrelationships depends on underlying organization theory. If one accepts the work-centered approach to organization theory, the role of the leadership function and subsequent interpersonal relationships are different from the role and relationships implied by a people-centered approach to organization theory. In the discussion of organization theory, Chapter 9, a third approach is presented—a systems approach. Similarly, there is a third approach to understanding the role of leadership; however, it is termed a revisionist approach rather than a systems approach. The three approaches to the role of leadership—work-centered, people-centered, and revisionist—and the consequent function of leadership that results from each role definition are discussed in turn.[1]

Scientific Management—A Work-Centered Approach

Scientific management is discussed in Chapter 2, "The Development of Management Concepts," and some of its implied assumptions concerning the nature of human behavior are presented as Theory X

---

[1] Warren G. Bennis, "Revisionist Theory of Leadership," *Harvard Business Review,* Vol. 39, No. 1, (January-February, 1961), pp. 26-36, 146-150. The discussion of theories of leadership is based largely upon the excellent review of the revisionists' work in organization theory written by Mr. Bennis.

in Chapter 9, "Organization Theory." The role of the leader is determined as a result of these assumptions concerning human behavior. Since men are assumed to be slothful and prone to make errors, such behavior must be corrected so that the organization may survive. Scientific management offers as a means of correction the strengthening of the organization. This may be accomplished in two ways—by improving the structure and definition of the organization, and by improving the methodology of the organization. Improvements in structure and definition are directed toward management itself. Policies, procedures, and standard practices are established to minimize the chance for error resulting from human frailty. The manager is taught to respect and revere the organization at all times. Thus, the bureaucrat, the organization man, emerges. The reward for subservience to the organization is economic security in the form of continued employment, advancement through a well-defined path of promotions, and the acquisition of status symbols to denote rank to others in the organization.

Improvements in methodology are directed toward controlling the behavior of lower echelons. If problems of quality control appear, the answer lies in engineering the product so that errors in production are reduced to an absolute minimum, not in training the worker to perform with greater skill. Quantity of production is controlled by measurement, not motivation. Under these conditions many of the problems of leadership disappear. All questions are resolved in favor of the organization. What is best for the organization is, by definition, best for the individual, for is he not a member of the organization and dependent upon its welfare for his own survival?

Human Relations—A People-Centered Approach

The human-relations approach to leadership emphasizes the potential strength and contribution of each member of the organization rather than the organization's structure and methodology. Instead of tinkering with the organization, management motivates the members of the organization to reach their full potential. Man is viewed as an individual with basic psychological needs that must be satisfied; further, it is believed that these needs can be satisfied within the framework of the modern industrial organization. Man needs recognition, the feeling of belonging to a group, and the opportunity to develop his capacities so that he may realize his full potential. The role of the manager-leader changes with these assumptions of human behavior. He must recognize that there is both a formal and an informal organization and deal with both, but his prime task is one of developing and guiding the members of the organization in order that they may reach their full potential. The leader's function is that of a catalyst. Questions are resolved in favor of the individual, since individual needs must be satisfied in order that he may reach his full potential and maximum contribution as a leader.

The Revisionists—Expressions of Doubt

Admittedly, the above descriptions of the work-centered approach and the people-centered approach to the role of leadership are over-drawn. There has probably never been a successful organization either entirely work centered or completely people centered, but the exaggerated statements representing the scientific-management and the human-relations views of leadership serve a useful purpose. They bring into sharp focus a problem confronting all managers—balancing the needs of the organization with the needs and desires of its individual members. Expressions of doubt have arisen concerning the validity of either point of view. An interesting expression of doubt comes from Douglas McGregor, one of the first exponents of the human-relations approach, after six years as a college president:

> I believed, for example, that a leader could operate successfully as a kind of adviser to his organization. I thought I could avoid being a "boss." Unconsciously, I suspect, I hoped to duck the unpleasant necessity of making difficult decisions, of taking the responsibility for one course of action among many uncertain alternatives, of making mistakes and taking the consequences. I thought that maybe I could operate so that everyone would like me—that good "human relations" would eliminate all discord and disagreement.
>
> I couldn't have been more wrong. It took a couple of years, but I finally began to realize that a leader cannot avoid the exercise of authority any more than he can avoid responsibility for what happens to his organization.[2]

The revisionists, unlike the early proponents of either of the polar approaches described above, realize that there are distinct needs for the organization and for the individual. Three of the revisionists, Robert N. McMurry, Chris Argyris, and Douglas McGregor, deserve attention, for each recognizes organizational needs and the needs of individual members. Their differences lie in their assessment of human needs and capabilities.

---

[2] Douglas M. McGregor, "On Leadership," *Antioch Notes* (May, 1954), pp. 2-3.

A Benevolent Autocracy. McMurry's position results in a call for the organization to become a "benevolent autocracy" and for its head to be a "great man." He has no quarrel with participative management and the development of the individual to his fullest capacities. He simply believes, based upon many years of experience as a consulting psychologist working in an industrial setting, that the capacity for most humans to participate and contribute significantly to the organization is rather limited. The basic human need postulated by McMurry is a need for security and direction, a need that is readily met by the well-structured organization. Members of middle management need well-defined positions of authority derived from structure, since they are, for the most part, incapable of personal leadership. At the top of the pyramid there is room for a mere handful of dynamic individuals to direct the workings of the organization. Though this view is strikingly similar to the scientific-management approach there is a major difference; McMurry's "benevolent autocracy" not only satisfies the needs of the organization, it also satisfies the dependency needs of the individual members of the organization.[3]

Yes, But. Another revisionist, Chris Argyris, expresses a more optimistic view in his book, *Personality and Organization.*[4] To a degree Argyris is answering McMurry by saying "yes, but." He agrees that at present most workers are dependent, but they do not need to remain in a continued state of dependency. He disagrees entirely with McMurry as to the effect of the formal organization upon the individual. McMurry sees the organization as a means of answering dependency needs; for Argyris, the goals of the typical organization are in basic conflict with the needs and goals of the individual. By fragmenting jobs into discrete activities such as the assembly line and emphasizing the formal relationship, the organization creates dependency and restrains the development of the individual to his fullest capacities. But Argyris sees hope for the future through the enlargement of jobs, employee-centered leadership, and a reality leadership that recognizes the needs of the organization and the individual.

A Middle Ground. The position of the third revisionist, Douglas McGregor, is not so glum as that expressed by McMurry, nor is it so optimistic as the expression of Argyris. In his book, *The Human Side of*

---

[3] Robert N. McMurry, "The Case for Benevolent Autocracy," *Harvard Business Review,* Vol. 36, No. 1 (January-February, 1958), pp. 82-90.
[4] Chris Argyris, *Personality and Organization* (New York: Harper & Row, Publishers, 1957). The appendix, "Some Basic Categories of a Theory of Organization," pp. 239-250, summarizes Argyris' position.

Enterprise, McGregor outlines four steps as a possible solution to the problems confronting the leaders of organizations.[5] He suggests, first, that goals be determined jointly, a step that facilitates the second phase of his recommendations, which is collaboration between superior and subordinate. The third step, the development of self-control, is based upon the belief that people are capable of learning and exercising self-control. The last step is the integration of the goals of the individual and the organization, a bit of give and take on both sides, toward the solution of a mutual problem. McGregor does not claim that his approach will work; he only says that it *may* work.

COMPONENTS OF LEADERSHIP

The preceding discussion of the varying concepts concerning the function of leadership indicates a range from the belief that the primary purpose of leadership is to support the organization and its goals to the belief that the major function of leadership is that of supporting the needs of individual members. The middle ground offers hope that both the needs of the organization and the needs of individual members can be met simultaneously. A similar triad emerges when one examines the literature directed toward an understanding of the components, or factors, contributing towards effective leadership. The first studies were directed toward an understanding of the leader as the critical element in the leadership process, an emphasis usually designated as the trait approach to leadership. Next, the emphasis shifts to situational characteristics as being the more significant factors in determining effective leadership. Finally, there is the current approach to the components of leadership known as the contingency, or interactionistic, approach. Each of these approaches is discussed in turn.[6]

The Trait Approach to Leadership

There are many studies dealing with the traits required for successful leadership. Generally, the traits listed include such attributes as objectivity, judgment, initiative, dependability, drive, a liking for and understanding of people, and decisiveness. Also mentioned frequently are emotional stability and maturity, a strong desire to achieve, the ability to cooperate with others, and a high degree of personal integrity.

---

[5] Douglas McGregor, *The Human Side of Enterprise* (New York: McGraw-Hill Book Company, Inc., 1960).

[6] Edwin P. Hollander and James W. Julian, "Contempory Trends in the Analysis of Leadership Processes," *Psychological Bulletin,* Vol. 71, No. 5 (May, 1969), pp. 387-397.

After surveying the literature, R. M. Stogdill concludes that leadership is associated with the following personal factors: (1) intelligence including judgment and verbal facility, (2) a record of past achievement in scholarship and athletics, (3) emotional maturity and stability expressed in dependability, persistence, and a drive for continuing achievement, (4) the ability to participate socially and to adapt to various groups, and (5) a desire for status and socio-economic position.[7]

Another summary lists the following characteristics of a successful executive: [8]

> (1) the ability to meet people from all walks of life and talk with pleasure on a wide range of subjects, (2) the ability at all times to work at "a mad pace" and sometimes with the "reflectiveness and slow tempo of a Buddhist priest," (3) an interest in world affairs and events in the personal lives of those around him, (4) pleasure in talking and the confidence required for isolation and pondering, (5) the ability to drive people hard when necessary, yet be subtle and tactful at other times, (6) the ability to take a witty or serious approach, as circumstances may require, (7) the capacity to deal with both concrete and abstract problems, (8) the capacity for originality and willingness to follow precedent, (9) the willingness to be conservative but at other times to take risks no gambler would dare to take (that is, the executive must know when to take risks and when to seek security), (10) assurance in decision making and humility in advice seeking.

There are several shortcomings in the trait approach as a means of analyzing and understanding leadership: (1) Trait studies, as a general rule, do not assign weightings to each of the traits so that the relative importance of each trait as it contributes to leadership can be determined. (2) There is considerable overlap between the various traits mentioned. Seldom are they mutually exclusive. Also, there are many instances of conflicting or incompatible traits, such as the ten traits listed above. (3) An analysis of personality traits makes no differentiation between those traits of value in acquiring leadership positions and those traits necessary to hold or maintain leadership. (4) Trait analysis is based upon the rather shaky assumption that personality is a composite of discrete traits, rather than viewing personality as an integrated functioning whole with a continually shifting pattern of characteristics both

---

[7] R. M. Stogdill, "Personal Factors Associated with Leadership: A Survey of the Literature," *Journal of Psychology,* Vol. XXV (January, 1948), pp. 35-64. Another summary of the literature yielding similar results was prepared in 1959. R. D. Mann, "A Review of the Relationship Between Personality and Performance in Small Groups," *Psychological Bulletin,* Vol. 56, No. 4 (July, 1959), pp. 241-270.

[8] Zygmunt A. Piotrowski and Milton R. Rock, *The Perceptanalytic Executive Scale* (New York: Grune and Stratton, Inc., 1963), p. 4.

in respect to their significance and to their strength. (5) The trait approach to leadership ignores situational factors in the environment that influence the effectiveness of leadership. Let us discuss briefly how situational factors influence leadership.

Situational Factors in Leadership

Experienced executive recruiters are frequently confronted with the problem of determining whether an applicant is available for a new position because personality factors created an inability to function as an effective leader in his former position, or whether environmental factors beyond the applicant's control limited the expression of his leadership abilities. The following experiment conducted by Alex Bavelas shows the importance of situational factors as determinants of leadership.[9]

Each experimental group consisting of five subjects was arranged in the positional patterns shown in Figure 16-1. Each member of a group had a card on which there were printed five symbols from a total set of six; however, there was only one symbol that appeared on all five cards. The problem was completed when, as the result of passing information back and forth to each other, the group correctly determined the full set of six symbols. At the end of 15 trials each group was asked whether or not it had a recognized leader. The number of votes received by each member of each group is shown in the circles representing the individual members of each group. Note that in Group A every member receives at least one vote, yet no one member emerges clearly as the leader of the group; however, in Groups B, C, and D, there is definite recognition of one member of the group as the leader.

In order to solve the stated problem it is necessary for the members of each group to pass information; in other words, to function as a part of an information system. The positions of the members determine the pattern of the informational network, and, as the pattern changes, the strategic value of each position also changes. In Group A, arranged in the form of a circle, every member receives at least one vote, but there is no one person emerging without question as the leader. In Group B, arranged as a straight line, neither of the individuals on each end of the line receives a single vote. Each of the persons on either side of the middle member of the group receives several votes, while the central figure receives 12 votes as the recognized leader. In Group C

---

[9] Alex Bavelas, "Communications Patterns in Task-Oriented Groups," in D. Lerner and H. D. Lassell (eds.), *The Policy Sciences* (Palo Alto, California: Stanford University Press, 1951), pp. 193-202.

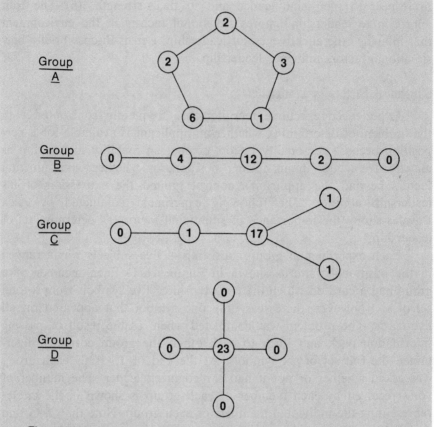

The number within each circle is the number of votes each person received as recognized leader of the group. (From Bavelas, "Communications Patterns in Task-Oriented Groups," *op. cit.*)

Figure 16-1
THE EFFECT OF POSITION AS A DETERMINANT OF LEADERSHIP

the person at the juncture of the Y receives the greatest number of votes, and in Group D, the person at the hub of the wheel is the only member receiving any votes as the recognized leader.

In Group B each of the members at the end of the straight line can communicate directly with only one other member of the group. The ones next to the end position can communicate directly with two members, but the one in the center communicates with two members directly and has only one intermediary when he desires to communicate with those on the end positions. Likewise, the person at the juncture of the Y communicates directly with three members of the group and is only one removed from the person at the end of the stem of the Y.

The person at the hub of the wheel can communicate directly with each of the other members and there is no need to pass information through an intermediary. Thus, the one in the center receives all the votes. The positioning of each member of the group was determined by chance, with no consideration given to personality factors; therefore, the conclusion of this study is inescapable: recognition as a leader is dependent upon the strategic value of one's position in a communication network—a situational factor—and not upon personality characteristics.

Other Situational Factors

In a study of employees of 88 companies, Professor J. C. Wofford, using multiple factor analysis technique, established five independent situational factors that influence the effectiveness of leadership behavior.[10] The first of these factors, centralization and work evaluation, refers to the degree of centralization of the decision-making functions in the organization and the extent to which work is closely controlled by supervision. Second is the factor of organizational complexity and the corresponding degree of technical knowledge required of organization members. Usually a high degree of group cohesiveness and high levels of technical skill are associated with high organizational complexity. The third factor is the size of the total organization which is associated with highly structured work tasks. The fourth situational factor refers to the structure of the work group itself. A high rating in this respect implies a small work group with the members preferring group meetings and participation in the decision-making process. The last factor, organizational layering and communications, refers to the number of levels in the organization and communication between peers in the organization.

Using the same multiple factor analysis techniques Wofford also develops five dimensions of managerial behavior. Group achievement is the first dimension and describes the manager who uses group processes in decision making and who organizes and plans the work carefully. The second dimension, personal enhancement, describes the

---

[10] J. C. Wofford, "Managerial Behavior, Situational Factors, and Productivity and Morale," *Administrative Science Quarterly,* Vol. 16 (March, 1971), pp. 10-17. This study clearly shows the effect of situational factors, as extracted by multiple factor analysis, upon the effectiveness of leadership styles with the criteria being productivity and morale. Professor Wofford indicates the probable reason for having more than two leadership styles is due to the fact that he included in his rating forms the managerial processes of planning, organizing, and controlling as well as the function of leading.

The entire March, 1971, issue of *Administrative Science Quarterly* is noteworthy as it is devoted entirely to organizational leadership.

manager whose primary means of influencing subordinates is the use of authority. Third is personal interaction, the dimension that describes the warm, friendly manager. Dynamic achievement is the fourth dimension and characterizes the manager who sets goals with his subordinates, then measures performance in relation to these goals. The fifth dimension, security and maintenance, describes the manager who is aloof and conscientious in that he continually checks with higher authority. By separating himself from his men he provides some freedom in their activities; however, standards of performance are not clearly defined.

The results of this study show that the manager whose behavior is best described by dimension five is most effective in large complex organizations, where apparently the people are skilled and competent, with little need for guidance. The manager whose forte is personal interaction is most effective in operations that are relatively simple and highly structured. If the manager's behavior emphasizes group achievement and order, he does best where he can work with small groups having relatively unstructured tasks and the need for group meetings. Dynamic achievement is also associated with small groups; however, there is evidence of manager job security. Personal enhancement, the direct reliance upon authority, is associated with relatively simple situations that can be controlled effectively by direct supervision.

Wofford's study is significant for several reasons. First, it shows clearly the effect of situational factors upon the effectiveness of certain styles of leadership behavior. Second, it clearly illustrates the interaction between situational factors and the personality and behavioral characteristics of the leader. Effectiveness, measured either in terms of productivity or morale, is the result of these two forces rather than the result of one or the other.

A CONTINGENCY MODEL OF LEADERSHIP EFFECTIVENESS

Before any definite statement can be made specifying the nature of the interaction between situational variables and the behavior of the leader it is necessary to develop a model and test the elements of that model by subjecting each element to objective scrutiny and verification. Such a model, capable of verification by objective research methods, has been developed by Professor Fred Fiedler and is known as *a contingency model of leadership effectiveness.*[11]

---

[11] The most complete statement of Fiedler's Contingency Model is found in Fred E. Fiedler, *A Theory of Leadership Effectiveness* (New York: McGraw-Hill Book Company, 1967). This book is the primary source of the contingency model discussion. For a briefer statement see Fred E. Fiedler, "Engineer the Job To Fit the Manager," *Harvard Business Review,* Vol. 43, No. 5 (September-October, 1965), pp. 115-122.

Assumptions and Definitions

In order to understand the contingency model it is necessary to define and examine the factors that contribute to effective leadership. First, the group in which leadership occurs is defined and a classification system is developed. Then the other factors—position power, the task structure, and leader member relationship—are discussed in turn. Finally, a group-task classification system is presented in model form.

The Group. Fiedler defines the small group within which most leadership occurs as "a set of individuals in face-to-face interaction who perceive each other as interrelated, or as reciprocally affecting each other, and who pursue a shared goal." [12] Groups vary considerably in respect to the degree and nature of the interaction between members, with the result that three types of groups emerge—*interacting, coacting,* and *counteracting*.

Interacting groups are characterized by a high degree of interdependence between members of the group. In interacting groups each member must complete his task in order that the other members may successfully perform their assigned tasks. Athletic teams, musical groups, airline crews, and restaurant employees are examples of interacting groups. The degree to which the goals of the group are shared by its members is high, and the leader must develop within such a group the coordination necessary to reach group goals.

The members of coacting groups may perform their respective individual tasks independently from those of other members of the group. The faculty of a university is a good example of a coacting group since each instructor can, and often does, conduct his teaching, research, or writing activities with little dependence upon other members of the faculty. Law firms and medical clinics are also typical of coacting groups. Coacting groups need coordination only in the achievement of group goals and in those instances where the goals of an individual member may be in conflict with those of another member.

A counteracting group, such as the labor-management bargaining team or a purchaser-vendor negotiating group, may not appear to be a group in that each side is pursuing separate goals. Yet, for ultimate success each is dependent upon the other in the solution of the problem at hand. Leadership in counteracting groups is very difficult, because in most instances there are two leaders—one for each side. Further, hostility and competition may be very marked. Leadership in these groups is primarily one of conflict resolution.

---

[12]*Ibid.*, p. 18.

To date, most of the work done in the development and validation of the contingency model is based upon interacting groups.

Position Power. Even a cursory examination indicates that one of the factors determining the effectiveness of the leader is the power associated with the position of leadership. Case Problem 16-B presents one of many scales that have been used to measure the position power of the leader. Indicators of high position power are the right to hire and fire, to reward or withhold promotions or changes in pay, the appointment to the position and designation of title endorsed by the organizational hierarchy, and the accompanying external signs that clearly indicate the position of the office within the organization. A leader with low position power might be designated as temporary or acting, be elected by and subject to removal by his peers or subordinates, have no power to select or retain subordinates, and no designation of rank or authority. An elected committee chairman or a working foreman are examples of leaders with low position power.

Though position power is usually recognized as one of the factors determining the effectiveness of leadership, its precise effect is not clear since the results of empirical studies are ambiguous. A leader with high position power has at least an initial advantage in that he has the support of the organization and consequently should feel more free to interact openly with the members of his group. On the other hand, the leader with low position power does not have such freedom initially, and he must first convince the members of the group to accept his leadership and direction. The situation is particularly critical for the leader with low position power if he may safely be ignored or even deposed by his subordinates.

The Task Structure. The second factor determining the effectiveness of leadership is the task itself. Some tasks by their very nature are relatively easy to define, to accomplish, and to measure. Such tasks are regarded as having a high degree of structure. There are also tasks that have a low degree of structure with the result that it is more difficult to define and to measure progress toward their accomplishment.

Fiedler uses four criteria in determining the degree of task structure. First is the extent to which the decision or solution may be verified. Those solutions that can be verified by comparison to a model or by subjecting them to an objective evaluation are regarded as structured. The work of an assembler may be verified by such means, but the conclusions of a research worker in the social sciences may not be as readily verified. The clarity of the goal and the extent to which it can be communicated to and understood by the members of the group is the second dimension of task structure. Third, multiplicity of available alternate pathways or solutions is significant. Usually there is only one way to correctly assemble a mechanical product, but there are many alternates, perhaps each being equally effective, available to the members of a research and development team in the development of a new product. Finally, there is the specificity of the solution. Most arithmetic problems have only one solution; others, such as a square root have two, a plus and a minus. At the other extreme, problems dealing with human relations, value judgments, and matters of opinion may have as many solutions as there are participants in the group. Consequently the structure of the task itself is a significant factor in determining the effectiveness of leadership.

Leader-Member Relationship. Third, there is the personal relationship that exists between the leader and the members of the group that is significant in determining leadership effectiveness. The personality characteristics of a leader are important, but of equal importance are the composition and history of the group. In most formal organizations a group exists prior to the advent of the designated leader. With legitimacy of position and the position power conferred by the organization most designated leaders are able to demonstrate some degree of effectiveness. If the leader succeeds in building a strong interpersonal relationship by demonstrating competence and achieving goals and at the same time by supporting the needs and desires of the group, his position is further enhanced, thus making subsequent leadership tasks easier to achieve. At the other extreme of the continuum of leader-member relationships is the mutinous rejection of the leader by the group. Under such conditions the leader has little or no influence upon the actions of the group.

There are several ways of measuring the nature of these leader-member relations. One way is to obtain the leader's rating of the group atmosphere. It is a rating based upon a scale quite similar to the one presented in Case Problem 16-A for the measurement of the characteristics of the Least Preferred Co-worker. A Group Atmosphere Scale appears in Case Problem 16-B. When measuring leader-member relations the leader is asked to describe the group atmosphere rather than the characteristics of the least preferred co-worker. Admittedly, there is the possibility of a difference between the leader's perception of the group and the groups perception of their leader; yet this potential discrepancy does not seem to be damaging to the effectiveness of the measure.

Group-Task Classification

These three characteristics—position power, task structure, leader-member relationships—are shown in Figure 16-2. Note that octants 1, 2, 3, and 4 represent those situations where the leader-member relationships may be termed as good while octants 5, 6, 7, and 8 describe those situations in which leader-member relationships are described as moderately poor. Table 16-1 summarizes the complete classification of group task situations on the basis on the three factors—leader-member relations, task structure, and position power.

Source: Fred E. Fiedler, "Engineer the Job to Fit the Manager," *Harvard Business Review,* Vol. 43, No. 5 (September-October, 1965), p. 117. (Reproduced by permission.)

Figure 16-2
A MODEL FOR CLASSIFYING GROUP-TASK SITUATIONS

Table 16-1
CLASSIFICATION OF GROUP TASK SITUATIONS
ON THE BASIS OF THREE FACTORS

Octant	Leader-Member Relations	Task Structure	Position Power
I	Good	High	Strong
II	Good	High	Weak
III	Good	Weak	Strong
IV	Good	Weak	Weak
V	Moderately poor	High	Strong
VI	Moderately poor	High	Weak
VII	Moderately poor	Weak	Strong
VIII	Moderately poor	Weak	Weak

Source: Fred E. Fiedler, A Theory of Leadership Effectiveness (New York: McGraw-Hill Book Company, 1967), p. 34.

Leadership Style

In addition to the task group situations which may be described by any one of the eight octants of Figure 16-2, the leadership style of the leader is also significant as a determinant of leadership effectiveness. Fiedler makes a clear distinction between leadership behavior and leadership style. Leadership behavior includes all the things that a leader might do in a work situation. It would include his efforts in the areas of planning, organizing, structuring the task, and controlling as well as his interpersonal relationships with his subordinates.[13] Leadership style refers to "the underlying need structure of the individual which motivates his behavior in various leadership situations. Leadership style thus refers to the consistency of goals or needs over different situations."[14]

It is difficult to summarize the terminology that has been used as descriptive of leadership style since the literature concerning leadership is so vast. Yet it seems the style of leadership is described most frequently as being either democratic, participative, supportive, or people oriented on the one hand, or autocratic, directive, or task oriented on the other. Fiedler's measure of leadership style follows a similar bipolar dichotomy.

---

[13] Wofford, loc. cit. It will be remembered that Wofford used such a definition in his measurement of the factors contributing to managerial behavior.

[14] Fiedler, op. cit., p. 36.

Least Preferred Co-worker (LPC). In Chapter 15, "Organizational Behavior," some of the problems associated with interpersonal perceptions are discussed. We know that a person's perception of another influences their interpersonal relationships. Further, it is known that interpersonal perceptions do not necessarily conform to an objective statement of the situation. Nonetheless, such perceptions are relatively enduring and stable over a period of time; e.g., a stereotype. We also know the kind of behavior that is most likely to occur in conjunction with a certain type of interpersonal perception. The mother who perceives her noisy, ill-mannered, spoiled brats as little darlings will have a smoother interpersonal relationship with them than the mother who perceives them as they are. Similarly, the leader who perceives his subordinates as cooperative, warm, friendly, and capable will have an interpersonal relationship different from that of the leader who perceives his subordinates as hostile, cold, antagonistic, and incompetent.

In Case Problem 16-A you are asked to describe the person with whom you can work least well, either someone you work with at present or someone that you know from the past. In order to obtain your average LPC score add each of the scaled values that you indicated for each of the 16 traits; then divide by 16 to obtain the average score. A high average LPC score ranges from 4.1 to 5.7 and a low LPC score ranges from 1.2 to 2.2.[15]

Leadership Style and LPC. Persons with a high LPC—those who rate their least preferred co-worker in favorable terms—are people-oriented and are interested in establishing good interpersonal relationships. They are usually more considerate and supportive in their relationships with their subordinates. Those with a low LPC—those who rate their least preferred co-worker in unfavorable terms—are more task-oriented than they are relationship-oriented. They are more punitive toward the inefficient worker, more goal-oriented, and more efficient. Fiedler summarizes the significance of high- and low-LPC scores as follows:

> "Thus, high-LPC leaders are concerned with having good interpersonal relations and with gaining permanence and self-esteem through these interpersonal relations. Low-LPC leaders are concerned with achieving success on assigned tasks, even at the risk of having poor interpersonal relations with workers. The behaviors of high- and low-LPC leaders will thus be quite different if the situation is such that the satisfaction of their respective needs is threatened. Under these

---

[15] *Ibid.*, pp. 43-44.

conditions, the high-LPC leader will increase his interpersonal interaction in order to cement his relations with other group members while
the low-LPC leader will interact in order to complete the task successfully. The high-LPC person is concerned with gaining self-esteem
through recognition by others, the low-LPC person is concerned with
gaining self-esteem through successful performance of the task. Both
types of leaders may thus be concerned with the task and both will use
interpersonal relationships, although the high-LPC leader will concern
himself with a task in order to have successful interpersonal relations,
while the low-LPC leader will concern himself with the interpersonal
relations in order to achieve task success." [16]

Leadership Style and Effectiveness

In view of the complexity of the task-group situation portrayed in
Figure 16-2, it seems highly unlikely that one leadership style would
be equally effective in all task situations and with all groups. Figure
16-3 shows how the style of effective leadership varies with the situation. In all cases the groups studied are performing well, and as the
task-group situation varies so does the effective style of the leader. Note
that for situations described by octants 1, 2, 3, and 8 a controlling,
active, structuring form of leadership (low-LPC) is most effective while
in situations represented by octants 4, 5, 6, and 7 the relations-oriented
(high-LPC) style of leadership appears to be the most effective.

Fiedler's contingency model of leadership effectiveness is presented
in considerable detail since it offers a way of showing the interaction
between situational factors and the characteristics and needs of the
leader, termed leadership style. The model is so constructed and presented that the tentative conclusions shown in Figure 16-3 are subject
to verification or modification by subsequent research.[17] To date, the
studies that have been reported are based on interacting groups; little
is known of the leadership requirements for co-acting or counteracting
groups. Further, the effectiveness of leadership style is based only upon
studies that include those with a high-LPC or a low-LPC score. What
is the effectiveness of those leaders who have an intermediate LPC
score?[18] In spite of these shortcomings, the contingency model of

---

[16] *Ibid.*, pp. 45-46.

[17] The following review is highly critical of the contingency model of leadership
effectiveness. George Graen, Kenneth Alveris, James B. Orris, and Joseph A. Martella,
"Contingency Model of Leadership Effectiveness: Antecedent and Evidential Results,"
Psychological Bulletin, Vol. 74, No. 4 (October, 1970), pp. 285-296.

[18] Fiedler, *op. cit.,* pp. 261-265. In the concluding chapter, Professor Fiedler
presents a concise statement of conclusions that may be drawn to date and problems
that remain unanswered by a contingency model in its present state of development.

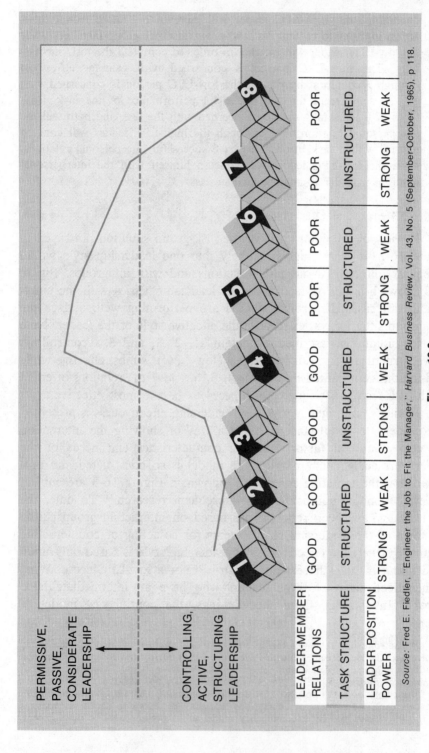

PERMISSIVE, PASSIVE, CONSIDERATE LEADERSHIP

← →

CONTROLLING, ACTIVE, STRUCTURING LEADERSHIP

LEADER-MEMBER RELATIONS	GOOD	GOOD	GOOD	GOOD	POOR	POOR	POOR	POOR
TASK STRUCTURE	STRUCTURED		UNSTRUCTURED		STRUCTURED		UNSTRUCTURED	
LEADER POSITION POWER	STRONG	WEAK	STRONG	WEAK	STRONG	WEAK	STRONG	WEAK

Source: Fred E. Fiedler, "Engineer the Job to Fit the Manager," *Harvard Business Review,* Vol. 43, No. 5 (September–October, 1965), p 118.

Figure 16-3

HOW THE STYLE OF EFFECTIVE LEADERSHIP VARIES WITH THE SITUATION

leadership effectiveness provides a useful way of thinking about and analyzing leadership situations.

SELECTING A LEADERSHIP PATTERN

As indicated, one of the shortcomings of the contingency model of leadership effectiveness in its present state of development is that it reports effectiveness only for those leaders with either a high- or low-LPC score. To this extent it perpetuates the extreme positions discussed in the first part of this chapter, "Theories of Leadership." One of the weaknesses of dichotomizing leadership style into two distinct categories is that we build stereotypes of each style—the inflexible "autocrat" making decisions without regard for human values and the permissive "democrat" working with fully satisfied subordinates. The discussion that follows emphasizes that leadership style is better described as points along a continuum instead of viewing the style of the leader as falling into one of two dichotomous classifications.

Leadership, a Continuum

Managerial leadership involves much more than the kind of interpersonal relationship between superior and subordinate. The situation must be appraised by the manager in respect to available resources and the possible actions of external forces, such as the action of competitors or governmental agencies. There is also need to assess the capabilities of the personnel of the organization. The nature of the decision or the problem to be solved has to be evaluated, and lastly, the capabilities and personality of the manager influence the type of leadership. With so many factors determining successful executive action, it seems highly unlikely that the interpersonal relationships between superior and subordinate can be neatly classified into one of two categories— autocratic or democratic. Instead, the relationships between superior and subordinate follow a continuum as shown in Figure 16-4.[19] Let us describe briefly each of the seven gradations of leadership behavior.

Manager Makes Decision and Announces It. This form of leadership represents the most autocratic form: i.e., there is no chance for the subordinate to express his thoughts either in the formulation or the solution of the problem. The superior formulates the problem, solves it,

---

[19] Robert Tannenbaum and Warren H. Schmidt, "How to Choose a Leadership Pattern," *Harvard Business Review*, Vol. 34 (March-April, 1958), pp. 95-101. In addition to the discussion concerning the seven leadership patterns that form a continuum, the authors discuss the factors which determine the pattern of leadership: forces in the manager, forces in the subordinates, and forces in the situation.

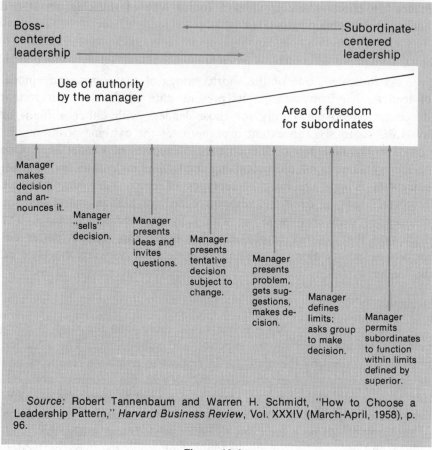

Source: Robert Tannenbaum and Warren H. Schmidt, "How to Choose a Leadership Pattern," *Harvard Business Review*, Vol. XXXIV (March-April, 1958), p. 96.

Figure 16-4
CONTINUUM OF LEADERSHIP BEHAVIOR

and announces his decision. Coercion, to assure the execution of the decision, is not necessarily implied since subordinates may be willing to follow such directions.

Manager "Sells" Decision. At this stage the manager recognizes the feelings of subordinates and the possibility that there might be resistance to his decision. Consequently, he attempts to persuade them to recognize the merits of his decision. However, the manager is still in control of all phases of the decision-making process.

Manager Presents Ideas and Invites Questions. The third form of managerial behavior marks the beginning of a degree of participation on the part of subordinates—at least they are being asked to express their ideas. However, the manager has in his own mind made the decision. Nonetheless, the presentation of his ideas to subordinates with the opportunity of their expressing themselves opens up the possibility that the decision may be modified.

Manager Presents a Tentative Decision Subject to Change. Here, at the midpoint of the range of leadership styles, there is definite participation on the part of subordinates in shaping a final decision. Although the manager's decision is tentative, he still defines the problem and works out the initial solution.

Manager Presents Problem, Gets Suggestions, Makes Decision. This is the first time the manager comes to the group without having at least a tentative solution to the problem; however, he still defines the problem in general terms. Consultation with the group prior to making a tentative decision increases the number of possible solutions.

Manager Defines Limits, Asks Group to Make Decision. Up to this point the decision is made by the manager with varying degrees of participation on the part of subordinates in influencing his decision; but this is the first time that the group makes the decision. However, the manager still states the problem and the limits within which the decision must be made. Usually these limits are expressed in terms of either cost or time, or both.

Manager Permits Subordinates to Function within Limits Defined by Superior. The last stage of managerial behavior on the scale represents the maximum degree of subordinate participation within formal organizations. The manager, himself a subordinate, is limited in the extent to which he may permit participation by the limits of authority granted to him. The greatest degree of subordinate participation is possible within the framework of a functional-teamwork or task-force type of operation (described in Chapter 11); even so, the objectives of the organization are stated by higher authority, but subordinates may define and solve problems consistent with the attainment of company objectives.

Determinants of Effective Leadership

The discussion above of patterns of leadership shows the varying degrees of understanding and participation on the part of subordinates in the decision-making process. The process ranges from the completely authoritarian situation with no subordinate participation to the maximum degree of democratic leadership that enables the subordinate to participate in all phases of the decision-making process. The problem is one of determining how to select an effective pattern of leadership. Tannenbaum and Schmidt suggest that there are forces in the manager, in subordinates, and in the situation that must be weighed in order to select the most effective form of leadership.[20] In Chapter 9, Theory Z, a systems approach to organization, is presented and in subsequent chapters it is applied to the organizational problems of departmentation, span of management, and determining the optimum degree of decentralization. Let us examine the forces in the manager, in subordinates, and in the situation within the framework of Theory Z as a means of understanding those factors that determine an effective pattern of leadership.

Size of Organization. As size (defined as number of people) increases, organization structure becomes more formal and complex, with the result that the appropriate processes of motivating employees toward the achievement of organizational goals become more formal and directive—rather than participative—in nature.

There is a positive relationship between the size of organizations and the formalization of organization structure and relationships as evidenced by the presence of organization charts and position descriptions. Also, as organizations grow, there is greater dependence upon written rather than oral communications, a development that tends to restrict the degree of freedom of subordinates. As relationships in an organization become more formalized, there is a clearer definition of areas of responsibility and lines of accountability, with the result that a supervisor may find his authority to delegate decision-making functions to his subordinates severely limited. For example, in a small company with a single plant it is quite possible for a foreman to invite employee participation in the placement of a piece of production equipment. However, in a large company with many plants it is likely that the layout of production facilities for all plants would be determined by a central production engineering department.

Degree of Interaction. As the need for interaction between members of an organization increases in order to accomplish the prescribed work, the organization structure should permit a free flow of information and ideas, and the accompanying process of motivation should become more participative and informal in nature.

The degree of interaction between the members of a group may be a function of the specialized knowledge that each member is capable of contributing toward the solution of a problem, or interaction may be

---

[20] *Ibid.*

a function of structural or situational factors in the problem-solving situation. In instances where subordinates have little or no knowledge of the problem, the need for participation is slight and the leadership exercised in these instances tends to be authoritative. Research and development teams composed of highly skilled technicians frequently are most productive when the manager participates as a member of the group in solving their common problem. Even so, if the problem is extremely complex, decision making may be reserved for the manager since he is the only one with complete knowledge of all phases of the work.

The need for interaction arising from structural characteristics of the problem-solving situation poses a rather interesting question: Should the situation be redesigned so that the need for interaction is minimized? In another experiment similar to the one conducted by Alex Bavelas (see Figure 16-1), it was found that people arranged in the pattern of Group D, four persons communicating with the fifth who forms the hub of a wheel, offered the most efficient problem-solving arrangement.[21] Next in efficiency were those arranged as Group B, with one man in the center and two on either side; while the least efficient group was structured similar to Group A, which forms a circle. Remember, when selecting a leader, Group D unanimously selected the person in the center; the leader for Group B was selected by a substantial margin; and in Group A, the circle, there was no clear choice of a leader. However, we find that a structure similar to Group A, although the least efficient, results in a group whose members are "happier" than the members of either Group D or B. Of greater significance is the fact that Group A was able to incorporate new ideas for the solution of the problem much more readily than either of the other groups and was also able to solve modified or new problems more readily.

What is the criteria for organizational effectiveness? Is it happiness and the ability to solve new problems, or is it efficiency in solving routine problems? Or, putting the question another way, how much interaction among members is needed? Apparently, if the problems to be solved are routine, similar to those found in the daily operations of most business firms, little interaction is needed. But if the problems

---

[21] Harold J. Leavitt, "Unhuman Organizations," *Harvard Business Review,* Vol. 40 (July-August, 1962), pp. 90-98. Professor Leavitt describes another experiment similar to the one conducted by Alex Bavelas. The original reference for the study is: L. Christie, D. Luce, and J. Macy, "Communication and Learning in Task Oriented Groups," Research Lab of Electronics, MIT (Tech Report No. 231, May, 1962). Professor Leavitt emphasizes organizations as systems that may be dependent upon humans or they may be "unhuman."

are continually changing and dependent upon new ideas for their solution, the need for interaction—and a corresponding shift in leadership patterns—is critical.

Personality of Members. Effective organizational structure and processes conform to the personality and expectations of members of the organization. Members who do not expect participation and who are dependent upon others for motivation react best to formal patterns of structure and motivation, while those who expect participation and are motivated largely from within react best to participative processes and informal organizational structure.

In the first section of this chapter, "Theories of Leadership," the position of several revisionists is stated. If McMurry is correct in assuming that the organization answers the dependency needs of people, the leadership pattern of a benevolent autocrat is appropriate; however, if one adopts Argyris' view that man is capable of development and self-direction, a participative or democratic style of leadership is desirable. In either case, emphasis is placed upon the personality and capabilities of subordinates as the determining factors in choosing a pattern of leadership.

Congruence of Goals. When the goals of the organization and those of its members are congruent, participative processes and a less formal structure are appropriate; but when organizational goals and members' goals are divergent, greater reliance must be placed upon external controls and formal structure so that adequate control is assured.

There is little question concerning the validity of the assumption above, yet the implications of this assumption that call for a variety of leadership patterns within the same company are often overlooked. The degree to which the goals of members and of the organization are congruent is a function of organization level. Among the members of top management, the president and his staff, the goals are usually congruent and result in an informal relationship with a high degree of participation. (Review "How Rathbone Runs Jersey Standard," Case Problem 13-B.) For lower levels of management there are committees, staff meetings, and training programs, all of which contribute to an understanding of the goals of the organization and the member's role in achieving these goals. However, most industrial organizations routinize jobs at the clerical and hourly levels, thereby widening the gap between organizational and individual goals. Consequently, leadership at these levels tends to be more authoritative and a greater reliance is placed upon formal controls. Thus, within a single organization there should be a differentiation in the pattern of leadership from one level of the organization to another, dependent upon the degree of congruency between organizational and members' goals.

Level of Decision Making. The hierarchical level of decision making is primarily a function of the technology of the organization. When technology permits and decision-making functions are retained within the primary work group of an organization, participative processes and informal structure are effective. As the decision-making processes moves upward in the organizational hierarchy and away from the work group affected by those decisions, formal structure and directive processes are more appropriate.

The level of decision making within an organization is in part a function of the organization's information system and in part the result of organizational policy. Information necessary for decision making may be available within the work group; for example, the knowledge needed to solve a quality control problem occurring in a production department. In such cases, participation in the decision-making process by the group may be the most effective means of solving the problem. But, as the result of a policy statement, a higher level of authority such as a company-wide quality control office may be established. Directives from this office are authoritative in nature and, in turn, affect the pattern of leadership at lower levels of production by removing a possible area of participative decision making. In many companies decision making at high levels is not the direct result of a policy statement; instead, it is due to the complexity and nature of the information needed to make decisions. A multiplant manufacturer supplying materials to customers with many plants must make decisions concerning production scheduling and purchasing on a companywide basis. Leadership in such an organization tends to be directive rather than participative in nature.

In judging extent of participative decision making and degree of participative leadership, the importance and scope of the decisions made should be given more weight than the sheer number of decisions.

State of the System. When the performance of an organization is relatively poor in respect to the achievement of organizational goals (thereby creating a state of system imbalance), directive processes of motivation and formalized structure become necessary to initiate corrective action. As the organization achieves stated goals, however, participative processes and informal patterns of organization become more effective and are expected by the members of the organization.

An extreme example of an organization failing to meet its goals is a company showing a loss, rather than a profit, at the close of the fiscal year. Under these circumstances the pattern of leadership of the president tends to be authoritative. Although he may have long-range plans for improving the company's profit position, his immediate reaction is to reduce variable costs, and the greatest potential of variable cost reduction is achieved by reducing payroll costs.[22] To ask subordinates to participate in eliminating their positions is unrealistic; consequently, such decisions are made without participation, and the means of communicating the decision is directive in nature.

Organizations in a continual state of crises, either real or imaginary, often cite the limitations of time as the reason for directive leadership. Admittedly, participative processes of decision making are more time consuming than the decision of a single individual, but there are instances when increased cooperation in the execution of the decision amply offsets the additional time taken in reaching the decision.

The preceding discussion emphasizes that there is no one successful pattern of leadership. Many factors contribute to the effectiveness of leadership. The personality and expectation of subordinates are important. Also important are the situational or environmental factors. However, of greatest importance is the leader himself, for he brings to his position a definite concept of the role of the leader, and he should be able to assess accurately the potentials of the situation and the capabilities and needs of subordinates.

Case Problem 16-B offers an opportunity to test the contingency model of leadership effectiveness. For those of you who now hold a position of leadership, the model may provide insights that will enable you to improve your leadership effectiveness. For those not presently in a position of leadership, the contingency model may provide a better understanding of those situations in which you served as a subordinate.

CASE PROBLEM 16-B

PREDICTING LEADERSHIP EFFECTIVENESS

In Case Problem 16-A you completed a rating form descriptive of your least preferred co-worker. It is also a measure from which certain inferences may be drawn concerning your style of leadership. Criteria for evaluating the structure of a task are discussed on pp. 492-493. Using Fiedler's Contingency Model of Leadership Effectiveness as a guide, there are two more measures

---

[22] See Chapter 5, "Planning for Profit and Sales," for a review of the significance of variable and fixed costs.

necessary for the prediction of leader effectiveness in a given situation. One of these is leader-member relations, a relationship that can be inferred by the leader's rating of group atmosphere. The other measure, the leader's position power, is found by completing a checklist of items descriptive of the power of the position. These instruments are included as Exhibits II and III for you to complete.

PROBLEMS

1. Recall some recent task oriented situation in which you had a position of leadership. Rate this situation in respect to group atmosphere and the power accorded the position. Now, rate the task in accordance with the criteria presented in the text in Figure 16-3. How successfully does the model predict the effectiveness of your leadership? Discuss.

2. If you are unable to recall a situation in which you had a position of leadership, describe the task, the position power, and the group atmosphere from your position as a subordinate. It will be necessary for you to assume the style of the leader. Again, prepare a model containing all of the information presented in Figure 16-3. Does the model predict the effectiveness of leadership as it actually occurred? Discuss.

Exhibit II
GROUP ATMOSPHERE SCALE

Describe the atmosphere of your group by checking the following items.

	8	7	6	5	4	3	2	1	
1. Friendly	:	:	:	:	:	:	:	:	Unfriendly
2. Accepting	:	:	:	:	:	:	:	:	Rejecting
3. Satisfying	:	:	:	:	:	:	:	:	Frustrating
4. Enthusiastic	:	:	:	:	:	:	:	:	Unenthusiastic
5. Productive	:	:	:	:	:	:	:	:	Nonproductive
6. Warm	:	:	:	:	:	:	:	:	Cold
7. Cooperative	:	:	:	:	:	:	:	:	Uncooperative
8. Supportive	:	:	:	:	:	:	:	:	Hostile
9. Interesting	:	:	:	:	:	:	:	:	Boring
10. Successful	:	:	:	:	:	:	:	:	Unsuccessful

Source: Fred E. Fiedler, A Theory Of Leadership Effectiveness, (New York: McGraw-Hill Book Company, 1967), p. 269.

Exhibit III

MEASURE OF POSITION POWER

1. Compliments from the leader are appreciated more than compliments from other group members.

2. Compliments are highly valued, criticisms are considered damaging.

3. Leader can recommend punishments and rewards.

4. Leader can punish or reward members of his own accord.

5. Leader can effect (or can recommend) promotion or demotion.

6. Leader chairs or coordinates group but may or may not have other advantages, i. e., is appointed or acknowledged chairman or leader.

7. Leader's opinion is accorded considerable respect and attention.

8. Leader's special knowledge or information (and members' lack of it) permits leader to decide how task is to be done or how group is to proceed.

9. Leader cues member or instructs them on what to do.

10. Leader tells or directs members what to do or what to say.

11. Leader is expected to motivate group.

12. Leader is expected to suggest and evaluate the members' work.

13. Leader has superior or special knowledge about the job, or has special instructions but requires members to do job.

14. Leader can supervise each member's job and evaluate it or correct it.

15. Leader knows his own as well as members' job and could finish the work himself if necessary, e.g., writing a report for which all information is available.

16. Leader enjoys special or official rank and status in real life which sets him apart from or above group members, e.g., military rank or elected office in a company or organization. (+5 points)

17. Leader is given special or official rank by experimenter to simulate for role-playing purposes, e.g., "You are a general" or "the manager." This simulated rank must be clearly superior to members' rank and must not be just that of "chairman" or "group leader" of the group during its work period. (+3 points)

18. Leader's position is dependent on members; members can replace or depose leader. (−5 points)

Note: The dimension of leader position power is defined by the above checklist in which all "true" items are given 1 point, except for items 16, 17, and 18, which are weighted +5, +3, and −5 points respectively.

Source: Fred E. Fiedler, *A Theory of Leadership Effectiveness,* (New York: McGraw-Hill Book Company, 1967), p. 24.

Chapter Questions for Study and Discussion

1. Do you believe that there has ever been a successful organization that was entirely work centered or entirely people centered? Why?
2. Much of the literature of management equates management with leadership. Do you believe that managing is necessarily leading? Discuss.
3. From your own experience describe a manager (or a teacher) whom you would characterize as typifying the scientific management approach to leadership. Describe one who typifies the human relations approach. Which one was more effective? Why?
4. How would you describe the revisionists' approaches to leadership?
5. What are some of the characteristics of leadership as revealed by the trait approach to the study of leadership? What are the shortcomings of this approach?
6. Describe a business situation that supports the situational aspects of leadership.
7. Certain positions in an organization, such as the presidency, carry with them a traditional prestige. Could this be considered similar to a situational factor? How?
8. What is meant by a *contingency* model? Evaluate fully Fiedler's Contingency Model of Leadership Effectiveness. Does it successfully integrate the trait and situational approaches to leadership?
9. Why is there a need for flexibility in leadership patterns?
10. Discuss in your own words the application of Theory Z to the choice of an appropriate leadership pattern.

Communications

John Thurman, president of the Thurman Manufacturing Company, recognizes the importance of keeping employees informed in respect to the economic problems of the company. He realizes that his company is entering a difficult competitive period resulting from a steady decline in prices. Thurman knows that he must lower prices in order to retain his share of the market.

He believes that his monthly letter, entitled *From The President's Desk,* which is sent to all employees, is adequate as a means of transmitting information. However, when a major crisis arises, he summons all department heads to the austere oak-paneled board room, an action which, in his opinion, assures them that they are a part of management and participating in major decisions. The established protocol for these meetings requires that all attending personnel be seated prior to the scheduled time and that they arise when Mr. Thurman enters the room and remain standing until asked to be seated again. John Thurman has made his entrance and has indicated by a curt nod of his head that all may be seated.

"I have called you together to explain our dire economic situation. We are face to face with competitive wolves who are snapping at our heels. They are making us sell at prices which are too low and delivery schedules that are utterly impossible to meet. If this great company of ours—one of the bulwarks of free enterprise—is to survive, we must all pitch in and pull together. Let me tell you what I mean."

CASE PROBLEM
17-A

A MESSAGE
FOR MANAGEMENT

510

Following his opening remarks, John Thurman glared at everyone in the room as though he were daring them to speak. No one spoke, since all knew that any expression of opinion would be classified as negative thinking by Mr. Thurman.

"First, what we need here is imagineering. We need positive thinkers and everyone has to play on the same team. We have to optimize production and nothing can be left out of account when we are considering cost reduction. To implement this crash program of cost reduction, I have gone outside the company and hired a top-drawer production manager.

"The second thing we have to do is maximize quality. Quality means everything in this business. Every machine has to be inspected on a regular schedule by the foreman of the department and when that machine starts up in production, it means that he has given it his stamp of approval. Nothing is too small to overlook when we are thinking of quality.

"Third on my list of items deserving serious consideration is beefing up our sales force. Customers are the lifeblood of this business, and even though they are not always right, they still must be handled with kid gloves. Our salesmen have to learn how to put themselves across and make every call count. Our method of compensating salesmen is eminently fair, but even so, we're going to try to sweeten the pot by upping the commission rates on slow-moving items. We would do it across the board, but we have to hold the line on costs.

"The last thing on my list is teamwork. This we need more than anything else. Unless we all pull together, we can't make it. Leadership is teamwork, and teamwork is striving and straining for the same goal. You are the representatives of management, you are the leaders, and you know what our goals are. Now let's all put our shoulders to the wheel and wrap up the whole ball of wax immediately. Remember, we're one big happy family."

As John Thurman concluded, all arose and stood by their chairs while he gathered his papers and left the board room through the connecting door to his office.

PROBLEMS

1. What was the purpose of this meeting?
2. What is John Thurman trying to say? Rewrite his remarks in simple, direct language. Do you think his analysis was correct?

3. What factors other than language cause a communication barrier in this case problem?
4. How would you arrange the above meeting so that two-way communication is assured?

The word, communication, as it is used in management literature has two distinct, yet compatible, meanings. One of these meanings emphasizes the dissemination of information and is commonly referred to as formal communication. The other meaning of the term refers to interpersonal communications between two or more persons. Interpersonal communications transmit much more than information since psychological needs, motives, and feelings are often revealed that may be in conflict with the expressed verbal message.

Since formal communication is based on the science of semantics, we examine some of the fundamental concepts of semantics. Next, formal communications are considered, then problems inherent in interpersonal communications are examined, and lastly, the means of improving both formal and interpersonal communications are discussed.

THE MEANING OF MEANING

Communication is defined in its broadest sense as *the transmission of meaning to others*. However, the definition as it now stands does not mean or signify much, since two words used in the definition—*transmission* and *meaning*—need further elaboration. The word *transmission* as used in the definition is broad and does not limit the methods of communication to the use of language in either spoken or written form. The word *meaning* is also broad. It includes information consisting not only of facts and descriptive statements of objects and other people but also attitudes and feelings that may be conveyed to others. For purposeful communications, such as those in a business organization, it is necessary to restrict our definition further by stating that communication is the transmission of *intended* meaning to others. The above restriction implies that the sender of the communication has a clear concept of the meaning that he wishes to convey; and in order for the communication to be purposeful, the receiver must interpret the message in such a manner that he receives the intended meaning.

The scientific study of meaning is known as *semantics,* a word derived from the Greek term, *semantikos,* which means significant. Semantics is concerned with the relationship between (1) objects and/or events, (2) the thought processes involved in interpreting these objects and/or events, and (3) the signs and/or symbols used to express a given thought or to describe a specific object or event. First, let us discuss these three aspects of semantics and then apply the lessons learned in analyzing Case Problem 17-A.

The Triangle of Meaning

The relationship between objects and events, their interpretation, and the development of signs and symbols are shown in Figure 17-1, The Triangle of Meaning.[1] Objects and events are known as the *referent*; thoughts, interpretations, and emotions are called the *reference*; and devices used to express the reference are called *signs* or *symbols*.

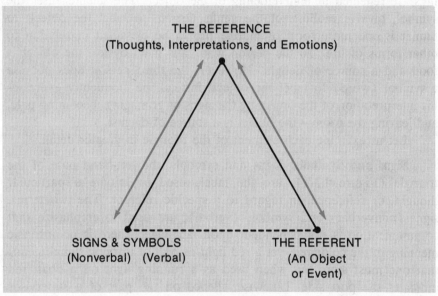

THE REFERENCE
(Thoughts, Interpretations, and Emotions)

SIGNS & SYMBOLS
(Nonverbal)   (Verbal)

THE REFERENT
(An Object
or Event)

Figure 17-1
THE TRIANGLE OF MEANING

---

[1] C. K. Ogden and I. A. Richards, *The Meaning of Meaning* (8th ed.; New York: Harcourt, Brace & Company, Inc., 1956). *The Meaning of Meaning*, first published in 1923, still stands as one of the basic works in the field of semantics. Figure 17-1 is adapted from a figure on page 11 entitled Thoughts, Words, and Things. *The Meaning of Meaning* is a good reference for the serious study of semantics.

Stuart Chase, *The Tyranny of Words* (New York: Harcourt, Brace & Company, Inc., 1938). Mr. Chase's book is based largely upon the writings of Ogden and Richards and the work of Korzybski (listed below) and is an excellent popularization of the field of semantics.

Alfred Korzybski, *Science and Sanity: An Introduction to Non-Aristotelian Systems and General Semantics* (Lancaster, Pa.: The Science Press Printing Company, Distributors for The International Non-Aristotelian Library Publishing Company, 1933). Count Korzybski, a mathematician, applies general semantics to all fields of science as they existed in 1933. *Science and Sanity* is recommended only for the advanced student.

The following example shows the relationship between a referent, a reference, and the way in which meaning is attached to a sign or a symbol. The object in question is taken from the ocean; it is elliptical in shape, three inches long, an inch and one half in width, an inch thick. The surface is a rough, brown, shell-like substance. Three persons are observing (thinking about) this object. One of them, a scientist, recognizes the object immediately and labels it a bivalve mollusk of the genus *Ostrea*. The second observer "sees" a dozen such objects on the half shell ringing a platter full of ice; to him it is an object to be eaten, an oyster. The third person takes one look, grimaces, turns pale, and leaves the room. All have seen the same object, yet three distinct meanings are reflected in their labeling of the object. The scientist uses the symbol, bivalve mollusk of the genus *Ostrea,* to label the object; to him it is one more form of marine life to be classified in relation to other forms of life. To the person who calls it an oyster, the object is food and a source of delight. However, the third person does not use a symbol (word) to label the object; instead, he eloquently expresses his interpretation of the object by the signs of grimacing, becoming pale, and leaving the room—the object is a source of disgust.

Let us examine each element of the triangle in greater detail.

Signs and Symbols. Signs and symbols, the left-hand base of the triangle (Figure 17-1), are the labels used to initiate a particular thought, or reference, in regard to a specific referent. The two terms, signs (nonverbal) and symbols (verbal), are used to emphasize that communication is not dependent upon language. There is no intrinsic meaning in the color red, yet a red light as part of a traffic signal means that one must stop; but when used as a running light on a boat, red indicates the port side. Likewise, silence on the part of a supervisor may express disapproval as effectively as a dozen words. Status in an organization is conveyed almost entirely by signs; for example, a carpeted office, special parking privileges, punching a time clock, and the hour at which one reports for work all designate status.

Note that the base of the triangle is a dotted line and that the two sides of the triangle are solid. There is a direct relationship between the referent that calls up a certain thought and between the thought and the symbol used in its expression. Similarly, there is a direct relationship between symbol and thought and between thought and referent. There is, however, no such direct relationship between the label (symbol) and the object itself. The label, either a sign or a word, is *not* the object; it is used only to identify a specific object. Labels are arbitrary, and to be meaningful they must establish the same reference (thought) in both the sender and the receiver of a communication. Yet, one of the commonest causes of misunderstanding results from filling in the base of the triangle and assuming that the label is the referent. Loyalty oaths are a good example of filling in the base of the triangle. The act of signing an oath does not make one loyal; yet, the assumption underlying such oaths is an identity between loyalty and the act of signing an oath.

Verbal symbols vary considerably in respect to their value as tools for communication. All words are abstractions; they are not the object or event itself. As words become more abstract; i.e., further removed from the specific object or event, their meanings become more difficult to transmit and their value as instruments for communication decreases. Words as names of things may be classified as follows:

1. *Names for objects* are a table, a chair, a milling machine, a lathe, an automobile, a truck, a machinist, and a clerk. When naming an object, we are at a relatively low level of abstraction, and there should not be too much misunderstanding since the referent may be seen and touched, and its characteristics detailed with a high degree of accuracy.

2. *Events* are more complex in their nature since action and time, in addition to an object, are implied. A table turning over, a milling machine cutting metal, a moving automobile, and a machinist reporting late for work are all statements of events—something happening to a specific object at a specified time.

3. Labels may be used to designate *clusters*, *groups*, or *collections of objects or events* composed of elements that have varying degrees of similarity. We refer to furniture, machine tools, motor vehicles, and employees.

4. At the highest level of abstraction, the referent may not be an object or event at all; instead, the referent is an *essence* or *value judgment* of an object or event. The furniture is described as beautiful, machine tools are valuable, motor vehicles are either necessities or luxuries, and the employee is lazy (the machinist reported late for work). Also in this category of high-order abstractions are such labels as democracy, free enterprise, truth, and honesty.

Reference and Referent. There are at least two persons involved in communication—a sender and a receiver. Symbols should create within the receiver a thought process (call it a mental image, if you wish) that leads him down the right-hand side of the triangle to the desired referent. Conversation has been described as the art of saying something when there is nothing to be said. In contrast, communication is saying something when there is something to be said and saying it clearly. The purpose of communication is to influence the behavior of

another person. Behavioral changes may consist of additional knowledge, a change in attitude, or action on the part of the receiver. Conversation takes place almost entirely on the left side of the triangle, from
symbol to thought and back to another symbol again. There is no need
for a common meaning between sender and receiver because the purpose
of conversation is merely to occupy time. In communication, however,
there is a purpose; and in order for the intended meaning to reach
the receiver, both sender and receiver must travel the same route around
the triangle from symbol, to reference, to referent.

A Semantic Analysis

A great deal can be told about how much meaning is transmitted
through a given communication by answering these questions:

1. What is the purpose of the communication?
2. Do the symbols used by the sender have a precise meaning understandable to the receiver?

Let us ask these two questions in our semantic analysis of Case Problem 17-A, A Message for Management. At the same time we must keep
in mind the triangle of meaning—symbol, reference, and referent.

What Is the Purpose of the Communication? Before there can be
any communication, the sender must determine the purpose of the communication. Why has John Thurman called his department heads together? In the first paragraph of his talk, he states that he has called
them together to explain "our dire economic situation." He closes his
opening remarks with the statement that he is going to explain what he
means. Apparently, Thurman is trying to state four things that the
company needs in order to survive the dire economic situation. These
needs are imagineering, which he does not define; instead, he talks about
cost reduction. The second need is quality, the third is beefing up the
sales force, and the last is teamwork. The conclusion is inescapable;
Thurman is not sure of what he wants to say or why he wants to explain
an economic condition to his department heads.

The purpose of the meeting is not to explain; instead, it is to influence or modify the behavior of the department heads—to direct their
actions so that the company may make a profit and at the same time
lower the prices of its product to the level established by competition.
Information concerning the actions of competitors and the development
of attitudes resulting in teamwork and effective leadership are necessary

if management is to do its job well. The purpose of the meeting is to change behavior.

Do the Symbols Have a Precise Meaning for the Receiver? Look at the first paragraph of Thurman's speech again. It is filled with abstractions having no precise meaning. He starts with a high-order abstraction, "dire economic situation," and does not bother to define what he means. Somehow he manages to drag into his remarks "the bulwarks of free enterprise," again without definition. Further, his use of metaphors indicates that he is not thinking clearly. How can he be "face to face with wolves snapping at his heels?" Prices are too low, but what does too low mean? If the delivery schedules are utterly impossible, how does the company manage to stay in business? The remainder of his talk is nothing but a collection of worn-out, meaningless words and phrases. What is "imagineering"? What is "positive thinking"? Are they going to play on the same team or are they working for the same company? What does he mean by "beefing up" the sales force? Does he want the salesmen to gain weight? Is leadership teamwork? If so, leadership is striving and straining for the same goals. How does one simultaneously "put his shoulder to the wheel" and "wrap up a ball of wax"?

John Thurman is having a wonderful time running up and down the left-hand side of the triangle—from symbol to reference and back to symbol without once attempting to go down the right-hand side of the triangle to a common referent. To some of you, Thurman's *Message for Management* may seem overdrawn and exaggerated. It is not. It is hoped that you will not have to sit through many such meetings as a member of management and that you *never* conduct a meeting as John Thurman did. Remember this case as an example of how *not* to communicate.

The above analysis of A Message for Management answers two questions. When the questions are recast as statements, they form a guide for effective communication.

For effective communication the sender must determine the purpose of the communication and use symbols having the same meaning for sender and receiver.

The following guides are presented to aid in developing effective communication:

1. Determine and state the purpose of the communication.
2. Develop a plan of presentation. Consider the information to be transmitted and the interests and abilities of the receiver.

3. Eliminate unnecessary words.
4. Use words known to the receiver. Establish the meaning of abstractions by referring to objects and events within the experience range of the receiver.[2]

FORMAL COMMUNICATIONS

Although the transmission of intended meaning is the central problem in formal communications, there are areas other than the lack of agreement on intended meaning that contribute to communication problems. Discussed first is the problem of determining the amount and kind of information needed for the managerial functions of planning and control. Another source of difficulty in formal communications is that all too often managers are not aware of the media available for communications; hence, a brief analysis of commonly used media is presented.

Communication and Information Systems

In Chapter 7, "Management Information Systems," the functions and characteristics of information systems are discussed. Case Problem 7-A, The Parable of the Spindle, describes an information system used in a restaurant and shows the positive relationship between system design and effective communication. Prior to the introduction of the spindle there was a complete breakdown in communications. Steps in the design of an integrated data processing (IDP) system and the functioning of an IDP system are illustrated by the experience of Westinghouse in Case Problem 7-B, The Short-Order Economy. Although the

---

[2] It is beyond the scope of this book to develop a manual of style. The following references are presented for the student who wants additional help in improving his ability to express his thoughts clearly:

George Orwell, "Politics and English Language," from *Shooting an Elephant and Other Essays* (New York: Harcourt, Brace and World, Inc., 1950). Reprinted in N. R. F. Maier, L. R. Hoffman, J. J. Hooven, and W. H. Read, *Superior-Subordinate Communication in Management* (New York: American Management Association, 1961), AMA Research Study 52, pp. 78-88. Mr. Orwell's essay is one of six presented in the AMA research study. Orwell presents six rules for clarity of expression and although his essay is concerned primarily with the language of politics, it is applicable to all subject matter. The annotations of George H. Hass provide many examples of hackneyed expressions used in business communications.

William Strunk, Jr., and E. B. White, *The Elements of Style* (New York: The MacMillan Company, 1959), pp. xiv and 71. This book should be in the personal library of every student of management. *The Elements of Style* deals with English usage and style. Professor Strunk had the book privately printed and for many years used it in his English classes at Cornell University. The 1959 edition, revised by E. B. White includes a chapter on how to write. *The Elements of Style*, dubbed "the little book" by Professor Strunk, reduces English rhetoric to 18 rules with examples of correct and incorrect usage to illustrate each rule.

emphasis in Chapter 7 is upon the concept and design of information systems, such systems must be considered as part of the communication process since their function is to transmit meaning. Of particular importance to management is securing and transmitting information for the functions of planning and control. The type of information needed for these functions is shown in Figure 17-2, Anatomy of Management Information.[3]

Planning Information. As shown in Figure 17-2, planning information comes from the environment, from competitors, and from internal sources. Environmental data include information about population level, trends, and the demographic characteristics of age, sex, and economic status. General economic factors such as price trends and predicted levels of consumer and capital goods expenditures are also reported. Although most environmental information is readily available, an interpretation of its meaning is necessary before the data can be used for management planning. In addition to determining the validity and reliability of information, there is a selective process, a matter of judgment and semantics, to determine the amount and type of information needed by the company. Wrong information or a false interpretation fed into a communication system leads to failure as quickly and surely as no information at all.

Sales personnel frequently furnish information about the present and future plans of competitors. The information may be presented in formal written reports, during sales meetings, or in conversation with an immediate superior. Information passed through the chain of command, whether it be written or oral, runs the risk of distortion as the result of superior-subordinate relationship. Quantitative data from internal sources relating to level of sales, costs, share of the market, and productivity may be developed for planning with a high degree of accuracy and minimum distortion; but nonquantitative internal information runs the same risk of distortion when passing through the superior-subordinate relationship. The subordinate may tell only what he believes his superior wants to hear, or the superior may hear only what he wishes to believe.

Control Information. Figure 17-2 classifies the types of control information as financial or nonfinancial data. In general, control data

---

[3] D. Ronald Daniel, "Management Information Crisis," *Harvard Business Review*, Vol. 39 (September-October, 1961), pp. 111-121. Figure 17-2 appears as Exhibit I on page 114. Mr. Daniel's discussion of information required for planning and control emphasizes the need for multiple sources and types of information. He presents the flow of information within the framework of a systems concept.

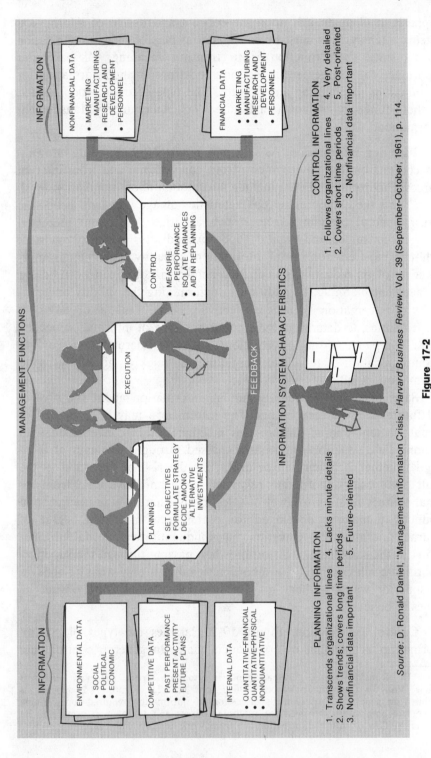

Figure 17-2
ANATOMY OF MANAGEMENT INFORMATION

Source: D. Ronald Daniel, "Management Information Crisis," *Harvard Business Review,* Vol. 39 (September-October, 1961), p. 114.

are more detailed than planning information, and this flow follows organizational lines. In order for information to be of use for control, it must be timely and accurate, requirements that call not only for the clarification of organizational lines of communication but also for the establishment of well-defined procedures and methods. Nonfinancial data from the areas of personnel, marketing, manufacturing, and research and development are often expressed as high-order abstractions with all the difficulties normally associated with the problem of assigning meaning to these symbols. Examples are the evaluation of the success of a labor-management relations program or determining the worth of a research and development project.

In small- and medium-size companies, the flow of management information is a manual process—a subordinate collecting, interpreting, and transmitting information to his superior and the superior asking his subordinate directly for information. Even when management information systems become as highly automated as the integrated data processing system of Westinghouse, determining the amount and type of information to be fed into the computer and determining the significance of the printed output are a process of attaching meaning to signs and symbols—a problem in communication.

Communication Media

Communication media within a company may be classified either in respect to the method used to transmit information or according to the directional flow of the communication. Using the means of transmission as a basis for classifying media, communications are either *written* or *oral*. When directional flow is the basis for classification—defining direction in terms of the organizational hierarchy—communications flow *downward, upward, horizontally,* and *diagonally.* Examples of written and oral communications are discussed briefly below.

Written Communications. Letters, memos, and reports are examples of written communications used to transmit information either downward, upward, or horizontally within an organization. Formal statements of policies, procedures, and methods are designed primarily for downward communications. Bulletin boards, house organs, annual reports, and handbooks are also directed downward. Written grievances, suggestion systems, and union publications serve as a means of upward communication. The information gained from attitude and morale surveys provides another means of directing information to higher levels of the organization. Letters and memos between department heads are examples of the horizontal or diagonal flow of communications. The distribution of carbon copies of written materials to all interested parties may be used as a means of directing information in several directions at one time.

Oral Communications. Even though a business may consume tons of paper during the course of a year in written communications, by far the greater percentage of information is transmitted by informal oral communications, either face to face or by telephone. Oral communications may involve as few as two people or as many as hundreds attending a training session or conference. All oral communication offers the potential of two-way information flow; and, depending on the relative organizational positions of the participants, the communication may be directed either vertically or horizontally. Most members of an organization prefer oral to written communications because they seem quicker and offer an immediate feedback in the form of questions and expressions of approval or disapproval. The advantages of speed and feedback may be more imagined than real, since oral messages are notoriously subject to misinterpretation and to the effects of barriers arising from interpersonal relationships.[4]

INTERPERSONAL COMMUNICATIONS

Thus far the discussion has been directed to one of the meanings of communication, the dissemination of information, with the emphasis upon the type of information needed. Interpersonal communications permit not only the transfer of information but also the expression of psychological needs and motives. Superior-subordinate communications are considered first with an assessment of the degree of understanding and the common barriers to effective communications that exist between superior and subordinate. Next, some of the problems encountered in horizontal communications are reviewed; and finally, the ubiquitous grapevine and its role is examined.

Superior-Subordinate Communication

It is generally assumed that superior-subordinate communication operates as a two-way information system permitting a free flow of information in an upward direction as well as downward. Yet, there are barriers in the superior-subordinate relationship that markedly interfere

---

[4] Keith Davis, "Success of Chain-of-Command Oral Communication in a Manufacturing Management Group," *Academy of Management Journal,* Vol. XI, No. 4 (December, 1968), pp. 379-387.

with the free two-way flow of information. Before discussing these barriers, it is well to determine the effectiveness of superior-subordinate
communication in a relatively objective and limited area—in relation
to a subordinate's job.

Superior-Subordinate Understanding. The American Management
Association conducted a statistical research project to determine the
extent of agreement between superior and subordinate concerning the
subordinate's specific job duties.[5] Fifty-eight superior-subordinate combinations from the upper management levels of five different companies
were selected for this study, and the information from both members of
each pair was obtained by patterned depth interviews. The following
specific areas of the subordinate's job were discussed:

1. Job duties—a descriptive statement of what the subordinate does in
   the performance of his job.
2. Job requirements—a statement of the skills, background, experience,
   formal training, and personal characteristics needed for the job.
3. Future changes in job duties—anticipated changes in either job
   duties or requirements that might be anticipated in the next several
   years.
4. Obstacles in the performance of the job—problems that interfere
   with getting the job done, as seen by the subordinate and as viewed
   by the superior.

The results of the study are presented in Table 17-1. An analysis
of Table 17-1 shows that 85 percent of the pairs interviewed agree on
one half or more of the subordinate's job duties (Columns 2, 3, 4), but
the extent of the agreement in respect to subordinate qualifications drops
to 63.7 percent. Only 53.3 percent of superiors and subordinates agree
upon anticipated changes in the subordinate's job within the next few
years. In interpreting the obstacles in the way of subordinate success,
68.2 percent showed either no agreement or agreement on less than half
of the obstacles. The following is a narrative summary of the study by
the authors:

> If a single answer can be drawn from this detailed research study
> into superior-subordinate communication on the managerial level in
> business, it is this: If one is speaking of the subordinate's specific job—
> his duties, the requirements he must fulfill in order to do his work well,

---

[5] Norman R. F. Maier, L. Richard Hoffman, John J. Hooven, and William H.
Reed, *Superior-Subordinate Communication in Management* (New York: American
Management Association, 1961), AMA Research Study 52. In addition to the presentation and interpretation of the statistical results of the study, there are six interpretative
comments on the project and its findings in Part 2 of the report.

his intelligent anticipation of future changes in his work, and the obstacles which prevent him from doing as good a job as is possible—the answer is that he and his boss do not agree, or differ more than they agree, in almost every area. Also, superior and subordinate very often disagree about priorities—they simply don't see eye to eye on which are the most important and the least important tasks for the subordinate.[6]

Table 17-1

COMPARATIVE AGREEMENT BETWEEN SUPERIOR-SUBORDINATE PAIRS ON BASIC AREAS OF THE SUBORDINATE'S JOB

	0 Almost No Agreement on Topics	1 Agreement on Less than Half the Topics	2 Agreement on About Half the Topics	3 Agreement on More Than Half the Topics	4 Agreement on All or Almost All Topics
Job Duties	3.4%	11.6%	39.1%	37.8%	8.1%
Job Requirement (Subordinate's Qualifications) ..	7.0%	29.3%	40.9%	20.5%	2.3%
Future Changes in Subordinate's Job	35.4%	14.3%	18.3%	16.3%	18.7%
Obstacles in the Way of Subordinate's Performance .	38.4%	29.8%	23.6%	6.4%	1.7%

Source: Norman R. F. Maier, L. Richard Hoffman, John J. Hooven, and William H. Read, *Superior-Subordinate Communication in Management* (New York: American Management Association, 1961), AMA Research Study, p. 10.

Barriers to Communication. The effect of communication barriers, whether they arise from semantic problems or from one of the specific superior-subordinate relationships discussed below, results in either a distortion of meaning because of embellishment or a filtering of information by suppression or withholding. Semantic barriers usually result in a distortion of meaning. Distortion also occurs as the result of introducing errors into a message. Filtering information results in only a part of the message getting through. Filtering of communications by either the sender or the receiver of the message may be intentional or unintentional. The following barriers are frequently found in superior-subordinate communications; nonetheless, it must be remembered that these same barriers may occur in any two-way personal communication.

SEMANTIC PROBLEMS. One barrier to communication, not limited to superior-subordinate relationships, is a semantic problem—determining

---
[6] *Ibid.*, p. 9.

a common referent and meaning for the symbols used in communication. In the research study described above, descriptions of the subordinate's job, of necessity, require the use of high-order abstractions. These are middle management jobs and, unlike operative jobs, they cannot be described as movements to be completed in a given sequence. Judgment, the interpretation of data, anticipation of future events, and skill in interpersonal relations are the important requisites for managerial jobs, and all of these characteristics are abstractions. Rudolf Flesch, in his comment on the study, believes that the problem of superior-subordinate communication as presented in Table 17-1 presents a somewhat exaggerated view of the inability of superior and subordinate to communicate effectively.[7] According to Flesch, who interpreted the same data, the lack of agreement is no greater than what might be expected when the subject is abstract and viewed from two entirely different positions; i.e., superior and subordinate. In brief, Flesch is saying that to some extent the results of the study are due to the methodology used in the study.

STATUS. Another barrier arises from the relative positions of the superior and subordinate in the organization. There is a strong tendency in formal organizations to express hierarchical rank through the use of signs known as status symbols. Status symbols within an organization, such as a better type of office furniture, may be deliberate as an attempt to reinforce the superior's position of authority. However, too much emphasis upon status may increase a subordinate's perception of organizational distance and consequently widen the communication gap between him and his superior.

PRESSURE OF TIME. In business organizations the pressure of time plays an important role as a communication barrier. The busy superior with many subordinates simply does not have the time to see all of them as frequently or to talk with them as fully as might be desired. Also, a busy subordinate does not have the time nor the inclination to report every detail of every problem to his superior. Supporting the subordinate's position is the concept of delegation. He has been assigned responsibilities, and the authority to fulfill these responsibilities has been delegated. In addition, he is accountable to his superior. One might argue quite properly that as the effectiveness of the process of delegation increases, the need for detailed communication between superior and subordinate decreases. The pressure of time and the presence of an

---

[7] *Ibid.*, "Is the Problem Exaggerated?" pp. 60-67. Mr. Flesch discusses the results of the study as a semantic problem.

effective delegation process may decrease the amount and frequency of superior-subordinate communication; but even so, communication may be more than adequate because information necessary for the operation of the business is being transmitted.

VALUE JUDGMENTS. Making value judgments of a message prior to receiving the entire communication interferes with receiving the intended meaning of the message. A value judgment is the assignment of overall worth to a message and may be based upon its origin, its reliability, or its anticipated meaning. When value judgments are made too hastily, the receiver hears only that part of the message that he wishes to hear. Closely related to hearing only selected parts of a message is the lack of sensitivity to the emotional content of the communication, which is often reflected by the mannerisms and tone of voice of the sender. In many instances the real message is conveyed not by the words of the sender, but by the emotions and feelings accompanying his expression of the message.

SUBORDINATE'S MOBILITY. A specific characteristic of the superior-subordinate relationship is the dependency of the subordinate upon his superior for advancement within the organization, either more pay for his present job or attaining a higher position. A study by Read supports the hypothesis that the more a subordinate desires to advance in an organization, the more he tends to filter by selecting the information he sends upward to his boss.[8] If he desires to advance, he passes upward only the good news and the positive aspects of his achievement and suppresses (filters) the problem-oriented aspects of his work. However, Read does report that the amount and nature of the information transmitted upward, even by the subordinate strongly desiring advancement, is influenced greatly by the degree of trust that he has in his superior and the extent to which he perceives the influence of his superior. As trust in the judgment and understanding of his superior increases, and as the perceived influence of the superior on the subordinate's advancement becomes greater, the amount of problem-oriented information communicated upward increases.

Horizontal Communication

Traditional organization theory with its concepts of line authority and the chain of command emphasizes vertical lines of communication

---

[8] William H. Read, "Upward Communication in Industrial Hierarchies," *Human Relations*, Vol. XV (February, 1962), pp. 3-15.

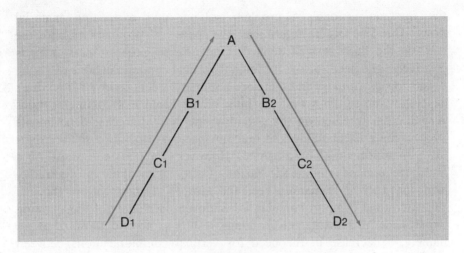

Figure 17-3
TRADITIONAL VERTICAL COMMUNICATION

between superior and subordinate. Figure 17-3 shows in schematic form the transmission of a message from D_1, foreman of production department 1, to D_2, foreman of production department 2, using the chain of command as a channel of communication. The advantage claimed for this formalized line of communication is that A, who is responsible for both production departments, is better able to coordinate the functioning of the two departments when he is fully informed of the activities of each department. The obvious disadvantages of following these formal lines of communication are the amount of time taken to transmit a message, the increased risk of error and distortion, and the loss of flexibility necessary to meet emergencies. The extent to which an organization insists that its lines of communication conform to the organizational lines of authority depend to a large extent on the technology of that organization. Failure to recognize communication needs arising from and depending on technology often results in poor communications.[9]

There are several empirical studies that show the need for horizontal and diagonal communications between first-line supervisors as a function of the technology, or method, of production. In a study of an automobile assembly line, Blau finds that the role of

---

[9] Frank J. Jasinski, "Adapting Organizations to New Technology," *Harvard Business Review*, Vol. 37 (January-February, 1959), pp. 79-86. Although Mr. Jasinski's article is concerned primarily with the adaptation of organizations to technology, much of what he writes is also applicable to the need for adapting communications to technology.

the foreman is one of problem solving and expediting material flow. The line itself determines the pace of production, and the jobs on the line are well defined. Under these circumstances there is relatively little need for the traditional vertical communications of giving orders to subordinates and there are not many orders received from one's superior. The result is that the bulk of the foreman's communications is with other foremen on the assembly line and with other departments such as material handling and maintenance.[10] All of these relationships are either horizontal or diagonal. However, Faunce in a study of a highly automated automobile factory finds, in an apparent contradiction, that there is a marked need for vertical communications through the traditional chain of command.[11] Simpson, in a study of the spinning department of a textile mill, obtains results similar to those of Blau; namely, a decrease in the need for vertical communications between superior and subordinate and an increase in the need for communications between supervisors on the same level.[12] In Simpson's study, the primary direct communication between the general foreman of the department and his subordinate foremen consists of a written message stating the type and amount of material to be produced on each machine for each shift.

Simpson also resolves the apparent discrepancy between his findings, similar to those of Blau, and the findings of Faunce. He describes three broad types of technology used in production and suggests that the relative need for vertical or horizontal communication is determined by the technology. First, in unmechanized operations there is a relatively greater need for vertical communications than there is for horizontal communications. In this situation the various production departments are relatively independent, and the amount of work produced is determined by the effectiveness of the supervisor of the department. The manager responsible for coordinating the work of all departments needs detailed information from each supervisor. Second, when technology is characterized by mechanization, such as a textile mill or an automobile assembly line, separate departments are bound together by that technology. The success of the foreman of an assembly line depends on the right part arriving at a certain place in the line at a scheduled time and on the reliable functioning of the tools used in production.

---

[10] Peter M. Blau, "Formal Organization: Dimension of Analysis," *American Journal of Sociology*, Vol. LXII (July, 1957), pp. 58-59.

[11] William A. Faunce, "Automation in the Automobile Industry," *American Sociological Review*, Vol. 23 (August, 1958), pp. 401-407.

[12] Richard L. Simpson, "Vertical and Horizontal Communication in Formal Organizations," *Administrative Science Quarterly*, Vol. IV (December, 1959), pp. 188-196.

Providing the necessary parts for assembly is the function of the production control and material handling departments, and the proper operation of the tools for production is the function of the maintenance department. Rate of output is determined by the speed of the assembly line or other automatic equipment. Under these circumstances the need for horizontal communications among the foremen of the various departments increases. Third, in highly automated plants where the breakdown of a single machine may result in the shutdown of all production facilities, the need for control becomes greater and the need for vertical communications also increases.

In summary, no mechanization or a low degree of mechanization emphasizes vertical communications; moderate mechanization (such as the assembly line) requires a greater emphasis upon horizontal communications; and highly automated production facilities reestablish the need for vertical communications.

The Grapevine

Our discussion of the problems of communication has been directed toward formal channels and methods of communication. It is necessary for management to recognize that there are also informal methods of communication that may be far more effective in some respects than the formal means of transmitting information. An informal system of communication is generally referred to as the *grapevine*. As the name suggests, the grapevine is entwined throughout the entire organization with branches going in all directions, thereby short-circuiting formal vertical and horizontal channels.

Two characteristics of communications via the grapevine are noted by those who have studied it. First, the grapevine is often an exceedingly rapid form of communication; and second, the information transmitted is frequently subjected to a great deal of distortion. Formal channels of communication, particularly those following the vertical chain of command, usually pass information from one person to another—a time-consuming process. In contrast, the grapevine transmits information along a pathway described as a *cluster chain*.[13] Instead of passing information from one person to another, as in superior-subordinate communication, information is passed to a group of three or four persons, and from this initial link in the cluster chain, one or two individuals

---

[13] Keith Davis, "Communication Within Management," *Personnel*, Vol. XXXI (November, 1954), pp. 212-217. In this article Professor Davis discusses a method of communication analysis and applies the method to the communications of one company. He also discusses the characteristics of the grapevine in management communications.

inform other groups. Thus, there is an ever-increasing rate in the flow of information. In part, this is due to the makeup of the grapevine; people who work near each other or whose work regularly brings them in contact with others are frequently on the same grapevine. The grapevine that includes the mail clerk, the switchboard operator, or any other person whose work requires contact with several groups transmits information much more quickly than formal channels of communication. Another factor encouraging rapid communication is that the information carried by the grapevine reflects the interests and personal concerns of its members; for example, news of an impending layoff, an increase in pay, or news about other people.

The grapevine is notorious for distorting information, so much so that information received from this source is often referred to as rumor. In the discussion of superior-subordinate communications, the filtering of information—passing on only certain parts of a message—is mentioned as one of the causes of distortion. The grapevine information at its source is often fragmentary and incomplete, with the result that there is a strong tendency to fill in the missing parts. Since the grapevine is informal, there are no formal lines of accountability. Consequently, a member of the grapevine does not have to answer to his superior for any misstatement of facts. Further, the elaboration of a fragment of news into a full-blown story offers to some people an opportunity to express feelings of self-importance and to compensate for feelings of insecurity.

The characteristics of the grapevine are summarized by Davis as follows:

1. People talk most when the news is recent.
2. People talk about things that affect their work.
3. People talk about people they know.
4. People working near each other are likely to be on the same grapevine.
5. People who contact each other in the chain of procedure tend to be on the same grapevine.[14]

IMPROVING COMMUNICATIONS

There are two approaches available for the improvement of communications. The first of these approaches is from the point of view of the sender of the message. Recognize the purpose of the communication, the significance of the symbols used, the organizational lines through which the communication travels, and its possible

---

[14] *Ibid.*, p. 212.

effect on the receiver. These and other ways of improving one's ability to communicate clearly as a sender of messages are discussed below as ten general rules for improving communications. The last of these rules states that in order to achieve effective communication it is necessary to learn how to listen. It is a listening to the feelings and emotional content of messages expressed by others as well as being able to understand the factual information that is being presented. The process of learning how to detect the emotional content of communications is discussed under the heading, *empathetic listening*.

Rules for Improving Communications

The American Management Association refers to the following rules as the Ten Commandments of Good Communication:

1. *Seek to clarify your ideas before communicating.* The more systematically we analyze the problem or idea to be communicated, the clearer it becomes this is the first step toward effective communication. Many communications fail because of inadequate planning. Good planning must consider the goals and attitudes of those who will receive the communications and those who will be affected by it.

2. *Examine the true purpose of each communication.* Before you communicate, ask yourself what you really want to accomplish with your message—obtain information, initiate action, change another person's attitude? Identify your most important goal and then adapt your language, tone, and total approach to serve that specific objective. Don't try to accomplish too much with each communication. The sharper the focus of your message the greater its chances of success.

3. *Consider the total physical and human setting whenever you communicate.* Meaning and intent are conveyed by more than words alone. Many other factors influence the overall impact of a communication, and the manager must be sensitive to the total setting in which he communicates. Consider, for example, your sense of timing—i.e., the circumstances under which you make an announcement or render a decision; the physical setting—whether you communicate in private, for example, or otherwise; the social climate that pervades work relationships within the company or a department and sets the tone of its communications; custom and past practice—the degree to which your communication conforms to, or departs from, the expectations of your audience. Be constantly aware of the total setting in which you communicate. Like all living things, communication must be capable of adapting to its environment.

4. *Consult with others, where appropriate, in planning communications.* Frequently it is desirable or necessary to seek the participation of others in planning a communication or developing the facts on which to base it. Such consultation often helps to lend additional insight and objectivity to your message. Moreover, those who have helped you plan your communication will give it their support.

5. *Be mindful, while you communicate, of the overtones as well as the basic content of your message.* Your tone of voice, your expression, your apparent receptiveness to the responses of others—all have tremendous impact on those you wish to reach. Frequently overlooked, these subtleties of communication often affect a listener's reaction to a message even more than its basic content. Similarly, your choice of language—particularly your awareness of the fine shades of meaning and emotion in the words you use—predetermines in large part the reactions of your listeners.

6. *Take the opportunity, when it arises, to convey something of help or value to the receiver.* Consideration of the other person's interests and needs—the habit of trying to look at things from his point of view—will frequently point up opportunities to convey something of immediate benefit or long-range value to him. People on the job are most responsive to the manager whose messages take their own interests into account.

7. *Follow up your communication.* Our best efforts at communication may be wasted, and we may never know whether we have succeeded in expressing our true meaning and intent, if we do not follow up to see how well we have put our message across. This you can do by asking questions, by encouraging the receiver to express his reactions, by follow-up contacts, by subsequent review of performance. Make certain that every important communication has a "feed-back" so that complete understanding and appropriate action result.

8. *Communicate for tomorrow as well as today.* While communications may be aimed primarily at meeting the demands of an immediate situation, they must be planned with the past in mind if they are to maintain consistency in the receiver's view; but, most important of all, they must be consistent with long-range interests and goals. For example, it is not easy to communicate frankly on such matters as poor performance or the shortcomings of a loyal subordinate—but postponing disagreeable communications makes them more difficult in the long run and is actually unfair to your subordinates and your company.

9. *Be sure your actions support your communications.* In the final analysis, the most persuasive kind of communication is not what

you say but what you do. When a man's actions or attitudes contradict his words, we tend to discount what he has said. For every manager this means that good supervisory practices—such as clear assignment of responsibility and authority, fair rewards for effort, and sound policy enforcement—serve to communicate more than all the gifts of oratory.

10. *Last, but by no means least: Seek not only to be understood but to understand—be a good listener.* When we start talking we often cease to listen—in that larger sense of being attuned to the other person's unspoken reactions and attitudes. Even more serious is the fact that we are all guilty, at times, of inattentiveness when others are attempting to communicate to us. Listening is one of the most important, most difficult—and most neglected—skills in communication. It demands that we concentrate not only on the explicit meanings another person is expressing, but on the implicit meanings, unspoken words, and undertones that may be far more significant. Thus we must learn to listen with the inner ear if we are to know the inner man.[15]

Empathetic Listening

The tenth rule admonishes us to listen to others—listen to the explicit meaning and also the implicit meaning. Explicit meaning is conveyed by the meaning of the words used by the sender; and in order to understand, it is necessary that we pay careful attention to what is being said.[16] However, we must also listen with the "inner ear" if we are to hear the "inner man." Hearing the inner man, the implicit meanings of the message, calls for *empathy*—the ability to put oneself in the other person's place, to assume his role, his viewpoint, and his emotions. *Empathetic listening* is hearing and understanding the emotional content, the feelings, and the mood of the other person. Empathetic listening requires a special technique of listening.

Case Problem 17-B, A Case of Misunderstanding, should be read now, for it is the basis of our discussion of empathetic listening. As stated in the third paragraph of the case, we do not know exactly what Hart, the foreman, said to Bing, the workman. We do know what each said to the personnel representative. With this information, let us reconstruct the conversation between Hart and Bing.

---

15 "Ten Commandments of Good Communication," (New York: American Management Association, Copyright, 1955).

16 Ralph G. Nichols, "Listening Is Good Business," *Management of Personnel Quarterly,* Vol. I (Winter, 1962), pp. 2-9. Professor Nichols discusses ten bad habits of listening and suggests the positive steps that should be taken to overcome these bad habits. He also touches slightly upon the problem of emphatic listening.

Hart: "Bing, I want to talk to you."

Bing: "Yeah?"

Hart: "Listen, why don't you try to get along here like other people do for a change?"

Bing: "How?"

Hart: "Well, for one thing, stop deliberately upsetting this department by going to lunch early and asking others to go with you."

Bing: "I haven't been to lunch early for a week."

Hart: "You have, too. And another thing, I want you to stop carrying three panels at one time over to your bench for inspection—you know the rules on that."

Bing: "That's what I want to talk to you about. I've got an idea . . ."

Hart: "Never mind your ideas, just follow the rules and you'll get along better."

Bing: "I want a transfer."

Hart: "We'll see about that. In the meantime, stop singing around here. What do you think this is, a nightclub, and you're Frank Sinatra?"

The above conversation and the comments made by Hart and Bing to the personnel representative show quite clearly that Hart is not listening to Bing. It appears that he is more interested in telling Bing off than he is in trying to determine the reasons for Bing's behavior. Hart is *not* using the techniques of empathetic listening. Without empathetic listening there cannot be two-way communication.

Listen with Understanding. Empathetic listening as a part of two-way personal communications is a concept borrowed from the methods of nondirective psychotherapy that have been highly developed by Dr. Carl Rogers.[17] In this form of psychotherapy the role of the therapist is one of encouraging not only good communications between himself and the patient, but also good communications within the patient himself. The patient must learn how to express himself and have the opportunity for that expression. Although a foreman and other members of management are not therapists, if they are to have successful two-way communications with another, that other person must have the

---

[17] Carl R. Rogers and F. J. Roethlisberger, "Barrier and Gateways to Communications," *Harvard Business Review*, Vol. 30 (July-August, 1952), pp. 46-52. The first part of the article is written by Dr. Rogers, who suggests that the major barrier to communication is the tendency to evaluate and that the main gateway to communication is listening with understanding. In the second part of the article, Dr. Roethlisberger analyzes a communications situation and suggests positive steps that may be taken to improve communications.

For a full discussion of Dr. Roger's views on therapy, see: Carl R. Rogers, *Client-Centered Therapy* (Boston: Houghton Mifflin Company, 1953).

opportunity to express himself. In order to encourage such expression, nondirective techniques are employed. The one conducting the interview encourages the expression of the feelings, emotions, and desires behind the words of the other person. In order to do this he listens—he does not talk. In the conversation above, Hart does most of the talking, not Bing. If he were listening with understanding, his comments would have been designed to encourage Bing to talk and the following conversation might have occurred:

Hart: "Bing, I want to talk to you."
Bing: "Yeah?"
Hart: "I've noticed that you have been carrying three panels over to your bench for inspection. Do you have a new idea for a methods change?"
Bing: "Well, maybe."
Hart: "Um-hum."
Bing: "Well, maybe it won't work all the time, but with these smaller panels there is no reason why three of them can't be carried at once."

With this approach to communication, Hart is encouraging Bing to talk, not to defend himself. The problems caused by his leaving for lunch early and his singing may be explored in the same easy manner.

Guides for Listening. The following guides for empathetic listening have been found to be as effective in industrial settings as in their original clinical setting.

1. *Avoid Making Value Judgments.* Value judgments are global in nature and made from the point of view of the listener, not from the frame of reference of the person doing the talking. Such judgments place a single value—good or bad, desirable or undesirable, true or false—on a series of complex statements, each of which varies considerably in respect to any given characteristic. In addition, the origin of value judgments is often derived from an earlier judgment of the source of the statement. How can Bing say anything worthwhile to Hart when he is prejudged by Hart as being mentally deficient and a sow's ear? Once the value judgment is made, the mind is closed and it becomes impossible to understand the other's point of view.

2. *Listen to the Full Story.* In the first interview, Bing started to say that he has an idea, but is stopped abruptly by Hart. In order to understand, listen to the whole story. Time is a critical factor in empathetic listening, and arrangements must be made for adequate time and a place where there will be no interruptions. Ask the other

person to be seated; if he smokes, offer him a cigarette. Do everything you can to put the other person at ease.

3. *Recognize Feelings and Emotions.* Remember, empathetic listening is putting yourself in the position of the other person. Try to pinpoint the meaning of the feelings and emotions behind the statements being made, rather than the meaning of the words being said. Look for signs of eagerness, hesitancy, hostility, anxiety, or depression. At the same time watch for evasions, the things left unsaid, or areas of discussion consistently avoided.

4. *Restate the Other's Position.* As a test of your understanding, restate the other person's statement from his point of view, not yours. For example, Hart might say, "You believe that I'm watching you like a hawk, treating you like a naughty kid, and as a result you feel like a marked man." Imagine the change in Hart's behavior if he can make the statement above with the same feeling that Bing would put into it.

5. *Question with Care.* The simplest way to keep the conversation going is to use the noncommittal "um-hum." If this is insufficient, phrases such as "and then what happened" or "what did you do" may start the story again. Occasionally restatements such as the one mentioned in (4) may be rephrased as questions. Avoid argumentative statements such as "that isn't true" or "I don't believe you." These statements not only cause you to lose your objectivity and become emotionally involved, but also put the other person on the defensive, thus making it impossible for him to express his true feelings.

The guides for empathetic listening are relatively easy to remember; however, their application requires a skill that may take years to develop. As a manager you will have to develop these skills to achieve two-way communication. Solving the problems for Case Problem 17-B [18] is the first step in learning the techniques of emphathetic listening and effective communicating.

CASE PROBLEM	In a department of a large industrial organization,
17-B	there were seven workers (four men and three women)
A CASE OF MIS-	engaged in testing and inspecting panels of electronic
UNDERSTANDING	equipment. In this department one of the workers, Bing,

---

[18] F. J. Roethlisberger, "The Administrator's Skill: Communication," *Harvard Business Review,* Vol. 31 (November-December, 1953), pp. 55-57. Reproduced by permission of *Harvard Business Review.* This case (names and places disguised) is adapted from a case in the files of the Harvard Graduate School of Business Administration.

was having trouble with his immediate superior, Hart, who had formerly been a worker in the department.

Had we been observers in this department we would have seen Bing carrying two or three panels at a time from the racks where they were stored to the bench where he inspected them together. For this activity we would have seen him charging double or triple setup time. We would have heard him occasionally singing at work. Also, we would have seen him usually leaving his work position a few minutes early to go to lunch, and noticed that other employees sometimes accompanied him. And had we been present at one specific occasion, we would have heard Hart telling Bing that he disapproved of these activities and that he wanted Bing to stop doing them.

However, not being present to hear the actual verbal exchange that took place in this interaction, let us note what Bing and Hart said to a personnel representative.

WHAT BING SAID

In talking about his practice of charging double or triple setup time for panels which he inspected all at one time, Bing said:

"This is a perfectly legal thing to do. We've always been doing it. Mr. Hart, the supervisor, has other ideas about it, though; he claims it's cheating the company. He came over to the bench a day or two ago and let me know just how he felt about the matter. Boy, did we go at it! It wasn't so much the fact that he called me down on it, but more the way in which he did it. . . . I've never seen anyone like him. He's not content just to say in a manlike way what's on his mind, but he prefers to do it in a way that makes you want to crawl inside a crack on the floor. What a guy! I don't mind being called down by a supervisor, but I like to be treated like a man, and not humiliated like a school teacher does a naughty kid. He's been pulling this stuff ever since he's been . . . promoted, he's lost his friendly way and seems to be having some difficulty in knowing how to manage us employees. He's a changed man over what he used to be like when he was a worker on the bench with us several years ago.

"When he pulled this kind of stuff on me the other day, I got so damn mad I called in the union representative. I knew that the thing I was doing was permitted by the contract, but I was intent on making some trouble for Mr. Hart, just because he persists in this sarcastic way of handling me. I am about fed up with the whole damn situation. I'm trying every means I can to get myself transferred out of his group. . . . He's not going to pull this kind of kid stuff any longer on me. When the union representative questioned him on the case, he finally had to back down, because according to the contract an employee can use any time-saving method or device in order to speed up the process as long as the quality standards of the job are met.

"You see, he knows that I do professional singing on the outside. He hears me singing here on the job, and he hears the people talking about my career in music. I guess he figures I can be so cocky because I have another means of earning some money. Actually, the employees here enjoy having me sing while we work, but he thinks I'm disturbing them and causing them to 'goof off' from their work. Occasionally, I leave the job a few minutes early and go down to the washroom to wash up before lunch. Sometimes several others in the group will accompany me, and so Mr. Hart automatically thinks I'm the leader and usually bawls me out for the whole thing.

"So, you can see, I'm a marked man around here. He keeps watching me like a hawk. Naturally, this makes me very uncomfortable. That's why I'm sure a transfer would be the best thing. I've asked him for it, but he didn't give me any satisfaction at the time. While I remain here, I'm going to keep my nose clean, but whenever I get the chance, I'm going to slip it to him, but good."

WHAT HART SAID

Here, on the other hand, is what Hart told the personnel representative:

"Say, I think you should be in on this. My dear little friend, Bing, is heading himself into a showdown with me. Recently it was brought to my attention that Bing has been taking double and triple setup time for panels which he is actually inspecting at one time. In effect, that's cheating, and I've called him down on it several times before. A few days ago it was brought to my attention again, and so this time I really let him have it in no uncertain terms. He's been getting away with this for too

long and I'm going to put an end to it once and for all.
I know he didn't like my calling him on it because a few
hours later he had the union representative breathing
down my back. Well, anyway, I let them both know I'll
not tolerate the practice any longer, and I let Bing know
that if he continues to do this kind of thing, I'm going to
take official action with my boss to have the guy fired
or penalized somehow. This kind of thing has to be
curbed. Actually, I'm inclined to think the guy's mentally
deficient, because talking to him has actually no meaning
to him whatsoever. I've tried just about every approach
to jar some sense into that guy's head, and I've just about
given it up as a bad deal.

"I don't know what it is about the guy, but I think
he's harboring some deep feelings against me. For what,
I don't know, because I've tried to handle that bird with
kid gloves. But his whole attitude around here on the job
is one of indifference, and he certainly isn't a good influence on the rest of my group. Frankly, I think he pur-
posely tries to agitate them against me at times, too.
It seems to me he may be suffering from illusions of
grandeur, because all he does all day long is sit over
there and croon his fool head off. Thinks he's a Frank
Sinatra! No kidding! I understand he takes singing lessons
and he's working with some of the local bands in the city.
All of which is o.k. by me; but when his outside interests
start interfering with his efficiency on the job, then I've
got to start paying closer attention to the situation. For
this reason I've been keeping my eye on that bird and if he
steps out of line any more, he and I are going to part ways.

"You know there's an old saying, 'You can't make
a purse out of a sow's ear.' The guy is simply unscrupu-
lous. He feels no obligation to do a real day's work.
Yet I know the guy can do a good job, because for a
long time he did. But in recent months he's slipped, for
some reason, and his whole attitude on the job has
changed. Why, it's even getting to the point now where
I think he's inducing other employees to 'goof off' a few
minutes before the lunch whistle and go down to the
washroom and clean up on company time. I've called
him on it several times, but words just don't seem to make
any lasting impression on him. Well, if he keeps it up
much longer, he's going to find himself on the way out.
He's asked me for a transfer, so I know he wants to go.

But I didn't give him an answer when he asked me, because I was steaming mad at the time, and I may have told him to go somewhere else."

PROBLEMS

1. Based upon Hart's (and Bing's) report to the personnel supervisor, what are the factors that would make empathetic listening difficult for Hart to achieve?
2. Reconstruct in full the conversation as it probably occurred.
3. Reconstruct in full an interview between Bing and Hart utilizing the techniques of empathetic listening.
4. Discuss Bing's responsibility to listen empathetically to Hart.

Chapter Questions for Study and Discussion

1. Explain in your own words the triangle of meaning. Why is it important that the triangle have a dotted line for its base?
2. What are some of the things transmitted by an oral face-to-face message other than facts descriptive of a situation? Can these other things be transmitted as effectively in written form? Discuss.
3. Does highly effective and efficient communication between people eliminate conflict between them? If not, why not?
4. Why is conversation not necessarily communication?
5. Why are superior-subordinate communications more susceptible to certain types of communication problems than communication between two persons on the same organizational level?
6. Differentiate between embellishment and filtering. Are communications directed downward in an organization likely to be filtered or embellished? Explain.
7. Develop an argument that supports the thesis that sound processes of delegation minimize the need for face-to-face communication between superior and subordinate.
8. What are the major differences between planning information and control information? Is a discussion of this type of information properly a subject for communications? Why?
9. Develop several examples showing how the technology of the organization influences the need for and the type of formal communications.
10. How can the grapevine be used effectively as a communications device?
11. Since communication is primarily the sending of a message, why is it necessary to be able to listen empathetically?
12. What is meant by a value judgment? Why are value judgments often barriers to effective communication?

CHAPTER 18

Motivating Employees

Acme Manufacturing Company, located in an eastern metropolitan area, produces a complete line of small household electrical appliances such as toasters, blenders, coffee percolators, and electric can openers. The products are of good quality and are distributed through department stores and mail-order houses under private labels. The small fractional horsepower motors and heating elements used in the products are purchased; however, the company does its own stamping, machining, plating, painting, and assembly. Two hundred hourly paid workers perform these operations.

The personnel policies of Acme Manufacturing are not stated in writing, nor is there an employee handbook. The company conducts an annual wage survey and maintains its wage level at the average of the area for similar jobs. There has not been the same effort to maintain fringe benefits at a competitive level. Surveys concerning employee benefits are not conducted on a regular basis, the last survey having been completed about five years ago. The company never conducted an attitude or morale survey.

John Rider, the general manager, is somewhat puzzled by one aspect of the monthly personnel department activity report. For the second successive month there are 10 production jobs to be filled. To the best of his knowledge there have been no changes in production schedules, nor has he authorized any additional factory personnel. Consequently, Rider wonders why the 10 openings exist. He has called the personnel manager to determine the reasons for the vacancies.

As the personnel manager, Frank Stevens, entered his office, Mr. Rider said, "Frank, I notice that for the second straight month we have 10 vacancies in our plant labor force. If this rate of turnover continues, we will be replacing over half of our labor force within a year. What is the reason for our hiring so many new employees?"

"Part of the reason is that we still have four vacancies to be filled from the preceding month, and the other six are vacancies created by employees with less than six months' service who quit last month," Frank answered.

"About the four jobs remaining from last month, why haven't we filled them?"

"Well, these are all skilled jobs. Even so, we managed to hire two people, but they didn't report for work. Both called and said that they had taken better jobs somewhere else."

"Do you know where they went to work?" Rider asked.

"Yes, and neither company has a higher wage rate than we have." Anticipating the next question, Stevens continued, "The only reason for their going to these other companies is that they offer better employee benefits than we do; and in a tight labor market like the one we have now, that kind of difference is significant."

"I also notice from your report that our absentee rate is running about eight to ten percent a day—about twice what it was this time last year. Is that part of the same pattern?"

"I believe it is," Frank answered.

"In that case I suggest that we take a good look at our fringe benefits. After you have determined what is happening in the area, summarize the results and recommend the level that we should adopt for our company. I know that we have more or less paid the average in regard to wages, but in view of our increasing quality problems and our productivity rate per man-hour, I'm willing to pay more for fringe benefits if they will help quality and production. Let me have the summary of the survey and your recommendations as soon as possible," Rider concluded.

Frank returned to his office and took from his files a partial list of fringe benefits. The list is shown in Exhibit I.

I. For Added Leisure and Income

Call-back pay
Call-in pay
Clean-up time
Clothes-change time
Coffee breaks
Cost-of-living bonus
Downtime pay
Family allowances
Holidays
Hour limits
Jury duty pay
Leave, for illness
Leave, death of relative
Leave, for grievances
Leave, for negotiation
Leave, for voting
Lonely pay
Military bonus
Overtime pay
Portal-to-portal pay
Reporting pay
Rest pauses
Room and board allowances
Setup time
Shift differentials
Standby pay
Supper money
Travel pay
Vacations
Voting time

II. For Personal Identification and Participation

Anniversary awards
Athletic activities
Attendance bonus
Beauty parlor service
Cafeteria
Canteen
Car wash service
Charm school
Christmas bonus
Counseling
Credit union
Dietetic advice
Discounts
Educational aids
Financial advice
Food service
Home financing
Housing
Income tax aid
Information racks
Laundry service
Legal aid

Loan association
Moving aid
Music with work
Orchestra
Parking space
Quality bonus
Recreational programs
Savings bond aid
Safety clothes
Scholarships
Suggestion bonus
Thrift plans
Transportation aids
Year-end bonus

III. For Employment Security

Death benefits
Layoff pay
Leave for maternity
Retraining plans
Technological adjustment pay
Severance pay
Supplementary unemployment benefits
Unemployment insurance

IV. For Health Protection

Accident insurance
Dental care
Disability insurance
Health insurance
Hospitalization
Illness insurance
Life insurance
Medical care plan
Medical examinations
Optical services
Plant nursing service
Sickness insurance
Sick benefits
Sick leave
Surgical care plan
Temporary disability insurance
Visiting nurse service
Workmen's compensation

V. For Old Age and Retirement

Deferred income plans
Old age assistance
Old age counseling
OASDI
Private pension plans
Profit sharing plans
Rest homes
Retirement counseling
Stock ownership plans

Source: Dale Yoder, *Personnel Management and Industrial Relations* (5th ed.; Englewood Cliffs, New Jersey: Prentice-Hall, Inc., 1962), p. 494.

Exhibit I
A PARTIAL LIST OF EMPLOYEE BENEFITS AND SERVICES

PROBLEMS

1. Would you include all the items listed in Exhibit I in your survey of fringe benefits for Acme Manufacturing Company? If all items are not included in the survey, which should be included?

2. What is your recommendation in regard to the level of fringe benefits that should be paid; i.e., below average, average, or in the upper quartile?

3. What can Acme expect as the result of a competitive employee benefit program in regard to turnover, absenteeism, productivity, and product quality?

4. How can a company measure the effectiveness of its employee benefit program?

5. Is there any justification for using the phrase, fringe benefits, to describe employee benefit programs?

One of the most difficult tasks of an organization is that of motivating its employees—managerial and nonmanagerial alike—to perform the work assigned to them in a manner that meets or surpasses expected standards of performance. Many methods are used to encourage employees to put forth their best effort. Among those commonly found in industrial firms are a variety of formulas intended to relate pay to performance, provisions for security on the job and during the later years of retirement, praise and reproof, and recognition in the form of special awards or promotion. The existence of so many different approaches to motivation suggests the complexity of the problem. Many factors are capable of motivating employees. Some of these factors are a normal part of the industrial situation and, as independent variables, can be controlled in some measure by the company; other factors have their origin in the individual employee, in his home, or in his community, and are beyond the company's control. Also, those forces that motivate a person today may be of little value as motivators next month or next year. Fundamental to the success of any plan for motivating employees is the extent to which the intended motivators meet the needs of the individual employees for whom they are designed.

In this chapter we discuss first the basis of motivation as a means of developing certain concepts that will enable us to better understand the worth of intended motivators. Next, specific problems of motivation in an industrial situation are presented. In the last part of the chapter the concept of morale is developed and the relationship between job satisfaction and productivity is reviewed.

THE BASIS OF MOTIVATION

The study of motivation attempts to answer the *why* of human behavior. Why do people behave as they do? Why does John Jones consistently complete his work on time while Pete Smith has to be urged to meet the minimum requirements of his job? When we speak of motivation or, in more precise terms, motivated behavior, we are referring to behavior having three distinguishing characteristics. First, motivated behavior is sustained; that is, it persists for relatively long periods of time. Second, motivated behavior is directed toward the achievement of a goal; and third, it is behavior resulting from a felt need. The third characteristic, behavior resulting from a felt need, introduces a concept requiring further explanation.

Various terms have been used to describe the motivating forces of human behavior. Some of the terms are need, drive, aspiration, and desire. Although each term has a precise meaning in psychological theory, they may be grouped together for our purpose, since each is felt and recognized by the individual as a motivating force. As a result of perceiving a need, a tension or imbalance is created within the individual that leads to activities intended to reduce the tension thus created. The process may be diagrammed as follows:

A Perceived ⟶ Tension ⟶ Activity ⟶ Reduction of Tension
   Need   (Motivating   (Achievement of Goal)
             Force)

The importance of the discussion above is this: If the efforts of organizations to motivate employees are to be successful, management must either create felt needs within the individual or offer a means of satisfying needs already in existence within the individual. Thus, in order to motivate employees, we must know something about the fundamental needs of man.

A Hierarchy of Needs

Numerous systems have been developed for the classification of human needs, ranging from those that attempt to explain all human motivation as the result of satisfying one basic need or drive to classifications that list 25 or more separate needs. Among those who have sought to explain behavior in terms of a single need is Freud, who stressed the libido—a broad concept of the sex drive—as the basic motivator of man. Two of his students, Adler and Jung, also postulated single motives; the former designated the desire for power as the primary motivator, while the latter believed that a desire for individuality served as the basic source of motivation. The economists also have had a hand in trying to describe human motivation as evidenced by Marx's description of economic determinism as a primary motivator. However, one of the most useful and widely quoted classifications of human needs is that developed by Maslow who recognizes five basic needs. These are: [1]

1. Physiological needs.
2. Safety needs.
3. Affection needs.
4. Esteem needs.
5. Self-actualization needs.

Each of these needs is discussed briefly below.

Physiological Needs. Hunger and thirst are considered classic examples of physiological drives. Also included in this category are the tissue needs such as maintenance of the proper water content of the blood; maintenance of proper amounts of salt, sugar, protein, fat, calcium, oxygen, and acid-base balance; and the maintenance of the proper temperature for the tissues and the blood stream.[2] Satisfaction of the physiological needs is necessary for the preservation of life, and in most industrial economies these needs are satisfied relatively easily. Once satisfied, they cease to operate as the primary motivators of behavior and are replaced by motivational forces of a higher order.

Safety Needs. When considered as a goal of motivated behavior, the meaning of the term, safety, is broad because it includes the desire for psychological security as well as the need for physical security. Factors such as clothing, shelter, and protection from attack contribute to physical safety, thereby preserving and reinforcing the satisfaction of physiological drives. Much of the effort of organized society at the community level, such as police and fire departments, is directed toward the maintenance of security needs.

The desire for psychological security is of particular interest to management since the safety needs may become the predominant motivators when the physiological needs are fulfilled. Psychological safety takes the form of ordering the environment into a predictable pattern

---

[1] A. H. Maslow, "A Theory of Human Motivation," *Psychological Review,* Vol. L, (July, 1943), pp. 370-396. The theory of motivation, first presented in 1943 as a journal article, is treated in greater detail in *Motivation and Personality* (New York: Harper and Brothers, 1954).

[2] W. B. Cannon, *Wisdom of the Body* (New York: W. W. Norton and Company, 1932.) W. B. Cannon describes the functioning of the human body as a homostatic system.

and attempts to cope with anticipated difficulties of the future. Demands for supplemental unemployment benefits, pension plans, termination pay, and other forms of economic insurance stress the need for predictability and security. The desire for the familiar and the predictable goes a long way toward explaining the resistance to change found in many organizations. It is not the direction or nature of the change being resisted; it is the fact that change implies something new and unfamiliar —a psychological threat.

Affection Needs. Some writers combine physiological needs and safety needs into one category and call them the primary needs. They then refer to the needs for affection, esteem, and self-actualization as secondary needs. Such a classification is misleading because in our society the needs for survival and safety may be satisfied to a large extent. Consequently, the predominant needs are those of affection, esteem, and self-actualization. Need for affection and love is best described as the need to belong, not only as a wanted member of a family unit but also as a member of other relatively small groups such as work groups. Loyalty to a small work group and the need to belong to that group often outweigh the financial incentives and the logical appeals of management.

sense of belonging

Esteem Needs. The esteem needs, like the needs for affection and group belonging, are particularly significant as motivators in the industrial setting. Esteem needs may be summarized as the need for self-respect, for accomplishment, and for achievement. An important corollary to the need for esteem and achievement, perhaps as important as the need itself, is that the achievement must be recognized and appreciated by someone else. Few people are able to continue a pattern of achievement and success without the added encouragement and additional motivation provided by recognition of success by others. The desire for prestige and status (in reality, a form of recognition by others) is an important aspect of the drive for achievement. Attaining goals leads to feelings of self-respect, strength, and confidence. On the other hand, continued failure, frustration, and defeat can result in feelings of inadequacy and a withdrawal from competitive situations.

Self-Actualization Needs. Self-actualization, the capstone of the hierarchy of needs, is self-fulfillment. Maslow's original statement— "what a man can be, he must be"—may be paraphrased to state that *what a man can do, he must do.* Self-actualization takes many forms. We usually think of the creative works of painters, musicians, composers, and authors as expressions of self-fulfillment; however, the realization of

have ideals

one's full potential is not limited to expression in the creative arts. The woman who desires to be the ideal mother, the professional athlete, and the dedicated teacher are all doing what each must do. Complete self-actualization is rare, perhaps because all the other needs—physiological, safety, affection, and esteem—must reach a level of minimal satisfaction before the self-fulfillment needs become the dominant motivation in one's life.

Variations in the Hierarchy

The discussion of Maslow's hierarchy of needs serves a useful purpose, provided we recognize that the concept of a hierarchy is used only as a model and is not intended to imply that the emergence and the strength of needs follow a rigid pattern. There are many reversals and substitutions of needs. For some persons the sole goal in life seems to center upon the esteem needs, the acquisition of prestige, wealth, and status, to the exclusion of the needs for love and affection. Closer examination often reveals a thwarting of the love needs early in life, with a permanent dampening and suppression of those needs; thus, the drive for self-esteem may serve as a substitute for the need for love. There is evidence that needs for esteem and self-actualization may be blocked to such an extent that seemingly they disappear and do not emerge. Those who have faced a life of unemployment, or at best marginal economic adjustment, are often motivated mainly by the desire for safety and security to protect basic physiological needs.

There is probably no universal motivator for all mankind, nor is there a single motivating force for any one individual. Needs are relative in their strength, and it is not necessary to satisfy a "lower" need fully before a "higher" need may emerge and operate as a motivator. Assume that 90 percent of a person's physiological needs are satisfied, that 80 percent of his safety needs are fulfilled, and that 55 percent of his needs for love and affection are being met. This does not mean that there are no needs for esteem or self-actualization. Needs are felt gradually and may become motivators along with the other needs, even though the earlier needs are not completely satisfied. The complexity of the problem of motivation can be fully grasped when it is realized that the hypothetical percentages stated above vary from one person to another, that the significance of each need also varies, and that within the same person the relative degree of satisfaction and the significance of each need vary. In addition, there are factors other than the variable characteristics of the basic needs that influence motivation. Among those factors are a person's evaluation of himself and his interpretation of his environment.

Concepts of Self and Environment

A person's concept of himself and his interpretation of his environment provide a source of consistency to behavior throughout his entire life and determine to a large extent those motives that influence him the most. The image of self is formed relatively early in life and is reflected to the outer world by the manner of dress, speech, posture, and actions. The reflection remains fairly constant throughout life, thereby enabling others to predict with considerable accuracy one's behavior under a given set of circumstances. In this sense it is true that clothes do not make the man; indeed, clothes (along with actions, posture, and speech) are the man.

There are many dimensions to the self-image. Of particular concern in respect to the problems of motivation in industry is a person's perception of his degree of competence and his ability to achieve. Biographical studies show that patterns of achievement appear early in life. Initial successes lead to later successes and reinforce one's estimate of his competence and ability to achieve. By the same token, failures, either imagined or real, deflate one's self-image of competence and achievement. Achievement, or the lack of it, shapes the environment in which man lives. Those who achieve develop a sense of *power* over their environment, for they are able to cope with that environment and seemingly control it to their advantage. A person who exercises power and control over his environment learns to expect a high degree of *reward* from that environment, and when received, the reward tends to make him feel that he is master of his own destiny. On the other hand, persistent lack of reward leads to an environmental image that is hostile and unrewarding. There are also the possible combinations of the person who believes that he has a low degree of power to control his environment, yet has expectations of relatively high rewards, and the person who feels that he can control his environment but expects little reward in return for his effort.

The potential combinations of a person's perceptions of the extent to which he can control his environment and his expectations of reward are shown in Figure 18-1. It must be remembered that there are many possible shadings and combinations of these two factors and that the four-cell table of Figure 18-1 represents only an outline of possible combinations.[3]

---

[3] Saul W. Gellerman, *Motivation and Productivity* (New York: American Management Association, Inc., 1963), pp. 194-197. *Motivation and Productivity* presents in very readable form a summation of the outstanding research in the field of motivation and its applications to the industrial setting. A complete bibliography is included. The four-cell classification in Figure 18-1 is based on Dr. Gellerman's discussion.

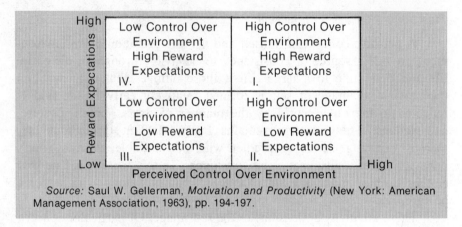

Source: Saul W. Gellerman, *Motivation and Productivity* (New York: American Management Association, 1963), pp. 194-197.

Figure 18-1

RELATIONSHIPS BETWEEN PERCEIVED CONTROL OVER ENVIRONMENT AND EXPECTATIONS OF REWARD

MOTIVATION IN INDUSTRY

The preceding discussion of needs and the way in which they are influenced by the concepts of self and the environment is presented in general terms with little specific reference to the application of these concepts to the day-to-day motivation of employees in an industrial situation. At the beginning of this chapter it is stated that in order to motivate employees management must either create felt needs within the individual or must offer a means of satisfying those needs already in existence within the individual. Undoubtedly the most widely used incentive to motivate employees is money, yet the evidence is overwhelming that more money does not necessarily mean greater productivity. The factors limiting the usefulness of money as a tool for motivating employees and the research findings concerning employee motivation are discussed below.

Money and Motivation

Money has no intrinsic value, yet we recognize the economic worth of money in that it can be exchanged for goods and services. There is also a psychological emotionally toned worth attached to money. The economic worth of money enables it to serve as a means of satisfying the basic physiological and safety needs. Its psychological value is that for many persons money may symbolize achievement, success, prestige, or power—a way of fulfilling the higher social needs.

Control Over Environment. However, not all people are capable of regarding money as an incentive. Refer to the four combinations of expected rewards and perceived power over one's environment shown in Figure 18-1:

1. High perceived control over environment and high reward expectations.
2. High perceived control over environment and low reward expectations.
3. Low in both perceived control over environment and reward expectations.
4. Low perceived control over environment and high reward expectations.

Those persons who are best characterized by either the first or second category are the ones capable of responding to money as an incentive. These are the people who perceive themselves as having a high degree of power in shaping their environment; the magnitude of the expected reward is secondary in importance. Those belonging to the first group are highly trained in either technical or professional fields, a training that by its very nature represents a pattern of success. For these people money readily becomes a symbol of success and achievement and can be exchanged for desired goods and services. Those in the second category who expect little but believe that they can effectively control their environment are likely to respond to money, not for its own sake, but as additional evidence of ability to control and shape the environment. Entrepreneurs (including successful managers) often belong to the second group. People characterized by groups three and four generally do not respond to money as an incentive since they do not perceive themselves as having an effective control over their environment.

Conflicting Needs. The belief that money is and should be a strong motivator is deeply rooted, and not without foundation, as evidenced by those who believe that they can control their environment. For the most part these people respond well to monetary incentive plans in sales and managerial jobs, but similar plans for hourly production workers experience questionable success at best. Whyte estimates that only 10 percent of the hourly production workers in the United States respond to a financial incentive plan by producing to capacity, thereby increasing their earnings.[4] What about the other 90 percent? Why don't they produce more, particularly when greater productivity means more money? Zaleznik and his co-workers at Harvard University offer some

---

[4] William F. Whyte, *Money and Motivation* (New York: Harper and Row, Publishers, Inc., 1955).

sound answers to this question; albeit the answers are not encouraging for management.[5]

Before discussing Zaleznik's work we must take another look at groups one and two mentioned above. These are the people—the physician, the lawyer, the accountant, the salesman, or the entrepreneur—capable of responding to financial incentives, people who believe that they can shape their environment and control it to a large extent. To them the world is not a foreboding place in which to live since there are more successes than there are failures. Further, success is the result largely of individual effort. Although any one of these people may work as a member or a leader of a group, each is usually recognized as an individual having a unique contribution to make to the group. Admittedly, membership in a small work group is necessary and highly prized, but it is not the key to success. Instead, success is attributable largely to individual effort. Members of groups one and two usually satisfy to a considerable extent their need for belonging; but even more important, the esteem needs—prestige, achievement, power, and recognition—also have a measure of satisfaction. Many are realizing a degree of self-actualization in that they are doing and being what they must do and be.

The environment of the production worker, as described by Whyte and Zaleznik, is one of sharp contrast to the environment described above. First, let us consider the production worker as an individual, then a group of production workers, and finally the statistical exceptions—Whyte's 10 percent who respond as individuals to incentives.

THE PRODUCTION WORKER. It is often said that all generalizations are false, including this one. Nonetheless, the following generalizations help to place in perspective some of the problems of motivation in an industrial society. For some reason, or perhaps a combination of reasons, the production worker (think of the man on the assembly line) has not become highly skilled. His lack of progress may be due to a lack of ability, lack of physiological drive and stamina, poor environmental factors, inability to acquire training in his youth due to economic conditions, or any one of a host of other reasons. Whatever the cause, the environment has not surrendered much over the years, with the resultant feelings of frustration and the conviction that the world is hostile and

---

[5] Abraham Zaleznik, C. R. Christensen, and F. Roethlisberger, *The Motivation, Productivity, and Satisfaction of Workers: A Prediction Study* (Boston: Harvard Business School, 1958). Both the Harvard study and Whyte's work emphasize the limitations of money as a means of motivating production workers and stress the importance of the work group as a motivating force.

unyielding. Expectations of reward may have been high in his youth, but early socio-economic forces may have permanently limited his expectations to a minimal level. If expectations were high, the years of frustration and lack of anticipated rewards serve to emphasize the hopelessness of ever achieving original goals.

The basic physiological and safety needs of the worker described above are, in all probability, fairly well satisfied. But what about the higher needs? It is difficult for most of us to imagine self-actualization or self-fulfillment on an assembly line. Punching a clock, being identified by number, and performing a routine task are not conducive to feelings of status, prestige, or high esteem in the eyes of others. Since these esteem needs are not satisfied, the next step in descending order of the hierarchy of needs is the need for belonging—for belonging to a group.

THE GROUP. Imagine our hypothetical worker accepting a new job and a new clock number with a different employer. The new job is not much different than several previous jobs, nor are the opportunities for advancement appreciably different, at least as the worker sees the situation. Since the job is the same, the possibilities for satisfying the esteem and self-actualization needs are effectively blocked, but the opportunity is present to become a member of a group. The informal group is composed of men with similar backgrounds and perceptions of self and control over the environment. At the beginning our new employee is not a "regular" member of the group (he may never become a member of the inner circle), but he aligns himself with the group as a means of satisfying a basic need—the need to belong. Zaleznik refers to these groups as "frozen groups"; Gellerman calls them "sick." Frozen or sick, these are the groups that set patterns of behavior and shape the attitudes of workers in the plant.

Conformity in respect to both overt behavior and attitudes is the price of membership in the group. One of the most noticeable aspects of the group's behavior is the restriction of output, in reality a reflection of attitudes toward management. Management is viewed with suspicion, and any change is regarded as ultimately resulting in an increase in the amount of work required from each member of the group or a reduction in the size of the work force. The objective of the group is to maintain a *status quo* since expectations of high reward and the belief that the environment can be shaped no longer exist. At least, present conditions assure the satisfaction of the physiological and safety needs, and membership in the group satisfies the need for belonging. For the new worker, joining or not joining the group may be a difficult choice in terms of satisfying his needs. Conformity to the group's standards of behavior and attitudes usually means giving up satisfying the esteem and self-actualization needs while on the job; but his prior experience shows that the satisfaction of these needs is difficult and in the distant future. To pursue the higher needs could mean rejection by the group, with the resulting frustration of the belonging needs. For many workers the dilemma exists only in theory; the choice is made early in life to belong to the group, thus satisfying the belonging needs and foregoing the higher esteem and self-actualization needs. Yet for some, the rate buster for example, needs other than belonging to the group are more important.

THE RATE BUSTER. A small percentage, Whyte's estimate is 10 percent, rejects the group's demand for conformity and responds to money as an incentive. These people are known as *rate busters*. Conceivably they could be responding to management's plan to reduce costs and improve productivity, but it is seldom that such is the case. For the rate buster who sought membership in the group and was rejected by the group, his behavior may be a form of revenge, a means of showing up the group by outproducing them. Others who excel in production do so as the result of their socio-economic background rather than as the result of responding to the merits of a specific incentive plan. Socially the rate buster tends to be a "loner" both inside and outside the industrial organization. Further, he generally comes from a home that stresses the virtues of individual achievement and economic independence. He still believes that as the result of his own efforts he can shape his environment and improve his lot in life. Either reason, revenge against the group or socio-economic background, points up the irony of incentive plans. The 10 percent who respond to incentives are not responding to the plan itself; instead, they are motivated by forces seldom recognized by and far beyond the control of management.

When Money Works. The above discussion shows the shortcomings of monetary incentives as a means of motivating the vast majority of production workers. Nonetheless, many companies are satisfied with incentive plans and attribute a reduction in cost and an increase in productivity to these plans. Admittedly, many such plans work, but they are not working as the result of the effectiveness of money as an incentive. There are other reasons why incentive plans often attain management's desired results. First, the presence of a realistic standard tends to motivate employees since it defines a goal to be reached within a specified period of time. In this respect a standard is the same as par in golf or a 200 game in bowling. Second, without stated standards, supervisors do not know what is expected of them and often reflect their unrest through aggressive attitudes toward production workers. When standards are in effect, the production worker who meets these goals assures himself of a more pleasant working relationship with his supervisor. A third reason is that prior to the installation of production standards there is usually a period of intensive methods analysis which improves the mechanics of actually performing the job, with the result that more work can be done with less effort and fatigue. Fourth, the introduction of standards forces management to improve the production control function so that the flow of work is at a more even pace with fewer periods of idleness due to waiting for materials.[6]

A Two-Factor Theory of Work Motivation

The discussion of money and motivation should not lead us to the conclusion that money is unimportant in the total process of motivating employees; it is important. However, according to the two-factor theory of motivation, money is a *hygenic factor,* not a *motivator.* The two-factor theory differentiates between hygenic factors and motivators and is the result of research conducted by Dr. Frederick Herzberg and his associates of the Psychological Service of Pittsburgh.[7]

Several hundred engineers and accountants were interviewed and asked to recall incidents related to their work and to indicate the effect of these incidents upon their productivity and attitudes toward their jobs. The subjects of the Pittsburgh studies were also asked to indicate the duration of the feelings aroused by each incident.

Herzberg found that experiences which create positive attitudes toward work arise from the job itself and function as *motivators*. These incidents are associated with feelings of self-improvement, achievement, and the desire for and the acceptance of greater responsibility. The

---

[6] The following observation was made by Morris S. Viteles many years ago. Morris S. Viteles, *Motivation and Morale in Industry* (New York: W.W. Norton & Company, Inc., 1953), pp. 29-30. "In practice, the installation of a wage incentive plan is generally accompanied by other changes in working conditions, personnel policies, and practices which are frequently major in character . . . as a result, management and industrial engineers have frequently been unable to present clear-cut and unequivocal evidence as to the specific effect of wage incentive."

For a review of the literature concerning the effect of money as a motivator the following is recommended. Robert L. Opsahl and Marvin D. Dunnette, "The Role of Financial Compensation in Industrial Motivation," *Psychological Bulletin*, Vol. 66, No. 2 (August, 1966), pp. 94-118.

[7] Frederick Herzberg, Bernard Mausner, and B. Snydeman, *The Motivation to Work* (2d ed.; New York: John Wiley & Sons, Inc., 1959).

For a more recent statement of Herzberg's position the following is recommended: Frederick Herzberg, *Work and the Nature of Man* (Cleveland: World Publishing Company, 1966).

feelings thus generated are of a relatively long duration and result in increased productivity. Since the subjects of the Pittsburgh studies were engineers and accountants, the change in productivity was more qualitative than quantitative in nature. The second set of factors related to productivity on the job are conditions peripheral to the job itself. Pay, working conditions (such as heating, lighting, and ventilation), company policy, and the quality of supervision are all part of the environment but peripheral to the job itself. When these factors are believed to be inadequate they function as _dissatisfiers;_ but when present, they do not motivate employees to greater productivity. Instead, they are _hygienic_ in character in that their presence makes it possible for the motivators to function. Positive feelings aroused by these peripheral conditions of work, such as a word of encouragement from a supervisor or an increase in pay, are relatively brief in duration. Another finding of the Pittsburgh study is significant. When employees are highly motivated and find their jobs interesting and challenging, they are able to tolerate considerable dissatisfaction with peripheral factors; however, a full measure of all hygienic factors does not make the job interesting.

One obvious limitation of Herzberg's work is that his subjects were engineers and accountants, people who have had the motivation to acquire professional training, who believe that they can shape their environment, and who expect considerable reward from that environment. Does the same hold true for the nonprofessional worker?

Hygienic and Motivating Factors at Work. Dr. M. Scott Myer, Manager of Personnel Research for Texas Instruments Incorporated, using essentially the same technique employed by Herzberg, raises and answers the three following questions concerning employee motivation.

1. *What motivates employees to work effectively?* A challenging job which allows a feeling of achievement, responsibility, growth, advancement, enjoyment of work itself, and earned recognition.

2. *What dissatisfies workers?* Mostly factors peripheral to the job— work rules, lighting, coffee breaks, titles, seniority rights, wages, fringe benefits, and the like.

3. *When do workers become dissatisfied?* When opportunities for meaningful achievement are eliminated and they become sensitized to their environment and begin to find fault.[8]

---

[8] M. Scott Myer, "Who Are Your Motivated Workers?" *Harvard Business Review,* Vol. XXXXII (January-February, 1964), p. 73. Dr. Myer's report, pp. 73-88, presents in detail the findings of his research conducted at Texas Instruments. The article contains many pictorial presentations well worth careful study.

Myers' study is not limited to the analysis of the professionally trained, since it is a representative sample of 282 employees from five different job classifications, three of which are salaried and two are hourly classifications. The salaried classifications included are scientists, engineers, and manufacturing supervisors; the hourly classifications include technicians (male) and assemblers (female). Although the answers to the above questions apply to all job classifications, the differences in the importance ascribed to various motivational factors other than achievement warrant a brief analysis of the responses of each group.

SCIENTISTS. For scientists, 50 percent of the favorable incidents reported are related to achievement on the job. The most intense feelings of satisfaction; i.e., those feelings that endure for at least two months, are related to "work itself." The most frequently mentioned source of dissatisfaction stems from company policy and administration, implying that rules and regulations sometimes interfere with the achievement of scientific goals. However, the most intense feelings of dissatisfaction come from a feeling that their work lacks full responsibility.

ENGINEERS. Engineers show a motivational pattern much like that shown by the scientists in respect to the importance of achievement and the satisfaction derived from work itself. Yet they differ from scientists in that advancement and pay are also predominant sources of feelings of intense satisfaction. In addition to reporting a lack of responsibility and poor company policy as causes of dissatisfaction, the engineers report that incompetence and lack of friendliness on the part of supervision and inadequate pay (in their estimation) create dissatisfaction.

MANUFACTURING SUPERVISORS. Although achievement is mentioned most frequently as a source of satisfaction, manufacturing supervisors—a nonprofessionally trained group—show a pattern distinctly different from that of the scientists and engineers. Advancement, recognition, and the possibility of growth create the intense feelings of satisfaction, with advancement being by far the greatest single source of intense satisfaction. Lack of responsibility, inadequate pay, and failure to advance are causes of dissatisfaction among manufacturing supervisors. The designation of advancement as the major source of satisfaction is not surprising since supervisors are frequently promoted from hourly classifications and seek such promotions because of their strong desire to achieve through advancement within the organization.

HOURLY TECHNICIANS. Hourly electronic technicians, like manufacturing supervisors, do not mention work itself as either a frequent or intense source of satisfaction; to them, work itself is the greatest dissatisfier. Increased responsibility is by far the strongest motivator of technicians and is followed by advancement. It is quite possible that enlarged responsibilities and successfully achieving these responsibilities are considered a means of advancing.

FEMALE ASSEMBLERS. The preceding groups—scientists, engineers, manufacturing supervisors, and hourly technicians—are all characterized by Myers as motivation seekers or, at the very least, potential motivation seekers. These people can be motivated by factors within the job itself, but the female assemblers are described as *maintenance seekers* in that factors peripheral to the work itself are dominant in creating either strong positive feelings of satisfaction or negative feelings of dissatisfaction. Although achievement is mentioned most frequently as a source of satisfaction, the competence and friendliness of supervision along with pay offer the most intense feelings of satisfaction. By the same token, lack of recognition by supervision and lack of security (the threat of layoff) are the chief causes of dissatisfaction. Increased responsibility and advancement are not motivators; instead, recognition and understanding by the immediate supervisor motivate the female assembler.

Management's Choice. The results of Dr. Myer's study are presented in pictorial form in Figure 18-2, Employee Needs. Note that the inner circle—motivational needs—contains those factors directly related to the job, while the outer circle is composed of maintenance needs. Employees seek satisfaction in the area of maintenance needs—those factors peripheral to the job itself—when the motivational needs of growth, achievement, responsibility, and recognition are not satisfied. The relative importance of maintenance needs diminishes when motivational needs are satisfied. Thus, management has two broad alternatives: (1) directing its efforts toward the satisfaction of motivational needs by designing jobs having the capability of fulfilling those needs, or (2) directing its efforts toward the satisfaction of those needs peripheral to the job itself. Acme Manufacturing Company, Case Problem 18-A, has apparently decided to choose the second alternative and satisfy the peripheral needs. Let us discuss this alternative and the results that might reasonably be expected from this approach to employee motivation.

EMPLOYEE BENEFIT PROGRAMS. In all probability no company has a vice-president in charge of fun and games, yet most companies of any size have several highly paid administrators in their personnel departments in charge of various phases of employee welfare and benefit

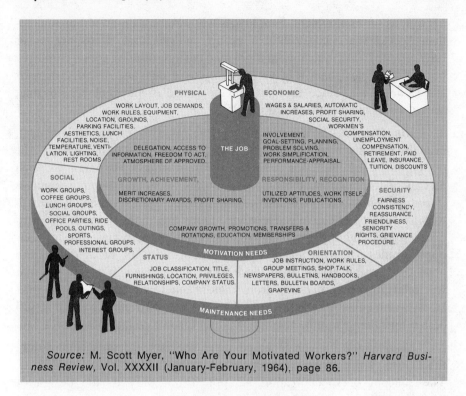

Source: M. Scott Myer, "Who Are Your Motivated Workers?" *Harvard Business Review*, Vol. XXXXII (January-February, 1964), page 86.

Figure 18-2

EMPLOYEE NEEDS—MAINTENANCE AND MOTIVATIONAL

programs. These programs are concerned with those items shown in the outer circle of Figure 18-2. Such activities are costly, not only in terms of dollars spent but more importantly because of their inefficiency as motivators. The dollar cost of maintaining these extrinsic factors at competitive levels is rising in a never-ending spiral. Unions have traditionally directed their bargaining efforts toward improvement of the physical and economic factors shown in the outer circle. Managements have, perhaps unwittingly, aided unions in their efforts to raise the level of employee benefits. Most companies take considerable pride in their benefit and welfare programs and in most instances are forced to keep them at competitive levels in order to attract needed personnel.

In addition to the ever-mounting total cost of these programs, a hidden cost lies in their inefficiency as motivators. When hygienic factors are absent, or not present in sufficient quantity, they function as dissatisfiers and can actually interfere with productivity. However, when present, they do not motivate personnel to greater productivity. They merely form a floor or base and represent the minimum acceptable conditions of employment. Employees who are best described as maintenance seekers are an insatiable group; maintenance needs are never fully satisfied. There is always a greener pasture offering more employee benefits. The designation of various employee benefits as fringe benefits is peculiarly apt, since they are on the fringe of the real benefits that should be derived from the job itself.

JOB DESIGN. If we are to tap the motivators of achievement, growth, responsibility, and recognition, we must examine closely the design of the job itself, for these factors are intrinsic. In some jobs, such as that of the scientist, the engineer, or the accountant, minor changes in company policy and administration might permit the potential motivators to operate effectively. However, there are many jobs in industry characterized by highly repetitive, monotonous activities offering few opportunities for growth, additional responsibility, or recognition. The obvious question arises: Can these jobs be designed in a manner that will offer greater motivation from factors inherently a part of the job? In answering this question, let us look first at current practices in job design and then examine two alternatives for increasing job satisfaction.

Current Job Design is based upon the concept of specialization, the nature of the production process, and the goal of lowest unit cost.[9] The concept of specialization is applied not only to the design of machinery used in the production process but also to the jobs performed by the workers. Jobs are composed of a sequence of individual tasks or operations that are grouped and then assigned to a single individual. Usually a particular method for performing each of the separate tasks of a job is specified. In many instances the tasks performed by the worker are determined by the characteristics of the machine; for example, the bag catcher who removes and boxes bags made by a machine designed to produce a single product.

When there is a choice in determining which tasks should be combined into a single job, the criterion of lowest unit cost is applied. Since cost is to be minimized, it seems only logical to design tasks and combine them in such a fashion that the lowest level of skill is required. The application of this procedure usually results in a highly repetitive operation, composed of relatively simple movements requiring little skill, and capable of being learned by a large number of workers in a comparatively short period of time. Thus, training costs are at a minimum and an

---

[9] Louis E. Davis, "Job Design and Productivity: A New Approach," *Personnel,* Vol. XXXIII (March, 1957), pp. 418-430. Dr. Davis' article presents an excellent analysis of specialization and job design. It also contains a detailed review of the study conducted by Marks that is cited in footnote 12.

adequate potential of labor is assured. Assembly operations are typical of jobs composed of repetitive, unskilled tasks capable of being learned by most industrial workers.

How valid are these assumptions? Judging by this nation's level of productivity, consumption, and pay, the assumptions underlying the design of production processes and fitting jobs to these processes are quite effective. Yet it remains to be answered whether or not current practices of job design utilize the best available means of designing jobs since there are relatively few instances in which jobs have been designed to be more complex and challenging to the worker.

Job Enrichment, sometimes referred to as *job enlargement,* is the process of making industrial jobs more challenging and interesting by increasing personal responsibility for one's work and the opportunity for personal achievement and recognition, and by providing expanded opportunities for psychological growth and development.[10]

One of the main reasons for job enrichment is found in the results of the work conducted by Walker and Guest of the Institute of Human Relations at Yale University.[11] Their studies reveal a very low level of job satisfaction on the part of automobile assembly-line workers; in fact, the workers despise their jobs even though most of them indicate that pay, supervision, and working conditions are more than satisfactory. The reasons for the intense dislike of the work is reported to be due to the anonymity of the worker himself and the complete depersonalization of the job. Feelings of anonymity and depersonalization arise because the pace is determined mechanically by the speed of the line, the low level of skills required, the highly repetitive nature of the tasks performed, the lack of choice or control over methods and tools to be used, and the lack of social interaction resulting from an isolated and fixed position on the line.

---

[10] The following book is recommended as a comprehensive statement of job enrichment practices currently employed in industry. The cases presented cover a wide range of companies and also a wide range of industrial jobs that have been modified successfully through the process of job enrichment. John R. Maher (ed.), *New Perspectives in Job Enrichment* (New York: Van Nostrand Reinhold Company, 1971).

For another summary of seven case studies from manufacturing and non-manufacturing firms and a governmental agency of experiences with job enrichment the following report which contains a complete bibliography is recommended. The name of the author is Harold M. F. Rush, *Job Design for Motivation: Experiments in Job Enlargement and Job Enrichment* (New York: The Conference Board, Inc., 1971).

[11] C. R. Walker and R. H. Guest, *The Man on the Assembly Line* (Cambridge, Mass.: Harvard University Press, 1952). C. R. Walker and R. H. Guest, "The Man on the Assembly Line," *Harvard Business Review,* Vol. XXX (May-June, 1952), pp. 71-83. *The Harvard Business Review* article presents a summary of feelings and attitudes of automobile assembly-plant workers as revealed by carefully conducted depth interviews.

An experimental approach to enriching the job content of an assembly operation is described in a study completed by A. R. N. Marks.[12] The total number of employees in the department was 35, of which 29 were female assemblers engaged in assembling a hospital appliance, and six performed supporting jobs of inspecting and supplying materials. Each assembler performed one of nine operations at a station on a conveyor-paced assembly line. Every two hours positions on the line were rotated to lessen fatigue and break the monotony. The speed of the conveyor determined the output for the group, and since positions on the line were rotated, there was no individual responsibility for quality. The experiment consisted of four stages:

1. Line Job Design—The normal method of assembling, performed on a conveyor-paced line with six workers supporting the 29 assemblers.
2. Group Job Design—The conveyor is eliminated but other conditions remain the same. In effect, the pace of the operation and consequently the output are determined by the worker.
3. Individual Job Design No. 1—Each worker performs all nine operations at her own station and is responsible for procuring her own parts, inspection of the parts, and quality of the final assembly. This stage of the experiment was conducted in a room near the main production area to provide training in the new method. Each worker spent two days in this phase. The conveyor is eliminated.
4. Individual Job Design No. 2—Following the two-day training period, each worker performs the assembly operation using the method of individual job design No. 1 in the main production area for six days. (In discussing the results of the experiment, individual job designs Nos. 1 and 2 are treated as a single method since design No. 1 served as a training period for design No. 2. The method is the same; the only variable is the location in which the work is performed.)

With the group job design method, which lasted only two days, productivity was considerably lower than the normal production of the line job design. Individual job design No. 1 resulted in a higher level of productivity than that attained from the group job design, and the level of production of individual job design No. 2 continued to rise, with the average for the group being about 95 percent of the amount produced using the original line job design. These results are quite remarkable considering that the total number of days' experience in using the individual job design methods is only eight, while the average length of time on the line job design is over four years.

---

[12] A. R. N. Marks, "An Investigation of Modifications of Job Design in an Industrial Situation and Their Effect on Some Measures of Economic Productivity" (Ph.D. dissertation, University of California, 1954).

A detailed analysis of the production records of the individual job design method shows that production increased each consecutive day, and on the sixth day the average production for the group exceeded the average for the line design method. Further, as a result of each assembler operating independently of the others, individual differences in productivity were noted, with some of the women producing 30 to 40 percent more than the average for the line job design. In addition, the level of quality improved considerably—a 75 percent reduction in kinked (wiring) assemblies—and the six supporting workers who normally inspected final assemblies and procured parts were eliminated. Marks also found that those who participated in the experimental individual job design developed a more favorable attitude toward their jobs in that they desired more responsibility and were willing to put forth more effort, and when returned to the line job design method at the end of the experiment, they disliked the loss of personal responsibility inherent in a conveyor-paced assembly operation.

The experiment in job enrichment described above raises some provocative questions. The level of production on the sixth day of individual job design No. 2 exceeded the average of the line production method, thus challenging the assumption that the highly engineered assembly-line operation is the *optimum* arrangement for producing at the lowest unit cost. We do not know whether or not the individual job design method would result in productivity equal to that of the line job for a sustained period of time; in other words, did the high production of the assemblers on the sixth day result from the job design itself, or did it result from their awareness that they were participating in an experiment? How applicable are these results to other industries? Assume that individual job design does yield a higher degree of productivity; what is the capital investment required for individual job design as compared with line job design in assembling a complex product such as an automobile? Can the same procedures be applied to the routine, repetitive clerical jobs of a bank or an insurance company? And finally, how important are feelings of job satisfaction and productivity? [13]

---

[13] In a review of the literature concerning job enrichment Professors Hulin and Blood conclude that positive relationships between job size and job satisfaction cannot be assumed to be general; instead, the success of job enlargement programs are greatly dependent upon the backgrounds of the workers involved. Charles L. Hulin and Milton R. Blood, "Job Enlargement, Individual Differences, and Worker Responses," *Psychological Bulletin,* Vol. 69, No. 1 (January, 1968), pp. 41-55.

Professor Hulin has modified the above paper and presents it as a chapter in Mayer (ed.), *op. cit.,* Chapter 9, "Individual Differences and Job Enrichment—The Case Against General Treatments," pp. 159-191. A complete bibliography is presented in both sources.

JOB SATISFACTION AND PRODUCTIVITY

The preceding discussion utilizes Herzberg's two factors with intrinsic job characteristics acting as motivators and peripheral job characteristics functioning as satisfiers or dissatifiers but not as motivators. The two-factory theory is useful as a means of discussing the alternate courses available for motivating employees.[14] Implied in the above discussion, though not stated explicity, is the assumption that job satisfaction is an independent variable with production the resultant dependent variable. However, such is not the case.

In order to place job satisfaction in its proper role as a dependent variable—the result of the total work situation—let us examine the concept of morale, and some of the studies of job satisfaction that utilize methods other than the interview. Then we review a part of the literature relating to job satisfaction and productivity and finally an instrumentality approach to the understanding of the causes of job satisfaction is presented.

Morale

Morale is a word with many meanings. Definitions include statements that morale is the absence of conflict, a feeling of happiness, good personal adjustment, those attitudes pertaining to work, and the extent of ego-involvement in one's job. Some definitions would limit the concept of morale to only those persons working in a group by defining morale as the extent of cohesiveness or "we feeling" of a group or the extent to which there is personal acceptance of the goals of the group. Dr. Robert Guion offers a definition of morale that includes most, if not all, of the attributes previously mentioned. *"Morale is the extent to which an individual's needs are satisfied and the extent to which the individual perceives that satisfaction as stemming from his total job situation."* [15] Guion's definition is of value since it stresses the importance of need satisfaction and applies equally to individuals as well as to those who are members of groups. It also emphasizes the complexity of the

---

[14] A criticism of the two-factor theory of job satisfaction and motivation is the following: Robert J. House and Lawrence A. Wigdor, "Herzberg's Dual-Factor Theory of Job Satisfaction and Motivation: A Review of the Evidence and a Criticism," *Personnel Psychology,* Vol. 20, No. 4 (Winter, 1967), pp. 369-389.

An alternate view, and one more in accord with current research findings, is presented in the last section of this chapter—"A Concluding View."

[15] Robert M. Guion, "Industrial Morale (A Symposium) 1. The Problem of Terminology," *Personnel Psychology,* Vol. XI (Spring, 1958), p. 62. This symposium was presented at the 1957 meetings of the Midwestern Psychological Association in Chicago. Dr. Guion's article, pp. 59-61, summarizes varying concepts of morale.

sources of morale by referring to the total job situation rather than to job satisfaction alone.

Other Studies of Job Satisfaction

There have been many studies showing that intrinsic job satisfaction is only one factor of the total job situation. An analysis of the job attitudes of 6,000 industrial workers in a midwestern tractor factory shows that there are four relatively independent factors contributing to satisfaction derived from the total job situation. They are: intrinsic job satisfaction, satisfaction with the company, satisfaction with supervision, and satisfaction with rewards and the opportunity for mobility.[16] Another study using the technique of multiple-factor analysis—a statistical tool for determining independent factors—investigated the needs to be satisfied by the total job situation. There is a general factor of morale resulting from overall satisfaction as a result of need fulfillment, the need for social recognition of status, and the need for self-respect.[17]

By far the most comprehensive study of job satisfaction, known as The Cornell Studies of Job Satisfaction, uses a carefully constructed checklist of items descriptive of the total job situation. The Cornell studies show that job satisfaction is composed of five relatively independent aspects of the work environment. They are the work itself, pay, supervision, opportunity for promotions, and the characteristics of co-workers. Further, it is shown that any one of these factors may serve as a source of satisfaction for a given group of employees and as a source of dissatisfaction for another group. Also, these factors shift in their significance to a given individual; that is, what is satisfying today may be dissatisfying tomorrow as the individual's needs and goals change.[18]

---

[16] Robert L. Kahn, "Productivity and Job Satisfaction," *Personnel Psychology* Vol. XV (Autumn, 1960), pp. 275-287. In addition to reporting the results of a multiple-factor analysis of employee attitudes, Kahn summarizes the major findings of the Survey Research Center of the University of Michigan in their studies of job satisfaction and productivity.

[17] Oakley J. Gordon, "A Factor Analysis of Human Needs and Industrial Morale," *Personnel Psychology,* Vol. VIII (Spring, 1955), pp. 1-18. This work complements the study of Kahn. Gordon's analysis is concerned with needs, while Kahn's is concerned with the job situation. Note that the definition of morale offered by Guion ties these two aspects of morale together.

[18] Patricia Cain Smith, Lorne M. Kendall, Charles L. Hulin, *The Measurement of Satisfaction in Work and Retirement: A Strategy for the Study of Attitudes* (Chicago: Rand McNally & Co., 1969). As indicated by the title, the Cornell studies measure satisfaction in retirement as well as satisfaction in work. The items measured in the Retirement Description Index (RDI) are activities and work, financial situation, health, and people you associate with. *The Measurement of Satisfaction in Work and Retirement* offers a detailed insight into carefully planned research strategy.

Productivity and Job Satisfaction

Psychologists have devoted a great deal of time and effort to studying the effects of reward and punishment upon human behavior. In general, it seems that situations that reward a person are satisfying and those situations that punish a person are dissatisfying. Further, people have a tendency to prolong or return to satisfying situations and to avoid those situations that are not satisfying. This line of reasoning is applied to the interpretation of morale as a factor in turnover and absenteeism. Thus, people with high morale (a high degree of perceived satisfaction of needs through the total job situation) can be expected to continue their job with a minimum amount of absenteeism, and those who quit or are chronically absent do so because the situation is not satisfying to them. Although this reasoning is plausible in explaining turnover and absenteeism, it does not follow that satisfaction with the job should or does result in a high level of productivity.

All individuals are simultaneously members of several social systems and the attainment of goals within each of these social systems serves to satisfy the needs of the individual. High productivity is seldom a goal, but high productivity may lead to the fulfillment of a goal, thereby creating a feeling of satisfaction. In this case, productivity is varying concomitantly with satisfaction (goal attainment); there is no causal relationship.

Katz and Kahn suggest that the industrial worker is a member of four social systems: (1) A system outside the plant and within the plant, (2) a system of relationships with other workers, (3) a system of the formal union structure, and (4) an organizational system of the company itself.[19] It might be argued that higher productivity is a means of achieving prestige, recognition, and higher status in the social system outside the plant. But evidence does not show that the majority of industrial workers are strongly motivated toward social achievement outside the plant.[20]

---

[19] D. Katz and R. L. Kahn, "Some Recent Findings in Human Relations Research in Industry." From G. E. Swanson, T. M. Newcomb, and E. L. Hartley (eds.), *Readings in Social Psychology* (New York: Henry Holt and Company, 1952), pp. 650-665.

Arthur H. Brayfield and Walter H. Crockett, "Employee Attitudes and Employee Performance," *Psychological Bulletin*, Vol. LII (September, 1955), pp. 415-422. Brayfield and Crockett present an excellent survey of the literature on employee attitudes in relation to productivity and use the four social systems suggested by Katz and Kahn as a format for their presentation.

[20] W. L. Warner and P. S. Lunt, *The Social Life of a Modern Community* (New Haven, Conn.: Yale University Press, 1941).

Further, many industrial workers are in Gellerman's classifications of those who perceive little chance of control over their environment. In analyzing the relationships of industrial workers among themselves, we must remember Zaleznik's "frozen groups," groups that have pegged production at minimal levels, and the desire to belong to the group—an impossibility with high levels of production. Workers who have aspirations of achieving rank and position within the formal structure of the union may do so without resorting to high production; in fact, high levels of productivity frequently serve as a detriment for advancement within the union. Seemingly the employee desirous of advancing within the company organization by receiving increased pay, a promotion, or a higher position in the hierarchy would be motivated to produce more. Yet, productivity is only one of several factors considered for advancement; quality, ability to get along with others, and dependability may outweigh productivity in determining advancement within the company.

In 1947 the newly founded Survey Research Center of the University of Michigan undertook a series of investigations to determine the relationships between supervisory practices, employee satisfaction, and productivity.[21] In the first study of the relationships of these three variables, the setting is the home office of a large insurance company. As might be expected, most of the employees are young women new to the labor force. Three indexes of satisfaction are used in this study. They are satisfaction with the company as a whole, satisfaction with pay and job status, and satisfaction with the job itself. The results show that there is no significant relationship between any of these indexes of satisfaction and the productivity of the work group. However, members of high-producing work groups recognize their groups as high producers; but this may not be satisfaction. Rather, it is a perception of the situation as it exists.

The design of the second study is the same as the first; however, the setting is as different as night from day. The work situation is the right-of-way maintenance jobs of approximately 300 railroad laborers and 72 foremen. The tasks performed are manual labor, not clerical functions; and the subjects are men, not young girls. Yet, the results are the same. No consistent relationship is found between productivity and the three indexes of job satisfaction. Again, the members of high-producing work groups are able to perceive their groups as high producers, but

---

[21] Robert L. Kahn, "Productivity and Job Satisfaction," *Personnel Pyschology,* Vol. XV (Autumn, 1960), pp. 275-287. Dr. Kahn also summarizes the results of the insurance study, the study of railroad workers, and the tractor study.

this ability to perceive a situation as it exists is not necessarily job satisfaction.

The third study is different in several respects from the first two. Instead of using group measures of productivity, individual production records for 6,000 production workers of a midwestern tractor company were examined and compared against known time study standards for each job. Also, instead of assuming indexes of job satisfaction, a factor analysis of data obtained from a carefully constructed questionnaire was performed to determine the dimensions of job satisfaction. These dimensions—presented in the discussion of morale—are: intrinsic job satisfaction, satisfaction with the company, satisfaction with rewards and mobility. Again, none of these measures of satisfaction are related to productivity.

A Concluding View

The search for the relationships between job satisfaction and productivity is frustrating to say the least. The Michigan Studies show that there is no clear-cut relationship between satisfaction and productivity. Also, an early review of the literature concludes that there is little evidence that there is either a simple or an appreciable relationship between employee attitudes toward their jobs and productivity.[22] Yet a later review of 23 studies shows that 20 of these studies result in a low but positive relationship; the average correlation being .14 between job satisfaction and productivity.[23] Remember, a coefficient of correlation is not a statement of causal relationship; it is merely a statement of covariance. Nonetheless, it is interesting to speculate why such a relationship exists.

Perhaps the best explanation for understanding the relationship between job satisfaction and productivity is offered by the concept of *perceived instrumentality*. Assume that an employee has clearly defined goals and that the performance of his job leads to certain rewards, either intrinsic to the job itself or extrinsic. If these rewards are perceived as equitable (defining equity as a balance between perceived inputs and perceived rewards), and if they are perceived as being instrumental as a means of attaining desired goals, then satisfaction from the work situation will result. However, if the individual does not

---

[22] Arthur H. Brayfield and Walter H. Crockett, "Employee Attitudes and Employee Performance," *Psychological Bulletin*, Vol. 52, No. 5 (September, 1955), pp. 415-422.

[23] Victor H. Vroom, *Work and Motivation* (New York: John Wiley & Sons, Inc., 1964).

have clearly stated goals or goals that can be satisfied by the work situation, or if there is a perceived inequity in the rewards, or if the rewards are not perceived as being instrumental in attaining goals, then satisfaction does not result from the work situation. These relationships are shown in Figure 18-3.[24]

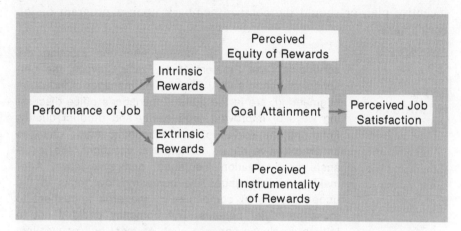

Figure 18-3

RELATIONSHIP BETWEEN JOB PERFORMANCE, INTRINSIC AND EXTRINSIC REWARDS, PERCEIVED EQUITY AND INSTRUMENTALITY OF REWARDS IN GOAL ATTAINMENT, AND PERCEIVED JOB SATISFACTION

Despite the fact that job satisfaction is best regarded as a dependent variable resulting from the performance of the job rather than causing the level of performance, the study of job satisfaction and the creation of satisfaction in jobs is a legitimate function of management. It does not seem likely that it is possible to achieve maximum organizational effectiveness for a long period of time with a low level of job satisfaction. Therefore, in designing motivational systems—the environment in which work is performed—a balance must be maintained between the goals and needs of the organization and the goals, needs, and capabilities of its members. To do otherwise could result in the depletion of one of the organization's most valuable resources—its people.

---

[24] The following references are suggested for a more complete discussion of instrumentality theory.

Ibid., Chapter 9, pp. 271-288.

Edward D. Lawler and Lyman W. Porter, "The Effect of Performance on Job Satisfaction," *Industrial Relations, A Journal of Economy and Society,* Vol. 7, No. 1 (October, 1967), pp. 20-28.

George Graen, "Instrumentality Theory of Work Motivation: Some Experimental Results and Suggested Modifications," *Journal of Applied Psychology,* Vol. 53, No. 2, Part 2 (April, 1969), pp. 1-25.

Case Problem 18-B describes the results experienced by Acme Manufacturing Company after having raised the level of its employee benefit program and poses another question to be resolved by the same management group: Should the company install a monetary incentive plan or should the company embark upon a program of job enrichment?

CASE PROBLEM 18-B

PART II: INCENTIVES OR JOB DESIGN?

Approximately 18 months after the meeting described in Case Problem 18-A, Frank Stevens, the personnel manager, and Al Conrad, the manager of industrial engineering, are in the general manager's office discussing ways of improving productivity and product quality. Following the survey of fringe benefits, Acme changed its practices in regard to holidays, vacations, life insurance, hospitalization insurance, and sick leave. After making these changes the company now ranks in the upper quartile of companies in the area in respect to these particular benefits. The company decided not to initiate employee services such as legal aid, counseling, a credit union, and a receation program because these benefits are offered by very few companies in the area. There has been no change in the policy of setting wage levels equal to the average of the area.

Since increasing the level of its fringe benefits, the company has been able to hire replacements without undue delay; turnover, which had been most noticeable among employees with less than six months' service, has declined to its previous level; and absenteeism has been reduced. However, there has been no change in productivity per man-hour, nor has there been any improvement in product quality. An analysis by the quality control department shows that about 80 percent of the quality problems can be traced to errors in assembly.

Because of the persistent quality problem and the lack of improvement in productivity, Mr. Rider, the general manager, requested two feasibility studies. One of these, prepared by industrial engineering, discusses the feasibility of an incentive plan for hourly employees; the other is a report by the personnel department concerning job enlargement. After reading these reports, Rider asked for a conference with the heads of the industrial engineering and the personnel departments.

Rider turned to Conrad and said, "Apparently your department questions the value of incentives as a means of increasing productivity. Would you summarize your position for Frank's benefit?"

"As you know," Conrad began, "we now have a measured day work plan; that is, we have time standards in most departments, but we do not have an incentive pay plan. The plant average is about 90 percent of stanard for those departments that have standards. The press room, where we form the metal parts of our appliances, and the machining department average about 93 percent; the plating and painting departments run about 95 percent; the assembly department, about 85 percent; and in shipping and receiving the packers are the only ones on standards and they average about 85 percent also."

At this point Stevens commented, "It seems that assembly and the packers are the ones pulling the plant average down."

"That is right," Conrad continued. "Even so, a plant average near 90 percent is not too bad. Frankly, I question how much we would gain with an incentive. In the press room and the assembly departments, the big factor in determining the output is the engineering design of the equipment and the manner in which it is maintained. Also, chrome plating requires a specified length of time for a given thickness of plate, and the capacity of the drying ovens is the limiting factor in our paint department. Improvement in production in these departments would be relatively small and the net gain in terms of earnings might be even smaller."

"Why is that?" Rider asked.

"To maintain standards for an incentive pay plan, I would have to double the size of my department. We would have to set additional standards for jobs that are run only infrequently. Complaints about standards would have to be answered promptly. All of this takes more people—I estimate at least an additional $50,000 a year in salaries alone. Sooner or later we would be forced into the position of paying the plant average to all workers—maintenance men, janitors, shipping and receiving—because they will contend that they are having to do more work since more units are being produced; yet, actually their workload would change very little."

Looking at Frank Stevens, Mr. Rider said "It seems to me that it is questionable whether we would actually gain very much from an incentive pay plan in view of what Conrad has said. What about your recommendation of job enlargement?"

"Since most of our difficulty is in the assembly department, I would suggest that we start there by eliminating the assembly lines and having each person assemble the entire product and do his own packing. There have been several instances where this approach has worked. If we had each person assemble the entire unit, inspect that unit, then insert an inspection slip into the box after packing the unit, we would have a much better control over quality."

"But assembly accounts for only one department," Conrad said. "What about the departments?"

"In the press room and the machining departments we could have the operators learn how to make their own setups and make minor repairs instead of having the tool room make the setups and the maintenance department making all repairs, even the minor ones."

"You do that and we will have to pay all the machine operators a much higher rate since they will be classed as skilled rather than semiskilled," Conrad interrupted. "Also, we would be undertaking a tremendous training program, and at present we don't have that kind of staff."

Rider realized that he was no nearer a solution after talking to Conrad and Stevens than he had been before the conference. He decided to meet with them again in a week.

PROBLEMS

1. As the general manager of Acme, would you accept the recommendations of the personnel department? Why?
2. What additional information would you need to make a decision?
3. Is the industrial engineering department correct in not recommending an incentive plan? Discuss.

Chapter Questions for Study and Discussion

1. Why is it necessary for managers to know something about the fundamental needs of man in order to motivate employees successfully? From

your own experience, describe an intended motivator that did not correspond to your own personal needs.

2. Of what significance are the physiological and safety needs in our economy today? Under what conditions would these needs become more significant?

3. What is meant by variations in the hierarchy of needs? Why is it necessary to recognize that such variations exist? In your opinion, which is the most important single variation in the hierarchy that can occur?

4. Evaluate the four categories of perception of one's self in relation to his environment as described by Gellerman. What is the probable outcome of using money as a means of motivation for each of Gellerman's four categories?

5. Give an example of conflicting needs in an industrial situation and show how this conflict affects employee motivation.

6. Why do monetary incentive plans achieve the desired goal of increased production in some companies if money is not a true motivator?

7. Differentiate between hygienic factors and motivators. Why is this distinction important?

8. What reasons can you advance to support the present practice of job design?

9. What is meant by job enrichment? What factors limit the opportunity for job enrichment?

10. Describe in your own words the meaning of the phrase "industrial morale."

11. Does it seem reasonable to you that whenever possible a company should strive to provide an industrial situation that will result in high morale on the part of its employees even though productivity is not increased? Discuss.

CHAPTER 19

The Supervisor and Productivity

The managers of Apex Manufacturing, a company with approximately 750 employees, prided themselves in running what the company called a "tight ship." They are satisfied with the results of a recent attitude survey which shows that most employees believe that supervision is "strict, but fair." Like most of the other members of management, John Sweeney has come up through the ranks and is currently assigned to Department #40, the lacquer department, where he supervises 35 hourly employees. He has been with the company for 20 years, and for the last 10 years he has been a foreman. John tries to be fair to the men working for him, and at the same time administer company policies in accordance with the wishes of the general superintendent who is very strict in his interpretation of company rules and regulations. John is waiting in his office for the arrival of Joe Adams, the union steward for Department #40.

"John, I'd like to talk to you about Jim Wilson, the man you discharged yesterday afternoon."

"Not much to talk about, Joe," John replied. "You know he was smoking in restricted areas."

"That's just the point, John. The rules don't say that you have to discharge him. All they say is that anyone who violates any of the Group One rules is *subject to* immediate discharge. That's a long way from saying that you *have* to discharge him."

"Look, Joe, I know that you have your job to do with the union and that you have a perfect right to question any action that I may take. But look at this

CASE PROBLEM 19-A

NO SMOKING

case. Jim was with the company for over 12 years; certainly in that length of time he should know what the company rules mean. They are there for a reason. You know that this department could blow up the whole plant if there was a fire in here, what with this lacquer we have to work with. There are *No Smoking* signs all over the place and the men in the spray booths even wear rubber soles so there is no chance for sparks. Sorry, there's nothing I can do about it; one mistake here would blow us all to hell and back."

"You say that Jim has been with us 12 years. That's true, but he's only been in your department for three months. He just forgot, maybe worried or something."

"I can't help that. Maybe it was some guy down the street last month who was just worried, or new, or something, and you know what happened. That fire took the lives of three employees in that plant and cost millions of dollars, and none of them are back to work yet. We don't want that happening here, and it won't if I have anything to do about it."

"John, you aren't leaving me much choice. I'm going to file a grievance, and I promise you this one will go all the way to arbitration. Twelve years of service without a single reprimand ought to mean something." With that remark, Joe Adams, the steward, left the foreman's office.

PROBLEMS

1. Do you agree with the action taken by John Sweeney, the foreman? Explain.
2. Has the steward presented his case well? Is he quibbling when he says that the words "subject to" do not mean that the foreman must discharge an employee?
3. The next step of the grievance procedure in Apex Manufacturing calls for a decision by the general superintendent. If he reverses Sweeney's stand, what effect will this have on Sweeney's relations with his men?
4. Of what significance are the "fire down the street" and the "12 years of service without a reprimand"?

Many statements have been made concerning the importance of the first-line supervisor because of his role in the attainment of the production goals of the organization and because his position in the managerial hierarchy results in his being the only member of management who directs the work of nonmanagerial employees. In the preceding chapter doubt is cast upon the value of monetary incentives *per se* or employee benefit programs as a means of motivating employees to higher levels of productivity. Further, the Michigan studies show that there is no consistent relationship between productivity and job satisfaction or morale. However, these studies do reveal a predictable relationship between supervisory practice and productivity; hence the importance of the supervisor in the achievement of the production goals of the organization.

This chapter is intended to provide an insight into the problems encountered by a supervisor. Most of the examples of supervisory practices refer to the manufacturing supervisor; however, it should be recognized that the supervisor of an accounting section or an order processing group has essentially the same problems. In order to provide insight into supervisory practices the following topics are discussed: (1) The Supervisor's Job, (2) Selection and Training of Supervisors, and (3) Improving Supervisory Performance.

THE SUPERVISOR'S JOB

The terms *supervisor* and *foreman* are frequently used interchangeably; however, in this chapter the term supervisor is used since it is somewhat broader in its application and also implies one of the major functions of supervision—to supervise. The term foreman is usually limited to supervisors in manufacturing organizations or to those supervising semiskilled or unskilled workers. The title supervisor is applicable to those who direct the work of others in laboratories, offices, retail establishments, and sales organizations as well as to those directing the work of hourly paid employees in manufacturing concerns. By definition, a supervisor is a part of management. His position in management is unique—his is the only level of management charged with the responsibility of directing the work of nonmanagerial employees. Members of middle and top management perform various administrative tasks, and if they do direct the work of others it is the work of other managers.[1] The supervisor's position, between the upper levels of management and the hourly nonmanagerial employees has been described rather caustically, if not disparagingly, as the "man in the

---

[1] It is recognized that many members of middle and top management may have secretarial employees reporting to them, but the direction of these employees is incidental to their primary function which is usually administrative or the performance of a staff duty.

middle" [2] and the "marginal man of industry." [3] The supervisor has also been referred to as both "master and victim of double talk" as well as being "victim, not monarch, of all he surveys." [4] It is important to recognize that the supervisor is the man in the middle and because of his sometimes ambiguous position we have the key to the primary function of his job—"the linking-pin function." [5] Before developing the concept of the linking-pin function, let us review the legal definition of the supervisor's job.

Legal Definition

As defined by federal legislation, a supervisor is:

. . . any individual having authority, in the interest of the employer, to hire, transfer, suspend, lay off, recall, promote, discharge, assign, reward, or discipline other employees, or responsibility to direct them, or to adjust their grievances, or effectively to recommend such action, if in connection with the foregoing the exercise of such authority is not of a merely routine or clerical nature, but requires the use of independent judgment. [6]

Another federal law, the Fair Labor Standards Act of 1938 (as amended) is often called the minimum wage law; one of its tests in determining whether or not a person is a supervisor is the amount of time spent performing work that is the same as that performed by the people under his direction. Supervisors are expected to spend no more than 20 percent of their time doing the same kind of work that is performed by employees whom they are directing. In effect, the National Labor-Management Relations Act determines who is eligible to join an employees' union, and the Fair Labor Standards Act determines whether or not an employee is paid to be on an hourly basis (usually with overtime for hours in excess of a specified number) or whether he is to be paid a salary with no compensation required for overtime. Supervisors cannot join a union of production or clerical employees; however, they can form a union composed entirely of supervisors. With

---

[2] B. B. Gardner, and W. F. Whyte, "The Man in the Middle: Postions and Problems of the Foreman," *Applied Anthropology,* Vol. IV (Winter, 1945), pp. 1-28.

[3] D. E. Wray, "Marginal Man of Industry: The Foreman," *American Journal of Sociology,* Vol. LIV (January, 1949), pp. 298-301.

[4] F. J. Roethlisberger, "The Foreman: Master and Victim of Double Talk," *Harvard Business Review,* Vol. XXIII (September, 1945), pp. 283-298.

[5] Rensis Likert, *New Patterns of Management* (New York: McGraw-Hill Book Company, Inc., 1961), p. 113. Chapter 8, "An Integrating Principle and an Overview," pp. 97-118, presents a detailed discussion of the linking-pin function of supervision.

[6] National Labor-Management Relations Act (Taft-Hartley), 1947 (as amended), Section 101, Subsection 2 (11).

respect to pay, supervisors are paid a salary and are exempt from the provisions of the law requiring compensation for overtime. Hence, supervisors are commonly called "exempt" employees.

The net result of these two pieces of legislation is that the supervisor is by definition a part of management, but the supervisor does not always view himself as being the same as the other members of management.

How the Supervisor Sees Himself

We have mentioned that the supervisor's position is unique in that it requires him to interact with nonmanagerial employees as well as with management. There is also a personal history characteristic that tends to set the supervisor apart from other members of management. Typically the first-line supervisor is promoted from the hourly ranks, and it is not at all unusual for him to supervise men whom he has known for years and with whom he has worked as an equal. At other levels of management, men usually start their careers as managers and are not in the position of having to change their attitudes toward former associates as they advance in the organization. With this difference in background, it is worthwhile to ask whether the supervisor sees himself in the same light as other members of management see themselves or whether he views himself as being more like the hourly group from which he was promoted.

Lyman W. Porter administered a self-description inventory consisting of 64 pairs of adjectives to 172 first-level supervisors, 291 upper-level management personnel, and 320 hourly production employees.[7] Each person was required to check one adjective of each pair that in his opinion offered the best self-description. The results of this study show that supervisors most frequently see themselves as planful, deliberate, calm, fair minded, steady, responsible, civilized, self-controlled, logical, judicial, and honest. Upper-level management personnel, a group including department heads, staff personnel, and vice-presidents, see themselves as resourceful, sharp witted, sincere, thoughtful, sociable, reliable, dignified, imaginative, adaptable, sympathetic, and generous. The hourly worker believes himself to be ambitious, industrious, sharp witted, efficient, thoughtful, sociable, pleasant, reliable, and adaptable.

Note that there is a clear differentiation between each of the three groups. The supervisor sees himself as a moderate, if not conservative,

---

[7] Lyman W. Porter, "Self-Perception of First-Level Supervisors Compared with Upper-Management Personnel and with Operative Line Workers," *Journal of Applied Psychology,* Vol. VIL (June, 1959), pp. 183-186.

individual who acts as a stabilizing influence—an image not at all unsuited for "the man in the middle." The upper levels of management picture themselves as the successful entrepreneur who is imaginative, resourceful, and sharp witted; yet thoughtful, sympathetic, and dignified. The hourly worker is clearly on the way up. There does not seem to be any trend in self-image from the hourly ranks, through the supervisory group, to the upper levels of management. The supervisor's image of himself does not retain the elements of the hourly image, nor has it acquired the outgoing self-confident characteristic of the higher levels of management. A look at a typical day in the life of a supervisor shows us why a calm, judicial attitude is the safest perception of self.

A Typical Day

We know that the supervisor's primary function is to direct the efforts of hourly personnel reporting to him. The data presented below are a composite of many supervisors and many days in an automobile assembly plant; however, the results are typical of supervisory activities in most of the mass-production industries—cans, glass containers, appliances, etc. The method employed in the research study described is applicable to any industrial setting and should be used by any organization interested in improving the performance of its supervisors.

The Method. Walker, Guest, and Turner decided to follow up their work on the man on the assembly line by studying the foreman on the assembly line.[8] Fifty-six foremen were observed for a full eight-hour day. On the day before the actual observation, the observer spent approximately three hours with the foreman becoming acquainted with the layout of the department, the nature of the operation, and the names and duties of key personnel. Starting the next morning at the beginning of the shift each of the foreman's activities was recorded and classified as follows: *Time*—the time the incident occurred; *Topic*—what the incident concerned, what it was about; *Activity*—what the foreman did; *Place*—where the incident occurred; *Contact*—who was involved in the incident; and *Interaction*—what was the nature of the contact. At the end of the day the observations were dictated and transcribed, then the typewritten record (some 40 to 70 pages in length) was reviewed with the foreman for interpretation and corrections. The results of the

---

[8] C. R. Walker, R. H. Guest, and A. N. Turner, *The Foreman on the Assembly Line* (Cambridge, Mass.: Harvard University Press), 1956.

56 observations were tabulated and analyzed. A total of 32,652 incidents was recorded. The following is a sequence of 14 incidents during an 11½-minute interval for a foreman named Pat.

Time	*Description*
2:15 p.m.	Pat checks with scheduler, S. Looks at hourly report of number of cars coming through body shop.
2:16	Walks over to R (repair man) on pickup line and checks to see if earlier repair trouble was corrected.
2:17	Calls over inspection foreman to show him a hole missing in a piece. Inspection foreman acknowledges he will notify the trim department.
2:19	Pat tells the repair man to locate the hole by eye until it comes through all right.
2:19½	Pat has a drink of water.
2:20	Pat walks over to station 5 and asks his utility man how many men he still has to relieve.
2:20½	Moves along the line—stations 5, 6, 7—checking visually on the quality of work.
2:21	Checks a loose nut on a fixture at station 7. Speaks with operator.
2:22	Man at station 3 calls for materials.
2:22¼	Pat tells man at subassembly bench E to make up more material.
2:23	Walks over to MH (stock man). Tells stock man the line is getting low on hinges. They discuss the number short and agree there is enough for tomorrow.
2:25	Pat walks from MH to station 1 and makes visual inspection of the car body to check on the hole discussed earlier at the pickup line.
2:26	Pat sees foreman from preceding section and tells him about the missing hole.
2:26½	A hand signal from welder, W.[9]

The range in the number of incidents for each foreman during an 8-hour day is from a low of 237 to a high of 1,073. The average number of incidents is 583; thus during a 480-minute workday a foreman does something different every 48 seconds. It requires a great deal of flexibility to move from one problem to another at the rate of more than one every minute. The supervisor's perception of himself as a calm and moderate person is no accident—he must believe and act like a

---

[9] Robert H. Guest, "Of Time and the Foreman," *Personnel*, Vol. XXXII, (May, 1956), p. 480. This article, pp. 478-486, shows clearly the pressures of time on a supervisor and points up the difference between what he should do and what he can do.

moderate; otherwise the pressures of his job could cause a complete psychological breakdown.

Let us now look more closely at the nature of the foreman's work, the topics; the actions he must take to accomplish the work, the activities, and the persons involved in these activities, the contacts.

Topics. Table 19-1, Average Amount of Time Spent by Foreman on Each Topic, shows that almost one third of his time, 31.4 percent, is directed toward the product—quality and progress of work. These figures are averages; there is a wide variation in the allocation of time between foremen, and for the same foreman from day to day. It is noted that when emergencies arise, the first activity to suffer is the amount of time spent on personal relations, normally 10.2 percent, or about 50 minutes a day. When an emergency arises—a shortage of materials, a change in schedule, a defective jig or fixture—the problem must be solved immediately. Consequently, two or three hours may be spent on the problem. One conclusion is inescapable from reviewing the nature of the topics—the foreman has little control over where he spends his time from day to day or minute to minute. The amount of effective planning a foreman can do is limited by the work situation.

Activities. Table 19-2 reveals that almost half of the foreman's time is spent talking, thereby emphasizing the importance of communication. There is a lot of walking, between four and six miles a day, and very little sitting, less than a minute a day. The need for health and stamina is obvious. The high percentage of time spent in looking, 20.9 percent, is related to the first two topics of Table 19-1, quality and work progress. Looking, as it is used in Table 19-2, means interpreting the work situation. If showing is considered an instructional activity, there is very little time spent in instructing personnel. The small amount of time spent in reading and writing is significant; it shows that nearly all clerical work has been eliminated from the foreman's job, thus freeing his time to observe the operations under his direction.

Contacts. Over 57 percent of the foreman's time is spent in face-to-face contacts, as indicated in Table 19-3. The percentage of time spent in contacts is somewhat higher than the percentage of time spent talking since some of the contacts involve a sign or gesture as a means of communication. Remember, the average amount of time spent on each topic is only 48 seconds; therefore, contacts and verbal exchanges with others are brief and sometimes fragmentary. Only a fourth of the

Table 19-1

AVERAGE AMOUNT OF TIME SPENT BY FOREMAN ON EACH TOPIC

Topic	Percent of time
Quality	18.2
Work progress	13.2
Personnel administration	11.2
Personal relations and other nonjob-related topics	10.2
Foreman performance of an operation	8.1
Tools, jigs, and fixtures	8.1
Materials	8.0
Employee job performance	7.6
Production schedule	5.2
Grievances	2.0
Injury, illness	1.2
Housekeeping	.5
Work standards	.4
Safety	.2
Meeting	.1
Miscellaneous	2.4
Topic unknown	2.4

Source: Robert H. Guest, "Of Time and the Foreman," *Personnel,* Vol. XXXII (May, 1956), p. 481.

Table 19-2

AVERAGE AMOUNT OF TIME SPENT BY EACH FOREMAN ON EACH ACTIVITY

Activity	Percent of time
Talks	46.6
Looks	20.9
Manipulates	9.6
Walks	6.9
Hands, carries	5.6
Reads	2.9
Telephones	2.4
Writes	2.1
Stands	1.0
Signals	.8
Listens	.6
Shows	.4
Sits	.2
	100.0

Source: Robert H. Guest, "Of Time and the Foreman," *Personnel,* Vol. XXXII (May, 1956), p. 482.

Table 19-3

AVERAGE AMOUNT OF TIME SPENT BY FOREMAN ON EACH CONTACT

Contact	Percent of time
Own operators	26.4
Other foremen	7.0
General foreman	4.6
Department superintendent	1.1
Other superiors	.4
Service personnel:	
Maintenance	2.5
Inspection	2.3
Material	2.6
Work standards	.4
Other operators	3.8
All Others	6.2
	57.3

Source: Robert H. Guest, "Of Time and the Foreman," Personnel, Vol. XXXII (May, 1956), p. 482.

foreman's day is spent in contact with his own operators. Yet training programs emphasize superior-subordinate relationship, even though most contacts are with other foremen, supportive personnel, and superiors.

In our discussion of the method used by Walker, Guest, and Turner in analyzing the foreman's job, it is stated that the incidents were also classified in respect to the place where each occurred and the type of interaction involved. Fourteen percent of the incidents normally occur outside the work area under the foreman's supervision, and 60.3 percent of the contacts are initiated by the foreman himself. Thirty-seven percent are the result of someone else wanting to contact the foreman.

In conclusion, the study of the foreman on the assembly line shows the variety of tasks that go to make up a foreman's job and the extent to which the job is structured by the nature of the operation, the objectives, the plans, the controls of top management, and the facilities provided to do the job. Although the supervisor is the one member of management in direct contact with operating employees, he spends relatively little time directly supervising subordinates.[10]

---

[10] The following study suggests that the amount of time spent by the supervisor in the direct supervision of subordinates is a function of technology; i.e., as the technology of an organization moves away from the concept of a craft and toward highly automatic or automated technologies the supervisor spends less time in the direct supervision of subordinates. Elmer H. Burack, "Technology and Some Aspects of Industrial Supervision: A Model Building Approach," *Academy of Management Journal*, Vol. 9, No. 1 (March, 1966), pp. 43-66.

Dimensions of Supervisory Performance

The preceding discussion illustrates the variety of tasks a supervisor must perform during the course of a typical day in a mass-production industry. It tells us little about the broad aspects of supervision or those factors that determine effective supervisory performance. Sandia Corporation of Albuquerque, New Mexico, wanted to know the independent dimensions, or factors, of administrative and general supervisory positions. Four hundred and fourteen supervisors were asked to write an essay describing the performance of the best supervisor that they knew at Sandia Corporation. The descriptive statements were tabulated and a questionnaire containing 303 items describing supervisory performance was constructed. Three hundred and seventy-two supervisors then applied this questionnaire as a checklist to develop a descriptive rating of the best and the worst supervisor they knew. These ratings were analyzed by means of multiple-factor analysis, and six independent dimensions of supervisory performance were obtained: [11]

1. Establishment of work climate.
2. Management ethics.
3. Self-development and subordinate development.
4. Personal maturity and sensitivity.
5. Knowledge and execution of corporate policies.
6. Technical job knowledge.

Establishment of Work Climate. Descriptive statements characteristic of this factor are: expects a day's work, disciplines when necessary, and expects only the best. A supervisor rating high in this respect establishes and maintains high performance standards. He is goal oriented and if necessary will put the attainment of stated objectives above the likes and dislikes of subordinates.

Management Ethics. The essence of this dimension is ethical behavior on the part of a supervisor in his dealings with other supervisors and members of top management. The same ethical behavior is also shown in his relationships with subordinates. Statements characterizing this trait are: gives credit where due, honest in discussing development of subordinates, no under-the-table deals, and doesn't promise anything he can't do.

---

[11] Sherwood H. Peres, "Performance Dimensions of Supervisory Positions," *Personnel Psychology*, Vol. XV (Winter, 1962), pp. 405-410. Seven factors were isolated; however, the seventh factor is a bias factor resulting from the halo effect present in rating scales. It is not a true factor of supervisory performance.

Self-Development and Subordinate Development. The effective supervisor is interested in personnel development—the growth of subordinates as well as his own. He attempts to make assignments interesting and challenging and tries to know his subordinates better so that he may direct their growth. He encourages outside study and pursues such activity himself. He tries to keep up with the professional aspects of management through reading and participation in outside groups.

Personal Maturity and Sensitivity. Two elements are closely related in this factor; one is personal maturity and emotional stability, and the other is empathy—a sensitivity to the feelings of others. Supervisors strong in this dimension maintain an "open door" policy, they have a knack of saying the right thing at the right time, do not lose control under pressure, and seem to lighten serious situations with a sense of humor.

Knowledge and Execution of Corporate Policies. Note that knowledge of policy is not sufficient; there must also be execution of policy. Strong supervisors keep up with changes in policy and procedures and keep their subordinates informed of such changes. Those strong in this characteristic are orderly and tend to follow the "letter of the law." The result of this trait is that it gives a supervisor's behavior consistency and predictability.

Technical Job Knowledge. This dimension of supervision suggests not only technical knowledge but also the drive and willingness to get the job done. The supervisor has sufficient background and information to understand a new problem quickly. He is technically competent and does more than is expected of him.

The "Linking-Pin" Function

The legal definition of a supervisor cited at the beginning of this chapter details only the relationships between a supervisor and his subordinates. If questioned, many managers would also answer that a supervisor's job is to direct the work of those who report to him. The breadth of contacts of the assembly-line foreman shows the narrowness and inadequacy of a definition that stresses the direction of subordinates. Only 26 percent of the assembly foreman's time is spent in contact with personnel under his direction; the balance of his time is in contact with superiors, service personnel, other foremen, and operators other than his own who contribute to the work of his department.

The analysis of supervisory positions at Sandia Corporation reveals that successful performance requires a person capable of much more than directing the efforts of others. Successful performance requires a structuring of the work situation; ethical behavior in personal relationships with superiors, peers, and subordinates; and effective execution of company policy.

The key to the supervisor's primary function is his singular position in the organization—the only member of management in direct contact with nonmanagerial personnel. He is the one member of management capable of linking management to operative personnel. For this reason his major function is best described as a *linking-pin* function.[12]

SELECTION AND TRAINING OF SUPERVISORS

Now that we have some insight into the nature of the supervisor's job, let us examine some of the problems associated with the selection and training of supervisors.

Selection of Supervisors

As the first step in the selection of personnel for any position in an organization, whether it be the job of janitor or president, it is necessary to know the job requirements for the position in question. One way of stating job requirements is by preparing a job description such as those shown in Chapter 14. However, the usual job description with its statement of responsibilities and duties to be performed leaves much to be desired as a measure of personal characteristics needed to meet the demands of a given position. What is needed is a statement of job requirements using a terminology applicable to both the job and its incumbent. A *job complexity profile* performs both functions.[13]

Job Complexity Profile. Based upon several hundred interviews with supervisors at different levels of many organizations, psychologists have come to the conclusion that supervisory positions—and also executive jobs in the upper levels of management—require six different activities for their successful performance. These activities, arranged in approximate chronological sequence, are:

---

[12] Likert, *op. cit.*, p. 113.

[13] Harold F. Rothe, "Matching Men to Job Requirements," *Personnel Psychology*, Vol. IV (Autumn, 1951), pp. 291-301. A detailed statement of job complexity analysis may be obtained from Dr. Rothe, or the author, or Stevenson, Jordan, and Harrison, Inc., 205 W. Wacker Drive, Chicago. Similar approaches to the analysis of jobs have been prepared by L. R. Gaiennie and J. C. Flanagan.

L. R. Gaiennie, "An Approach to Supervisory Organization Control in Industry," *Personnel Psychology*, Vol. III (Spring, 1950), pp. 41-52.

J. C. Flanagan, "A New Approach to Evaluating Personnel," *Personnel Psychology*, Vol. XXVI (July, 1949), pp. 35-42.

1. Planning an activity.
2. Deciding what to do or not to do.
3. Organizing a group of persons to carry out the plans.
4. Communicating the plan to the organization.
5. Leading a group to fulfill the plan.
6. Analyzing progress being made so that plans may be revised if necessary.

These are not discrete independent activities; instead, one leads into another and several may be performed at the same time. Their value is that they are readily understandable and can be used to describe both job requirements and the personal qualifications of any candidate being considered for the job. Each job is analyzed and graded on a 16-point scale for each of these activities in the same manner that jobs are rated in a job evaluation program.

When presented in profile form, the factors are rearranged and abbreviated so that they appear in the following order: plan, communicate, analyze, lead, delegate, and decide. The first three activities—planning, communicating, and analyzing—draw upon the intellectual capabilities of a person. Planning requires the ability to reason, to perceive relationships; communicating requires verbal skills and the ability to express ideas that range from the simple to the very complex; and analyzing, as the term is used here, is dependent upon the ability to understand mathematical relationships. There are very few managerial jobs not requiring the ability to understand numerical concepts. The next three activities—lead, delegate, and decide—demand certain personality characteristics for their performance. Leadership is defined primarily in terms of the degree of social dominance or aggressiveness required and is dependent to a large extent upon the characteristics of the group being led. Delegation requires a sense of personal security and the willingness to accept responsibility for the work of others. The making of decisions is considered as dependent upon personality, not the intellectual ability of planning and arriving at a "correct" solution. To decide is to make a mature, responsible choice and be willing to follow that choice through to its conclusion. It is the characteristic of decisiveness.

Figure 19-1 shows the job profiles for the positions of section supervisor, general supervisor, and superintendent of a manufacturing firm. Note the requirements for leadership and delegation of the general superintendent position. The size of the group being led is large and heterogeneous, and leadership must be accomplished by working through several levels of supervision. The section foreman does very little

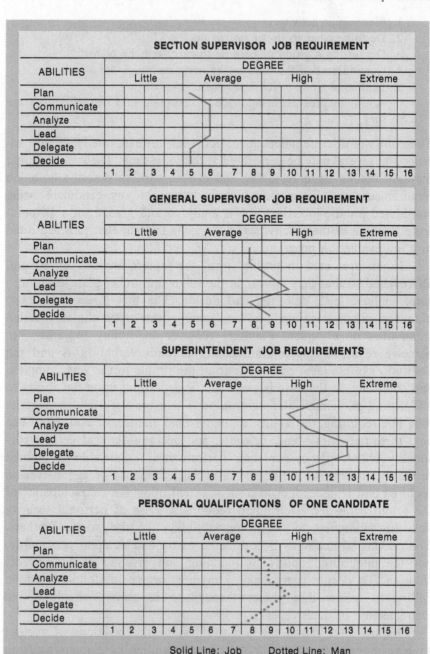

Solid Line: Job   Dotted Line: Man

Source: Harold F. Rothe, "Matching Men to Job Requirements," *Personnel Psychology,* Vol. IV (Autumn, 1951), p. 297.

Figure 19-1

**COMPARISON OF QUALIFICATIONS OF ONE CANDIDATE
WITH REQUIREMENTS OF THREE JOBS**

delegating and his group is relatively homogeneous in character, conditions that require only an average ability to lead and to delegate. The personal qualifications of a candidate, also shown in Figure 19-1, may be matched against the requirements of the job as an aid in making the final choice in the selection process. One of the methods used in preparing the personal qualification profile of the candidate is discussed later in this chapter under the heading, "The Personnel Evaluation."

Sources of Supervision. Most companies fill vacancies in supervisory ranks by promoting personnel from hourly jobs; however, some supervisors are recruited from other companies, and there is a growing tendency to recruit college graduates for these positions. Promotion from within aids in building the morale of an organization since it satisfies employee needs for recognition and mobility. In addition, there is reasonable assurance that the candidate has the necessary technical knowledge and skills for the position. When supervisors are sought from other companies, it is usually because an organization is in a period of rapid expansion and does not have a sufficient number of trained hourly personnel.

Companies that promote from within may be able to identify the successful supervisor rather early in his career and establish a pool of potential supervisors through the use of peer (buddy) ratings. Weitz investigated the use of peer ratings as a means of identifying supervisors prior to their promotion to supervisory positions.[14] The company in question was a large insurance company with 2,200 agents (salesmen) in 127 sales districts. Each district was headed by a district manager who had reporting to him several assistant managers. Each assistant manager supervised an average of four agents. Each agent rated the other agents with whom he worked by completing a questionnaire; total scores for each agent were then computed and for those promoted to assistant manager the scores were later compared with ratings obtained in supervisory positions. Weitz concludes that there are characteristics which differentiate between successful and unsuccessful supervisors and that these characteristics can be identified prior to promotion to a supervisory position by obtaining ratings from peers performing the same nonsupervisory job.

College graduates may be recruited and assigned supervisory positions in several different departments as part of a training program

---

[14] Joseph Weitz, "Selecting Supervisors with Peer Ratings," *Personnel Psychology*, Vol. XI (Spring, 1958), pp. 25-35. Weitz's article contains the questionnaire used by insurance agents in nominating their peers for supervisory positions and the rating form used by district managers which served as the criterion for the study.

designed to acquaint them with the various phases of a company's operations. The graduate generally spends three to six months in a department as an assistant supervisor and is then assigned to another section. Upon completion of the training program, which usually takes two years, he may be assigned full supervisory responsibilities. The college-trained supervisor who has the personality characteristics necessary for supervision does surprisingly well despite his lack of technical knowledge. The reason for his success is probably due to his "influence" with upper levels of management.[15] Though presently in a supervisory position of the lowest level of management, he is hired with the expectations of advancing to the upper levels of the organization. His subordinates are aware of his potential in the company and, if they perceive his influence with his superiors and like him personally, they supply the necessary technical knowledge. Subordinates are also capable of making the trainee appear a dismal failure.

Selection Methods. The methods used in selecting supervisors range from an informal interview to the highly sophisticated personnel evaluation. Each of the tools used in selection is capable of contributing to the selection process, provided it is used with skill and there is a clear concept of the requirements of the job. In our discussion of the methods used in selecting supervisors, it is assumed that the candidate is from within the organization; however, the same methods are applicable to the selection of personnel from outside the company.

THE INTERVIEW. In its simplest form, an interview is an informal discussion between the candidate and a general supervisor or a representative of the personnel department in which the candidate is informed that there is a supervisory position available and is asked whether or not he would like the job. With this form of interview there is little opportunity to learn more about the candidate, nor does he have much opportunity of becoming acquainted with the advantages and disadvantages of the job. The interview should provide a free exchange of information so that the candidate knows fully the requirements and opportunities of the position. At the same time, the interviewer should attempt to understand the motivation of the candidate in seeking the position and form an estimate of the personal characteristics of the candidate. A series of interviews conducted by present members of supervision and upper levels of management is often helpful when the

---

15 Donald C. Pelz, "Influence: A Key to Effective Leadership in the First-Line Supervisor," *Personnel*, Vol. XXIX (November, 1952), pp. 209-217. This study of employee attitudes of employees of the Detroit Edison Company shows the importance of influence as a factor in effective supervision.

impressions gained from the interviews are compared so that the best judgment of the group can be determined. Having the candidate appear before a group offers the possibility of observing his reactions to the pressures of an unfamiliar situation and inferences may be drawn concerning the way in which he might react under the stress of a supervisory job. The interview is a good means of assessing speech, gestures, personal appearance, persuasiveness, and the sincerity of a potential supervisor.

COMPANY RECORDS. Job titles of previous positions held in the company indicate the breadth of technical skills and knowledge that may have been acquired by the candidate. Previous jobs also show rate of progress, and from the pattern of progression certain inferences may be drawn in regard to the candidate's ability and interests. If the company has a merit rating plan, the record of merit reviews should also be examined and summarized. The application form completed at the time of employment usually provides information pertaining to age, education, prior experience, community activities, and other outside interests. Personal history items recorded in the application for employment should be supplemented with current information concerning outside activities and interests at the time of the interview.

TESTING PROGRAMS. Psychological tests may be used as part of the total program for selecting supervisors. When tests are used, the test battery usually includes a measure of intelligence, interests, personality, and mechanical or other special aptitudes. The usefulness of tests depends upon the skill of the interpreter and the extent to which the tests have been validated for the particular job in question. If the company has administered the test battery to its present supervisors and has found a clear relationship between performance on the job and performance on the tests, then the tests are considered valid; i.e., they measure what they purport to measure.[16] If a validating procedure has not been carried out, the use of tests borders on wishful thinking. All too often management looks to tests as a magic formula for improving supervisory performance, yet the real reason for inadequate performance is usually in the design of the job, not the capabilities of the supervisor.[17]

---

[16] Hubert Clay, "Experiences in Testing Foremen," *Personnel,* Vol. XXVIII (May, 1952), pp. 466-470. Dr. Clay presents a step-by-step approach to the introduction of a testing program for the selection of supervisors. He discusses the reaction of supervisors to tests and makes suggestions for the interpretation of test results.

[17] Mason Haire, "Use of Tests in Employee Selection," *Harvard Business Review,* Vol. 28 (January-February, 1950), pp. 42-51. Professor Haire discusses the difficulties of establishing a testing program and reviews many of the problems of performance that are not related to the capabilities of employees but which are the result of the structure of the situation in which they are working.

THE PERSONNEL EVALUATION. The personnel evaluation—or as it is sometimes called, the psychological evaluation—is of special value in the selection process when a candidate is being considered for a position requiring skills and abilities he has not had the opportunity to demonstrate, or when a man is being recruited from another company. The personnel evaluation is an extensive analysis in depth conducted by a professional psychologist who has had training in both clinical and industrial psychology. The evaluation may begin with the development of a personal history that includes education, prior vocational experience, early life, aspirations, and views on current problems. A brief intelligence test may be administered to check the present level of intellectual functioning against work history items and educational background. Personality characteristics are usually evaluated by means of tests and a clinical interview. From the information thus obtained, the psychologist is able to describe in dynamic, motivational terms the personality structure and function of the candidate. If the psychologist is familiar with the demands of the job in question, a combined job-man profile may be constructed as in Figure 19-1, page 588. The worth of the personnel evaluation is dependent upon the clinical judgment and skill of the psychologist and management's insight into the demands of the job.[18]

A COMPOSITE APPROACH. The following suggested procedure combines each of the methods above into an integrated selection process.

1. Prepare a job complexity profile of the position to be filled. It is essential that the traditional job description be rephrased so that personal requirements and job requirements are clearly understood.

2. A trained representative of the personnel department should compile and summarize all available company records for each candidate.

3. Separate interviews with each candidate should be conducted by interested supervisors and personnel from other levels of management. The impressions gained from these interviews should be stated in written form.

4. An interview conducted by a group may be desirable as a check on the impressions gained from individual interviews and as a means of observing the candidate under moderate pressure.

5. If the personnel department is adequately staffed with professionally trained personnel, psychological tests may be utilized. If the

---

[18] Charles D. McDermid, "The Psychological Evaluation," *Advanced Management-Office Executive,* Vol. I (November, 1962), pp. 22, 23-25. Dr. McDermid's article is one of the very few descriptive statements of the personnel evaluation written by a professional psychologist.

personnel department is not adequately staffed, psychological tests
should not be used in the selection of supervisors.

6. A personnel evaluation prepared by a professionally trained psychologist may be obtained for each candidate. The confidential report
prepared by the psychologist should be sent to the personnel department or to a member of top management.

7. The personnel department should prepare a written record of all
proceedings (including company records, test results, interview impressions, and the personnel evaluation) and forward the applicant's
completed file to the appropriate line executive for final decision.

Training of Supervisors

*"You could dispose of almost all the leadership training courses
for supervision in American industry today without anyone knowing the
difference."* [19]

The above statement, made by Robert H. Guest, is not intended
as a criticism of the content or methods of leadership training programs
for supervisors; instead, it is intended to emphasize that the conditions
of the supervisor's job—refer to Tables 19-1, 19-2, and 19-3—are
often such that it is difficult, if not impossible, to exercise the type of
leadership expected. Despite the very real limitations on supervisory
leadership imposed by the structure of the job, much effort and money
are spent on supervisory training. In addition to training in leadership,
programs are designed to improve other skills necessary for effective
supervision.

The content of supervisory training programs is geared to the
needs of the supervisor. Thus, there is considerable variation in content
and method from one organization to another and within the same
organization from one level of supervision to another. Figure 19-2 shows
a useful classification proposed by Georgopoulus and Mann of the skills
needed for supervision.[20] Note that the range of supervisory positions
included in Figure 19-2 is from the first level of supervision, through
department heads, and includes the highest level of administrators.
With each step upward in the organizational hierarchy, the "mix" of
supervisory skills changes. Technical skills are the skills and knowledge
necessary for the performance of a given supervisory position in a

---

[19] Robert H. Guest, "Of Time and the Foreman," *Personnel*, Vol. XXXII (May,
1956), p. 478.

[20] Basil S. Georgopoulus and Floyd C. Mann, *The Community General Hospital*
(New York: The Macmillan Company, 1962), Chapter 9. Reprinted in Robert A.
Sutermeister, *People and Productivity* (New York: McGraw-Hill Book Company, Inc.,
1963), pp. 381-385.

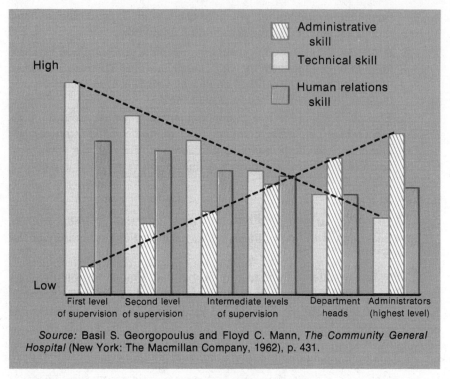

High

Administrative skill

Technical skill

Human relations skill

Low

| First level of supervision | Second level of supervision | Intermediate levels of supervision | Department heads | Administrators (highest level) |

Source: Basil S. Georgopoulos and Floyd C. Mann, *The Community General Hospital* (New York: The Macmillan Company, 1962), p. 431.

Figure 19-2
RELATIVE IMPORTANCE OF DIFFERENT SUPERVISORY SKILLS

specific industry. For the first-line supervisor, technical skills include the knowledge and skill required to perform jobs at the operational level. He must know the technology of his industry so that he can train the operators working for him. Administrative skills require a concept of the entire organizational system and the coordination of the component parts of the system. Planning, organizing, assigning work, and the establishment and exercise of necessary controls are administrative skills. For the first-line supervisor these skills are relatively less important than the technical and human relations skills. Human relations skills require a knowledge of the principles of behavior and an ability to work with subordinates, peers, and superiors. Let us examine briefly some of the content and methods of technical and administrative training.

Technical and Administrative Skills. Technical training has as its goal the understanding of the technical aspects of a supervisory position. The supervisor in manufacturing must understand the design, operating principles, and maintenance of production equipment; the specifications of raw materials and component parts; and the quality standards of the finished product. The technical phases of a data processing supervisor's position include a working knowledge of the principles used in the design of electronic equipment, an understanding of the binary number system, and the ability to prepare computer programs. Training in the administrative area acquaints the supervisor with company policies and procedures as they apply to his department. The supervisor must know purchasing procedures, production scheduling methods, and the company's cost accounting system. He must also know how to apply and interpret company personnel policies. If there is a labor union, he should be familiar with the provisions of the labor agreement.

The content of training programs in the technical and administrative areas is dependent upon the technology and administrative procedures of each individual company. As a result, most training programs are designed and conducted internally. The methods used are traditional in nature and rely heavily upon written materials such as technical manuals and statements of company policy and procedure. Formal classes are held at periodic intervals and may be supplemented by departmental meetings. In many large companies supervisors are furnished bound volumes of company policies and operating procedures to serve as a basis for technical and administrative decisions.

Training in Human Relations. Training in human relations poses problems not present in the development of skills in the technical and administrative fields. First, there is no concise definition of subject matter to be mastered. Second, there is typically a marked disparity between responses given in answer to written questions and the ability to transfer knowledge into effective supervisory patterns. Third, training in human relations requires the use of teaching methods quite different from those employed in the technical and administrative areas. Training programs in human relations stress: (1) communications, with particular emphasis placed on empathetic listening—the perception of the meaning and feeling of communications from subordinates, (2) the making of decisions involving people based upon the perceptions gained from empathetic listening, and (3) overcoming resistance to change, usually through the use of a participative leadership style.

Training Methods in Human Relations. In this section we present a brief overview of the methods used in human relations training and review experimental studies illustrative of specific problems in human relations encountered by all supervisors. The methods used in developing skills in human relations include the *case method,* the *incident process,* and *role playing.* Each of these methods is discussed briefly below.

CASE METHOD. The case method of leadership training utilizes case problems much like those contained in this book. The case problem usually sets forth a sequence of events in such a manner that a question calling for a solution is posed. Or, as in Case Problem 19-A, No Smoking, the solution is provided as part of the case and the learner is asked to evaluate the given solution. In order to solve a case problem it is necessary to acquaint the participant with the principles or procedures to be applied, a task usually accomplished by lectures or assigned readings. Case problems should describe a situation that is part of the learner's background or a situation that is understandable to all learners. The case method arouses greater interest than that created by answering questions not related to a specific situation. Also, a case problem offers a chance to apply the principles and methods to be learned. Thus, the case problem offers an opportunity to increase interest, to participate in discussion, and to illustrate the application of principles, policies, or methods to simulated or real situations.

INCIDENT PROCESS METHOD. The incident process method, a variation of the case method, is used in small discussion groups. If Case Problem 19-A were rewritten as an incident, the incident described could be the fact that the foreman discharged a worker for violating the no smoking regulations of the company. A bare statement of the facts—discharge for violation of a no smoking rule—cannot be evaluated without additional information. In the incident method, participants draw from the discussion leader all the information necessary to make a sound evaluation of the action taken and to recommend alternative courses that might have been available. Skill in questioning is developed by the incident method and experience is gained in gathering information needed for sound decisions in the area of human relations.[21]

ROLE PLAYING. The role playing method offers the advantages of the case method and, in addition, provides training in the perception of the attitudes and feelings of other persons. As the name suggests, role playing is the assignment of a definite role to each member of a training group. There is usually a brief explanation and discussion of the supervisory problem under study prior to the assignment of roles.

Case Problem 19-A may be adapted for role playing in the following manner. The supervisors of the plant in which the smoking incident occurred might attend a company training session concerned

---

[21] Paul Pigors and Faith Pigors, *Director's Manual: The Incident Process* (Washington, D. C.: The Bureau of National Affairs, 1955). For a brief article describing the incident method see James L. Centner, "The Incident Process," *Advanced Management*, Vol. XXI (December, 1956), pp. 15-20.

with the enforcement of company rules. The rules may be explained, the need for their enforcement stated, and the duties of the union steward described. Following this general session for all supervisors, groups of three or four meet separately and each member of the small groups is assigned a specific role. One is selected to be the supervisor, another the steward, and the remaining members assume the role of the employee in question who, in this instance, acts as an observer and evaluates the effectiveness of the steward in representing his case and the equity of the supervisor's decision. Each member is given a written statement describing the role to be assumed and is not aware of the details of the roles of the others in the group. The supervisor's statement may indicate that he *must* discharge the employee and cite as a reason the fire in a neighboring plant and the need to enforce company rules. He may or may not be informed of the employee's long service record. The steward's role emphasizes that one who violates the rule is only "subject to" discharge, and the long, faithful record of the employee may be outlined for the steward. Remaining members of the small group—no more than one or two—are asked to evaluate the behavior of the supervisor and the steward from the standpoint of an employee with a long seniority who has admittedly violated a rule. Roles may be rotated either within the same group or by forming new groups. Either way, each participant has the opportunity to assume the role of the supervisor, the steward, and to evaluate the incident as the employee. Role playing is particularly effective in developing empathy—the understanding of the other person's feelings and attitudes.[22]

Specific Problems in Leadership Training. Let us study in detail two specific problems in the area of leadership training. The first is concerned with discipline; the second, with the effectiveness of training in group decision making.

DISCIPLINE. Maintaining discipline is one of the perennial problems of supervision. In general, there are two approaches to disciplinary problems: (1) a *judicial* approach—determining the rightness or wrongness of an act as defined by a specific rule and applying the penalty prescribed, and (2) a *human relations* approach—an emphasis on problem solving with an ultimate goal of improving the employee's

---

[22] Norman R. F. Maier and Lester F. Zerfoss, "MRP: A Technique for Training Large Groups of Supervisors and Its Potential Use in Social Research," *Human Relations,* Vol. V (May, 1952), pp. 177-182. This article is a relatively brief statement of the multiple role playing technique. For a more detailed treatment of role playing, see Norman R. F. Maier, Allen R. Solem, and Ayesha A. Maier, *Supervisory and Executive Development, A Manual for Role Playing* (New York: John Wiley & Sons, Inc., 1957).

behavior.[23] A judicial approach may be forced upon a supervisor by his superior as intimated in Case Problem 19-A. Some supervisors by reason of personality may be rigid, insecure, and incapable of flexibility. These persons find in the rule and its prescribed penalty a ready-made justification for their own rigidity. Still others would prefer the human relations approach but are fearful of where it may lead—they envision an ultimate state of complete anarchy. The studies described below show how supervisors tend to enforce company rules and point up the need for training in human relations.

The subjects of the study were approximately 500 supervisors from a variety of industries attending the Foremen's Conferences held at the University of Michigan.[24] Following a lecture on attitudes and how to understand them, the supervisors were divided into workshop groups to study a "No Smoking" case using the role playing method. Each of the 172 role playing units consisted of three men: the foreman, the steward, and the employee. The case was much like Case Problem 19-A, with one important exception—the penalty for violating the rule was a three-day layoff rather than a discharge. The roles assigned made it clear that a violation of the rule had occurred, the worker knew he had violated the rule, and he knew the penalty involved. The worker acted as an observer in the role playing situation, with the interaction occurring between the foreman and the steward who was instructed to press the worker's case. A 20-minute time limit was placed on the discussion between the foreman and the steward.

Maier and Danielson found that slightly over half of the foremen (52 percent) used the human relations approach and resolved the problem with an adjusted solution not calling for the three-day layoff penalty. Adjusted solutions ranged from no penalty, a warning or reprimand, or a one- or two-day layoff. Thirty-five percent of the foremen followed the judicial approach and found the worker guilty, invoked the penalty, and refused to change their positions. The problem was not settled in the allotted time by 13 percent of the foremen. The human relations approach resulted in greater satisfaction as judged by all three participants with a problem-solving type interview rather than argumentative, and the worker seemed more satisfied with the actions of the steward and less inclined to restrict future production. In another study the same authors found that only seven percent of the supervisors in a similar role playing situation laid off a worker who violated a safety

---

[23] Norman R. F. Maier and Lee E. Danielson, "An Evaluation of Two Approaches to Discipline in Industry," *Journal of Applied Psychology* Vol. XL (October, 1956) pp. 319-323.
[24] *Ibid.*

rule.[25] In the safety case the situation was ambiguous: i.e., the foreman was not sure that the employee, a lineman for a utility company, was wearing his safety belt and the penalty was much more severe—a three-week layoff. Despite the fact that 45 percent of the participants who played the role of the lineman admitted violating the safety rule, only seven percent were laid off in accordance with the prescribed penalty.

These two studies indicate that foremen are inclined to use the human relations approach to discipline. Further, the formulation of strict rules with no latitude in their interpretation poses a dilemma for the supervisor. If he uses his judgment and modifies the penalty, he is not carrying out the wishes of a higher echelon; but if he enforces the letter of the law, he is demonstrating a lack of understanding and harshness toward his subordinates.[26]

TRAINING FOR DECISION MAKING. In another study Maier investigated the effect of training in group decision making.[27] Forty-four role playing groups of supervisors were given an eight-hour presentation of the methods of group decision making. These experimental groups also participated in four hours of discussion that permitted them to ask questions and to express their attitudes toward the role playing problem which was introduced as part of the training. The 36 control groups were given no training in group decision methods, but were given one-half hour of instruction explaining the role playing situation. The problem is a proposed change in method—a change sure to arouse resistance—for a group of three workers who normally rotate three production jobs among themselves at the end of each hour during an eight-hour day. There is a variation in the length of time it takes each man to perform the duties of each position as shown in Table 19-4, Time Per Operation. A methods man has suggested that the work be assigned on a permanent basis as follows: Jack to the first position, Steve to the second position, and Walt to the third position. The reduction in time would amount to 2¼ minutes per cycle, a savings of 17 percent or 80 minutes per eight-hour day. In other words, compared to the "optimum" solution, the men are now loafing 80 minutes a day.

In the role playing situation, the foreman desires to install the solution recommended by the methods man and is met with varying degrees of

---

[25] Lee E. Danielson and Norman R. F. Maier, "Supervisory Problems in Decision Making," *Journal of Applied Psychology,* Vol. XL (October, 1956), pp. 319-323.

[26] For another statement of the human relations approach to discipline the following is recommended: John Huberman, "Discipline Without Punishment," *Harvard Business Review,* Vol. 42, No. 4 (July-August, 1964), pp. 62-68.

[27] Norman R. F. Maier, "An Experimental Test of the Effect of Training on Discussion Leadership," *Human Relations Journal,* Vol. VI (May, 1953), pp. 161-173.

Table 19-4
TIME PER OPERATION

	Position 1	Position 2	Position 3	Total
Jack	3 min.	4 min.	4½ min.	11½ min.
Walt	3½ min.	3½ min.	3 min.	10 min.
Steve	5 min.	3½ min.	4½ min.	13 min.
				34½ min.

Source: Norman R. F. Maier, "An Experimental Test of the Effect of Training on Discussion Leadership," *Human Relations Journal,* Vol. VI (May, 1953), p. 164. This table was originally published by John Wiley and Sons in Norman R. F. Maier's *Principles of Human Relations,* 1952.

resistance on the part of each of the three men. The results of the role playing situations for trained and untrained supervisors, Table 19-5— Percentage of Successes, Failures, and Compromises of Trained and Untrained Groups—shows clearly the effect of training. Only 4½ percent of the trained foremen experience failure—with failure being defined as no solution, no change, or open rebellion against the foreman's imposed solution. On the other hand, 50 percent of the untrained leaders experienced failure. However, the striking result is that the untrained leader did not produce a single compromise. It must be pointed out that many compromise solutions might in practice be the "optimum" or best solution, since the compromises contained varying plans for rotation of jobs to minimize the effects of monotony and boredom on production.

IMPROVING SUPERVISORY PERFORMANCE

In Chapter 18, "Motivating Employees," it is stated that no consistent relationship is found between measures of employee morale and productivity. Fortunately there is a distinct positive relationship between supervisory practices and productivity. There are many characteristics of effective supervisory action; however, four stand out above all others. The first factor determining effective supervision, *organizational climate,* is largely beyond the control of the supervisor and determines how effectively he may exercise the other three characteristics of sound supervision. Good practices in *delegation,* the second factor, are necessary for effective supervision. The third requisite for effective supervision is an orientation toward his job, best described as a *contingency* approach, with a balanced emphasis upon the task and the maintenance of good relations with subordinates.[28] The fourth requirement is an ability to use *employee participation* skillfully to introduce change.

---

[28] See Chapter 16, A Contingency Model of Leadership Effectiveness, pp. 490-499.

Table 19-5
**PERCENTAGE OF SUCCESSES, FAILURES, AND COMPROMISES
OF TRAINED AND UNTRAINED GROUPS**

	Failures	Compromises	Successes
Trained leader	4.5	36.4	59.1
Untrained leader	50.0	0	50.0

Source: Norman R. F. Maier, "An Experimental Test of the Effect of Training on Discussion Leadership," *Human Relations Journal,* Vol. VI (May, 1953), p. 168. This table was originally published by John Wiley and Sons in Norman R. F. Maier's *Principles of Human Relations,* 1952.

Organizational Climate

The quotation from Guest's "Of Time and the Foreman," appearing at the beginning of the preceding section on training, dramatizes the limiting effects of organizational climate upon the efficacy of training. Fleishman also emphasizes the limitations of training unless the "leadership climate" is such that the supervisor can readily put to use his newly found skills.[29] Organizational or leadership climate is made up of the attitudes and practices of top management and is reflected by the extent that management practices delegation, the degree that they recognize the organization as a system, and their use of participation as a method of introducing change. Yet the chief advantage gained by a supervisor from the organizational climate created by his superiors is *influence* or power within his own department.

Pelz and others of the University of Michigan's Survey Research Center show that a supervisor's influence or power has a great deal to do with productivity and employee satisfaction.[30] In work groups having high production records, promotions recommended by supervisors were generally approved by higher management; or no recommendations were made at all. On the other hand, the supervisors of low-producing groups frequently made recommendations for promotion that were not approved by higher authority. Three factors seem to contribute most

---

[29] Edwin A. Fleishman, Edwin F. Harris, and Harold E. Burtt, "Leadership and Supervision in Industry." Reprinted in Robert A. Sutermeister, *People and Productivity* (New York: McGraw-Hill Book Company, Inc., 1963), pp. 410-425. This reading is a re-edited and up-to-date version of Chapter 9 of *Leadership and Supervision in Industry* (Columbus, Ohio: Bureau of Educational Research, Ohio State University, 1955) by the same authors.

[30] Donald C. Pelz, "Influence: A Key to Effective Leadership in the First-Line Supervisor," *Personnel,* Vol. XXIX (November, 1952), pp. 209-217.

A recent study by Ronan indicates that direct supervision is significant as a determinant of positive relationships between job satisfaction and behavior on the job. W. W. Ronan, "Individual and Situational Variables Relating to Job Satisfaction," *Journal of Applied Psychology Monograph,* Vol. 54, No. 1 (February, 1970), pp. 1-29.

to a supervisor's influence: (1) the contribution that he makes to decisions made by his superior, (2) the freedom and autonomy that he possesses in the operation of his own department, and (3) his salary, interpreting salary as a measure of responsibility and status within the organization. Note that these conditions determining the amount of supervisory influence are not the direct result of a supervisor's actions within his own department or something that may be asked for and received; these traits are a reflection of the supervisor's position and status in the organization—the result of organizational climate.

Improved Delegation

One of the keys to effective supervision, as measured by productivity and employee satisfaction, is the ability to delegate responsibility to subordinates and to allow as much leeway in the performance of assigned duties as the situation permits. Improvement in delegation requires that the supervisor have a clear perception of his role as leader and that he make a careful determination of how closely he should follow and oversee the work of subordinates. Let us discuss, first, the differentiation of the supervisor's role.

Differentiating the Supervisor's Role. Drs. Robert L. Kahn and Daniel Katz, in a summary of much of the work of the Survey Research Center of the University of Michigan, report that supervisors of groups with high production records assume a role that is more differentiated from the work of those supervised than the role assumed by the supervisors of low-producing work groups.[31] High-producing supervisors perform those tasks traditionally associated with the managerial functions of planning, organizing, directing, and controlling. The differentiation between the task of the worker and the supervisor begins with the supervisor's perception of himself as a member of management and an understanding of the functions of management; at the same time, subordinates have an unusually acute perception of what their supervisor is doing in comparison to what he should be doing. The supervisory task perceived most readily by subordinates is that of planning the work to be done. Members of high-producing railroad section gangs and departments in a tractor manufacturing company rate their supervisors as superior in planning work, providing materials, and watching or supervising the performance of the work. Supervisors

---

[31] Robert L. Kahn and Daniel Katz, "Leadership Practices in Relation to Productivity and Morale," from Derwin Cartwright and Alvin Zander (eds.), *Group Dynamics, Research and Theory* (New York: Harper and Row, Publishers, Incorporated, 1961), pp. 554-570.

with better than average production records also spend more time than their low-producing counterparts in solving the interpersonal problems arising in the work group. Low-producing supervisors are prone to get lost in paper work and spend too much of their time doing the same type of work performed by subordinates. Supervisory tasks include not only the planning function but also directing on-the-job training.

Closeness of Supervision. The supervisor who spends most of his time performing those tasks normally associated with supervision is delegating authority and assigning responsibility and, in the case of hourly workers, it is primarily the assignment of responsibility to perform work. However, the delegator still remains accountable to his superior for the performance of the assigned duties. Close supervision is associated with excessively detailed instructions, constant checking on progress, and insistence that all decisions be approved before being put into effect. However, a careful engineering of the work to be performed and the establishment and exercise of necessary controls to assure proper progress are not considered excessively close supervision; instead, they are part of the normal supervisory function. Closeness of supervision refers primarily to the personal conduct of the supervisor, and when supervision becomes too close, it is a reflection of the supervisor's own insecurity and inability to delegate.

In studies of clerical workers in an insurance company and production workers manufacturing tractors, it is found that there is an inverse relationship between closeness of supervision and productivity; i.e., the closer the supervision, the lower the productivity. Also, the closeness of supervision has a great deal to do with the three factorial dimensions of employee morale. Employees not closely supervised are more likely to have a high degree of satisfaction with their jobs, their supervisors, and the company than those who are closely supervised. However, there is evidence that closeness of supervision is in many instances a reflection of the type of supervision received by the supervisor. If a superior fully delegates authority, the supervisor is likely to do the same; but when he is closely supervised, it is difficult for him to delegate as freely as he should. Thus, organizational climate exerts its influence on the supervisor's ability to delegate effectively.

A Contingency Approach

Much has been written about supervisors being either production-centered or employee-centered in respect to attitudes concerning the work of their departments and their subordinates. Early research in the area of job satisfaction and morale implicitly assumed that the orientation of the supervisor is best described in terms of a continuum with production-centered concepts at one pole and employee-centered concepts at the other extreme. However, later studies, particularly those conducted at the tractor company, cast doubt upon the usefulness of a continuum as a model for describing supervisory orientation. High-producing workers at the tractor company reported, as might be expected, that their supervisor took an interest in them, that they got along well with him, and that he was easy to talk to. Yet, they also stated that production was important to their supervisor and that he supervised them in such a manner that production standards were met— a situation quite impossible to describe on a continuum model.[32]

Dr. Robert L. Kahn suggests that we use a four-celled table to describe the orientation of the supervisor.[33] In one cell are those supervisors who are high in their interest in production and at the same time have a high interest in the welfare of their employees. Another cell would best describe those with a high orientation toward production but low in employee-centered attitudes. The third square would fit those low in production but high in employee-centered interests. The fourth possibility consists of those supervisors with low interests in both production and employees. In effect, the four-celled table represents a systems orientation, with the most effective supervisor recognizing simultaneously the goals and needs of the organization and its members.

At first glance it may seem quite impossible to be production-centered and employee-centered at one and the same time, but such is not the case. Martin Patchen suggests that in order to achieve morale and at the same time a high level of productivity, the supervisor must do three things.[34] First, he must make it clear that he expects high but realistic and attainable standards of performance. By so doing he establishes the tenor of the operation. Second, he must have the power to deliver appropriate rewards or punishment if his statement of goals is to mean anything. Third, the supervisor must demonstrate to the satisfaction of his subordinates that he is capable of using this power effectively. One of the best ways of demonstrating a wise use of power

---

[32] The following two review articles are recommended as summaries of the literature concerning supervisory style.

Stephen M. Sales, "Supervisory Style and Productivity: Review and Theory," *Personnel Psychology,* Vol. 19, No. 3 (Autumn, 1966), pp. 275-286.

Abraham K. Korman, " 'Consideration,' 'Initiating Structure,' and Organizational Criteria—Review," *Personnel Psychology,* Vol. 19, No. 4 (Winter, 1966), pp. 349-361.

[33] Robert L. Kahn, "Productivity and Job Satisfaction," *Personnel Psychology,* Vol. XIII (Autumn, 1960), pp. 275-287.

[34] Martin Patchen, "Supervisory Methods and Group Performance Norms," *Administrative Science Quarterly,* Vol. VII (December, 1962), pp. 275-293.

and influence is a willingness to "go to bat" for a subordinate when the need arises; but a supervisor does not stand alone in carrying out the suggestions of Patchen. He is part of an organization, and the management he represents must create the climate to enable him to exercise effectively a contingency approach toward production and subordinates.

Participation and Change

Overcoming resistance to change is a problem confronting all levels of supervision. The proposed change in method or content may have little direct effect upon the worker's ability to perform his job, or the change may be of such a nature that the learning of new skills or the transfer of existing skills to a new work situation is required. Regardless of the amount or type of change, there are varying degrees of resistance that are manifested by an extremely long period of time to learn the new job, open expressions of hostility toward management, or an increase in the number of voluntary terminations of employment. One explanation that has been offered for resistance to change is that the rate of learning for the new job is inhibited because of its similarity to the old job. For example, an expert typist might experience greater difficulty initially in learning the finger movements required in playing a piano than one with no skill in typing. However, research indicates that resistance is caused by psychological factors and may be controlled by using participation when introducing change.[35]

The Coch and French experiments concerning resistance to change were conducted in the Marion, Virginia, plant of the Harwood Manufacturing Company, a garment manufacturer. Harwood's employees are paid on a piece-rate incentive system, with 60 units representing the standard production for one hour. Further, the company normally tries to cushion the effects of change by conducting orientation programs and by paying a special bonus to those affected by change. Despite these efforts, any change in production methods usually results in failure to meet production standards in the same length of time required by a new employee to learn the job, an increase in the number of resignations, and expressions of hostility toward the management of the company.

In the experiments, four groups of employees were studied. Group One, the control group, had the change introduced in the usual fashion, with no participation on the part of employees in the change. However,

---

[35] Lester Coch and John R. P. French, "Overcoming Resistance to Change," *Human Relations*, Vol. I (August, 1948), pp. 512-532. This study contains a discussion of the theoretical aspects of resistance to change as well as reporting in detail the results of the experiments.

the reasons for the change were presented to them in a meeting. Group Two elected representatives who participated in developing the change and were trained as "special operators" to work out the details of the change prior to its being adopted by the entire group. In Groups Three and Four, the total participation groups, all employees participated from the very beginning in developing the need for the change and working out the details of how the changed jobs should be performed. Though the changes made in the jobs varied for each group, they were comparable and minor in nature. Group One, pajama pressers, formerly stacked their finished work in lots of one-half dozen on pieces of cardboard. The change required them to stack their finished work in one-half dozen lots in boxes. Group Two had to alter their method of folding pajama coats, while Groups Three and Four, inspectors, were required only to cut certain threads from the garment and inspect all seams instead of cutting all loose threads and inspecting all seams.

Resistance developed in the control group immediately. There was conflict with the methods engineer, grievances were filed, and 17 percent of the group quit during the first 40 days after the change. As a group they did not reach the standard of 60 units an hour. Group Two, the one with elected representation, produced 61 units per hour at the end of 14 days; also, there was only one act of aggression against a supervisor and no layoffs during the first 40 days after the change. The two total participation groups recovered faster than Group Two. There was a slight drop in production the first day of change, but it immediately rose to 14 percent above prechange levels. There were no acts of agression, nor any quits during the first 40 days. Later the remaining members of the control group were reassembled as a unit and a change was introduced in their work; but this time they participated in the change. As expected, they performed in the same way as the total participation group had.

The results of these experiments are clear—participation reduces resistance to change. Yet, two limitations must be presented. Participation in the introduction of change is not decided by the supervisor; it is an expression of organizational climate. Second, at the present time there is no record of a company that has used total participation to introduce change over an extended period of time. Thus, the question arises as to how effective participation would be in overcoming resistance to change if it were normal operating procedure.[36]

---

[36] For an interesting account of how an organizational climate conducive to change was established for two companies brought together as a result of a merger the following is recommended: Alfred J. Marrow, David G. Bowers, and Stanley E. Seashore, *Management by Participation: Creating a Climate for Personal and Organizational Development* (New York: Harper & Row, Publishers, 1967), pp. xvi and 264.

Case Problem 19-B, The New Truck Problem, is different from the other cases you have analyzed in that its solution calls for role playing.[37] You may be asked to assume the role of the foreman or one of the repairmen. If you are not a participant, you will be asked to observe and evaluate the decision made by the foreman.

CASE PROBLEM
19-B

THE NEW TRUCK
PROBLEM

"General Instructions for Crew.

"You are repairmen for a large company and drive to various locations in the city to do your work. Each of you drives a small truck and you take pride in keeping it looking good. You have a possessive feeling about your trucks and like to keep them in good running order. Naturally, you like to have new trucks, too, because a new truck gives you a feeling of pride.

"Here are some of the facts about the trucks and the men in the crews who report to Walt Marshall, the supervisor of repairs.

"George—17 years with the company, has a 2-year-old Ford truck.

"Bill—11 years with the company, has a 5-year-old Dodge truck.

"John—10 years with the company, has a 4-year-old Ford truck.

"Charlie—5 years with the company, has a 3-year-old Ford truck.

"Hank—3 years with the company, has a 5-year-old Chevrolet truck.

"Most of you do all your driving in the city, but John and Charlie cover the jobs in the suburbs.

"In acting your part, accept the facts as given as well as assume the attitudes supplied in your specific role. From this point on let your feelings develop in accordance with the events that transpire in the role playing process. When facts or events arise which are not covered by the roles, make up things which are consistent with the way it might be in a real-life situation."

---

[37] Norman R. F. Maier and Lester F. Zerfoss, "MRP: A Technique for Training Large Groups of Supervisors and Its Potential Use in Social Research," Human Relations, Vol. V (May, 1952), pp. 180-181.

Note to Instructor: Since role playing requires that participants be unaware of hidden motivations of others in the role playing situation, the roles of the crew are not included in the case. They are in the instructor's manual and should be reproduced on separate sheets of paper and distributed prior to the role playing.

Chapter Questions for Study and Discussion

1. The supervisor has been described as being "the man in the middle." Is this characterization borne out by the two legal definitions of the supervisor? How?

2. What inferences could you make concerning the organizational climate of a company whose supervisors petitioned for a union of their own? As a member of middle or top management, what action would you recommend upon receiving notification of such petition?

3. What is the relationship between the results of Porter's study of how supervisors perceive themselves and the description of a typical day of a supervisor as provided by Walker, Turner, and Guest? Why does such a relationship exist?

4. Recognizing that most supervisors are promoted from the hourly ranks, why is there such a cleavage between the way in which the hourly worker describes himself and the manner in which the supervisor sees himself?

5. Discuss and give an example showing the significance of each of the dimensions of supervisory performance as described by Peres.

6. What is meant by the "linking-pin" function? How is this function related to the supervisor's position in the organization? Is it of significance in the motivation of employees? How?

7. Discuss the advantages and disadvantages of each of the several sources of supervision.

8. Describe and evaluate a composite approach to the selection of supervisors showing the contribution of each selection method that is utilized.

9. Comment on the following statement: "You could dispose of almost all of the leadership training courses for supervision in American industry today without anyone knowing the difference."

10. Describe and give an example illustrating the methods commonly used for training in human relations.

11. Define in your own terms the meaning of organizational climate.

12. Evaluate each of the factors that contributes to a supervisor's influence. Which do you believe to be the most important? Relate the concept of influence and the performance of college graduates in training positions.

13. What major factor limits the applicability of participation as a means of introducing change? What is the next step if the employees fail to see the need for change?

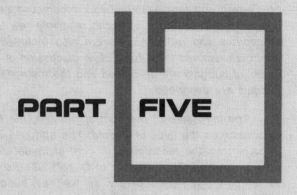

PART FIVE

The Control Function

The first three chapters of this last section discuss the control func-tion, and the last chapter is a summing up of our study of management. The control function is a three-step process of setting standards, measuring current performance against standards, and taking corrective action when necessary to bring performance in line with standards. The characteristics of good control are summarized. Commonly used nonbudgetary controls ranging from personal observation and reports to the more complex break-even and time-event-network techniques are examined. Internal audit programs with emphasis upon the relatively new human resource accounting procedures and ratio analysis are also included among the nonbudgetary controls examined in Chapter 21. A discussion of budgetary controls follows. Types of budgets are discussed and the methods of securing flexibility with budgets are described.

The third step of the control process, the taking of corrective action, touches upon the lives of people. The attitudes held toward control are as important as the techniques of control in determining the success of the control function. The last part of Chapter 22 discusses behavioral reactions to all controls, nonbudgetary as well as budgetary. The typical control procedure, a seemingly endless cycle of control, resistance, and more control, is analyzed in terms of its effect upon people. The reasons for resistance to controls and the unfavorable responses to controls are presented in detail. The chapter closes with recommendations for the effective use of controls.

Each of the functions of the management process—planning, organizing, leading, and controlling—has been discussed in sequence; the task remains to integrate these functions. The first part of Chapter 23 reviews the functions of planning and control as a planning-control-planning cycle. Interrelationships between this cycle and the functions of organizing and leading are described. A discussion of management and the systems concept is a means of furthering the concept of management as an integrated process. A hierarchy of systems and the characteristics of open systems are presented in tabular form. Organizations are social systems and as such are open systems. Some of the major characteristics and functions of business organizations are reviewed within the framework of open systems characteristics. A brief discussion of current issues confronting today's managers, to be resolved by the managers of tomorrow, follows. The chapter closes with a statement that relates the introductory course in management to subsequent courses in the business administration curriculum.

CHAPTER 20

The Basis of Control

Standard Building Service Company of St. Louis is a 15-year old company that provides janitorial services for office buildings and industrial plants. Standard was purchased five years ago by Leslie Waller and, at the time of the purchase, annual sales were approximately $500,000. In three years he was able to double the sales volume to the present level of $1,000,000, but for the past two years sales volume has remained relatively constant. Waller attributes the lack of growth for the past two years to his being unable to call on new accounts because the business has grown to such an extent that his full energies and time are required in solving the myriad of problems that arise each day. He recognizes that the few new accounts he does obtain do no more than offset the normal turnover of accounts lost each month.

Janitorial services are usually performed after the tenants have left the building for the day; consequently, very few of Standard's employees start work before 6 p.m. Waller has found from experience that in order to keep employees, he must offer them at least 20 hours of work a week. On the other hand, very few people seem willing to work more than 25 hours a week. As a result, the work force of approximately 275 men and women are part-time employees. Waller also found that by hiring persons presently employed he is assured of stable, motivated employees. However, since his employees are working full-time elsewhere, there is considerable resistance when supervisors expect an above-average amount of work from them.

611

A recent analysis of the 121 accounts serviced by the company shows that 40 customers require the services of only one person working a maximum of 25 hours a week. Thirty-five accounts require two people with total man-hours ranging from 35 to 50 hours a week. Fifteen accounts require an average of 100 man-hours a week, thus utilizing the services of up to four employees. There is one large industrial plant that requires 500 hours of service each week and approximately 20 workers. The remaining 30 accounts range between 100 and 400 man-hours each week, and require between four and sixteen employees.

Mr. Waller is not sure which size job yields the most profit. Jobs are priced on a rule-of-thumb basis and depend upon the type of floor surfaces, the amount of building traffic, number and types of offices, and other similar factors. Mr. Waller and one of his two full-time supervisors estimate the man-power requirements for each new job. An analysis of company records shows that for the past five years variable costs—direct labor and materials (waxes, detergents, etc.)—average about 80 to 85 percent of total revenue.

The full-time organization consists of Mr. Waller, two supervisors, a secretary, an accountant, and a supply man who also maintains some of the larger pieces of cleaning equipment such as the floor polishers. In addition, there are five part-time supervisors, each of whom supervises 40 to 50 workers in a given geographic area of the city. Most of their time and energy is spent in delivering supplies and materials to the various buildings within a given geographic area of the city. They also reassign personnel as the need arises and collect the weekly time cards. The two full-time supervisors have no specific duties assigned to them nor is either one responsible for the work of any particular part-time supervisor.

At the present time Mr. Waller has only two sources of information to guide him in the operation of his business. One of these is customer complaints, which serve as a check on the quality of the work. The other source is the weekly payroll, which is prepared by a local bank. Each week time cards are submitted to the bank and from these records payroll checks are prepared. The bank also maintains the necessary social security and income tax records. In addition, a summary is prepared showing the total man-hours per week for each job. At present, no consistent use is made of this information. However, on the occasions when he has examined these weekly reports, Mr. Waller has found that the total hours per week run as much as 400 hours in excess of the number of hours used in computing the price of the services. There is no record of the use of supplies for each job.

PROBLEMS

1. Is there a need for control in this company? Why?
2. If controls are needed, what areas of the business are most in need of control?
3. What type of standards are now being used? What kind would you recommend?
4. How can the organization be modified to improve the control function?

The control function is one of the four major functions of the process of management. The usual sequence assigned to these functions places planning first, next is organizing, the third is the human relations function—frequently called leading or directing—and the last function is control. The word, control, and its position in the management process sequence are indicative of the nature of the control function. In this chapter we will examine, first, the nature of the control function, and second, we will study in detail the steps of the control process. The characteristics of effective controls are then discussed and from this discussion several principles of control are developed.

THE NATURE OF CONTROL

If plans were never in need of revision and were executed flawlessly by a perfectly balanced organization under the direction of an omnipotent leader, there would be no need for control. However, as Robert Burns observed years ago, "The best-laid schemes o' mice an' men gang aft agley." [1] In addition, organizations do not always work smoothly and need revision to meet changing conditions. Also, the effectiveness of leadership is often open to question. It is the

---

[1] The closing stanza of Robert Burns "To A Mouse" is a statement that could be made by many of today's executives:
"Still thou art blest, compared wi' me!
The present only toucheth thee.
But och! I backward cast my e'e
    On prospects drear!
And forward though I cannot see,
    I guess an' fear!"

purpose of the control function to take the corrective action necessary to assure the fulfillment of organizational objectives. Although control denotes corrective action that may be objective in all respects, the reactions of those subjected to controls may be highly emotionalized and tinged with resentment. The reason for this reaction is that control always touches upon the people who make up organizations, for they are charged with responsibilities and are accountable to their superiors for the performance of these duties. When determining whether or not goals are being met, it is the performance of the people of the organization that is actually being reviewed. One way of developing an understanding of the nature of control is to place the control function in perspective within the framework of a systems concept.

Cybernetics and Control

The study of how dynamic systems maintain a state of equilibrium, or steady state, though subject to changing envionmental conditions is called *cybernetics*.[2] Examples of cybernetic systems are numerous and familiar. The thermostat maintains the temperature of a room at a predetermined level by making or breaking an electrical circuit that starts or stops the furnace. The rotating arms of a steam-engine governor rise or fall with changes in centrifugal force, thereby controlling the input of steam into the cylinders of the engine with the result that a constant speed is maintained under varying load conditions. Another example is a photoelectric cell placed in a circuit to turn on lights in the evening when daylight illumination decreases to a predetermined level and to turn off the artificial lighting the next morning when natural illumination is sufficient.

The above examples of cybernetic systems illustrate the major characteristics of such systems. First, there is a predetermined steady state or equilibrium to be maintained. In the first example, a constant temperature is the state of equilibrium to be maintained; the second illustration focuses upon speed as the steady state, and the third example uses a predetermined intensity of light as the state of equilibrium. Second, in all of the above instances there is constant change in the

---

[2] For a complete discussion of cybernetics, see:

Norbert Weiner, *Cybernetics,* Control and Communication in the Animal and the Machine (New York: John Wiley & Sons, Inc., 1948).

Norbert Weiner, *The Human Use of Human Beings* (New York: Doubleday Anchor Books, 1954).

W. R. Ashby, *An Introduction to Cybernetics* (New York: John Wiley & Sons, Inc., 1956).

environment within which the system operates, thus forcing adjustments within the system in order to maintain an equilibrium; hence, the term "dynamic system." Third, there is a transfer of information from the external environment to within the system. The "information" that activates the thermostat is a change in temperature; centrifugal force is the information transmitted by the steam-engine governor, and the intensity of light is the information received by the photoelectric cell. Fourth, there is a mechanical device so designed that corrective action is taken, with the result that the equilibrium of the system is maintained. The bimetal of the thermostat makes or breaks the electrical circuit, the moving arms of the governor open and close a valve regulating the flow of steam, and the photoelectric cell responds to the intensity of light by opening or closing the circuit. In each of these instances the control device is engineered to perform the specific function necessary to maintain the system's equilibrium.[3]

All living organisms are by definition cybernetic systems, for they must maintain equilibrium in order to survive. It is useful to apply the concept of cybernetics—the maintenance of a steady state through the interpretation of information and subsequent corrective action—to organizations. The concept of cybernetic systems is not being introduced for the first time in this chapter. The systems concept is first discussed in Chapter 1. In Chapter 6, Figure 6-3 (reproduced here as Figure 20-1) shows how the major business functions of finance, production, sales, and personnel form a self-correcting system with a feedback loop to the external environment between the sales department and the external environment, the customer. Feedback loops with outside forces could also be shown between finance and sources of capital, between production and vendors, and between personnel and the labor supply. There is also a continual exchange of information internally between the major functions of an organization.

The Parable of the Spindle, Case Problem 7-A, illustrates how the cook performs a control function by selecting the most efficient combination of orders from information contained on tickets stored on a spindle. Further, the tickets can be used as a control device by the waitress and can be checked against the order received. At the close of the day the tickets may also be used as a control measure when compared with cash receipts. The schematic concept of a business as shown

---

[3] Robert Chin, "The Utility of System Models and Developmental Models for Practicioners," from W. G. Bennis, K. D. Benne, and Robert Chin, *The Planning of Change* (New York: Holt, Rinehart and Winston, Inc., 1961). This article discusses several types of models and their application to business situations.

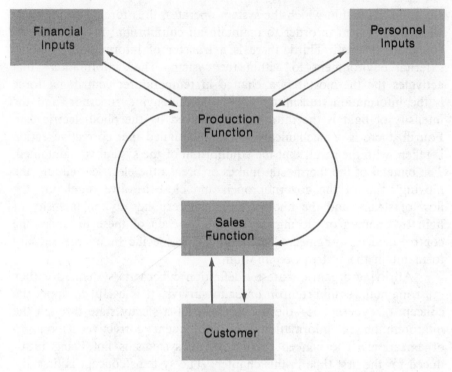

Figure 20-1
MAJOR BUSINESS FUNCTIONS AS A CYBERNETIC SYSTEM

in Figure 20-1 and the specific illustration of the experience of a restaurant illustrate that control is the interpretation of information, from both internal and external sources, so that corrective action may be taken in order to reach desired objectives.[4]

Steps in the Control Process

There is agreement among students of management concerning the three steps of the control process:

1. Establishing standards of performance.
2. Measuring current performance in relation to established standards.
3. Taking corrective action.

Let us now interpret these three steps of the control process in the light of what we know about cybernetic systems. The establishment of standards

[4] For a more complete discussion of the systems concept as applied to control, see the following:

Richard A. Johnson, Fremont E. Kast, and James E. Rosenzweig, *The Theory and Management of Systems* (New York: McGraw-Hill Book Company, Inc., 1963), Chapter 4, "Control and Systems Concepts," pp. 57-72.

defines the desired state of equilibrium. Standards are definitions of the objectives of an organization, but it must be remembered that objectives can and do change. The second step, measurement of current performance, requires that information be processed and interpreted by someone so that a conclusion can be drawn concerning present position, or performance, relative to the desired position as defined by the standards. The information used in measurement is not limited to financial data reflecting the economic condition of the company; it also includes reports on the quality of the product, the amount of inventory, the morale of personnel, or even the intuitive judgment of a manager that all is not going well. Taking corrective action intended to bring performance in line with predetermined standards requires executive decision making and a realignment of company resources. The person who makes the decision corresponds to the control device of the mechanical cybernetic system.[5]

The next major section of this chapter discusses in greater detail each of the three steps of the control process; first, however, there is one more question to answer for a more complete understanding of the nature of control. Who does the controlling?

Who Controls?

Many students, particularly those majoring in accounting, consider as a personal career objective the position of controller of a business organization. Figure 20-2 presents two typical position descriptions—one, the controller of a large company, and the other, the combined position of treasurer and controller in a medium-size company. In general, the controller is closely associated with the finance function of the company, though he may or may not report to the vice-president for finance. If he does not report to the financial officer, he reports to the president or chief executive officer of the company. He is usually responsible for designing the systems and procedures necessary for management control; thus, in companies having integrated data processing systems the controller may be responsible for the design and maintenance of such systems. Traditionally the controller's function is concerned with those aspects of the business that can be reduced to dollars and cents; for this reason he is usually concerned with the

---

[5] Douglas S. Sherwin, "The Meaning of Control," *Dun's Review and Modern Industry* (January, 1956), pp. 45, 46, 83, 84.

Edward L. Anthony, "Effective Control for Better Management," from *Management Aids for Small Manufacturers*, Small Business Administration (January, 1957), pp. 1-4.

These two articles present general discussions of the control function.

FUNCTIONS OF THE CONTROLLER IN THE LARGE COMPANY

Objectives

The Controller (or Comptroller) of Accounts is responsible for the effective financial and cost controls of the company's activities.

Functions

1. Prescription of principles and methods to govern accounting controls throughout the enterprise
2. Provision of adequate protection against loss of the company's money and property
3. Prescription of principles of accounting determining cost of product, and normal volume of production in order to compute costs and install appropriate systems
4. Verification of the propriety of expenditures
5. Providing comparison of capital expenditures and appropriations
6. Preparation of the accounts of the corporation
7. Determination of income and expenditure allocation among plants and departments
8. Proposals regarding the nature of the corporation's financial statements
9. Preparation of the financial statements
10. Preparation of analyses assisting others to improve the earnings of the enterprise
11. Observation of the manner of performing accounting responsibilities

Relationships

The Controller of Accounts reports to the Vice-President for Finance.

Figure 20-2
FUNCTIONS OF THE CONTROLLER

efficiency of production and the cost of sales. Few companies require that the controller secure information concerning morale of employees, the status of innovations in the organization, or the quality of management; yet these factors are legitimate areas of control.

We still have not answered the question, who controls? Note in Figure 20-2 there is no statement saying that it is the duty of the controller to control by taking corrective action. Control, the act of taking corrective action, is a function of the line manager. The controller, a member of the staff organization, may design the information system, secure and interpret data concerning performance, and even make recommendations as to what might constitute the most appropriate

**FUNCTIONS OF THE TREASURER AND CONTROLLER
IN THE MEDIUM-SIZE COMPANY**

1. Accountability for the safekeeping and custody of corporate funds, securities owned by the company, and the corporate seal

2. Establishment of a General Accounting Department with the following duties:
   a. Post-audit of plant transactions
   b. Installation and maintenance of primary books of accounts
   c. Setting the policies, procedures, and standards of accounting and cost records and reports
   d. Setting up methods of cash disbursement, accounts receivable, plant and equipment records
   e. Cash management
   f. Preparation of financial statements and reports
   g. Credit approval

3. Establishment of a cost accounting department with a view to:
   a. Prescribing and administering factory timekeeping and payroll procedures
   b. Maintaining inventory controls
   c. Supervision of timekeeping methods
   d. Setting up a cost system in each plant

4. Establishing a budget department to present standards of performance to management with a view to:
   a. Showing the results of operations
   b. Establishing standards of performance
   c. Proposing a budget forecast
   d. Informing executives of variations from the budget
   e. Continuous revision of the budget

Source: Ernest Dale, *Planning and Developing the Company Organization Structure* (New York: American Management Association, Research Report No. 20, 1952), pp. 200-201.

Figure 20-2 (Continued)

corrective action. However, the final decision and the request for corrective action are the responsibility of the line manager. Nor is control by the line organization limited to any level of management; indeed, for effective control all levels of management must exercise control over those functions assigned to them. There is much that the first-line supervisor can control in his department that cannot be controlled directly by anyone else in the organization.

THE CONTROL PROCESS

We have described the control process as consisting of the following steps: (1) establishing standards of performance, (2) measuring current performance in relation to the established standards, and (3) taking corrective action. Standards are the basis of the control process, for without adequate standards the subsequent steps of measurement and corrective action are meaningless. Let us examine, first, the nature of standards; then, problems encountered in the measurement of performance; and last, the kind of corrective action that should be taken.

Establishing Standards

The dictionary definition of standards includes two concepts. First, a standard is a rule (unit) for measuring. It is intended to serve as a model or criterion. Second, a standard is established by authority. *Thus, a standard may be defined as a unit of measurement established to serve as a model or criterion.* The 72-stroke par for an 18-hole golf course is an excellent example of a standard. Par is a recognized level of performance or achievement established by authority —custom and the various golfing associations. Second, par demonstrates clearly that a standard is not perfection—many professional golfers consistently exceed, or break, par. Nor is par the average of the level of performance for all golfers; indeed, the average would be considerably higher than 72. Thus, par is a difficult, but attainable, level of performance. It serves as a criterion for comparing the proficiency of one golfer against that of another in terms of an objective unit of measurement—the number of strokes required to complete the course. Par is analagous to the work standards established by a company for its employees.

Scope of Business Standards. Standards in business organizations are not limited to establishing levels of performance for individual workers; instead, they are applicable to all phases of the operation. Ralph C. Davis suggests that standards be set for all activities that contribute to the primary service objectives of the organization. He recommends establishing standards of service, including the development of criteria for the particular good or service being offered by the organization. Standards of policy and function include an evaluation of the organization structure and its method of operation. Standards should also be determined for the evaluation of the physical facilities of the organization, for determining the characteristics of the kind of personnel required, and for determining the level of performance of personnel.[6]

---

[6] Ralph C. Davis, *The Fundamentals of Top Management* (New York: Harper & Brothers, Publishers, 1951), pp. 28-29. Chapter 2, "Standards and Standardization," pp. 21-42, presents a complete discussion of standards in business organizations.

Another approach to describing the scope of standards is to set standards for each of several key result areas. General Electric uses this approach and establishes standards for each of the following eight key result areas:

1. Profitability
2. Market position
3. Productivity
4. Product leadership
5. Personnel development
6. Employee attitudes
7. Public responsibility
8. Balance between short-range and long-range goals.[7]

Some of the major considerations necessary to establish standards for each of the key result areas are discussed below.

PROFITABILITY. The standard for profitability may be expressed by means of the widely used rate of return ratio, percent of profit to sales, or total dollar volume. The expression of profit as a ratio between profits earned and capital employed is useful in comparing the contribution of each of several decentralized units in respect to current performance and is also of value in determining which of several alternatives to select for future operations. Deviations from expected profit expressed as a percent of sales may indicate variations in cost or the need for changing the price of the product or service. However, profit expressed as a ratio —either return on investment or percent of sales—is not necessarily a valid measure of the contribution of personnel to the profitability of a given operation. For example, the profit of a retail store expressed as a percent of sales may be a function primarily of the cost of goods sold and the cost of renting physical facilities, factors that may be beyond the control of the manager. The expression of profits in terms of total dollars earned is a measure of the effectiveness of sales effort on the part of store personnel over a period of time. Standards of profitability should reflect the contribution of personnel in controlling costs and

---

[7] Robert W. Lewis, "Measurement, Reporting, and Appraising Results of Operations with Reference to Goals, Plans, and Budgets," from the report, *Planning, Managing, and Measuring the Business:* A Case Study of Management Planning and Control at General Electric Company (New York: Controllership Foundation, Inc., 1955), pp. 29-41. Mr. Lewis discusses the problems inherent in the measurement of performance in each of the eight key result areas.

The student should also review the eight major objectives of an organization described by Peter Drucker and note the similarity between Drucker's objectives and the key result areas of Lewis. Drucker suggests objectives for each of the following eight areas: market standing, innovation, productivity, physical and financial resources, profitability, manager performance and development, worker performance and attitude, and public responsibility. See Chapter 3, "Objectives and Ethics," and the following:

Peter F. Drucker, "The Objectives of a Business," from *The Practice of Management* (New York: Harper & Brothers, Publishers, 1954).

expanding volume as well as the utilization of physical and financial resources.

MARKET POSITION. The position of a company in a chosen market is a measure of the extent to which its product or service is accepted by the customer and an indication of the effectiveness of its sales-promotion techniques. Standards intended to measure a company's market position must be expressed in terms of the total market. A company may, for example, increase its sales at the rate of two percent a year and be the largest in its field; yet, if the total market for the good or service offered is increasing at the rate of four percent a year, that company's market position is deteriorating.

PRODUCTIVITY. Measures of productivity are immediately associated with the production function, but standards of productivity should be set for administrative and sales functions as well as for production. Typically, productivity is expressed as the relationship between total output, measured in respect to dollar volume or units produced, and units of input—for example, the number of man-hours required for a stated level of output. Standards of productivity should be determined for other units of input as well as for man-hours. Efficiency of production may be expressed in relation to the number of machine hours, and a retail establishment is interested in the dollar volume produced per square foot of floor space. The use of total payroll dollars as an index of input indicates whether or not the rate of productivity is keeping pace with the increasing cost of labor—sometimes a more significant measure than the number of man-hours employed.

PRODUCT LEADERSHIP. Standards for profitability, market position, and productivity are not too difficult to express in relatively objective, quantitative units of measurement, but corporate achievement must be measured in areas where the criteria are qualitative in nature rather than quantitative. A company's position in respect to product leadership is difficult to express quantitatively; yet an estimate of position is necessary if it is a company objective to become or remain a leader in its field. A simple count of new products or services introduced is not sufficient. The significance of new contribution should also be weighed. Standards of quality and performance for current products should be compared with those of competitors. Determination of the significance of research in the development of new products and an evaluation of research effort offer a means of estimating potential leadership capabilities. Customer surveys indicate the degree of product acceptability and may furnish suggestions for product improvement. Finally, a value judgment must be made as to whether the company is meeting its goals of product leadership.[8]

PERSONNEL DEVELOPMENT. Standards for measuring the effectiveness of management development programs are also qualitative in nature. Since management development is usually the result of long-range planning and intended to meet future needs, it is difficult to assess the success of any such program on a year-to-year basis. However, an annual reporting of developmental activities establishes a trend in this area, and when compared with projected managerial needs resulting from expected growth, an estimate may be made concerning the need for expanding the management development program. The number of people participating in formal developmental programs, the success of those who have received training compared with those who have not been trained, and the number of managers hired from outside the company should be included in annual reports of personnel development. A current inventory of personnel skills when compared with forecasts for immediate personnel needs may indicate the short-range effectiveness of a management development program.

EMPLOYEE ATTITUDES. Although there is some question in regard to the existence of a positive relationship between employee attitude and short-range production goals (Chapter 18), there is no doubt that employee attitudes have their effect upon the success of an organization over a long period of time. Attitudes may be measured operationally by an analysis of labor turnover, absenteeism, grievances, and safety records. Measurement of these factors can be accomplished in an objective, quantitative manner; the difficulty lies in establishing the standard, or criterion, of what is acceptable or desirable. Year-to-year figures and comparisons between different units in the same organization or with industry experience may be used as a guide to determine expected results. Product quality, if within the control of employees, and the number of suggestions for improvements in operating methods may be used as measures of employee attitudes. Attitude surveys conducted at periodic intervals indicate the degree of progress being made in the improvement of employee attitudes. The determination of employee attitudes is significant for the company desirous of maintaining a position of respect and leadership in its community.

---

[8] Barry M. Richman, "A Rating Scale for Product Innovation," *Business Horizons*, Vol. V (Summer, 1962), pp. 37-44. Mr. Richman presents a method of screening and selecting new products.

PUBLIC RESPONSIBILITY. The fulfillment of goals in the area of public responsibility is highly intangible and difficult to measure. Included are contributions to the life of the community in the form of stable employment, participation in community affairs, and the leadership supplied for community activities. Standards of performance are not readily expressed in quantitative terms; consequently, the results obtained in the area of public responsibility are appraised in terms of their broad contribution to the public.

BALANCE BETWEEN SHORT-RANGE AND LONG-RANGE GOALS. Again, the measure of success is subjective in nature. Implied in this measurement is the existence of long-range goals, say 15 or 20 years from now; and the existence of intermediate and short-range plans to achieve the objectives of those long-range goals. The inclusion of a measurement of the balance between short-range and long-range goals forces a company to review its entire planning process and emphasizes that future success is dependent upon the execution of carefully developed plans.

Methods of Establishing Standards. It is apparent from the number and kinds of the areas for which standards may be established that one method of establishing standards cannot be applied to all areas. There are three methods used to determine the level of expected performance. One is to develop statistical, or normative, data from sources internal and external to the company; another is to appraise results in the light of experience and judgment; and the third method is to develop engineered standards.

STATISTICAL STANDARDS. Statistical standards, sometimes called historical standards, are standards based upon an analysis of past experience. The data used may be drawn from the company's own records or they may be a reflection of the experience of several companies. The particular statistic selected for the criterion may be the average or it may be a stated point above or below the midpoint, for example, the upper quartile. While an analysis of past experience may be helpful in setting standards of performance in some areas, the statistical approach has many pitfalls in setting production standards. The following example illustrates the weakness of a historical analysis.

> The accounting department of a rebuilder of automobile parts kept a careful, complete record of the number of labor hours, broken down into direct and indirect labor hours, required to rebuild each of several parts. At the end of each fiscal year, the average number of hours required to rebuild each part was determined. Thus, the average

for the past year became the standard for the current year and deviations from the average were reported as above or below standard. Despite the fact that this company was producing parts well within the limits set by its own standards, its labor costs were considerably in excess of those of its competitors. A consultant called in to review the situation discovered that there were many bottlenecks in the production control department and that the output per man-hour was only 70 percent of what could reasonably be expected based upon sound time study standards.

The lesson is clear: meeting standards of past performance is not sufficient, particularly when past performance is only a fraction of potential performance.

Yet, if used as an adjunct to other sources of information, statistical data are not only helpful but sometimes the only guide available. Indexes of profitability vary widely from one industry to another, and an analysis of industry data may prove helpful in setting criteria of profitability. Analysis of the experience of competing firms and one's own historical records of growth aid in setting realistic goals relative to market position. Companies choosing to set standards in the area of employee attitudes may find it useful to analyze the results obtained by other firms using the same attitude or opinion survey. The average contribution to charities and educational institutions may be significant in setting goals of public responsibility. In all of these instances before a final criterion can be set, the information gained from statistical sources is combined with another factor—judgment.

STANDARDS SET BY APPRAISAL. Standards do not have to be expressed in units of measurement accurate to the third decimal place. Some areas of corporate performance are, in the last analysis, appraised primarily in terms of a manager's past experience and judgment. As indicated in our discussion of statistical standards, normative data are a useful adjunct in setting standards of performance in regard to profitability, market position, employee attitudes, and to some extent in the area of public responsibility. However, the final determination of what constitutes a satisfactory level of performance is a judgment based upon management's past experience. Standards set by appraisal are essentially *value* judgments and can be as realistic and attainable as statistical or engineered standards. In the absence of standards determined by formal study and analysis, every manager is expected to appraise the output of his subordinates in terms of what he, as a manager, believes to be a satisfactory day's work. In so doing, standards are being set by appraisal.

ENGINEERED STANDARDS. Engineered standards, so called because they are based upon an objective, quantitative analysis of a specific work situation, may be developed for the measurement of machine output and for measuring the output of individual workers. Machine output standards express the production capabilities of a given piece of equipment and are determined by mechanical design factors. Machine capacity figures are developed by the designers of the equipment and represent the optimum output of the equipment in normal production use. Machine capacities are significant in determining output standards in industries using automatic equipment; for example, the metal and glass container industry.

Engineered standards developed to measure the output of individual workers, or groups of workers, are called either *time standards* or *time study* standards. The reason is that time is the element of measurement and is almost always measured by means of a stopwatch.[9] The first time studies in this country were completed by Frederick W. Taylor in 1881 at the Midvale Steel Company.[10] His studies were directed toward an analysis of the productivity of hourly workers in a steel mill. Since then, time study techniques have been applied to all types of production jobs—including material handling and maintenance—clerical positions, and even sales jobs.

In setting time standards the actual time taken to perform a given job is determined. This value is termed the *actual* time. The standard time is the time that should be required to perform the job under certain specified conditions. These conditions are usually defined as an average worker, trained in the skills of the job, working at normal pace (rate of speed), and following the prescribed methods for the job. Determining effort, or pace, is a matter of judgment and is related to the effort expended—and the speed required—to walk three miles an hour on level ground. Standard times are usually developed for a normal eight-hour

---

[9] The student is referred to the following references for a more complete discussion of time study methods:

Marvin E. Mundel, *Motion and Time Study Principles and Practice* (3d ed.; Englewood Cliffs, N. J.: Prentice-Hall, Inc., 1960).

Claude S. George, Jr., *Management in Industry* (Englewood Cliffs, N. J.: Prentice-Hall, Inc., 1959), pp. 394-416.

Franklin G. Moore, *Manufacturing Management* (3d ed.; Homewood, Illinois: Richard D. Irwin, Inc., 1961), pp. 508-542.

Richard N. Owens, *Management of Industrial Enterprises* (4th ed.; Homewood, Illinois: Richard D. Irwin, Inc., 1961), pp. 362-393.

For a point of view highly critical of time study methods, the following book is suggested:

William Gomberg, *A Trade Union Analysis of Time Study* (2d ed.; Englewood Cliffs, N. J.: Prentice-Hall, Inc., 1955).

[10] See Chapter 2, "The Development of Management Concepts," page 29.

workday and include allowances for fatigue, unavoidable delays, personal time, and other interruptions of work that occur at predictable intervals. A worker who performs his work according to the standards set for his job is said to be working at 100 percent of standard. The use of the expression, 100 percent of standard, causes much of the initial misunderstandings of time study. The term, 100 percent, normally conveys the idea of perfection, of maximum effort and maximum output. A more acceptable expression would be to use the term, par.

Time study standards are essential if incentive plans are to be installed, but it does not follow that incentives are necessary to make effective use of time study. On the contrary, time standards can be used quite effectively as a means of increasing production without the introduction of incentives. The presence of time standards alone tends to increase production.[11] Time standards also form the basis of standard costs. Standard costs are composed of the cost of labor performing at standard plus standard allowances for materials and allocated overhead.

The need for establishing standards varies widely from one company to another, but any company that has labor costs greater than 30 percent of its total product or service cost should investigate the possibility of establishing time standards to serve as the basis for control when measuring human output.

Measuring Current Performance

There is an intermediate step in the control process between the first step of the process, establishing standards, and the final phase of the process, the taking of corrective action. The middle step is that of measuring current performance. To a degree, the problems of measurements are defined, and sometimes partially solved, by the manner in which standards are defined. Standards of profitability, for example, imply that the measuring unit be one of dollars; but the statement of criteria in the areas of product leadership and public responsibility requires ingenuity in developing satisfactory methods of measurement. The variety and the number of performance factors for which standards may be set make it virtually impossible to discuss problems of measurement by describing units of measurement applicable to all business situations. Nonetheless, there are certain characteristics of effective control measurements to be examined. In addition, further elaboration of the significance of the measurement of current progress to the entire control process is helpful in assessing the worth of measuring devices.

---

[11] See Chapter 18, "Motivating Employees," pages 541-573.

Fundamental to sound control measures is recognition that management control systems are cybernetic systems, defining cybernetics as the processing and the interpretation of information. Thus, control systems are best regarded as information systems. The appropriateness of corrective action, the end point of the control process, is dependent almost entirely upon the kind of information received. Information intended to measure and describe current performance can be evaluated by seeking answers to the following five questions:

1. Is the information timely?
2. Are the units of measurement appropriate?
3. How reliable is the information received?
4. Is the information valid?
5. Is information being channeled to the proper authority?

Let us discuss each of these questions so that the problems of measuring performance are better understood.

Timeliness of Information. Control information, to be of greatest use, must reflect present position. Typically, managers rely too much on data supplied by the accounting department and as a result fail to develop other sources of information. Accounting statements are prepared at the end of a given time period, for example a calendar month, and, even with efficient procedures, seven to ten working days are required to prepare statements of the preceding month's operations. Though this information may have historical significance and be of value in the preparation of annual reports, it is of little or no value to the manager responsible for the efficiency of day-to-day operations. Ideally, the manager of each operating unit should have information presented to him during the course of each working day so that he might have an adequate basis for corrective action. Is such timeliness possible? The following example suggests that it is.

> The manager of a plant producing stamped automobile parts devised the following method of securing information concerning the quantity produced by each of several production departments on an hourly basis. Departments were designated by the operations performed and included the following: shearing, stamping, chrome plating, and buffing and polishing. The manager placed in his office a large blackboard ruled into vertical columns for each production department. Horizontal lines were drawn for each hour of the day. A production clerk checked with the foreman of each production department at the end of each hour, received the quantity produced by each department, and posted the information on the board in the manager's office. In this

way the manager became immediately aware of trouble spots and could anticipate future difficulties likely to arise resulting from a shortage of parts or from a breakdown in earlier operations in the production sequence.

Another result of the control procedure described in the above incident is that the foremen of the various departments confer more frequently with each other and with the plant manager to minimize delays in production. Timely control information can be obtained through telephone calls, daily reports, or personal observation without having to wait for information prepared and distributed by formal reporting systems.

Appropriate Units of Measurement. One of the most difficult tasks in measuring current performance is the selection of an appropriate unit of measurement. Occasionally the use of several different units offers a partial solution to this problem. For example, profit is expressed as a percentage of sales, the percent return on capital invested, and as total dollars. Similarly, production may be measured and described as a ratio of output to input or as total units produced. Market position is also measured by several different methods. The use of multiple measures to describe performance is sound because each measure serves as a cross check on the information provided by the other measures and at the same time emphasizes one particular aspect of the performance under review.

The measurement of performance against standard for profits, productivity, and sales utilizes quantitative units of measurement. However, much of the evaluation of a company's progress depends on qualitative, rather than quantitative, units of measurement. In the absence of quantitative measures, the manager, drawing upon past experience and his own set of values, must judge for himself whether or not standards are being met. Such judgments must be made in the areas of personnel development, public responsibility, and determining the balance between long-range and short-range goals. Attempting to express achievement in these areas by relying solely upon quantitative units can be misleading. For example, measuring personnel development by a head count of the number of persons who have completed a given training program does not answer the question of the effectiveness of the program in improving performance on the job. Even though qualitative measures are difficult to apply and generally unreliable when compared with quantitative units, it is a mistake not to set standards in those areas where measurement must be made in qualitative terms.

Reliability of Information. Reliability of information pertains to its degree of accuracy. It is assumed that the data are free from clerical errors. Thus, the accuracy referred to by the term reliability is in respect to the consistency of data and the extent to which all aspects of the problem are measured. Almost always a compromise must be made between reliability and timeliness. Usually the reliability of information is positively related to its completeness. Computer predictions of election returns illustrate the increasing accuracy of predictions as more and more data are reported and interpreted. However, most managerial interpretations of operations—and the subsequent corrective action—are based upon incomplete information. A sales manager having reports for only the first two weeks of a calendar month may be required to take corrective action even though his data are not fully reliable because they are not a complete description of the month's activities. Even so, partial information on recurring time cycles, such as monthly sales and production reports, can be analyzed and related to the entire cycle and provide a relatively accurate basis for analysis and action.

In addition to decreased reliability of information when using data for only a part of the reporting period, there is a marked decrease in the reliability of data covering initial phases of an operation. The reason for this type of loss in reliability is best explained by the adage, "practice makes perfect." At the start of a new operation quality and quantity of performance are at their lowest point; but with time, there is improved individual performance and better methods are usually developed. Graphic representations of improved performance are called *learning curves*. The aircraft industry, constantly faced with changing products, short runs, and the threat of contract cancellation, has developed techniques to predict with considerable accuracy the average level of performance by projecting an improvement or learning curve. Data from the beginning of an operation are not characteristic of the entire operation or its latter phases and are a highly unreliable source of information unless interpreted as part of a learning curve. Though the use of learning curves is most highly developed in the aircraft industry, the same techniques are applicable to the prediction of final performance in maintenance operations, in building heavy equipment, in construction, and in the performance of salesmen introducing a new product. The danger lies, not in using the initial data of a new operation, but in failing to recognize that there is a predictable improvement factor.[12]

---

[12] Winifred R. Hirschmann, "Profit from the Learning Curve," *Harvard Business Review*, Vol. XXXXII (January-February, 1964), pp. 125-139. Mr. Hirschmann's article discusses the characteristics of the learning curve, the reasons why it has not been accepted widely, and suggests some practical applications of the concept.

Validity of Information. It is possible for information to be highly reliable, yet not valid. Likewise, the appropriate unit of measurement, either quantitative or qualitative can be established, and yet the information received may not be valid. The validity of a measurement refers to the degree that a measurement actually reflects the phenomenon that it is intended to measure. An example of a highly reliable, quantitative measure with virtually no validity is the experience of a printing company in trying to determine the quantity of daily production. The figure used was the total number of pounds of finished materials shipped each day. There are several reasons why the total number of pounds shipped is not a valid measure of the company's productivity. First, the total number of pounds bore no consistent relationship to dollar volume of sales, profitability, or man-hours required for production because of the diversity of product line, which included cellophane and pliofilm packaging materials, lithographed products, foil wrappings, and fibre board cartons. Second, the pounds shipped bore only an indirect relation to production for any given day since up to 40 percent of the orders shipped on any given day came out of a warehouse and not directly from that day's production. Thus, the number of pounds shipped did not measure what it was intended to measure—the amount of goods produced in a given day.

Another example of a measurement that may or may not be valid is the use of gross sales as an index of profitability. Whenever the performance being reviewed is complex and composed of many different elements, it is extremely difficult to develop one single unit of measurement that adequately portrays what it is intended to portray. In these situations it is best to measure each segment of performance separately rather than use a single indicator that may not be valid.

Channeling Information to Proper Authority. The timeliness of information, the appropriateness of the unit of measurement, and the reliability and validity of control data are directed toward having the right information at the right time. A fifth requirement must be met, the channeling of information to the proper authority. Only then do we have all ingredients of a good information system for control—the right information at the right time and at the right place. What constitutes the proper channel for information flow varies with each company organization structure, the kind of information to be interpreted, and the kind of corrective action required to attain expected standards. Even so, the following generalization can be made: control information should be directed toward the individual assigned responsibility for the operation and at the same time having authority to take corrective action.

There is much discussion concerning the effect of integrated data processing systems upon the flow of information. Some argue that integrated systems encourage centralized control, with the result that the control of an organization ultimately rests in the hands of a few at the top of the organization. Others point out that the speed with which information can be handled and the variety of information processed make it possible to supply control information to first-line supervisors and middle management never available to them before. Although there seems to be a trend toward centralized control, the trend is not necessarily a function of integrated data processing systems. Rather, it may be an expression of a desire to place control information in the hands of those possessing the authority to take action.[13]

In summary, the measurement of organizational performance in respect to stated standards is not precise; yet, measure we must if we are to improve the quality of corrective action. An awareness of the difficulties inherent in measuring current position eventually leads to the development of meaningful control information.[14]

Taking Corrective Action

The third and last step of the control process, taking corrective action, epitomizes the busy, efficient executive. Here is a man making things happen and getting things done. Without action there is no control. The actions taken are the result of executive decisions and as such reflect the personality of the person taking the action as well as being determined by situational, or environmental, factors. Thus, the personality of the person in control has much to do with the kind of control. Before discussing the range of action available to the controlling executive, it is well to examine more closely the influence of personality upon corrective action, to determine who should take corrective action, and to make sure that causes—not symptoms—are being corrected.

Personality and Control. Personality factors, rather than the demands of the situation, are the cause of the extremes in control. One

---

[13] Garry E. Morse, "Pendulum Swing of Management Control," *Harvard Business Review*, Vol. XXXXIII (May-June, 1965), pp. 158-160, 162, 164. Mr. Morse discusses the trend toward more centralized control and stresses that information systems do not necessarily determine the degree of centralization.

[14] Paul Kircher, "Fundamentals of Measurement," *Advanced Management*, Vol. XX (October, 1955), pp. 5-8. Mr. Kircher's article contains a thorough discussion of the theoretical problems involved in establishing any system of measurement. As yet we have not developed for business organizations a system of measurement comparable in effectiveness to the systems used in the measurement of length.

extreme is typified by the Captain Queeg approach to management—
too much control. The other extreme might be called the Will Rogers
approach to management—too little control.[15] Captain Queeg, as
described by Herman Wouk in the *Caine Mutiny*, hewed to the letter
of the law and insisted that his men do the same. He had to know every
detail of what every man aboard his ship did and rationalized such
excessive control as a means of assuring himself, and the Navy, that all
regulations were being carried out. The same approach in an industrial
organization results in a mass of paper work, so much so that the real
work of the organization is neglected.

What motivates a Captain Queeg to check on every last detail? The
answer is simple: The same personality that makes it impossible to
delegate effectively. When effective delegation is practiced, there is little
need for tight control. In Chapter 12, four personality characteristics
that interfere with effective delegation are discussed. They are worth
recounting at this point. First, there are those who by vocational choice
—notably engineers and accountants—are trained to attend to details
and as a result find it difficult to delegate effectively when placed in
a supervisory position. Next, there are those managers who want to avoid
the major issues and occupy themselves by attention to petty detail.
Third, there are those who, for either real or imagined reasons, fear
failure; and last, there are those who have a mistrust of others.[16] These
are the traits that prevent effective delegation and at the same time result
in excessive control over the relatively unimportant. The effect on an
organization is stultifying. Initiative, innovation, and creativity on the
part of subordinates are stifled.[17]

The other pole in control, the Will Rogers approach, is equally
ineffective in achieving organizational goals. Here everything is assumed
to be going along just fine, there is no need to check because these are
wonderful people in the organization, and things are bound to work out
just right in the long run. Also, there is a hesitancy about offending
someone by questioning him about his performance. The Will Rogers

---

[15] Arnold F. Emch, "Control Means Action," *Harvard Business Review*, Vol.
XXXII (July-August, 1954), pp. 92-98. Mr. Emch uses Captain Queeg and Will Rogers
as the extremes in control. His article sets forth rules and guides for effective control
and emphasizes good delegation as the key to good control.

[16] See Chapter 12, page 352, for a more complete discussion of these personality
traits.

[17] Lyman K. Randall, "Organizational Paradox," *Harvard Business Review*, Vol.
XXXXIII (July-August, 1965), pp. 86-87, Mr. Randall presents a little quiz to determine
whether one is control oriented or creatively oriented. He also mentions Captain Queeg
as typical of excessive control and suggests the architect, Howard Roark, of Ayn Rand's
The Fountainhead as typifying the creative personality.

type is a defender of the Theory Y approach to organization. Eventually, however, he wants to know more about the operation than the mere fact that he has a certain amount of money in the bank at the end of each month. With no clearly defined organization, the inevitable happens —he creates an "assistant-to" to do his controlling for him. It is quite possible that the assistant-to might become another Captain Queeg. But more importantly, the creation of an assistant-to leads us again to the question, "Who controls?"

Who Controls? The payoff of the control process is not the setting of standards, nor is it the measurement of performance against standards. It is taking the corrective action necessary to bring performance in line with the standards. The logical person to take this action is the manager who has had assigned to him the responsibility of managing a particular aspect of the business and who has had delegated to him the authority necessary to fulfill the assigned responsibilities. Thus, effective control is the result of sound organizational structure and the practice of an important organizational process—delegation. Taking corrective action is executive action and as such is in the hands of the line manager. The controller's office may be involved in the setting of standards and almost always participates in the measurement of current position against standard, but the taking of corrective action belongs to the manager of an organizational unit.

Symptoms or Causes? Prior to taking corrective action it is necessary to differentiate between symptoms and causes. Most of us have had the experience of taking an antihistamine drug at the first sign of a cold, and after a day or so we stop taking the medicine. Sometimes, much to our disgust, the sniffling and sneezing return and we discover that we have done an excellent job of treating symptoms but not getting at the cause of the cold. A manager must learn to recognize a symptom for what it is and to devote his attention to the cause of the problem. Cost control, or the control of expenses, often falls into the category of treating symptoms rather than causes.

Excessive costs are an indication that something has gone wrong; they are the result of someone's performance and if costs are to be brought in line it is the performance that must be corrected. First, it is wise to examine the standard to determine whether or not the costs in question are in fact excessive. Next, try and determine the contribution of each factor that makes up the total cost. How much of total cost is attributable to direct labor, to materials, and to overhead? Finally, examine each of these factors separately and determine how performance can be improved in each area. The same analytical procedure can be applied to the sales function. The answer to a declining sales volume is not necessarily more salesmen or better performance on the part of the present sales force; instead, the decline in sales may be the result of a poorly designed product or the failure to meet the challenge of competitors.

The Management Process Cycle. After determining the cause for poor performance, corrective action is in order. It is impossible to formulate a list of actions available to the manager; each situation is unique and calls for its own solution. There is, however, a frame of reference of value to the manager in evaluating his proposed action. That framework is the management process cycle—replanning, reorganizing, redirecting, and continued control since in a going organization all these functions have been performed in one way or another. Failure to meet expected levels of performance is sometimes unavoidable and calls for the development of new plans with the possibility of revised standards of performance. Though there is merit in the adage, "the difficult we do immediately; the impossible we do tomorrow," there are times when one must recognize that the impossible cannot be accomplished in accordance with present plans. Delays in a construction schedule resulting from inclement weather necessitate a revision of plans. Failure to meet a marketing objective may mean allocating more money for advertising or a restatement of expected results.

The present organization may need revising. Is the organization structured in such a manner that there is clear-cut responsibility for each organizational unit, or is there need for the creation of a new unit? What about the people in the organization? Are they performing their assigned duties satisfactorily? A change in either organizational structure or personnel may be necessary to correct the causes of poor performance. Or the difficulty may lie in directing. Sometimes a restatement of what is expected brings the desired results. Finally, there is the control process itself—it must be exercised continually. The management cycle is not composed of the four discrete steps of planning, organizing, directing, and controlling; instead, it is a continuous process, with control functioning as a catalyst to produce an integrated continuous process.

CHARACTERISTICS OF GOOD CONTROL

In the preceding discussion of the steps of the control process, many of the characteristics of an effective control system are implied and touched upon briefly. Control is an extremely critical factor in the achievement of organizational objectives, with the effectiveness of the control function dependent upon the information received. Control systems, to be of greatest use, must possess certain characteristics. Again, we are unable to describe all control systems since each control situation is unique. Despite this difficulty, there is general agreement that good control has the following characteristics: timeliness, follows organizational lines, strategic, economical, shows both trends and status, and stresses the exception.[18] Each of these characteristics is discussed separately.

Timeliness

Accounting records are relatively precise, detailed statements of a company's activity for a stated period and are historical in nature since they are prepared after the period has closed. Frequently these reports are of great value to the planning process, but they are often inadequate as control reports because they are not timely. Ideally, the optimum form of control information should forecast deviations from standard prior to its occurrence. In practice, such forecasting is seldom achieved, but every effort should be made to report deviations from standard while the event in question is still in process. We mentioned the control device developed by the plant manager of an automobile parts manufacturer that enabled him to keep abreast of the output of each production department at hourly intervals. Supervisors of production departments frequently find it necessary to develop control information during the course of the day. One supervisor in a large printing company placed a small blackboard at the end of each press, with the cumulative standard production posted for each hour. He requested the pressmen to post actual production for each hour alongside the posted standard. One immediate result of this procedure was that the pressmen called the supervisor when trouble began to develop, thereby permitting the rescheduling of work to other presses.

Another means of focusing upon timely information is to require unit managers, such as plant managers and sales managers, to prepare monthly forecasts and to submit revisions of these forecasts on either a weekly or a biweekly basis. While it is true that the information used in these forecasts may not be accurate when compared with the accounting

---

[18] John Richard Curley, "A Tool for Management Control," *Harvard Business Review*, Vol. XXIX (March, 1951), pp. 45-86. General characteristics of tools for control based upon the experience of RCA are presented. A brief discussion of accounting controls and their limitations is also included.

records prepared at the close of the period, the process of forecasting and revising forces the manager to develop and rely upon timely information. If a choice must be made between timeliness and accuracy of control information, timeliness should be emphasized for the control of current operations.

Follows Organizational Lines

The excessive control of a Captain Queeg and the hands-off attitude of a Will Rogers, with the eventual inevitability of an assistant-to, reflect the same organizational shortcoming—a failure to delegate. Responsibility is not assigned nor is authority delegated, with the result that clear-cut accountability to superiors in the organization is not established. The control function can in no way substitute for poor organizational practices and structure. Good controls are closely related to organizational structure and reflect organizational structure and processes in their design and function.

Accumulated total product costs are of great significance to the sales department in the pricing of a given product, yet such figures may not be meaningful to manufacturing personnel charged with the responsibility of controlling costs. To be meaningful to manufacturing departments, cost data must reflect the portion of total cost added to the product by each department. Only then is the manager aware of the costs chargeable to his department and in a position to control those costs. Defects in quality should be traced to component parts and reported to the operating department responsible for the production of the defective part. Wage and salary plans can be utilized for control by reporting the average rate paid for each job classification and each salary grade. The information should be prepared for each organizational unit as well as for the entire company. Directing information to the responsible manager is an effective way of making it possible to exercise control at the lowest possible echelon of the organization.

Strategic Placement

It is impossible to establish controls for every aspect of even a small to medium-size business because of its complexity. Thus, it becomes necessary to establish controls at certain points of the operation selected because of their strategic value. A company whose primary contact with customers is through letters written by the correspondents in the sales order department may experience difficulty in maintaining good customer relations as the result of inconsistencies from the many sources of contact with customers. A strategic control of correspondence is the requirement that all letters be prepared for the signature of the sales manager, a step that permits the manager to sample all outgoing correspondence. Most governmental agencies require the signature of the chief administrator on all outgoing mail.

Quality control programs rely heavily upon the selection of strategic points where inspection approaches the 100-percent level as a means of meeting quality standards. A major appliance, such as a refrigerator, is checked after final assembly by connecting it to a test circuit to see if it cools properly. Also, the components of the compressor are subjected to complete dimensional checks prior to assembly to insure proper fit. Establishing key control points prior to the assembly of a critical component and after final assembly minimizes the likelihood of expensive rework and the possibility of defective products reaching the customer.

A few well-chosen measures of performance are often sufficient for the overall control of medium-size business operations. The owner-manager of a firm manufacturing trays for use in cafeterias and drive-in restaurants received weekly reports containing the following information: the backlog of orders, finished goods inventory, number of units shipped, and total hours of factory labor. A change in the order backlog with the other measures remaining relatively constant indicated the effectiveness of sales effort, and the number of units shipped was closely related to gross sales for the month. Total labor hours when balanced with inventory and units shipped let him know something about manufacturing efficiency, and a rising inventory indicated the need for either increasing sales effort or decreasing direct labor hours. To this manager, changes in the interrelationships of these four measures revealed potential trouble spots and enabled him to take immediate corrective action.

Economical Administration

In addition to its stifling effects on human effort, the excessive control of a Captain Queeg can be expensive. The story is often told of a consultant encountering strategic controls similar to those used by the manager of the tray manufacturing company. The consultant suggested that in addition to these overall controls there was a need to control overhead costs. The recommended controls were put into effect. At the end of several months a marked decline in profits was noticed, and the amount of the decline corresponded to the additional costs of administering the new controls. Figure 6-1, page 183, presents a graphic model showing the relationships between total cost, the cost of taking managerial action—for example, quality control—and decreasing costs resulting from managerial action. This model serves well as a means of judging the economic cost of proposed controls.

There is an old saying, "You can inspect yourself out of business." Yet, failure to detect defective products results in the loss of customers. One method of balancing the cost of quality control against the cost of not taking action is the use of sampling techniques where every 10th or 100th item is checked thoroughly. Another area deserving careful attention is the use of incentives as a means of reducing unit labor costs. Although incentives may reduce the cost of direct labor, the indirect costs of maintaining up-to-date time studies by the industrial engineering department may more than counterbalance any savings in direct labor. Some companies have found measured day work—the use of time standards to determine a fair day's work—to be satisfactory since the standards do not have to be maintained with the same degree of accuracy as required when standards are used as the basis for incentive pay. Accuracy of measurement is an important factor in determining the cost of a given set of controls. Sometimes the presence of a deviation from standard and its direction, rather than the precise amount of the deviation, is sufficient for control purposes.

Reveals Trends As Well As Status

Controls that show the current status of a specific phase of an operation are relatively easy to prepare since all that is needed are periodic statements of the particular activity in question. Although such measures show present status, they do not necessarily reveal the trend of performance; i.e., monthly production reports do not show whether production is increasing or decreasing. This limitation of periodic reporting is overcome by using a graphic method of presentation that shows successive measures, thus forming a trend line, or by presenting the data in tabular form and including year-to-date or month-to-date figures. However, establishing and showing the trends of specific business functions do not always provide sufficient control information. It is necessary to include supporting information that is closely related to the primary function under observation. In the case of production, concentration on the number of units produced without the inclusion of a measure of the units of input gives no indication of the cost or efficiency of production—an aspect of production that may be more important for control purposes than the total produced.

Interpreting trends in the light of related happenings is of special significance in the development of control information for the measurement of market position. There is the well-known example of a soap manufacturer who recorded continuous gains in the sales of soap, but neglected to focus attention on the increasing share of the home-laundry market claimed by detergents, with the result that the company discovered too late that it was last in the newer and larger market. One of the largest and oldest manufacturers of men's suits measured market position not only in respect to the market for suits but also in respect to the total amount spent for men's outer wear. As a result, the company discovered that an increasing share of the money spent for outer wear was spent on sports clothes and thus established plants for the manufacture of men's sportswear. Control data showing market position should show position in relation to competitive items as well as the market position relative to that of competitors.

Stresses the Exception

In Chapter 2, "The Development of Management Concepts," Jethro's recommendations to Moses are presented. The three recommendations are: teach "ordinances and laws" to the people; select leaders and assign them "to be rulers of thousands, and rulers of hundreds, and rulers of fifties, and rulers of ten"; and those rulers should administer all routine matters and bring to Moses only the important questions. The third suggestion is often referred to as the *principle of the exception*. There are two reasons why effective systems of controls stress the exception. First, the amount of information generated in even small organizations is so great that it becomes difficult, if not impossible, to determine the significance of all information. To review every action of subordinates or to consult with them prior to taking action consumes too much of the time and energy of the manager. Second, when information stressing the exception is presented to the manager, his attention is directed toward those items that require corrective action.

Examples of controls that point up the exception are numerous in all functions of management. The sales data presented to a national sales manager should specify those districts that deviate from predicted standards of performance beyond a predetermined range; for example, those districts that vary more than plus or minus 5 percent. The exceptions must include those areas that exceed expected performance as well as those that fail to meet the standard. It is quite possible that the reasons for successful performance can be applied to those districts whose performance is below par. The reporting of the exception is of value in the control of quality, cost, production, or any other measure of performance for which standards have been set. Usually acceptable performance is defined as performance within the limits of a predetermined range, with the breadth of the range varying for each performance factor, rather than satisfactory performance as a point value with no tolerance allowed.

Control by exception is closely related to the process of delegation and is not necessarily the exercise of corrective action after the function in question has been performed. Instead, effective control is exercised by either approving or disapproving the exceptional action prior to its occurrence. When responsibilities are assigned, authority within prescribed limits is delegated in order that these responsibilities may be fufilled. Occasionally a manager requires greater authority so that he may fulfill his responsibilities. When need arises, he requests his superior to recognize the exception and grant additional authority. For instance, the supervisor of a manufacturing department may have the authority to spend $100 for the repair of any one piece of equipment in his department and $1,000 per month for total repairs in the department. Deviations beyond these maintenance cost standards require prior approval from his superior, the plant manager. The plant manager, in turn, may be permitted to spend $1,000 on any single item of general plant maintenance and $5,000 in any month. For the expenditure of sums exceeding these limits, he must secure prior approval from his superior, the manufacturing vice-president. Clearly defined limits of authority and the requirement of prior approval to exceed these limitations permit the control of the exception prior to its happening. Thus, the concept of control by exception is used to control deviations from standard before the exception occurs as well as to emphasize those areas in need of corrective action.

Each of the six preceding characteristics of an effective control system—timeliness, follows organizational lines, strategic placement, economical administration, showing both trends and status, and stressing the exception—is important to the control of operations. These characteristics are descriptive of two different aspects of the control process and as such can be condensed and stated as two principles of control.[19] The establishment of controls that present information while

---

[19] Harold Koontz and Cyril O'Donnell, *Principles of Management*, 4th ed. (New York: McGraw-Hill Book Company, Inc., 1968), pp. 731-73. Professors Koontz and O'Donnell present 12 principles of control grouped into three general categories: (1) those reflecting the purpose and nature of control, (2) those emphasizing the structure of control, and (3) those emphasizing the control process. The following reference presents a more complete discussion of control principles:

Harold Koontz, "Management Control: A Suggested Formulation of Principles," *California Management Review*, Vol. I (Winter, 1959), pp. 47-55.

it is still timely, that reveal information that is of strategic value in the control of operations, and that follow established organizational lines is descriptive of the purpose and structure of the control system. The characteristics of economy of administration and the reporting of trends as well as current status are also a function of the purpose and structure of the control system. The last of the six characteristics, stressing and reporting the exception, leads directly to the essence of control—corrective action. Thus, logically there are two fundamental principles of control. The *principle of control design* emphasizes the nature and design of the control system and states:

> Effective control systems are designed to be economical in their administration and to reflect organizational structure. Such systems should provide management with information that is timely, of strategic value, and descriptive of the trends of operations as well as current status.

The *principle of the exception* emphasizes the essence of the control process—taking corrective action:

> The most efficient use of managerial time and energy is possible when control information stresses the exception and focuses attention upon those functions that need corrective action.

Case Problem 20-B, Controlling Sales Expense, describes two widely divergent degrees of control within the same organization and offers an opportunity to determine the proper degree of control that is needed and the methods to be utilized in establishing such control.

CASE PROBLEM
20-B

CONTROLLING
SALES EXPENSE

Frank Anchor, a district manager for Paper Products Company, has been in charge of the Chicago district sales office for two months. Prior to his transfer to Chicago to replace Tom Aderly, who has been in Chicago for 30 years as a salesman and for the last 20 years as sales manager, Anchor had been assistant manager of the New York sales district. When reviewing his new assignment with the vice-president in charge of sales, Anchor was told that the Chicago sales expenses were 50 percent higher than those in New York and that sales volume had not kept pace with the rate of increase shown by other large offices. He was advised that he should first reduce the cost of operating the Chicago office and that as soon as costs were under control he should take steps to increase sales volume.

Anchor arrived in Chicago a month prior to Aderly's retirement and had occasion to review with him the operations of the office. Aderly recognized that the Chicago expenses were higher than those for New York but attributed this difference to the size of the district, which covered many more square miles than New York. When Anchor asked to see the records of daily calls made by each salesman, a list of potential customers, and the names of the new customers for each month, Tom Aderly answered as follows:

"Frank, I don't bother much with things like that. Every morning I visit with each of my eight salesmen when they come into the office. I've known every one of these men since the first day he started to work here. I know that they have the best interests of the company at heart, and I'm sure that each man is doing his very best. I help them when they ask for it, but otherwise I let each man follow his own lead. Makes for a nice friendly atmosphere."

After Aderly formally retired, Anchor had the opportunity to examine more closely the salesmen's expense accounts. He found that the average expense advance was $250 instead of the $100 maximum allowed by company policy, and that one salesman had drawn a $500 expense advance. Anchor realized that, in order to bring expenses and sales volume in line with those of other districts in the company, a radical change in the method of managing the Chicago office was needed. He decided to present these changes in memo form and to discuss the changes in the first of the newly instituted weekly meetings scheduled for Friday afternoons. The following is a copy of the memorandum.

To: Salesmen, Chicago District, Paper Products Company.

Re: Expense Control.

You are all aware that the expenses of the Chicago District sales office are much higher than those of offices in other large cities. For example, our expenses are 25 percent higher than those of Los Angeles, a district of comparable size. It is necessary that we get our expenses in line with those of similar offices in the company. The following procedures are effective beginning next Monday.

1. Expense advances will be limited to the $100 per week as outlined in the company sales policy manual.

Those of you who have outstanding balances of more than $100 will not be permitted to draw additional advances; further, the amount in excess of $100 must be paid by the end of this month. If not paid by that time, authorization will be asked for to deduct the balance in excess of $100 in three equal monthly installments from your salary.

2. Salesmen will no longer report to the office each morning; instead, each of you is expected to telephone the office between 9 and 9:30 each morning and give my secretary a schedule of the calls you intend to make that day. You are also asked to call between 1 and 1:30 p.m. so that we may relay messages from customers that have been received during the morning.

3. Each salesman is expected to report to this office in person between 4 and 5 p.m. every day to review with me the calls made during the day and arrange appointments for calls on large accounts so that I can make the calls on these customers with you.

4. Daily expense records will be kept and are to be completed each afternoon when you are in the office.

5. Prior approval must be obtained for any entertainment expense exceeding $25.

6. Monthly time and expense reports must be summarized by the 25th of each month, showing total number of sales calls made, total expense, and total dollar volume of orders received. These summaries will then be forwarded to New York. No salary checks will be issued to any salesman until monthly time and expense reports have been received by the New York office.

PROBLEMS

1. How would you characterize Mr. Aderly and Mr. Anchor in respect to their methods of exercising control?
2. Is there need for stricter controls in the Chicago office? Why?
3. Do you agree that there is need for the controls set forth in Anchor's memo? Do you approve of the method he is using in establishing these controls?
4. How would you have handled this situation? Explain.

Chapter Questions for Study and Discussion

1. Define in your own terms the meaning of the word "cybernetics." Give an example of a cybernetic system and show why it is so classified.

2. Comment on the following statement: All dynamic systems involve the transmission of information.

3. Relate the three steps of the control process to the concept of a cybernetic system.

4. What are the major functions of a person holding the title of controller in an organization? In an organization, whose responsibility is it to take the corrective action?

5. Describe the relationship between the controller and the manager of an organizational unit.

6. What are the characteristics of a standard? Does the concept of par, borrowed from the game of golf, provide a good analogy for the understanding of the concept of standard? Why?

7. How are standards and objectives related? Illustrate by example.

8. Evaluate the three methods for establishing standards by indicating which methods are most likely to be appropriate in establishing standards for each of the eight key result areas.

9. Discuss each of the major problems encountered in the measurement of performance.

10. What relationship, if any, exists between the process of delegation and the control process? Explain fully.

11. As a manager, what steps would you take to assure yourself that you were able to distinguish symptoms from causes?

12. If it is true that each control system is unique, how is it possible to develop the characteristics of a good control system? State briefly why each of these characteristics is necessary.

13. How are the principle of control design and the principle of the exception related to the characteristics of a good control system? What are the likely results when these principles are violated?

CHAPTER 21

Nonbudgetary Control

Tom Olafson, long a manager for a Chicago-based national moving and storage company, has recently been assigned the position of manager of a newly acquired company, Sunshine Moving and Storage Company. Sunshine's annual sales are approximately $850,000. Though the company is not as profitable as similar companies in the national system, Sunshine was considered a good buy because it is well located in a West Coast city of one million persons, the rolling equipment is relatively new, and the two warehouses are modern and well kept. The parent corporation believes that increased sales efforts should produce an annual sales volume of at least $950,000 and a net profit before taxes of six percent of annual sales.

After studying the operating statement for the previous year, shown in Exhibit 1, Tom prepared a summary of the major operating ratios used as guides by the parent company in evaluating the performance of company-owned moving and storage facilities and in advising those privately owned companies that operate under a franchise system. In regard to revenue sources it is recommended that companies located on the West Coast derive no more than 25 percent of their revenue from long-distance moving, with at least 27 percent of their revenue coming from local moving. It is important to control the ratio between long-distance and local-moving revenues because the direct operating expenses incurred by long-distance moving approximate 80 percent of long-distance revenue, while local-moving operating expenses are about

Exhibit I
ANNUAL OPERATING STATEMENT
Sunshine Moving & Storage Company

Revenue Sources:

1. Long distance	$301,750
2. Local moving	204,850
3. Commissions	85,000
4. Storage & warehousing	128,350
5. Packing and crating	130,050
Total revenue	$850,000

Expense Items:

6. Traffic & sales

Supervision, sales, and clerical salaries	$ 34,000
Advertising	12,750
Other expenses	12,750
Total traffic & sales	$ 59,500

7. Administrative & general expense

Salaries (officers & managers)	$ 42,500
Other administrative salaries	45,900
Other general administrative expense	90,950
Total administrative & general expense	$179,350

8. Trucking expense (includes long distance and local moving)

Equipment maintenance	$ 39,515
Insurance and safety	19,757
Depreciation	20,264
Taxes and licenses	15,705
Transportation—supervisor, wages, fuel oil	331,316
Total trucking expense	$426,557

9. Storage & warehousing expense

Supervision and clerical employees	$ 5,519
Building expense	34,783
Insurance, taxes, maintenance, & supplies	11,423
Wages	25,625
Total storage & warehousing expense	$ 77,350

10. Packing & crating expense

Supervision & office employees	$ 2,601
Depreciation, insurance, taxes	11,835
Materials and supplies	22,499
Wages	41,265
Total packing & crating expense	$ 78,200

Profit or loss:

11. Profit	$ 29,043

77 percent of local-moving revenue. It is also recommended that storage and warehousing revenue account for at least 18 percent of total revenue, with 20 percent of total revenue from this source being entirely possible. Similarly, packing and crating revenues should range between 14 and 16 percent of the total, and commissions earned from business booked for vans from other terminals should account for at least 10 percent of total revenue. Commissions are regarded as a particularly valuable source of revenue because little capital equipment is utilized and there is usually additional income resulting from required packing and crating.

Recommended ratios for major expense items are summarized as follows:

Department	Percentage of Total Revenue
Traffic and Sales:	
Supervision, sales, and clerical personnel...	5.7%
Advertising	3.0
Other expenses	.9
	9.6%
Administrative and General:	
Salaries (officers and managers)	4.5%
Other salaries	5.5
Other general expenses	10.5
	20.5%

Department	Percentage of Departmental Revenue
Trucking Department:	
Equipment and maintenance	6.0%
Insurance and safety	3.5
Depreciation	3.5
Taxes and licenses	2.5
Transportation (including fuel, wages, and subsistence)	62.0
	77.5%
Storage and Warehousing:	
Supervisory and office personnel	4.5
Building expense	28.0
Depreciation, insurance, and taxes	9.5
Wages	20.0
	62.0%
Packing and Crating:	
Supervision and office personnel	3.1%
Depreciation, insurance, and taxes	9.5
Materials and supplies	15.0
Wages	29.0
	56.6%

PROBLEMS

1. Are company expectations for sales and profits reasonable? What action would you take to increase sales?
2. Analyze each of the operating departments—trucking, storage and warehousing, and packing and crating—in

respect to company recommendations for such operations and indicate the steps you would take as manager
of Sunshine Moving and Storage Company in order to
bring performance in line with expected results.
3. How profitable is each of the four sources of revenue—
commissions, trucking, storage and warehousing, and
packing and crating—when traffic and sales expense
and administrative and general expense are appor-
tioned to each in the same percentage amount that
the source is of total sales?

In Chapter 20, "The Basis of Control," it is stated that standards
may be set for each of the following key result areas: (1) profitability,
(2) market position, (3) productivity, (4) product leadership, (5) personnel development, (6) employee attitudes, (7) public responsibility,
and (8) balance between short-range and long-range goals. Since the
nature of the goals and the kind of performance required to meet stated
objectives in each of these areas are different, it seems highly unlikely
that a single control device can be used with equal effectiveness in all
areas. Such is the case. Budgets, discussed in Chapter 22, are a very
effective means of controlling expense and revenue items; thus, they are
particularly useful in controlling performance in the areas of profitability
and productivity. However, there are other means of control, conveniently referred to as *nonbudgetary,* that are necessary to establish
an effective and complete system of control. These techniques of nonbudgetary control, arranged in order from the simple to the more
complex, are as follows: personal observation, reports, audit programs,
ratio analysis, break-even analysis, and time-event-network analysis.

PERSONAL OBSERVATION

Personal observation is a means of securing control information
applicable to all key result areas and is used by all levels of management. The supervisor in charge of a manufacturing department or a
clerical section relies to a great extent upon impressions gained as
the result of personal contact with subordinates. He is able to judge
output by observing the pace of his workers; quality can be evaluated by
personally inspecting the work in progress; and an estimate of morale
and attitudes results from seeing employees, listening to their spontaneous
remarks, and obtaining responses to questions. The plant manager who
makes a daily tour of the plant is able to obtain firsthand information
concerning conditions in the plant that are not revealed by formal

reports. Similarly, many presidents and chief executive officers visit all company installations at least once each year so that the personal impressions thus gained may become a part of the basis for their decisions.

Personal observation as a means of gaining information is time consuming and is often criticized for this reason. Also, there is the possibility that subordinates may misinterpret a superior's visit and consider such action as meddling or failure to delegate. Finally, the value of firsthand information obtained from personal contact is limited by the perceptual skills and interpretative ability of the observer. Even so, personal observations are often the only means of substantiating impressions gained from other sources, and personal contacts almost always have a salutary effect upon subordinates since the presence of one's superior reveals his interest in the operation.

REPORTS

In designing or evaluating control reports, two closely related questions arise: (1) What is the purpose of the report? and (2) Who should receive the report?

Purpose of Control Reports

The primary purpose of control reports is to supply information intended to serve as the basis for corrective action if needed. At the same time, the significance of control reports must be kept in proper perspective. Control reports are only a part of the planning-control-planning information cycle that is necessary for a complete management information system. Refer to Figure 17-2, Anatomy of Management Information, on page 520. Note that control information includes nonfinancial as well as financial data, that it measures performance, and isolates variances from standard. Control information also provides feedback so that planning information may be updated and corrected.

An example of a set of relatively simple control reports that contribute to the control process as well as provide a basis for updating the planning process is presented in Chapter 20, page 638. In this illustration the owner of a company manufacturing trays for cafeterias and drive-in restaurants receives reports containing information that shows the current backlog of orders, finished goods inventory, number of units shipped, and total hours of factory labor. A decline in the backlog of current orders, with the other three measures remaining relatively constant, indicates the need for corrective action resulting in increased sales. In this instance, the information provided serves primarily the control function. However, an increase in the order backlog, again with all other measures remaining constant, signals the need for additional planning so that production may be increased to meet the increased demand. Whenever possible, control reports should be designed so that they provide feedback for the planning process as well as provide information of immediate value to the control process.

Distribution of Control Reports

Since the culmination of the control process is the taking of necessary corrective action to bring performance in line with standards, it follows that control information must be directed to the person who is organizationally responsible for taking the required action. Usually the same information, though in a somewhat abbreviated form, is given to the responsible manager's superior. The supervisor of a manufacturing department requires detailed information that describes the performance of equipment and personnel in his department, but the plant manager may receive condensed summary statements showing performance in relation to standard, expressed as a percentage, for each of several operating departments. A district sales manager needs a complete daily record of the performance of each of his salesmen; yet, the report forwarded to the regional sales manager summarizes only the performance of each sales district in his region. In preparing reports for higher echelons of management, summary statements and recommendations for action should appear on the first page; substantiating data, usually the information presented to the person directly responsible for the operation, may be included if needed.

Characteristics of Good Reports

Since control reports are an integral part of a control system, they should incorporate the characteristics of an effective control system as described in Chapter 20, pages 635 to 642. They should be timely, particularly those prepared for a unit supervisor. When reports provide information intended primarily for the purpose of control, they should follow organizational lines; yet, it must be remembered that for the same information to become effective as a basis for additional planning, it is necessary to cross organizational lines. Reports should be prepared to reveal activity in the more sensitive or strategic areas of the business. In organizations where progress depends upon new products, frequent periodic reporting of research and development activities may be required. A firm whose chief concern is manufacturing efficiency may emphasize a detailed reporting of the production process.

Reports should be economical, and their costs should be measured in terms of the extent to which they actually contribute to the control process. In preparing reports, sufficient data should be included so that trends as well as current status are reflected. Finally, reports should be prepared so that the exception is emphasized. Summary statements should stress performance that deviates from standard and show clearly both the direction and magnitude of the deviation.

AUDIT PROGRAMS

Traditionally, auditing, an independent appraisal of a company's financial records, seeks to test the reliability and validity of financial records by determining the degree of accuracy and the extent to which financial statements reflect what they purport to represent. As a result, audit programs are often regarded as a means of encouraging honesty on the part of employees and safeguarding the company's financial resources. This concept of auditing, the verification of company financial records, is limited in scope and is associated with *external audits* conducted by outside agencies such as bank examiners or a firm of public accountants. When conducted by a specialized staff made up of company personnel, auditing can be an effective means of control as well as a means of verifying financial records, and is known as the *internal audit*. It is possible also to apply the techniques of auditing as a means of assessing the overall effectiveness of management, an application often referred to as the *management audit*. In addition, *human resource accounting* can be used by companies whose production depends primarily on the creativity of its personnel. Each of these forms of auditing, the external audit, the internal audit, the management audit, and human resource accounting is discussed in turn.

External Auditing

The external audit is usually conducted by a firm of public accountants. Its primary purpose is to determine whether or not company records of financial transactions present a true statement of the company's financial condition. It is essentially a verification of the accuracy of the records and a determination of the consistency of application of accepted accounting procedures. In order to make a summary statement of the financial condition of a company, it is necessary for the auditors to spot check all types of basic financial transactions to determine their accuracy. It is the checking phase of the auditing process that causes many to regard external auditing as a means of encouraging honesty on the part of employees. For example, a review of inventory records, a part of the process of verifying assets, may reveal shortages that may be the result of dishonesty.

The contribution of the external audit to the control process is indirect and limited in its nature. For instance, a company might wish to allocate certain capital expenditures as expense items, but independent auditors will not certify such allocations unless they are consistent with previously established accounting procedures. The same indirect form of control may be exerted if a company attempts to modify its statement of assets by altering established practices of evaluating finished goods or raw material inventories. The value of the external audit as a means of assessing financial position is limited by the appropriateness, or validity, of existing accounting procedures. When the summary information of the audit—usually a verification of the balance sheet items of assets, liabilities, and net worth—is used as a basis for formulating the corrective action of the control process, its worth is no greater than the validity of the accounting techniques used to record the financial condition of the company.

Internal Auditing

As the phrase, internal auditing, implies, the internal audit is conducted by a specialized staff made up of company personnel. Like the external audit conducted by an outside source, the internal audit verifies the accuracy of company records and determines whether or not such records are what they purport to be. However, the purpose of the internal audit is to provide a means of internal control. It seeks to determine the effectiveness of other controls; consequently, the internal audit may be regarded as a master control over all other forms of control.[1]

The potential benefits of an effective internal auditing program are many; however, there are three contributions that stand out above all others. First, internal auditing provides a way of determining whether established procedures and methods are effective in meeting stated company objectives and insuring compliance with stated policies. If, for example, it is the objective of a company to build a product having the highest possible quality, procedures are established to insure that component parts of the product are the best available. In reviewing purchase requisitions, the internal audit team goes beyond the accuracy

---

[1] William T. Jerome, III, "Internal Auditing As an Aid to Management," *Harvard Business Review,* Vol. XXXI (March-April, 1953), pp. 127-136.

of the records of the purchasing department and seeks to determine whether or not, in fact, components are of the highest available quality. The determination of the extent to which company policies are observed leads directly to the second major contribution of internal auditing— formulating recommendations for the improvement of policies, procedures, and methods so that they are more effective in the attainment of stated objectives. It may be necessary to modify existing controls, establish new controls, or change present procedures or methods. Deviations from established procedures may arise because someone believes that he has discovered a short cut, or there may have been an honest misunderstanding of the procedure due to its complexity. Whatever the reason, it is the task of the internal auditor to recommend those changes necessary to insure compliance, including the recommendation for additional or improved controls.

The third benefit of an internal auditing program may seem paradoxical at first glance. Internal auditing provides a means of providing a greater degree of delegation of authority and, if desirable, a means of facilitating the decentralization of operations. Delegation of authority and its broader organizational counterpart, the decentralization of authority to operating units, do not imply an absence of centralized control. On the contrary, the extent of delegation and decentralization is dependent to a large measure upon the effectiveness of central control. Internal auditing offers a means of continually checking the effectiveness of established controls and recommending needed improvements.

The use of the internal audit as a means of control has been increasing, particularly in large companies. One study reveals that in 1920 only 9 of 132 large companies had internal auditing departments; in 1940, only 58 of these companies had such departments; but by 1950, all of the 132 companies studied had internal auditing departments.[2] Even though many small and medium-size companies do not have internal auditing departments, the functions of internal auditing can still be accomplished to a degree by emphasizing that one of the functions of control is to determine the extent to which procedures and methods are being observed and to recommend improvements.

The success of internal auditing is dependent not only upon the attitude of top management but also upon the degree of acceptance accorded the audit team by lower and middle echelons of management. Acceptance by other members of management is more readily attained

---

[2] F. A. Lampert and J. B. Thurston, *Internal Auditing for Management* (Englewood Cliffs, N. J.: Prentice-Hall, Inc., 1953), pp. 84-86.

when internal auditors perform the functions of consultants and act as special staff advisors concerned with the improvement of all operations rather than appearing as custodians of company resources.

The Management Audit

The external audit is concerned chiefly with verifying the reliability and validity of financial records. Internal auditing goes a step further and determines the degree of compliance with company policies, procedures, and methods, and, if necessary, makes recommendations to insure the observance of established company practices. An even broader form of auditing is the *management audit,* a systematic approach to the appraisal of the overall performance of management.

One of the better known methods of appraising managerial performance is the management audit developed by Jackson Martindell of the American Institute of Management (AIM).[3] The AIM management audit evaluates the performance of a company in relation to the performance of other companies in the same industry and in relation to the performance of outstanding companies in other industries. Some of the information needed for the management audit is a matter of public record, but much of it comes from the answers to a 300-item questionnaire. Point values for the answers given to each question are assigned, with the maximum number of points being 10,000. Managerial performance in each of the following 10 categories is evaluated: [4]

1. Economic Function
2. Corporate Structure
3. Health of Earnings
4. Service to Stockholders
5. Research and Development
6. Directorate Analysis
7. Fiscal Policies
8. Production Efficiency
9. Sales Vigor
10. Executive Evaluation

---

[3] Jackson Martindell, *The Scientific Appraisal of Management* (New York: Harper and Row, Publishers, Incorporated, 1962). This book is a revised statement of Martindell's original program that was first published under the same title and by the same publisher in 1950.

Jackson Martindell, "Management Audits Simplified," *The Corporate Director,* Special Issue, No. 15 (December, 1951), pp. 1-6.

[4] Jackson Martindell, "The Management Audit," *The Corporate Director,* Vol. IX (December, 1962), pp. 1-4. This is a paper presented to the Academy of Management at the annual meeting held at Pittsburgh in December, 1962.

There has been much criticism of the AIM audit. For many, it is oriented too much toward the investment concept of business management. Of the 10,000 total points, only 500 are allowed for corporate structure; 2,200 for executive evaluation; and 800 for directorate analysis—making a maximum of 3,500 points for these categories. Production efficiency and sales vigor comprise a maximum of 2,000 points; the remaining 4,500 are distributed among the categories of economic function, health of earnings, service to stockholders, research and development, and fiscal policies. Another criticism is that the audit rates past performance too heavily and does not attempt to evaluate future performance.[5] In support of these criticisms, instances are cited of companies with recent ratings of "excellent" that have experienced severe financial difficulties. For example, Douglas Aircraft Company received the rating of "excellently managed" for 1957, 1958, and 1959, and then suffered severe financial reverses during the latter part of 1959 and 1960. In 1957 Allis Chalmers Manufacturing Company and Olin Mathiesen Chemical Company received "excellently managed" ratings that were immediately followed by marked financial difficulties.[6]

Despite the shortcomings of the management audit, the audit program developed by the American Institute of Management establishes firmly the concept that the performance of management can and should be subject to evaluation as a part of an overall control program. The management audit focuses attention upon many aspects of managerial performance rather than upon one or two easily measured performance areas. Second, the audit emphasizes the measurement of the results of managerial performance rather than appraising the purpose of managerial performance. Third, individual companies that work seriously with the concept of auditing management's performance may develop as the result of experience within their own organization a means of assigning weight to the various performance categories that will prove a valid predictor of future performance.

Human Resource Accounting

An approach that offsets some of the major shortcomings of the AIM management audit, particularly its inability to predict future

---

[5] Robert B. Buchele, "How to Evaluate a Firm," *California Management Review*, Vol. V (Fall, 1962), pp. 5-16. Mr. Buchele presents a method for evaluating a firm that attempts to weight the future more than the past.

[6] The ratings are presented in *Manual of Excellent Managements* (New York: American Institute of Management, 1957). See *Business Week* (April 9, 1960), p. 79, and (April 15, 1961), pp. 147-149 for a discussion of the companies mentioned.

performance, is human resource accounting. Fundamental to the concept of human resource accounting is the positive relationship that exists between the performance of an organization and the quality and quantity of its human resource capability. The quality of human resources is highly significant for those companies whose product or service relies upon knowledge, research, and creativity. Traditionally the expenditure of funds for recruitment, training and development, and other items associated with the acquisition and upgrading of personnel are treated as expense items. Human resource accounting regards these expenditures as an investment in assets. Conventional accounting practices do not offer a true picture of an organization's effectiveness or potential. For the firm that is building human resources faster than they are being consumed, conventional accounting understates net income; conversely, the firm that is consuming its human resources faster than the replacement rate has an overstatement of its profits. Also, in the budgeting process expenditures for physical facilities are regarded as capital expenditures and are not necessarily justified in terms of revenue for the current year. Yet the manager who wishes to invest in human resources is forced to justify expenditures in this area in terms of additional revenue for the current year since costs associated with people are considered an expense. Human resource accounting seeks to treat expenditures in human resources as an investment in assets thereby enabling one to predict future performance as the rate of consumption of human resources relative to the rate of replacement of human resources becomes known.[7]

The R. G. Barry Corporation, a leisure footwear manufacturer headquartered in Columbus, Ohio, instituted a plan to develop human resource accounting in conjunction with William C. Pyle, Director of Human Resource Accounting Research of the University of Michigan. As noted by Robert J. Woodruff, Jr., vice president—human resources, of R. G. Barry Corporation the company has a technology comparable to the apparel industry with one of the lowest ratios of capital investment per employee of any industry and with labor representing a significant portion of total product costs. Further, the R. G. Barry Corporation has long had a strong philosophical commitment to the recognition of the importance of people to its operations. The seven

[7] William C. Pyle, "Human Resource Accounting," *Financial Analysts Journal*, Vol. 26, No. 5 (September-October, 1970), pp. 69-77.

Rensis Likert, *The Human Organization, Its Management and Value* (New York: McGraw-Hill Book Company, 1967). The reader's attention is directed to Chapter 9, "Human Asset Accounting."

functional accounts developed by the R. G. Barry Corporation for use in its human resource accounting are: [8]

1. *Recruiting outlay costs*—costs associated with locating and selecting new (management) personnel. This category includes search fees, advertising, interviewer or interviewee travel expenses, allocations of personnel, and acquiring department time for internal screening, interviewing, testing, and evaluation expenses. Outlay costs for unsuccessful candidates are allocated to the cost of obtaining the candidate hired.

2. *Acquisition costs*—costs incurred in bringing a new man "on board." This category includes placement fees, moving costs, physical examination, allocation of personnel, and acquiring department time in placing a man on the payroll and situating him with the necessary equipment to perform his job.

3. *Formal training and familiarization costs*—costs normally incurred immediately after hire or possible transfer from one location to another. These refer to formal orientation programmes, vestibule training, etc.

4. *Informal training costs*—costs associated with the process of teaching a new person to adapt his existing skills to the specific job requirements of his new job. The costs related to this process are normally salary allocations only and vary with each position depending upon the level of the job in the organization, number of subordinates, interaction patterns outside the department, etc.

5. *Familiarization costs*—costs associated with the very complex process of integrating a new manager into the organization to the point where he can be a fully effective member. Such costs include learning the company's philosophy, history, policies, objectives, communications patterns, past practices, precedents, understanding of the people with whom the new position-holder will regularly interact. These costs, which can be sizable, depending upon the level and scope of the position, include salary allocations.

6. *Investment building experience costs*—costs associated with investments in on-the-job training which occur after the initial familiarization period and which are expected to have value to the company beyond the current accounting period. Investment building experience is the development of a capability which would not reasonably be expected as a normal part of the person's job.

7. *Development costs*—costs associated with investments in increasing a manager's capabilities in areas beyond the specific technical skills

---

[8] R. L. Woodruff, Jr., "Human Resource Accounting," *Canadian Chartered Accountant,* Vol. 97, No. 3 (September, 1970), pp. 156-161. The functional accounts are stated on pp. 157-158.

required by the position. In this category are management seminars, university programmes or courses, etc. Costs are collected by means of a "Training & Development Requisition," and are modified by the participant's evaluation of the pertinency of the study.

The R. G. Barry Corporation has since developed a pro forma balance sheet, an income statement that shows the effect of human resource accounting concepts upon the conventional accounting statement.[9] In effect, human resource accounting provides internal control over the long-term management of human resources.

RATIO ANALYSIS

A *ratio* is a way of expressing the proportional relationship that exists between two measures. Ratios may be expressed as:

1. A proportion, by using a colon to separate the two measures—1:2.
2. A fraction—½.
3. A percentage—½ $\times$ 100 = 50%.

Whatever the method of expression—proportion, fraction, or percentage —a ratio shows the magnitude of the relationship between two measures. The analysis of ratios existing between various measures of organizational performance is a useful and necessary control technique.

Single measures of organizational performance seldom have much meaning. For example, the statement that a company earned $100,000, after taxes, during the past fiscal year expresses only the dollar volume of earnings. For a statement of earnings to have more meaning, it is necessary to compare and describe the earnings of a competitor. In a like manner, the fact that a salesman sold $5,000 worth of goods last month or that a production worker produced 50 units yesterday conveys little information. We have to know the performance standards for salesmen and production workers before drawing conclusions concerning the adequacy of their performance.

Ratio analysis is not new, and much has been written about it as a control technique.[10] It is beyond the scope of this chapter to survey all or even a majority of the ratios used in analyzing and controlling business operations since there are many of them and the usefulness of a given set of ratios varies considerably from one industry to

[9] *Annual Report 1968* (Columbus, Ohio: R. G. Barry Corporation.)
[10] Spencer A. Tucker, *Successful Managerial Control by Ratio-Analysis* (New York: McGraw-Hill Book Company, 1961). Mr. Tucker discusses the relatively simple first-degree ratios obtained by comparing two variables and also reviews the analysis of relationships between more than two variables.

another. However, a few of the most frequently used ratios are presented and discussed briefly. For convenience, the ratios discussed are classified as *financial ratios*—contributing primarily to a greater understanding of the financial condition of a company—and *operating ratios*—providing greater understanding of the operational aspects of a company. Some of the difficulties encountered in interpreting ratios are also presented.

Financial Ratios

Admittedly, financial ratios tell us something about the manner in which a company is operated as well as reveal financial condition. Yet, these ratios may be regarded as primarily financial in nature since much of the basic data is derived from the balance sheet and the information provided by these ratios is descriptive of a company's financial condition. The first and second ratios discussed below are statements of profitability; the last two ratios are statements of liquidity and are of particular significance to creditors.

Profit As a Percentage of Capital Invested. Many consider the relationship between profit (after taxes) and invested capital to be the most important single ratio. In the use of this ratio, profit is expressed as a percentage of invested capital, and when computed annually, a trend line is established. Profit as a percent of invested capital reveals how well the capital resources are being utilized. Comparisons may be made with other companies in the same industry, but the value of such comparisons is limited because the method used in evaluating invested capital varies from one company to another. Although there is no means of determining the optimum level of profitability, a realistic minimum level can be defined. The return on invested capital, after taxes, should be greater than the return guaranteed by other forms of investment— for example, tax-exempt municipal bonds. In addition to the basic rate of return offered by securities, there should be some compensation for risk and managerial effort.

Profit As a Percentage of Sales. Again, it is necessary to compute profitability from year to year so that a trend may be established. Also, comparisons with other companies in the same industry are valuable. Expressing profit as a percentage of sales volume is particularly helpful when analyzing the possible contribution of new product lines or when considering the deletion of current products. The profit-to-sales ratio is of value in measuring managerial effectiveness in the control of variable or controllable costs. For instance, within a retail chain, units of similar sales volume and fixed costs can be compared and differences in profitability may be attributed to the control of variable costs.

Current Ratio. The *current ratio* is of particular significance to credit men because it is an indication of a company's ability to pay its bills promptly. Current ratio is determined by dividing current assets by current liabilities as stated on the balance sheet. Unlike the measures of profit, which are usually expressed as a percentage, current ratio is expressed as a ratio; i.e., 2:1 or 2.5:1. Although there seems to be general agreement that a company should have a current ratio of assets to liabilities of at least 2:1 to insure ability to pay current obligations, the determination of what constitutes a satisfactory ratio is much more complex than it appears to be. Some of the problems encountered in interpreting the current ratio are discussed later under the heading, "Interpreting Ratios."

Quick Ratio. The *quick ratio,* sometimes called the *acid test ratio,* is found by dividing the company's quick assets, usually cash and negotiable securities, by current liabilities. Accounts receivables and inventory, generally a part of current assets and used in computing the current ratio, are excluded since there may be considerable time required to convert these items into cash. A minimum quick ratio of 1:1 indicates that there is sufficient cash to meet maturing obligations.

Operating Ratios

There are several ratios that contribute more to an understanding of the operations of a company than they do to an appreciation of the financial structure of a company; thus, they are referred to as operating ratios. Three of these ratios contribute to our knowledge of the sales function of a company. The fourth ratio is a generalized concept of input-output functions.

Net Sales to Average Inventory. Dividing net sales by average inventory value yields a measure of inventory turnover. For instance, net sales of $600,000 with an average inventory evaluation of $200,000 indicates that the inventory turnover rate is three times a year. If desired, the average number of days required for a complete inventory turnover can be computed as follows: $\dfrac{\text{Average Inventory} \times 365}{\text{Net Sales}}$.
In the example above, the average number of days is 121. The net sales to average inventory ratio is an indication of how well the working capital invested in inventory is being utilized; consequently, the

ratio should be interpreted in conjunction with profitability expressed as a percentage of sales. A profit of two percent on net sales, typical of many retail food operations, does not seem very great; but with an average inventory of $100,000 and an annual inventory turnover rate of 35, the absolute dollar volume of profit is considerable in relation to the amount of capital invested in inventory. The sales to inventory ratio provides the control information that is needed to insure maximum inventory turnover.

Net Sales to Total Market. Expressing net sales as a percentage of the total market—defined either geographically or by product line—indicates whether or not a company is maintaining its share of an ever-changing market potential. Dollar volume of sales does not provide such information since it is quite possible for a company's sales to show an annual increase, yet the rate of increase may be less than the market's rate of growth. Thus, a firm with an annual sales increase of four percent in a market expanding at a rate of six percent shows an increasing sales volume and a decreasing share of the potential market.

Selling Expense to Net Sales. Expressing selling expense as a percentage of net sales offers a means of determining the efficiency of the selling function. Selling expense may be broken down into greater detail by specifying the costs of maintaining a sales force, of advertising, or of administrative costs.

Input-Output Ratios. The number and the kind of input-output ratios used as control measures vary a great deal from one company to another. Such ratios are almost always expressed as percentages and are measures of efficiency in the utilization of inputs. Some of the more common measures of inputs and outputs are as follows:

Inputs	*Outputs*
Payroll dollars	Net sales
Man-hours worked	Units produced
Square feet of floor space	Units sold
Advertising costs	

Each input can be paired with any one of the outputs.

Interpreting Ratios

Although ratios are widely used, there are three difficulties encountered in their interpretation that limit their value as a means of providing precise control information. First, a ratio is a quotient obtained by the arithmetic process of dividing a numerator by a denominator. A change in the value of a quotient may result from a change in the value of either the numerator or the denominator. There is no way of determining which member of the fraction changed in value by noting the change in the quotient. An analysis of the current ratio illustrates this point. Assume that a company has current assets of $60,000 and current liabilities of $30,000, thereby producing a comfortable current ratio of 2:1. Do we know what has happened if we read that the company now has a current ratio of 3:1? Fixed assets may have been sold in the amount of $30,000 and added to current assets to yield the 3:1 ratio. Or the amount realized from the sale of assets may have been $10,000 and applied to the reduction of current liabilities, again creating a 3:1 ratio. When changes occur in a ratio, it is necessary to inspect the original data used in arriving at the numeric values of the numerator and the denominator in order to have a sound basis for determining the significance of the change that has occurred.

Second, it must be realized that there is no precise means of determining what constitutes a good or a satisfactory ratio. Ratios should be used over a period of time so that trends may be established. Only then can a determination be made as to which ratios offer significant information for the control process. Occasionally it is helpful to compare ratios with those of similar companies in the same industry. Even so, there must be some assurance that the accounting systems used by the several companies are comparable.

The third danger inherent in the use of ratios is that of inferring causal relationships that are not warranted. A sales manager may conclude that an increase in selling expense as a percentage of sales indicates a decrease in the number of units sold by the sales force, but the real reason could be due to a decrease in unit price. Most faulty inferences result from a failure to examine closely the direction and magnitude of change in both the numerator and denominator and failure to evaluate the validity and reliability of the data used in computing the ratio.

Despite the difficulties encountered in interpreting ratios, they remain a useful control device when there is a thorough understanding of the manner in which they are developed and when there are several related ratios presented so that the significance of any one ratio may be checked by comparing it with another.

BREAK-EVEN ANALYSIS

Break-even analysis utilizes the same concepts employed in the construction of variable budgets (Chapter 22, pages 684 to 687).

There are striking similarities between the break-even chart (Figure 21-1) and the graphic representation of a variable expense budget shown in Figure 22-1, page 686. However, there are two important differences: First, the vertical axis of the break-even chart is designated as a revenue-expense axis rather than being labeled an expense axis; and second, the sales revenue line of the break-even chart shows the expected revenue for each level of sales volume. The point where the revenue line intersects the total cost line is the break-even point.

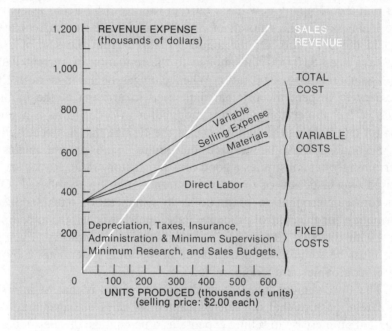

Figure 21-1

BREAK-EVEN CHART

Break-even analysis is discussed in considerable detail in Chapter 5, "Planning for Profit and Sales," as a means of analyzing the interrelationships of various factors that influence the profitability of a company. An understanding of the dynamic relationships existing between the factors included in the break-even chart enables one to forecast and plan for profit. We know that the break-even point and consequently the amount of profit vary with changes in any one of four factors: unit volume, fixed cost, variable cost, and unit selling price. Further, the precise effect upon the break-even point resulting from a change in one or any combination of these variables can be determined by means of the following formula:

$$\text{Break-Even Point} = \frac{\text{Fixed Expense}}{P/V \text{ ratio}}$$

$$\text{when } P/V = \frac{\text{Sales} - \text{Variable Costs}}{\text{Sales}}$$

The ability to predict changes in profits under various operating conditions has obvious applications to the process of planning. A knowledge of the relationship of the factors that influence profit is equally applicable to the control process, a re-emphasis of the continuous nature of the planning-control-planning cycle. Specifically, break-even analysis provides information that aids in the control of costs and underscores the importance of sales volume.

Cost Control

Break-even charts can be prepared so that they contribute to overall control by showing both fixed and variable costs for the entire company. They can also be prepared for smaller operating units such as manufacturing departments or sales districts. In either case, fixed costs are segregated from variable costs. Fixed costs move slowly and show little variation as the result of changes in sales volume. Variable costs, on the other hand, vary directly as a function of volume. By their very nature, variable costs are subject to some degree of control. By clearly separating these variable costs, attention is directed toward those areas where corrective action is possible. When presented in the graphic form of a break-even chart, deviations from budgeted expenses are readily recognized.[11]

Sales Volume

An analysis of the break-even formula above shows clearly the effect of sales beyond the break-even point upon profit. The P/V ratio, the denominator of the fraction on the right side of the equation, expresses the profitability of an operation after the break-even point has been reached. Too many small and medium-size firms tend to express profitability as a percentage of total sales rather than as a percentage of sales beyond the break-even point. The following operating statement indicates a net profit of 10 percent of total sales:

[11] Fred V. Gardner, "Breakeven Point Control for Higher Profits," *Harvard Business Review*, Vol. XXXII (September-October, 1954), pp. 123-130. Mr. Gardner discusses the need for flexible control and develops the specific control data needed so that the break-even point can be used as an effective means of control.

Revenue from sales $1,000,000
    Variable costs $500,000
    Fixed costs 400,000
    Total costs 900,000
Net profit .... $ 100,000

However, the P/V ratio $\dfrac{\$1,000,000 - \$500,000}{\$1,000,000}$ indicates that the profitability of each unit sold beyond the break-even point is 50 percent. By emphasizing the contribution to profit of additional sales beyond the break-even point, there is greater incentive to stimulate and control sales effort.

TIME-EVENT-NETWORK ANALYSIS

To meet the requirements of what has been called "an age of massive engineering"—in contrast to repetitive production—a number of fairly sophisticated techniques for the analysis of networks have been developed.[12] Two time-event-network analysis techniques were developed separately and published in 1959. The Program Evaluation Review Technique—commonly called PERT—was developed by the Special Projects Office of the U. S. Navy Bureau of Ordnance, with the assistance of staff members of the management consulting firm of Booz, Allen, and Hamilton. It was first used in the development of the Polaris Fleet Ballistic Missile.[13] The Critical Path Method—CPM—of network analysis was developed by DuPont to reduce downtime for periodic maintenance.[14] PERT is credited with saving two years in the development of the Polaris missile, while the CPM method cut DuPont's downtime for maintenance in the Louisville plant from 125 to 93 hours.[15] Before discussing the relative merits and applications of PERT and CPM, let us review some of the fundamentals of network analysis.[16]

---

[12] See "Thinking Ahead: The Age of Massive Engineering," *Harvard Business Review,* Vol. XXXIV (January-February, 1961), p. 138.

[13] Donald G. Malcolm, John H. Rodrboom, Charles E. Clark, and Willard Fazar, "Applications of a Technique for Research and Development Program Evaluation," *Operations Research,* Vol. VII (September-October, 1959), pp. 646-699.

[14] James E. Kelley, Jr., and Morgan R. Walker, "Critical Path Planning and Scheduling," *Proceedings of the Eastern Joint Computer Conference* (December, 1959).

[15] F. K. Levy, G. L. Thompson, and J. D. Wiest, "The ABCs of the Critical Path Method," *Harvard Business Review,* Vol. XXXXI (September-October, 1963), p. 100. On pp. 102-103 there is a discussion of how to determine the critical path through the use of a relatively simple algorithm.

[16] The term, review, is used advisedly since network analysis required by PERT and CPM is similar to the analysis of information systems required in the design of an integrated data processing system. See p. 219, Chapter 7, "Management Information Systems."

Fundamentals of Network Analysis

In order to use network analysis for purposes of planning and control, several conditions must be met:

1. *A clearly recognizable end point or objective.* One-of-a kind projects, such as developing and building the first prototype of the Polaris missile or the construction of a shopping center, meet this requirement. The installation of a data processing system, the construction of a highway interchange, or the building of a piece of special machinery all have clearly definable and recognizable end points. In contrast, the 100,000th car from an assembly line is difficult to distinguish from its immediate predecessor or successor.

2. *A series of events.* There should be a series of clearly defined, separate, but interrelated, events leading up to the completion of the final project. In constructing a highway interchange, temporary routes must be built, bridges constructed, drainage facilities installed, service roads prepared, and many other distinct subprojects completed before the interchange is ready for use.

3. *Time for each activity.* The time required for the completion of the work or activity preceding each event must be calculated. Herein lies one of the major differences between PERT and CPM. PERT employs a method of estimating probable time, even though there has been no prior experience to serve as a basis for estimating time. CPM implies some prior experience or knowledge of the time estimated for the completion of activities leading to each event.

4. *A starting point.* There must be a recognizable starting point—the issuance of a sales order for a piece of special machinery, notification from the government to begin the development of a weapons system, or the date of a scheduled plant shutdown as the beginning of an annual maintenance program.

Figure 21-2 is a schematic diagram of a network analysis. Each event is designated by a square, although circles may be used. In each square there is a number and a letter. The number is a statement of the amount of work, expressed in days, that must be completed so that the event in question can occur. Events, as such, require no time; they merely serve as milestones. The letter in each square designates the event and is explained in the legend included on the chart. The arrows indicate the sequence of events. Unlike vector analysis, the length of the arrow has no particular significance. The shaded area is the *critical path,* the longest route in time from start to finish. If the duration of the project is to be shortened, it must be shortened by reducing the time intervals necessary for the completion of each event along this pathway. To

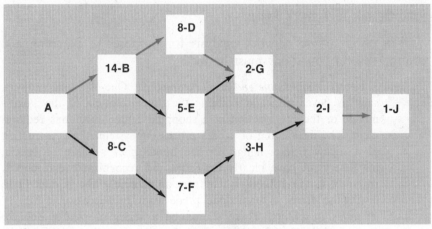

Figure 21-2
SCHEMATIC NETWORK ANALYSIS

reduce the work time along another path would not reduce the total time required for the project; instead, it would merely create more "slack"—excess time in the other pathways.

Let us assume that the project represented by the network in Figure 21-2 is a piece of special-purpose machinery including both electrical and mechanical components. In charting a network, the analysis of the project commences with the end result, the finished machine, and then works backwards, step by step, until the origin of the project is reached, the issuance of a sales order. The machine is ready for shipment when it has passed final inspection (J), a process that takes one day after the completion of final assembly (I). Thus, the number 1 and the letter J are entered in the square designating the completion of the project. Final assembly takes two days to complete but cannot be started until the subassembly of all electrical components (H) and all mechanical components (G) is finished. To perform the mechanical subassembly, components must be released by the milling department (D) and the lathe department (E). The largest single requirement for time in this network is the 14 days needed to procure mechanical components (B). The project starts with the issuance of the sales order (A). The same procedure is followed in analyzing the sequence of operations in the production of the electrical components of the manufacturing process.[17]

---

[17] E. ,T. Alsaker, "The Basic Technique: Network Analysis," in Gabriel N. Stilian *et al., PERT: A New Management Planning and Control Technique* (New York: American Management Association, No. 74, AMA Management Reports, 1962), pp. 37-60. *PERT* presents in concise form a series of papers on PERT theory, the applications of PERT, and a discussion of related techniques such as the CPM and the Line of Balance system of control.

Two major advantages result from the use of time-event-network analysis techniques. In the first place, breaking a project down into its component events, specifying the time required for the completion of each event, and designating the sequence of events force a degree of planning that improves any production process. Presenting this information pictorially as a network offers the second advantage—a clear understanding of the interdependence and relationships that exist between the various events. We know that the critical path, by definition, is the longest route in time. In the example discussed, and shown in Figure 21-2, the critical path is 27 days. If the duration of the project is to be shortened, attention and control effort must be directed toward the critical path.

With this introduction to network analysis, let us examine PERT in more detail.

PERT

PERT in its original form stresses the time required to perform the activities necessary for a given event to occur. The unique contribution of PERT as a form of network analysis is that it provides a means of obtaining a probability estimate of the expected time to complete activities that have not been performed previously and, therefore, have not been measured. The building of the Polaris missile, the first application of PERT, is a case in point. None of the activities leading up to the specified events had been performed before; consequently, there were no historical records or time study standards to serve as a basis for estimating expected times.

To determine the probable expected time for activities leading up to an event, PERT requires three time estimates. First is the most optimistic time—the time that is required if everything goes right. The probability of a most optimistic set of circumstances occurring is about 1 out of 100. Second, the most likely time is estimated—the time required in the normal course of events. The third time estimate is the most pessimistic—the time required if everything that could go wrong does go wrong. Again, the probability for the most pessimistic set of circumstances occurring is 1 out of 100; however, catastrophies such as floods, fires, and strikes are excluded. Designating the most optimistic time as a, the most likely time as m, and the most pessimistic time as b, the expected time, T_e, is found by substituting estimated times in the following formula:

$$T_e = \frac{a + 4m + b}{6}$$

There is also a formula to determine the standard deviation of the expected time, thus making it possible to state a statistical probability that the expected time will fall within a stated range.[18]

CPM

The difference between PERT and CPM (Critical Path Method) is one of degree rather than kind. PERT emphasizes time and provides a way of computing the most probable time; however, CPM emphasizes cost as well as time.[19] CPM differs from PERT in three respects. First, only one time estimate is given for each set of activities leading up to a given event, instead of the three time estimates required by PERT. Second, with CPM, a cost estimate is included along with each estimated time for both *"normal"* and *"crash"* operating conditions. Normal operating conditions are usually defined as the least-cost method for the performance of an activity; and "crash" conditions represent the time and cost incurred in the performance of activities in less than the normal time. For example, under normal operating conditions two men assigned to the day shift take three days to complete a job. The time can be shortened under "crash" conditions by assigning two men to each of three consecutive shifts—a reduction in elapsed time but with a resultant increase in cost because the men on the second and the third shifts will receive premium pay. Third, CPM assumes some previous experience with the work necessary for the completion of each event; otherwise, it would be impracticable to state a single time and cost estimate.

These differences explain to a large degree why PERT is used primarily for one-of-a-kind projects involving an extensive amount of research and development prior to the building of a prototype and for similar projects where time is of greater importance than cost. CPM, on the other hand, is widely used in complex construction and maintenance

---

[18] There has been much discussion concerning the mathematics of the PERT time estimate. The following report discusses the Beta distribution, a fundamental assumption of the estimated time computation.

PERT Summary Report, Phase I, (Washington, D. C.: Special Projects Office, Department of the Navy, July, 1958).

A brief description of the mathematics of PERT, along with a discussion of its application, is presented in the following article:

Robert W. Miller, "How to Plan and Control with PERT," *Harvard Business Review,* Vol. XXXX (March-April, 1962), pp. 93-104.

[19] Levy, Thompson, and Wiest, *op. cit.,* pp. 98-108.

For another discussion of the critical path method, see Walter Cosinuke, "The Critical Path Method," in Stilian *et al., op. cit.,* pp. 147-163.

projects where cost is a significant factor and prior experience offers a basis for making a reliable estimate of both time and cost.[20]

Evaluation of PERT and CPM

There are three major benefits to be derived from the use of either PERT or CPM in the planning and control of certain production functions. First, the application of network analysis techniques forces a high degree of planning and results in plans that are objective, structured, and flexible. In so doing, either PERT or CPM approaches the optimum conditions summarized in Chapter 4, page 114. The second advantage of network analysis is that the establishment of a network system makes it possible to determine the critical path. The significance of the critical path to the control process is that knowledge of the key elements in a complex production system makes possible the design and administration of a set of forward-looking controls so that corrective action may be taken before serious deviation from schedule occurs. Third, network analysis shows clearly the interrelationships between the various organizational components of a complex production system, thereby making it possible to improve both communications and organizational structure.

Nonetheless, there are two limiting conditions that must be fulfilled before the advantages described above can be realized. First, network analysis is most effective when applied to one-of-a-kind projects that include several subprojects. Further, both the main project and the various subprojects must be fairly well defined and recognizable. They cannot be too nebulous. Examples of activities amenable to network analysis are construction projects, research and development programs, the installation of an integrated data processing system, the design and construction of a weapon systems, and the design and manufacture of special machinery or equipment. The second factor that limits the effectiveness of network analysis is organizational structure. Experience

---

[20] The above discussion refers to PERT in its original form. Since its original introduction, there have been many variations of PERT. For this reason the original PERT is often referred to as basic PERT or PERT/Time to differentiate it from later variations such as PERT/Cost. The following article discusses the application of PERT/Cost.

Hilliard W. Paige, "How PERT-Cost Helps the General Manager," *Harvard Business Review*, Vol. XXXXI (November-December, 1963), pp. 87-95.

For a discussion of the application of PERT to the control of production activities see the following: Peter P. Schoderbek and Lester A. Digman, "Third Generation, PERT/LOB," *Harvard Business Review*, Vol. XLV, No. 5 (September-October, 1967), pp. 100-110.

has shown that a task force or project form of organization is necessary to obtain maximum benefits from either PERT or CPM (See Chapter 11, page 335). Task force organization requires organizational flexibility and highly trained personnel. In summary, both the project and the organization must be appropriate if full benefit is to be realized from the application of either PERT or CPM as a means for planning and control.[21]

    Case Problem 21-B offers an opportunity to determine how the critical path in building a house can be shortened. Though a contractor might include more separate events than shown in the case problem, there are sufficient events presented to enable you to see for yourself how CPM points up the interrelationships of the various phases of a complex process.

CASE PROBLEM 21-B

SHORTENING THE CRITICAL PATH

Ralph Billings, an independent building contractor, has completed building the fifth house of a projected development of 25 homes in the $30,000 price range. Recently he read of an application of the Critical Path Method to the building of a shopping center and became interested in applying the method to his own business. Currently he employs four carpenters and two laborers. Much of his work, such as excavating, plumbing, grading, cement work, bricklaying, and electrical work, is performed by subcontractors who base their charges on a combination of materials and man-hours required for each job. Ralph hopes that the application of CPM to his operation will result in a reduction of the total number of days required to build a house and in better utilization of the labor he now has.

    As a first step in applying the critical path method to his own building efforts, Ralph determined the average time required for each phase of the building of the first five houses. These values, along with the sequence of each building operation, are shown in Exhibit I.

---

[21] There have been relatively few reports in the literature concerning the limitations of network techniques and difficulties encountered in their application. The following two studies indicate some of the limitations.

    Lawrence S. Hill, "Perspective: Some Possible Pitfalls in the Design and Use of PERT Networking," *Academy of Management Journal,* Vol. VIII, No. 2 (June, 1965), pp. 139-145.

    Peter P. Schoderbek, "A Study of the Applications of PERT," *Academy of Management Journal,* Vol. VIII, No. 3 (September, 1965), pp. 199-209.

Exhibit I
SEQUENCE AND TIME REQUIREMENTS OF JOBS

Job No.	Description	Immediate Predecessors	Normal Time (Days)
a	Start		0
b	Excavate and Pour Footers	a	4
c	Pour Concrete Foundation	b	2
d	Erect Wooden Frame Including Rough Roof	c	4
e	Lay Brickwork	d	6
f	Install Basement Drains and Plumbing	c	1
g	Pour Basement Floor	f	2
h	Install Rough Plumbing	f	3
i	Install Rough Wiring	d	2
j	Install Heating and Ventilating	d, g	4
k	Fasten Plaster Board and Plaster (including drying)	i, j, h	10
l	Lay Finish Flooring	k	3
m	Install Kitchen Fixtures	l	1
n	Install Finish Plumbing	l	2
o	Finish Carpentry	l	3
p	Finish Roofing and Flashing	e	2
q	Fasten Gutters and Downspouts	p	1
r	Lay Storm Drains for Rain Water	c	1
s	Sand and Varnish Flooring	o, t	2
t	Paint	m, n	3
u	Finish Electrical Work	t	1
v	Finish Grading	q, r	2
w	Pour Walks and Complete Landscaping	v	5
x	Finish	s, u, w	0

Source: F. K. Levy, G. L. Thompson, and J. D. Wiest, "The ABC's of the Critical Path Method," *Harvard Business Review*, Vol. XXXXI (September-October, 1963), p. 100.

PROBLEMS

1. Using the information presented in Exhibit I, construct a schematic network analysis similar to Figure 21-2 and determine the critical path.

2. What recommendations would you make to shorten the critical path?

Chapter Questions for Study and Discussion

1. What factors in the situation and what factors in the manager would tend to either increase or decrease the value of personal observations as a means of securing control information?
2. What points should be considered when designing or using control reports? Develop examples to illustrate both effective and ineffective control reports.
3. Comment on the following statement: Control reports are primarily a part of an information system rather than a control system.
4. Differentiate between internal and external auditing and show by example the strengths and weaknesses of each type of audit.
5. State in your own words the basic assumptions underlying the concept of human resource accounting. Is there a relationship between the technology used by a firm and the potential value that might result from the use of human resource accounting? If so, state the relationship.
6. Give an example of each of the more common forms of operating ratios and financial ratios.
7. How can the difficulties encountered in interpreting ratios be minimized?
8. How do the techniques of break-even analysis contribute to the effectiveness of the control process?
9. In your opinion, does break-even analysis and P/V analysis have greater impact in the area of manufacturing through cost control than in the area of sales planning? Why?
10. Under what conditions would you recommend the use of PERT as opposed to CPM?

CHAPTER 22

Budgetary Control

Ray Barr retired from the Air Force and within a month found himself in the retail business as the result of the unexpected death of his father-in-law, who owned and managed the Avenue, a men's clothing and furnishings store. Barr was appointed acting manager by the executor of the estate and served in that capacity during the peak sales period that normally occurs during the last three months of the calendar year. When the estate was settled in mid-December, Ray and his wife decided to continue managing the store rather than selling it. The records kept by Ray's father-in-law were rather sketchy and incomplete, but they did indicate that net sales had been $200,000 a year for the past three years and that net profit before taxes had varied between 4 and 5½ percent of net sales for the same period.

Ray had worked with budgets as an officer in the management control section of the Air Force and decided that development of a revenue and expense budget would serve as a useful guide during the coming year. After studying the information made available to him by the Small Business Administration and the publications of the National Association of Retail Clothiers and Furnishers, he decided to use the percentages for revenue and expense items as shown in Exhibit I. He considered dividing the total for each of these accounts by 12 to develop a budget for each month, but later decided that the variation in sales volume and advertising costs from month to month was great enough to require that these items be computed on the basis of the variations shown

Exhibit I

BUDGETED OPERATING REVENUE AND EXPENSES
FOR ANNUAL NET SALES OF $200,000

Account	Percentage of Net Sales
Sales:	
1. Gross sales	102.6
2. Customer returns and allowances	2.6
3. Net sales	100.0
Cost of goods sold:	
4. Beginning inventory	30.9
5. Net purchases plus transportation charges paid	66.1
6. Total cost of merchandise handled	97.0
7. Ending inventory	32.3
8. Net cost of merchandise sold	64.7
9. Net busheling (alterations) cost	2.1
10. Total cost of merchandise sold	66.8
11. Gross margin	33.2
Operating expenses:	
12. Payroll:	
A. Salary of owner	7.3
B. Salaries and wages of employees	9.0
Total payroll	16.3
13. Rent expense	2.9
14. Taxes and license fees (omit real estate, Federal income and sales taxes)	1.1
15. Insurance	.6
16. Depreciation and amortization	.8
17. Repairs	.2
18. Supplies (omit repair materials)	1.0
19. Services purchased	.9
20. Traveling (business trips)	.3
21. Communication (include parcel post)	.4
22. Advertising and publicity	2.8
23. Professional services (outside professional agencies)	.2
24. Unclassified (all expenses not under headings):	
A. Losses from bad debts	.3
B. Other unclassified expenses	.5
Total unclassified expenses	.8
25. Total expenses	28.3
26. Net profit (or loss) before Federal income taxes	4.9

in Exhibit II. Both Exhibit I and Exhibit II are based upon an annual net sales volume of $200,000.

PROBLEMS

1. Develop an annual monthly revenue and expense budget for the store owned and operated by Ray Barr.
2. What additional information would you need to prepare a cash budget? a balance sheet budget?
3. What kind of standards has Ray used in determining budgeted performance?
4. Would flexible budgets be of any value in allocating monthly sales volume and advertising expenses?
5. Of what value will this budget be in succeeding years?

Exhibit II
BUDGETED NET SALES AND ADVERTISING
COSTS FOR EACH MONTH

Month	Percentage of Annual Net Sales	Percentage of Annual Advertising Costs
January	8%	9%
February	5	7
March	6	6
April	6	7
May	8	7
June	9	8
July	7	7
August	7	8
September	7	9
October	9	8
November	10	10
December	18	14

The budget is without doubt the most widely used control device in both business and government; indeed, it is used so extensively that for many persons the word budget is synonymous with control. Yet, the preparation of budgets originates as part of the planning process, and the budget itself is the end point of the planning process—the statement of a plan. Some companies, in order to avoid the negative reactions often associated with the concept of control, refer to their budgetary controls as either *profit plans* or *profit paths*.

In our discussion of budgetary controls we shall examine, first, the nature of budgets and review the types of budgets used most frequently. The success or failure of either budgetary or nonbudgetary controls (discussed in the previous chapter) depends on their acceptance by the people in an organization; consequently, consideration is given to behavioral reactions to control.

THE NATURE OF BUDGETS

A *budget* may be defined as a plan expressed in quantitative terms. However, this overly simplified definition of a budget does not tell us much about the nature of budgets or of budgetary control. The process of preparing a budget is planning in every sense of the word, and the budget itself is the resultant plan. As such, the budget, like any other plan, should possess the characteristics of objectivity, structuralization, and flexibility. The extent to which a budget reflects these characteristics is a measure of its probable success.[1]

Even so, there are certain aspects of budgets that differentiate them from other plans. First, the reason for preparing a budget is to provide a means for controlling operations. Second, as a means of controlling operations effectively, a separate budget is usually prepared for each organizational unit, and individual budgets may be prepared for each of the several functions within an organizational unit. Third, a budget is designed to cover a specific period of time. The fiscal year is the unit of time used most frequently, but this unit may be subdivided into semiannual, quarterly, or monthly periods. Also, budgets may be prepared for periods of time greater than one year; for example, capital expenditure budgets. Finally, budgets are expressed in financial terms since dollars serve well as a common denominator and thereby permit the comparison and coordination of all phases of a company's operations.

Though planning is an essential ingredient in the process of preparing budgets, the preparation of budgets is more closely related to the control process than it is to the planning process. The budget itself is the stated standard of performance. Thus, preparing budgets is, in effect, setting standards—the first step of the control process. The measurement of current performance against standards, the second step in the process of control, is facilitated because the budget expresses standards of performance in quantitative terms—dollars. Deviations from budgeted or expected results are readily identified and show the need for corrective action, the last step in the process of control.

---

[1] See Chapter 4, pp. 109-114.

Undoubtedly, the preparation of budgets refines the planning process necessary for the establishment of standards, or goals; however, the greater value of budgeting lies in its contribution to improved coordination and control. When budgets are prepared for all organizational units and the various functions performed by these units, a basis is provided for the coordination of the efforts of the organization. At the same time, budgets establish a basis for the corrective action of control since deviations from expected results are more readily identified and measured. Thus, the preparation of budgets may be expected to result in better planning and improved coordination, and to provide a basis for control— the primary purpose for establishing budgets.

Types of Budgets

Virtually every aspect of the operations of an organization can be budgeted. A business firm may prepare budgets for sales, inventory, shipments, production, maintenance, direct labor, and indirect labor. Budgets may also be used to forecast the operations of the industrial relations department, the cost of industrial engineering, and the needs for research and development. The list of organizational units and functions susceptible to budgetary control is almost endless. Fortunately, there is a logical framework that provides an easily remembered classification of budgets. This classification follows roughly a time sequence in the operation of a business and results in the following four types of budgets:

1. Revenue and expense budget
2. Cash budget
3. Capital expenditure budget
4. Balance sheet budget

As we shall see, each of these major types of budgets may be further subdivided so that the individual needs of each company may be fully met.

Revenue and Expense Budget. If one were starting a new business or beginning to prepare the initial set of budgets for a going concern, his first need would be a summary statement of the company's operations. The *revenue and expense budget,* sometimes called an *operating budget,* provides a bird's eye view of operations. Since revenue from the sale of products or services is the main source of income, the revenue budget is often referred to as the *sales budget.* All other budgets must be coordinated with the sales forecast since revenue from sales defines the upper limits of expenses and profits.

SALES BUDGET. In preparing a sales forecast, careful consideration must be given to external environmental factors as well as to conditions within the company itself. General economic conditions, the availability of credit, and the action of competitors are illustrative of the external factors that influence a company's level of sales. Accurate sales forecasts are difficult to achieve, at best, but the experience gained from the preparation of successive annual sales budgets gradually narrows the gap between budgeted and actual sales.

The content and the format of the sales budget vary with each company; however, certain generalizations are possible. For companies with multiple products or services, the expected revenue from each product or service should be stated separately. For large companies, a breakdown of expected sales by territory is essential. Sometimes the forecast should reflect expected sales for each class of customer. Since sales are seldom the same for each month of the year, the expected revenue for each calendar month should be stated to show clearly the seasonal variations. A forecast of revenue by month is necessary for the preparation of cash budgets.

EXPENSE BUDGET. The second part of the revenue and expense budget is a statement of expected expenses. Two considerations guide the preparation of expense budgets. First is a determination of the classification of items to be included in expense budgets; and second, the allocation of expense items according to organizational unit. Expense budgets may be prepared for every item listed in the expense division of the company's chart of accounts. In manufacturing firms, a manufacturing budget is prepared to show the expenses anticipated in the manufacture of the company's product. Included are the cost of material, the cost of inventory, direct and indirect labor charges, factory overhead including the cost of supervision, and the cost of maintaining equipment and other manufacturing facilities. General administrative costs and the cost of sales are shown separately.

If the budget is to be an effective tool in the control of expenses, a budget must be prepared for each organizational unit and placed in the hands of the managers of those units. Manufacturing budgets are prepared for operating departments and become a statement of expense responsibilities for the manager of each department. Managers of territorial or product divisions of the sales department are charged with the responsibility of keeping the cost of sales within budgeted limits. Difficulties encountered in controlling expenses are often a result of ill-defined organizational structure rather than an unwillingness on the part of departmental managers to cooperate in reducing expenses.

Cash Budget. The *cash budget,* derived from the basic data included in the revenue and expense budget, shows the cash requirements needed for the operation of the business during the budget period. The need for a specific budget detailing cash requirements arises from the fact that rarely does the flow of cash into the firm from sales coincide with the amount and frequency of disbursements necessary to pay expenses. For example, if too little cash is on hand to purchase materials in order to increase inventory levels to meet seasonal sales requirements, it may be necessary to borrow and thereby incur the added cost of interest. Also, having sufficient cash on hand makes it possible to take advantage of cash discounts offered by suppliers. On the other hand, excess cash may be used for short-term investments, or it may make possible an earlier than expected fulfillment of capital expenditure plans. When the amount of cash falls below budgeted expectations, it may be an early warning that accounts receivable are running too high. Budgeting cash requirements may not alter significantly the amount of profit earned by a firm, but it does assure a liquid position and is considered one of the hallmarks of prudent management.

Capital Expenditure Budget. If the planning and the control of the revenue and expense budget are successfully managed, revenue should exceed expenses. A part of this balance is reinvested in the company to insure the continued existence and growth of the firm. Since these expenditures produce revenue, they are classed as capital expenditures and are included in the *capital expenditure budget.* Typically, one finds in the capital expenditure budget allotments for the replacement of present facilities, including plant and equipment, and funds for the expansion of facilities for increased production of the present product line or the development and manufacture of a new product.

However, there are expenses other than those for physical facilities and equipment that require the appropriation of fairly large sums of money and the passage of a relatively long period of time before the anticipated results become apparent. Executive development programs, including the recruitment of college graduates, require support on a continuing basis; and it may take many years before the results of such personnel programs can be assessed. The decision to spend a greater than usual amount in advertising in order to develop new markets is another long-range investment of company funds. Research and development plans for new and improved products require continued appropriations for their completion. Institutional advertising intended to establish a desired public image also requires special budgetary appropriations. Consequently, some companies develop a single *appropriation budget* to reflect intended expenditures for capital equipment, personnel development, the development of new markets, research and development programs, and institutional advertising.

Budgeting capital or appropriation expenditures poses some rather difficult problems not directly related to the control of expenses. Since emergency needs in the five areas mentioned above arise infrequently, the control of expenses is relatively easy to achieve—one simply does not spend more than the budgetary allowance. Instead, the difficulty in preparing budgets for special appropriations arises from the long-term nature of these investments and the limited amount of money available for such expenditures. Because these projects are long term, their true worth cannot be computed until completed or until their useful life, in the case of capital equipment, is exhausted. Even then one is not sure that the course selected is of more value than some of the rejected alternate courses of action. But alternate courses must be weighed and choices made since the funds available to a company are never unlimited. Difficult as the appraisal of the results of capital expenditure budgeting may be, there are, nonetheless, several important benefits to be gained from this class of budget. First, capital or appropriation expenditures should be controlled and can be controlled relatively easily once they are budgeted. Second, budgeting the major appropriations forces an improvement of the planning process in each of the functional areas so that a careful weighing of alternate forms of investment may be accomplished. Third, capital expenditures require cash and as a result must be budgeted if the cash budget is to be of maximum value as a control device. Fourth, special appropriations must be included so that the greatest degree of coordination of the company's resources, especially financial, is achieved.

Balance Sheet Budget. The *balance sheet budget* is a forecast of expected financial status as of the last day of the budget period, usually the close of the fiscal year. The balance sheet forecast, a statement of the relationships between assets and liabilities, does not require the preparation of any additional budgets; rather, it is a consolidation of all preceding budgets. Preparing a balance sheet forecast shows what might be expected if performance meets the standards defined in the other budgets. By preparing a forecast of anticipated financial position, management may discover that the other budgets when consolidated do not result in an entirely favorable financial condition as revealed by certain key ratios. For example, the ratio between current assets and current liabilities or expected earnings and current market price per share may be such that the value of the company's stock would be adversely affected. When this happens, the other budgets have to be recast. The balance sheet showing the actual financial position at the close of the budget period serves as a useful check on the accuracy of preparation and the degree to which all other budgets have been met. Also, deviations between the actual and the forecasted balance sheets may show the need for preparation of special budgets to improve control over performance in certain areas; for instance, accounts receivable, accounts payable, or finished goods inventory.

Securing Flexibility with Budgets

Several disadvantages may arise as the result of an overzealous application of budgetary controls. In the administration of budgetary controls, it is all too easy to emphasize conformance to the budgetary goals of the organization. For example, a regional sales manager who is experiencing difficulty in meeting sales objectives may have every reason to believe that a market research study would be of help in solving his problem; yet, he may find it impossible to conduct such a study because there is no provision for it in his budget. Another criticism arising from the use of budgets is that the statement of objectives in numeric terms lends a degree of precision and exactness that is seldom warranted. After all, goals stated numerically are no more reliable than the original estimates from which they are drawn. However, the greatest potential danger of budgetary control is that it may lead to inflexibility. Budgets are statements of plans and, like any other plan, if they are to be successful, they must be flexible as well as possess the characteristics of objectivity and structuralization. Flexibility in budgetary control may be achieved by either one of two methods: *periodic budgetary reviews* and *flexible budgets*.

Periodic Budgetary Review. Normally, budgets are prepared in advance for a 12-month period. However, changes in operating conditions may occur that make the attainment of stated bugetary goals a virtual impossibility. Some of the factors frequently subject to change during the course of the budget period are labor costs, selling price, and the predicted volume of business. Periodic budgetary reviews are intended to incorporate and reflect changes in any of the first two factors, while flexible budgets are designed specifically to reflect changes in the anticipated volume of business.

Periodic budgetary reviews may be prepared on a monthly basis, prior to the beginning of the new month. Then, during the third month of the budgetary period, a revised quarterly estimate is prepared. For example, a company whose fiscal year is the same as the calendar year would prepare revised estimates of the budget for the months of January, February, and March prior to the beginning of each of these months. During the month of March, a revised quarterly budget for the second quarter might be prepared in addition to the revised estimate for April. Also, revised quarterly budgets may be prepared for the third and fourth quarters prior to their beginning, along with the usual monthly revisions.

However, there is a danger inherent in the use of periodic budgetary reviews as a means of recognizing changing conditions. If changes are made too frequently and if the magnitude of these changes is too great, it is quite possible for the original budget to become meaningless. Also, the other extreme is possible; that is, periodic reviews of the budget, backed by ample evidence, may show the need for a restatement of budgeted goals but may not be permitted because the original budget is considered inviolate. One way of minimizing the variation between the annual budget and the revised budget resulting from periodic reviews is to anticipate in the preparation of the annual budgets the changes that might reasonably be expected in labor rates, raw materials, and selling prices. Past experience is a good guide in these areas. Changes suggested as the result of periodic reviews must not only be substantiated, but reasons must also be given showing why it was impossible to anticipate these changes in the preparation of the original budget. In this manner the accuracy of the original budget is improved over a period of years.

Flexible Budgets. Periodic budget reviews allow management to compensate for changes in labor costs, selling price, the cost of raw materials, a change in technology, or the method of operation. In many respects the amount of change resulting from these factors is unpredictable, with the result that the extent of their effect on the budget can be determined only after the change has begun. However, the effect of changes in the volume of business of a company upon the revenue and expense budgets can in many instances be predicted in advance. When budgets are prepared for the coming fiscal year, they are prepared on the basis of an assumed or predicted level of revenue or volume— a statement of expected expenses for an expected amount of revenue. Flexible or variable budgets show the effect of changes in the volume of business upon certain expense items in the revenue and expense budget.

From our study of break-even analysis (Chapter 5), we know that some costs regarded as fixed or standby do not vary proportionately with the volume of business and that other costs vary proportionately with changes in volume. Good examples of fixed and variable costs are the costs incurred in operating an automobile. The costs of depreciation, insurance, and garaging the automobile are not a function of the number of miles driven (volume). Rather, these costs are incurred at the time the car is purchased and do not change appreciably as a result of the number of miles driven. For this reason these costs are termed fixed, or standby, costs. On the other hand, the costs of tires, oil, gasoline, and repairs vary directly with the number of miles driven; hence, these costs are called variable costs. Similarly, a company's costs for depreciation, insurance, and administration remain relatively unchanged within wide ranges of volume and are termed fixed costs. Labor costs, the cost of materials, and variable selling expenses such as commissions are representative of those costs that vary directly with changes in volume and are called variable costs.

Figure 22-1 shows in graphic form the relationship between the fixed and the variable expenses of a flexible budget. Determination of the nature of the relationship between variable costs and volume level may be accomplished by: (1) a historical analysis of costs incurred at varying levels of volume and (2) the development of standard costs.

HISTORICAL ANALYSIS OF COSTS. The historical approach is an effective tool for determining the relationship between variable costs and volume when the company's product line is limited to a few products and when each product contributes a relatively constant percentage to total sales volume. In its simplest form, historical analysis may consist of determining actual costs incurred in producing the company's historical maximum volume and the costs incurred for the lowest point of the sales record. These two points, the high and the low, may be plotted on a graph and a straight line drawn to connect them; thus, by interpolation, a prediction may be made concerning expected costs for each level of volume between the historical high and low points. More sophisticated techniques include plotting sales and cost data for each year and determining by the method of least squares the line of best fit. For those companies with diverse product lines, it becomes necessary to analyze the variable costs for each product.

STANDARD COSTS. Standard costs for each product may be developed and may show the predicted cost for labor, materials, and supplies that might be expected for each unit produced. The predicted standard costs become the budgeted amount of variable costs, and the total cost for varying levels of volume can be readily computed.

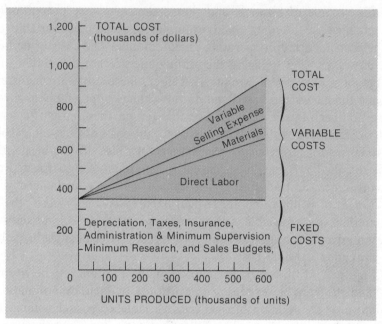

Figure 22-1
GRAPHIC REPRESENTATION OF A VARIABLE EXPENSE BUDGET

Evaluation of Flexible Budgets. Variable budgets, particularly those utilizing standard costs, are often criticized as being too costly from the standpoint of both time and money in their preparation. Another criticism of variable budgets is that in practice they are extremely difficult to apply in a manner that results in savings in variable expenses. Part of the difficulty arises from an inability to predict short-term variations in volume. Even when this can be done, it is sometimes impracticable to take advantage of this information. For example, a department supervisor may normally supervise a work force of 15 machinists. A decline in volume for a period of two months does not necessarily result in a reduction in force since it may be more economical in the long run to retain highly skilled employees instead of running the risk of losing their services as a result of a layoff. Also, a sudden upturn in business may be handled more efficiently by assigning overtime work rather than incurring expenses resulting from training new employees. An advantage of variable budgets is that there is a budgeted goal for varying levels of volume without having to rework the entire budget each time a significant change in activity occurs. However, a greater advantage comes not from the variable goals feature of the flexible budget but from the study and analysis necessary for the preparation of a flexible budget.

In addition to focusing attention upon the variable costs that contribute to the total cost of each unit, the preparation of flexible budgets requires a closer analysis of all costs in separating fixed and variable costs.[2]

Advantages of Effective Budgetary Control

Although budgets are one of the most widely used control techniques, it must be remembered that they are but one of several control devices. There are potential dangers as well as distinct advantages resulting from the use of budgets. Oddly enough, one of the strengths of budgets—the conversion of all aspects of organizational performance into a single comparable unit of measurement, dollars—can become its greatest weakness because it may result in measuring only those things that are easy to measure; i.e., those aspects of organizational performance readily converted into dollars. Equally important factors, such as manager performance and plans for organizational development, may be ignored because achievement in these areas is not readily convertible into dollar units. Second, there is a danger of identifying symptoms as causes. A decline in revenue from sales does not necessarily call for greater sales effort; instead, the real cause may result from a poor product, the action of competitors, or general economic conditions. And finally, there is a danger of autocratic control by the staff organization. The function of the controller or the budget director is to coordinate and guide the development of budgets, but the actual control of performance must remain in the hands of the line managers.

The obvious advantage of budgetary control is that a comparable statement of goals is provided for all organizational units; and since the budget serves as a standard of performance, deviations from this standard are readily measurable and provide the basis for necessary corrective action. However, there are indirect advantages resulting from the proper use of budgets. The consistent and uniform application of budgets results in a more clearly defined organizational structure since budgets measure the performance of organizational units. Second, more meaningful accounting systems and terminology are developed. Traditionally, accounting has a deep preoccupation with the preparation of historical and tax records rather than focusing upon the reporting of current operations and the forecasting of future performance. Third,

---

[2] Adolph Matz and Othel J. Curry, *Cost Accounting,* 5th ed. (Cincinnati: South-Western Publishing Company, 1972), pp. 405-496. The three chapters on budgets, Chapters 15, 16, and 17, provide a discussion of the nature of budgets and offer many problems and examples of budgetary controls.

better planning of all phases of the company's operations results from the use of budgets. Budgets are carefully structured plans and serve to emphasize the continuous nature of the planning-control-planning cycle. Lastly, a clearer statement and understanding of organizational goals comes from the use of budgets because each manager is forced to develop and state attainable goals for his organizational unit. Wishful thinking in respect to organizational objectives is minimized.

BEHAVIORAL REACTIONS TO CONTROL

The application of any control device, whether it is one of the nonbudgetary controls (discussed in the preceding chapter) or a budget, bears directly upon the people of an organization. The success or failure of a control program depends to a greater degree on the attitudes of those subjected to control—members of middle management as well as hourly employees—than it does on the accuracy and kind of technique used in its preparation. Attitudes and overt responses to controls vary from open hostility and resentment, through indifference and tolerance, to complete understanding and appreciation of the need for controls. Before discussing the commonly observed reasons for resistance to controls and the usual reactions to controls, let us examine a procedure that is usually followed in the establishment and administration of controls.

Typical Control Procedure

All too often the establishment and the administration of controls seemingly follow an endless cycle destined to have little chance of success. Top management determines objectives and sets the standards of performance required to meet these objectives; however, middle management and hourly employees react with attitudes and responses of hostility and resentment or indifference and bare tolerance. Such reactions are interpreted by top management as evidence of the need for additional and firmer controls. Robert Katz describes this cycle of control, resistance, and more control as follows:[3]

1. The predetermined program is implemented. It is characterized by general, nonpersonal rules, division of labor, specialized competences, and continuous checking to assure compliance.
2. Here the program immediately encounters unsought-for behavior as employees and subordinate managers seek to maintain their feelings

---

[3] Robert L. Katz, "Toward a More Effective Enterprise," *Harvard Business Review*, Vol. XXXVIII (September-October, 1960), pp. 86-87.

of self-worth, their potential for self-determination, and their needs to have others acknowledge these capabilities.

3. Employees' reaction—Management's unilateral imposition of rules and detailed programming of behavior conflicts with employees' needs for self-determination and self-respect.

Employees feel misunderstood, unappreciated, manipulated. They develop behavior patterns which enable them to resist rigid task pressures and permit some degree of self-regulation through informal social relationships.

Performance stabilizes at the minimum level tolerated by management. Employees tend to produce well below their capacities, have low involvement in their tasks, show little initiative, do only what they are directed to do.

4. Subordinate manager's reaction—Expected by top management to obtain the employees' compliance in the program without deviation, subordinate managers are likely to feel helpless, asked to do the impossible, and misunderstood. They try to escape their feelings of inadequacy by blaming "unreasonable and uncontrollable" employees or "unreasonable and unsympathetic" superiors.

Depending on their temperament, individual managers will tend either to (a) insist on more precise performance of the program, instituting closer controls, closer supervision, more rigorous use of rewards and punishments, or (b) abdicate, contacting subordinates as little as possible, giving instructions, and then busying themselves elsewhere.

5. In either case, whether the subordinate manager cracks down or withdraws, his employees tend to react to his response by developing new behavior patterns. These patterns tend to stabilize at a new level of minimal performance and minimal satisfaction so that all of the old problems remain while new anxieties are created.

6. At this point, top management becomes apprehensive and convinced that things are "out of control." Seeing widespread deviation from its predetermined program, top management is likely to respond to its anxieties by replacing the subordinate manager, applying more pressure for compliance, establishing more elaborate controls, or trying to train the subordinate manager in "how to get people to do what he wants them to."

7. Top management's action only serves to heighten the subordinate manager's anxieties and feelings of inadequacy. The proverbial "man in the middle," he finds his superiors expecting that he *should* be able to get his employees to perform strictly according to plan, and his subordinates expecting that he should attend to *their* needs which underlie their deviation.

8. No matter what the subordinate manager does, the likely outcome is that employees will feel more unappreciated and misunderstood than before, the subordinate manager more helpless and insecure, and top management more anxious about its lack of control.

9. Top management responds by devising new predetermined programs, installing new controls, shuffling personnel, but *not* by questioning any of its original assumptions. Thus, the cycle of unanticipated consequences starts all over again.

Obviously something is wrong. The cycle of control, resistance, and more control cannot go on endlessly. Usually a compromise, or more accurately, a stalemate, is reached. Top management settles for standards of performance that fall short of budgeted expectations; and subordinates, including middle management, tacitly recognize but do not wholly accept or understand the need for control. An understanding of the reasons for resistance to controls enables us to prepare and install them in such a manner that the cycle of control, resistance, and more control never begins.

Why Resistance Develops

Seemingly, most of us have a built-in resistance to any form of control; perhaps such reactions are necessary for the preservation of one's own individuality. Nonetheless, as managers, we must learn not only to cope with our own reactions to control but also to meet and minimize the resistance of subordinates to control. The three steps of the control process—setting standards, measuring performance, and taking corrective action—provide a logical outline for our discussion of resistance to controls.

Standards Are Too Tight. A frequent initial reaction to budgets and other forms of control is the complaint that the standard of performance is unreasonable or too tight. There are several reasons why people respond in this manner. There may be no understanding of or desire to meet organizational objectives expressed by the standard. Such reactions occur when standards are imposed without any explanation concerning their need. Unless the reasons for standards can be presented in such a way that they become personal objectives for persons who are expected to meet such standards, complaints that the goals are unreasonable are sure to arise.

Another reason for objecting to standards is that historically they have a way of moving in only one direction—up. Consequently, is it any wonder that the initial reaction to them is the belief that they are unreasonable or too tight? A sales budget may show that a higher dollar volume is expected from each salesman for the current year; however, the increased volume may be the result of higher prices rather than the result of an increase in the number of units sold. In a like manner, an increase in the number of units expected from a production worker is often the result of improved methods or more efficient production equipment that actually call for less effort on the worker's part. Since budgets are prepared annually and usually show a steady increase in expected performance, it is necessary that those affected by standards understand not only the reasons for the changing objectives but also how the new standards can be met.

The third reason for resistance to standards lies in the way in which they are administered on a day-to-day basis. Regardless of how carefully standards may have been developed, unexpected conditions arise that make their attainment impossible. Materials that fail to meet stated specifications or machine breakdowns lower the output of the production worker. Unexpected product developments by competitors or even unseasonable variations in the weather can affect the performance of a salesman. In such cases the wise administrator notes the reasons for variances from standards and does not place undue pressure upon subordinates.

Measurements Not Accurate. Many times standards of performance are accepted, but the methods used in measuring performance are considered inaccurate. When control measures are criticized as not being accurate, more often than not factors other than accuracy are involved. The real complaint on the part of a supervisor operating under budgetary controls may be that the information provided is not timely enough to be of use to him in the operation of his department. Also, a supervisor's superior may criticize control measurements because they are not timely enough to aid in the coordination of the activities of several departments.

The comment is often heard that the measures used are satisfactory as far as they go, but they do not begin to measure all that is being done. The implication is that the measurements being used are not measuring those things that are important. The production foreman may agree that the unit count is an accurate statement of what is produced but reveals nothing about the decline in the number of units rejected by final inspection and the consequent decrease in the cost of rework. A salesman may readily admit that the dollar volume statement of his sales is correct and at the same time complain that the information used to measure his performance is unfair because it does not reflect the number of new accounts or the miles that he has to travel in his territory in order to call on customers. Before corrective action is taken, it is well to make sure that all the significant aspects of performance are being measured.

However, the bitterest complaint of all concerning measurements used in the control process is that they do not measure effort. Students may receive a grade of C on an assignment that in their opinion was worth at least a B in terms of the amount of effort expended. Unfortunately, for those whose work is subjected to measurement and comparison to standard, the information required for control purposes is an accurate statement of the amount of variance from standard. A good supervisor will note the effort spent in doing a job and should commend his subordinates for such effort. By so doing, he may be able to minimize the normal resistance of subordinates to having their work measured— particularly when performance does not meet expected goals.

Dislike of Corrective Action. In the first paragraph of this section on behavioral reactions to control, it is stated that the administration of controls bears directly upon the people of an organization. Specifically, it is the corrective action taken as the result of failure to meet standards that is disliked and sometimes even feared. Somehow there is the belief that where there are no controls there is always the possibility that poor performance will not be noticed and, if detected, plausible excuses can be offered and will be accepted.

One reason for disliking corrective action, even a mild form of admonition, is that it is a form of criticism directed toward an individual. Criticism of a person can never be completely impersonal even though such criticism might be based upon an objective analysis of all the facts. Consequently, we all have a tendency to reject at least a part of any criticism and interpret what is said with some degree of animosity.

Another reason for disliking corrective action is that it exposes a person's shortcomings to his peers and sometimes to subordinates and superiors in the organization as well. Such exposure is practically unavoidable when demotion or discharge is the corrective action taken. It is the dislike and the fear of potential corrective action more than resistance to standards and criticisms of the methods of measurement that lead to most of the undesirable reactions to controls.

Unfavorable Responses to Controls

Our analysis of resistance to controls shows that any of the three steps of the control process may serve as a focal point for resistance.

To some observers, resistance is regarded as a reaction to the pressures created by application of controls. Before studying the specific form of resistance demonstrated by either an individual or a group, let us find out why controls are commonly regarded as pressure devices.

Controls As Pressure Devices. There are two major reasons why controls, especially budgets, are commonly regarded as pressure devices. First, controls are standards of performance. Standards, like the 72-stroke par of golf, should be difficult but attainable. It is expected that the amount of effort expended by an individual in attaining a standard is somewhat greater than the amount he would expend if there were no stated standard. Thus, a certain degree of pressure is inherent and intended in any statement of standards. The second source of pressure arises from the procedures frequently followed in the installation and administration of controls. More often than not, controls are developed solely by top management and imposed upon the middle and the lower echelons of the organization. Supervisors and hourly employees alike cannot help but believe that top management is not entirely satisfied with the usual level of performance. Many times top management affirms their subordinates' view of controls as a means of pressure by pointing to the increases in productivity that occur after the installation of controls. Often the reaction to control imposed from above results in the control, inadequate response, more control cycle described earlier.

Improperly conceived and administered controls can result in serious human relations problems. One writer has summarized what may happen when budgets are improperly applied.[4]

1. Budget pressure tends to unite the employees against management, and tends to place the factory supervisor under tension. This tension may lead to inefficiency, aggression, and perhaps a complete breakdown on the part of the supervisor.
2. The finance staff can obtain feelings of success only by finding fault with factory people. These findings of failure among factory supervisors lead to many human relations problems.
3. The use of budgets as "needlers" by top management tends to make each factory supervisor see only the problem of his own department.
4. Supervisors use budgets as a way of expressing their own patterns of leadership. When this results in people getting hurt, the budget, in itself a neutral thing, often gets blamed.

---

[4] Chris Argyris, "Human Problems with Budgets," *Harvard Business Review,* Vol. XXXI (January-February, 1953), p. 108. Argyris' article is a report of a research study undertaken for the Controllership Foundation to determine the effects of budgets on human relationships in an organization and the extent to which budgets accomplish their purpose. Suggestions are given to improve the effectiveness of budgets.

Note that the pressure of budgets can affect both individuals and groups in an organization.

Effects on Individuals. Unfavorable individual responses to budgets or other controls on the part of supervisors are essentially reactions resulting from their failure either to understand or to meet stated budgetary goals. Occasionally the tensions and pressures created by budgets may result in a supervisor suffering a complete breakdown. Apathy, loss of interest in the job, and compliance to "the letter of the law" are forms of behavior that reflect a withdrawal from an unpleasant situation. Some supervisors respond with overt aggressiveness that is intended to shift the responsibility for failure to meet standards from themselves and their department to other departmental managers or to members of the staff organization.

Budgetary controls always contain the potential threat of disrupting cooperative relationships between members of the line and staff organizations. When imposed from above, the budget is developed and administered by a specialized staff group—usually a part of the controller's office. The measure of success of the budget staff is the extent to which the line managers meet the budgeted goals. Failure to meet these goals is interpreted as failure on the part of the line organization rather than the result of poorly stated or unattainable goals by the budget group. When budgets are fulfilled, ensuing budgets can be tightened so that they are more difficult to attain; thus, the line manager is once again faced with the threat of failure. Under these conditions, it is understandable why the relationships between the line manager and the controller's staff are in a state of perpetual conflict.

The departmental supervisor may generalize his conflict with the controller's staff and attempt to shift the blame for his difficulties to other staff groups. The personnel department may be criticized for failure to enforce disciplinary action and for not supplying qualified and sufficient manpower. Quality control may be accused of setting quality specifications that make it impossible to meet budgeted cost and production standards. The production control staff comes under attack for failure to schedule long production runs and for scheduling unreasonable sequences in the production of different products. Plant maintenance departments receive their share of criticism for not maintaining production equipment and other facilities at peak levels of efficiency.

The reactions discussed so far are descriptive of how the individual supervisor might react when controls are interpreted as a means of exerting pressure. He may withdraw from the situation through sickness or apathy or he may become aggressive and strike out in any and all directions. He may try to shift the blame to other operating departments, to the controller's staff, or to other staff groups. Unfavorable reactions to controls do not remain individual reactions indefinitely; instead, individuals form cohesive groups and the strength of the group is utilized to combat the pressures of control.

Group Reaction to Pressure. Organized group resistance to any kind of external control pressure, does not develop immediately; nor is it planned. However, the formation of group resistance is inevitable and follows a consistent evolutionary pattern. Argyris describes this process well:[5]

1. First, the individuals sense an increase in pressure.
2. Then they begin to see definite evidences of the pressure. They not only feel it, they can point to it.
3. Since they feel this pressure is on them personally, they begin to experience tension and general uneasiness.
4. Next they usually "feel out" their fellow workers to see if they too sense the pressure.
5. Finding out that others have noted the pressure, they begin to feel more at ease. It helps to be able to say, "I'm not the only one."
6. Finally, they realize that they can acquire emotional support from each other by becoming a group. Furthermore, they can "blow their top" about this pressure in front of their group.

When leadership crystallizes and emerges, the group is ready to act in unison. Let us see what happens; first, on the hourly level; then, within the ranks of management.

THE HOURLY LEVEL. Assume that the production of a manufacturing department, or the output of a clerical section, is stabilized at a rate that time study shows to be 65 percent of standard. Certain conditions or forces are holding production at this level. Perhaps supervision is satisfied, and an output of 65 percent of standard may be the most comfortable pace considering the methods used in performing the work. The individual worker has no reason for deviating from this pattern since conformance assures continued membership in the group and enables him to assume the protective coloring of the group. Now, incorporate the time study data into standards and express these standards as part of a budget—unannounced and imposed from above. Pressure is felt first by the supervisors, who, in turn, attempt to enforce the newly stated standards by requiring an increased level of production. The development of group cohesiveness as described by Argyris begins. Eventually

---

[5] *Ibid.*, p. 100.

a static state of balance between the pressures of the budget and the pressures of the group may be reached; a level higher than the original 65 percent but still short of the budgeted 100 percent. These are the *frozen* groups of Zalesnik or the *sick* groups described by Gellerman.[6] When the informal group achieves cohesiveness and adopts the leadership and resources of a formal organization—the union—the groundwork is laid for labor-management strife.

GROUPS WITHIN MANAGEMENT. The formation of groups whose primary purpose is to combat the pressures exerted by top management is not limited to groups composed of hourly or clerical employees. Informal groups may develop within the ranks of management as well. The first-line supervisors of a plant may feel themselves caught between the pressure of the budget from above and the resistance of their subordinates from below. They are literally caught in the middle and seek the support offered by others who are in the same position. When talking to subordinates, the supervisor blames the "budget people" for the pressures of production. When reporting to his superior, the incompetence and the uncooperativeness of his subordinates are offered as the cause for failure to meet budgeted expectations. There are instances of supervisory groups having become so firmly solidified that they eventually became formal unions of supervisors. Many supervisory or management clubs have been formed to nullify the cohesiveness of informal groups of supervisors and forestall their becoming formal union organizations. The labor unions of engineers and scientists, though not directly the result of budgetary controls, are another example of resistance to top management that has led to the formation of groups so that group pressure may be applied in opposition to the pressure exerted by management.

Informal groups may develop within either the line or the staff organization and make it almost impossible to achieve the benefits that might be realized from the application of budgets or other forms of control. When line management unites as a group and opposes the recommendations of the staff organization, one can be sure that the staff, as a group, will oppose any suggested modifications of their programs that come from members of the line organization.

Effective Use of Controls

Our review of those aspects of the control process that cause resistance, the concept of pressure associated with the administration

---

[6] See Chapter 18, "Motivating Employees," p. 553.

of budgets, and the responses of individuals and groups to pressure does not seem to offer much encouragement for the successful application of controls. Fortunately, there are ways to minimize resistance to controls. The following suggestions have been found helpful in making the application of controls more effective.

Establish Proper Attitudes. The attitudes of the members of an organization toward controls depend on the underlying motivation of top management. Controls can be established as a device to goad managers into better performance, or they can be used by the managers themselves as an instrument for measuring and guiding performance. These two divergent uses of controls are analagous to the uses that may be found for two long pieces of wood. At the end of one piece of wood, there is a sharp point. This piece of wood is used as a prod to keep managers in line and moving in the right direction. Another piece of wood—the same length, is divided into 36 equal segments and becomes the familiar yardstick, a tool that can be used to measure progress. For controls to be most effective, they must be regarded as yardsticks developed to measure performance rather than prods intended to keep people in line.[7]

Place Controls in the Hands of Managers. One of the best ways top management has of expressing its understanding of controls is by placing the responsibility for their preparation and administration in the hands of departmental managers. True, a well-trained controller's staff is valuable in company-wide consolidation and coordination, but the preparation and administration of controls at the operating level are best accomplished by the responsible manager. In preparing controls, managers should make the first draft; then if revisions are needed, cooperative effort between the controller's office and line management is required to reach a final statement of goals. In order to administer controls properly, managers must have adequate standards of performance, timely information concerning their performance, and freedom to manage. Standards serve as a measure of performance and form the backbone of any control. In manufacturing departments, standards should be developed for labor, materials, supplies, and the maintenance of equipment. Standards of performance and cost can also be determined for administrative and sales units. The controller should provide departmental managers with timely information so that necessary corrections

---

[7] James L. Pierce, "The Budget Comes of Age," *Harvard Business Review,* Vol. XXXII (May-June, 1954), pp. 58-66. Mr. Pierce discusses some of the problems encountered in improving budgetary controls.

may be made and so that performance conforms to budgeted expectations. Controls are not intended to restrict the activities of a manager; he must have freedom to manage. So that freedom in operations may be increased, some companies state only the total of the expense items and leave to the discretion of the manager the allocation of the amount to be spent for each item. Finally, procedures must be clearly stated to set forth steps to be followed in securing revisions, and practice must demonstrate that such revisions are possible.

Follow Organizational Lines. Fundamenal to effective budgetary control is a clear concept of organization structure. The manager of each department must know the superior to whom he reports and the subordinates who report to him, and his relations with other departments must be clearly defined. When organizational lines are clearly stated, the budgets become the yardstick capable of measuring performance; however, when organizational lines are fuzzy and ill defined, there is a tendency to use the budget as a prod since there is no means of defining duties and assigning responsibilities. The clarity of organizational definition marks the upper limit of the effectiveness of controls as a determinant of organizational performance.

Case Problem 22-B is a continuation of Case Problem 22-A. All did not go as planned, and now there is need for corrective action. Two points are illustrated in this closing case. First, even though performance did not measure up to expectations, the presence of a budget pinpoints the areas requiring corrective action. Second, each variation from a budget may be small, but the aggregate can sometimes be alarming.

CASE PROBLEM
22-B

A NEED FOR
CORRECTIVE
ACTION

It was the latter part of January before Barr completed the proposed revenue and expense budget described in Case Problem 22-A. Only then did he know he would not make a profit during the first quarter of the year and that the best he could expect would be to break even by the end of June. In an attempt to offset the normally slow months of February, March, and April, he decided to increase advertising outlays and to gain a competitive advantage by lowering his prices slightly. During the year he hired additional sales personnel to offset his own lack of sales experience and knowledge of the men's clothing business. Also, the lease expired during the year, and a new one was negotiated at a somewhat higher figure. The results of Barr's first full year as manager of the store are shown in Exhibit III.

Exhibit III
BUDGETED AND ACTUAL PERFORMANCE
Avenue Men's Store

Account	Budgeted % of Net Sales ($200,000)	Actual Dollar Rev./Exp.	Actual Percentage of Budgeted Net Sales ($200,000)
Sales:			
1. Gross sales	102.6	$206,000	103.0
2. Customer ret. & allow. ..	2.6	5,000	2.5
3. Net sales	100.0	201,000	101.0
Cost of goods sold:			
4. Beginning inventory	30.9	61,800	30.9
5. Net purchases plus transportation charges paid ..	66.1	137,000	68.5
6. Total cost of merchandise handled	97.0	198,000	99.4
7. Ending inventory	32.3	66,800	33.4
8. Net cost of mdse. sold .	64.7	132,000	66.0
9. Net busheling (alterations) cost	2.1	6,000	3.0
10. Total cost of mdse. sold .	66.8	138,000	69.0
11. Gross margin	33.2	62,000	31.0
Operating expenses:			
12. Payroll:			
A. Salary of owner ...	7.3	14,600	7.3
B. Salaries and wages of employees	9.0	21,000	10.5
Total payroll ..	16.3	35,600	17.8
13. Rent expense	2.9	6,000	3.0
14. Taxes and license fees (omit real estate, Federal income and sales taxes).	1.1	2,200	1.1
15. Insurance	.6	1,200	.6
16. Depreciation & amort. ...	.8	1,600	.8
17. Repairs	.2	200	.1
18. Supplies (omit rep. mat'ls.)	1.0	2,400	1.2
19. Services purchased	.9	1,400	.7
20. Traveling (business trips) .	.3	400	.2
21. Communications (include parcel post)	.4	1,200	.6
22. Advertising and publicity .	2.8	6,400	3.2
23. Professional services (outside professional agencies)	.2	200	.1
24. Unclassified:			
A. Losses from bad debts	.3	800	.4
B. Other classified	.5	1,200	.6
Total unclassified expenses	.8	2,000	1.0
25. Total expenses	28.3	60,800	30.4
26. Net profit (before Federal income taxes)	4.9	1,200	.6

PROBLEMS   1. Are the results shown in Exhibit III attributable to poor
                       budgeting techniques or to poor management? Explain.
                    2. What corrective action would you take as manager of
                       this store?

Chapter Questions for Study and Discussion

1. How are budgets different from other kinds of business plans? Show why
   each of these differences is necessary.
2. Are the terms budget and standard synonymous? If so, what type of
   standards are utilized in the development of the four major types of
   budgets?
3. Discuss the following statement: Flexible budgets make periodic
   budgetary reviews unnecessary.
4. Should expense budgets be stated at a lower figure than that actually
   computed in order that final expenses will not exceed the budgeted
   amount? Support your answer.
5. Why are budgets or other controls often regarded as "pressure devices"?
6. Of what worth would a control be if it did not create pressure? Discuss.
7. What are the attitudes essential for the effective use of controls?
8. Describe the steps you would take to offset the usual resistance that
   develops when controls are installed.
9. Describe the steps you would take in establishing an effective sales budget.

CHAPTER 23

A Summing Up

The four functions of the management process—planning, organizing, leading, and controlling—are utilized as a broad framework for the study of management. These functions should not be regarded as discrete steps in the management process; instead, they should be regarded as interdependent subsystems with each subsystem contributing its share to the total system of management. In the last paragraph of Chapter 22, the interdependence between the control function and the organizing function is indicated by the statement that clear organization structure is fundamental to effective control. The control function is also dependent upon sound planning and effective leadership.

The first step in summing up our study of management is an integration of the four functions of the management process. Next, there is a summary of the systems concept and its application to the management of systems. Some of the major issues confronting today's managers, to be resolved by the managers of the future, are presented, and we conclude with a brief epilogue that discusses the introductory course to management in relation to other courses in the business administration curriculum.

INTEGRATING MANAGEMENT FUNCTIONS

A major assumption underlying the management of formal organizations is that such organizations are teleological in nature. The extent of commitment to purpose is in large measure the result of the clarity and manner in which objectives are stated. Without objectives there is no need for a formal organization; and were it possible to create a formal organization without a stated purpose, it would soon deteriorate and dissolve. Similarly, an existing organization that no longer has a goal to fulfill—e.g., one whose product or service is no longer needed nor desired by society—must recast its objectives if the organization is to survive. It is axiomatic that without an organization there is no need for managers or the management process. Hence objectives are considered fundamental to the process of management.

Admittedly there are differences of opinion concerning whether the setting of objectives should be considered as part of planning or regarded as an activity distinct from and preceding the planning function. There is no right or wrong answer concerning the inclusion of objectives as a part of planning or the consideration of objectives as a distinct activity. Those who favor the inclusion of objectives as a part of the planning process point out that planning activities are sometimes needed to clearly define an objective and that stated objectives are sometimes modified as the result of undertaking the development of plans for the fulfillment of previously stated goals. Those who view the setting of objectives as being apart from and preceding the planning function do so to add emphasis to the importance of setting objectives and to stress the need for a clear-cut goal before undertaking any activity. Further, objectives may result from individual desires or needs neither related to nor dependent upon planning. In this text objectives are considered apart from the function of planning, yet susceptible to modification as the result of subsequent planning. Regardless of the inclusion or exclusion of the setting of objectives as part of the planning function, it is agreed that objectives are basic to the management process. We now review the functions of that process.

Planning—Control—Planning Cycle

Most introductory textbooks of management discuss the planning function first and follow with a treatment of the functions of organizing and leading in that sequence, then close with a discussion of the control function. However, it is more in keeping with the performance of managerial functions to regard the planning and control functions as a continuous cycle. The chief reason for presenting the functions separately is that such separation provides a convenient framework for organizing the functions of the process of management in a manner that facilitates the analysis of each function. Also, it is difficult to discuss the control function immediately after a discussion of planning since control is dependent so much upon the structure of the organization. Without knowledge of the organizing function and familiarity with the terminology used to describe organizational processes and relationships, the concept of control can be presented only in vague and general terms. In addition, the nature of and the manner in which the leadership function is executed is a major variable in determining the effectiveness of any control procedure. Before discussing the planning—control—planning cycle, let us examine briefly each function separately.

Planning. Planning is generally accorded a position of primacy among the management functions since logically it is the first function that should be performed. Also, planning is considered pervasive in its nature because planning is required to form the organization, to determine the patterns of leadership, and to design the control system. The results of planning are plans that serve as guides for the actions of the members of the organization in the achievement of stated objectives. In addition to those plans that are developed to serve a given project, such as locating and building a new plant, some plans become relatively permanent in nature and are sometimes called standing plans. These plans, depending upon their breadth or scope, are classified as policies, procedures, or methods.

In its simplest form planning is an activity that can be executed by any member of an organization as illustrated by the planning of one's activities for a day, several days, or a week. As the nature of the problem under consideration becomes more complex, so do the methods of planning. In medium and large organizations the volume of data gathered to be analyzed and evaluated prior to making a final choice has increased significantly with the utilization of electronic data processing equipment in the planning process. Part of the increase in the amount of data evaluated in the planning process is the result of a desire to improve the quality of the final plan by developing and examining many alternative courses of action, and part is due to the capabilities of information processing equipment. Because of virtually unlimited capabilities for storage, retrieval, and processing of data, there is a tendency to examine more data than needed simply because they are available.

Control. The purpose of the control function is to insure the proper execution of plans. Control is accomplished through a three-step process —the determination of expected standards of performance, the measurement of current performance in relation to expected standards, and the taking of corrective action when necessary to insure that standards are met. The sequence of events, the date each event is to be completed, and the organization responsible for the completion of a given event are quite evident when plans are developed in detail and are highly structured. Budgets, the instrument most frequently associated with the control function, are plans for profit that have been converted into dollars to be received, spent, and earned during a specified period of time. Similarly, the time-event-network analysis used as a means of control is a statement of the sequence and timing of activities to be accomplished so that a given project may be completed.

The Cycle. The planning and control functions of management are best described as a planning-control-planning cycle since each of these functions is a different aspect of the same continuous management information system. Information for planning is drawn from external environmental sources such as socioeconomic data. Financial and other internal resources available in the form of physical plant and personnel are also utilized in planning. Control relies heavily upon internal data developed as the result of the execution of plans; yet changes in the external environment, for example the actions of competitors and customers, are also signlficant. More often than not, when corrective action is required the modification of plans is a part of that action. The interlocking nature of the information utilized in the planning and control functions is illustrated in Figure 17-2, page 520.

However, the planning-control-planning cycle is but one phase of the management process. Organizations are required to develop and execute plans, and organizations must be actuated in order to achieve the desired level of effectiveness.

Organizing

The classical approach to the study of organization reveals two major themes. The first is concern for the structuring of work and results in the creation of roles that guide and limit the behavior of people. Closely associated with and a part of the process of structuring is the subsequent arrangement of work into manageable units. The structuring and arranging of work into units is known as departmentation. The arrangement of these units of work under the jurisdiction of a single manager creates a span of management. The second theme that appears in the classical discussions of the organizing function is the concept of authority. There are two major opinions concerning the source of authority—the institutional source which states that authority is derived from society and the subordinate acceptance view which holds that authority is granted by subordinates.

Another facet of authority is its transfer within the organization. Superior-subordinate relationships are referred to as the chain of command, and the process of transferring authority from superior to sub-ordinate is known as the delegation of authority. When the subordinate is a manager of a lower level organizational unit, the process of delegating authority to that manager is known as the decentralization of authority. Although the phrase, decentralization of authority, is used frequently to describe the authority relationships between a plant manager and a vice-president manufacturing or between a district sales manager and a vice-president sales, it is best to reserve the term decentralization for those instances where the decentralized unit is of sufficient scope so that there is a clear responsibility for profits. Such a limitation requires that the unit manager must have responsibility for both the production function and the sales function.

It is apparent that there is an obvious need for an organization—defining an organization as people with assigned and interrelated roles—to execute the planning function. Of equal significance are the benefits obtained for the well defined organization in executing the control function. A clearly defined organization aids in the flow of information necessary for the measurement of performance. The corrective action of the control function is accomplished by the managers responsible for the variance from expected standards. It is difficult to designate the responsible managers without a clearly defined organization.

Leading

The leadership function is termed variously as leading, directing, actuating, or motivating. Despite the variation in terminology used to designate the function, it is agreed that the purpose of the function is to elicit desired forms of behavior on the part of the members of the organization. Within the context of independent, intervening, and dependent variables leadership is best regarded as an independent variable—an input into the organization intended to influence behavior. The results of effective leadership are expressed in many ways. The statement of objectives may be an expression of the goals of one person, or it may represent a consensus of the top echelon of the organization. The quality of leadership is reflected in the development and execution of plans, in the clarity and appropriateness of the organizational structure, and in the design and administration of control systems.

Leadership in formal organizations includes not only those characteristics of interpersonal relationships known as leadership style; it also includes all of the actions of a manager necessary for the performance of the managerial functions of planning, organizing, and controlling, as well as the selection of the appropriate style of leadership. Consequently, the concept of managing is broader in scope than the concept of leading. Similarly, the managerial function known as leading is broader than the interpersonal relationships between manager and subordinate. Among the managerial functions associated with the function of leadership are the design and administration of motivational systems, planning and executing formal communication programs, and the staffing and development of the organization on a continuing basis. The performance of these managerial functions is a major contribution to the formation of organizational climate, which in turn becomes a significant determinant of behavior of the members of the organization.

MANAGEMENT AND THE SYSTEMS CONCEPT

Utilization of the systems concept is another means of emphasizing the integrative nature of the management process. In Chapter 2, "The Development of Management Concepts," an integrative view outlining the parts of a system and the processes that link a system is presented. In Chapter 6, the major business functions—finance, sales, production, and personnel—are examined within the context of a servo system, and in Chapter 9 the parameters of a systems approach to organization theory are presented. The development of information systems is discussed in Chapter 7, "Management Information Systems," and in Chapter 17, "Communications." The control function and its contribution as a part of a cybernetic system is presented in Chapter 20.

Since the systems concept is utilized as a way of describing the management process, it is helpful to present in summary form two aspects of systems theory that are of particular significance to managers. First is recognition that there is no single system; instead, there is a wide range in the complexity of systems with the result that systems are best regarded as forming a hierarchy. The hierarchical arrangement of systems is shown in Figure 23-1. The second aspect of systems theory significant to managers is an understanding of the characteristics of open systems since managers are concerned primarily with the management of social systems, a form of open system. The characteristics of open systems are shown in Figure 23-2.

A Hierarchy of Systems

Boulding's classification of systems into a hierarchy of levels of complexity is in effect a "system of systems." [1] His classification is of

---

[1] Kenneth E. Boulding, "General Systems Theory—The Skeleton of Science," *Management Science,* Vol. II, No. 3 (April, 1956), pp. 197-208.

1. *Static structure* is a level of *frameworks*; for example, the geography and anatomy of the universe, the pattern of structure of atoms, genes, cells, and the solar system.
2. *Dynamic systems* are known as the level of *clockworks*; machines, ranging from a simple lever to complex steam and gasoline engines, fall into this category.
3. *Cybernetic systems*, known as the level of the *thermostat*, are capable of maintaining a dynamic relationship within specified limits.
4. *Open systems* are the beginning of life and may be termed the level of the *cell*. There are self-maintaining characteristics and the ability to reproduce.
5. *Genetic-societal systems* are the level of the *plant* and are characterized by a division of labor among the cells with differentiated yet dependent parts such as roots, leaves, seeds, etc.
6. *Animal systems* are the next level and are characterized by increased mobility, purposeful behavior, and self-awareness. Also, specialized receptors for receiving outside information are developed.
7. *Human systems* incorporate all of the characteristics of animal systems and in addition there is self-consciousness and the ability to interpret and manipulate symbols.
8. *Social systems* are composed of humans and at this level the concept of values, the development of historical records, and the expression of the arts appear.
9. *Transcendental systems* are in the words of Boulding "the ultimates and absolutes and the inescapable unknowables, and they also exhibit systematic structure and relationship."

Source: Kenneth E. Boulding, "General Systems Theory—The Skeleton of Science," *Management Science*, Vol. 2, No. 3 (April, 1956), pp. 202-205.

Figure 23-1
A HIERARCHY OF SYSTEMS

value because it is one more step toward a general systems theory intended to unify the many diverse fields of knowledge. It is also useful in that it shows the evolutionary nature of systems as well as the differences and similarities that exist among the many types of systems.

The first systems level, static structure, is descriptive in nature. An accurate descriptive statement of the phenomenon being studied is a necessary first step in the development of knowledge. An accurate description is also necessary to progress to the second level which is an analysis and description of simple dynamic relationships. Simple

1. *Importation of Energy.* Open systems import energy from the external environment; for example, the cell imports oxygen, food, and water from the external environment.

2. *The Through-put.* Open systems convert energy into a form that can be utilized, thus within the system work is accomplished with part of the imported energy utilized to maintain the system itself.

3. *The Output.* Open systems export a product or service to the external environment.

4. *Cycles of Events.* Social systems, a form of open systems, are best regarded as cycles of events rather than being considered as things or objects.

5. *Negative Entropy.* Entropy is the tendency for systems to disentegrate or die; in order to survive systems must develop negative entropy.

6. *Feedback.* An open system must maintain a continuing source of information concerning its relationship with the external environment; the feedback of this information to the system enables the system to measure its relationship to the external environment and make necessary corrections in order to survive.

7. *Dynamic Homeostasis.* Open systems maintain a steady state or a condition of homeostasis. Since a homeostatic condition presents a continual energy exchange between inputs and outputs the term dynamic homeostasis is utilized.

8. *Differentiation.* As open systems develop there is a tendency toward differentiation and specialization so that the system may operate in a more efficient manner.

9. *Equifinality.* The concept of equifinality states that a given end condition may be attained from several different starting points and by means of different pathways to the end condition.

Source: Daniel Katz and Robert L. Kahn, *The Social Psychology of Organizations* (New York: John Wiley & Sons, Inc., 1966), pp. 19-26.

Figure 23-2
CHARACTERISTICS OF OPEN SYSTEMS

dynamic systems may evolve into cybernetic systems capable of maintaining a balanced dynamic relationship within specified limits. Although dynamic systems, such as the solar system, maintain a dynamic relationship due to gravitational forces, the cybernetic system marks the beginning of the utilization of information as a means of keeping the system in balance.

The fourth, fifth, sixth, and seventh levels of the systems hierarchy show gradations in the complexity of living organisms. The cell, level number four, clearly marks the beginning of open systems. Open systems must interact with their environment in order to survive. Energy is imported from outside; a through-put or conversion of that energy occurs with part of the energy being used by the organism to sustain life itself and part being exported to the environment as an output. One of the outputs of animal life, carbon dioxide, is imported by plant life, and during the through-put is converted then exported as oxygen, to be imported by animal life. Recognition of the symbiotic relationships that exist between the many forms of life is the basis for the current drive to improve the quality of our environment.

Note that social systems are eight in the hierarchy of complexity. This is the level of greatest interest to students of management because managers manage and are members of social systems. Obviously man (also a system) is a component of social systems, yet it is doubtful that man is the unfying aspect of social systems. Instead, it appears that roles—expected and prescribed behavior—are the basis for the continuity and predictability of organizations.

Perhaps the greatest value of Boulding's classification is that it clearly shows the nature of our problem in studying the management of organizations. It is doubtful that there are any thoroughly tested theoretical models beyond level four. We have fairly accurate models of dynamic and cybernetic systems, borrowed from the physical sciences, that we try to apply to level eight, social systems. Such applications have inherent and obvious shortcomings, yet they are all that is available at the present time. With these limitations in mind, let us examine the characteristics of open systems as shown in Figure 23-2.

Characteristics of Open Systems

The elements of the basic model of open systems are expressed in the first three open systems characteristics—the importation of energy, the through-put, and the output. The fourth characteristic offers a way of viewing open systems. The next three characteristics—negative entropy, feedback, and dynamic homeostasis—are attributes that contribute to the continuity, or life, of open systems. The remaining characteristics—differentiation and equifinality—are helpful in understanding the functioning of complex social organizations. Each of these three groups of open system characteristics is examined.[2]

The Model. The basic open system model is that of an energic input-output system. Energy is imported from the external environment;

---

[2] Daniel Katz and Robert L. Kahn, *The Social Psychology of Organizations* (New York: John Wiley and Sons, Inc., 1966). This work is a major theoretical contribution to the study of social organizations as systems. The discussion above is based upon Chapter 2, "Organizations and the System Concept," and Chapter 3, "Defining Characteristics of Social Organizations," pp. 14-70.

there is a transformation of that energy in the through-put with part of the energy being used to maintain the system itself and part being exported as an output to the external environment. The fourth characteristic is an admonition that it is best to regard the three steps of importation, transformation, and exportation as events rather than objects or things.

For the manufacturing firm the production function is one of creating a product. The product is exported to the external environment where it is exchanged for cash which, in turn, is exchanged for raw materials so that the cycle of procurement, production, and sales begins anew. However, not all of the money realized from the sale of the product is utilized for the purchase of raw materials. Part must be used to maintain the system itself. People must be paid, capital equipment must be maintained and replaced, and the costs of promotional efforts in the selling of the product must be met.

The production function, or through-put, is present in all formal social organizations. For the air transport industry it is the transportation of passengers and freight; for the educational institution it is the education of people; and for the charitable organization it is the distribution of benefits to its recipients. In each case there is a definite sequence of events—importation, transformation, and exportation.

Sustaining Characteristics. Entropy is the tendency for systems to disintegrate and die. Open systems, by importing more energy than required for the conversion process in the through-put and the maintenance of the system, can theoretically arrest entropic processes. To a degree biological systems import more than is required for immediate needs and are able to store energy; however, the quality of the energy imported is not of the type required to forestall entropy indefinitely.

However, formal social organizations have potentially an unlimited duration. Yet few have succeeded in lasting more than a century or so. Among those that have succeeded are the Roman Catholic Church, Harvard University, and the Hudson Bay Corporation. Maintenance subsystems must be created if social organizations are to arrest entropy. One such subsystem is the financial function of organizations. There must be sufficient monetary inputs so that the system can perform its production function and have enough energy (money) remaining to bring new people into the organization; to prepare these people to perform necessary organizational roles; and to make these roles so rewarding that the people do not voluntarily leave the organization. When the personnel function is viewed as the development of the characteristic of negative entropy, its importance becomes obvious. The human asset accounting used by the R. G. Barry Corporation (Chapter 21) tacitly recognizes that organization development is the development of negative entropy.

Adaptive systems are necessary to sustain the open system. There must be provision for an informational feedback between the system and its environment and between the subsystems of the total system. The internal feedback of information between the financial, personnel, production, and sales functions are shown within the context of a servo system in Figure 6-3 (page 202). The sales function is a part of the feedback loop with the customer. The financial and personnel functions must also maintain informational circuits with organizations outside the system and provide the information necessary for the system to adapt to both internal and external changes. Management information systems are an adaptive mechanism.

Systems must maintain a steady state, or equilibrium, to survive. However, a steady state is not a constant; instead, it is a prescribed range of variation. Hence the term, dynamic homeostasis. Open systems undergo constant change in the process of adapting to internal changes as well as to external changes, yet the change is within prescribed limits and occurs over a period of time with the result that there is seldom a loss of identity. The growth of plants and animals is an example of continuous change with the retention of identity. Formal organizations lose members who must be replaced; products and services are modified to meet the changing needs of customers; and changes must be made within the system itself in respect to both structure and function if it is to survive in an ever changing environment. Market research, product development, and long-range planning are some of the adaptive functions that contribute to the maintenance of a dynamic homeostasis in business firms.

Differentiation and Equifinality. As open systems become more complex there is a differentiation of functions with specialized resources being developed for each function. The one-man hamburger stand is illustrative. In the beginning the one man performs the four functions of the management process; in addition, he performs the business functions of finance, production, sales, and personnel. He is an undifferentiated organization. As the business grows, limitations imposed by time and knowledge force the process of differentiation and specialization. The need for a subsystem known as management develops long before the hamburger stand becomes a chain of restaurants. Plans must be made for the continuity of the business, an organization must be created and directed, and a control function must be established. In this sense, management is a subsystem whose function is to coordinate, control, and direct the activities of the other subsystems.

The concept of equifinality may be paraphrased by the old saying, "there is more than one way of skinning a cat." The process of attaining a stated dollar sales volume offers an example of equifinality in business firms. The stated sales volume may be attained by expanding existing facilities, by developing new products, and by increasing one's share of the market. It is a method often referred to as internal growth or growth from within. The same sales objectives may be reached by the acquisition and merger route. Although there is a measure of equifinality in all organizations, there is some evidence that as the degree of differentiation and specialization of open systems increases there is a corresponding decrease in the characteristic of equifinality.

CURRENT ISSUES IN MANAGEMENT

One of the favorite topics of those writers who popularize management are predictions of what managers of the future will do. Such forecasts are often extrapolated from a superficial examination of one aspect of management and based upon somewhat tenuous assumptions. Rather than predict the future, it seems more prudent to discuss current issues confronting today's managers since these are the issues to be resolved by the managers of tomorrow. Admittedly, not all students of management would select the three issues discussed below; however, these three would in all probability be included in a ranking of the ten most significant issues by serious students of management. The issues discussed are related to information technology, organization development, and the social value issue in business.

Information Technology

With the advent of the computer there has been a change, not only in the method of processing information, but also in the significance of information *per se* in the management of formal organizations. We have moved from the laborious transcription of data by hand and decisions based largely on intuition and personal experience to electronic data processing and its seemingly limitless capability to process, store, and retrieve information to be used in the decision-making process. Virtually all medium and large business organizations utilize electronic data processing to some degree, and many are well along the way toward the development of a completely integrated data processing system designed to integrate all information necessary for planning and control. Implied in the development of integrated data processing is a centralized information processing function. What effect will the establishment of integrated data processing have on the degree of centralization of authority to make decisions, and what effect will it have on the functions of the middle manager?

Traditionally some positions, such as district sales manager, have considerable authority to make decisions since the manager is the one person in the organization who knows the customer and his needs. When a company installs an information system that permits the customer to order directly through a remote terminal to an information center that processes the order, prepares billing and shipping instructions from the coded input, and notifies the warehouse to ship the item, such procedures are bound to affect the functions of the field sales force. Another typical middle management position, the production control manager, has considerable influence and decision-making authority in many plants. However, when the information system is extended to correct the inventory balance automatically and, when necessary, to notify a plant to replenish the item to a predetermined inventory level, the role of the production control manager is changed significantly.

There is no single criterion that can be used to predict the effect of integrated data processing upon the degree of centralization or decentralization of authority to make decisions within a given company or the effect that it will have upon middle management positions such as those described above. Arguments have been developed that have equal force in predicting either a greater degree of centralization or a greater degree of decentralization of authority to make decisions as the result of integrated data processing. However, two factors seem highly significant in determining the probable effects of integrated data processing within a given company. First is the basic philosophy of the company. If it is the desire of the company to place decision making at the lowest possible level of the organization, information technology can serve as an effective means of placing complete information for the decision-making process in the hands of lower eschelon managers. However, if the desire is to centralize decision making as much as possible, information technology can be used for that end. The second factor is the technology of the organization, and that technology may limit the philosophical desires of management. For some organizations, the technology may be such that the need for a high degree of centralization outweighs the philosophical inclinations of management to decentralize. For other companies, technology may be such that decentralization of the authority to make decisions may be realized, provided management has the desire to move in that direction.

Another aspect of information technology, and one seldom treated in discussions of the subject, is its effect upon what may be termed human values or the quality of life. Almost everyone has had the frustrating and discouraging experience of trying to correct a billing error. As yet there seems to be no effective way for a customer to have a computerized billing error corrected. Another example, and one most students will appreciate, is the tendency to identify people by number rather than by name. A student in a college or university uses his social security number as a means of identification. The same number is used when opening a bank account, when seeking employment, and when applying for retirement benefits. There is a recent serious proposal that each child entering the first grade be issued a social security number—it could be argued that the number should be issued at birth, thereby assuring the collection of more accurate vital statistics. Surely, such a process of reducing names to numbers has its effect on the quality of life.

Organization Development

Formal development programs are not uncommon in business firms. As a first step many programs utilize color coded charts as a basis for determining manpower needs arising from anticipated growth and attrition resulting from retirement. In such manner, the managerial needs of the organization may be determined quite accurately. Some companies establish formal training programs that utilize facilities manned by company personnel; in addition, programs offered outside the company by universities may be used. Also, managers may be encouraged to seek advanced degrees through tuition rebates and other financial incentives. The goals of organization development programs range from the supplying of needed managerial manpower to that of changing the management style of the organization. Despite widespread interest in and support of organization development, it is highly doubtful that many companies define organization development within the context of open system characteristics. Until organization development is viewed as a process of developing the characteristic of negative entropy, the full potential of organization development programs cannot be realized.

Though the phrase, organization development, indicates that it is the organization that is being developed, the actual means of such development is the development of individual members of the organization. Yet, there is a serious question to be resolved concerning the degree of compatibility that exists between the individual and the organization. Written records indicate that man has always been a social creature and that he has lived and functioned as a member of a group. However, in recent years much has been written concerning conflicts that result from the pressures of the organization and its demands upon the individual and the needs for fulfillment and self-actualization on the part of the individual. Such expressions of doubt concerning the compatibility of the individual and the organization are not confined to the ranks of managers as evidenced by interest in job enrichment and job satisfaction at the hourly level. Thus one of the major issues in organization development is that of striking a balance between the needs of the organization and the needs of the individual; further, it is a problem that exists at all levels of the organization.

Social Value Issues

Perhaps the most significant issues confronting today's corporate managers—to be resolved by the managers of tomorrow—are in the broad area of social values. One issue in size. Is size, defined as a combination of sales volume and number of employees, sufficient grounds for subjecting a corporation to the antitrust divestiture procedure? What is the role of the corporation vis-a-vis community, state, and national government agencies? What responsibility does the corporation have for improving the blighted areas of our cities or for employing and training the disadvantaged? These and similar questions require value judgments in their solution.

As a first step in answering questions requiring value judgments in their solution, it is necessary to develop an appropriate model of the present day corporation. At one extreme there is the traditional economic model of the corporation. Within this framework the corporation is an instrument that is designed primarily to serve the stockholders. The welfare of employees is, at best, a secondary goal. Customers are included in the model, but in its extreme form the guide for relationships with customers is *caveat emptor*. Using this model the criterion provided for the resolution of social issues is the welfare of the stockholder. The model provides no clearly defined relationship with community, state, or national government. The other extreme is the metrocorporation. Here the managers, not the stockholders, are the decisive group. Managers must consider not only the wishes of the stockholder, but in addition those of the government, employee groups, customers, and the needs of society as a whole. The firm is regarded as a "citizen" of society with obligations to other "citizen groups." Government is accepted in full partnership so that the general welfare of society may be enhanced. If hard choices are to be made between the welfare of the firm and the welfare of society, consideration of the number of persons who might benefit would be a dominant factor in making the decision rather than the welfare of the stockholder.

The shortcomings of either extreme model presented above are obvious. Corporations can no longer—if for that matter they ever did—operate as purely economic institutions. At the same time it is highly doubtful that the extreme form of the metrocorporation could meet the minimal economic requirements necessary for survival. Thus one of the major challenges is the development of a viable corporate model that can both fulfill the economic needs of the corporation and its investors and meet the demands placed upon to fulfill the needs of society.

EPILOGUE

The introductory course to any field of study introduces and discusses a broad range of topics. As might be expected neither all students nor all instructors are in complete agreement with the amount of space assigned to each topic by the author. In the field of management the problem of selecting content is compounded by the various approaches (sometimes called schools) to the study of management. The texts of 10 or 15 years ago are representative of the classical approach to management. Presently there are texts with titles that indicate a behavioral approach, a systems approach, or a quantitative approach. One way of lending some order to the diversity of opinion concerning the content and emphasis of the introductory course is to examine the introductory course within the context of the sequence of courses normally taught in the business administration curriculum.

Most authors of management textbooks define management as a process. As a result their books have, in addition to an introductory section, four major sections—planning, organizing, leading or directing, and controlling. The execution of the planning function and the control function rely more heavily upon mathematical techniques than the other two functions of the management process. The development and application of quantitative techniques to the problems of management, primarily related to the functions of planning and controlling, has emerged as an academic field of study known as management science. It is questionable whether it is either desirable or possible for the introductory course to do more than indicate the problems that may be resolved by mathematical techniques. The interested student may explore the quantitative aspects of managerial problem solving and decision making in subsequent management science courses.

The origin of that body of knowledge discussed in the organizing function is lost in antiquity; however, much of it does come from the writings of military leaders. Most introductory courses confine the discussion of the organizing function to the level of description. The chapter titles of the section concerned with organizing in this text are typical of the material presented in most texts. Beyond the introductory course there are advanced courses in organization theory and detailed studies of specific organizational forms such as the bureaucratic model.

The behavioral sciences—especially psychology, sociology, and anthropology—are the academic disciplines that provide the subject matter content to be applied to the leadership function. Most business schools offer additional courses in organization behavior, industrial and organizational psychology, and industrial sociology so that the interested student may explore the behavioral sciences in depth.

At the same time that the student is studying the discipline of management he is also, in most colleges and universities, specializing in one of the functional areas of business management so that he can perform one of the specialized jobs in the business organization. He may complete a major in accounting, personnel, finance, marketing, or production. Or he may receive special training for positions in quality control, industrial engineering, or purchasing. Since these are the traditional majors within schools of business administration, they are not explored in depth in the introductory course to management.

When the introductory course to management is viewed as the beginning course within the emerging academic discipline known as management and when it is recognized that the student is acquiring necessary skills and knowledge so that he can perform a specific function within the modern industrial organization, it seems best to adopt an eclectic approach to the study of management. Consequently, the concepts of planning and control that draw heavily upon management science in their more complex applications are introduced in their simpler forms. Systems theory, organization theory, and the major findings of the behavioral sciences are presented in the discussions of the functions of organizing and leading. The breadth of an eclectic approach best meets the needs of those students who will have no additional courses in management and at the same time best prepares students who have opportunity for further study in the field of management.

Chapter Questions for Study and Discussion

1. Discuss briefly the reasons for considering the setting of objectives as an action apart from the planning process. What are the reasons for

including the setting of objectives as a part of planning? Which position do you prefer? Why?

2. Describe in your own words the interrelationships that exist between the four functions of the management process. Is it possible to rank these functions in order of significance within the management process? Discuss.

3. Comment on the statement in the text that the concept of managing is broader in scope than the concept of leading. Do you agree with this statement? Why?

4. What is meant by an open system? Differentiate between an open and a closed system? Can inanimate; i.e., non-living, systems properly be considered as open systems?

5. Why are social systems considered open systems? Discuss the major implications of considering formal organizations as open social systems?

6. Of the three current issues presented in the text, which do you consider to be the most significant? Why?

7. What are the shortcomings and the strengths of the traditional economic model of the firm? What are the advantages and disadvantages of the metrocorporation model?

8. We hear much concerning the quality of the environment in which we live. To improve it will cost money. Who is to bear this burden—the corporation, the customer, government, or society as a whole? Discuss.

CUES II
College & University Environment Scales[1]

DIRECTIONS: Colleges and universities differ from one another in many ways. Some things that are generally true or characteristic of one school may not be characteristic of another. The purpose of the College & University Environment Scales (CUES II) is to help describe the general atmosphere of different colleges. The atmosphere of a campus is a mixture of various features, facilities, rules and procedures, faculty characteristics, courses of study, classroom activities, students' interests, extracurricular programs, informal activities, and other conditions and events.

You are asked to be a reporter about your school. You have lived in its environment, seen its features, participated in its activities, and sensed its attitudes. What kind of a place is it?

There are 160 statements in this booklet. You are to answer them *True* or *False,* using the answer sheet given you for this purpose.[2]

As you read the statements you will find that many cannot be answered True or False in a literal sense. The statements contain qualifying words or phrases, such as "almost always," "frequently," "generally," and "rarely," and are intended to draw out your impression of whether the situation described applies or does not apply to your campus as you know it.

---

[1] C. Robert Pace, *College & University Environment Scales: Technical Manual* (2d ed.; Princeton, N.J.: Educational Testing Service, 1969). Directions and CUES II are copyrighted by C. Robert Pace and are published and distributed by ETS, Princeton, N.J. These materials are reproduced with the permission of the author and publisher. They should not be used in any manner other than as a part of Case Problem 15-A. College and universities desiring to conduct a formal evaluation using CUES II as the measuring instrument should write directly to Institutional Research Program for Higher Education, Educational Testing Service, Princeton, N.J.

[2] Answer sheets for CUES II, form x-2s, are in the *Student Study Experiences.*

As a reporter about your college you are to indicate whether you think each statement is *generally characteristic,* a condition that exists, an event that occurs or might occur, the way people generally act or feel—in short, whether the statement is more nearly True than False; or conversely, whether you think it is *not generally characteristic,* does not exist or occur, is more nearly False than True.

The CUES II is not a test in which there are right or wrong answers; it is more like an opinion poll—a way to find out how much agreement or disagreement there is about the characteristics of a campus environment.

1. Students almost always wait to be called on before speaking in class.
2. The big college events draw a lot of student enthusiasm and support.
3. There is a recognized group of student leaders on this campus.
4. Frequent tests are given in most courses.
5. Students take a great deal of pride in their personal appearance.
6. Education here tends to make students more practical and realistic.
7. The professors regularly check up on the students to make sure that assignments are being carried out properly and on time.
8. It's important socially here to be in the right club or group.
9. Student pep rallies, parades, dances, carnivals, or demonstrations occur very rarely.
10. Anyone who knows the right people in the faculty or administration can get a better break here.
11. The professors really push the students' capacities to the limit.
12. Most of the professors are dedicated scholars in their fields.
13. Most courses require intensive study and preparation out of class.
14. Students set high standards of achievement for themselves.
15. Class discussions are typically vigorous and intense.
16. A lecture by an outstanding scientist would be poorly attended.
17. Careful reasoning and clear logic are valued most highly in grading student papers, reports, or discussions.
18. It is fairly easy to pass most courses without working very hard.
19. The school is outstanding for the emphasis and support it gives to pure scholarship and basic research.
20. Standards set by the professors are not particularly hard to achieve.
21. It is easy to take clear notes in most courses.
22. The school helps everyone get acquainted.
23. Students often run errands or do other personal services for the faculty.
24. The history and traditions of the college are strongly emphasized.

25. The professors go out of their way to help you.

26. There is a great deal of borrowing and sharing among the students.

27. When students run a project or put on a show everybody knows about it.

28. Many upperclassmen play an active role in helping new students adjust to campus life.

29. Students exert considerable pressure on one another to live up to the expected codes of conduct.

30. Graduation is a pretty matter-of-fact, unemotional event.

31. Channels for expressing students' complaints are readily accessible.

32. Students are encouraged to take an active part in social reforms or political programs.

33. Students are actively concerned about national and international affairs.

34. There are a good many colorful and controversial figures on the faculty.

35. There is considerable interest in the analysis of value systems, and the relativity of societies and ethics.

36. Public debates are held frequently.

37. A controversial speaker always stirs up a lot of student discussion.

38. There are many facilities and opportunities for individual creative activity.

39. There is a lot of interest here in poetry, music, painting, sculpture, architecture, etc.

40. Concerts and art exhibits always draw big crowds of students.

41. Students ask permission before deviating from common policies or practices.

42. Most student rooms are pretty messy.

43. People here are always trying to win an argument.

44. Drinking and late parties are generally tolerated, despite regulations.

45. Students occasionally plot some sort of escapade or rebellion.

46. Many students drive sports cars.

47. Students frequently do things on the spur of the moment.

48. Student publications never lampoon dignified people or institutions.

49. The person who is always trying to "help out" is likely to be regarded as a nuisance.

50. Students are conscientious about taking good care of school property.

51. The important people at this school expect others to show proper respect for them.

52. Student elections generate a lot of intense campaigning and strong feeling.

53. Everyone has a lot of fun at this school.

54. In many classes students have an assigned seat.

55. Student organizations are closely supervised to guard against mistakes.

56. Many students try to pattern themselves after people they admire.

57. New fads and phrases are continually springing up among the students.

58. Students must have a written excuse for absence from class.

59. The college offers many really practical courses such as typing, report writing, etc.

60. Student rooms are more likely to be decorated with pennants and pin-ups than with paintings, carvings, mobiles, fabrics, etc.

61. Most of the professors are very thorough teachers and really probe into the fundamentals of their subjects.

62. Most courses are a real intellectual challenge.

63. Students put a lot of energy into everything they do in class and out.

64. Course offerings and faculty in the natural sciences are outstanding.

65. Courses, examinations, and readings are frequently revised.

66. Personality, pull, and bluff get students through many courses.

67. There is very little studying here over the weekends.

68. There is a lot of interest in the philosophy and methods of science.

69. People around here seem to thrive on difficulty—the tougher things get, the harder they work.

70. Students are very serious and purposeful about their work.

71. This school has a reputation for being very friendly.

72. All undergraduates must live in university approved housing.

73. Instructors clearly explain the goals and purposes of their courses.

74. Students have many opportunities to develop skill in organizing and directing the work of others.

75. Most of the faculty are not interested in students' personal problems.

76. Students quickly learn what is done and not done on this campus.

77. It's easy to get a group together for card games, singing, going to the movies, etc.

78. Students commonly share their problems.

79. Faculty members rarely or never call students by their first names.

80. There is a lot of group spirit.

81. Students are encouraged to criticize administrative policies and teaching practices.

82. The expression of strong personal belief or conviction is pretty rare around here.

83. Many students here develop a strong sense of responsibility about their role in contemporary social and political life.

84. There are a number of prominent faculty members who play a significant role in national or local politics.

85. There would be a capacity audience for a lecture by an outstanding philosopher or theologian.

86. Course offerings and faculty in the social sciences are outstanding.

87. Many famous people are brought to the campus for lectures, concerts, student discussions, etc.

88. The school offers many opportunities for students to understand and criticize important works of art, music, and drama.

89. Special museums or collections are important possessions of the college.

90. Modern art and music get little attention here.

91. Students are expected to report any violation of rules and regulations.

92. Student parties are colorful and lively.

93. There always seem to be a lot of little quarrels going on.

94. Students rarely get drunk and disorderly.

95. Most students show a good deal of caution and self-control in their behavior.

96. Bermuda shorts, pin-up pictures, etc. are common on this campus.

97. Students pay little attention to rules and regulations.

98. Dormitory raids, water fights, and other student pranks would be unthinkable.

99. Many students seem to expect other people to adapt to them rather than trying to adapt themselves to others.

100. Rough games and contact sports are an important part of intramural athletics.

101. The vocational value of many courses is emphasized.

102. Most people are aware of the financial status of students' families.

103. Student organizations are required to have a faculty adviser.

104. There are good facilities for learning vocationally useful skills and techniques.

105. Most faculty members really know the regulations and requirements that apply to student programs.

106. There is a well-organized and effective job placement office for the graduating students.

107. Many faculty members are involved in services or consulting activities for outside groups—business, adult education, etc.

108. Professors will sometimes increase a student's grade if they think he has worked especially hard and conscientiously.

109. Most students want to get a degree because of its economic value.

110. Vocational guidance is a main activity of the counseling office.

111. New ideas and theories are encouraged and vigorously debated.
112. Students who don't make passing grades are quickly dropped from school.
113. Students are allowed to help themselves to books in the library stacks.
114. Excellence in scholarship is the dominant feature of this institution.
115. There are lots of quiet and comfortable places for students to study.
116. Even in social groups students are more likely to talk about their studies than about other things.
117. There are many excellent facilities for research on this campus.
118. The main emphasis in most departmental clubs is to promote interest and scholarship in the field.
119. Most students are pretty dissatisfied if they make less than a B grade.
120. The library is one of the outstanding facilities on the campus.
121. The campus design, architecture, and landscaping suggest a friendly atmosphere.
122. Student groups often meet in faculty members' homes.
123. Counseling and guidance services are really personal, patient, and helpful.
124. There are courses which involve students in activities with groups or agencies in the local community.
125. Most of the students here are pretty happy.
126. There are courses or voluntary seminars that deal with problems of marriage and the family.
127. In most classes the atmosphere is very friendly.
128. Groups of students from the college often get together for parties or visits during holidays.
129. Most students seem to have a genuine affection for this school.
130. There are courses or voluntary seminars that deal with problems of social adjustment.
131. There is a regular place on the campus where students can make speeches about controversial issues.
132. Students are free to cut classes at their own discretion.
133. Many faculty members have worked overseas or frequently traveled to other countries.
134. There is a lot of variety and innovation in the way many courses are taught.
135. Many professors permit, and sometimes welcome, class discussion of materials that are outside their field of specialization.
136. Many students are interested in joining the Peace Corps or are planning, somehow, to spend time in another part of the world.

137. Many student groups invite faculty members to lead special discussions.

138. Groups of students sometimes spend all evening listening to classical records.

139. Student chorus, orchestra, and theater groups are really excellent.

140. Students like to browse in book stores.

141. Many professors require students to submit an outline before writing a term paper or report.

142. The Dean of Students office is mainly concerned with disciplinary matters.

143. Faculty members always wear coats and ties on the campus.

144. A major aim of this institution is to produce cultivated men and women.

145. In literature, drama, and music the main emphasis is on the classics.

146. Nearby churches have an active interest in counseling and youth programs.

147. Proper standards and ideals are emphasized in many courses.

148. Most professors think of themselves as no different from other adults in the community.

149. Faculty members are always polite and proper in their relations with students.

150. In most exams the emphasis is on knowing the correct answers rather than on being able to defend a point of view.

151. There are students on many academic and administrative committees.

152. Students have real authority to determine some campus policies and procedures.

153. Some faculty members are active in experimenting with new methods of teaching, new courses, and other innovations.

154. There is much student interest and activity about social issues—such as civil rights, justice, peace.

155. The administration is receptive and active in responding to student proposals for change.

156. There is an "experimental" college or program where a variety of new courses are offered (whether for credit or not).

157. Massive disruption, force, or violence by students would be unthinkable on this campus.

158. The attitude of most college officials about drugs is generally patient, flexible, and tolerant.

159. The response of most college officials toward student sit-ins or other "confrontations" is (or would be) firm, forceful, and unsympathetic.

160. Due process considerations are expected by students who are accused of violating laws or college rules.

Comprehensive Case
—Buying and Operating a Motel[1]

The accommodation industry with annual sales in excess of seven billion dollars provides the industrial setting for this comprehensive case study.[2] There are several reasons for selecting a 95-unit motel as the specific setting of the case. First, almost every student has been a guest in a motel; consequently there is some knowledge of the characteristics and services provided. Second, motels and motor hotels are the growth segment of the accommodation industry. Further, the modern motel is a complex operation and offers a career opportunity for the professionally trained manager.

The format of the case parallels the major parts of the text. The first part of the case presents a discussion of the nature of the industry and offers an opportunity to formulate specific internal and external business objectives. The second part examines the planning required to determine whether or not the purchase of the property in question is a sound decision. Next, you are asked to determine the optimum organization necessary for the efficient, long-term operation of the motel. Questions concerning the most effective type of leadership and means of motivating employees are considered. Finally, the controls normally used in the operation of a motel are developed. Each major part of the case

---

[1] The author wishes to thank the following persons of the Ramada Inn organization who gave generously of their time in supplying information for the preparation of this case: Mr. Prentiss R. Moore, Regional Manager; Mr. James Daniels, Manager of the Arlington, Texas, Inn; and Mr. Charles Steadman, Assistant Director of Training, Management Developemnt Center, Phoenix, Arizona.

[2] *Trends in the Hotel/Motel Business: Thirty-fifth Annual Review* (New York: Harris, Kerr, Forester & Company, 1971). Much of the information concerning the operation of the hotel-motel industry was drawn from this report which was provided by Mr. Eric Green, partner, Harris, Kerr, Forester & Company, Certified Public Accountants.

may be considered as an integrating case to be studied in conjunction with the corresponding part of the text, or the case may be regarded as a comprehensive case drawing upon all of the functions of the management process. However the case is used, it is suggested that the student read the entire case before analyzing each of the five parts. Also, the information presented and the experience gained in analyzing the case should enable you to evaluate a motel in your area as either an investment opportunity or for employment as a manager.

THE NATURE OF THE MOTEL BUSINESS

It is axiomatic that if one is to fulfill the accommodation needs of the traveler such facilities must be located so that they are readily accessible. The earliest accommodation facilities established in this country were for those who traveled on foot or horseback and are typified by the colonial inns of New England.[3] As stagecoach routes developed so did the way station and the coffee house. In the mid-nineteenth century the railroad system of this country began its development, and in time the inn, the way station, and the coffee house diminished in importance and were replaced by the downtown hotel. The major hotels of Chicago, New York, St. Louis, and Philadelphia are all located near the rail terminals of these cities. With the advent of the automobile, and highways that make their use possible, the mode and pattern of transportation shifted again. Tourist cabins appeared along the highways to accommodate those who used this mode of transportation.

The development of the tourist cabin, soon followed by the tourist court and the motel, marks the completion of a full circle that began with the New England inn to accommodate the individual traveler, followed by the downtown hotel for those using the mass transportation of the railroads, and back to roadside facilities for the individual traveling in his own automobile. However, change in the mode and pattern of transportation still continues. The large jet airport, the result of mass air transportation, is away from the central city and has created the need for a new type of lodging facility readily accessible from the airport.

Types of Facilities

For many years the mainstay of the accommodations industry has been the transient hotel. Although most of these hotels were built prior

---

[3] George O. Podd and John D. Lesure, *Planning and Operating Motels and Motor Hotels* (New York: Ahrens Book Company, Inc., 1964). Much of the background information of the industry was obtained from this source, which is a comprehensive treatment and analysis of the problems encountered in operating a motel or motor hotel.

to 1930, new transient hotels have been built in recent years. These are full service hotels and provide all the services that a traveler needs, whether he be on business or pleasure, or attending a convention. There are resort hotels which are located in resort areas and characterized by marked seasonal fluctuations in business. In addition, some hotels are classed as residential since the majority of their guests are permanent residents rather than transients.

The modern motel had its beginnings in the tourist cabin and the tourist court. In the 1920's, mainly in the South, Southwest, and California, roadside tourist cabins made their appearance to serve those who were traveling by automobile. These early facilities were in rural areas and offered minimal services. Private baths, telephone service, food, and linen service were unknown. Tourist cabins soon developed into the tourist court and many services associated with hotels were added. Sometime during the 1930's the descriptive term, motel, made its appearance and was readily accepted. The motel of this period was a relatively modest establishment and did not pose a serious threat to the well established hotel industry. For the most part there was individual ownership, often husband and wife, who could and did perform all of the work necessary for its operation. The capital investment was small, $2,000 to $3,000 per unit with an average of ten units, and units could be added as desired. Managing a motel became a way of life for many retired persons.

With the development of the interregional highway system and the construction of new airports the characteristics of the motel industry, again adapting to the mode and pattern of transportation, changed significantly. The number of guest rooms increased sharply with the result that motels with 300 units are not unusual. Also, full hotel services, including public meeting rooms and facilities for conventions, made their appearance. One is tempted to describe the modern motel as a horizontal hotel, but that description is not accurate since many so-called motels are multi-story buildings, and some are even located in the central city. If a differentiation must be made between the full service motel and the traditional hotel, it is in the availability and accessibility of parking facilities. Usually the motel has a parking lot or parking garage which is adjacent to and is an integral part of the building complex.

The Tradition of Innkeeping

Since the primary function of the accommodation industry is to provide a service, it may be considered as a part of that broad segment of industry known as the service industry. It is also a part of the retail industry since services are sold to the customer who is also the consumer. However, the accommodations industry differs from other service and retail establishments in that there is a distinguishing relationship between the customer and the seller. It is a relationship that is best described by the terms "guest" and "host." A guest is more than a traveler away from home; he is there by invitation. The manager or owner does more than merely provide service; he must, in the tradition of innkeeping, provide the personal attention, warmth, and courtesy that makes the traveler a truly welcomed guest. It is not an easy task. The guest-host relationship is not easily attainable with corporate ownership and professional management, yet the traditional innkeeping relationship of guest and host should be one of the major objectives of any motel.

The Business Aspects

In addition to formulating service objectives within the tradition of innkeeping, there are significant financial considerations in the operation of a motel. A motel is a long-term investment in real estate. The initial land investment is improved with the construction of a special purpose building. If the real estate improvement does not succeed as a motel, the only value that normally remains is the value of the land. Further, the capital investment per room is significant. Construction costs of $15,000 per guest unit are not uncommon. Though the rewards are great, the risk is high. The construction of a new highway, a new airport, the closing of a major industry in the area, or the building of additional rooms by competitors can all spell disaster. Thus the need arises to determine a reasonable rate of return on equity capital invested in an enterprise having a substantial degree of risk which is often due to factors beyond the control of the investor. Return on other investments having a lower degree of risk, such as corporate and tax free municipal bonds, must be examined. For these reasons a rate of return on equity capital of 10 to 12 percent a year is considered minimal.

PLANNING TO BUY

The Apex Motel, which is readily accessible and visible from the interstate highway, is located 40 miles from a major city with a population of 850,000. The motel property is within the city limits of a town that has a population of 50,000. The metropolitan area is one of the 10 largest in the United States and ranks sixth in respect to expected population growth. The motel was built eight years ago and opened with

98 guest rooms, an apartment for the manager, a lobby newsstand and sundries shop, and a large swimming pool. At the present time there are 95 rooms available to guests since one of the intended guest rooms is used as an employee's lounge, one for storage, and another is equipped as a maintenance shop. Shortly after opening, a separate restaurant with three public meeting rooms was built adjacent to the motel. The present owner intends to retain and operate this property; however, the purchase agreement includes an option to buy the restaurant in three years. There are adequate parking facilities for both motel and restaurant guests, and the courtyard and pool area are attractively landscaped. The rooms are comfortably furnished and most of the carpeting has been replaced, but there is need for a planned refurnishing of all guest rooms. The present owner is asking $950,000 and is willing to finance 50 percent of this amount for 15 years at an annual rate of 9 percent.

How does one determine a fair price for an existing motel? When building a new motel, the first step is a feasibility study to show immediate and expected market potential, the cost of land and construction, and projected operating revenues and expenses. However, when purchasing an existing property, current operating statements are of primary significance; yet the feasibility study must be updated to obtain a reliable forecast of the future.

Current Operations

The primary source of income for motels without restaurants is almost entirely room sales revenue which should range between 92 and 95 percent of total income.[4] Telephone service (usually operated at a loss) should provide two to five percent of gross sales, and miscellaneous income derived from vending machines and space rentals such as a lobby sundries shop and newsstand usually contributes between one and two percent. The direct costs of operating the rooms—wages for the rooms department employees, linens, cleaning supplies, glassware and other supplies—and the cost of providing telephone service are deducted from total sales. The result is defined as gross operating income, which

---

[4] The classification of accounts used in this discussion and presented in Exhibit I, Table I, and Exhibit II are based upon the following industry sources.

Edward F. Chirhart, Kemper W. Merriam, and Robert W. McIntosh, *Uniform Classification of Accounts for Motels, Motor Hotels, or Highway Lodges* (Temple, Texas: Tourist Court Journal, 1962).

Uniform System of Accounts and Expenses Dictionary for Motels, Motor Hotels, and Small Hotels (New York: American Hotel and Motel Association, 1962). This publication was prepared under the direction of Co-Chairman Thomas. J. Hogan, C.P.A., and John D. Lesure, C.P.A., and is approved by the American Hotel and Motel Association.

should be between 67 and 75 percent of total income. Administrative
and general expenses, including the manager's salary and the cost of
front office personnel; advertising; heat, light, and power; and the cost
of repairs and maintenance are subtracted from gross operating income
to determine gross operating profit, an amount that should range between
40 and 50 percent of total income. Fire insurance, approximately one
percent of total income, and real estate taxes—from four to nine
percent of total income—are deducted from gross operating profit to
determine operating profit before other capital expenses. Profit after
real estate taxes usually ranges between 35 and 45 percent of total
income. The most recent operating statement of Apex Motel is shown
in Exhibit I.

An examination of the operating statement shows an operating
profit, after real estate taxes but before other capital expenditures, of 30
percent of total revenue. Though many buyers assume that they have the
management skill to improve operating ratios, the prudent buyer makes
no such assumption and forecasts net profit based upon current operations and projected capital expenses. Counsel advises that the proposed
selling price of $950,000 may be distributed on the following basis
expressed as cost per guest room:

Land	$ 1,000.00
Buildings	7,600.00
Pool	200.00
Furnishings	1,200.00
Total	$10,000.00

Counsel indicates that the buildings may be depreciated on a 20-year
basis and that the pool and furnishings may be depreciated on an
8-year basis. Both depreciation schedules are computed by the straight-
line method. The nine-percent, 15-year mortgage with fixed monthly
payments, including payments on principal, results in an interest charge
of $42,180.00 and payments on principal of $15,675.00 for the first
year. Total debt service is $57,855.00 per year. Proposed capital ex-
penses are shown in Table 1 on page 734.

When interest on mortgage and depreciation charges, 11.8 percent
and 14.7 percent of total income respectively, are deducted from profit
after real estate taxes, profit before federal and state income tax is 3.5
percent, a return of 2.6 percent on the equity capital of $475,000.00.
It is difficult to project income taxes as each buyer's situation differs;
however, assume that Apex is being bought by a newly formed corporation and that there are no other properties. The federal tax of 22 percent

Exhibit I

APEX MOTEL

CURRENT OPERATING STATEMENT

For Year Ending December 31, 19—

			Percentage of Total Income
Total Sales & Income			
Rooms	$339,815.00		95.0
Telephone	14,300.00		4.0
Other	3,577.00		1.0
Total		$357,692.00	100.0
Departmental Expenses			
Rooms Department			
Salaries & Wages	73,320.00		20.5
Payroll Taxes & Employee Benefits	5,132.00		1.4
Laundry	16,096.00		4.5
Other—China, glass, cleaning supplies	14,308.00		4.0
	108,856.00		30.4
Telephone	17,884.00		5.0
Total		126,740.00	35.4
Gross Operating Income		$231,225.00	64.6
Deductions from Income			
Administrative & General Expenses			
Salaries & Wages	33,408.00		9.3
Payroll Taxes & Employee Benefits	2,339.00		.6
Other A&G Expenses	13,092.00		3.7
	48,839.00		13.6
Advertising & Sales Promotion	10,731.00		3.0
Heat, Light & Power	21,461.00		6.0
Repairs & Maintenance	21,461.00		6.0
Total		102,492.00	28.6
Gross Operating Profit		$128,733.00	36.0
Fire Insurance & Franchise Taxes	3,577.00		1.0
Profit Before Real Estate Taxes and Other Capital Expenses		$125,156.00	35.0
Real Estate Taxes	17,885.00		5.0
Profit After Real Estate Taxes but Before Other Capital Expenses		$107,271.00	30.0

Table 1
APEX MOTEL
PROPOSED CAPITAL EXPENSES

		Percentage of Total Income
Interest on Mortgage	$42,180.00	11.8
Depreciation on Buildings & Furnishings	$52,725.00	14.7
Profit Before Income Taxes	$12,366.00	3.5

on the first $25,000 of corporate earnings amounts to $2,720.00 which must be paid out of the $12,366.00 profit. From the balance, $9,646.00, repayment of principal, $15,675.00, is deducted and results in a net loss of $6,029.00. Any state income tax creates a greater loss.

An obvious first step in determining the reasonableness of a proposed selling price for real estate is to request a professional appraisal. Such an appraisal has been made in respect to Apex Motel, and the report indicates that the asking price is equitable; that is, the appreciation sought by the original owner is in line with similiar properties in the area. Further, with proper maintenance, the building is expected to have a useful life of 20 years with minimal risk of obsolesence. Nonetheless, there is a question concerning the true worth of the room furnishings, and the appraiser's report strongly recommends that all room furnishings be replaced within three years. It is estimated that the cost of refurnishing will average $1,500.00 per room.

A motel is more than bricks and mortar on a parcel of land; it is an ongoing business. Rules of thumb have developed and serve as guides in evaluating the worth of a given property. The gross income multiplier is obtained by dividing the selling price by gross income. The normal range of gross income multipliers is three to seven, with four being the average. The net operating profit multiplier is another index. Net operating profit is defined on a cash-flow basis and shows the amount of money available from net profit and depreciation after debt service which includes payments on principal and interest. This value is also termed net spendable and when divided into the equity investment the result is the pay out period for the recovery of equity capital. It is estimated that a buyer should recover equity capital in four to five years.

The Feasibility Study

A remark attributed to Mr. E. M. Statler, founder of the Statler Hotels, states that there are three factors that determine the success of a hotel. They are: location, location, and location. The original feasibility study indicates that the site selected for Apex Motel was the last available motel site within the city limits and that there were no planned changes in either the state highway system or the interregional system. At the request of the present owner of Apex the consultants who did the original feasibility study have recently brought the earlier study up to date. The favorable economic forecast for the entire metropolitan area remains the same. The university in the town where Apex is located has grown and now has an enrollment of 15,000 students. In addition, there are plans for a community college scheduled to open within a year. Four additional manufacturing plants have located within five miles of Apex during the past five years. The nearby major city has built a convention center and now has an American Conference team of the NFL and a National League baseball team. There are also professional basketball, hockey, and soccer teams. Two seasonal amusement parks, similar to Disneyland, have been established in the last eight years.

The current survey of the occupancy rates of the five motels (there are no hotels) competing directly with Apex is presented by month in Table 2. The current annual occupancy rate for the area is 70 percent, the same occupancy rate that Apex experienced during the last full year of operation. The consultants believe that Apex could increase its occupancy rate by replacing room furnishings. They also recommend an evaluation of the current rate structure so that the average revenue

Table 2

AREA OCCUPANCY RATES

Month	Occupancy Rate	Month	Occupancy Rate
January	55%	July	82%
February	60	August	85
March	70	September	68
April	79	October	76
May	78	November	58
June	80	December	49

Annual Occupancy Rate—70%

per room may be increased from the present $14.00 to $15.00 per room, an amount that would put Apex in line with the immediate area. No decrease in occupancy rate is foreseen, provided the rooms are well maintained.

THE ORGANIZATION

The organizing function for small service organizations is primarily a manning problem rather than one of creating a managerial hierarchy. Apex Motel is large enough to warrant the services of a full-time manager who lives on the premises. He is classified as an exempt employee; all others are non-exempt and their base pay is computed on a 40-hour week. Determining an optimum organization is complicated by the need for maintaining a 24-hour day, 7-day week operation and by daily and seasonal fluctuations in the occupancy rate.

It is difficult to set precise manning standards because of variations in physical layout, service objectives, and the availability and quality of labor. Even so, normative data indicate that total payroll costs, excluding payroll taxes, for motels without restaurants range between 22 and 28 percent of total sales and income. The average is 26 percent and results in an annual cost of $924.00 for each available room and $1,273.00 for each occupied room. Payroll costs (excluding the cost of payroll taxes) for the rooms department should be between 14 and 18 percent of room sales. A labor cost of 16 percent is acceptable. The total cost of operating the rooms department, including payroll taxes and the cost of supplies, should be about 25 percent of room sales.

The present manning of the rooms department is considerably above the recommended average and is the result of the present owner's method of allocating restaurant and motel labor costs. An analysis of the payroll costs, excluding payroll taxes and other benefits, charged to the rooms department shows a total of $73,320.00, or 21.6 percent of room sales. These costs are distributed as follows:

12	Maids	$43,680.00
1	Housekeeper (working)	4,056.00
1	Houseman	3,744.00
6	Porters	21,840.00
	Total	$73,320.00

It is difficult to determine how many maids are required to service a motel effectively. Under normal conditions a maid is expected to clean a room in approximately 30 minutes, and during the course of an eight-hour day she can be expected to clean 14 rooms. In addition to the seasonal variations in occupancy, shown in Table 2, there are variations in the daily occupancy rate with Friday, Saturday, Sunday, and Monday showing a lower rate than the days in the middle of the week. Also, there are the factors of absenteeism and the need to maintain a seven-day week operation. Proposed manning, allowing for these factors, results in a monthly average of eight maids. If labor costs remain constant, $1.75 per hour, total annual projected payroll costs for maid service is $29,130.00. The working housekeeper, who schedules the maids and is responsible for maintaining the cleaning supplies inventory, is expected to be retained at her present rate of $1.95 per hour. The houseman picks up the clean linen and delivers the soiled linen to the local linen service, cleans the hallways, and performs other services as required. His annual pay, at $1.80 an hour, is $3,744.00. Three porters, with an hourly rate of $1.75 earn a total of $10,920.00. The total annual cost of the proposed manning for the rooms department is $47,840.00, excluding payroll taxes.

There are relatively few persons allocated to the administrative and general payroll account. There are four desk clerks, one of whom works as relief and on weekends. Payroll cost for each person is $346.00 per month and the annual cost for desk clerks is $16,608.00. All of the clerks know how to operate the switchboard and can perform the duties of cashier when assigned that duty. The layout of the front office is such that a full-time telephone switchboard operator is not needed. The night auditor, who works from 11:00 p.m. to 7:00 a.m., has agreed to remain at his present monthly salary of $550.00. The manager also indicates that he will continue at his present salary of $10,200.00 per year. It is highly doubtful that any significant changes can be made in the operations of the front office; thus, projected payroll costs shown in Exhibit II, page 738, for A&G personnel are the same as in Exhibit I.

The total payroll costs for maintenance personnel are $9,336.00. The maintenance man is a good mechanic and is capable of handling all minor repairs and painting. The yardman fills in occasionally as a porter and also helps the maintenance man. On a monthly basis the payroll cost (including payroll taxes) for the maintenance man is $475.00, and for the yardman the amount is $303.00. Considering the age of the motel and the need for refurnishing all rooms, it seems wise to retain both of these employees. If the number of persons assigned to maintenance and administrative and general expenses remains constant, and if the

Exhibit II

PROPOSED BUDGET

(Assuming No Change in Occupancy Rate or Average Rate per Room)

			Percentage of Total Income
Total Sales & Income			
Rooms	$339,815.00		95.0
Telephone	14,300.00		4.0
Other	3,577.00		1.0
Total		$357,692.00	100.0
Departmental Expenses			
Rooms	81,593.00		22.8
Telephone	17,884.00		5.0
Total		99,477.00	27.8
Gross Operating Income		$258,215.00	72.2
Deductions from Income			
Administrative & General Expenses	48,839.00		13.6
Advertising & Sales Promotion	10,731.00		3.0
Heat, Light & Power	21,461.00		6.0
Repairs & Maintenance	21,461.00		6.0
Total		102,492.00	28.6
Gross Operating Profit		$155,723.00	43.6
Fire Insurance & Franchise Tax	3,577.00		1.0
Profit Before Real Estate Taxes and Other Capital Expenses		$152,146.00	42.6
Real Estate Taxes	17,885.00		5.0
Profit After Real Estate Taxes but Before Other Capital Expenses		$134,261.00	37.6
Interest on Mortgage	42,180.00		11.8
Depreciation on Building and Furnishings	52,725.00		14.7
		94,905.00	26.5
Profit Before Federal Income Tax		$ 39,356.00	11.1

proposed manning for the rooms department is achieved, total payroll costs at present hourly rates are $96,272.00, including all payroll taxes.

THE PROBLEM OF LEADERSHIP

In Chapter 16 and again in Chapter 23 a differentiation is made between leadership style and leadership behavior. Leadership style pertains to the interpersonal relationships that exist between a leader and the members of his group. Leadership behavior encompasses all of those actions normally associated with the management process and includes formal and informal communications, methods of motivating and compensating employees, and supervisory practices. In addition to those characteristics necessary for effective interpersonal relationships, the manager of a motel must have the ability to establish the guest-host relationship discussed earlier. The purpose of this section of the case is to offer you an opportunity to crystallize your thinking in regard to the leadership function in a motel. The recommendations that you make to the manager of Apex Motel and the standards used to judge his performance as a leader may or may not apply to other forms of business organizations.

Leadership Style

Whether an authoritarian personality, one who is highly directive in his relationship with subordinates, can establish and maintain an optimum guest-host relationship is open to question. If one assumes that it is possible for the authoritarian manager to maintain an effective guest-host relationship, the effect of such a personality upon subordinates must be considered. How effective would their performance be, what attitudes would they demonstrate toward guests, and how would they react to control?

As one moves away from the authoritarian pattern of leadership, there are varying degrees of participative leadership. What is the optimum degree of participation? In discussing the organization structure of a motel it is noted that problems arise in manning a 24-hour day, 7-day week operation with a fluctuating work load. Should work schedules be fixed or should they be rotated? More important, who should make the determination, the manager or the employees? Also, how much should employees participate in setting the standards used for control? Your answers to these and similar questions are indicative of your own leadership style and influence your judgement of the effectiveness of managerial performance.

Leadership Behavior

Now let us consider the formal actions of the manager in determining and administering personnel policies. As noted in Chapter 18, there is marked interest in the measurement of job satisfaction. Although many studies show a consistent, but low, correlation between job satisfaction and performance, a conclusion that there is a causal relationship between job satisfaction and performance is not warranted. Considering these findings and also considering the nature of the motel business, what steps would you take as a manager to determine the level of job satisfaction of your employees?

The present owner of Apex Motel has not formulated any clear statement of personnel policy; however, during preliminary discussions he stated that he believed that the large motel chains with formal policies and retirement plans were able to attract a better quality employee than he did. Thus the question arises concerning the advisability and nature of a formal statement of personnel policy for an independent operation such as Apex Motel.

ESTABLISHING CONTROLS

Exhibit II presents the optimum operating ratios that the group considering the purchase of Apex Motel have developed as a basis for establishing a budget. They believe that these ratios are attainable since they are virtually the same as those presented in Exhibit I. The major difference between Exhibit I and Exhibit II is that the latter reflects a reduced manning in the rooms department.

The proposed budget must be evaluated in respect to the extent to which it fulfills the financial objectives of the purchasers and the probability that it can be attained. If the financial objectives of those desiring to purchase Apex Motel are not fulfilled by the budget proposed in Exhibit II, there are additional steps that may be taken before making a decision to withdraw and invest their capital elsewhere.

INDEX

AUTHOR INDEX

751